BY

AUGUST MEIER AND ELLIOTT RUDWICK

The Making of Black America (editors)   1969
*From Plantation to Ghetto: An Interpretive History of
American Negroes*   1966

BY

AUGUST MEIER

Negro Protest Thought in the Twentieth Century
(editor, with Francis Broderick)   1966
Negro Thought in America, 1880–1915   1963

BY

ELLIOTT RUDWICK

Race Riot at East St. Louis, July 2, 1917   1964
W. E. B. Du Bois: A Study in Minority Group Leadership   1960

THE
MAKING OF
BLACK AMERICA

VOLUME I

The Origins of Black Americans

THE MAKING OF BLACK AMERICA

Essays in Negro Life & History

EDITED BY

AUGUST MEIER & ELLIOTT RUDWICK

VOLUME I

The Origins of Black Americans

STUDIES IN AMERICAN NEGRO LIFE
August Meier, General Editor

Atheneum   NEW YORK

1974

For Paul and Sey

FOREWORD

SLIGHTLY over a half century ago, in 1915, the late Carter G. Woodson organized the Association for the Study of Negro Life and History. A year later he founded the *Journal of Negro History*. Due to his efforts, the study of the American Negroes' past was placed on modern scholarly foundations. Later, in the 1930's and early 1940's, appeared a number of notable sociological monographs dealing with the Negro community and race relations.

In choosing essays for *The Making of Black America*, we have included a substantial selection of materials from the behavioral sciences, particularly sociology and political science, as well as history. We have for the most part limited ourselves to the periodical literature, and only in unusual cases have we excerpted passages from books. Nearly all of the selections from learned journals are reprinted in their entirety. Space limitations, however, necessitated excisions in a few instances.

Unfortunately the periodical literature is uneven in its coverage of the many and varied aspects of American Negro life, and we have been unable to include materials on several subjects, such as the history of Negro colleges and Negro business since the Civil War. Conversely we have found that certain areas, such as Negro political participation, have received a relatively large amount of attention from scholars. Our selection reflects the weaknesses and strengths of the scholarly literature. Moreover, because of our inclusion of articles from sociology and political science, the twentieth century is naturally heavily represented in this book.

For the most part we have chosen articles that concern themselves entirely or in large part with what Negroes were doing, rather than with what white Americans were doing about Negroes. Inevitably we have been compelled to omit many excellent studies. Nevertheless, we believe that the ones included in this book illustrate most of the major themes in the making of black America.

We have made the headnotes brief, preferring to let the selections speak for themselves.

AUGUST MEIER
ELLIOTT RUDWICK

ACKNOWLEDGMENTS

WE ARE grateful for leaves of absence provided by Roosevelt and Southern Illinois Universities, which greatly facilitated the preparation of these volumes. We also wish to acknowledge with appreciation the splendid cooperation given by the Princeton University Library and particularly by the Newark, New Jersey Public Library and the Dana Library of Rutgers University (Newark).

CONTENTS

III   THE ANTE-BELLUM FREE PEOPLE OF COLOR

IV CIVIL WAR AND RECONSTRUCTION

VOLUME II:

The Black Community in Modern America

V THE FOUNDATIONS OF THE TWENTIETH-CENTURY BLACK COMMUNITY

VI   THE MAKING OF THE BLACK GHETTO

VII   THE NEW MILITANCY AND THE ENDURING GHETTO

PART ONE

FROM AFRICA
TO AMERICA

Joseph Greenberg

THE NEGRO KINGDOMS OF THE SUDAN

The overwhelming majority of Africans brought in slave ships to the New World came from West Africa—from a belt of land stretching from the Senegal River to modern Angola, and extending inland from the coast for about two or three hundred miles. This territory encompassed parts of the African tropical rain forest and, in its northern section, of the vast grasslands known as the Sudan.

In political structure the ancestral societies of New World Negroes ranged from tribal organizations, through city-states in the Niger Delta area, to large and complex kingdoms. The earliest West African monarchies, located in the Sudan and going back at least to the fourth century A.D., were the prototypes for the kingdoms of the Guinea and southern Sudan—such as Dahomey, Ashanti, Yoruba and Benin—with whom the Europeans traded during the height of the transatlantic slave traffic between the sixteenth and eighteenth centuries.

For many years it was generally held that the political organization of the West African kingdoms was based upon Caucasoid models. In his seminal article on "The Negro Kingdoms of the Sudan," Joseph Greenberg not only summarized existing knowledge about the development of kingdoms in the western Sudan, but demonstrated conclusively that the institution of African kingship was of indigenous African origin.

Monarchical patterns are widespread in Negro Africa and have been reported from peoples as distant from each other as the Shilluk of the Upper Nile Valley, the Zulus of South Africa and the Wolofs of Senegal on the Atlantic Coast. Among African kingdoms, those of the Sudan, particularly in its western portions, have been conspicuous for their size, in which they are without rival in Negro Africa. Their early date of historical attestation is only

Joseph Greenberg, "The Negro Kingdoms of the Sudan," reprinted with permission from *Transactions of the New York Academy of Sciences*, Ser. II, Vol. II, February, 1949, pp. 126–134. Copyright 1949 by The New York Academy of Sciences.

surpassed by Ethiopia and by the kingdoms of the Nile Valley known from Egyptian records. Moreover, the cultural contributions of these Sudanese kingdoms, under the aegis of Islam, are unique in African history. What follows is a brief attempt to consider some of the factors operative in the rise of these empires and to evaluate those theories, found frequently in this literature, which assign a predominant part in their foundation and expansion to Caucasian influences of one kind or another.

The Sudan is the term applied to that vast portion of the African continent which stretches between the Sahara Desert on the North and the tropical rain forests of the Guinea Coast and the Belgian Congo on the south. In keeping with its transitional nature, it is predominantly steppe in its northern portions and savannah towards the south. Rainfall is generally adequate and both agricultural and pastoral populations are found. A conspicuous trait of the area is the relative ease of west-east movement over its open terrain, a facility intensified by the use of the horse as a riding animal, which is at least as old as the introduction of Islam in this region and perhaps older. At the exit of the last century, Rabeh, an adventurer who had been a lieutenant of Zubeir Pasha, active in a rebellion in the Anglo-Egyptian Sudan, fled across the entire eastern and central Sudan and carved out an empire for himself in the shores of Lake Chad. What has occurred so recently in the full light of history may have happened many times in the past also. Certainly, in this ease of communication in the open lands of the Sudan, we have an encouraging factor for the formation of large territorial units.

The great importance of the Sudan in the commercial history of Africa is its position as an entrepôt for goods crossing the Sahara, and for their exchange with the products of the Sudan itself and of the frost area farther south. The Sudan first enters written history, in this guise, with the activities of Mohammedan merchants from the cities of North Africa. Whether this trade first began after Islam had made its conquest of North Africa in the seventh century, or whether it existed even earlier, has been the subject of some speculation. The Romans, to whom is usually assigned the introduction of the camel into North Africa, without which this trade would have been seriously handicapped, if possible at all, are not likely to have bothered to assure themselves of the control of the oases of the Fezzan in southwestern Libya, had not some trade existed. There is no evidence concerning the Carthaginians before them, though some have thought that Carthage maintained such trans-Saharan routes.

It is clear, at any rate, that the large size of the Negro empires of the western Sudan, their stability over centuries, and the security of travel which they provided, were powerful factors in the development of this trade, while the prosperity which it engendered was, in turn, the *raison-d'être* for their expansion and wealth. The mere need for such a route is, however, not adequate as an over-all explanation of the existences of these kingdoms. In the seventeenth century, the old organization of the Niger areas in the western Sudan collapsed under the impact of the Moroccan conquest and was never re-established, in spite of the continued operation of the geographical and economic factors which tended to favor this portion of the Sudan. It was the shortness of the route from Morocco, the great bend of the Niger in western Sudan, which led to its early prominence. Islam spread into the interior of Africa along this western path of penetration, trade and religion proselytization going hand-in-hand. The eastern route via the Nile Valley was far less prominent, not only because of its greater length, but because of the persistence of Christian kingdoms in Nubia, which throughout the Middle Ages blocked the southward expansion of Islamic trade and religious conversions.

Our knowledge of the great empires of the western Sudan rests first upon accounts furnished by Arab travelers and by geographers who utilized the reports of Islamic merchants who traded in these regions. Arab materials commence with the tenth century and continue through the Middle Ages. They are sparse in ethnographic detail, but they at least furnish the main outlines of political history. A second source is the Negroes themselves, who borrowed writing and the exercise of historiography, along with other branches of literature from Islam. The records range from mere lists of kings, with the length of their reigns, to such lively and detailed accounts as the *Tarikh-es-Sudan* of *es-Sa'di*, a native of Timbuctoo. They are an invaluable supplement to the information furnished by Modern European explorers and ethnographers, beginning with the exploration of Mungo Park at the end of the eighteenth century.

The first large kingdom which these sources disclose is that of Ghana, whose existence is attested as early as the tenth century by Ibn-Haukal and is described by El-Bekri, in the eleventh century. The exact location of Ghana is disputed, but it is generally agreed that it was west and north of the great bend in the Niger River, so that it stood as a kind of outpost in the desert for the transmission to the Sudan of goods from the south Moroccan city of Sijilmassa. The rulers of Ghana were pagan throughout its history, although Moslems were welcomed as traders and held important official posts. The capital was divided into two distinct parts, a Moslem city and a pagan city. From El-Bekri's account, it is clear that Islam had spread to the ruling class of other kingdoms of the western Sudan as far west as the Senegal Basin, and eastward to the region of Kukia or Kaokao on the lower Niger, the center of the later Songhoi empire. Ghana became engaged in a struggle with the Almoravids in the eleventh century. These Almoravids were a Berber group from north of the Senegal who, moved by the familiar combination of religious reforming zeal and desire for plunder, finally advanced into Spain, for a time controlling a vast empire, stretching from the Sudan almost to the Pyrenees. They captured Ghana, which subsequently lost most of its commercial as well as political importance although it was not abandoned until the fourteenth century.

With the decline of Ghana, empire and trade both moved to the east and the hegemony which it had enjoyed passed to the Mandingo empire of Mali. Its racially Negroid rulers spoke a Mandingo dialect, affiliated with the western Sudanese linguistic stock. Its capital, whose exact location is disputed, was certainly somewhere on the Niger, southwest of the great bend. The great commercial center, however, was now Timbuctoo, which, located on the Niger bend, was beginning to establish the reputation for learning and commerical prosperity that made it eventually a name to be conjured with in Europe. The height of its prosperity was attained in the fourteenth century, to which period belongs the celebrated pilgrimage of Mansa Musa to Mecca, recorded by contemporary Arab writers, and the visit of the great Moslem traveler, Ibn Batutah, to Timbuctoo and to the Mandingo capital.

The Mandingo empire, in its turn, entered a period of decline and its position of leadership fell to the Songhoi, formerly a vassal state. In 1468, the Songhoi ruler, Sonni Ali, entered Timbuctoo and under his successor, Askia-El-Hajj, the Songhoi empire became the largest in the history of Negro Africa, extending from the Atlantic almost to Lake Chad and controlling the important oases of the western Sahara. Timbuctoo, also, attained its greatest intellectual importance during the sixteenth century, especially the university associated with Dyingerey Bey, the great Mosque.

In 1590, a trans-Saharan expedition, launched by the Sultan of Morocco, put an end to the Songhoi empire and with it to the prosperity of Timbuctoo and the pre-eminent position enjoyed for so long by Negro political units in the Niger area. The Moroccan pashas' power soon declined until it was limited to the city of Timbuctoo. The distant ties with Morocco were dissolved and the activities of the Moroccan soldiery, which deposed and set up pashas at will, prevented the re-establishment of public security and the remarkable safety of travel in these regions noted by such earlier travelers as Ibn Batutah.

As a consequence of this situation, the main lines of trade moved more eastward to the Hausa States, a series of city units bound together by language and traditions of common origin for the ruling class, but without any wider political organization. Native records, if their chronology is to be trusted, put the founding of these States in the eleventh century. Subsequently, the rulers of most of them became at least nominally Moslem. For a time, the western Hausa States were under the rule of the Songhoi Empire, when it was at the zenith of its power under Askia-el-Hajj early in the sixteenth century. The great period of prosperity for the Hausa States dates from the Moroccan conquest of Songhoi, after which the route from the great Hausa cities of Kano and Katsina to Tripoli became the chief avenue of trans-Saharan commerce.

The last important political events in the western Sudan before the advent of the European colonial powers involve the people known variously in the literature as Ful, Fula, Peul, Fulani, and Fellata. An essentially pastoral people, they spread, in historic times, eastward from the Senegal basin in scattered groups, often of considerable size, as far east as Waldai, almost half the distance across the entire African continent. All through these regions they lived as politically impotent, often oppressed groups. Some, at least, became enthusiastic and learned Moslems, while others stayed in the bush as pagans or near-pagans. At the beginning of the nineteenth century under the leadership of Osman-dan-Fodio, and a decade later in the Niger basin under Ahmadu, they proclaimed a holy war against the existing political rulers of the Sudan, whom they called pagans. This crusade was, in general, successful and two great confederations were organized, one, in the east, embracing the Hausa States in a loose confederation with its capital at Sakato, and the other at Hamdallahi in the upper basin of the Niger. These political aggregates were in the process of dissolution when the European colonial powers appeared upon the scene. There were other important political units in the western Sudan in the period under consideration: for example, the cluster of kingdoms with related rulers, the most important of which was Mossi, in the basin of the Volta River south of the Songhoi Empire. The Mossi remain stubbornly resistant to Islam up to the present day and have formed a bulwark against the spread southward to the frost belt of the Guinea Coast. Another notable kingdom is that of Kanem, later Bornu, on the shores of Lake Chad. It has existed with many vicissitudes from the eleventh century, according to native records. Its ruler was converted to Islam in the twelfth century. At times, this kingdom has been of enormous extent and at one time it controlled a portion of the Hausa States. It successfully resisted the Fulani onrush in the nineteenth century, but finally succumbed to Zubeir Pasha's lieutenant, Rabeh, just before the arrival of the French. In the central Sudan, we find the kingdom of Bagirmi, southeast of Lake Chad, Wadai, east of the same lake, and further east still, Darfur, within the boundaries of the Anglo-Egyptian Sudan. All these kingdoms are authenticated by native records from a more recent period than those of the western Sudan, approximately from the sixteenth century onward, but it is probable that at least small material states existed in this area previously. There are local traditions to this effect almost everywhere.

There are a number of theories in regard to the great empires of the Sudan whose history we have just traced in general outline, attributing their origin or their main features to Caucasian influence.

One intepretation in regard to these kingdoms is that they owe their existence to the application of Mohammedan political patterns by racially Caucasoid groups. An early and explicit statement is that of Leo Africanus, the well-known sixteenth century scholar and traveller, who attributes the introduction of political organization in the Sudan to the Berber Moslem Almoravids. In a statement which forcibly reminds us of the pre-Rousseau conception of the primitive we read:

> Our ancient chroniclers of Africa, to wit, Bishri and Meshudi, knew nothing of the land of the Negroes but only the region of Guechet and Cano, for in their times all other places of the land of the Negroes were undiscovered. But in the year of the Hegira 380, by means of a certain Mohumetan which came into Barbary, the residue of the said land was found out, being as then inhabited by great numbers of people which lived a brutish and savage life, without any king, governour, commonwealth or knowledge of husbandry.

Clad they were in skins of beasts; neither had they any peculiar wives
... using hairy skins for beds and each man choosing the leman he
had any fancy unto ... These Negroes were first subject to Joseph, the
founder of Morocco, and afterwards under the five nations of Libya.[1]

Elsewhere we find less baldly stated the suspicion that these kingdoms
are essentially the result of Moslem influence. Thus Delafosse, a standard
authority, tells us that there are legitimate doubts concerning the purely
Negro character of the great Sudanese kingdoms, by way of contrast with
Mossi, which, in his opinion, is purely Negro. The writer in the *Enciclopedia
Italiana* mentions "the very interesting hypothesis of the purely Negro origin of
these monarchical institutions." P. C. Meyer in his historical survey of the
Sudan distinguishes four periods. The first is that of the numerous small
heathen kingdoms, which last into the eleventh century, to be followed by the
large empires coincidental with the spread of Islam in the Middle Niger. He
thus attributes the growth of large states, even if not of political institutions in
general in this area, to the influence of Islam.

All these views attributing, in whole or in part, the organization of the
large, west Sudanese kingdoms to direct Moslem influences are easily refuted
by reference to the known facts about these kingdoms, some of which have
already been adduced. On grounds of simple chronological priority, it can
be pointed out that each one of them had centuries of stable political organization and wide territorial expansion before the introduction of Islam among
the ruling group. For the first of these, Ghana, the evidence is indisputable,
inasmuch as its rulers were never converted and it remained pagan throughout
its history. So also for Mali, Songhoi, and Bornu the evidence is clear that
there was a period of pagan political rule before the introduction of Islam and
that the continuity of political institutions was not seriously interrupted by
the conversion. The Negro character of Mossi, which was never converted, was,
we have seen, emphasized by Delafosse, who is willing to entertain theories of
Islamic origin regarding the other states. Indeed, the changes wrought by Islam
in the domain of political institutions in this area is very small, and it is
striking, that, despite the sparseness of the sources at our disposal, the
essentially African nature of Sudanese kingship stands out clearly.

Thus, in the brief account of Ghana by el-Bekri, we find the throwing of
dust on the head in greeting the king, the use of royal "interpreters" to repeat
everything the king says, the beating of drums to summon a royal audience,
the sacrifice of the king's attendants at his death, and sacrifices to the royal
ancestors. All of these are clearly African traits and none of them are found
in the Islamic kingdoms of North Africa and the Near East. In the Mandingo
Empire of Mali, we have likewise the throwing of dust on the head in
saluting the king, which struck Ibn Batutah as a characteristic Negro custom,
the use of royal "interpreters," and the important position accorded to the

---

[1] By Joseph is meant Yusuf ibn Tashfin, the Almoravid leader. The five nations of
Libya are the Berbers. In this division, Leo follows Ibn-Khaldun.

king's wife. Similarly in the Songhoi State we find the throwing of dust on the head as a mode of salutation and the office of royal interpreter. We hear on one occasion that a prince regards as a deadly insult the threat on the part of a rival to destroy his drum. This points clearly to the widespread African connection between royal position and the possession of specific drums. In the Songhoi Empire there is present, at least since the time of Askia-el-Hajj, fixed territorial division, each with an associated title and specific privilege and duties, another usual feature of African Monarchial organization absent in the Moslem areas of the Near East. In Bornu, we have, in addition to most of the features already mentioned, the institution of the queen-mother and the queen-sister, each with her own court and officials, which finds its exact parallel in the Uganda kingdom of East Africa.

If the evidence for the essentially Negro character of these kingdoms is so clear, one may well ask why there has been so much hesitation or opposition to this view. Outside of the general tendency to deprecate the Negro which permeates the literature on Africa, there are certain superficial data which lend credibility to a theory of direct Moslem origin. For example, the use of the term "Sultan" and "Vizier" in the literature gives the impression that we are dealing with Moslem political institutions of the Near Eastern type. Our suspicions should be aroused regarding the validity of such deduction when we read that "in Dar-Fur the use of the term Sultan is connected with the possession of certain drums." Sometimes Sultan, Emir and Vizier have been borrowed into a language of the Sudan from Arabic, most frequently as an alternative to an already existing native word. More frequently, when we find such expressions in secondary sources, they have been drawn from Arab accounts in which Sultan would designate any ruler and Vizier any minister. It no more indicates Moslem origin or influence than the title "king of the Zulus" found in an English account would indicate the British origin of Zulu kingship. Occasionally an Arabic term is borrowed and a new office created, but even in this instance, the institutions remain African. Typical in this respect is the Hausa adoption of the word *waziri*, "*vizier*," to designate an additional position of nobility. It is but one of a large number of varied titles without any special pre-eminence. The *waziri*, just as other Hausa noblemen, has his territorial fief and fixed prerogatives. The addition of this office has not produced any significant alteration in the existing political system. The only important Moslem influences on political life of which I am aware is the Fulani establishment of an Amiru l-Mu'minina, "Commander of the Faithful," on the model of the caliphate, and the office of the Alcali or judge (from the Arabic *gadi*), who judges in accordance with Moslem law in many Sudanese states.

That it is through Islamic influence that writing was introduced into this region and with it a certain development of intellectual life is indisputable. Impressed with the contributions of Negro intellectuals, particularly those of Timbuctoo and Jenne during the Songhoi period, there is a tendency to attribute all developed institutions, whether intellectual, economic, or political, to Moslem influence. However, as the data already adduced indicate, political organization was Negro in structure before Islam and remained so after its diffusion through the Sudan. It is not legitimate to argue from the undoubted Moslem influence on intellectual life to a Moslem origin for political. So, in early Medieval England, intellectual life was Latin and Christian, but political organization was based on Germanic tradition.

Perhaps more than any other factor, the native African traditions regarding the origin and migration of ruling groups have lent credibility to theories of Moslem origin. These reports have not usually been treated with the scepticism they deserve. In spite of Mohammed's admonition that 'the noblest among you is the most pious," the view has always had some currency in Islam that nobility depends upon nearness of kinship to the Prophet. Hence, the constant attempt in the Islamic world to demonstrate descent from the Prophet or at least from a well-known Arab tribe or ruling family. For this reason, the accounts of migrations from Arabia and of Arabian descent found among practically all Moslem Negro ruling groups are to be discounted. Thus, the founder of the old Sefawa dynasty of Bornu is said to be the celebrated Saif ibn Dhu Yazan, a pre-Islamic ruler of Yemen in southwestern Arabia. The first ruling house of the Songhoi attribute their origin to the same area. The pre-Fulani rulers of the Hausa states trace their descent from Abu-Yazid of Baghdad. Many other examples could be cited of this general tendency. It is amusing to note what short shrift the Arabist, Basset, gives to some of the most cherished views of Africanists on the subject, in his reply to the African student, Carbou's queries regarding the credibility of these accounts. Whenever the specific individuals mentioned in native tradition as ancestors are known from Arabic literary documents, the evidence is clear that they died in the Near East without ever having migrated to Sudan. Were all African native accounts of this nature true, Near Eastern history would be filled with the exodus of eminent men to the Sudan. But not a trace of these movements is authenticated from Arab sources.

The vogue of these stories in the Sudan is so great that they have on occasion been adopted by non-Moslem Negro groups. The royal house of the pagan, Mossi, tell the same story as their Moslem Songhoi neighbors concerning their origin from Za-Alyamen, a migrant from Yemen in Arabia. It is a corollary of this view of migration from Arabia that in at least two instances, Ghana and Songhoi, we hear of an early dynasty of "white kings." Both of these accounts lack all historic authentication and so must be accepted or rejected along with the accounts of migration from Arab with which they are connected.

Since writing did not exist in this area until the introduction of Islam, all our written accounts come from those areas which are already Islamic and "they try to forget ... their predecessors, because they are ashamed of the pagan period." Our narratives are all written by members of the learned class, who are the most enthusiastic Moslems among the population and anxious to develop the theme of the connection with the land and kin of the Prophet.

An allied but distinct point of view does not specifically stress Moslem influence but attributes the establishment of these kingdoms to Negroes with a large Caucasoid racial admixture which supplies the leaven for cultural achievement. This view is clearly stated by A. H. Keane. "Standing out in marked contrast to all these primitive peoples are the relatively civilized Hamito-Negro or Semito-Negro nations, such as the Mandingo, Songhois, and Fulahs in the west; the Hausas, Kanuri, Baghirmi, and Mabas of the Wadai in the centre; and the Furs and Nubians in the east.... From these striking contrasts between the pure Negro and the mixed Negroid peoples, the inference has been drawn that the Negro, left to himself, remains a Negro in every sense of the term, and without miscegenation is incapable of making any advances beyond a low social and intellectual level." Another statement of similar import is that of Meyer that "all these data point to the impulse for the building of States originating from Hamito-Semites who influenced the Negroid elements by mixing with them." Seligman, in his standard work "Races of Africa," describes this process in the following terms: "The mechanism of the origin of Negro-Hamitic peoples will be understood when it is realized that the incoming Hamites were pastoral Caucasians—arriving wave after wave—better armed as well as quicker witted than the dark agricultural Negroes." In the same work, we find the common view that the Bantu languages are the result of a linguistic mixture between a Hamite stratum and a Negroid stratum similar to the Sudanic languages of West Africa, while the Masai and similar pastoral peoples of East Africa are called half-Hamites and stated to reflect an even greater Hamitic linguistic, cultural, and racial preponderance.

It will be observed in these statements that there are both a physical anthropological and a linguistic side to the question. Negroes are declared to be incapable of founding advanced political structures except through physical mixture with racially Caucasoid groups. Such groups are identified with those Negroids or half-Negroids who speak either Hamitic or Semitic languages, presumably imposed on them by Caucasoid speakers of these languages.

With considerable diffidence, inasmuch as I am not a physical anthropologist, I should like to enter a demurrer to the views which dominate the literature on the physical anthropology of the Negro. We are told that only the "forest Negro of the forest zone of the West African Guinea Coast is the true Negro," since it is only here that the dark-skinned, fuzzy haired, broad-nosed and dolichocephalic type is found in his pure form. All other Negroid types are the result of intermixture with Caucasoid peoples, producing such varieties as the Nilote, the Nilo-Hamite, and the Bantu-speaking groups which dominate the southern part of the continent. It would seem just as logical to assert that only the Nordic show the full Caucasoid characteristics of blond hair, blue eyes and tall stature. We could then attribute classical and oriental civilization to Negroid intermixture and state that the leaders of western European civilization—England, France, and Germany—were only so by virtue of admixture with Negroid types producing the Alpine and Mediterranean types found in large or dominant numbers in England, France and Germany.

Even were we to restrict the term Negro to those of the West African tropical forests, we would find such important Negro political structures as the kingdoms of Dahomey, Ashanti, Benin, and the Yoruba states as evidence of the political abilities of the "pure Negro."

The linguistic side of this doctrine is notable chiefly for its reliance on an extension of the term Hamitic, particularly by Meinhof, to many languages beyond the established Hamitic groups of ancient Egyptian, Berber, and Cushite langauges of Ethiopia, without adequate and convincing proof of linguistic relationship. A conspicuous case is Fulani. The political successes of this people have perhaps been the point of departure, whether consciously or not, for declaring them to be Hamitic. The linguistic evidence, which would take us too far afield to discuss here, clearly points to Fulani being simply another of the vast group of West-Sudanese languages, all spoken by Negroes. It shows special points of resemblance to the Serer language of Gambia and the Biafada of Portuguese Guinea. Again, the view espoused by Meinhof, that the Bantu languages are a result of intimate fusion of Hamitic with languages of the Sudanese "Negro," is in a relation of mutual support to the doctrine that the Bantu physical type is the result of admixture between Negroes and Hamitic speaking Caucasoids. Here again the technical linguistic problems cannot be treated adequately at this point. However, languages do not "mix" after this fashion, or at least such views are looked upon with extreme suspicion by linguists as unusual and requiring real proof, which has not been offered in this case. The clear fact seems to be that the Bantu languages are related to those of the Western Sudan and that the "Hamitic" features are illusory.[2] Likewise, the Masai and other so-called half Hamitic languages are not Hamitic at all, but clearly related to the Nilotic languages of the Shilluk and other tribes of the White Nile as well as the Nuba farther north.[3]

The independence of language and physical type is a fundamental theoretical achievement of contemporary anthropology and there is no wish to sacrifice it here. It is interesting to see, however, that if we grant the premise that Hamitic and Semitic speech are evidence of Caucasoid racial descent, we can then ask what has been accomplished by peoples of the Sudan who speak indisputable Hamitic and Semitic languages. If infusion of the precious Hamitic and Semitic 'blood' has such civilizing effects on the Negro, it should be most manifest in those groups which speak languages of the Semitic and Hamitic group. Actually, the record is most uninspiring. The Tuareg, a Berber Hamitic group, has been present in the Niger bend region since the Middle Ages in large numbers without overcoming surrounding Negroid groups, or founding any political structure of note. The Moroccans, Semitic-speaking

[2] This relationship has been noted particularly by D. Westermann without affecting standard doctrine regarding African linguistic relationship. Proof of this extremely obvious connection will soon be published by the writer.

[3] This was clearly demonstrated by G. W. Murray (1920) in a common-sense demonstration.

Caucasoids, as we saw, conquered the Songhoi Empire, but brought in its stead chaos. The Tunjur Arabs, found throughout the central Sudan, were apparently either pagan or very loosely Moslem Arabs, and yielded political sovereignty to the Mohammedanized Negro people of the Fur in Dar-Fur and of the Negro Maba of Wadai. Other Arabs of the Sudan, for example, the Shuwa of Lake Chad, have been politically impotent and contributed scarcely anything to Islamic culture. All this is not meant to prove that Hamitic and Semitic speaking peoples in Africa are incapable of political organization, but to demonstrate the *reductio-ad-absurdum* of the coventional arguments.

Our conclusion, then, is that the great empires of the Sudan were instances of a widespread Negro pattern of political structure and that, stimulated by the trans-Saharan trade and taking advantage of the open terrain afforded by the Sudan, territorial organization on a wide scale and of considerable stability became possible.

Finally, the remarkable degree to which Negro institutions survived under a Moslem exterior may be documented from the example of Dar-Fur. Although under Moslem rulers since approximately 1600, all of the characteristic features of Negro kingship already enumerated were found in a flourishing condition by Nachtigal in the middle of the nineteenth century, although the country was then raided by the Mohammedan governor of the Sudan. There was a keeper of the sacred stool, as in the West African kingdom of Ashanti. The Queen Mother had her own troops and courtiers. An aboriginal compilation of customary law was in alternative use in place of the Moslem Maliki law. The great annual festival was the feast of the drums in the Mohammedan month of Rajab. On this occasion, the slaves devoted to each of the past kings sacrificed animals to the royal souls. For those kings who were Mohammedans, learned men read chapters of the Koran, while, for the ancient pagan line, all proceeded to a pre-Islamic sacred place at Jebel Kora where animals were sacrificed to the pagan royal ancestors.

The skins of the slain animals were employed to cover anew the royal drums for the succeeding year. These are just a few of the observances which convince us that the institution of Darfur resemble those of Ashanti, Dahomey, Uganda, and other Negro kingdoms in a thoroughgoing fashion.

There are indications that the traits of Negro political structure also continued with great persistency under a Christian façade in Ethiopia and under Egyptian influence in ancient Cush and Meroe.[4]

4 See, for example, the account of king-killing Diadorus's account of the Nubian Kingdom of Napata (iii, 6). King-killing, a widespread African trait, is unlikely to have been borrowed from Egypt in this instance, since it was already abolished in the early dynastic period, more than two thousand years earlier, and is postulated by Egyptologists from such survivals as the Sed-festival.

K. O. Dike

TRADE AND POLITICS IN THE NIGER DELTA

In Trade and Politics in the Niger Delta, 1830–1885, *the African scholar K. O. Dike produced a tour de force based upon years of work in English colonial archives and a thorough mastery of local African oral tradition. In the passages reprinted here, K. O. Dike examines the political and social structure of the city states of the Niger Delta, and describes the mechanics of the slave trade in this part of the Guinea Coast.*

FROM Lagos to the Cameroons lies the low country of the Nigerian coastal plain. The Niger Delta occupies the greater part of this lowland belt and may be described as the region bounded by the Benin river on the west and the Cross river in the east, including the coastal area where the Cameroon mountains dip into the sea. It covers an area of some 270 miles along the Atlantic coast and is 120 miles in depth. The two mouths of the Niger are the Forcados and the Nun, but the rivers Benin, Brass, Bonny, Kwa-Ibo, the Cross, and other separate streams are linked to these by a labyrinth of creeks and lagoons. "I believe," wrote Mary Kingsley, "the great swamp region of the Bight of Biafra [Niger Delta] is the greatest in the world, and that in its immensity and gloom, it has a grandeur equal to that of the Himalayas." [1] There remains, however, the intriguing paradox that this area, notorious among nineteenth-century travellers for its unhealthiness, with a soil too poor "to produce a ton of oil" as Macgregor Laird put it in 1832, and practically uninhabited by the tribes of the Nigerian interior before the Portuguese adventure to the Guinea coasts began had become by 1830 the greatest single trading area in West Africa.

It was as navigable waterways that the rivers of the Niger Delta became so important in the economic history of modern Nigeria. A canoe could be taken from Badagry on the west coast of Nigeria to Rio del Rey in the east without going into the open sea. This "Venice of West Africa," as Winwood Reade

From K. O. Dike, *Trade and Politics in the Niger Delta, 1830–1885* (London: Oxford University Press, 1956), pp. 19–21, 30–41. Reprinted with permission of the Clarendon Press, Oxford.

[1] *Travels in West Africa* (1897). Cf. A. C. C. Hastings, *The Voyage of the Day Spring* (London, 1857), pp. 73–74.

described it in 1867, linked together not only places in the Delta but towns and villages along the 2,600 miles of the Niger valley. "The Oil Rivers are chiefly remarkable among our West African possessions," wrote Sir Harry Johnston in 1888, "for the exceptional facilities which they offer for penetrating the interior by means of large and navigable streams and by a wonderful system of natural canalization which connects all the branches of the lower Niger by means of deep creeks. There are hardly any roads existing in the Delta; the most trivial distance that a native requires to go, he generally achieves in a canoe." This water system links the Delta with "the markets and sources of production far inland." [2]

Geographically the Delta divides easily into two sections. The northern section is comparatively drier and higher than the area of swampland to the south. Even in the lowland belt the dank and humid surroundings are interspersed with vast stretches of dry land, a maze of islands intersected by creeks and rivers, and on these settlements have been built. Some of these southern colonies, being placed on points of control for internal and external commerce, quickly grew in importance and became the trading centres on the Atlantic seaboard. Just as the growing volume of Atlantic commerce drew Europe irresistibly to the lands of Guinea, so the natives of tribal areas, impelled by the urge "to traffic and exchange," flocked to the coast to do trade. From now on the coastland became the frontier of opportunity. As in medieval West Africa trade with the Arabs by way of the Sahara caravans led to an outcrop of commercial cities on the Niger bend such as Jenne, Timbuktu, Gao, and others, so the rise of Lagos, Accra, Dahomey, and the Delta states must be attributed to the development of maritime commerce. The seaboard trading communities which emerged with this commerce transcended tribal boundaries; their history belongs both to Atlantic and to tribal history.

Every item of the export trade in the ports of Biafra was a product of the tribal interior, and the carrying-trade on which the prosperity and greatness of the Delta states rested linked their fortunes decisively with those of the producers in the tribal locations. The coastal communities united in their blood and institutions elements of the Atlantic and tribal societies which fashioned them. Each of the adventurous groups that pioneered these settlements was different in language and culture and in political and social organization. The Jekris of Warri (on the Benin river) could not understand the Ijaws on the Brass river. These migrants represented many Nigerian tribes in movement— Ibos, Binis, semi-Bantus from the Cameroons Highlands, Ijaws, Efiks, Ibibios, to name only a few and the most important. This fact must be noted. It helps to explain the haphazard way in which the Delta communities grew. Down to the nineteenth century this movement of populations continued. Opobo, the main centre of trade and politics in the eighties, was founded in 1870....

In the peopling of the Delta the points occupied by the migrants were widely separated from each other. Usually they were islands like Bonny

[2] F.O.84/1882, Memorandum by Consul H. H. Johnston on the British Protectorate of the Oil Rivers, Part II.

dominating the mouth of a river which linked the hinterland to the sea. In time each community developed the independence and individualism so typical of island dwellers. Every river mouth, every centre of trade, and, in some areas, every town had its overlord. Each city-state had all the apparatus of rule which enabled it to maintain law and order, administer justice, make war and peace, organize and prosecute peaceful commerce for four centuries. The term "city-state" as applied to the Delta communities embraces not only the settlements on the coast but also their extensions (by way of trading posts) in the interior. This is in line with the Greek idea of city which means a community of people rather than an area of territory; for although the Delta trading colonies were all outside her political boundaries, they were indissolubly bound by strong economic ties. Moreover "city-state" is a more appropriate designation than "tribal-state," since the period of migrations disorganized the tribal entities and the slave trade further accentuated the mingling of peoples. In the nineteenth century, therefore, the Delta states were grouped not by considerations of kinship but by contiguity, and in the period under survey citizenship came increasingly to depend not on descent but on residence.

The city-states divide broadly into two political groupings—the monarchies and the republics. The former include Bonny (Ibani), New Calabar (Kalabari), and Warri, not to mention petty monarchies such as those of Bell Town and Aqua Town in the Cameroons. The republics were in reality single trading units with divided political authority as in Old Calabar, Brass, and the Cameroons. Bonny and Old Calabar best illustrate these two types of political systems.

Bonny was the economic and political centre of the Niger Delta during the greater part of the nineteenth century, and even its successor from the 1870's, Opobo, was an offshoot of the older kingdom. The former has always been a monarchy as far as can be ascertained; a list of her kings from the foundation of the monarchy to the end of the nineteenth century was recorded by A. G. Leonard in 1906.[3] A more detailed list and a fuller account of their

[3] Leonard, op. cit., p. 47.

Kings of Bonny

1. Alagbariye.	6. Edimini.
2. Opkraindole.	7. Kamalu.
3. Opuamakubu.	8. Dappa (Great or Opu).
4. Okpara-Ashimini.	9. Amakiri
5. Ashimini.	10. Appinya.

11. Warri

King Holliday Owsa
           (Igbani.   Short quartumvirate—
           (Bupor.   all princes of the blood.
12. Perekule, (Ipor.
    afterwards King Pepple.

13. Foubra (Agbaa).	16. Bereibibo.
14. Foubra) Sons of	17. Dappa (William).
15. Opobo) Perekule.	18. George.

reigns, corroborating Leonard, is preserved by the descendants of the Pepples at Bonny.[4] If, as is generally supposed, the monarchy was founded around the mid-fifteenth century, in 1830 that institution was almost 400 years old.

The reigning king in that year was Opubu (of the House of Pepple). The first king of this House was Pelekule or Perekule (anglicized Pepple) and although Opubu was the third of the Pepples he was the fourteenth king (Ama-nya-na-bo) in an unbroken line of succession. The monarchy was therefore a deep-rooted institution at Bonny. Moreover, the Royal House of Pepple which reigned from the eighteenth to the nineteenth centuries had a knack of producing remarkable men. In the Pepples Bonny found, New Calabar excepted, a focal point for unity and strength unknown to the other Delta communities.

Impressed by the might of the Pepple monarchs European observers have tended to credit them with autocratic powers; indeed, Adams's statement in 1790 that the power of the king of Bonny "is absolute" and that "the surrounding country, for a considerable distance, is subject to his dominion" represents the general contemporary opinion.[5] Nor was this view altogether unfounded. The Pepples sought by alliance and conquest to gain ascendancy over the entire Delta and the markets of the interior. In this they well nigh succeeded but for the stubborn opposition of the kingdom of the Kalabaris (New Calabar) which refused to accept subjection. The recurrent wars between the two kingdoms not infrequently ended in the defeat of New Calabar, yet that state's powers of recuperation were demonstrated time and again.

In 1790 it was reported that the king of Bonny had "destroyed the town of New Calabar twice," had compelled its "inhabitants...to take their merchandise to Bonny for sale," and had not permitted them "to have any communication whatsoever with the shipping." [6] In 1826 Captain Owen noted that one of the titles of the reigning Pepple was "Conqueror of the Callabar," a title "he derived from his grandfather, who subdued that country, but which has long since been independent, although the present king threatens again to reduce it to his dominion." [7] Notwithstanding this threat New Calabar was a thriving independent state in 1830.

Even in home affairs the powers of a Bonny king were limited by the country's constitution. This did not altogether escape the attention of contemporary European observers and one of them made this significant comment: "The Kings of Bonny, although in many respects they appear to exercise absolute power unrestrained by any fixed principles, may be properly termed heads of an aristocratic government. This is evinced by having a grand palaver house, in which they themselves presided, but the members of which composed

---

[4] In 1949 I was permitted to study several well-preserved documents and other relics relating to the Bonny monarchy in the possession of the present Head of the Royal House.

[5] Talbot, *Peoples of Southern Nigeria*, i. 250–1.

[6] Ibid., p. 250.

[7] Owen, op. cit., p. 345.

of the great chiefs or great men, were convened and consulted on all matters
of state urgency." [8] The king was nothing if not king in council, and as the
analysis of the social organization will reveal the king's powers were everywhere
limited by the peculiar political system of the city-states.

In contrast to the hereditary monarchies of the Pepples at Bonny and
of the Amakiris at New Calabar there was the divided authority of the Efik
community on the mouth of the Cross river. At Old Calabar, from the
eighteenth century onwards, there were four trading towns—Creek Town,
Henshaw Town, Duke Town, and Obutong, each—except on questions of
common interest—under separate and independent rulers. As an eyewitness
put it in 1847, "The towns of Calabar, are, in fact, a number of small republics,
each with its own chief and council, united only by the Egbo confraternity." [9]
The Egbo Society was a sort of freemasonry, a secret cult, uniting the ruling
classes in all four towns; membership was open to freemen only. This "confraternity" came into being because the nobility felt the need for "a bond
of union," a "supreme authority" for "enforcing peace and order among equals
and rivals," and for safeguarding the interests and privileges of the nobility. "It
seemed especially designed to keep" women, slaves, and the masses of the
population in subjection. [10]

For all practical purposes the Egbo Order was the supreme political power
in Old Calabar; it exercised not only executive and legislative functions but was
the highest court of appeal in the land. Its President became the first citizen
of the community. Hutchinson reported that at Duke Town (the seat of Egbo
power) there was in 1856 a "Palaver-House, a species of senatorial forum, where
all matters public or private, are discussed and settled by the Egbos." [11] Similar
organizations existed in communities of divided authority, such as the Cameroons, primarily to protect the privileges of the nobility against the insurrection
of the lower orders.

The pivot of Delta social organization was the "House System" or "House
Rule." This peculiar constitution is common to all the trading states and was
the direct result of the trade with the Europeans. As used in the Delta it is a
European term and a descriptive one at that. The mixture of peoples often
meant that African law and custom vanished and a new law and order was
evolved based partly on African precedent and experience and partly on the
lessons of the contact with Europe. In its full development the House became
at once a co-operative trading unit and a local government institution. As a
rule every trader of any importance owned so many slaves bought from various
tribes. These, along with the trader's family, formed the nucleus of a "House."
Even in the hey-day of the slave traffic the Delta middlemen retained the best
slaves in their personal service, some of whom manned the fleet of canoes

[8] H. Crow, op. cit., pp. 215–16.
[9] Waddell, op. cit., p. 314.
[10] Ibid., pp. 313–15.
[11] T. J. Hutchinson, *Impressions of Western Africa* (London, 1853), p. 119.

indispensable for the trade with the interior or engaged in agricultural work on the farms. The smaller Houses numbered anything from 300–1,000 members; others, such as the royal Houses, numbered many thousands. In 1847 King Eyo of Creek Town, Old Calabar, "had in his House many thousand slaves, and four hundred canoes with a captain and crew for every one. Besides his extensive trade, which amounted to several puncheons annually, he employed his people reclaiming waste land, founding towns, and planting farms in well-selected positions which gave him command of the rivers and channels of trade." [12] Along with the king's House there would be scores of smaller Houses, each presided over by a wealthy merchant.

The House system, which grew out of the needs of Delta society, followed, in a measure, the pattern of social organization of the interior tribes. Among the Ibos and Ibibios each town or village is composed of a group or of several groups, at the head of which is the eldest member of the group. Such a group among the Ibos is called "Umunna" and among the Ibibios "Ekpuk," i.e., an extended family. In each group all the members are related by blood. It is significant that with the emergence of the "House" the words "Umunna" and "Ekpuk" disappeared from the vocabulary of the extribal Ibibio and Ibo-speaking peoples in the Delta; in their place we have "Ulo" and "Ufok"— House, expressing the new coast relationship based not on kinship but on common interests and economic necessities. Master and servant, the bond and the free, all became members of one House, a veritable hierarchy, with numerous gradations, each rank with its duties and responsibilities, its privileges and rewards.

But, unlike the "Umunna" and the "Ekpuk" the House system did not make for "excess of democracy"; the House Head, unlike the Elder of the interior, was not just a mere figurehead, registering the people's will. He was in theory absolute, with powers of life and death over his subordinates. How far this power was exercised is another matter. It cannot be denied, however, that the element of autocracy in House rule was very strong: it had to be, particularly if the discordant and often rebellious elements composing a House in the semi-military society of Delta were to be welded into a coherent whole.

Estimates of the House system vary considerably. There are some, like Dr. Jeffreys, who would declare that "the authority of the Head of a House" was based on the principle that "might is right." He spoke of the "iniquitous reign of the Houses" and from his account one would derive the impression that the system was all darkness and no light.[13] It cannot be denied that an element of cruelty and even brutality was ever present. A cruel master could, on occasion, take the life of his slave for very trifling offences. de Cardi enumerated punishments that could be inflicted on the domestic slaves:

> ear cutting in its various stages, from clipping to total dismemberment; crucifixion round a large cask; extraction of teeth; suspension

[12] Waddell, op. cit., p. 320.
[13] Jeffreys, op. cit., pp. 55–62.

by the thumbs; Chilli peppers pounded and stuffed up the nostrils, and forced into the eyes and ears; fastening the victim to a post driven into the beach at low water and leaving him there to be drowned with the rising tide, or to be eaten by the sharks or crocodiles piece-meal; heavily ironed and chained to a post in their master's compound ...and reduced to living skeletons; impaling on stakes; forcing a long steel ramrod through the body until it appeared through the top of the skull.[14]

These speak plainly of the dark side of the system.

Yet, as he himself emphasized, these extremities were resorted to only in exceptional circumstances, and he admitted that the chances of a slave "improving his condition are manifold." While allowing, therefore, that the life of a slave before he "gets his foot on the first rung of the ladder of advance-ment" could be terrible, once he had graduated beyond the domestic hierarchy progress was usually rapid. In the nineteenth century, European observers, who were by no means uncritical of some aspects of House rule, did not over-look its merits. This peculiar system defies definition and does not lend itself to generalization. It cannot be assessed apart from the context of the society which produced it. Delta society in the nineteenth century rested on a founda-tion of slavery; terror and despotism were normal features of a system that had to keep the masses in subjection. Yet if House rule may be judged from its practical results, on the whole it met the needs of the day. "Absolute authority on the one part, and entire subjection on the other, is the theory; but in practice both the authority and subjection are checked and limited in many ways ... the harsh terms master and mistress are not in the Calabar language. The sweet and precious names, father and mother, alone are used to express the relation. The children of both classes (slave and free) grow up together as playmates, and equally regard the Head of the House as their father. In our schools they sat side by side, read in the same classes, and were treated as they deserved, without reference to their relation." [15] Another observer declared that "it is remarkable how clannish the slaves belonging to the same house become. Each one considers that he partakes of the honour of the house, and is zealous in maintaining it. Any slight upon his master or father [the one word 'ete' signifying both] is resented as a personal offence." [16]

The British Consul to the Bight of Biafra, T. J. Hutchinson, declared in 1861 that "in many of the palm oil trading rivers slavery is purely mythical. In Bonny, the men who rule the roost in political debate, as well as on the palm oil change, are of the slave class." [17] "The best thing in it" [the House system], said another, "is that it gives to the poorest boy who paddles an oil canoe a chance of becoming a king." [18] That many slave boys rose to the rank of the

---

[14] M. H. Kingsley, West African Studies (London, 1899), p. 535.
[15] Waddell, op. cit., p. 315.
[16] Goldie, op. cit., pp. 19–20.
[17] Ten Years Wandering Among the Ethiopians (London, 1861), pp. 2–6.
[18] M. H. Kingsley, op. cit., p. 427.

nobility in the city-states is writ large in Delta history of the nineteenth century. Forceful and energetic Ibo slaves such as JaJa and OkoJumbo took advantage of the peculiar constitution of the House system and became the Heads of the Houses to which they were attached.

It was in the interest of every House Head to foster and increase the trade of his people: as trade cannot flourish under conditions of terror, the Heads must have used their absolute power with great discretion and restraint. Discipline might have been severe and brutal in certain cases,[19] but as a general rule, loyalty from the slaves and confidence from the master (father) was the prevalent mood. For the difference between the plantation slavery of the New World and the domestic slavery as practised in the Niger Delta lies in this: whereas in the former the slaves performed, on the whole, an indirect and impersonal service and were regarded as some form of capital goods, in the latter the wealth produced by a slave eventually set him free, for the master knew his slave intimately and the value of his work and rewarded him accordingly. It was this incentive, ever present in the House system, that made it in the nineteenth century an institution full of vitality, flexible, and in a large measure beneficial to all.

The "House" was primarily the unit of local government in the Delta, and as each occupied a separate quarter in the community the Head of the House was responsible for law and order in his section. It followed then that in a place like Bonny the king, who was as a rule the leading merchant in the state, had no direct power over the Houses of his chiefs. He could intervene to resolve a conflict between one house and another, to confirm the election of new House Heads and to determine the rank a chief might occupy in the state. But although he was in direct control of foreign relations, war and peace, and was the initiator of commercial policies, he always acted within his authority as king in council.

The trading organization of the hinterland was closely linked with the Delta states. No tribe in eastern Nigeria achieved a highly centralized political organization in the nineteenth century; and the clans, local government units, recognized few authorities higher than themselves. Although this "excess of democracy" was the characteristic feature of the political organization, it must not be imagined that there were no threads of unity in the commercial and cultural spheres nor that the fragmentation of authority necessarily impeded the flow of trade.

Two types of trading organization operated in the hinterland. The first, centered upon the Aros, obtained mainly in the period of the slave trade. Their influence was based on the Aro Chuku Oracle which was universally respected and feared throughout Iboland, and in fact by every tribe in eastern Nigeria. This Oracle was supposed to reside in the territory of the Aros, a section of the Ibo tribe. In 1854 Baikie wrote of the "noted City of Aro where there is the

---

[19] M. H. Kingsley, op. cit., pp. 533–8.

celebrated shrine of Tshuku [God], to which pilgrimages are made, not only from all parts of Igbo proper, but from Old Calabar, and from the tribes along the coast, and from Oru and Nembe. The town is always mentioned with great respect, almost, at times, with a degree of veneration, and the people say 'Tshuku ab yama,' or 'God lives there.' " [20] Aro people (whom the Ibos call "Umu-Chukwu"—the Children of God) exploited this belief in their Oracle in many ways, principally in order to dominate the life of the region economically, and they made themselves the sole middlemen of the hinterland trade. This they did by establishing Aro colonies along the trade routes of the interior [21]—like the Greeks, the course of whose colonizing expeditions was largely directed by the priests of the Delphic Oracle. In its wake they organized a trading system which had its ramifications throughout practically the whole of the country between the Niger and the eastern side of the Cross river. Every quarter of Aro Town had its "sphere of influence" in matters of trade. "For instance, the country between AroChuku and Awka belonged to the quarters of Utari, Amove and Ndizioggu." [22] Acting as mediators between God and the clans and assuming themselves to be the spokesmen of the Almighty, they held a privileged position throughout the land, erecting what amounted to a theocratic state over eastern Nigeria. Aro colonies became the divinely ordained trade centers in the interior; Aro middlemen the economic dictators of the hinterland. During the time of the slave trade and in the period of legitimate commerce they acquired immense wealth through a monopoly all believed to be divinely appointed, and with wealth came great political influence.[23]

The numerous political units represented by the clans, admirable as organs of local government, proved inadequate for handling matters of common interest such as commerce and justice. A central organization was needed to facilitate inter-tribal trade, and provide a "pax" without which commerce could not flourish.[24] It was this vacuum existing at the centre of the tribal organization that the Aros, working through the medium of their Oracle, filled. The trading settlements they established at the crossing of rivers and at the intersection of the main routes became the "free cities" to which all who

---

[20] Baikie, op. cit., pp. 310–11.

[21] See K. Umo, *The Aro Settlements* (Lagos, 1945). The author traced more than twenty-five of these settlements.

[22] Talbot, *Peoples of Southern Nigeria*, i. 182–3.

[23] The predominant position held by the Aros during the slave-trade period is acknowledged by all sections of Ibo country. Today sites of Aro colonies exist, and although no longer trade routes, are still inhabited by descendants of the Aros. The great Oracle, known to Europeans as "Long Ju Ju," was destroyed by the British in 1900.

[24] In *The Ibo People* S. R. Smith describes the conditions requisite for the establishment and development of oracles. These are (1) A quiet place remote from main routes. (2) Some natural features which inspire the sense of dread, such as rocks, caves, steep valleys with water, groves, or dense bush. (3) A system by which travelling agents get to know local disputes and encourage reference for settlement to their own oracles. (4) An easy and secret method for the disposal of the victims of the oracles. As an example a victim sold in slavery would be announced as having been "eaten" by the Oracle.

wished to "traffic and exchange" safely repaired, international courts where individuals and clans in conflict sought justice from the undisputed authority of the Oracle.[25] "From most parts of the Niger Delta and the Cross River litigants proceed to invoke the aid of the oracle in the settlement of their claims and disputes," wrote Sir Harry Johnston in 1888. That the astute Aros abused the use of this Oracle and diverted it to their own ends must not obscure the need which called it into being.

The position of power the Aros occupied was of course dependent on the universal belief in their Oracle as the supreme deity. This belief they sought by every means at their disposal to sustain. They hired the services of the famous professional warriors of Iboland—"the Abam, Abiriba, Awhawfia, and Edda" (or Ada)—whenever there was fighting to be done—arming these mercenaries with "the guns obtained from the white traders" and "conquered all the people who resisted their influence or killed their agents." [26] Thus to the supernatural powers of the Oracle was added the military might of its adherents. This explains the contemporary fear and dread of the Aro name. Even in the Niger Delta the fear for this hinterland deity was great. "The terror inspired by the threat that if a slave gave trouble to his master he would be sent to Chukwu [the Oracle] was sufficient to enable the numerically inferior people of the Delta to hold thousands of slaves in subjection, and herein probably lies one of the reasons for the establishment and maintenance of the Oracle at Aro-Chukwu." [27]

The intimate link between the interior trade organization and that of the Delta led many writers to suggest that the Aros might have emigrated originally from the Delta itself and founded the towns of Aro-Chukwu "primarily for the supply and forwarding of slaves to the coast," and that the Oracle was a device in the name of religion for attracting people from the surrounding country, and so kept up a steady flow of human beings whose lot was represented as being "eaten by Chukwu." [28] The theories of Aro origin are legion. Their close economic ties with the Delta have never been disputed. There is no doubt that "they sold most of the slaves at Bonny" [29] and that the Obi-Nkita quarter (the leading Aro town) monopolized the trade with that city-state. Thus it was that Bonny became a leading slave market in West Africa.

The system of obtaining slaves by use of oracular devices was fairly widespread in the Ibo country and, apart from the Chukwu at Aro-Chukwu, there were other oracles such as the Agballa at Awka, the Igwe at Umunora in the Owerri district, the Onyili-ora near Nri, and Ogba, a cave in the Nkisi

[25] F.O.84/1882, Memorandum of Sir Harry Johnston on Oil Rivers.
[26] Talbot, *Peoples of Southern Nigeria*, i. 184. Cf. Smith, op. cit., pp. 135–45.
[27] Smith, op. cit., p. 136, where he also states that the Aro Oracle "was some 80 miles from Bonny, 60 miles from Kalabar [New Calabar], and 70 from the mainstream of the Niger above Abo, it was sufficiently remote for its purpose, while at the same time it was in close touch with the dense populations of the Ibo people, and the neighbouring tribes, the Ibibio, Ijo, Isokos, Jekiri, Usobos, and the Benis of the Niger Delta."
[28] Ibid., p. 136.
[29] Talbot, op. cit., pp. 184–5.

stream at Ogbunike in the Onitsha district,[30] all of which merely supplemented the work of the all-powerful Aro Oracle, undoubtedly the dominating power in the country.

The belief that the bulk of the slaves handled in the Atlantic trade were captives from tribal wars or that kidnapping and raids were the normal methods of obtaining the human victims is now seen to be but a half truth when applied to the tribes east of the Niger. The Oracle, directed by the Aros, was the medium through which the slaves exported from Delta ports were largely recruited. As the highest court of appeal, this deity was supposed to levy fines on convicted individuals and groups. These fines had to be paid in slaves who were believed to be "eaten" by Chukwu (the Oracle), although in fact they were sold to the coast middlemen. This recruiting campaign, carefully staged under conditions of awe and reverence, was rarely attended by violence. Only when the injunctions of the Oracle were defied did the Aros, in his name, turn their fierce mercenaries on the offending party. Then the process of terrorizing the victims began and with their superior arms and immense wealth they invariably emerged victorious. But the dominant power of the Oracle was widely understood and rarely opposed, so that the slaves obtained by violence and kidnapping could not have greatly exceeded, and may even have been fewer than, those who surrendered to the dictates of the Oracle. Nevertheless, both methods of recruitment—whether by violence or the invocation of superstitious fears—led to unsettlement and terror, and exposed the interior tribes to exploitation by the middlemen.[31]

[30] Smith, op. cit., p. 135.
[31] In *Tribes of the Niger Delta*, p. 289, Talbot confirmed the statements already quoted and declared that the greatest source of Aro wealth was the slave trade.

Richard R. Wright

NEGRO COMPANIONS OF THE
SPANISH EXPLORERS

Europeans first engaged in the slave trade with sub-Saharan Africa during the latter part of the fifteenth century. Both then and later many Africans were held as slaves in Spain and Portugal. It was not unnatural, therefore, that black bondsmen were to be found in the expeditions that explored the Americas. Richard R. Wright, in his early article, was the first scholar to inform the public of the role of Negroes in the exploration of the New World. Even two generations later his research, except for minor details, has not been superseded.

THE fact seems to be well established that Negroes were introduced into the New World with the first discoverers and explorers. Indeed, there is evidence which leads to the surmise that some of the pre-Columbians may have been Negroes. Peter Martyr, a learned historian and an acquaintance of Columbus, mentions "a region, not two days' journey from Quarequa's territory, in the Darien district of South America, where Balboa, the illustrious discoverer of the Pacific ocean, found a race of black men, who were conjectured to have come from Africa and to have been shipwrecked on this coast.[1] In connection with this statement may be noted a report by the Bureau of Ethnology which describes "early American pottery with physiognomies of decided African lineaments." [2] The late Justin Winsor stated in a letter to the writer that "there is a possible chance that at some early time the ocean currents may have swept across from the Canaries and the African coasts canoes with Guanches and other African tribes from which some considerable strains of Negro blood may have mixed with the pre-Columbian peoples of tropical

Richard R. Wright, "Negro Companions of the Spanish Explorers," reproduced by permission of the American Anthropological Association from *American Anthropologist*, IV, No. 2 (1902), pp. 217–228.

[1] Helps, *Spanish Conquest in America*, I, p. 360.
[2] *Fourth Annual Report*, Bureau of Ethnology, p. 407.

America. The skulls found in caves in the Bahamas seem to be very like those in the early burial places of the Canaries."

The good Bartolomé de las Casas, the "Protector of the Indians," is often charged with the introduction of Negro slavery into this continent.[3] It is claimed that he introduced Negro slaves to relieve the hard-worked natives, and it is charged that "at one inauspicious moment of his life he advised a course which has ever since been the one blot upon his well-earned fame, and too often has this advice been the only thing which has occurred to men's minds respecting him, when his name has been mentioned. He certainly did advise that Negroes should be brought to the New World." "I think, however," wrote Sir Arthur Helps, "I have amply shown in the Spanish Conquest that he [Las Casas] was not the first to give this advice and that it had long before been largely acted upon."[4] It is said again that Las Casas, as early as 1498, with his father, accompanied Columbus and was therefore familiar with the companions of the latter and especially with Ovando, the successor to the Discoverer in the government of the Indies. It was during the year 1501 that Columbus was deposed from the government of the Indies, and he may probably himself have been cognizant of the fact that Negro slaves had been introduced into the new Spanish possessions. But there seems to be no positive evidence either way as to the great admiral's attitude toward the introduction of African slavery into the New World. There is a letter of Columbus in which he refers to Negroes in Guinea, and it is known that he gave an Indian slave to Las Casas' father, but all beyond this seems to be mere surmise.[5]

The year 1501 is the date of the earliest reference in American history to Negroes coming from Spain to America.[6] Sir Arthur Helps, in his Spanish Conquest in America, states that, in the year mentioned, instructions were given to the authorities that while Jews, Moors, or new converts were not to be permitted to go to the Indies or to remain there, "Negroes born in the power of Christians were to be allowed to pass to the Indies, and the officers of the royal revenue were to receive the money to be paid for these permits.[7]

From this time forward Negroes were more or less familiar personages in the West Indies.[8] On September 15, 1505, King Ferdinand of Spain wrote to Ovando, then governor of Hispaniola, a letter of the following tenor: "I will send more Negro slaves as you request; I think there may be a hundred. At each time a trustworthy person will go with them who may share in the gold they may collect and may promise them ease if they work well.[9] Some time prior to this, soon after he had become governor, Ovando had objected to the importation of Negro slaves into Hispaniola on the ground that "they fled

[3] Helps, Spanish Conquest in America, III, p. 210.
[4] Helps, Life of Las Casas, preface.
[5] Ellis in Winsor's Narrative and Critical History, II, p. 304.
[6] Helps, Spanish Conquest, I, p. 180. Irving, History of Columbus, III, p. 162.
[7] Helps, ibid.
[8] Helps. Navarrete, Coleccion, I, p. 233. Herrera, Historia de las Indias, dec. I, lib. 5. Irving, History of Columbus, III, p. 162.
[9] Helps, Spanish Conquest, I, p. 219 (Coleccion de Muñoz, MS., tomo 90).

among the Indians and taught them bad customs and never would be captured." [10]

In 1510, according to Antonio de Herrera, the royal historiographer to Philip II, King Ferdinand informed Admiral Don Diego Columbus that he had given orders to the officials at Seville that they should send fifty Negroes to work in the mines of Hispaniola.[11] The next year, 1511, the king complained in language like this: "I do not understand how so many Negroes have died; take much care of them." [12]

Again, on September 27, 1514, King Ferdinand, in response to a request of the Bishop of La Concepcion, in Hispaniola, that more Negroes should be imported, said that there were already many Negroes and it might occasion inconvenience if more males of the race should be introduced into the island.[13] There seems, therefore, to have been no cessation, but rather a yearly increase in the number of Negroes sent to the New World. On his accession to the Spanish throne, Charles V granted "license for the introduction of Negroes to the number of four hundred." [14] From this time onward the importation of Negroes into the West Indies became a considerable industry, and the monopoly was greedily sought by Cortés and more eagerly bestowed by King Charles in 1523.[15] There were sent to Hispaniola, 1500 (half of these males); to Cuba, 300; to Jamaica, 300, and 500 to the province of Costilla del Oro on the mainland.[16] By 1528 there were in the New World, according to Herrera's account of the Indies, nearly 10,000 Negroes. It is said that the treatment of the Negroes was injudiciously lenient; they had four months' holiday.[17]

In Honduras, in 1539, Francisco de Montejo sent a Negro of his, who knew the Indian language, to burn a native village.[18] In 1554, in Peru, 30 Negroes accompanied a military force of 70 Spaniards, under Francisco Hernandez.[19] In 1541, in Tolanite, a settlement in New Galicia, Mexico, the Indians killed a Negro, "de Bovadilla," perhaps the name of the owner, and robbed him of his cattle and hacienda—his establishment—and everything he had.[20] On April 14, 1559, the *cabildo* or town council of Santiago de Chile, voted to grant a petition of one Tomé Vasquez, a free or enfranchised Negro, by allowing him possession of a lot of land in the town, provided this was found to be vacant and unclaimed.[21] The wording of the record seems to

[10] Herrera, *Historia de las Indias*, dec. I, lib. 5, cap. 12.
[11] Ibid., *Hist. West Indies*, Stevens' trans., I, p. 374.
[12] Helps, *Spanish Conquest*, I, p. 245 (Coleccion de Muñoz, MS., tomo 90).
[13] Ibid., I, p. 491.
[14] Ibid., I, p. 505.
[15] Helps, *Spanish Conquest*, III, p. 210 (Coleccion de Muñoz, MS., tomo 90).
[16] Ibid.
[17] Ibid., tomo 81.
[18] Pacheco-Cardenas, *Coleccion de Documentos de las Indias*, II, 216.
[19] Ibid., III, p. 319.
[20] Ibid., III, p. 37.
[21] *Coleccion de Historiadores de Chile*, Santiago, 1898, XVII, p. 66.

show that Vasquez received precisely the same treatment as the white applicants for permission to settle in the town.

On St. Luke's day, October 18, 1526, Lucas Vasquez de Ayllon died. According to Navarrete he was among the first to bring Negroes to the present confines of the United States.[22] He explored our eastern coast and attempted to found a colony at San Miguel de Gualdape, since known as Jamestown, Virginia.[23] In this colony, under his successor, a Porto Rican, the Negroes were so grievously oppressed that they arose in insurrection against their oppressors and fired their houses.[24] The settlement was broken up and the Negroes and their Spanish companions returned to Hayti, whence they had come. This ended the first introduction and the first insurrection of Negroes on our eastern shores. Thus Hayti, the place where Negro slaves were first introduced into the New World, was strangely enough the first to manifest an awful retribution against human slavery. It would be interesting to know what part Ayllon's fugitive Negroes, in the persons of their descendants, took in the dreadful revolution which swept over that island nearly three centuries later under the lead of Toussaint L'Overture, Dessalines, and their associates. A singular incident connected with Ayllon's expedition along this coast is the fact that he, with the assistance of his Negro slaves, built the first ships constructed on our coast. This fact is made more interesting when it is known that Vasco Balboa had with him some thirty Negroes who in 1513 assisted in building the first ships on the Pacific coast of America.

The introduction of Negroes into the western portion of the United States was about as early as the coming of the Spaniards. George Bancroft thinks that there was no part of the United States into which the Spanish explorers did not land Negroes. Cortés had with him three hundred Negro slaves in 1522.[25] Under date of July 19, 1537, the governor of Mexico wrote: "I have written to Spain for black slaves because I consider them indispensable for the cultivation of the land and the increase of the royal revenue." [26] Also Gustav Adolf Bergenroth, the collector of Spanish papers, has shown that Negroes at an early date were considered and called the "strength and sinew of the western world." [27] The Great Antilles especially had already been crowded with Negroes on the plea that they were sent thither with a view of facilitating the christianization, and to relieve the toil and suffering of the unfortunate natives; [28] but their advent into the western portion of America

---

[22] Shea in Winsor's *Narrative and Critical History*, II, 241.

[23] Ibid. [For a discussion of the location of the settlement of San Miguel, see Lowery, *Spanish Settlements within the Present Limits of the United States*, pp. 448–452.—EDITOR.]

[24] Ibid.

[25] Prescott, *Conquest of Mexico*, III, p. 350.

[26] Pascual de Gayangos, *Calendar of Spanish State Papers*, Col. V. p. 441.

[27] State Papers of Spain in British Museum, collected by Gustav Adolf Bergenroth. Revetus Enys to Secretary Sir Henry Burnet. Paper Col. Entry Bk., vol. XI, p. 82.

[28] Winsor, Letter to author, July 9, 1894.

was fraught with a good deal of concern. Before 1530 there were enough Negroes in Mexico to warrant an attempt at self-liberation from the Spanish yoke.[29] Their plan was to massacre the Indians friendly to the Spanish, form an alliance with the others, elect a ruler, and set up a government for themselves in the City of Mexico. H. H. Bancroft, speaking of this event, says that "the Negroes neither gave nor accepted quarter." [30] Their enterprise, however, failed, the ringleaders being betrayed, captured, and executed. In this connection there is another interesting story of the followers of a certain Bayano, a Negro insurgent captured and sent back to Spain, whose followers in 1570 founded the town of Santiago del Principe.

There is, however, some reason for the belief that many of the Negroes imported by the Spaniards were not savages nor ignorant; that many of them were nominally Mohammedans or Spanish Catholics. One writer mentions his Mandingo servant who could write the Arabic language with great beauty and exactness.[31] The Guinea or Gold-coast Negroes were bold, brave, and liberty-loving, as the history of the Pacific states will attest.

Bandelier says that the most interesting period in the history of the discoveries on the American continent was during that part of the sixteenth century when the efforts of the Spaniards were directed from the already settled coasts and isthmuses into the interior of both North America and South America. It was during this interesting period that certain Negroes connected with the Spanish explorers rendered conspicuous service on various expeditions.[32] Mr. George Parker Winship mentions, in his *Coronado Expedition*,[33] a Negro slave of Hernando de Alarcon who, in the expedition of 1540, was the only one in the party who would undertake to carry a message from the Rio Colorado across the country to the Zuñis in New Mexico when Alarcon wished to open communication with Coronado.

In 1527, some time prior to Coronado's expedition to New Mexico and the buffalo plains, we are introduced to another Negro who was, perhaps, the most conspicuous of those who took part with the Spaniards in the early expeditions and discoveries on this continent. Reference is here made to him who was one of the four survivors of the ill-fated expedition to the New World made by Pamfilo de Narvaez who sailed from Spain, June 17, 1527, having received from King Ferdinand a commission as governor of Florida, Rio de las Palmas, and Espiritu Santo. This is the best authenticated case at hand, however, of a Negro participating in exploring this continent. Estevanico, or Estevanillo, the Negro here referred to, was most likely not the only Negro who accompanied Narvaez from Spain in 1527, but he was the only one whose identity has been made known. That he was the discoverer of the Zuñi Indians and of New Mexico is, I think, a fact now well known. It has often been

---

[29] H. H. Bancroft, *History of the Pacific States*, III, p. 384.
[30] Ibid., II, p. 385.
[31] Bryan Edwards, *History of the British West Indies*, II, p. 72.
[32] Bandelier, Letter of February 4, 1900.
[33] Bureau of Ethnology, *Fourteenth Annual Report*, p. 406.

claimed that Alvar Nuñez Cabeza de Vaca, the treasurer of the ill-starred expedition of Narvaez, was the discoverer of that country; but Bandelier has shown quite conclusively that Cabeza de Vaca never saw New Mexico, and that he was absent from the country at the time of the exploration of the New Mexican territory in 1539.[34] The evidence which this authority adduces to show that the Zuñi Indians and New Mexico were not discovered by Cabeza de Vaca is, in the opinion of the writer, equally conclusive against the claim of discovery by any other man than the Negro Estevanillo. Bandelier's historical researches show beyond doubt that only one of two men can possibly be credited with the discovery—Fray Marcos de Niza or his Negro guide and interpreter, Estevanillo, or Estevanico; for a careful reading of his own narrative does not reveal any evidence upon which the discovery can be attributed to Cabeza de Vaca.

The only claimant worthy of consideration against Estevanillo is the friar Marcos de Niza. Bandelier ably supports Fray Marcos' claim to the honor of the discovery, but this claim can certainly have no foundation except as it is based upon the fact of the guidance and information which Niza received from the Negro Estevanillo. While it is true, therefore, that Estevanillo disobeyed Niza's order to "stop and send messages," it is likewise a fact, supported by all authorities, that Estevanillo saw the territory of New Mexico some days before the arrival of the friar. According to the information, Fray Marcos followed days in the rear of his ambitious guide.

Later historians, in writing of this discovery, have not only ignored any right which Estevanillo, or Estevanico, had to the discovery, but have charged him with undue ambition and avarice. In writing of Fray Marcos, Cortés called the monk "a common impostor" and declared that he claimed to discover countries that he never saw. While it may not be proper to accept this wholesale charge, it is safe to say that Fray Marcos was too far in the rear of his Negro guide to lay claim to the discovery of New Mexico.

Fiske, in his *Discovery of America*, writes rather slightingly, in our opinion, of this interesting episode of American history, laying particular stress on the "illo" or "ico" in Estevanillo's, or Estevanico's, name.[35] Although it would perhaps be improper to charge so distinguished a historian with flippancy in his reference to "poor silly little Steve," [36] it would not, perhaps, be pretentious to suggest that the termination alluded to in Estevan's name does not warrant such a reflection on the man. Indeed, it seems clear that a fair interpretation of the facts related in Dr. Fiske's work (II, pp. 500–508) would warrant the conclusion that a "man [Estevanillo] who visited and sent back reports of a country," is more entitled to the honor of its actual discovery than one who, according to Dr. Fiske's own statement, "from a hill only got a Pisgah's sight of the glories of the country, and then returned with all possible

[34] Bandelier, *Contributions to the History of the Southwestern Portion of the United States*, chap. IV.

[35] Fiske, *Discovery of America*, chap. IV, p. 500.

[36] Fiske, *Discovery of America*, chap. IV, p. 505.

haste"—without having set foot actually within the Cibolan settlements of New Mexico.

Dr. Henry W. Haynes treats Estevanico with greater justice. He says: "The Negro was ordered to advance in a northerly direction fifty or sixty leagues, and to send back [to Fray Marcos] a report of what he should *discover*." [37] This the Negro did; he sent back information that he had *discovered* "a country, the finest in the world." It was Cibola, one of the long-sought-for "Seven Cities." [38] Now, instead of giving credit to his guide, who had been killed in prosecuting his discoveries,[39] Fray Marcos claimed all the honor for himself, and subsequent historians, if they have not sustained the friar have not placed the honor where it belongs.

It is a pity that we have no connected narrative of this important Negro discoverer. An account of his connection with the ill-fated expedition of Narvaez in 1527, and of his association with Marcos de Niza in 1539, may be found in the various writings bearing on this period. But aside from these little is known of his early history. Estevan was born in Azamor,[40] one of the principal cities of Morocco, Africa, and may be supposed to have been about twenty-eight or thirty years of age when he joined the expedition of Narvaez, which sailed from San Lucas de Barrameda, Spain, June 17, 1527. With the first fleet were 506 persons. After landing on the coast of Florida they wandered through the country, harassed by the Indians until they had lost all but 240 of their number; then, about September 22, they set sail, in a number of boats, in the Gulf of Mexico. Narvaez, as usual, proved a poor leader; misfortune befell him and his men. At the end of the year only four survived [41] —three whites and the Negro Estevanico. These four men discovered and landed upon the coast of Texas. They strove to keep together so that they might render mutual aid, but found this to be impossible. For eight years [42] they wandered among the savages, and it is evident that the Negro manifested fully as much tact and ability as the white men for self-maintenance among the savages and for exploration. Each of these unfortunate Spanish wanderers labored as a slave, and all finally became "medicine-men" of distinction among the natives. They are reported to have become so expert in healing the sick that the savages came from great distances to be cured, and crowds followed them from place to place.[43]

[37] Winsor, *Narrative and Critical History*, VII, p. 477.

[38] It was called "Cibola" by mistake, this being the name of the seven Zuñi settlements collectively. The pueblo in ruins near the Zuñi summer village of Ojo Caliente, is the pueblo meant.—EDITOR.

[39] For the Zuñi account of the killing, see Lowery, *Spanish Settlements*, pp. 280, 281.

[40] Buckingham Smith, *Narrative of Alvar Nuñez Cabeza de Vaca*, chap. XXXVIII, p. 123.

[41] Ibid., chaps. XVII and XXXVIII. Bryant and Gay, *Popular History of the United States*, vol. I. Bancroft, *History of the United States*, I, p. 20.

[42] Herrera, op. cit., Stevens' trans., V, p. 105.

[43] Smith, *Narrative of Cabeza de Vaca*, op. cit., chap. XXII, p. 74.

The black explorer was as successful as his white brothers; he became familiar with the Indian dialects and characteristics, and the experience gained in these eight years of wandering afterward proved valuable to him. At the conclusion of their marvelous journey Estevan's three white companions left for Spain,[44] but Estevan remained in Mexico, where he was held in esteem by those who were interested in extending the Spanish dominion.

Accordingly it was not long before Estevan was selected as guide for an expedition into the northern country, a selection which gave him the opportunity of his life. He evidently had a strong ambition to become an explorer and a discoverer, as is shown by the fact that he risked disobedience to instructions in order that he might be the first to find Cibola. The story of the search for this supposed El Dorado is most interesting, but it is sufficient here to say that though he lost his life, the Negro succeeded in discovering the famous "Seven Cities" of the Zuñi Indians of New Mexico.

The importance of the discovery of Estevan to his time, and its influence on the early progress of Spanish America, may be judged from the fact that various expeditions had been planned for this discovery, but had failed. Cortés had vainly spent nearly twelve years in trying to push an expedition into the northern country, and following Estevan's discovery there was a wild desire on the part of explorers to find the now famous Seven Cities of Cibola. Coronado longed to be the discoverer, and he did visit the country the year following the discovery made by Estevan and which resulted in the latter's death. Bandelier, who gives all the credit of the discovery to Niza, asserts that this journey, which he acknowledges to have been led by Estevan, was of the greatest value to Christendom, and to Spain in particular. The value of the discovery was such that we can only rightfully accord to Estevan an important place among the early explorers of America.

It is not inappropriate to add testimony from Sir Clements R. Markham, the noted historian, who writes: "Owing to information brought to Mexico by Cabeza de Vaca in 1528 [1536], the viceroy, Don Antonio Mendoza, determined to send an expedition to search for the powerful towns reported to exist in the north of Mexico. A friar named Marcos de Niza was sent in search of these towns. A Negro named Estevan, who had previously served in the expedition of Cabeza de Vaca, accompanied Niza; and they set out from Culiacan, on the Gulf of California, in March, 1539. Niza and his Negro companion met with a good reception everywhere. They crossed deserts and came to Indians who had never heard of the Spaniards. Here they received tidings that in an extensive plain some days' journey to the north there were several large towns. Niza sent his faithful Negro companion *alone*, and *waited* for his return with news. Estevan sent back word to Niza that he had found the way to the great city called Cibola. Niza then followed; but after a few days he received news from an Indian that Estevan had reached Cibola, but had been killed by the natives. Niza fled back to Mexico. This," concludes the English

---

[44] Herrera, op. cit., Stevens' trans., V, p. 105.

historian, "is one instance of a Negro having taken an important part in the exploration of the continent. Estevan was the discoverer of Cibola," the territory of New Mexico.

It may be asked, Why is it that this Negro's name has remained practically in obscurity for more than three and a half centuries? The answer is not difficult. Until recently historians were not careful to note with any degree of accuracy and with due credit the useful and noble deeds of the Negro companions of Spanish conquerors, because Negroes were slaves, the property of masters who were supposed to be entitled to the credit for whatever the latter accomplished. The object of this paper is to direct attention to this apparent injustice, and if some one more competent will undertake a thorough investigation of the subject, the purpose of the writer will have been accomplished.

William R. Bascom

ACCULTURATION AMONG THE
GULLAH NEGROES

In 1941 Melville J. Herskovits published his path-breaking volume,
The Myth of the Negro Past. He maintained that, contrary to gen-
eral scholarly opinion, substantial survivals of African culture existed
in the culture of the black population of the United States (and
that, indeed, some of these Africanisms had diffused into the culture
of white Americans). Herskovits based his conclusions on substantial
ethnographic work in Africa, the Caribbean, and Brazil, as well as
drawing upon empirical data from the sub-culture of Negroes in the
United States. While it was agreed that the evidence for African
survivals in the Latin-American societies was incontrovertible, con-
troversy raged over his assertions about Negro life in the United
States. Certainly African survivals to the extent that they persist in
this country are greatly attenuated. The strongest evidence for them
exists among the Negroes who live on the Sea Islands along the coast
of South Carolina and Georgia. William R. Bascom, who was a close
associate of Herskovits, has described the cultural traits from Africa
which were retained by these Gullah Negroes. His article should be
supplemented with Lorenzo J. Turner's definitive work, Africanisms
in the Gullah Dialect *(1949).*

T̲HE analysis of the accommodation of African and European customs in
the New World presents a particularly difficult problem in the United States
because the processes of acculturation have gone much farther here than in
other regions. In dealing with the Negro cultures in South America and the
West Indies, the African traits that have been retained are specific enough

William R. Bascom, "Acculturation Among the Gullah Negroes," reprinted by
permission of American Anthropological Association from *American Anthropologist,*
XLIII, No. 1 (1941), pp. 43–50.

and numerous enough to make possible the identification of the tribes whose cultures have been involved. But even among the Gullah in the coastal regions of South Carolina and Georgia,[1] where the Negroes have been as isolated as anywhere in the United States, resemblances to specific African tribes are very rare. For the most part the similarities are to those elements which are common to West Africa as a whole—to the common denominators of West African culture—and not to those aspects of culture which are distinctive of the tribes within that area. It is therefore extremely difficult to determine what particular West African cultures have contributed to the present situation.

It is now recognized that the differences in the general pattern of the cultures of Africa and Europe were not great; in fact their fundamental similarity justifies the concept of an Old World Area which includes both Europe and Africa. There were a number of institutions common to both regions, including a complex economic system based on money, markets, and middlemen, as well as a large number of crafts among which iron-making was important; a well developed system of government based on kings, and courts of law in which cases were tried by specialists (lawyers) and in which ordeals were employed to decide certain cases; a religious system with a complex hierarchy of priests and deities; a common stock of folklore and a common emphasis on moralizing elements and proverbs. Aside from writing, the wheel, the plow, and Christianity, most of the distinctive traits of Western civilization seem to have followed the industrial revolution.

This similarity between the fundamental patterns of Europe and Africa has further complicated the problem of assessing the relative influences of these areas in the culture of the Gullahs. Since most African traits of a specific nature have disappeared, what is to be found is, for the most part, a series of institutions which differ from the European forms only in their African flavor. To a person who is not familiar with West African cultures, it might seem possible to explain Gullah customs entirely in terms of European influence. The resemblances that are to be found might well be rejected as too general and too indefinite to prove diffusion from Africa to the Sea Islands, if taken by themselves. But we have the historical record of contact with Africa through the importation of African slaves into this region, so that the problem becomes not one of proving that there has been contact, but of assessing the importance of a known factor.

The result of the contact of the Negroes with the whites, both in slavery and in the period of freedom, seems to have been that in those cases where there was a difference or a conflict between African and European customs, the African customs have for the most part disappeared. But those institutions which were present in similar forms in both Africa and Europe, while manifesting a great many specifically European details, have retained an African

[1] Field work in Georgia and South Carolina during the summer of 1939 was made possible by a grant-in-aid from the Social Science Research Council of Northwestern University.

stamp and have had a place in Gullah life the importance of which cannot be explained in terms of European forms alone. In these cases the two streams of tradition have reinforced one another.

An excellent example of the operation of this process is to be found in the institution of cooperative work among the Gullahs. In West Africa, cooperative work is a widespread and important institution, which among the Yoruba,[2] for example, takes two forms. There is first of all the *aro* which is a simple labor exchange between two or three farmers who have small families and are too poor to own slaves or "pawns." Such men work a certain amount of time on the farm of one, and then the same amount on the farms of the second and third. The other form of cooperative work is the more spectacular social event, *owe*, in which a man calls upon his friends, relatives, or society members to help him with the work he is required to do for his father-in-law: hoe the fields, thatch the house, build its mud walls, or whatever may be required. On such occasions a large number of men work together while the host directs the activities. Meanwhile the wife, who has called her friends and society together to help her, prepares a large feast for the men with palmwine or gin, if her husband can afford it. In this case there is no attempt to keep track of the amount of work accomplished or time spent, as is done for *aro*.

In Dahomey,[3] besides the cooperative work done by members of the same guild, there is the *dokpwe* which is the equivalent of the Yoruba *owe* or working bee. The *dokpwe* is apparently even more closely associated with the society, however, and it differs in that the host hires a drummer to set the pace for the men working in the field, so that all the workers keep step and finish their rows at the same time. The Yoruba work in a line, so that each man hoes his own row, but they do not work in unison to music, although they are familiar with this procedure from contact with the Hausa. This Dahomean form of cooperative work, complete with hoeing in unison to a drummer, is a pattern which has been retained among other New World Negro cultures. It has been observed by Herskovits in Haiti,[4] by J. C. Trevor in the Virgin Islands,[5] and by Miss Katherine Dunham in Jamaica.[5]

Cooperative work, on the other hand, is not foreign to the European pattern. Certainly it played an important part in American colonial life in the form of house-raisings, quilting bees, log-rollings, husking bees, and the general pattern of neighborliness. According to informants, the white masters frequently loaned their slaves to one another for occasions of this sort, so that the Gullah had first hand contact with the European forms. Memories of the house-raisings, log-rollings, quilting bees, and even the associated candy pulls which the Negroes held on their own accord after freedom are still vivid

---

[2] Discussion of Yoruba material is based on field work in Nigeria, carried on during 1937–38 under terms of a fellowship grant from the Social Science Research Council of New York City.
[3] M. J. Herskovits, *Dahomey* (Augustin, New York, 1938), Vol. I, pp. 63–77.
[4] M. J. Herskovits, *Life in a Haitian Valley* (Knopf, New York, 1937), pp. 70–76.
[5] From unpublished field notes.

in the minds of the older individuals. But at the same time certain forms of cooperative work show a closer correspondence to the West African pattern, especially with regard to hoeing side by side, hoeing in unison to music, and the association between cooperative work and the societies.

On Sapeloe Island in Georgia informants remember large groups, apparently of between 30 and 50 persons, hoeing side by side in the fields. This in itself is significant, since, during the period of slavery, work was assigned by the task in this region so that each slave worked out a separate area by himself. Furthermore, after freedom when a man got behind in his work, he would call on his neighbors or his society for help; and even today, on Sapeloe, people will still "jump right into the field and help you out." In the old days the man would give a big dinner on a long table under a tree, but nowadays people are invited into the house. In hoeing each person takes his own row, and while the host did not hire a drum for use in the fields, the people frequently sang church songs and worked in unison, finishing their rows at the same time. When they worked without singing, couples talked and fell behind so that they did not all finish together. As in Africa, working together is said to make the work more pleasant and to make it go faster; as one informant put it, "You're really cuttin' grass then."

Similarly, if a man needed help, he might call upon a neighbor, and this favor would be returned when requested. This resembles the Yoruba *aro* except that no strict account was kept of the amount of work done. The person called upon might be a relative, or a good friend, or just a neighbor. Significantly, these arrangements were more or less permanent, so that a man would always call upon the same person to help him out. Usually the host gave the helper a meal; but if he were alone and ill, this was omitted.

On the island of Hilton Head, South Carolina, cooperative work has disappeared, but shortly after slavery it existed in two forms. In the first place neighbors might help each other even when they were not ill, working first in the fields of one family and then in the fields of the other. In the second place, the societies such as Mutual Friendly Aid would come without being asked to help a member who fell behind in his work. In this case they did not take note of the amount of work done, but just went in and "hoed him out," while the host provided a dinner for his helpers, serving whatever he could afford. When several people hoed the fields together, each took his own row, and when they sang their hoeing was in unison and was said to go faster and with less effort. In recent times the Hilton Head societies have been primarily "policy clubs" of the type so common in the South, and the function of working in the fields has been abandoned.

African elements are not so evident in other parts of the coastal regions as they are in Hilton Head and Sapeloe. On St. Simons Island, Georgia, neither neighbors nor societies helped in the fields; and while several members of the same family might hoe side by side, each taking his own row, even when they did sing they did not work in unison. On St. Helena, South Carolina, it is said that neighbors never worked each other's fields, but on this island the society called Knights of Wise helped members who were not well and fined those who did not show up to work. Members of the Sisters of Zion were likewise expected, but not forced, to turn out to work the fields of a sick member; if the man proved to be lazy instead of ill, he was given a mock whipping. There was no singing while farming on St. Helena, where they say they had to "sing with the hoe." About Darien and on Harris Neck, on the Georgia mainland, the pattern of cooperative work was once strong, but the forms it took were mainly European, with log-rollings, quiltings, and the like. People would come to hoe the fields of a neighbor who was not well, but the work was not done in unison to music, and while societies were important shortly after slavery, they did not help their members with their work.

It is difficult to explain these local variations in terms of the information at hand, but explanations are probably to be sought in differentials in isolation, the rules laid down by individual slave owners, and perhaps the African sources of the slaves and the dates at which slaves were last imported directly from Africa. While cooperative work persisted in these localities for a long time, it has disappeared in all of them except Sapeloe Island. In all these places except St. Simons, informants respond with conviction to the suggestion that people were more neighborly in the old days than they are now.

Friendship is another institution which is common to both the European and African tradition, but in West Africa it takes a slightly different form and is considerably more formalized than it is in our society. Among the Yoruba there is a distinct emphasis on the best friend (*korikosun*) with whom every contemplated undertaking is discussed, and whose advice in financial matters, or affairs with women, or any matter whatsoever is very seldom disregarded. The best friend is told how a man wants his property to be divided and is called in by the family to see that these wishes are carried out when his partner dies. There are folktales which show that a man's best friend is more to be trusted than his own mother; and the best friend is told things which a man does not confide to his wife. A man's wife or members of his family would attempt—supposedly always without success—to find out a man's plans by "pumping" his best friend.

The affection between best friends is legendary. A man speaks of loving his best friend "like a woman," and there are stories of men dying of grief at the passing of their friends. The Yoruba belief is that women's mouths are "too big" to keep a secret; they do not remain faithful to any friend, but go through life with a series of them. In Dahomey [6] the same general pattern holds but the institution is itself more elaborate in form. Each man has a first best friend in whom he confides everything; a second best friend to whom he tells slightly less; and a third best friend who receives only a part of his confidence.

In the Sea Islands the European practice of writing wills has been accepted completely so that an important and distinctively African function of

[6] M. J. Herskovits, *Dahomey* (Augustin, New York, 1938), Vol. I, pp. 239–242.

friendship has disappeared. At most a man asks his friend's advice about the way his property should be divided. A few informants in their discussion of friendship, did, however, give an emphasis to the institution which seems characteristically African.

On Hilton Head men used to have one or two "sworn friends" upon whom they could depend and to whom they told all their secrets. These friends interpreted each other's dreams, gave advice on financial ventures, and criticized each other's behavior, for instance, in such matters as having "affairs" with women. A man's wife or even his parents might go to his sworn friend in an attempt to find out what plans he had in mind, and in some cases a wife's persistence in this led to a gradual breaking up of the friendship, since the man would stay away from the house rather than be forced to betray his confidence.

Such friendship had a special importance in the time of slavery when slaves banded together against the master. They continued for a time after slavery, but in succeeding generations people came to confide in too many individuals—having too many sworn friends—so that secrets soon spread. The inability of women to keep a secret was blamed in part for the disappearance of the institution, for "as soon as you tell a girl, your secret is gone."

An African influence can be seen in the present form of a number of other institutions which will simply be enumerated. It is apparent in the functions of the local clubs or societies such as the Mutual Friendly Aid, the Jolly Boys, the Golden Link, the Seaside Branch, and the Union Gospel Travellers on Hilton Head. In most other regions these local societies were followed by the well-known, national, chartered lodges, which in turn have almost disappeared. In the structure of the Gullah family there seems to be a certain matrilineal emphasis for which there are counterparts in West Africa. For example, there is the feeling that an individual is somehow more closely related to his mother than to his father. There are several rationalizations for this, but one is the same as that offered in Africa, namely that a person is fed on his mother's milk.

The emphsis on special circumstances of birth is characteristically African. Parsons [7] has already pointed out how children born with a caul, children born "foot fo'mos'," twins, and the seventh child are all believed to have special qualities or abilities. The Gullah, like the West Africans, bury the naval cord in the yard, and frequently nursed their children for one, two, or three years in the old days. One woman was said to have nursed her child after it was old enough to help her in the fields. And people today remember women who carried their children on their backs, in some cases when working the fields. Certain Gullah beliefs are obviously comparable to the taboos of the West Africans; for example, the idea that a nursing mother should not eat beans, green corn, crabs, prawns, or net fish (channel fish caught with hook and line are all right), because it is not good for the baby's stomach.

---

[7] E. C. Parsons, *Folk-Lore of the Sea Islands, South Carolina* (Memoirs of the American Folk-Lore Society, Vol. XVI, Cambridge and New York, 1923), pp. 197–198.

The interpretation of dreams in order to predict the future is important in West African as well as in European tradition and it is wide-spread in the Sea Islands. Magic likewise is not foreign to the European tradition, but certain details of the practice are specifically African; the importance of "graveyard dirt," of "foot track dust," and of hair and nails in working conjure; and the importance of "frizzled chickens" as a means of detecting charms buried in the earth.[8]

The belief in multiple souls, the very vivid belief in ghosts, the special burial rites for persons who die by drowning, lightning, small-pox, and suicide, all resemble African beliefs more closely than they do European. A baby that is taken to a funeral must be passed across the coffin so that its soul will not accompany that of the deceased.[9] When a mother starts home after a visit she takes her baby in her arms, and then calls its name so that its soul will not be left behind.[10] As in Africa, a distinction is made between ghosts and witches, who take off their skins and can be caught either by sprinkling pepper and salt about the room in good African tradition,[11] or by the distinctly European method of putting a Bible under the pillow.

Turning once more to agriculture, we find that a specifically West African form of motor behavior has been retained widely in this region. In the planting of several crops, and especially of rice in the old days, the hole into which the seed was dropped was first made with the heel and then covered over with the foot. Moving pictures taken in West Africa and in Haiti by Herskovits [12] show very plainly this West African procedure which, as far as can be ascertained, was entirely foreign to European tradition.

Gullah speech, which has long been recognized as distinctive among Negro dialects in the United States, has a number of African idioms and grammatical peculiarities. A detailed analysis may show African influences in the phonetic system as well. Dr. Turner of Fisk University has listed several thousand words which he believes to be of West African origin.[13] These are mainly in the form of nicknames and words for plants and animals, and are used only within the family circle so that they would not be noticed unless someone set out to look for them. Lastly there are the very specific correspondences between the animal tales of the Gullah and those of West Africa, the first aspects of Gullah culture to be recognized as having an African origin.

In conclusion then, while it is impossible in the case of the Sea Island Negroes to assign African influences to particular tribes, and while we are

[8] Cf. *Drums and Shadows* by the Savannah Unit of the Georgia Writers' Project (University of Georgia Press, Athens, 1940).

[9] Cf. E. C. Parsons, *op. cit.*, p. 213; G. B. Johnson, *Folk Cuture on St. Helena Island, South Carolina* (Chapel Hill, The University of North Carolina Press, 1930), p. 172.

[10] Cf. E. C. Parsons, *op. cit.*, p. 199; G. B. Johnson, *op. cit.*, p. 172.

[11] Cf. J. Peterkin, *Black April* (Grosset & Dunlap, 1927), p. 100.

[12] See M. J. Herskovits, *Life in a Haitian Valley* (Knopf, New York, 1937), illustrations facing p. 100.

[13] By personal communication.

dealing with the problem of the relative influence of European and African culture on institutions common to both traditions, rather than with African origins of non-European institutions, these influences can be recognized in many aspects of present-day Gullah life. It would thus seem historically incorrect as well as methodologically unsound to explain Gullah customs by reference only to European culture. It is quite true that, as elsewhere in the United States, the European elements outnumber by far the African elements which have been retained, yet that Africanisms can be traced indicates the importance of the study of this society as an aid in the analysis of acculturation.

Hollis R. Lynch

PAN-NEGRO NATIONALISM IN THE
NEW WORLD, BEFORE 1862

Throughout their history most American Negroes have felt some degree of identification with Africa. As early as the end of the eighteenth century, a few had advocated migration to that continent. Not until the middle of the nineteenth century, however, did this interest become a major theme in Negro thinking. At that time the status of the ante-bellum free Negroes was declining in most parts of the Union. In the North, the passage of the Fugitive Slave Act of 1850 and economic competition from the rising tide of Irish immigrants were prominent factors causing Negroes to become more despairing for their safety and their rights. In the South, increasingly restrictive legislation made life ever more difficult. Under these conditions, colonization—i.e., emigration to Africa, to Haiti, or to some part of Central America—became increasingly attractive to many free Negroes.

Hollis Lynch's essay describes these early efforts and the rising nationalism that flourished among articulate Negroes in the years before the Civil War.

Pan-Africanism and pan-Negro nationalism are historically related phenomena with similar origins.[1] Both grew out of resentment at the treatment of black-skinned peoples, whether as slaves in the West Indies and in the American South, as "free persons of color," or, later, as subjects of new European

Hollis R. Lynch, "Pan-Negro Nationalism in the New World, Before 1862," reprinted by permission of the publishers from *Boston University Papers on Africa*, Volume II, *African History*, pp. 149–179, Boston, Massachusetts: Boston University Press. Copyright © 1966 by the Trustees of Boston University.

[1] This article on Pan-Africanism and pan-Negro nationalism is based on a paper given at the University of Massachusetts on December 13, 1962. I am grateful to Professor Gwendolen Carter for her assistance. Research was made possible by a travel grant from the Central Research Fund of the University of London, and by the British Commonwealth Scholarship Commission; to both of these bodies I am grateful.

empires in Africa. Pan-Africanism as an organized movement, concerned with the grievances of all black-skinned peoples, and particularly involving an attack on colonialism in Africa, is a twentieth-century phenomenon: the term came into use in 1900 when Henry Sylvester Williams, a West Indian barrister from Trinidad, organized a Pan-African conference in London, attended by delegates from the West Indies and the United States.[2]

Five other conferences were held, largely through the efforts of the American Negro scholar, W. E. B. Du Bois, at which delegates met to articulate their grievances and to devise means of removing them.[3] These delegates were almost entirely from the New World; indeed, it was only at the last of the extra-African conferences—at Manchester in 1945—that Africans were adequately represented.[4] No meetings had been held on African soil, though African issues were discussed at every conference. After Ghana gained its independence in 1957, the Pan-African movement began to take on a more African character, largely because it had the support of the first of the new African states created after World War II. Though New World Negroes had played, and continued to play, a part on the African continent, the movement passed finally into the hands of African leaders.[5]

This specifically named and organized Pan-Africanism was not the first Negro movement with "African" and "all-African" aspirations. There were at least two earlier such manifestations of thought and feeling, the most recent— Marcus Garvey's "Back to Africa" movement in the nineteen-twenties—being the best known.[6] But early in the nineteenth century there developed among Negroes in the West Indies and in the United States a movement preoccupied with the promotion of emigration and the creation of new states, most of them in Africa. As in the case of Garvey's movement, these early pan-Negro nationalists were concerned with the plight of Negroes in the New World. They failed, however, to produce a charismatic leader or a mass movement. Nevertheless, in their statements and actions these pan-Negro leaders anticipated many of their twentieth-century successors,[7] particularly in their interest in Africa, their belief in a great African past, and their dilemma of

---

[2] The Times, July 24, 25, 26, 1900; also the account by an American delegate, Bishop Alexander Walters, My Life and Work (New York, 1917), xx.

[3] See W. E. B. Du Bois, The World and Africa (New York, 1947), 7–12, 236–242; George Padmore, Pan-Africanism or Communism? (London, 1956), 137–151; American Society of African Culture, ed., Pan-Africanism Reconsidered (Los Angeles, 1962), 37–52; and Vernon McKay, Africa in World Politics (New York, 1963), 93–108.

[4] For a list of the delegates of the 1945 Pan-African conference, see George Padmore, ed., History of the Pan-African Congress (Manchester, n.d.), 71–73.

[5] For Pan-Africanism since 1958, see Colin Legum, Pan-Africanism (London, 1962); also McKay, Africa, 109–133.

[6] See Edmund David Cronon, Black Moses (Madison, 1955).

[7] See George Shepperson, "Notes on American Negro Influences on the Emergence of African Nationalism," Journal of African History, 1.2:299–312 (1960); Nnamdi Azikiwe, "The Future of Pan-Africanism," Présence africaine, 12:11 (1962).

choice between reform of the New World and "regeneration" of their ancestral home.

I

Haiti had a chance to be the first state to provide a base for a pan-Negro program. The slaves of Haiti revolted in 1804 and gained their independence from the greatest military power in Europe, to become the second modern sovereign state in the Americas. The rulers of the Negro "empire" were aware of a responsibility to the Negro race when they invited Negroes to cooperate in building a model state as the final, convincing answer to assertions of Negro inferiority.[8] However, because of internal division, Haiti failed to fulfil its promise.[9] Even so, its continued existence remained for many Negroes proof of Negro ability, and a source of hope for a better future for the race.

Of course, many New World and British Negroes had maintained a sentimental attachment to, and interests in, Africa. It is noteworthy that practically all Negro organizations formed in the United States up to about the third decade of the nineteenth century had the word "African" in their titles.[10] And among the Negroes in Britain, set free by Lord Mansfield's judicial decision in 1772, there were a few who advocated what was essentially the point of view of British evangelicals and humanitarians, namely, that Britain should exert itself to stop the slave trade, replace it by legitimate commerce, and help to christianize and civilize Africa.[11] These Negroes of Britain also played a part in inducing British humanitarian groups to found the colony of Sierra Leone in 1787. The Negroes themselves formed the great majority of the emigrants who embarked from Britain.[12] Less than two years after the first emigrants landed, the Free African Society of Newport, Rhode Island, showed an interest in the colony and in 1795 sent out a delegate to prospect.[13] Sierra Leone also attracted Negroes from Nova Scotia, where they had been settled after fighting on the side of the British in the American revolution. Anxious to leave behind an uncongenial climate and society, 1,131 of them—

[8] James Redpath, ed., *A Guide to Hayti* (Boston, 1861), see preface and 104.

[9] See James G. Leyburn, *The Haitian People* (New Haven, 1941), *passim*.

[10] Some examples are: Prince Hall's African Lodge No. 1, the Free African Societies of Philadelphia and Newport, the African Institutions of New York and Philadelphia, various independent African Baptist churches, and the African Methodist Church. From about the third decade on, when American Negroes became convinced that the American Colonization Society (founded in 1817) wished forcibly to deport them to Africa, the title "African" became less popular among them and was replaced by "Colored."

[11] See Ignatius Sancho, *Letters* (London, 1782); Ottobah Cugoano, *Thoughts and Sentiments on the Evil of Slavery* (London, 1787); and Gustavus Vassa, *The Interesting Narrative of the Life of Olaudah Equiano, or Gustavus Vassa, the African* (London, 1789).

[12] R. R. Kuczynski, *Demographic Survey of the British Colonial Empire* (London, 1948), 40–43; also Christopher Fyfe, *History of Sierra Leone* (London, 1962), 13–19.

[13] *Ibid.*, 112.

led by Thomas Peters, a millwright, who had negotiated with the directors of the Sierra Leone Company, and David George, a zealous Baptist preacher— emigrated to the "Colony of Freedom" in 1792. Both Peters and George can be regarded as prototypes of those Negro leaders who sought to lead Negroes out of "bondage" and back to the "fatherland" in Africa.

Moreover, the arrival of the Nova Scotians saved the colony from complete dissolution. Further reinforcements came in 1800 in the form of 532 Maroons who had taken part in a revolt in Jamaica, had been transported to Nova Scotia, and had then elected to emigrate to Sierra Leone. In 1807, the British government outlawed the slave trade and on January 1, 1808, assumed from the Sierra Leone Company direct control of the colony, which was to be used as a center for the suppression of the slave trade in West Africa as well as for settling and civilizing liberated Africans. In 1804, the Church Missionary Society began work in the colony, and Sierra Leone became the center of British humanitarian activities in West Africa. By 1808, Sierra Leone had a population of nearly two thousand westernized Negroes and had become an obvious focus for further Negro emigration to Africa. Sierra Leone might do what Haiti was failing to do.

In the early years of the nineteenth century, there were already signs that the freed American Negro might have to seek a home outside the United States. Those years marked a sharp decline in his fortune. The invention and use of the cotton gin in the last years of the eighteenth century, and the subsequent remarkable spread of the cotton kingdom to the south and southwest, had served to revive the waning institution of slavery. Manumission of slaves, which had been frequent in the years following the American revolution, had come to a virtual end in the South by the turn of the century. The relatively large free Negro population that had grown up was regarded by many white Southerners as an anomaly and a threat to its society.[14] In the North, Negroes fared no better: although by 1804, all slavery there had been abolished, Negroes were not accepted as an integral part of American society.[15] And as the Southern states began taking measures intended to return free Negroes to slavery or to drive them out, the North, fearful of an influx, seemed to vie with the South in making their lives difficult.

Despite the growing discrimination against them, however, many American Negroes continued to assert their rights as American citizens. Many, for instance, began to look upon the efforts of the American Colonization Society,[16] founded in 1817 as a barely disguised attempt on the part of slaveholders, who

[14] In 1800, there were 108,435 free Negroes in the United States. By 1830, this had risen, mainly by natural increase, to 319,599, and to 488,070 by 1860. The free Negro population remained at roughly one tenth of the entire Negro population. See Negro Population of the United States, Bureau of Census (Washington, 1918), 57.

[15] For an elaboration of this thesis, see Leon F. Litwack, North of Slavery: The Negro in the Free States, 1790–1862 (Chicago, 1962).

[16] For the history of the society, see Earle Lee Fox, The American Colonization Society, 1817–1840 (Baltimore, 1919); and P. J. Stadenraus, The African Colonization Movement, 1816–1865 (New York, 1961).

were prominently associated with the organization, to rid the United States of a potentially troublesome element and thus make secure the Southern system of slavery.[17] From 1830 on, Negroes met in national conventions to denounce slaveholders and the American Colonization Society, and to declare their determination to fight for their civil rights.[18]

II

While many Negroes in the United States sought to achieve complete integration within American society, others became pan-Negro nationalists. Despairing of becoming first-class citizens in their own country, they became advocates of Negro emigration to Africa and elsewhere, and held visions of new states on a continent regenerated by their efforts. Prominent among them were Paul Cuffee, Daniel Coker, Lott Cary, and John Russwurm.[19] All but Cuffee died in the newly established Negro settlements in West Africa.

Cuffee was a devout Quaker from Massachusetts, a prosperous trader and shipowner who, as a young man, had fought for the rights of Negroes in his native state.[20] When this met with little success, he turned to Africa, and particularly to Sierra Leone, to work for the "improvement and civilization of the blacks" of Africa, to provide selective emigration to Sierra Leone, and to seek the suppression of the slave trade and its replacement by legitimate commerce. His trader's mind was excited by the possibility of extensive commerce between Negro America and West Africa, to raise the wealth and prestige of the race. In 1808, he obtained the support of the African Institution, a British humanitarian organization comprised mainly of former directors of the Sierra Leone Company and still influential in directing the affairs of the colony. Three years later he visited Sierra Leone, where he showed considerable care in making plans for emigration. Finally, he founded the Friendly Society of Sierra Leone "to open a channel of intercourse" between Negro America and Sierra Leone; as an earnest of his good faith, he bought a house in Freetown.[21]

Long interested in Negro education in America, Cuffee also showed interest in promoting education in Sierra Leone: "Africa calls for men of character

[17] See Louis B. Mehlinger, "The Attitude of the Free Negro Toward Colonization," *Journal of Negro History*, I (July 1916).

[18] See John W. Cromwell, "The Early Negro Convention Movement," *Occasional Papers* [of the American Negro Academy], IX (Washington, 1940); August Meier, "The Emergence of Negro Nationalism," *Midwest Journal*, IV (Winter 1951–52), 96–104; and Howard H. Bell, "A Survey of the Negro Convention Movement, 1830–1861" (unpublished dissertation, Northwestern University, 1953).

[19] This is not, of course, meant to be an exhaustive list: these were chosen because they were articulate or outstanding men of action. For a discussion of American Negro procolonization views in this period, see Mehlinger, "Attitude." For an example of a project for colonization outside Africa, see the discussion of Delany and Holly below.

[20] For Cuffee's biography, see Henry Noble Sherwood, "Paul Cuffee," *Journal of Negro History*, VIII (April 1923), 153–229.

[21] *Ibid.*, 176.

to fill stations in the Legislature," he wrote.[22] On his return to America, he sought personally to persuade Negroes in such centers as Baltimore, Philadelphia, New York, Boston, and his own town of Westport to support colonization in Africa. In 1815 Cuffee made his second trip to Sierra Leone, taking, largely at his own expense, thirty-eight Negroes in family groups. In letters to America these emigrants urged other Negroes to follow their example.[23] When Cuffee returned, he made his experience available to the founders of the American Colonization Society. Indeed, he was chosen to lead emigrants to be sent out by the society, but he died before the first expedition left for West Africa. However, shortly before this he expressed the widespread feeling Negroes shared against the society by cautioning against too eager an acceptance of its scheme.[24]

Despite Cuffee's warning, the society won the support of his friend Daniel Coker. A runaway slave who as a boy had acquired a rudimentary education, Coker had become schoolmaster and religious leader in the free Negro community of Baltimore. As a young man, he had angrily denounced the institution of slavery and asserted that, despite its handicap, "the African Race ... had given proof of talents." [25] Coker had played a leading role in the break with the Methodist Episcopal Church, which resulted in the formation of the African Methodist Episcopal Church.[26] Elected its first bishop, he had declined the honor. Intent on emigrating to West Africa, he was among the first eighty-eight emigrants sent out by the Colonization Society. Although the expedition was led by three white officials, it seems that in the eyes of the emigrants Coker was the leader.[27] His journal shows him as keenly conscious of the possibilities of the enterprise and of some responsibility for its success. In the two years of hardship and uncertainty that followed before the emigrants finally settled at Cape Mesurado—the first beginnings of Liberia—the leadership devolved mainly on him. He later settled in Sierra Leone.

Lott Cary, who was among the second group of emigrants, played a versatile role as clergyman, doctor, militiaman, builder, and pioneer in agriculture.[28] He regarded himself as primarily a missionary to the native Africans, and from the start he was concerned that the colonists should have friendly relations with the tribes and so exert a civilizing influence. He was born a slave, and,

[22] *Ibid.*, 206.

[23] *Ibid.*, 218.

[24] *Ibid.*, 213–221; also Henry N. Sherwood, "Paul Cuffee and his Contribution to the American Colonization Society," *Proceedings of the Mississippi Valley Historical Association*, VI (1913), 370–402.

[25] *A Dialogue Between A Virginian and an African Minister, Written by Daniel Coker, a Descendant of Africa, Minister of the African Methodist Episcopal Church in Baltimore* (Baltimore, 1810), 10.

[26] Daniel A. Payne, *History of the African Methodist Episcopal Church* (Nashville, 1891), 89.

[27] *The Journal of Daniel Coker, A Descendant of Africa ... in the Ship Elizabeth, on a Voyage for Sherbro in Africa ...* (Baltimore, 1820), 15–16.

[28] Harry Johnston, *Liberia* (London, 1906), I, 135; R. R. Gurley, *Life of Jehudi Ashmun* (Washington, 1835), 147–160; Alexander, *History*, 241–254.

though ignorant at twenty-seven, he acquired considerable learning and became a well-to-do Baptist preacher in Richmond, Virginia, by the age of thirty-three. Yet he gave up this relatively comfortable position to go to Liberia. He wrote: "I am an African; and in this country, however meritorious my conduct and respectable my character, I cannot receive the credit due to either. I wish to go to a country where I shall be estimated by my merits not by my complexion, and I feel bound to labour for my suffering race." [29] Cary died, in an accident, on November 10, 1828.

John B. Russwurm was born in Jamaica, and became one of the first two Negro graduates from an American college.[30] In March 1827, he founded and became the editor of the first American Negro newspaper, *Freedom's Journal*. He abandoned his opposition to the American Colonization Society, and in 1829 announced his conversion to the view that the free Negro could help himself and his race best by giving strong support to Liberia.[31] He soon left for Liberia and in 1830 founded the *Liberia Herald*. He also held the positions of superintendent of education and colonial secretary; from 1836 until his death in 1851, he was governor of Maryland, a colony adjacent to Liberia to the south, which was founded by the Maryland Colonization Society in 1834.[32] As the first Negro governor in West Africa, Russwurm felt that the conduct of his office was a test of the ability of the Negro: he seems to have ruled, with substantial justice to colonists, Africans, and missionaries alike.[33]

These four leaders in the early phase of the Pan-African movement had much in common. All were men of substance, in nearly every case through their own talent and industry. All of them, including Russwurm the Jamaican, were protesting against discrimination in the United States. Indeed, Coker had taken part in the setting up of an "African" church, an early example of the use of historical origins as the basis of a protest. Although Russwurm and Cuffee showed an understandable suspicion of the white-dominated American Colonization Society, they gave Liberia their support, perhaps on the good practical ground that, whatever the motive of the society's leaders and supporters, the society was creating a Negro state in Africa.

Between 1830 and about 1850, there seems to have been something of a falling off of activity among American Negroes. No new and effective leader appeared to take up the pan-Negro cause, although there is evidence that sentiment in favor of emigration continued to grow.[34] In the West Indies,

---

[29] Quoted in *ibid.*, 243.

[30] See William M. Brewer, "John B. Russwurm," *Journal of Negro History*, XIII (Oct. 1928), 413–422.

[31] See his editorials in *Freedom's Journal*, II (Feb. 14, 1829 *et seq.*).

[32] For a history of the founding of the colony, see *Journal of the Maryland Historical Society*, V (Feb. 1850), 129–152.

[33] Russwurm's letters and reports as governor, not used in Brewer's "Russwurm," are in the archives of the Maryland Historical Society.

[34] Carter G. Woodson, *The Mind of the Negro as Reflected in Letters Written during the Crisis, 1800–1860* (Washington, 1926), *passim*.

particularly in Jamaica and Barbados, there was widespread interest both in leaving the place of former bondage and continued discrimination and in taking Christianity to "benighted brothers" in Africa.[35] In Barbados, in the three decades after the abolition of slavery, at least three organizations were formed for promoting emigration to Liberia: the Barbados Colonization Society, the Fatherland Union Society, and the Barbados Company for Liberia.[36] But because of the lack of adequate financial resources among Negroes or external aid, the opposition of the still powerful West Indian sugar planters, and perhaps the absence of any oppressive discrimination, little emigration was organized.[37]

It is, however, interesting that groups in the West Indies should have looked to Liberia. After the emancipation of the slaves, there was less pressure on them in the form of discrimination than on the American Negro to seek a home elsewhere. It is significant that the three important West Indian advocates of pan-Negro nationalism discussed here—Russwurm, Edward W. Blyden,[38] and Robert Campell [39]—had all experienced and resented the discrimination against Negroes in the United States.

The desire of West Indian Negroes who wanted to emigrate for other reasons had important consequences for West Africa. It was these people who urged the start of missionary work in West Africa by both the British Baptist and the United Scottish Presbyterian societies. West Indians played an important role in their work, as well as in that of the Basel and Wesleyan missions. They accounted also for the formation of the West Indian Church Association, whose missionaries worked in the Rio Pongo area in West Africa. The association was an autonomous body which, unlike the other missionary societies, derived its support in money and men mainly from West Indian Negroes.[40] The West Indian missionaries and teachers worked, so they felt, for the regeneration of Africa and on behalf of the Negro race.[41] Men like Joseph Fuller,

---

[35] See A. E. Payne, *Freedom in Jamaica* (London, 1946), 73–74; C. P. Groves, *Planting of Christianity in Africa* (London, 1954), II, 54; *A General Account of the West Indian Church Association for the Furtherance of the Gospel in West Africa* (London, 1855), 5–7.

[36] *Maryland Colonization Journal*, IV (1848), 213; also American Colonization Society, *Forty-Ninth Annual Report* (Washington, 1866), 7.

[37] There is one exception to this. In 1865, 365 Negroes from Barbados emigrated to Liberia in an expedition sponsored by the Liberian government but financed mainly by the American Colonization Society. See American Colonization Society, *Fifty-Second Annual Report* (Washington, 1869), 53; and chap. 3 my book on Blyden cited below.

[38] See discussion of Blyden below; also Hollis R. Lynch, *Edward W. Blyden* (1832–1912), *Pan-Negro Patriot* (London, 1966).

[39] See discussion of Campell below; also Robert Campell, *A Pilgrimage to My Motherland* (New York, 1861), 11.

[40] A. Barrow, *Fifty Years in Western Africa: Being a Record of the West Indian Church on the Banks of the Rio Pongo* (London, 1900), *passim*.

[41] In addition, many West Indian artisans and professionals were attracted to West Africa, particularly to Sierra Leone, but primarily because of the better economic opportunities there. See Abioseh Nicol, "West Indians in West Africa," *Sierre Leone Studies*, N.S., no. 13 (June 1960), 14–23. Also from about 1840, Brazilian and Cuban

Henry Wharton, and John Duport respectively spent forty, twenty-eight, and eighteen years in Africa.[42]

In the eighteen-fifties, however, there was a rapid revival of interest among American Negroes, as the conflict over slavery became more intense. Negroes were, of course, deeply involved and, as events appeared to be set on a course against them, more wanted to emigrate. In 1850, the Fugitive Slave Bill was passed giving federal commissioners virtually unlimited power for the apprehension and return of alleged fugitives. This was only the first shock in a decade of "sorrowful and unmixed gloom." [43] There followed the Kansas-Nebraska Act, the Dred Scott decision, the failure of John Brown's raid, and an apparent blow from the Republican Party when Abraham Lincoln, a compromise candidate, assumed the presidency. It would be useful to study the period between 1850 and 1862 in detail because not until Garvey's "Back to Africa" movement of the 1920s did pan-Negro nationalism seem again to possess real vigor.

The independence of Liberia in 1847 could hardly have come at a more opportune time for the cause of emigration from the New World. Congratulations to the new republic came from all major Negro groups, and many hoped with John B. Hepburn of Port-au-Prince that Liberia's course was now "onward to empire and to fame." [44] In 1848, the American Colonization Society sent out delegates to report on Liberia's possibilities as a future home.[45] West Indian Negroes, too, showed interest: the Barbados Colonization Society "for assisting in the suppression of the Slave Trade, and the introduction of civilization into Africa" received the news of Liberia's independence with "inexpressible joy" and regarded it "as another demonstration to the world, that the descendants of Africa, when placed in a fair position, are not inferior in civilization, religion, and morality, to those nations amongst whom it was their lot to be cast for a given time." [46] The new interest in Liberia reflected itself in a substantial increase in the annual number of American emigrants, which rose from 51 in 1847 to 441 in 1848. This increase in emigration was maintained throughout the next decade.[47]

Negroes trickled back to Lagos and its hinterland where, as artisans, agriculturists, and traders, they formed an important section of the community.

[42] For biographical details on these three missionaries, see Robert Glennie, *Joseph Jackson Fuller* (London, 1925); G. G. Findlay and W. W. Holdsworth, *The History of the Wesleyan Methodist Society* (London, 1922), 164; and Barrow, *Fifty Years*, *passim*.

[43] The phrase is that of the American Negro leader, James McCune Smith. See his introduction to a *Memorial Discourse by Rev. Henry Highland Garnet, Delivered in the Hall of the House of Representatives* . . . (Washington, 1865), 56.

[44] *Maryland Colonization Journal*, IV (1848), 213.

[45] The American Colonization Society, *Thirty-Second Annual Report* (Washington, 1849), 8.

[46] *African Repository*, XXIV (Aug. 1848), 24.

[47] American Colonization Society, *Fifty-Second Annual Report* (Washington, 1869), 53.

III

The new Liberian republic, of which so much was hoped, had a disappointing beginning. In 1850, three years after independence, it was a country of roughly 13,000 square miles, with a coastline of approximately 300 miles. Its emigrant population, depleted by a high mortality rate, was about 6,000. Since 1827 the majority of those sent out by the Colonization Society had been slaves who were emancipated expressly for that purpose,[48] and many were unfit for pioneering.[49]

It is not surprising, then, that the sense of mission and destiny which inspired the early emigrants was largely missing among the later ones. Between its founding and 1850, Liberia seems to have produced only one outstanding champion of the pan-Negro ideology, the "poet and philosopher," Hilary Teage, son of Colin Teage, who had come from Lott Cary's congregation in Richmond, Virginia. He succeeded Russwurm as editor of the *Liberia Herald* in 1835, and for the next fourteen years used it to express his pan-Negro sentiments. He was certainly the first poet of pan-Negro nationalism: his poetry is concerned with the themes of the past achievements of his race and of a mission to fulfill.[50] He was also an accomplished orator. He said to a group of Liberians in 1846: "Upon you, rely upon it, depends, in a measure you can hardly conceive, the future destiny of the race. You are to give the answer whether the African race is doomed to interminable degradation—a hideous blot on the fair face of creation, a libel upon the dignity of human nature; or whether they are capable to take an honourable rank amongst the great family of nations." [51] In 1847 he was a representative at Liberia's constitutional conference.

On the whole, however, Liberians did not demonstrate much unity of purpose or public spirit. They were berated by their white governors and their progressive leaders for their "want of self-respect" and their easy dependence on foreign philanthropy.[52] Socially there had quickly developed in Liberia an American pattern of stratifications based on color, the mulattoes considering themselves superior to the black emigrants while the colonists, generally speaking, held the natives in contempt.[53] The Liberians exploited native labor on their plantations, but, on the whole, agriculture was neglected for trading,

---

[48] Up to 1850, 6,116 emigrants were sent out by the Society: 2,315 were born free, 165 purchased their freedom, and 3,636 were emancipated for emigration.

[49] Edward W. Blyden, *A Voice from Bleeding Africa* (Monrovia, 1856), 26.

[50] For quotations from his poems extolling the Negro past and urging Liberia to "press towards the prize in glory's race," see Edward W. Blyden, *From West Africa to Palestine* (Freetown, Manchester, London, 1873), 104; also Frederick Alexander Durham, *The Lone-Star of Liberia* (London, 1892), 1.

[51] Quoted in Wilson Armistead, *A Tribute to the Negro* (Manchester and New York, 1848), 532; also J. A. B. Horton, *West African Countries and Peoples* (London, 1868), 273.

[52] Johnston, *Liberia*, 149, 182–184.

[53] Abayomi Karrnga, *History of Liberia* (Liverpool, 1926), 45.

which brought quick profits without developing the productive capacity of the country.

Until its independence, the supreme authority in the colony was the American Colonization Society. Independence came from the demand by Liberians for, among other things, the sovereign power to deal with recalcitrant European traders scornful of the developing Negro nation.[54] And so on July 26, 1847, Liberia became a sovereign nation with a constitution modeled on that of the United States.[55] Unfortunately, the constitution contained a provision which was later to keep the young nation in a chaotic political condition: the president, the House of Representatives, and half of the senators were to be elected every two years. Moreover, the franchise was confined mainly to American colonists.

With renewed support from New World Negroes, however, the new nation could have retrieved itself. Such was the view of Edward Wilmot Blyden, probably the most articulate advocate of pan-Negro nationalism in the nineteenth century.[56] Born free [57] on the Danish West Indian island of St. Thomas in 1832, and educated at the local primary school and by private tuition from his American pastor, the Reverend John Knox, and his own mother, Blyden early decided on the ministry as a career. In May 1850, Knox took him to the United States and attempted to enroll him in Rutgers' Theological College, Knox's alma mater. Blyden was refused admission because of his race, and, aware of the operation of the Fugitive Slave Law, he accepted an offer from the New York Colonization Society to emigrate to Liberia.

Even before he left the United States, Blyden expressed pride in the newly independent Negro republic: Liberia, he thought, could "include within its limits the dark regions of Ashantee and Dahomey and bring those barbarous tribes under civilized and enlightened influence." [58] In his first letter to the United States he described his pleasure at being on African soil: "You can easily imagine the delight with which I gazed upon the land of Tertullian, ancient father in the Christian Church; of Hannibal and Henry Diaz, renowned generals; yes, and the land of *my* forefathers... The land here is teeming with everything necessary for subsistence of man." The skeptics, he wrote, should come and see for themselves.[59] He continued his studies at Alexander High School, a Presbyterian school in Monrovia. In 1858 he was ordained a minister and became principal of the high school. From the beginning of his time in Liberia, Blyden was active in public life, both as a correspondent for the *Liberia Herald* and as editor during 1855–56. Moreover,

[54] Johnston, *Liberia*, 187–195.

[55] The basic document was drafted by Simon Greenleaf, Professor of Law at Harvard University, but was somewhat revised at Liberia's constitutional convention; Liberians wrote the preamble.

[56] See Lynch, *Edward W. Blyden*.

[57] Slavery was not abolished in the Danish West Indies until 1848, but here, too, there was a small group of free Negroes before general emancipation.

[58] *New York Colonization Journal*, I (Dec. 1850).

[59] *African Repository*, XXVII (Sept. 1851), 266.

he remained an active propagandist for Liberia and the cause of emigration, writing often for the *African Repository* (the journal of the American Colonization Society) and for the journals of the New York and Maryland Colonization societies.

Blyden was an articulate and critical defender of his new home, and from an early stage he was concerned about diverting the expected flow of emigration from the United States to Africa, particularly to Liberia. It is probable that his first pamphlet, *A Voice from Bleeding Africa*, published in Monrovia in 1856, appeared just before the emigration conference of 1856 was scheduled to meet in Cleveland,[60] though there is no evidence that it was discussed there. In the pamphlet he appealed to "colored men of every rank and station, in every clime and country" to support the colonization movement. Moreover, he urged Negroes to take the name of the new state seriously: the object of the creation of Liberia was "the redemption of Africa and the disenthralment and elevation of the African race, objects worthy of every colored man." At the same time, he attacked Liberians for a lack of dedication to the cause:

> How painful is the reflection that there are but few of the young men of Liberia who seem to give the future of their country a moment's thought...! O young men and women of Liberia, arise from your lethargy, shake off your puerile notions and practices! It is high time to bestir yourselves to be men and women. Let the brave achievements and noble deeds of your fathers arouse you to effort. Let the future glory that awaits your country kindle within you an honorable ambition and urge you onwards.[61]

He wanted to see "the young men of Liberia, like the youth among the ancient Spartans, exercise themselves vigorously in all things which pertain to the country's welfare."[62]

An opportunity for him to act as a defender of Liberia came in 1852. Gerrit Smith, a veteran abolitionist and member of Congress from New York, in opposing a scheme to send Negroes to Liberia, dubbed the American Colonization Society "the deadliest enemy of the Negro race," and Liberia "a frightful graveyard."[63] Blyden attacked Senator Smith for "doing ... considerable harm ... by blinding the minds of colored men to their true interests." Colonization in Africa, he contended, was "the only means of delivering the colored man from oppression and of raising him up to respectability." He would not accept the advice of Smith and other abolitionists that, if necessary, free Negroes should retire to Canada to await the outcome of the issue of

---

[60] The conference is discussed below. See also Martin R. Delany, *Official Report of the Niger Valley Exploring Party* (New York, 1861), for a discussion of the conference.

[61] *New York Colonization Journal*, IV (Aug. 1854).

[62] *African Repository*, XXXI (April 1855), 18.

[63] Howard H. Bell, "The Negro Emigration Movement, 1849–54: A Phase of Negro Nationalism," *Phylon*, XX (Nov. 1959), 136.

slavery. Admitting that the mortality rate in Liberia was high, Blyden claimed that this was a temporary condition, common to all pioneer communities.[64]

While Blyden was rebuking Senator Smith, Martin R. Delany, a Negro doctor trained at Harvard and a former newspaper editor and abolitionist, was devising a scheme based on a Negro empire in the Caribbean and South and Central America. After the passage of the Fugitive Slave Bill, he despaired of American Negroes ever enjoying the full rights of citizenship in the United States. He had grown impatient even with the white abolitionists when he realized that Negroes were "occupying the very same position, in relation to our anti-slavery friends, as we do in relation to the pro-slavery part of the community—a mere secondary, underling position, in all our relations to them, and anything more than this comes by mere sufferance." He dismissed with "contemptuous indignation the absurd idea of the natural inferiority of the African," warned Negroes not to carry their religion to the point of hoping for a divine intervention on their behalf, and urged them to support him in constructive action.[65]

His projected empire was to be formed by American Negroes emigrating to South America, an area for which he made two doubtful claims: first, that it was predominantly Negroid and, second, that there had "never existed there an inequality on account of color or race." [66] His advocacy of a Negro empire in the Americas was partly for strategic reasons: by its proximity it would, either by moral or physical force, bring about the collapse of slavery in the United States. But he also believed that Negroes, as developers of the economic base of the New World, were entitled to their full share of its fruits. Still he did not overlook Africa, which he hoped would be "civilized and enlightened," with Liberia in a "high and elevated position ... among the nations of the earth." Yet he continued to regard the American Colonization Society as working to promote the interest of slaveholders and was, therefore, severely critical of Liberia's dependence on it.[67]

It is hardly surprising that Blyden and Delany came into conflict. Blyden defended the American Colonization Society and Liberia with some spirit. Delany's plan was a diversion, he wrote, and doomed to failure in any case. Only in Africa could the Negro race rise to distinguished achievement.[68]

Before Delany could act on his scheme, the largest Negro national conference up to that time was convened in Rochester, New York, in 1853, and

[64] *Liberia Herald*, n.s., III (July 7, 1852); also *Maryland Colonization Society*, VI (Nov. 1852), 277–280.

[65] See Martin R. Delany, *The Condition, Elevation and Destiny of the Colored People of the United States, Politically Considered* (Philadelphia, 1852).

[66] *Ibid.*, 27. Although Delany's statement was not strictly true, it is true that in Latin American countries Negroes were on the whole better treated than in Anglo-Saxon America. For a comparative study of the treatment of Negroes in the Americas, see Frank Tannenbaum, *Slave and Citizen* (New York, 1947); also Stanley M. Elkins, *Slavery* (Chicago, 1959).

[67] *Ibid.*, 169, 170.

[68] *Liberia Herald*, n.s. III (Oct. 6, 1852).

the persistent division between emigrationists and anti-emigrationists was forced into the open. The anti-emigrationists, led by the Negro leader Frederick Douglass, persuaded the conference to go on record as opposing emigration.[69] But as soon as the conference was over, the emigrationists, led by Delany, James M. Whitfield, a popular poet, and James T. Holly, an accomplished Episcopalian clergyman, called a conference for August 1854, from which anti-emigrationists were to be excluded. Douglass described this action as "narrow and illiberal," and he sparked the first public debate among American Negro leaders on the subject of emigration.[70]

The conference on emigration met in Cleveland as planned. It was, according to Delany, the most widely representative one ever convened by Negroes.[71] Shortly before it met, the passage of the Kansas-Nebraska Act had provided another triumph for the supporters of slavery. Understandably, the mood of the conference was militant. Delany repeated his call for the creation of a Negro empire in the New World, where "the inherent traits, attributes ... and native characteristics peculiar to our race could be cultivated and developed." [72] He warned that "submission does not gain for us an increase of friends nor respectability, as the white race will only respect those who oppose their usurpation, and acknowledge as equals those who will not submit to their rule." They were to take concerted action: "We must make an issue, create an event and establish for ourselves a position. This is essentially necessary for our effective elevation as a people, in shaping our national development, directing our destiny and redeeming ourselves as a race." A Negro empire was further necessary to put "a check to European presumption and insufferable Yankee intrusion and impudence." [73]

Although the conference adopted Delany's report, there were distinct territorial preferences among those who thought in terms of the Western hemisphere. Whitfield favored colonization in Central America, while Holly opted for Haiti. No public announcement about Africa emerged from the conference, but that too had been discussed. According to Delany: "The Convention ... in its Secret Session made Africa, with its inexhaustible productions and the great facilities for checking the abominable Slave Trade, its most important point of dependence; though our first gun was levelled, and the first shell thrown at the American continent driving the slave-holding faction into despair ... Africa was held in reserve." [74] As a result of the conference, the National Emigration Board was set up. Delany began negotiations with "several states of Central and South America as well as Jamaica and Cuba." [75] Holly left for

[69] Cromwell, "Early Negro Convention," 16.
[70] *Frederick Douglass' Paper*, VI (Oct. 6, 1853 *et seq.*).
[71] Delany, *Official Report*, 6.
[72] Martin R. Delany, "Political Destiny of the Colored Race of the American Continent," appendix no. 3, in *Report of the Select Committee on Emancipation and Colonization* (Washington, 1862), 37–59.
[73] *Ibid.*, 43.
[74] Delany, *Official Report*, 8–9.
[75] *Ibid.*, 10.

Haiti to conduct negotiations there, which, although inconclusive, were encouraging enough to cause him on his return to begin agitating for Negro
emigration to that territory.[76] In August 1856, the biennial meeting of the
National Emigration Conference convened again in Cleveland; delegates supported emigration again and decided to organize a publishing company for
propaganda purposes.

I V

As the conflict between Delany and Blyden shows, it was not merely a
dispute between emigrationists and their opponents that was preventing a
rapid flow of Negroes back to Africa. The emigrationists were quarreling among
themselves. Fortunately for those who wished emigration to Africa, Delany
abandoned his scheme for an empire in the Americas, soon after the National
Emigration Conference in Cleveland. Whitfield died in California on his way
to Central America, and Delany began to develop a positive enthusiasm for
Africa, stimulated by the publication in 1857 of works by Thomas Bowen and
David Livingstone.[77] In particular, it was Bowen's "intelligent and interesting
account of Yorubaland" which spurred him to explore the Niger Valley in
search of a base for a Negro nation.[78] Even when he turned to Africa, Delany
persisted in looking beyond Liberia. His enthusiasm for an expedition to Yorubaland was matched by that of his assistant, Robert Campell, a young Jamaica-
born chemist. When the third National Emigration Conference met in Chat-
ham, Ontario, in August 1858, Delany had his plans ready. The conference
endorsed the expedition to the Niger Valley as well as Holly's Haitian scheme.

Those interested in West Africa received further help in 1858 when the
African Civilization Society was formed, with Henry Highland Garnet as president, to support emigration to that region. Garnet was one of the most aggressive of the American Negro leaders. As early as 1843, he had called on slaves
"to rise in their might and strike a blow for their lives and liberties," a counsel
which, although it won the endorsement of John Brown, failed to win the
general support of Negroes.[79] He left the United States in 1850 for England,
where he lectured as an abolitionist for three years. On his return to the United
States in 1855, he became a strong supporter of emigration. He had no sym-

---

[76] James T. Holly, A Vindication of the Capacity of the Negro Race for Self-
Government, and Civilized Progress, as Demonstrated by Historical Events of the
Haitian Revolution; and the Subsequent Act of the People since their National Inde-
pendence (New Haven, 1857), preface.

[77] These were Thomas J. Bowen, Central Africa: Adventures and Missionary
Labors in the Interior of Africa, from 1849–1856 (Charleston, 1857), and Dr. Living-
stone's Seventeen Years' Explorations and Adventures in the Wilds of Africa, John
Hartley Coomb, ed. (Philadelphia, 1857).

[78] Delany, Official Report, 10.

[79] John W. Cromwell, The Negro in American History (Washington, 1916),
126; also William Wells Brown, The Black Man: His Antecedents, His Genius, and
His Achievements (Boston, 1863), 149–152.

pathy for those Negro leaders who opposed free emigration to Africa simply because slaveholders promoted it, and he castigated Frederick Douglass and his associates as "humbugs who oppose everything they do not originate."[80] The main object of Garnet's society was "to establish a grand center of Negro nationality from which shall flow the streams of commercial, intellectual, and political power which shall make colored people respected everywhere." [81] Though he preferred such a center to be founded in West Africa through select American Negro emigration, he was not averse to the building of a Negro state in the Americas. Furthermore, by 1858, a few Liberian trading vessels were plying regularly between the Negro republic and eastern American ports. Garnet was impressed by this; the establishment of a vast commercial network between West Africa and Negro America, he wrote, "would do more for the overthrowing of slavery, in creating a respect for ourselves, than fifty thousand lectures of the most eloquent men of this land." [82]

In turning to West Africa as the geographical center for their pan-Negro program, the Delany-Garnet groups were not overlooking one of their major objectives: the overthrow of slavery in the United States. The new plan, in theory, represented a more effective strategy: it would bring about the collapse of American slavery as well as annihilate the slave trade at its source. The first object was to be attained by the planting of cotton in the selected sites, with the object of underselling in world markets the cotton produced in the Southern states.[83] American Negroes, with their special knowledge of the cotton culture, so it was reasoned, were peculiarly well fitted to succeed in this.

Campell, Delany's assistant, reached West Africa before his leader. On June 24, 1859, he sailed from Liverpool aboard the "splendid ship, Ethiopia," in the company of an American Negro from New York, John Bennet, who had invested $125 in two cotton gins and was on his way to Lagos to start an independent venture in cotton growing.[84] Campell landed at Freetown, Sierra Leone, on July 12, and here met "several natives ... of respectability and ... education." [85] He made short stops at Cape Palmas and Cape Coast before arriving at Lagos on July 21. Through the acting British consul of Lagos, Lieutenant Lodder, Campell met Okukenu, the Alake of Abeokuta, and found him favorable to the idea of select Negro emigration into his territory. Already in the Alake's domains were several hundred emigrants—"semi-civilized" liberated Africans from Sierra Leone who had returned to their homeland or had been repatriated from Brazil and Cuba.[86] In Campell's view, these emigrants "had inaugurated a mighty work, which ... must be continued in a higher

---

[80] Weekly Anglo-African, I (Sept. 3, 1859).
[81] Ibid.
[82] Ibid.
[83] Ibid.; also Delany, Official Report, 14.
[84] Weekly Anglo-African, I (Sept. 3, 1859).
[85] Campell, Pilgrimage, 11.
[86] Ibid., 18. For the fullest treatment of this, see Jean F. Herskovitts, "Liberated Africans and the History of Lagos Colony to 1886" (unpublished dissertation, Oxford, 1960).

form by the more civilized of the race." He advocated that emigrants should organize on "municipal" lines. But his goal was that of a "national government" which would require the cooperation and support of native Africans. He therefore advised prospective emigrants to "remember that the existing rulers must be respected, for they alone are the *bona fide* rulers of the place. The effort should be to fit them up to the proper standard, and not to supersede or crush them." [87]

Delany, leader of the Niger Valley exploring party, sailed from New York aboard the Liberian vessel, *Mendi*, on May 24, 1859, and arrived in Monrovia early in July. Also aboard the *Mendi* as an emigrant to Liberia was William C. Monroe, an Episcopalian clergyman from Detroit, a former missionary to Haiti, and former president of the National Emigration Conference, who had come to believe that Liberia was "the chief instrument in determining the future destiny of the Negro race." [88] In Monrovia Delany received a hero's welcome as he reported to a large public meeting of Liberians, who had come "from all parts of the country," that "the desire of African nationality has brought me to these shores." [89] At Grand Bassa, a council of "the most eminent Liberians" approved Delany's mission and policy. This meeting gave Delany "one of the most happy hours of his life" and produced in him "an unforgettable and profound sensation." [90] On July 26, he participated in Liberia's twelfth annual Independence Day celebration, which "came off with grand effect." [91] On August 1, Delany and Blyden, now much closer together in policy, were speakers at the twenty-fifth anniversary of the emancipation of British West Indian Negroes, celebrated "with great spirit by the leading citizens of Liberia." [92]

Delany left Monrovia on August 4, 1859, for Cape Palmas, where he stayed six weeks. During his two and a half months' stay in Liberia, Delany moved even further toward Blyden's views: his opposition to the Negro republic had been transformed into support. He was especially impressed with the area up St. Paul's River—its beautiful location, its thriving sugar and coffee plantations, its "livestock of all kinds," and its neat brick houses.[93] Although still wishing to see the Negro republic more self-reliant, he was now able to recommend it to the "intelligent of the race." [94] Blyden had also been prominent in welcoming Delany. He hailed him as "the far-famed champion of the elevation of colored men," as the "Moses" who would "lead the exodus of his people from the house of bondage." [95]

Delany reached Lagos on September 20, spending five weeks there and

[87] Campell, *Pilgrimage*, 137.
[88] *Weekly Anglo-African*, I (Oct. 1, 1859). Holly's *Vindication* was dedicated to Monroe.
[89] *Weekly Anglo-African*, I (Oct. 1, 1859).
[90] Delany, *Official Report*, 23.
[91] *Weekly Anglo-African*, I (Sept. 24, 1859).
[92] *Ibid.*, I (Oct. 15, 1859).
[93] *Ibid.*, I (Sept. 24, 1859).
[94] *New York Colonization Journal*, IX (Oct. 1859).
[95] *Ibid.*

winning the confidence of Docemo, king of Lagos. Delany wrote to Garnet from Lagos:

> Lagos is a fine, and will be a great, commercial city. It is destined to be the great metropolis of this part of the world. Entirely under a black government, it only wants a few of the right stamp of black men to make it one of the most desirable cities in the world. They bid us come, and to that end the authorities have presented me with two acres of land in the heart of the city plot on which to build my residence . . .
>
> There will be for you and also Mr. J. T. Holly, after our return to Africa, a fine prospect in this rich city of Lagos, where Christians . . . desire to have black instead of white preachers.[96]

From Lagos he went to Abeokuta, where he joined his fellow commissioner, Robert Campbell, and together they spent six weeks touring the principal cities of Yorubaland. On their return to Abeokuta, they held talks with the obas and chiefs and, on December 27, signed a treaty that assigned to them as "Commissioners on behalf of the African race in America the right and privilege of settling in common with the Egba people, on any part of the territory belonging to Abeokuta, not otherwise occupied." [97] The signing of the treaty was witnessed by the famous African missionary, Samuel Crowther, and his son, Samuel, Jr. Delany had taken the first step, he felt, in "the grandest prospect for regeneration of a people that ever presented itself in the history of the world." [98]

The expedition had aroused great curiosity and interest in both humanitarian and commercial circles in England; men were deeply divided on the issues of the coming American civil war, and attention was turning to sources of supply of cotton in areas outside the United States.[99] On their way back to the United States, Delany and Campell arrived in London on May 17, 1860, and on the next day were invited to a meeting "of a number of noblemen and gentlemen interested in Africa's Regeneration," held in the parlor of Dr. Thomas Hodgkin. A series of meetings was subsequently called, from which grew the African Aid Society, founded to assist by "loans or otherwise" the emigration of Negroes from North America to Africa for the purpose of cultivating tropical products, including cotton, and of promoting "the Christian Civilization of the African Races and the annihilation of the slave trade." Though extremely cautious of any alliance with white men, Delany agreed to cooperate with the society after he had impressed upon its members that the relations between the two groups were to involve strictly business, and that Negro emigrants were to be completely free in managing their own affairs. "Our policy," Delany emphasized, "must be . . . Africa for the African race and black men to rule them." [100]

---

[96] *Weekly Anglo-African*, II (Jan. 1861).   [98] *Ibid.*, 30.
[97] Delany, *Official Report*, 27.   [99] *New York Times* (Dec. 20, 1860).
[100] Delany, *Official Report*, 64. Thomas Hodgkin was a prominent London physician and philanthropist; see *Dictionary of National Biography*, XXVII, 63–64.

V

Although Delany had abandoned his idea of an empire in Central America and Whitfield had died, James T. Holly was still active in promoting his
scheme for emigration to Haiti. The scheme began to gain support even before
Delany and Campell left for West Africa. The emigrationist position was
generally strengthened by the Dred Scott decision of 1857,[101] which led directly
to the founding of the *Weekly Anglo-African* and the *Anglo-African Magazine*
by Robert Hamilton, who in 1859 urged Negroes to "set themselves zealously
to work to create a position of their own—an empire which shall challenge
the admiration of the world, rivalling the glory of their historic ancestors." [102]
Meanwhile Holly was leading his campaign and in 1857 wrote of Haiti's revolution: "This revolution is one of the noblest, grandest and most justifiable outbursts against oppression that is recorded in the pages of history . . . [it] is also
the grandest political event in this or any other age . . . it surpasses the American revolution in an incomparable degree." [103] "Never before," he continued,
"in all the annals of the world's history did a nation of abject and chattel
slaves arise in the terrific might of their resuscitated manhood, and regenerate,
redeem and disenthral themselves: by taking their station at one gigantic
bound, as an independent nation among the sovereignties of the world."

His object in recounting this phase of Haitian history was to arouse
Negroes of the United States "to a full consciousness of their own inherent
dignity." They were to help in building up Haiti "until its glory and renown
overspread and cover the whole earth, and redeem and regenerate by its influence in the future, the benighted Fatherland of the race of Africa." As a
tactical measure, Holly was against immediate American Negro emigration to
Africa: for a start, efforts should be concentrated on building a "Negro Nationality in the New World." Such a successful state would then "shed its . . .
beams upon the Fatherland of the race." [104]

The Haitian emigration movement received a further fillip when the
Haitian government gave it official sanction. The Haitian "Call for Emigration" was issued on August 22, 1859, by R. E. DuBois, Secretary of State for
Justice and Public Worship.[105] Haiti's doors were now open to all Negroes
who wished to emigrate. Fabre Geffrard, the new president who seemed bent
on reforming Haitian society, joined in the appeal, inviting Negroes to bring
"their arms and minds." He predicted: "Haiti will soon regain her ancient
splendor . . . and . . . will be a formal denial, most eloquent and peremptory,
against the detractors of our race who contest our ability to attain a high degree
of civilization." [106] And F. J. Joseph, Secretary of State for Agriculture, who
was directly responsible for settling emigrants, said that "welcoming men of

101 John Hope Franklin, *From Slavery to Freedom* (New York, 1956), 264.
102 *Weekly Anglo-African*, I (July 23, 1859).
103 Holly, *Vindication*, 7.
104 *Ibid.*, 8.
105 *New York Colonization Journal*, X (July 1860); Redpath, *Guide*, 97-99.
106 *Ibid.*, preface.

our blood, the victims of these outrageous persecutions, is to continue the work of rehabilitation undertaken by the Founders of the Republic, and to remain faithful to the National Traditions." [107] Among the agents of the Haitian emigration bureau were Holly and Garnet, the latter showing his willingness to support emigration both within the New World and to Africa.

Events in the United States were continuing to give impetus to the emigration movement: the failure of John Brown's raid, the split in the Democratic Party, and the founding of the avowedly anti-slavery Republican Party had both exacerbated feelings against Negroes and increased the interest in emigration. By January 1861, the Haitian emigration campaign seemed to be succeeding. After five weeks in Philadelphia, Holly reported that "the choicest spirits among our people ... are thoroughly awake to the importance of the present movement and ready to give it their contribution." [108] Garnet also rejoiced "to see that there are more of the colored people ... in favor of this movement than they are of any other of the present age." [109] Indeed, by 1861 almost all American Negro leaders had given some expression of support to Negro emigration. Even the formidable Frederick Douglass gave in and accepted an invitation by the Haitian government to visit that country. [110]

Thus, when Delany and Campell returned to the United States in late December 1860, they found that the feeling for emigration was stronger than ever. But Delany did not become involved in a conflict with the Haiti group. He soon let it be known that he was preparing for "a hasty return to Africa where my duty calls me." He called for the cooperation in his venture "of intelligent persons ... of various occupations, among whom mechanics and cotton cultivators are acceptable." Select emigration was essential, he felt, to ensure the success of his plan; for "Africa is our fatherland, we, its legitimate descendants, and we will never agree or consent to see this ... step that has been taken for her regeneration by her own descendants blasted." [111]

Liberians, too, were encouraged by the steady, if moderate, flow of emigrants. In the 1850s, Liberia had settled a total of 5,029—almost as many as had been settled in the previous thirty years. The Negro republic's incorporation of Maryland in 1857 and purchase of territory in the area of the Mano and Gallinas Rivers had given it a coastline of 500 miles. Late in 1860, the Reverend James Payne wrote a series of articles in the *Liberia Herald* entitled "A Plea for Liberia," with a view to arresting the attention of American Negroes and directing their attention to the land of their fathers. And the vice-president, D. B. Warner, a close friend of Blyden's, wrote that he was gratified "that Liberia had begun to make a favourable impression abroad among whites and colored." He hoped American Negroes would "reestablish themselves in this our fatherland." [112]

---

[107] *Ibid.*, 104. [108] *Weekly Anglo-African*, II (Feb. 16, 1861).
[109] *Ibid.*, II (Jan. 26, 1861).
[110] Howard H. Bell, "Negro Nationalism: A Factor in Emigration Projects, 1858–61," *Journal of Negro History*, XLVIII (Jan. 1962), 43.
[111] *Weekly Anglo-African*, I (Jan. 26, 1861).
[112] *African Repository*, XXXVI (Jan. 1861), 87.

V I

There is one more Negro leader who should be mentioned here, Alexander Crummell. He left the United States in 1847 at the age of thirty-six; after graduating from Queens College, Cambridge, he went to Liberia in 1853. As in the case of Blyden, he sought to bring about reform in Liberian society and to impress upon his countrymen their high responsibility.[113] He wanted Liberia to extend its influence and jurisdiction over the inland peoples, and he took a leading part in organizing schemes for exploring and opening up the interior. In September 1860 he published an open letter to win the support of all the American Negro leaders, both emigrationists and anti-emigrationists, for Africa.[114]

To appease the anti-emigrationists, he rejected the idea that America could never be the home of the Negro, but he maintained that the task of civilizing Africa was peculiarly that of westernized Negroes: "without doubt God designs great things for Africa and ... black men themselves are without doubt to be the chief instruments." The civilizing process could be accomplished by voluntary emigration, by the pooling of economic resources and inauguration of trade between America and Africa, and by support of the missionary activities of American Negro churches. "From the port of Lagos in almost direct line through a crowded population, and passing by cities containing tens of thousands of people, a highway is now open reaching to Rabba on the banks of the Niger. All through this country the coloured churches of America can send their missionaries, build up Christian churches, and lay the foundation of Christian colleges and universities." [115] By utilizing this combination of commerce and Christianity, not only would Africa be civilized, but American Negroes would gain in wealth and respect:

> At an early date whole fleets of vessels, manned and officered from the United States and Liberia, would outrival all the other agencies which are now being used for grasping West African commerce. Large and important houses will spring into existence among you, all through the States. Wealth will flow into your coffers, and affluence would soon exhibit itself amid all your associations.
>
> The kings and tradesmen of Africa, having the demonstration of Negro capacity before them, would hail the presence of their black kinsmen from America and would be stimulated by a generous emulation ... To the farthest interior, leagues and combinations would be formed with men of commerce, and thus civilization, enlightenment and Christianity would be carried to every state and town, and village of interior Africa.[116]

[113] See, for example, Alexander Crummell, *The Duty of a Rising Christian State, Annual Oration Before the Common Council and Citizens of Monrovia, Liberia, July 26, 1855.* (London, 1856).

[114] Alexander Crummell, *The Relation and Duties of the Free Colored Men in America to Africa* (Hartford, 1861), 55.

[115] *Ibid.*, 45.   [116] *Ibid.*, 25.

Crummell, like Blyden and Delany, had strongly supported the founding of Liberia College, on which construction had begun by 1860. The college was to be the first modern, secular English-speaking institution of higher education in tropical Africa. Crummell and other Negro patriots hoped that the college would attract Negro scholars and students from all parts of the world.

Crummell and Blyden left Liberia in February 1861 for England and America, to win financial support for the college and to study institutions of higher learning. In England, Blyden met W. E. Gladstone, Chancellor of the Exchequer, with whom he had been in correspondence, and Lord Brougham, the great humanitarian, both of whom he sought to interest in the "little Republic" that was destined to "revolutionize for good that whole portion of Africa." [117]

When Blyden and Crummell arrived in the United States in June 1861, war had already begun between the Union and the Confederacy. But this seemed to make no difference to the plans of the emigrationists. By May, Delany and Campell had joined forces with Garnet's African Civilization Society in an attempt to raise funds to promote colonization in the Niger Valley.[118] Campell, "appearing in native costumes," lectured regularly on West Africa and vowed that "my home shall be in Africa though I be the only person from America." [119] Delany and Campell had each published a book describing the expedition to the Niger Valley and propagandizing for the cause of colonization.[120] In November the African Civilization Society increased its strength by gaining the support of men who held high offices in the African Methodist Episcopal Church.[121]

Blyden and Crummell joined with the other emigrationists. Blyden himself welcomed the civil war as the "purifier of a demoralised American conscience," [122] and no doubt as a means of bringing slavery to an end. However, he warned Negroes that they were deceiving themselves if they thought they could earn proper respect in the United States. He urged them to be makers and witnesses of history: "It need not imply any pretensions to prophetic insight for us to declare that we live in the shadows of remarkable events in the history of Africa."[123] Crummell asserted that "the free black man of this country . . . is superior to the Russian, the Polander, the Italian" and was now "in a state of preparedness for a new world's history, for a mission of civilization." He saw the decline of Anglo-Saxon civilizations in "the moral and political convulsion" within the United States. But "now the Negro is

[117] Blyden to Gladstone, May 3, 1861, British Museum Add. Mss. 44396/63; Blyden to Lord Brougham, May 24, 1861, Brougham Papers, University College, London.

[118] *Constitution of the African Civilization Society* (New Haven, 1861), 1.

[119] *Weekly Anglo-African*, II (March 16, 1861).

[120] Delany, *Official Report*, and Campell, *Pilgrimage*.

[121] *Constitution of the African Civilization Society*, 4.

[122] Blyden to Gladstone, June 16, 1862, British Museum Add. Mss. 44398/183.

[123] Edward W. Blyden, *Hope for Africa, A Discourse . . .* (tract no. 8 from the *Colonization Journal*, 1861), 16.

rising and will rise ... God has destined a great future for the Negro race ... On the continent of Africa, a civilization of a new type and more noble and generous ... than has ever existed, is on the eve of starting a new life." [124]

When Blyden and Crummell returned to Liberia in the fall of 1861, they reported the support of American Negroes for emigration. The Liberian government decided to act: legislation was passed by which Blyden and Crummell were appointed commissioners "to protect the cause of Liberia to the descendants of Africa in that country, and to lay before them the claims that Africa had upon their sympathies, and the paramount advantages that would accrue to them, their children and their race by their return to the fatherland." [125]

The action of the Liberian government had little effect. The outbreak of the civil war was the turning point after which there was a fairly sharp decline in pan-Negro nationalism. At the start of the war, Douglass canceled his trip to Haiti and urged American Negroes to stay and help to decide the outcome of the struggle, advice that apparently found quick response. The emigrationists, who had at first regarded the war as irrelevant to their plans, were unable to act because of lack of funds. The war apart, emigration to Haiti had by December 1861 virtually come to an end because of reports of the high mortality rate among the emigrants and unattractive living conditions. [126] There was a correspondingly swift decline in emigration to Liberia. By early 1862, Negro leaders were again united to work for the victory of the North. Indeed, when in the summer of 1862 Lincoln decided to put into effect his scheme for gradual Negro emancipation with colonization, he received no support from American Negro leaders. [127] Thus when Blyden and Crummell returned to the United States as official commissioners in the summer of 1862, to urge American Negroes to "return to the fatherland," they found "an indolent and unmeaning sympathy—sympathy which put forth no effort, made no sacrifices, endured no self-denial, braved no obloquy for the sake of advancing African interests." [128] Further, Lincoln's proclamation of January 1, 1863, ending slavery, and the use later in that year of Negro troops in the Union army, made American Negroes feel sure that a new day had dawned for them.

In this they were wrong, of course. Although Negroes were awarded political and civil rights during the period of Reconstruction (1867–1877), their hopes of full integration within American society were largely frustrated. This disappointment, continuing throughout the nineteenth century and into the twentieth, again resulted in a desire to leave for other parts of the Americas or for Africa. Many Negro leaders once more urged emigration to Africa:

[124] *African Repository*, XXXVII (Sept. 1861), 279.
[125] Cited in the American Colonization Society, *Forty-Sixth Annual Report* (Washington, 1863), 6.
[126] Benjamin Quarles, *Lincoln and the Negro* (New York, 1962), 120.
[127] Benjamin Quarles, *The Negro in the Civil War* (Boston, 1953), 147–149.
[128] Blyden, *Liberia's Offering*, 69.

Henry M. Turner, bishop in the African Methodist Episcopal Church; Pap Singleton; R. H. Cain, like Turner an AME bishop; J. McCants Stewart, a lawyer; and J. Albert Thorne, a doctor from Barbados. Their activities are, however, beyond the scope of this article.[129]

VII

Pan-Negro nationalists before 1862 did not succeed in creating and sustaining either a return to Africa on a large scale or any significant and persistent contact with African communities. The movement did not come to an end in 1862 and, in spite of the difficulties of the years following the American civil war, it is hardly likely that everyone at the first Pan-African conference of 1900 had forgotten the personalities and events of fifty years earlier. The twentieth-century Pan-Africanists were concerned that Negroes should mobilize to defend and extend their rights wherever they lived. They held their first congress in London, the most imperial of capital cities, in the middle of the South African War, and increasingly they identified themselves with the larger movement against imperialism.

Nineteenth-century pan-Negro nationalism and Garveyism had much in common. They both owed their existence almost entirely to discrimination against Negroes in the New World, particularly in the United States. They shared a preoccupation with emigration, with a great African past, and with an equally great future, and both relied heavily on leaders from the West Indies, particularly those who had lived in the United States. Nineteenth-century pan-Negro nationalism produced no leader to match Marcus Garvey in the emotional quality of his oratory, the scale of organization and mobilization of resources he achieved, or, indeed, the bitter disillusionment that followed his failure. Though the nineteenth-century movement did achieve a sustained, if limited, emigration, both movements failed to achieve a massive emigration to Africa or its "regeneration."

In their frequent references to the need for action to save Africa, and to prove by deeds the fundamental equality of Africans with other peoples, these Negroes from the New World showed their indebtedness to the societies from which they came. References to the effects of "commerce and Christianity," "the mission of civilization," the great resources of Africa, and the racial bases of society are found as much in the writings of the pan-Negro nationalists as in the writings of missionary groups and subsequently among some believers in imperial rule. It is, however, in reference to "regeneration," with its implication of a great African past, and to the frontal attack on notions of white superiority that the pan-Negro nationalists of the nineteenth century were pioneers.

[129] See August Meier, *Negro Thought in America, 1880–1915* (Ann Arbor, 1963).

St. Clair Drake

"HIDE MY FACE?"
ON PAN-AFRICANISM AND NEGRITUDE

I ran to the rocks to hide my face;
The rocks cried out, No hiding place,
There's no hiding place down here.

A SPIRITUAL

As the selection by Hollis Lynch indicates, identification with
Africa has been a persistent theme in American Negro thinking,
muted in some periods, heightened in others. This concern—often
laden, it is true, with considerable ambivalence toward the ancestral
continent—has ranged from an interest in the African past and
African culture to the advocacy of colonization as a solution for the
problems facing black men in America. In "Hide My Face?" St.
Clair Drake has explored with great sensitivity and subtlety the
attitudes of American Negroes toward Africa in the twentieth cen-
tury. Although written in 1965, before the current emphasis upon
"black consciousness," the essay perceptively predicted the swelling
sense of race pride and identification with Africa which exists today.

THE end of the Second World War marked the beginning of the liberation
of Africa and of racial integration in the United States. Although there is
no direct causal connection between the two momentous developments, they
are interrelated and they influence each other. That they occurred at approximately the same time has profound implications for Negro Americans, all of
whom are aware that they are "of African descent." In America, this "African
descent" is considered to be the only really socially relevant fact about Negroes,
and some states actually define a Negro as "anyone with an ascertainable trace of
Negro blood." Whether those who are defined as "American Negroes" like it
or not, history and the peculiar evaluations of American society have linked them

St. Clair Drake, "Hide My Face?" in Herbert Hill, ed., *Soon, One Morning* (New
York: Alfred A. Knopf, 1963), pp. 78–105. Reprinted with permission of St. Clair Drake.

with the fate of Africa and its peoples. This is a reality to which Negroes in the United States have always had to adjust.

In 1925, the distinguished American Negro literary critic Alain Locke presented an anthology to the public which bore the title *The New Negro*. The poets, essayists, and writers of fiction whose works appeared in the volume were participants in what came to be called the "Negro Renaissance," that remarkable outburst of literary creativity which followed the First World War. The dominant theme in the work of all these writers was "the Negro experience." The intellectual vanguard of ten million Negro Americans were expressing the moods and wishes, the aspirations and frustrations, the joy as well as the anger, of their ethnic group. They were also revealing their own sensitive reactions to reality, and laying bare the distinctive configurations of ideas and emotions which each had elaborated in order to cope with reality. For some of them, Africa was a part of this reality.

Alain Locke in his own essay, "The Negro's Americanism," dissociated himself from those who saw extensive evidence of African cultural survivals in the United States, insisting that "what there is today in Harlem distinct from the white culture that surrounds it is, as far as I am able to see, merely a remnant from the peasant days in the South. Of the African culture not a trace." But he did not mean by this that he was unconcerned with Africa or African culture. African art was one of his consuming interests.

The two most talented of the "New Negro" poets, Langston Hughes and Countee Cullen, felt impelled to speak of a sense of "kinship" with Africa. Langston Hughes's confrontation of the African reality was composed of bewilderment tinged with nostalgia, as these lines from "Afro-American Fragment" suggest:

> *So long,*
> *So far away*
> *Is Africa. . . .*
> *Through some vast mist of race*
> *There comes the song*
> *I do not understand . . .*

Apparently Langston Hughes could not bring himself to accept the kind of "understanding" which his fellow troubadour, a white man, Vachel Lindsay, had achieved. He too had heard the song "Boomlay, boomlay, boomlay, BOOM." Lindsay was so sure *he* understood that he gave his poem "The Congo" a subtitle, "A Study of the Negro Race." The poetic "study" was divided into three parts: "Their Basic Savagery," "Their Irresponsible High Spirits," and "The Hope of Their Religion." Vachel Lindsay had no doubts about the origin of the gusto which expressed itself in drunken table pounding by

> *Fat black bucks in a wine-barrel room,*
> *Barrel house kings with feet unstable.*

They had inherited the wild emotions of "tatooed cannibals." He could plainly see "the Congo creeping through the black," and this "insight" also explained to him why

> *Wild crap shooters with a whoop and a call*
> *Danced the juba in their gambling hall....*
> *Guyed the policemen and laughed them down...*

These American Negroes were simply blood kinsmen of "cake walk princes... fat as shotes" cavorting in the jungle, and putting "the skull-faced lean witch doctors" to rout with their exhuberant dancing. Both Africans and American Negroes such as these were under the spell of "Mumbo Jumbo, God of the Congo," the god who will "hoodoo you."

But Vachel Lindsay also saw a vision of hope for Negroes, in Africa and America:

> *A good old Negro in the slums of the town*
> *Preached at a sister for her velvet gown,*
> *Howled at a brother for his low down ways....*
> *And the people all repented a thousand strong*
> *From their stupor and savagery and sin and wrong.*

So Mumbo Jumbo died in the jungle, and "pioneer angels cleared the way for a Congo paradise... a singing wind swept the Negro nation... and redeemed were the forests, the beasts, and the men..."

Such eschatological anthropology was widely shared by Americans during the early years of the century, offensive as it may sound to modern ears. Both the image of African savagery and the implications of inherited African traits repelled many American Negroes, while others accepted the image, believed in the myths, and worked for the specific variety of "redemption" about which Vachel Lindsay wrote. The "New Negro" had to come to terms with the image and the popular Negro reaction to it.

Langston Hughes did not reject identification with Africa because he saw it as a derogation. He sought, rather, for the deeper understanding that comes from knowledge and empathy.

Countee Cullen, too, chose to grapple with the African reality and America's distortion of it. In his long, rich, image-laden poem "Heritage," Africa emerges as a romantic land of "wild, barbaric birds, Goading massive jungle herds," a land of supple cats and slithering snakes." Mumbo Jumbo was present too, for Cullen found "Quaint, outlandish heathen gods, Black men fashion out of rods." Africa was, to him, the setting for a D. H. Lawrence paradise where "Young forest lovers lie, Plighting troth beneath the sky."

Vachel Lindsay's evangelical Puritanism led him to reject Africa until it should have been "redeemed." Cullen not only accepts it as it is, but also rejects the vision of "redemption." He even expresses regret that he and other American Negroes have been subjected to such "redemption," for he sees them as having been symbolically castrated in the process:

My conversion came high-priced,
I belong to Jesus Christ....
Lamb of God although I speak
With my mouth thus, in my heart
Do I play a double part....
Wishing he I served were black ...?
Not yet has my heart or head
In the least way realized
They and I are civilized.

Cullen bemoans the fact that Christianity has forced him to "Quench my pride and cool my blood." This romantic, neo-pagan response to Africa was probably as shocking to most middle-class Negroes as Vachel Lindsay's was repulsive. The significant thing is that Countee Cullen felt he *had* to respond to Africa.

Langston Hughes heard "the song" through "some vast mist of race," and said frankly, "I do not understand." Countee Cullen, however, reported that he too felt "the Congo creeping through the black," or, as he phrased it, "The unremittent beat Of cruel padded feet Walking through my body's street." And like the feet in Thompson's "Hound of Heaven," they beat with "majestic instancy," and made him cry out, "Ever must I twist and squirm, Writhing like a baited worm." Cullen, in this mood, felt that American culture was stifling what the African poet Senghor would call his *negritude*. Cullen began his poem with a query:

What is Africa to me
Copper sun or scarlet sea,
Jungle star or jungle track,
Strong bronzed men, or regal black,
Women from whose loins I sprang
When the birds of Eden sang?
One three centuries removed
From the scenes his fathers loved,
Spicy grove, cinnamon tree,
What is Africa to me?

In 1951, Akinsola Akiwowo, a Nigerian student studying in the United States, wrote "Song in a Strange Land," which appeared in *Phylon*, a quarterly published by Atlanta University. His artistry is not so polished as that of either Langston Hughes or Countee Cullen, but the sentiments are significant:

Shall I sing your song, Africa,
In this strange land of hate and love?
Shall I sing to them whose forebears
Were torn away from you long ago?
For they know you not, but believe

All the strange and gory stories
They oft have read and seen in films:
Apes, thick jungles, and men with spears,
And nude women with pancake lips.
They have not seen how, what, you are;
That long estrangement shuts their eyes . . .
Some say you are a thing of shame!

                        •   •   •

But fill our hearts, Africa's sons,
With holy untiring zest to work,
And ask no rest till She is free
And great with true greatness from Thee.
Then make them see again, dear Lord;
Open their ears, unleash their tongues
And make them see, hear, proclaim
What they now refuse to apprehend!

Since "Song in a Strange Land" was sung, "holy untiring zest" has brought results. In 1961 African states were sitting in the United Nations. A new image of Africa was in the making.

The struggle for independence and for national development is something all American Negroes can understand, and it is a phenomenon with which they can all identify.

The wheel has come full circle, for when the Governor General of Nigeria was inaugurated, Langston Hughes was among the honored guests. (He had been a schoolmate of Governor Azikiwe at Lincoln University.) The governor ended his address by quoting Hughes's poem of optimism, "Dawn." Meanwhile, Langston Hughes had been hearing songs from Africa which he could understand. He had never abandoned the effort to understand. So he compiled an anthology, *An African Treasury: Articles, Essays, Stories, Poems by Black Africans*. Having understood, he was now taking it upon himself to interpret, and in the introduction to this volume he wrote:

> When I first began to gather this material, the term *negritude*—currently popular with African writers, especially poets influenced by Senghor—had not come into common use. But there was in most of the writing that reached me an accent of Africanness—blackness, if you will—not unlike the racial consciousness found in the work of American Negro writers a quarter of a century ago. The Harlem writers of that period, however, had to search for their folk roots. The African writer has these roots right at hand. . . . Evident in most African writing, of course, is a pride in country, which underlies everything that is thought and spoken south of the Sahara today. It is an African pride with a character all its own, which owes allegiance neither to West nor East but to its newly emerging self. . . . Perhaps

the phrase that best sums up this swelling pride and fierce insistence on individual identity is *African Personality*.... While it is a personality necessarily—and happily—as varied as the people of Africa, it is founded on a common bond, a common yearning... 'Come back, Africa!'

CULTURAL PAN-AFRICANISM

The term "negritude" was first used by the Haitian poet Aimé Césaire and by the Senegalese scholar-poet Léopold Senghor. The American Negro scholar Samuel Allen has pointed out in his essay "Tendencies in African Poetry":

> The term is not amenable to easy definition.... It represents in one sense the Negro African poet's endeavor to recover for his race a normal self-pride, a lost confidence in himself, a world in which he again has a sense of identity and a significant role.

But, in another dimension, the term denotes the assumption that there are impulses, traits, and conceptions of the world which are characteristic of Negroes everywhere. To Senghor, these include "softness" and a non-mechanical approach to men and things, "spirituality," and a direct but symbol-laden approach to sexuality. Senghor sees negritude as that quality of life in Harlem which "softens" the hardness of New York. And he recognizes it in the American soldiers on the streets of Paris, to whom he speaks as follows:

> *Behind your strong face, I did not recognize you.*
> *Yet I had only to touch the warmth of your dark hand—*
> *my name is Africa!*
> *And I discovered lost laughter again, and heard old*
> *voices, and the roaring rapids of the Congo.*
>   .   .   .
>
> *Oh black brothers, warriors whose mouths are*
> *singing flowers—*
> *Delight of living when winter is over—*
> *You I salute as messengers of peace!*

Allen points out that many American Negro intellectuals are

> inclined to feel that to affirm the rights and dignity of the Negro as a man among men is one, and a valid, thing but to acclaim a specific quality or a complex of traits or attitudes as peculiarly Negro... is distinctly another matter and smacks of the racism American social scientists have patiently been attempting to erase.

However, he notes that, in fact, negritude has a dialectical dimension, that it involves what Jean-Paul Sartre calls in his *Black Orpheus* anti-racist racism;

it accentuates differentness in order to win respect and abolish differences. Those who assert their negritude most vigorously have never isolated themselves from the main stream of French intellectual and political life and are "deeply aware that man, ultimately, is man and that his race is an attribute, only, of his more basic membership in the human community." One suspects that, had he lived to know them, Countee Cullen would have felt very much at home with "the poets of negritude." Langston Hughes, on the other hand, displays a depth of understanding but does not seem to have been caught up in the mystique of either negritude or the "African Personality."

Whatever one may think of the concept of negritude in its relation to modern social science, or as it applies to American Negroes, it is important to realize that it serves the function of reinforcing the self-esteem of an emergent Africa, and of investing the struggle for African liberation with meanings that transcend the continent—a struggle believed to benefit people of African descent everywhere. And it is significant, too, that those who developed the concept of negritude have been profoundly influenced by the "Negro experience" in America. The Haitian intellectuals of the early 1920's were influenced by the Negro Renaissance in the United States, and a most distinguished member of their ranks, Dr. Jean Price Mars, influenced Senghor, who in his essay "Que Sais-Je?" has written:

> Studying at the Sorbonne, I began to reflect upon the problem of a cultural renaissance in Black Africa, and I was searching—all of us were searching for a "sponsorship" which could guarantee the success of the enterprise. At the end of my quest it was inevitable that I would find Alain Locke and Jean Price Mars.

In 1947 an African intellectual from Senegal, Alioune Diop, established the magazine *Présence Africaine* in Paris, under the sponsorship of such patrons as Sartre, Camus, and Paul Rivet, as a medium for self-expression by Negroes everywhere. Richard Wright, the American Negro novelist, was a member of the sponsoring group. In 1956 the Society of African Culture, which had arisen to give organized expression to the objectives of *Présence Africaine*, convened the First International Congress of Negro Writers and Artists in Paris. A number of American Negroes accepted an invitation to attend, and as a result, an *American* Society of African Culture came into being.

When the poet-philosopher of negritude, Léopold Senghor, visited the United States in 1962 in his role as President of Senegal, the American President arranged a literary luncheon in his honor at the White House. In his introduction, President Kennedy referred to the 16,000,000 American Negroes as a bridge between the United States and Africa. Senghor, in turn, payed tribute to the poets of the American Negro Renaissance of the twenties as an early source of inspiration for him and his fellow intellectuals in Paris. Both men seemed to assume that something other than the color of the skin forms an enduring—and desirable—bond between Africans and Negroes in the United States. So long as white Americans and Africans act upon such an assumption, Negro American intellectuals will be forced to participate in what their Continental counterparts refer to as a "dialogue," an effort to discover what the "something" is. "What is Africa to me?" becomes an inescapable question.

The French-speaking "poets of negritude" feel that the bond between New World Negroes and Africans lies in the persistence of certain African behavior patterns and approaches to life which have survived in the New World. Senghor is very explicit about this when he speaks of *"the sense of communion, the gift of myth-making, the gift of rhythm"* as "the essential elements of negritude which you will find indelibly stamped on all the works and activities of the black man . . ." To him there is a Negro *élan*, the "active abandon of the African Negro toward the object" which is not only very real but is also a much-to-be-desired trait. He is convinced, furthermore, that Negroes differ fundamentally from white men in that "European reason is analytic through utilization; Negro reason is intuitive through participation." He even insists that "emotion is Negroid," and complains that he has been "wrongly reproached" for saying so, adding, "I do not see how one can account otherwise for our characteristics, for this negritude, which is the 'ensemble of cultural values of the black world' including the Americas, and which Sartre defines as 'a certain emotional attitude in respect to the world.'" As Sartre and Senghor see it, this Negro ethos expresses itself in various forms of art and ritual as well as in customs and institutions. It finds its purest expression, of course, in Negro-African cultures, but it is also evident in various aspects of Afro-Cuban, Afro-Brazilian, Afro-Haitian, and Afro-American cultural and social life. According to this view, where Negroes from Africa have been subjected to the influences of other cultures, they have borrowed and blended, rephrased and reinterpreted, but the end product always bears the stamp of negritude. (Senghor would probably cite the "swinging" of Anglo-Saxon hymn tunes in American Negro churches or the embroidering of Bible stories as vivid examples.) When groups or individuals try to suppress their negritude—and they can do so—they become "inauthentic Negroes, carbon copies of white men. They also thereby deprive the World Culture of the fructifying stimulus of 'Negro emotion.'"

In a paper prepared for the Second Congress of Negro writers and Artists, which met in Rome in 1959, Senghor presented an erudite and eloquent defense of his belief that the African tropical environment has, through the centuries, produced a human being with a special type of nervous and glandular system, "a being with open senses, permeable to all solicitations, even to the very waves of nature, without intermediary filtrants—I do not say without gaps —between subject and object. A thinking man to be sure, but first of all a man sensitive to forms and colors and especially to odors, sounds and rhythms." Such men are not confined to Africa. He writes:

What strikes me concerning Negroes in America is the permanence of non-physical but psychic traits of the African Negro, despite the mixture and despite the new environment. Some may try to explain this by segregation. To be sure, segregation explains partially the permanence of psychic traits, particularly the gift of emotion, but it does not explain all, especially not with Negroes of Latin America, where segregation is less real.

Certain of the reality of negritude and convinced that the African environment has produced it, Senghor falls back upon heredity for an explanation of both its tenacious persistence and the manner in which it changes. Speaking to a group of students at Oxford in 1962, he made an attempt to explain why negritude becomes diluted and attenuated when Negroes come in contact with other cultures, and revealed a Lamarckian view of inheritance in his comment that "as certain biologists point out, the psychological mutations brought about by education are incorporated in our genes and are transmitted by heredity." Thus, the negritude of New World Negroes has been changed through contact with a dominant culture (and by miscegenation), while the existence of negritude in Africa has been, and is, threatened by political and cultural imperialism.

It is not clear to what degree the so-called "apostles of negritude" agree with Senghor in detail, but all of them feel that the primary task of Negro intellectuals everywhere is to express negritude, proudly and without shame or apology, and to protect their cultures and literary and artistic traditions from being denigrated and disintegrated by bearers of "Western" culture (whether capitalist or communist). They feel that negritude should be cherished and cultivated and that enrichment from contact with other cultures should be carefully controlled. Negro Americans are summoned to participate along with Africans and West Indians in this historic task.

Most American Negro intellectuals have declined the invitation, although they have not broken off the dialogue. They feel that they have heard all of this before from the lips of enemies and patronizing white friends, and from Negro romantic primitivists of the twenties, such as Countee Cullen, as well as from less sophisticated members of their own group. It is disquieting to hear it now from a cultivated French-African savant. The concept of negritude elaborated by Senghor conjures up the ghost of Vachel Lindsay. It evokes unpleasant memories of Southern orators warning against the powerfulness of Negro blood that "always tells." It is a reminder of all the preachers—black and white (including Arnold Toynbee)—who espouse a peculiar kind of black messianism in which Negroes are said to have a mission to teach white men how to abjure materialistic goals and to demonstrate that patience and long-suffering are higher virtues than the iniquitous struggle for power. It presents an image of a kind of man they do not want to be, for they have no desire for "intuitive reason" in the place of "analytical reason." It rejects those values of the Western world which they have learned to prize—critical rationality, success in controlling the natural environment, Aristotle's Law of Measure, and, above all, individuality. It confuses race and culture, cause and effect, in a fashion they have learned to avoid. Senghor's voice seems to resound with echoes of Marcus Garvey, Mr. Mohammed, and Senator Bilbo. But above all, most Negro intellectuals reject this concept of negritude not only because they consider it undesirable but because they feel that it substitutes mysticism for science and ignores reality as they see it.

Yet, of the essential ingredients of negritude—a sense of communion, the gift of myth-making, and the gift of rhythm—they cannot deny their prevalence in the character structure and institutional expressions of thousands of American Negroes. Church services and political rallies, dancing and drama, as well as the songs and sagas of work and play and worship, are suffused with these characteristics. But modern social science has shown us that the presence of such traits has nothing to do with the inheritance of a special kind of nervous system or with inborn emotionality. In fact, there is nothing uniquely African about this particular combination of traits. They are to be found among peasant and tribal peoples everywhere. They are characteristic of what anthropologists call "folk societies." And until recently, most American Negroes were folk—rural and unsophisticated. Admittedly, the specific cultural forms through which these traits manifested themselves were, in the beginning, African; and African survivals are today perhaps more prevalent than many American Negroes wish to admit (although less widespread than some enthusiastic anthropologists would have us believe). No one denies that Negro American life has developed a "flavor" all its own. But it is Negro American not African. Even those who emphasize the presence of African survivals in American Negro life, such as Melville J. Herskovits in his *Myth of the Negro Past*, are careful to stress the fact that the culture of Negroes in the United States is Afro-*American* and not African, and that heredity has nothing to do with the retention of Africanisms.

Such African survivals as do exist, as well as a folk "sense of communion" and tendencies toward "myth-making," are rapidly disappearing as Negroes become predominantly urban and as participation in America's mass culture obliterates the ethos of the folk. Prosaic disenchantment and routine decorum are important earmarks of the constantly growing Negro middle-class, which has, moreover, set complete integration into American society as its goal. A "sense of communion" and the habit of "myth-making" still persist in lower-class churches in America, but as Senghor himself states, these are really characteristics of peasant societies. They will exist for decades to come in Africa and the West Indies, but in America, where Negroes are a numerical minority and share the values of the larger society, the processes of mobility and secularization are inexorable and irreversible. Negritude as Senghor defines it could not continue to persist in the United States even if all of the intellectuals desired it to do so.

One folk trait—"the gift of rhythm"—does persist, however, though not for the reasons Senghor would adduce. Rhythm is a salable commodity. It is marketed by members of jazz bands as well as by athletes of the Harlem Globetrotters variety. But it is a "gift" that has been acquired in large measure by the white Benny Goodmans in competition with the black Louis Armstrongs. It is probable that this aspect of negritude, expressed through music and dance, will persist in urban areas as well as rural, among white people as well as black. And insofar as it is not tied up with beliefs that "that's why darkies were born," it will be approved and treasured. But Langston Hughes's note of warning always sounds in the background:

> Because my mouth is wide with laughter
> And my feet are gay with song
> You do not know I suffer
> I've held my pain too long.

Although African cultural survivals and the folk character of American Negro life will become more and more attenuated, it is likely that an appreciation for African cultures and cultural products on the part of American Negroes will increase. Growing numbers of American Negroes, of all social levels, are learning to look at African art without laughing at the techniques of distortion or being puzzled by its stylization. They are beginning to face the bare bosoms and wild leaps of African concert artists without embarrassment and shame. They feel less threatened personally by the sight of sweating black bodies gyrating in magic rituals on screen and stage. They are beginning to feel that African cultural phenomena are not a "reflection upon the Negro race." Such transformations in attitude are taking place, in part, because of a growing awareness that white people of importance and influence think of African cultural products as important, beautiful, and acceptable. Negro American intellectuals can, perhaps, help to provide a more meaningful basis for acceptance.

But however much Negro Americans come to appreciate African cultures for what they are, it is likely that they will continue to think of the African folk and their products as different, non-Western, exotic, strange—as African. Some will come to understand what negritude means to the African intellectual, but they will not feel that it has any reference to them. They will identify but not emulate and will admire and appreciate without any desire to imitate. (And very, very few will feel the call to "return 'home.'") A few artists and intellectuals will "cash in" on the growing interest in Africa, but most will have more immediate American concerns to engage their time and attention. As familiarity with and appreciation of the poets of negritude grow among Negro Americans, they will feel a real sense of identity with the French-Guianese poet, Damas, who sings:

> The white man killed my father
> My father was proud—
> The white man seduced my mother
> My mother was beautiful—
> The white man burnt my brother
> Beneath the noonday sun—

My brother was strong
His hands red with black blood—
The white man turned to me
And in a conqueror's voice said,
"Hey boy, a chair, a napkin, a drink."

Every American Negro will know what this poet is talking about. Some will also understand what makes Damas write:

Give me back my black dolls
To disperse the image of pallid wenches, vendors of love
going and coming
on the boulevard of my boredom

But such words will have no personal significance except for those who have known a type of interracial sexual experience that is still rare in America. Most will even understand the psychology of rejection which appears in Aimé Césaire's poem which exalts black people as

. . . those who have never invented anything
They abandon themselves possessed to the essence of all things
Ignoring surfaces but possessed by the movement of all things.

But here American Negroes will begin to pull back emotionally. They are not prepared to glorify "those who have never invented anything"; they will be inclined to dismiss such sentiments as a "sour-grapes mechanism" which American Negroes no longer feel that mature sophisticated people should use. And they are likely to comment cynically that "Africans will sing another tune as soon as they have the sense of power that comes from independence and factories and dams." The mysticism and surrealism of Césaire is likely to leave them cold except for the enjoyment of words superbly handled:

My negritude is not a rock, its deafness
hurled against the clamor of the day

. . .

It plunges into the red flesh of the earth
It plunges into the burning flesh of the sky
It pierces the opaque prostration by its upright patience

Lovers of *avant-garde* poetry will enjoy Césaire and perhaps allow themselves to wish for a moment that they too had been born in a setting that could produce such an impassioned affirmation of identity.

In a sense the African writer stands today where the American Negro writer stood in the twenties. Now Sartre's *Black Orpheus* has overtones that echo what Carl Van Vechten used to say. This is nothing for Africans to be ashamed of or apologetic about, for the black man of letters has to go through this experience in a white man's world. But American Negroes have already passed through it. As Africans shake off colonial controls and confront the white world as political equals, as Negro poetry and fiction become more abundant, the concept of negritude itself will change. For instance, we already find Senghor in his Oxford address saying:

> Today our negritude no longer expresses itself in opposition to European values, but as a complement to them. Henceforth its militants will be concerned, as I have often said, not to be assimilated but to assimilate. They will use European values to arouse the slumbering values of negritude which they will bring as their contribution to the Civilization of the Universal.

As Senghor begins to think in these terms he is led to emphasize a dimension of negritude quite different from discussions of nervous systems and genes and the inheritance of acquired characteristics—negritude viewed as *myth*.

In defending his concept he reminded his English audience that all men live by myths. "For what are Free Enterprise, Democracy, Communism, but myths around which hundreds of millions of men and women organize their lives? Negritude itself is a myth (I am not using the word in any pejorative sense), but a living dynamic one, which evolves with its circumstances into a form of humanism ... it welcomes the complementary values of Europe and the white man, and indeed of all other races and continents. But it welcomes them in order to fertilize and reinvigorate its own values, which it then offers for the construction of a civilization which shall embrace all mankind." He himself has been working all along to weave Marxism and Catholicism into the fabric of negritude in order to produce an ideology of "African Socialism." Presumably negritude as myth can stand on its own feet without the prop of belief in the inheritance of acquired characteristics—as a body of belief about the nature of African society and its worth, including the cultural products of African society which have survived here and there in the New World.

Intellectuals are continuously involved in the process of making and remaking myths to replace those elaborated by the folk. American Negro intellectuals do not reject the dialogue with their African and West Indian counterparts as the process of remaking the myth goes on. They have the obligation, however, to submit the myth of negritude to ruthless critical analysis as a part of their contribution to the process. There is some evidence, for instance, that Senghor misunderstands some of the findings of modern science as well as the nature of race relations in the United States. For instance he writes:

> The Negro is quite different. American psychotechnicians have already confirmed that his reflexes are more natural, better adapted. That explains his utilization in industry and in the technical services of the armed forces in a higher percentage than that which he represents in the population of the United States of America.

What American Negroes know to be pseudo science in the service of those who are looking for rationalizations for segregation and discrimination is interpreted by Senghor as welcome fact! And he explains the consequences of a caste system in industry and in the armed services as a recognition of the Negro's anatomical uniqueness! This lack of familiarity with the natural and social sciences is prevalent to a surprising extent among British and Continental men of letters, but for African and West Indian writers to emulate them and to perpetuate their errors is a disservice to "the race" which they so passionately profess to defend and to advance.

Yet, if purged of its antiquated notions of biology and instinctual psychology, the concept of negritude has value in focusing our attention upon the cultural survivals and subtle African orientations which may still exist among us. It encourages serious consideration of African cultures and frees us from prejudices and distortions to which we have all been subjected. It opens up whole new vistas of appreciation for the great contributions which Africa has made to the stream of world culture. The myth of negritude—the belief that black men have developed cultures of worth, and that although these cultures may be different from those of the West they have values which all can appreciate and share—has important morale-building functions. It can give confidence to the masses in the West Indies and America, as well as in Africa, who smart under the stigma of their blackness and of being of African descent, although the intellectuals hardly need such a crutch.

Equally important is a recognition that *American* Negroes are involved in a struggle to become fully integrated into the nation and culture of their birth. This fight for equal rights does not mean that they deny their African heritage. It does, however, pose problems quite different from those faced in the West Indies and Africa, where dignity and equality are to be sought in a creative nationalism which leads toward sovereign states and federations of states. There is no danger that American Negroes will forget that they are Negroes, for no matter how much one may wish to be a Negro *American,* society forces him to see himself as an American *Negro.*

French-speaking African and West Indian writers have developed the concept of negritude as an ideology and a program to give meaning to their literary efforts. In its emphasis upon mystique, it is peculiarly French. Perhaps it is more than language which draws American Negro intellectuals closer to English-speaking writers and artists in Africa and the West Indies. They have no "program," no mystique, no ideology. They simply write and dance and sing and argue to express what they loosely and half-jokingly refer to as the African Personality.

In this era of African liberation, the myth of negritude should be, and probably will be subordinated to the broader myth of "Pan-African solidarity," viewed as the attempt to unite all Africans irrespective of race, creed, and color into some kind of functioning cohesive political unit. But negritude will live as an important subsidiary myth in the Pan-African movement, emphasizing that black Africans, West Indians, and Negro Americans *are* one people because they all suffer from the world's low estimation of Negroidness, blackness, African origins. They are bound together by memories of past suffering and by the hope of future triumphs. The success of one fragment of the dispersed peoples of African descent reflects credit upon all; the failure of one injures the reputations of all the rest. It is this common fate, not genes, which binds them together and reinforces the struggle against racism. It was the Negro folk in America who produced the spiritual "Walk Together, Children, Don't Ya Get Weary, There's a Great Camp Meeting in the Promised Land."

POLITICAL PAN-AFRICANISM

While preparations were being made in 1921 for the Second Pan-African Congress in London, a new and colorful leader burst upon the Harlem scene— the Honorable Marcus Aurelius Garvey, D.C.L., as he styled himself, a self-educated, eloquent, and fanatically zealous Jamaican who had come to the United States in 1915 to study Booker T. Washington's program and leadership. He had remained to organize his own Universal Negro Improvement Association with a doctrine of "Africa for the Africans," Black Zionism for picked cadres of New World Negroes, and racial solidarity for the rest so that they could carry on mutually beneficial trade with Africa through an African Communities League and the Black Star Line.

Garvey began to build up a following as the war ended, and on August 1, 1920, the First International Convention of the U.N.I.A. met in Harlem with evangelical fervor. A motto was proclaimed: "One God! One Aim! One Destiny." The U.N.I.A. welcomed everyone who desired "to work for the general uplift of the Negro peoples of the world." As the movement grew Garvey became the "Provisional President of Africa." The African Orthodox Church was organized with a black hierarchy and gave its blessings to the idea of a black God, a black Jesus, a black Madonna, and black angels. (Garvey gave Countee Cullen the black God he yearned for, but the poet could not accept Him on U.N.I.A. terms.)

The Universal African Legion rode on horseback in Harlem parades, the forerunners of the shock troops who would someday, at Garvey's call, hurl the white men into the sea, as "400,000,000 black men" rose under the banner of the red, black, and green. The Black Eagle Flying Corps marched in their uniforms, awaiting the day when the movement would supply them with planes to scourge those who had ravished "the Motherland." The Universal Black Cross Nurses studied first aid so they could give succor to black bodies everywhere. Pioneers were selected to begin what Garvey called Africa's "redemption." The uniforms, the parades, the speeches, the promises, and the hopes drew hundreds of thousands of urban Negroes to the Garvey movement in the immediate postwar years. How many actually dreamed of emigrating we shall never know.

There was a tone of superiority and condescension in the New World Negroes' U.N.I.A. manifesto, but the "Beloved and Scattered Millions," schooled as they were in church and lodge, knew no other idiom in which to speak:

To establish a universal confraternity among the race; to promote the spirit of love and pride; to reclaim the fallen; to administer to and assist the needy; to assist in civilizing the backward tribes of Africa; to assist in the development of independent Negro nations and communities; to establish a central nation for the race; to establish commissaries or agencies in the principal countries of the world for the representation of all Negroes; to promote a conscientious spiritual worship among the native tribes of Africa; to establish universities, colleges, academies, schools for the racial education and culture of the people; to work for better conditions among Negroes everywhere.

Garvey's collected speeches appeared in the *Philosophy and Opinions of Marcus Garvey*. Passionate in their espousal of black nationalism, they made such an impact upon Nkrumah when he was a student in America that he cites them as one of the primary sources of his "inspiration" as a developing nationalist leader.

The American Communist Party was founded the same year that Garvey called his first convention, and the Negro members of the Party received orders to bore from within and try to capture both the Garvey movement and the National Association for the Advancement of Colored People, which was founded in 1909. The N.A.A.C.P., the Pan-African movement, and the Communist Party were alike in one respect. They were all led by intellectuals whose problem was how to make contact with the masses. Garvey had no such problem, and while his movement grew apace in American cities and in the West Indies, another type of popular leader was emerging in Africa.

Just before the Second Pan-African Congress met in Brussels to chide the Belgians, a half-educated carpenter in the Congo, Simon Kimbangu, announced that he was "touched by the grace of God on the 18th March, 1921." His followers announced that the world would end in October, and fire from heaven would wipe out all white men. Some Kimbanguist preachers, however, declared that American Negroes would soon be coming to deliver their Congo brothers from white oppression. Kimbangu was immediately jailed, but the movement spread. (In 1958 eighteen years after Kimbangu's death, Belgian authorities in the Congo arrested over 3,000 Kimbanguists.) Similar "prophet movements" arose in the twenties in Kenya, the Rhodesias, and South Africa.

During 1923 the Garvey movement grew rapidly. Negotiations were proceeding for land in Liberia for the establishment of a colony. Steamships were being purchased for the Black Star Line. The ingathering of the exiles seemed about to begin. All the while, Du Bois and other Negro leaders were denouncing Garvey as a menace and a fraud and warning the Negro public against supporting him. But in 1924 a mission left for Liberia to complete arrangements for the settlement. Then, under pressure from Britain and France and fearful of Garvey's pretensions, Liberia suddenly broke off all negotiations. The Black Star Line ran into financial difficulties. The U.N.I.A. was facing the beginning of the end.

Although the Garvey movement was heading for disaster in the United States, its influence was spreading in Africa. In 1920, the President of the newly organized Congress of British West Africa said in his inaugural address that he had heard of the U.N.I.A. and charged his members to draw inspiration from it, and to be ready to welcome their "brothers" from overseas to share in the wealth of the country and to help in developing it. Nigerians slept on the beaches at Calabar with bonfires burning to light the ships of "Moses Garvey" in for the landfall. And Kadalie, leading the most powerful social movement South Africa had ever seen, said he had been profoundly influenced by Garveyism. George Padmore, a West Indian ex-Communist, in *Pan Africanism or Communism?* has called attention to the fact that

> In certain places the punishment for being seen with a *Negro World* [the U.N.I.A. paper] was five years at hard labor, and in French Dahomey it was life imprisonment. It was suppressed in such places as Trinidad, British Guiana, Barbados, etc., in the West Indies and all French, Italian, Portuguese, Belgian, and some of the British colonies in Africa.

Thomas Hodgkin, in his *Nationalism in Colonial Africa*, notes that "the impact of Garveyism can be traced in British and French West Africa as well as in South Africa, particularly during the period of unrest and revolt immediately following the First World War"; referring to the growth of African independent churches, he writes:

> Probably the most important single outside stimulus was the American-born Garvey movement, in which the strands of Ethiopianism and Pan Africanism were closely interwoven. Marcus Garvey...was successful in spreading the idea of Independent African churches as an instrument of African liberation.

About 1935 the African separatist churches among the Kikuyu in Kenya brought in one of Garvey's bishops to train and ordain preachers. It was this group of churches and their affiliated schools that formed part of the seedbed from which the Mau Mau eventually grew.

But in 1925, the year of the publication of *The New Negro*, the Garvey bubble burst. The Provisional President of Africa was sent to a federal prison, convicted of using the mails to defraud. As the gates closed upon him, he promised that if he died he would return in the wind and the rain to trouble the white man and lead the black man to victory. Garvey was an embarrassment to Negro intellectuals. (It is significant that none has ever chosen to write a biography of him.) But all of them concede that black folks were given a sense of pride and worth as a result of his efforts.

Du Bois convened his Fourth (and last) Pan-African Congress in 1927, in New York. Most of the 220 delegates represented American Negro women's organizations, but representatives of ten foreign countries were also present, including Chief Amoah II from the Gold Coast. It was in this year, too, that President Harding pardoned Garvey and deported him to Jamaica.

Garvey blamed the leaders of the N.A.A.C.P., the Communists, and the Jews for his downfall rather than his own business ineptitude and overweening arrogance. His charges were, of course, absurd. The Communists, on the other hand, after their failure to infiltrate the Garvey movement, denounced it. The Sixth Congress of the Communist International in 1928 made a slashing attack upon the movement in a formal ideological statement:

> Garveyism, which formerly was the ideology of the masses, like Gandhism, has become a hindrance to the revolutionization of the Negro masses. Originally advocating social equality for Negroes, Garveyism subsequently developed into a peculiar form of Negro "Zionism" which instead of fighting American imperialism advanced the slogan: "Back to Africa!" This dangerous ideology, which bears not a single genuine democratic trait, and which toys with the aristocratic attributes of a non-existent "Negro kingdom," must be strongly resisted, for it is not a help but a hindrance to the mass Negro struggle for liberation against American imperialism.

George Padmore, writing in *Pan Africanism or Communism?* in 1955, claims that

> Had the Communists succeeded in capturing the Garvey movement and in gaining control of other black nationalist groups, specially selected Negro militants were to have been recruited and trained in Moscow as cadres for colonial work in Africa.

Padmore was himself a leader in the colonial section of the Communist International during the period of which he writes. In 1935 he broke with the Communists, and went to London, where he organized the International African Service Bureau and the Pan-African Federation.

By the time the Second World War erupted, Padmore had developed a distinctive Pan-African theory, namely, that only Africans could liberate Africa, and that only "Pan-African Socialism" could prevent an eventual Communist takeover there. Kwame Nkrumah joined the small group of nationalists around Padmore in 1943, and the two of them, together with Jomo Kenyatta, did the preparatory political work for the Fifth Pan-African Congress.

When the Sixth Pan-African Congress (the All African Peoples Conference organized by Padmore and Nkrumah) met in Ghana in 1958, Nkrumah began his speech to the final session with these words:

> We are happy to see so many of our brothers and sisters from the New World here today. Before many of us were conscious of our own degradation, it was the New World Negroes who raised the banner of African liberation. Two names I must mention, Marcus Garvey and W. E. B. Du Bois.

NEW IMAGES IN THE MAKING

Both Countee Cullen and the church-oriented segment of the American Negro population shared Vachel Lindsay's widely accepted image of Africa. But whereas the Negro poet made a virtue of African "primitivism," the Christians deplored it. Negro Christians differed from white Christians, however, in their appraisal of what were, to them, the undesirable aspects of contemporary African reality. They saw Africa in a larger time perspective. They visualized a Golden Age in the remote past, before the present state of affairs had come to pass, as well as an Africa to be "redeemed" in the future. Du Bois, Garvey, and the Communists, too, were convinced that Africa would be "redeemed," but not in a religious sense. The Communists looked forward to the classless society that would emerge from a revolution led by New World Negroes. Garvey had an apocalyptic vision of a united Africa functioning as a powerful equal in the comity of nations. In his view, too, Negroes would play a messianic role. Some kind of African Socialism lay in the future, as Du Bois and Padmore conceived it, but African leaders would make their own revolution, with New World Negroes operating only as catalytic agents. Some Africans were influenced by all the varieties of "redemption" which emanated from the New World, but history did not assign a decisive role to any of them.

The African leaders who breached the bastions of colonialism in the 1950's and 1960's elaborated their own ideas of Pan-Africanism, negritude, and the "African Personality," ideas which reflect the influences of Marxism and Western democratic thought, but also acknowledge some intellectual indebtedness to New World Negro intellectuals and leaders. But the product is their own, based upon a fierce and passionate conviction that Africans alone must determine the goals and the strategies of their own liberation and development. It is this African "pride" that Hughes came eventually to understand. Du Bois understands it, too, but feels that the Communist world is more likely to respect it than is the West. The relation of New World Negroes to contemporary Africa is now in the process of redefinition.

For a very small group of American Negroes, the New Africa will offer a refuge from the race prejudice of the present or the integration of the future, but latter-day Garveyism is likely to have a very limited appeal. The African states will probably welcome the few exiles who want to be gathered in so long as they become peaceful and industrious citizens. There will not be, however, any campaigns urging them to "come home."

For a somewhat larger group, Africa will offer a focus for meaningful social action. It has served this function in the past for members of missionary societies. It does so today for a growing number of American Negroes who are interested in cementing intercultural ties or doing research. A "cult of Africa" has always existed within the Negro community. It will probably grow in size, and will include a mutually incompatible group of devotees ranging from Harlem's fanatical black nationalists who heckle at United Nations meetings, through middle-class families that specialize in entertaining African dignitaries, to members of the American Society for African Culture. Varied groups of Africans are beginning to cherish their relationships with these segments of the Afro-American world. Thoughtful American Negroes are aware of some of the dangers inherent in this type of close identification with Africa. Tendencies to gloss over, and even to suppress, the less favorable aspects of African life will appear. Temptations to claim a monopoly of understanding Africa will manifest themselves. There may even be sharp conflicts of loyalty if some African states veer away sharply from the West. There is also the risk of isolation from white friends and colleagues, although this has not happened to French-African intellectuals who emphasize their negritude. Despite the dangers, some American Negroes will continue to feel that the rewards of a close identification with Africa are worth the risks.

Increasing numbers of American Negroes, too, are likely to find careers in Africa with American church, government, or business institutions. African attitudes toward them, will, no doubt, always be a mixture of pride at seeing successful Negroes occupying high places and some measure of apprehension, wariness, and resentfulness over Negroes allowing themselves to be "used" by the white man in his contact with Africans. But insofar as Negroes are not involved in the exploitation of Africans or in attempts to frustrate their national aspirations, Pan-African sentiments of friendliness are likely to override antagonism. The fortunes of Negroes who represent the American government abroad, however, can be expected to vary with the twists and turns of both African and American foreign policy. As for missionaries, the "African Personality" is certain to reject any among them, whether they be black or white, who stand in the way of the development of Africa's own brand of Christianity or try to control Africa's churches.

For most American Negroes, however, Africa is likely to remain the far-off but inescapable fact that it has always been. It will become less and less a source of embarrassment, however, as the image of successful nations replaces that of "savages." Leaders cut in the heroic mold of Kenyatta and Lumumba will continue to stir the imagination and provide symbols of protest and courage with which American Negroes can identify, but there will be no ever-present sense of involvement with Africa. Feelings of shame and rejection, however, are likely to give way to pride over specific persons and events. At the same time, any attempts to suggest that they are Africans and not Americans will certainly be resisted. They will be interested in Africa, but not especially "concerned," and the idea that American Negroes have any mission to "redeem" Africa, in either a religious or a secular sense, will disappear.

When the executive secretary of the N.A.A.C.P., in welcoming Nkrumah to America, spoke of the "blood tie," everyone knew that he was using the term in symbolic and metaphorical sense, that he was talking about historical experiences and sentiments which bind American Negroes to the peoples of Africa. "Blood" will continue to function as a most inadequate verbal symbol for something else, and American Negro intellectuals must accept it as one of their never-ending duties to explain to less highly trained Americans, as well as to many of their European and African counterparts, that insofar as they accept the idea of negritude (as either a present reality or a convenient myth), they speak of qualities which have survived by virtue of the toughness of a culture, not through immutability of genes.

As the processes of integration in the United States proceed at an accelerated pace, many Negroes may find themselves wishing to cling to certain aspects of Negro life in America which seem to them rich, familiar, and warm, despite the fact that they will, at the same time, demand all of their civil rights. This is in no way inconsistent with the pluralistic conception of American society which is gaining popularity in some quarters. But, in any event, full integration into American life is a long way off, and amalgamation is even further away. There will be Negro Americans and a "Negro community" in America for many, many years to come. Their white fellow Americans are not going to let Negro Americans forget that they are of African descent even if they want to. Negro Americans will continue to confront the question: "What is Africa to me?" Seeing integration opening up before them, many will be inclined to answer: "Nothing!" Others will give Langston Hughes's answer of the 1920's—"So long, so far away"—and for them the song will be, forever, the song they cannot understand.

For others, however, because of the African friends they have made, or because they wish to be identified with the process of "poetic justice" now working itself out, or because of sentiments which became deeply imbedded in their youth, or because they smart under the continued impact of deprecatory definitions placed upon their own physical Negroidness, Africa will function as a "spiritual homeland." They will share the feelings which made a Nigerian who had studied in America, Mboni Ojike, write a book entitled *I Have Two Countries*. There is nothing "un-American" about this, for such identification has its parallel among the Poles and the Irish, the Jews and the Swedes, and numerous other groups who keep alive both memories and contacts with an "ancestral homeland."

Perhaps the most significant impact which the New Africa and America's changing image of it will have may be the reassurance it will give in regard to the capacity and worth of "blackness." Seeing successful and forceful Africans winning the respect of white Americans—people like Senghor and Azikiwe—will bolster the self-esteem of many American Negroes. For darker and more Negroid individuals whose self-esteem is frequently threatened by the derogatory appraisals which American aesthetic standards place upon their physical traits, the New Africa will have the same tonic effect that the Garvey moment had—an acceptance of their own physical image. There will be no need, however, for fantasy symbols such as black angels and Madonnas, for attractive black airline hostesses and African beauty queens competing in international contests, as well as the artists and the diplomats, will exist in reality.

Many American Negroes will feel no need for the psychological support that comes from identification with the New Africa. For those Negroes who do feel the need for "roots," however, the New Africa will, no doubt, excite emotions similar to those which stirred Jean Toomer, the American Negro poet of the "Renaissance," when he came to terms with his Southern background, and sang:

> Oh land and soil, red soil and sweet gum tree,
> So scant of grass, so profligate of pines
> Now just before an epoch's sun declines,
> Thy son, in time, I have returned to thee,
> Thy son in time I have returned to thee. . . .

PART TWO

AMERICAN NEGROES
AND THE
SYSTEM OF SLAVERY

Carl N. Degler

SLAVERY AND THE GENESIS OF AMERICAN
RACE PREJUDICE

Historians have long recognized that the first Negroes brought to Virginia in 1619 did not become slaves, but were assimilated into the existing system of indentured servitude. Carl Degler has written what is probably the definitive account of how, in the New England and Chesapeake colonies during the seventeenth century, Negro slavery evolved from indentured servitude.

Degler also concerns himself with another major theme: the relationship between slavery and race prejudice. As he points out, in a different cultural context enslavement of one racial group by another does not necessarily involve hostility and prejudice. Observers have noted that the character of slavery and race relations in Latin American countries stands in striking contrast to the situation in the United States. Degler, in a sharply revisionist interpretation, proposes the provocative thesis that in the United States, rather than slavery causing race prejudice, it was race prejudice that led to slavery. Going a step beyond Degler, we wish to suggest that the process was circular: as the majority of Negroes became assigned to a state of perpetual servitude, the fact that they were identified with a lowly status reinforced the prejudice existing among the whites.

O VER a century ago, Tocqueville named slavery as the source of the American prejudice against the Negro. Contrary to the situation in antiquity, he remarked: "Among the moderns the abstract and transient fact of slavery is fatally united with the physical and permanent fact of color." Furthermore, he wrote, though "slavery recedes" in some portions of the United States, "the prejudice to which it has given birth is immovable." [1] More modern observers of

Carl N. Degler, "Slavery and the Genesis of American Race Prejudice," *Comparative Studies in History and Society*, II (October, 1959), pp. 49–66. Copyright © 1959 by The Editorial Committee of the Comparative Studies in History and Society. Reprinted with the permission of the author and publisher.
    [1] *Democracy in America* (New York, 1948), I, 358–60.

the American past have also stressed this causal connection between the institution of slavery and the color prejudice of Americans.[2] Moreover, it is patent to anyone conversant with the nature of American slavery, particularly as it functioned in the nineteenth century, that the impress of bondage upon the character and future of the Negro in the United States has been both deep and enduring.

But if one examines other societies which the Negro entered as a slave, it is apparent that the consequences of slavery have not always been those attributed to the American form. Ten years ago, for example, Frank Tannenbaum demonstrated that in the Spanish and Portuguese colonies in South America, slavery did not leave upon the freed Negro anything like the prejudicial mark which it did in the United States.[3] He and others [4] have shown that once the status of slavery was left behind, the Negro in the lands south of the Rio Grande was accorded a remarkable degree of social equality with the whites. In the light of such differing consequences, the role of slavery in the development of the American prejudice against the Negro needs to be reexamined, with particular attention paid to the historical details of origins.

Tannenbaum showed that in the Portuguese and Spanish colonies there were at least three historical forces or traditions which tended to prevent the attribution of inferiority to the Negro aside from the legal one of slavery. One was the continuance of the Roman law of slavery in the Iberian countries, another was the influence of the Roman Catholic Church, and the third was the long history—by Anglo-American standards—of contacts with darker-skinned peoples in the course of the Reconquest and the African explorations of the fifteenth and sixteenth centuries. Roman law, at least in its later forms, viewed slavery as a mere accident, of which anyone could be the victim. As such it tended to forestall the identification of the black man with slavery, thus permitting the Negro to escape from the stigma of his degraded status once he ceased to be a slave. The same end, Tannenbaum showed, was served by the Roman Church's insistence upon the equality of all Christians and by the long familiarity of the Iberians with Negroes and Moors.

In North America, of course, none of these forces was operative—a fact which partly explains the differing type of slavery and status for Negroes in the two places. But this cannot be the whole explanation since it is only negative. We know, in effect, what were the forces which permitted the slave and the Negro in South America to be treated as a human being, but other than the negative fact that these forces did not obtain in the North American colonies, we know little as to why the Negro as slave or freedman, occupied a degraded position compared with that of any white man. A more positive explanation is

---

[2] Most recently, Oscar and Mary Handlin, "The Origins of the Southern Labor System," *William and Mary Quarterly*, 3rd Series, VII (April, 1950), 199–222.

[3] *Slave and Citizen; The Negro in the Americas* (New York, 1947).

[4] Gilberto Freyre, *Brazil: An Interpretation* (New York, 1945), pp. 96–101; Donald Pierson, *Negroes in Brazil* (Chicago, 1942), pp. 330–6.

to be found in an examination of the early history of the Negro in North America.

It has long been recognized that the appearance of legal slavery in the laws of the English colonies was remarkably slow. The first mention does not occur until after 1660—some forty years after the arrival of the first Negroes. Lest we think that slavery existed in fact before it did in law, two historians have assured us recently that such was not the case. "The status of Negroes was that of servants," Oscar and Mary Handlin have written, "and so they were identified and treated down to the 1660's." [5] This late, or at least, slow development of slavery [6] complicates our problem. For if there was no slavery in the beginning, then we must account for its coming into being some forty years after the introduction of the Negro. There was no such problem in the history of slavery in the Iberian colonies, where the legal institution of slavery came in the ships with the first settlers.

The Handlins' attempt to answer the question as to why slavery was slow in appearing in the statutes is, to me, not convincing. Essentially their explanation is that by the 1660's, for a number of reasons which do not have to be discussed here, the position of the white servant was improving, while that of the Negroes was sinking to slavery. In this manner, the Handlins contend, Negro and white servants, heretofore treated alike, attained different status. There are at least two major objections to this argument. First of all, their explanation, by depending upon the improving position of white servants as it does, cannot apply to New England, where servants were of minor importance. Yet the New England colonies, like the Southern, developed a system of slavery for the Negro that fixed him in a position of permanent inferiority. The greatest weakness of the Handlins' case is the difficulty in showing that the white servant's position was improving during and immediately after the 1660's.

Without attempting to go into any great detail on the matter, several acts of the Maryland and Virginia legislatures during the 1660's and 1670's can be cited to indicate that an improving status for white servants was at best doubtful. In 1662, Maryland restricted a servant's travel without a pass to two miles beyond his master's house; [7] in 1671 the same colony lengthened the time of servants who arrived without indenture from four to five years.[8] Virginia in 1668 provided that a runaway could be corporally punished and also have additional time exacted from him.[9] If, as these instances suggest, the white

[5] Handlin, "Origins of Southern Labor," p. 203.

[6] Virtually all historians of the institution agree on this. See U. B. Phillips, *American Negro Slavery* (New York, 1933), pp. 74–77; J. C. Ballagh, *History of Slavery in Virginia* (Baltimore, 1902), pp. 28–35. More recently, however, Susie Ames, *Studies of the Virginia Eastern Shore in the Seventeenth Century* (Richmond, 1940), pp. 101–10 and W. F. Craven, *Southern Colonies in the Seventeenth Century, 1607–1689* (Baton Rouge, 1949), pp. 217–19 have more than suggested that it is possible that slavery existed in Virginia almost from the very beginning of the Negro's history in America.

[7] *Maryland Archives*, I, 451.

[8] *Ibid*, II, 335.

[9] W. W. Hening, *Statutes at Large; being a Collection of all the Laws of Virginia...* (Richmond, 1809), II, 266.

servant's status was not improving, then we are left without an explanation for the differing status accorded white and Negro servants after 1660.

Actually, by asking why slavery developed late in the English colonies we are setting ourselves a problem which obscures rather than clarifies the primary question of why slavery in North America seemed to leave a different mark on the Negro than it did in South America. To ask why slavery in the English colonies produced discrimination against Negroes after 1660 is to make the tacit assumption that prior to the establishment of slavery there was none. If, instead, the question is put, "Which appeared first, slavery or discrimination?" then no prejudgment is made. Indeed, it now opens a possibility for answering the question as to why the slavery in the English colonies, unlike that in the Spanish and Portuguese, led to a caste position for Negroes, whether free or slave. In short, the recent work of the Handlins and the fact that slavery first appeared in the statutes of the English colonies forty years after the Negro's arrival, have tended to obscure the real possibility that the Negro was actually *never* treated as an equal of the white man, servant or free.

It is true that when Negroes were first imported into the English colonies there was no law of slavery and therefore whatever status they were to have would be the work of the future. This absence of a status for black men, which, it will be remembered was not true for the Spanish and Portuguese colonies, made it possible for almost any kind of status to be worked out. It was conceivable that they would be accorded the same status as white servants, as the Handlins have argued; it was also possible that they would not. It all depended upon the reactions of the people who received the Negroes.

It is the argument of this paper that the status of the Negro in the English colonies was worked out within a framework of discrimination; that from the outset, as far as the available evidence tells us, the Negro was treated as an inferior to the white man, servant or free. If this be true, then it would follow that as slavery evolved as a legal status, it reflected and included as a part of its essence, this same discrimination which white men had practiced against the Negro all along and before any statutes decreed it. It was in its evolution, then, that American colonial slavery differed from Iberian, since in the colonies of Spain and Portugal, the legal status of the slave was fixed before the Negro came to the Americas. Moreover, in South America there were at least three major traditional safeguards which tended to protect the free Negro against being treated as an inferior. In summary, the peculiar character of slavery in the English colonies as compared with that in the Iberian, was the result of two circumstances. One, that there was no law of slavery at all in the beginning, and two, that discrimination against the Negro antedated the legal status of slavery. As a result, slavery, when it developed in the English colonies, could not help but be infused with the social attitude which had prevailed from the beginning, namely, that Negroes were inferior.

It is indeed true as the Handlins in their article have emphasized that before the seventeenth century the Negro was rarely called a slave. But this fact should not overshadow the historical evidence which points to the institution without employing the name. Because no discriminatory title is placed upon the Negro we must not think that he was being treated like a white servant; for there is too much evidence to the contrary. Although the growth of a fully developed slave law was slow, unsteady and often unarticulated in surviving records, this is what one would expect when an institution is first being worked out.[10] It is not the same, however, as saying that no slavery or discrimination against the Negro existed in the first decades of the Negro's history in America.

As will appear from the evidence which follows, the kinds of discrimination visited upon Negroes varied immensely. In the early 1640's it sometimes stopped short of lifetime servitude or inheritable status—the two attributes of true slavery—in other instances it included both. But regardless of the form of discrimination, the important point is that from the 1630's up until slavery clearly appeared in the statutes in the 1660's, the Negroes were being set apart and discriminated against as compared with the treatment accorded Englishmen, whether servants or free.

The colonists of the early seventeenth century were well aware of a distinction between indentured servitude and slavery.[11] This is quite clear from the evidence in the very early years of the century. The most obvious means the English colonists had for learning of a different treatment for Negroes from that for white servants was the slave trade [12] and the slave systems of the Spanish and Portuguese colonies. As early as 1623, a voyager's book published in London indicated that Englishmen knew of the Negro as a slave in the South American

[10] John C. Hurd, *Law of Freedom and Bondage in the United States* (Boston, 1858–61), I, 163, points out that the trade "in negroes as merchandise was ... recognized as legitimate by European governments, without any direct sanction from positive legislation, but rested on the general customs among nations, known both in municipal and international private law." Furthermore, he reported that none of the colonies ever found it necessary to pass laws legalizing slavery. He quotes from the Connecticut Code of 1821: "Slavery was never directly established by statute; but has been indirectly sanctioned by various statutes and frequently recognized by courts, so that it may be said to have been established by law." I, 212 n.

[11] The Handlins, "Origins of Southern Labor," pp. 203–4, have argued that in the early years slavery meant nothing more than a low form of labor and that it had no basis in law. This is true insofar as statute law is concerned, but, as will appear later, in practice quite a different situation obtained.

[12] The Handlins, "Origins of Southern Labor," pp. 203–4, argue that the continental colonies could not have learned about a different status for Negroes from that of white servants from the slave trade because, they say, "the company of Royal Adventurers referred to their cargo as 'Negers,' 'Negro-servants,' 'Servants ... from Africa,' or 'Negro Persons' but rarely as slaves." They overlook, however, abundant references to Negro slaves in the correspondence of the contemporary Royal African Company. Thus in 1663 a warrant for that company refers to "negro slaves" as a part of its monopoly. *Calendar of State Papers, Colonial*, V, 121; see also p. 204. In that same year the Privy Council wrote that the Spanish were "seeking to trade with our island of Barbada for a supply of Negro Slaves. ..." And then the letter referred to a "supply of Negro Servants," and later still "for every Negro Person a Slave" and then "all such Negro Slaves." E. Donnan, *Documents Illustrative of the History of the Slave Trade* (Washington, 1930), I, 161–2.

colonies of Spain. The book told of the trade in "blacke people" who were "sold unto the Spaniard for him to carry into the West Indies, to remaine as slaves, either in their Mines or in any other servile uses, they in those countries put them to." [13] In the phrase "remaine as slaves" is the element of unlimited service.

The Englishmen's treatment of another dark-skinned, non-Christian people —the Indians—further supports the argument that a special and inferior status was accorded the Negro virtually from the first arrival. Indian slavery was practiced in all of the English settlements almost from the beginning [14] and, though it received its impetus from the perennial wars between the races, the fact that an inferior and onerous service was established for the Indian makes it plausible to suppose that a similar status would be reserved for the equally different and pagan Negro.

The continental English could also draw upon other models of a differentiated status for Negroes. The earliest English colony to experiment with large numbers of Negroes in its midst was the shortlived settlement of Providence island, situated in the western Caribbean, just off the Mosquito Coast. By 1637, long before Barbados and the other British sugar islands utilized great numbers of Negroes, almost half of the population of this Puritan venture was black. Such a disproportion of races caused great alarm among the directors of the Company in London and repeated efforts were made to restrict the influx of blacks.[15] Partly because of its large numbers of Negroes, Old Providence became well known to the mainland colonies of Virginia and New England.[16] A. P. Newton has said that Old Providence

> forms the connecting link between almost every English colonising enterprise in the first half of the seventeenth century from Virginia and Bermuda to New England and Jamaica and thus it is of much greater importance than its actual accomplishments would justify.[17]

Under such circumstances, it was to be expected that knowledge of the status accorded Negroes by these Englishmen would be transmitted to those on the mainland with whom they had such close and frequent contact.

Though the word "slave" is never applied to the Negroes on Providence, and only rarely the word "servant," "Negroes," which was the term used, were obviously *sui generis*; they were people apart from the English. The Company, for example, distrusted them. "Association [Tortuga island] was deserted thro' their mutinous conduct," the Company told the Governor of Old Providence in 1637. "Further trade for them prohibited, with exceptions, until Providence be

[13] Quoted in Donnan, *Slave Trade*, I, 125.

[14] See particularly, Almon Lauber, *Indian Slavery in Colonial Times Within the Present Limits of the United States* (New York, 1913), Chap. IV.

[15] A. P. Newton, *The Colonising Activities of the English Puritans* (New Haven, 1914), p. 258.

[16] *Ibid.*, p. 260.

[17] A. P. Newton, *The European Nations in the West Indies, 1493–1688* (London, 1933), pp. 173-4.

furnished with English." [18] In another communication the Company again alluded to the dangers of "too great a number" of Negroes on the island and promised to send 200 English servants over to be exchanged for as many Negroes.[19] A clearer suggestion of the difference in status between an English servant and a Negro is contained in the Company's letter announcing the forwarding of the 200 servants. As a further precaution against being over-whelmed by Negroes, it was ordered that a "family of fourteen"—which would include servants—was not to have more than six Negroes. "The surplusage may be sold to the poor men who have served their apprenticeship." [20] But the Negroes, apparently, were serving for life.

Other British island colonies in the seventeenth century also provide evidence which is suggestive of this same development of a differing status for Negroes, even though the word "slave" was not always employed. Though apparently the first Negroes were only brought to Bermuda in 1617,[21] as early as 1623 the Assembly passed an "Act to restrayne the insolencies of Negroes." The blacks were accused of stealing and of carrying "secretly cudgels, and other weapons and working tools." Such weapons, it was said, were "very dangerous and not meete to be suffered to be carried by such Vassals...." Already, in other words, Negroes were treated as a class apart. To reinforce this, Negroes were forbidden to "weare any weapon in the daytyme" and they were not to be outside or off their master's land during "any undue hours in the night tyme...." [22]

During the 1630's there were other indications that Negroes were treated as inferiors. As early as 1630 some Negroes' servitude was already slavery in that it was for life and inheritable. One Lew Forde possessed a Negro man, while the Company owned his wife; the couple had two children. Forde desired "to know which of the said children properly belong to himself and which to the Company." The Council gave him the older child and the Company received the other.[23] A letter of Roger Wood in 1634 suggests that Negroes were already serving for life, for he asked to have a Negro, named Sambo, given to him, so that through the Negro "I or myne may *ever* be able" to carry on an old feud with an enemy who owned Sambo's wife.[24]

There is further evidence of discrimination against Negroes in later years. A grand jury in 1652 cited one Henry Gaunt as being "suspected of being unnecessarily conversant with negro women"—he had been giving them pres-

---

[18] *Calendar of State Papers, Colonial*, I, 249.

[19] *Ibid.*, pp. 277–8.

[20] *Ibid.*, pp. 278–9.

[21] J. H. Lefroy, *Memorials of the Discovery and Early Settlement of the Bermudas or Somers Islands, 1515–1685* (London, 1877), I, 127.

[22] *Ibid.*, I, 308–9.

[23] *Ibid.*, I, 505. Cases in 1676 and 1685 indicate that this practice of dividing the children became the standard practice under slavery in a colony where the parcels of slaves were so small that few masters could have a spouse on their plantations for each of his adult Negroes. *Ibid.*, II, 427, 547–8.

[24] *Ibid.*, I, 539. Emphasis added.

ents. The presentment added that "if he hath not left his familiarity with such creatures, it is desired that such abominations be inquired into, least the land mourne for them." [25] The discrimination reached a high point in 1656 when the Governor proclaimed that "any Englishman" who discovered a Negro walking about at night without a pass, was empowered to "kill him then and theire without mercye." The proclamation further ordered that all free Negroes "shall be banished from these Islands, never to return eyther by purchase of any man, or otherwise...." [26] When some Negroes asked the Governor for their freedom in 1669, he denied they had such claim, saying that they had been "purchased by" their masters "without condition or limitation. It being likewise soe practised in these American plantations and other parts of the world." [27]

In Barbados Negroes were already slaves when Richard Ligon lived there in 1647–50. "The Iland," he later wrote, "is divided into three sorts of men, viz: Masters, servants, and slaves. The slaves and their posterity, being subject to their masters for ever," in contrast to the servants who are owned "but for five years...." [28] On that island as at Bermuda it was reported that Negroes were not permitted "to touch or handle any weapons." [29]

On Jamaica, as on the other two islands, a clear distinction was made between the status of the Negro and that of the English servant. In 1656 one resident of the island wrote the Protector in England urging the importation of African Negroes because then, he said, "the planters would have to pay for them" and therefore "they would have an interest in preserving their lives, which was wanting in the case of bond servants...." [30]

It is apparent, then, that the colonists on the mainland had ample opportunity before 1660 to learn of a different status for black men from that for Englishmen, whether servants or free.

From the evidence available it would seem that the Englishmen in Virginia and Maryland learned their lesson well. This is true even though the sources available on the Negro's position in these colonies in the early years are not as abundant as we would like. It seems quite evident that the black man was set apart from the white on the continent just as he was being set apart in the island colonies. For example, in Virginia in 1630, one Hugh Davis was "soundly

[25] *Ibid.*, II, 30.
[26] *Ibid.*, II, 95–6.
[27] *Ibid.*, II, 293. As late as 1662 the perpetual character of slavery for Negroes was being obscured by their serving for ninety-nine years. See *Ibid.*, II, 166, 184.
[28] Richard Ligon, *A True and Exact History of the Island of Barbados* (London, 1657), p. 43.
[29] *Ibid.*, p. 46.
[30] Quoted in Richard B. Morris, *Government and Labor in Early America* (New York, 1946), p. 499. As early as 1633, on the island of Tortuga, the separation of whites, servants or no, from Negroes was in evidence. At a time of anarchy on the island, "The eighty-odd Englishmen in the island had formed a council among themselves for the government of the colony and to keep in subjection the one hundred and fifty negroes, twenty-seven of whom were the company's property." Newton, *Colonizing Activities*, p. 214.

whipped before an Assembly of Negroes and others for abusing himself to the dishonor of God and the shame of Christians, by defiling his body in lying with a negro." [31] The unChristian-like character of such behavior was emphasized ten years later when Robert Sweet was ordered to do penance in Church for "getting a negro woman with child." [32] An act passed in the Maryland legislature in 1639 indicated that at that early date the word "slave" was being applied to non-Englishmen. The act was an enumeration of the rights of "all Christian inhabitants (slaves excepted)." [33] The slaves referred to could have been only Indians or Negroes,[34] since all white servants were Christians. It is also significant of the differing treatment of the two races that though Maryland and Virginia very early in their history enacted laws fixing limits to the terms for servants who entered without written contracts, Negroes were never included in such protective provisions.[35] The first of such laws were placed upon the books in 1639 in Maryland and 1643 in Virginia; in the Maryland statute, it was explicitly stated: "Slaves excepted." [36]

In yet another way, Negroes and slaves were singled out for special status in the years before 1650. A Virginia law of 1640 provided that "all masters" should try to furnish arms to themselves and "all those of their families which shall be capable of arms"—which would include servants—"(excepting negros)." [37] Not until 1648 did Maryland get around to such a prohibition, when it was provided that no guns should be given to "any Pagan for killing meate or to any other use," upon pain of a heavy fine.[38] At no time were white servants denied the right to bear arms; indeed, as these statutes inform us, they were enjoined to possess weapons.[39]

[31] Hening, *Statutes*, I, 146.

[32] *Ibid.*, I, 552.

[33] *Maryland Archives*, I, 80.

[34] It is not known whether there were any Negroes in Maryland at that date. J. R. Brackett, *The Negro in Maryland* (Baltimore, 1889), p. 26 found no evidence of Negroes before 1642.

[35] Handlin, "Origins of Southern Labor," p. 210; Hening, *Statutes*, I, 411, 539. This is not to say that some Negroes were not indentured servants, for there is evidence to show that limited service was enjoyed in the statutes. In October, 1673, for instance, the Council and General Court of Virginia ordered that "Andrew Moore A Servant Negro," who asserted he was to serve only five years, and who had the support of several "oathes," was declared free. Moreover, his erstwhile master was compelled to "pay him Corne and Clothes According to the custome of the country" and 400 pounds of tobacco and cask for the Negro's service since his time expired and to "pay costs." *Minutes of the Council and General Court of Colonial Virginia*, edited by H. R. McIlwaine (Richmond, 1924), p. 354.

[36] Hening, *Statutes*, I, 257; *Maryland Archives*, I, 80.

[37] *William and Mary Quarterly*, Second Series, IV (July, 1924), 147.

[38] *Maryland Archives*, I, 233.

[39] Handlin, "Origins of Southern Labor," p. 209, implies that these early restrictions were later repealed. "Until the 1660's," the Handlins write, "the statutes on the Negroes were not at all unique. Nor did they add up to a decided trend." In substantiation of this point they instance the "fluctuations" in the Negro's right to bear arms. Their cited evidence, however, does not sustain this generalization. Four references to the statutes of Virginia are made; of these four, only two deal with arms bearing. The first one, that

One other class of discriminatory acts against Negroes in Virginia and Maryland before 1660 also deserves to be noticed. Three different times before 1660—in 1643, 1644 and 1658—the Virginia Assembly (and in 1654, the Maryland legislature) included Negro and Indian women among the "tithables." But white servant women were never placed in such a category,[40] inasmuch as they were not expected to work in the fields. From the beginning, it would seem, Negro women, whether free or bond, were treated by the law differently from white women servants.[41]

It is not until the 1640's that evidence of a status for Negroes akin to slavery, and, therefore, something more than mere discrimination begins to appear in the sources. Two cases of punishment for runaway servants in 1640 throw some light on the working out of a differentiated status for Negroes. The first case concerned three runaways, of whom two were white men and the third a Negro. All three were given thirty lashes, with the white men having the terms owed their masters extended a year, at the completion of which they were to work for the colony for three more years. The other, "being a Negro named John Punch shall serve his said master or his assigns for the time of his natural Life here or elsewhere." [42] Not only was the Negro's punishment the most severe, and for no apparent reason, but he was, in effect, reduced to slavery. It is also clear, however, that up until the issuing of the sentence, he must have had the status of a servant.

The second case, also in 1640, suggests that by that date some Negroes were already slaves. Six white men and a Negro were implicated in a plot to run away. The punishments meted out varied, but Christopher Miller "a dutchman" (a prime agent in the business) "was given the harshest treatment of all: thirty stripes, burning with an "R" on the cheek, a shackle placed on his leg for a year "and longer if said master shall see cause" and seven years of service for the colony upon completion of his time due his master. The only other one of the seven plotters to receive the stripes, the shackle and the "R" was the Negro Emanuel, but, significantly, he did not receive any sentence of work for

referred to in the text above, indicates that Negroes were not to be armed. The other reference is at best an ambiguous statement about who is taxable and which of the taxables are to serve in the militia. It in no wise constitutes either a repeal or even a contradiction of the earlier statute, which, therefore, must be presumed to be controlling. Their evidence for "fluctuations" in the right of Indians to bear arms suffers from the same weakness of sources. The two statutes they cite merely confirm the right of certain Indians to possess guns and deny them to other Indians. No "fluctuation" in rights is involved.

[40] Hening, *Statutes*, I, 242, 292, 455; *Maryland Archives*, I, 342. The statement in Handlin, "Origins of Southern Labor," p. 217 n, that the "first sign of discrimination was in 1668 when white but not Negro women were exempt," is therefore erroneous.

[41] In his well-known emigrant pamphlet, *Leah and Rachel* (London, 1656), p. 12, John Hammond casts some interesting light on contemporary opinion regarding women who worked in the fields in Virginia. "The Women are not (as is reported) put into the ground to work, but occupie such domestique imployments and housewifery as in England . . . yet some wenches that are nasty, beastly and not fit to be so imployed are put into the ground . . ."

[42] *Minutes of the Council*, p. 466.

the colony. Presumably he was already serving his master for a life-time—*i.e.*, he was a slave.[43] About this time in Maryland it does not seem to have been unusual to speak of Negroes as slaves, for in 1642 one "John Skinner mariner" agreed "to deliver unto . . . Leonard Calvert, fourteen negro-men-slaves and three women-slaves." [44]

From a proceeding before the House of Burgesses in 1666 it appears that as early as 1644 that body was being called upon to determine who was a slave. The Journal of the House for 1666 reports that in 1644 a certain "mulata" bought "as a slave for Ever" was adjudged by the Assembly "no slave and but to serve as other Christian servants do and was freed in September 1665." [45] Though no reason was given for the verdict, from the words "other Christian servants" it is possible that he was a Christian, for it was believed in the early years of the English colonies that baptism rendered a slave free. In any case, the Assembly uttered no prohibition of slavery as such and the owner was sufficiently surprised and aggrieved by the decision to appeal for recompense from the Assembly, even though the Negro's service was twenty-one years, an unheard of term for a "Christian servant." [46]

In early seventeenth century inventories of estates, there are two distinctions which appear in the reckoning of the value of servants and Negroes. Uniformly, the Negroes were more valuable, even as children, than any white servant. Secondly, the naming of a servant is usually followed by the number of years yet remaining to his service; for the Negroes no such notation appears. Thus in an inventory in Virginia in 1643, a 22-year old white servant, with eight years still to serve, was valued at 1,000 pounds of tobacco, while a "negro boy" was rated at 3,000 pounds and a white boy with seven years to serve was listed as worth 700 pounds. An eight-year old Negro girl was calculated to be worth 2,000 pounds. On another inventory in 1655, two good men servants with four years to serve were rated at 1,300 pounds of tobacco, and a woman servant with only two years to go was valued at 800 pounds. Two Negro boys, however, who had no limit set to their terms, were evaluated at 4,100 pounds apiece, and a Negro girl was said to be worth 5,500 pounds.[47]

These great differences in valuation of Negro and white "servants" strongly

[43] *Ibid.*, p. 467.

[44] Catterall, *Judicial Cases*, I, 57 n. Mrs. Catterall does not think any Negroes came under this agreement, but the language itself testifies to an accepted special status for Negroes at that time.

[45] *Journals of the House of Burgesses of Virginia*, edited by H. R. McIlwaine (Richmond, 1914), II, 34.

[46] *Ibid.*, II, 34–5. His plea, however, was turned down, the Assembly not knowing "any Reason why the Publick should be answerable for the inadvertency of the Buyer. . . ."

[47] John H. Russell, *The Free Negro in Virginia, 1619–1865* (Baltimore, 1913), p. 36. Russell concludes from his survey of inventories of estates for this early period that Negroes were valued from 20 to 30 pounds sterling, "while white servants of the longest term . . . receive a valuation of not more than £15 sterling." *Ibid.*, p. 35. Catterall, *Judicial Cases*, I, 58 n, upon concluding her investigation of inventories of estates, picked 1644 as the date at which " 'servant' standing alone, had generally become synonomous with 'white servant' and 'negro' with 'negro slave,' . . ."

suggest, as does the failure to indicate term of service for the Negroes, that the latter were slaves at least in regard to life-time service. Beyond a question, there was some service which these blacks were rendering which enhanced their value—a service, moreover, which was not or could not be exacted from the whites. Furthermore, a Maryland deed of 1649 adumbrated slave status not only of life-time term, but of inheritance of status. Three Negroes "and all their issue both male and female" were deeded.[48]

Russell and Ames culled from the Virginia court records of the 1640's and 1650's several instances of Negroes held in a status that can be called true slavery. For example, in 1646 a Negro woman and a Negro boy were sold to Stephen Charlton to be of use to him and his "heyers etc. for ever." A Negro girl was sold in 1652 "with her Issue and produce . . . and their services forever." Two years later a Negro girl was sold to one Armsteadinger "and his heyers . . . forever with all her increase both male and female."[49] For March 12, 1655 the minutes of the Council and General Court of Virginia contain the entry, "Mulatto held to be a slave and appeal taken."[50] Yet this is five years before Negro slavery is even implied in the statutes and fifteen before it is declared. An early case of what appears to be true slavery was found by Miss Ames on the Virginia eastern shore. In 1635 two Negroes were brought to the area; over twenty years later, in 1656, the widow of the master was bequeathing the child of one of the original Negroes and the other Negro and her children.[51] This was much more than mere servitude—the term was longer than twenty years and apparently the status was inheritable.

Wesley Frank Craven, in his study of the seventeenth-century Southern colonies, has concluded that in the treatment of the Negro "the trend from the first was toward a sharp distinction between him and the white servant."[52] In view of the evidence presented here, this seems a reasonable conclusion.

Concurrently with these examples of onerous service or actual slavery of Negroes, there were of course other members of the race who did gain their freedom.[53] But the presence of Negroes rising out of servitude to freedom[54]

[48] Catterall, *Judicial Cases*, IV, 9.

[49] Russell, *Free Negro in Virginia*, pp. 34–5. He also reports the instance of a Negro by the name of John Casor who was claimed, in 1655, as a "Negro for his life," but he was rescued from such a status by two witnesses testifying that he had an indenture. *Ibid.*, pp. 32–3.

[50] *Minutes of the Council*, p. 504. Handlin, "Origins of Southern Labor," p. 216, in arguing the late development of a different status for Negroes as compared with whites in Virginia, says: "As late as the 1660's the law had not even a word to describe the children of mixed marriages. But two decades later, the term mulatto is used. . . ." Such a statement is obviously misleading, for though the Handlins presumably mean statute law, the decisions of the General Court were also "law." The *Oxford English Dictionary* cites references for the word "mulatto" for 1595, 1613 and 1657.

[51] Ames, *Eastern Shore*, p. 105.

[52] Craven, *Southern Colonies*, p. 219.

[53] See especially Russell, *Free Negro in Virginia*, pp. 36–9. See also Brackett, *Negro in Maryland*, p. 37.

[54] An indication that even freedom for the Negro carried certain disabilities is afforded by an instance reported by Ames, *Eastern Shore*, p. 107 from the Northampton County

does not destroy the evidence that others were sinking into slavery; it merely underscores the unsteady evolution of a slave status. The supposition that the practice of slavery long antedated the law is strengthened by the tangential manner in which recognition of Negro slavery first appeared in the Virginia statutes.[55] It occurred in 1660 in a law dealing with punishments for runaway servants, where casual reference was made to those "negroes who are incapable of making satisfaction by addition of time," [56] since they were already serving for life.

Soon thereafter, as various legal questions regarding the status of Negroes came to the fore, the institution was further defined by statute law. In 1662 Virginia provided that the status of the offspring of a white man and a Negro would follow that of the mother—an interesting and unexplained departure from the common law and a reversion to Roman law. The same law stated that "any christian" fornicating "with a negro man or woman . . . shall pay double the fines imposed by the former act." Two years later Maryland prescribed service for Negroes "durante vita" and provided for hereditary status to descend through the father. Any free white woman who married a slave was to serve her husband's master for the duration of the slave's life, and her children would serve the master until they were thirty years of age. Presumably, no penalty was to be exacted of a free white man who married a Negro slave.[57]

As early as 1669 the Virginia law virtually washed its hands of protecting the Negro held as a slave. It allowed punishment of refractory slaves up to and including accidental death, relieving the master, explicitly, of any fear of prosecution, on the assumption that no man would "destroy his owne estate." [58]

court records of 1654. For contempt of authority and abuse of certain persons, Anthony Longoe, a Negro, was ordered, almost twenty years after his release from service, to receive "thirty lashes now applied, and tomorrow morning thirty lashes more."

[55] A year earlier, 1659/60, a statute dealing with trade with the Dutch promised remission of a ten shilling tax if "the said Dutch or other forreiners shall import any negro slaves. . . ." This is the first reference in the Virginia statutes to Negroes as slaves. Hening, *Statutes*, I, 540.

[56] Hening, *Statutes*, II, 26. The equivalent Maryland statute (1663) referred to "Negroes and other Slaves, who are incapeable of makeing Stisfaction [*sic*] by Addition of Tyme . . ." *Maryland Archives*, I, 489.

[57] Hening, *Statutes*, II, 170: *Maryland Archives*, I, 533–4. Handlin, "Origins of Southern Labor," p. 215 sees the genesis of these prohibitions in concern over status rather than in objection to racial intermarriage. This seems to be true for Maryland. But in speaking of the Virginia circumstances they write: "It was to guard against the complications of status that the laws after 1691 forbade 'spurious' or illegitimate mixed marriages of the slave and the free . . ." Actually, however, the Virginia statue of 1691 (Hening, *Statutes*, III, 87) clearly aimed at the prevention of "abominable mixture and spurious issue" by forbidding marriage of "English or other white man or woman being free" with "a negro, mulatto or Indian man or woman *bond or free*." (Emphasis added.)

[58] Hening, *Statutes*, II, 270. The working out of the exact legal status of slave property, however, was a slow one. A Virginia law of 1705 (Hening, *Statutes*, III, 333–4), declared "Negro, Mulatto and Indian Slaves . . . to be real estate," but there were a number of exceptions which suggest the later chattel nature of property in slaves. In South Carolina slaves were decreed to be real estate in 1690 and not until 1740 were they said to be legally chattels. Hurd, *Law of Freedom*, I, 297, 303.

In fact by 1680 the law of Virginia had erected a high wall around the Negro. One discerns in the phrase "any negro or other slave" how the word "negro" had taken on the meaning of slave. Moreover, in the act of 1680 one begins to see the lineaments of the later slave codes. No Negro may carry any weapon of any kind, nor leave his master's grounds without a pass, nor shall "any negroe or other slave . . . presume to lift his hand in opposition against any christian," and if a Negro runs away and resist recapture it "shall be lawful for such person or persons to kill said negroe or slave. . . ." [59]

Yet it would be a quarter of a century before Negroes would comprise even a fifth of the population of Virginia. Thus long before slavery or black labor became an important part of the Southern economy, a special and inferior status had been worked out for the Negroes who came to the English colonies. Unquestionably it was a demand for labor which dragged the Negro to American shores, but the status which he acquired here cannot be explained by reference to that economic motive. Long before black labor was as economically important as unfree white labor, the Negro had been consigned to a special discriminatory status which mirrored the social discrimination Englishmen practiced against him. [60]

In the course of the seventeenth century New Englanders, like Southerners, developed a system of slavery which seemed permanently to fasten its stigma upon the Negro race. But because of the small number of Negroes in the northern provinces, the development of a form of slavery, which left a caste in its wake, cannot be attributed to pressure from increasing numbers of blacks, or even from an insistent demand for cheap labor. Rather it seems clearly to be the consequence of the general social discrimination against the Negro. For in the northern region, as in the southern, discrimination against the Negro preceded the evolution of a slave status and by that fact helped to shape the form that institution would assume.

References to the status of the Negroes in New England in this period are scattered, but, as was true of the Southern provinces, those references which are available suggest that from the earliest years a lowly, differential status, if not slavery itself, was reserved and recognized for the Negro—and the Indian, it might be added. The earliest date asserted in the sources for the existence of Negro slavery in Massachusetts is that of 1639. John Josselyn tells of a Negro woman held on Noddles Island in Boston harbor. Her master sought to mate her with another Negro, Josselyn says, but she kicked her prospective lover out

[59] Hening, *Statutes*, II, 481–2.

[60] Like Virginia, Maryland developed its slave law and status long before the Negroes had become an important aspect of the labor force. As late as 1712, Negroes made up only slightly more than 20 per cent of the population. Brackett, *Negro in Maryland*, pp. 38–9. If Virginia was slow in bringing her slave practices out into the open air of the statute books, the same could not be said of Carolina. In the Fundamental Constitutions, drawn up in 1669, it is stated in article CX that "Every freeman of Carolina shall have absolute power and authority over his negro slaves, of what opinion or religion so ever."

of the bed, saying that such behavior was "beyond her slavery...." [61] Though the first legal code of Massachusetts, the Body of Liberties of 1641, prohibited "bond-slavery" for the inhabitants, it clearly permitted enslavement of those who are "sold to us," [62] which would include Negroes brought in by the international slave trade.[63]

Such use of Negroes was neither unknown nor undesirable to the Puritans. Emanuel Downing wrote to John Winthrop in 1645 about the desirability of a war against the Indians so that captives might be taken who, in turn, could be exchanged

> for Moores, which wilbe more gayneful pilladge for us then [sic] wee conceive, for I doe not see how wee can thrive untill wee gett into a stock of slaves sufficient to do all our busines, for our children's children will hardly see this great Continent filled with people, soe that our servants will still desire freedome for themselves, and not stay but for verie great wages. And I suppose you know verie well how we shall maynteyne 20 Moores cheaper than one English servant.[64]

The following year the Commissioners of the United Colonies recommended that in order to spare the colonies the cost of imprisoning contumacious Indians they should be given over to the Englishmen whom they had damaged or "be shipped out and exchanged for Negroes as the cause will justly serve." [65] Negroes were here being equated with Indians who were being bound out as prisoners: this was treatment decidedly a cut lower than that visited upon white

[61] Massachusetts Historical Society, *Collections*, Third Series, III, 231. There is no doubt that there were Negroes at this time in Massachusetts, for in 1638 Winthrop reported that Capt. Peirce brought back from Old Providence "some cotton, and tobacco and Negroes...." John Winthrop, *History of New England*, James Savage, ed. (Boston, 1853), I, 305.

[62] Some events of 1645 indicate that those few words were of crucial importance to the Puritans. That year some Negroes were brought to Massachusetts by a Captain Smith and they were ordered by the General Court to be returned to Africa on the ground that their importation constituted "the hainous and crying sinn of man-stealing." But this was man-stealing only because Smith and his men had captured the Negroes in a raid, instead of buying them from traders. *Records of Massachusetts*, III, 48, 58, 84.

[63] Very early in New England history the concept of perpetual servitude—one of the distinguishing marks of slavery—appears in the records. In 1637 Roger Williams, in pleading for the lives of the captured Indians during the Pequot War, alludes to "perpetuall slaverie" as an alternative to their execution. Massachusetts Historical Society, *Collections*, Fourth Series, VI, 214. The will of John Winthrop, written in 1639, deeded to his son Adam "my island" and "also my Indians there and my boat and such household as is there" Robert C. Winthrop, *Life and Letters of John Winthrop* (Boston, 1869), II, 252. Though at least three white men were sentenced to "slavery" in Massachusetts in the early years, in at least two cases this did not, in fact, amount to perpetuity, for they appear to have been released in a short time. The use of the word as a special form of service, however, is most interesting. *Records of Massachusetts*, I, 246, 310, 269.

[64] Massachusetts Historical Society, *Collections*, Fourth Series, VI, 65.

[65] *Records of the Colony of Plymouth* (Boston, 1859), IX, 71.

servants.[66] That enslavement of Negroes was well known in New England by the middle of the century at the latest is revealed by the preamble to an act of Warwick and Providence colonies in 1652. It was said that it "is a common course practised amongst Englishmen to buy negers, to that end they may have them for service or slaves forever...." [67]

By mid-century, Negroes were appearing in the inventories of estates and, significantly, the valuation placed upon them was very close to that found in Virginia inventories of the same period. Their worth is always much more than that of a white servant. Thus in 1650 "a neager Maide" was valued at £25; in 1657 the well-known merchant, Robert Keayne left "2 negros and a negro child" estimated to be worth £30. "A negro boy servant" was set at £20 in an estate of 1661.[68] A further indication of the property character of Negroes was the attachment by the constable of Salem in 1670 of a Negro boy "Seasar" as the "proper goods of the said Powell." [69]

Despite the small numbers of Negroes in New England in this early period, the colonies of that region followed the example of the Southern and insular provinces in denying arms to the blacks in their midst—a discrimination which was never visited upon the English servant. In 1652 Massachusetts provided that Indians and Negroes could train in the militia the same as whites, but this apparently caused friction. The law was countermanded in 1656 by the statement "henceforth no negroes or Indians, altho servants of the English, shalbe armed or permitted to trayne." [70] Although as late as 1680 it was officially reported to London that there were no more than thirty "slaves" in Connecticut, that colony in 1660 excluded Indians and "negar servants" from the militia and "Watch and Ward." [71]

Edward Randolph in 1676 reported that there were a few indentured servants in Massachusetts "and not above two hundred slaves," by which he meant Negroes, for he said "they were brought from Guinea and Madagascar." [72] But it was not until 1698 that the phrase "Negro slave" actually appeared in the Massachusetts statutes.[73] The practice of slavery was preceding the law in

[66] John Cotton in 1651 clearly distinguished between slavery and servitude. He wrote Cromwell in that year in regard to the Scottish prisoners sent to New England, that "we have been desirous ... to make their yoke easy.... They have not been sold for slaves to perpetuall servitude, but for 6, or 7 or 8 yeares, as we do our owne." Quoted in George H. Moore, Notes on the History of Slavery in Massachusetts (New York, 1866), p. 17 n.

[67] Records of the Colony of Rhode Island ... (Providence, 1856), I, 243.

[68] Quoted in William B. Weeden, Economic and Social History of New England (Boston, 1891), p. 149 n. It was officially reported in 1680 by Connecticut colony that three or four "Blacks" were imported each year from the Barbados, and that they usually sold for £22 apiece. This was much more than the going price for servants. Public Records of the Colony of Connecticut (Hartford, 1850–90), III, 298.

[69] Quoted in Lorenzo Greene, The Negro in Colonial New England, 1620–1776 (New York, 1942), p. 172.

[70] Records of Massachusetts, III, 268, 397.

[71] Records of Connecticut, III, 298, I, 349.

[72] Quoted in Palfrey, History of New England, III, 298.

[73] Hurd, Law of Freedom, I, 262. Greene, Negro in New England, pp. 65–6, says that in 1670 slavery in Massachusetts became legally inheritable, for in that year the word

Massachusetts precisely as it had in the South. Though an official report to London in 1680 distinguished between Negro slaves and servants in Connecticut,[74] the law of that colony did not bother to define the institution of slavery. Indeed, as late as 1704, the Governor gave it as his opinion that all children born of "negro bond-women are themselves in like condition, i.e., born in servitude," though he admitted that there was no statute which said so. His contention was, however, that such legislation was "needless, because of the constant practice by which they are held as such...." [75]

During the last years of the seventeenth century, laws of Connecticut and Massachusetts continued to speak of Negroes as "servants," but it was very clear that the Negro's status was not being equated with that of the white servant. The General Court of Connecticut observed in 1690 that "many persons of this Colony doe...purchase negroe servants" and, since these servants run away, precautions have to be taken against such eventualities. It was therefore laid down that all "negroe or negroes shall" be required to have a pass in order to be outside the town bounds. Any inhabitant could stop a Negroe, free or slave, and have him brought before a magistrate if the black man were found to be without such a pass. Moreover, all ferrymen, upon pain of fine, were to deny access to their ferries to all Negroes who could not produce a pass.[76] Massachusetts in 1698 forbade trade with "any Indian, or negro servant or slave, or other known dissolute, lewd, and disorderly person, of whom there is just cause of suspicion." [77]

By the early years of the eighteenth century, the laws of Connecticut and Massachusetts had pretty well defined the Negro's subordinate position in society. Massachusetts acted to restrict the manumission of slaves by providing in 1703 that "molatto or negro slaves" could be freed only if security was given that they would not be chargeable upon the community. Another law set a curfew upon Indians, mulattoes and Negroes for nine o'clock each night. In 1705 Massachusetts became the only New England province to prohibit sexual relations between Negroes and mulattoes and Englishmen or those of "any other Christian nation." [78] Moreover, "any negro or mulatto" presuming to "smite or strike" an English person or any of another Christian nation would be "severely whipped." [79] In 1717 Negroes were barred from holding land in Connecticut.[80]

"strangers" was dropped from the Body of Liberties as a description of those who might be enslaved.

[74] Records of Connecticut, III, 298.

[75] Quoted in Bernard C. Steiner, History of Slavery in Connecticut (Baltimore, 1893), p. 18.

[76] Records of Connecticut, IV, 40.

[77] Hurd, Law of Freedom, I, 262–3.

[78] Ibid., I, 263, Massachusetts had prohibited marriages between whites and Negroes, mulattoes and Indians in 1692. Lauber, Indian Slavery, p. 253.

[79] Hurd, Law of Freedom, I, 263. Rhode Island, too, in 1728, provided that before a Negro or mulatto could be manumitted, security had to given that he would not become a public charge. Hurd, Law of Freedom, I, 276.

[80] Greene, Negro in New England, p. 312.

Thus, like the colonists to the South, the New Englanders enacted into law, in the absence of any prior English law of slavery, their recognition of the Negroes as different and inferior. This was the way of the seventeenth century; only with a later conception of the brotherhood of all men would such legal discrimination begin to recede; but by then, generations of close association between the degraded status of slavery and black color would leave the same prejudice against the Negro in the North that it did in the South.

It would seem, then, that instead of slavery being the root of the discrimination visited upon the Negro in America, slavery was itself molded by the early colonists' discrimination against the outlander. In the absence of any law of slavery or commandments of the Church to the contrary—as was true of Brazil and Spanish-America—the institution of slavery into which the African was placed in the English colonies inevitably mirrored that discrimination and, in so doing, perpetuated it.

Once the English embodied their discrimination against the Negro in slave law, the logic of the law took over. Through the early eighteenth century, judges and legislatures in all the colonies elaborated the law along the discriminatory lines laid down in the amorphous beginnings. In doing so, of course, especially in the South, they had the added incentive of perpetuating and securing a labor system which by then had become indispensable to the economy. The cleavage between the races was in that manner deepened and hardened into the shape which became quite familiar by the nineteenth century. In due time, particularly in the South, the correspondence between the black man and slavery would appear so perfect that it would be difficult to believe that the Negro was fitted for anything other than the degraded status in which he was almost always found. It would also be forgotten that the discrimination had begun long before slavery had come upon the scene.

Robert C. Twombly and Robert H. Moore

BLACK PURITAN: THE NEGRO IN

SEVENTEENTH-CENTURY MASSACHUSETTS

The institution of slavery actually appeared in New England before it had fully evolved in Virginia. Yet the character of New England slavery, both in law and in fact, was never as severe as bondage in the South. The description by Robert C. Twombly and Robert H. Moore of Negroes in seventeenth-century Massachusetts provides a case study that is representative of colonial New England as a whole.

Historians have assumed that seventeenth-century Massachusetts was no different from other American colonies in its treatment of Negroes.[1] It has

Robert C. Twombly and Robert H. Moore, "Black Puritan: The Negro in Seventeenth-Century Massachusetts," *The William and Mary Quarterly*, XXIV (April, 1967), pp. 224–42. Reprinted with permission of *The William and Mary Quarterly*.
    [1] Recent scholarship on early American slavery has ignored Massachusetts or assumed similarity with the South: Oscar and Mary Handlin, "Origins of the Southern Labor System," *The William and Mary Quarterly*, 3d Ser., VII (1950), 199–222, and Oscar Handlin, "The Origins of Negro Slavery," *Race and Nationality in American Life* (New York, 1957), 3–29, argue that discrimination developed because of the institutionalization of slavery. Carl N. Degler, "Slavery and the Genesis of American Race Prejudice," *Comparative Studies in Society and History*, II (1959), 49–66, reverses the Handlin thesis, attributing slavery to innate white discriminatory attitudes. Winthrop D. Jordan, "Modern Tensions and the Origin of American Slavery," *Journal of Southern History*, XXVIII (1962), 18–30, sees both slavery and discrimination as part of a worldwide debasement of the Negro. Other relevant works are: Jordan, "The Influence of the West Indies on the Origins of New England Slavery," *Wm. and Mary Qtly.* 3d Ser., XVIII (1961), 243–250; Lawrence W. Towner, " 'A Fondness for Freedom': Servant Protest in Puritan Society," *ibid.*, XIX (1962), 201–219; Towner, "The Sewall-Saffin Dialogue on Slavery," *ibid.*, XXI (1964), 40–52; Jules Zanger, "Crime and Punishment in Early Massachusetts," *ibid.*, XXII (1965), 471–477; Emory Washburn, "Slavery as It Once Prevailed in Massachusetts," in *Early History of Massachusetts: Lectures Delivered . . . Before the Lowell Institute, in Boston* (Boston, 1869), 199–225; and Lorenzo J. Greene, *The Negro in Colonial New England, 1620–1776* (New York, 1942).

been easy to overlook a colony where, as late as 1715, there were only 2,000 Negroes in a population of 96,000, and where whites seemed to hold racial views similar to those of other settlers. But an analysis of Negro life in the Puritan Commonwealth reveals the inaccuracy of this view.

Most authorities agree that Negroes first came to Massachusetts in 1638, but it seems clear to us that at least one Negro had arrived as early as 1633. Contemporaries estimated that there were between 100 and 200 in 1680 and 550 by 1708.[2] Although Negroes were numerous enough to be familiar in the everyday affairs of many communities by the 1660's, most Puritans regarded blacks as strange and exotic creatures. Despite the inconsistent terminology used to refer to Negroes,[3] Massachusetts whites held certain derogatory attitudes.

John Josselyn noted that some New Englanders thought Negro blackness resulted from the African climate, while others believed it came from Ham's curse. Blackness was commonly associated with evil. During the witchcraft hysteria many people claimed to have seen the Devil in the form of a "Blackman"; white women accused of having evil spirits were sometimes called "black witches." Blackness connoted ugliness as well as evil. "Sea-Devils," a fish found off the Maine coast, were popularly called "Negroes" because they were a very "ugly," "hideous" species, "having a black scale." [4]

[2] William Wood's 1634 *New-England's Prospect* . . . (1764 ed.), in *Publications of the Prince Society*, III (Boston, 1865), 86; and Deloraine P. Corey, *The History of Malden, Mass., 1633–1785* (Malden, Mass., 1899), 415, refer to a Negro living in Plymouth at least as early as 1633. Population estimates are taken from Simon Bradstreet to the Committee of Trade and Planations, May 18, 1680, in Elizabeth Donnan, ed., *Documents Illustrative of the History of the Slave Trade to America* (Washington, D.C., 1930–35), III, 14–15; Edward Randolph's Report to the Lords of the Committee of Trade of the Colonies, Aug., 1681, in Samuel G. Drake, *The History and Antiquities of Boston* . . . (Boston, 1856), 441; Joseph Dudley to the Council of Trade and Plantations, Oct. 1, 1708, in Cecil Headlam, ed., *Calendar of State Papers, Colonial Series, America and West Indies, June, 1708–1709* (London, 1922), 110; and Evarts B. Greene and Virginia D. Harrington, *American Population Before the Federal Census of 1790* (New York, 1932), 14.

[3] "Slave" was not precisely defined in seventeenth-century Massachusetts; its flexible usage permitted several meanings. The conventional definition was "one who is the property of, and entirely subject to, another person, whether by capture, purchase, or birth; a servant completely divested of freedom and personal rights." See W. A. Cragie, ed., *A New English Dictionary on Historical Principles* (Oxford, 1919), X, 182–184. The burden of this article is to demonstrate that Massachusetts never forced Negroes into this status. Puritans also used "slavery" to describe prisoners of war and criminals, and the term functional as a rhetorical device to indicate dissatisfaction with government or authority. "Slave" and "servant" were used interchangeably in reference to Negroes: John Noble and John F. Cronin, eds. *Records of the Court of Assistants of . . . Massachusetts . . .* (Boston, 1901–28), I, 74 and John Josselyn, *An Account of Two Voyages to New-England, Made during the Years 1638, 1663* (Boston, 1865), 139–140.

[4] The long history of black men in the European experience and the development of white racial opinion has been admirably treated in Winthrop D. Jordan, "White Over Black: the attitudes of the American colonists toward the Negro, to 1784" (unpubl. Ph.D. diss., Brown University, 1960), Ch. I. Puritan racial attitudes are illustrated in Josselyn, *Two Voyages*, 143; George L. Burr, ed., *Narratives of the Witch-*

If some derogatory attitudes found expression in metaphor, others appeared in social relations. Whites were insulted when compared closely with a Negro. "A Lieutenant of a Man of War," the perturbed Cotton Mather wrote, "whom I am a stranger to, designing to putt an Indignity upon me, has called his *Negro-Slave* by the Name of COTTON-MATHER." Samuel Sewall recorded in his diary that "Mr. Cotton Mather came to Mr. Wilkins's shop, and there talked very sharply against me as if I used his father worse than a Neger; spake so loud that the people in the street might hear him." Such opinions sometimes led to bizarre actions. Josselyn wrote that fish did not respond to herring as quickly as they did for a "waggish lad at Cape-porpus [Maine], who baited his hooks with the drown'd Negro's buttocks." Puritan racial attitudes do not seem appreciably different from those held by other contemporary white men.[5]

One might expect the Puritans to have treated Negroes with an indignity matching their attitudes. But the real test of the colony's race relations must be based not on what whites thought and said but on what they did. How the Negro fared in day to day activity is the best indication of the nature of Negro life in the Puritan Commonwealth.

II

Central to the maintenance of order and stability in any society is the administration of justice. This was particularly true in Massachusetts where respect for the law was primary in the colonists' conception of a vigorous, stable, and godly society. A profound commitment to the law and the judicial process overpowered antipathetical racial views and assured fair and equal treatment, guaranteeing the basic legal rights of Englishmen to free, servant, and slave Negroes. These rights—including police protection, legal counsel, trial by jury, fair and considered hearings, and impartial justice—are very much expected in the twentieth century. In the seventeenth they were incipient concepts in much of the western world. But Massachusetts guarded these liberties jealously, applying them without regard for skin color. The Puritans did not hold advanced racial views but they did place a high priority on the universality of justice. Throughout the century Negroes and whites received essentially equal treatment before the law.

Important principles were observed even in minor offenses. In 1680, for example, Goodman Wolland accused Daniel King's Negro boy of insulting him

craft Cases, 1648–1706 (New York, 1914), 309–310, 312, 425; and William S. Southgate, "History of Scarborough, from 1693 to 1783," Maine Historical Society, *Collections*, III (1853), 92.

[5] Dec. 10, 1721, in Worthington C. Ford, ed., *Diary of Cotton Mather* (New York, 1957), II, 663; Barrett Wendell, *Cotton Mather: The Puritan Priest* (New York, [1891]), 153, quoting Samuel Sewall, Oct. 20, 1701; Josselyn, *Two Voyages*, 159; Jordan, "White Over Black," Ch. I.

on a Boston street. When the boy denied the allegation, Wolland brought him to court where the case was thrown out for lack of witnesses. That the case went to court at all indicates a predilection to seek legal redress rather than to initiate private action. When, in 1653, "a contravercy" developed between John Smith of Plymouth and John Barnes's "neager maide servant," the Plymouth court listened to "whatsoever could bee saide on either side." Both were cleared of any misdemeanor, but they were admonished for public quarreling.[6]

Like whites, Negroes received police protection and were shielded from extralegal punitive action. When three Indians broke into the home of Angola, a free Negro, in 1672, he prosecuted. All three were given twenty stripes and ordered to remain in prison until they paid court costs. In another case Pelatiah Glover brought suit against Betty Negro for insulting his son and mother. Richard White and Tom, a Negro, testified against her. She was found guilty of slander and given ten stripes but by being taken to court Betty at least found a measure of protection. The principle of using judicial means rather than resorting to personal retribution extended to the colony's Maine jurisdiction where in 1686 George Norton prosecuted his own Negro for stealing his wool. Due process and a willingness to use the courts minimized expeditious extralegal punishment. Even masters recognized this principle.[7]

Other incidents establish that Negro testimony was admissible as evidence against whites. In 1673 a defendant challenged a witness's legal right to testify, but the plaintiff replied "that the negro was of such carriage and knowledge that her testimony had been accepted several times before this." Later, in 1679, Wonn Negro testified against Bridget Oliver, who was suspected

[6] George F. Dow, ed., *Records and Files of the Quarterly Courts of Essex County* (Salem, 1911–21), VII, 425; Nathaniel B. Shurtleff, ed., *Records of the Colony of New Plymouth in New England* (Boston, 1855–61), III, 39. To demonstrate racial equality before the law we shall compare the several kinds of criminal and civil offenses committed by Negroes to similar cases involving whites. We have appraised all the published records (falling between 1650 and 1690) in which Negroes appear; those presented here are not atypical. We believe these cases accurately reflect the temper of the Negro's participation in the legal process.

[7] The Angola case is in Samuel Eliot Morison, ed., *Records of the Suffolk County Court, 1671–1680*, 2 vols., in *Publications of the Colonial Society of Massachusetts, Collections*, XXIX–XXX (Boston, 1933), I, 119. The Glover incident is listed in Joseph H. Smith, ed., *Colonial Justice in Western Massachusetts (1639–1702): The Pynchon Court Record* ... (Cambridge, Mass., 1961), 375. A comparable case involving a white woman brought a penalty of twenty stripes and the order to wear a paper "pinned upon her forehead with this inscription in capital letters: 'A SLANDERER OF MR. ZEROBABELL ENDICOTT,'" in Dow, ed., *Essex Court Recs.*, I, 380. Norton and Peter appear in Robert E. Moody, ed., *Province and Court Records of Maine* (Portland, 1928–64), III, 226. Carl Degler, on the Southern administration of justice to Negroes, says: "As early as 1669 the Virginia law virtually washed its hands of protecting the Negro held as a slave. It allowed punishment of refractory slaves up to and including accidental death, relieving the master, explicitly, of any fear of prosecution ...," in "Slavery and the Genesis of American Race Prejudice," 61. Compare this situation also with the 1694–95 Nathaniel Cane murder case cited in Moody, ed., *Maine Recs.*, IV, 34–35.

of witchcraft. In 1680 Mingo the Negro was a witness in a suit involving warehouse arson. Instances of Negro testimony for and against both races are numerous.[8]

It is also evident from the records that Negroes had access to legal counsel. In 1679 Hannah, a Negro servant, was convicted for stealing a box of "Chyrurgions Jnstruments." From prison she persuaded three white men to post forty pounds bond for her release and petitioned the Suffolk County court for dismissal of her fines. Her appeal, a sophisticated legal argument, cited page and section numbers of the laws governing burglary. Although the jury dismissed it, Zachariah Chaffee, Jr., commenting on Hannah's appeal, noted the "refined distinctions" that could only have been "written by men accustomed to legal problems." [9]

An additional example of the many elements of justice accorded Negroes stemmed from the Salem witch controversy. In 1692 a warrant was issued for the arrest of Mary Black, a Negro owned by Lieutenant Nathaniel Putnam of Salem Village. Although maintaining her innocence, Mary was tried, convicted, and imprisoned for witchcraft. The next year, however, cooler heads had apparently prevailed, and Mary was not forgotten. Upon petition she was released from prison by proclamation of the Governor.[10]

These cases introduce important principles illustrating Negro legal rights. A Negro's word was admissible as evidence and his testimony could be as acceptable as that of whites. Charges against Negroes had to be documented and they received the thoughtful consideration of juries and magistrates. Negroes had police protection and were shielded from extralegal practices that would have denied them due process of law. They could appeal, use legal counsel, and receive gubernatorial pardons.

The principles operative in the cases described above were applicable when more abhorrent crimes were committed. Negroes were given the same judicial treatment as whites in all aspects of the case from indictment to punishment. Some crimes, like burglary, are impossible to analyze, for penalties were distributed on the basis of the kinds and amounts of items stolen; we were unable to find cases in which Negroes and whites appropriated exactly the same things. For this reason we have not attempted comparisons of thefts, but have analyzed arson, murder, manslaughter, and sexual offenses—the four main areas in which comparison between the races is possible.

Of the sexual crimes committed in Massachusetts, fornication, bastardy, and rape were most prevalent. According to the 1675 Laws and Ordinances of War—a compilation of previous statutes—rape, ravishment, and unnatural abuses were punishable by death. Fornication and other "dissolute lascivious-

[8] See Dow, ed., *Essex Court Recs.*, V, 179; VI, 255; VII, 329–330, 373, 410. For white testimony on behalf of Negroes see Noble and Cronin, eds., *Assistants Recs.*, III, 194.

[9] Morison, ed., *Suffolk Court Recs.*, II, 1153–1157. Chaffee's remarks are in the Intro., I, xxv.

[10] Charles W. Upham, *Salem Witchcraft* ... (Boston, 1867), II, 128, 136–137.

ness" were penalized at the judge's discretion, taking into account the severity and circumstances of the case. Fornication, by both Negro and white, was a considerable problem in early Massachusetts, and the many recorded cases provide ample opportunity for comparative analysis.[11]

Essex County punished its Negro fornicators by whipping or fine, the choice sometimes being left to the offender. In 1660, Captain White's Negro Jugg was whipped; Grace and Juniper, convicted in 1674, were "to be fined or whipped." In 1678, two "neager" servants, David and Judith, chose to pay a fine rather than feel the last ten and five times respectively. The whites in Essex County received similar treatment. Mary Dane, an indentured servant, was whipped. The same year, 1654, Elizabeth Osgood was given thirty stripes and her mate twenty-five. Most infringers, regardless of race, received from ten to twenty stripes or were ordered to pay from forty to fifty shillings.[12]

Representative of Suffolk County's treatment of fornicators was the case of Mary Plumb, a white, who was punished with fifteen stripes and court and prison fees for "Lascivious carriage by being seene in bed with a man." For the same offense, Phoebe Lovell received ten strips or a forty shilling fine plus court costs. Negroes in Suffolk County got the same penalties. Joan and her partner, Jasper Indian, were given their choice of fifteen stripes or a forty shilling fine plus court costs. In a significant case Robert Corbet, a white, and George, a Negro, both servants of Stephen French, received identical sentences for committing fornication with the Negro Maria: twenty stripes and court costs. Fornication between the races was not punished any more stringently than that between members of the same race. In Suffolk, as in Essex County, the most common penalty ranged from ten to twenty lashes or a forty to fifty shilling fine plus fees of court.[13]

Although there is no evidence that it was practiced, racial intermarriage was not illegal until 1705. Before then most miscegenation was illicit. If it led to bastardy, penalties for both races were generally the same as for simple

---

[11] The 1675 statutes are in Nathaniel B. Shurtleff, ed., *Records of the Governor and Company of the Massachusetts Bay in New England* (Boston, 1854), V, 49–50, Sections 13 and 14. Also see Jordan, "White Over Black," 119. Fornication and adultery were usually treated as one crime in the seventeenth century. Married men, engaging in sexual activity with women other than their wives, were often tried for fornication.

[12] For Essex County Negro fornication cases see Dow, ed., *Essex Court Recs.*, II, 247; V, 411; VI, 73, 135; VII, 141, 411; for whites see I, 71, 80, 82, 337, 347, 404, 414, 420; III, 17, 61, 198–199; VII, 377–378, 398, 406, 410; VIII, 375, 377, 424. This list is by no means exhaustive.

[13] Because the published records are incomplete, the only Suffolk County cases are from the 1670's. For Negro offenders see Morison, ed., *Suffolk Court Recs.*, I, 233; II, 991; for whites see, for example, I, 22, 80, 90–91, 114, 119, 185, 233–234; II, 885, 1012–1014, 1097–1099, 1102, 1153. The Courts sometimes required a couple fornicating before marriage to make public confession before the church. See I, 80, 90–91. In Maine fornicators usually received seven or more stripes or a fine ranging from fifteen to fifty shillings. See Moody, ed., *Maine Recs.*, IV, 268–269, 293, 340, 344–345, 358, 360, and 371 for examples.

fornication. In most cases the court sought to determine paternity in order to provide the child's support, and this led to additional costs for the father. Usually the woman was whipped from ten to twenty stripes or ordered to pay a forty to fifty shilling fine. The man was given a similar number of stripes and then bound to pay weekly support or a lump sum to be administered over the years. In 1682, for example, Richard Prior gave thirty pounds surety to save Ipswich from maintaining his illegitimate child. The same year John Tucker was fined six pounds and ordered to pay an undisclosed amount for birth and support. In 1679 the court ordered John Hunkins to give his partner's father one shilling per week. When the races mixed the penalties were about the same: William Rane, father of a child by the Indian servant Ann, paid three shillings a week. For "haveing a bastard," the white Hannah Bonny was "well whipt"; her mate, Nimrod Negro, was also whipped and made to turn over eighteen pence weekly for his offspring. Illegitimate Negro children were generally awarded financial support in amounts similar to those paid to white and mixed offspring. In 1673 the Negro Silvanus provided two shillings six pence per week for his son's upbringing.

A humorous episode took place in Maine in 1695. Alice Metherill, for being pregnant, was given a choice of ten stripes and fifteen shillings or five pounds and court costs; her alleged partner was ordered to pay eleven shillings six pence bond and two shillings six pence maintenance per week payable monthly. When the child was born, however, it was quite black. The "father," already punished by the court, quickly prosecuted Alice for falsely associating him with her "black bastard." Alice, by now known as a "whore" and a "witch," finally admitted that Black Will, a Negro slave, was her real consort. The province did not hold Black Will's past against him, however, for several years later when he was accused of fathering the baby of Elizabeth Brooks, a single white woman, he was acquitted.[14]

Rape, a more serious offense, could be punished by death. The two Negro cases in the published records reveal the severity dealt offenders. Basto Negro was convicted in 1676 of raping the three year old daughter of Robert Cox, his master. When Cox appealed Basto's death sentence, the jury substituted thirty-nine lashes and ordered him "allwayes to weare a roape about his neck, to hang doune two foot." If ever he was found without his rope Basto would feel an additional twenty lashes. Shortly thereafter John Negro confessed to "pulling Sarah Phillips of Salem off her horse and attempting to ravish her."

[14] As with fornication interracial bastardy was not punished more severely than bastardy between two members of the same race. For examples of penalties accorded illegitimate white births see Morison, ed., *Suffolk Court Recs.*, II, 1097–1099; Dow, ed., *Essex Court Recs.*, VII, 97, 187; VIII, 12–13, 279; Shurtleff, ed., *Plymouth Recs.*, I, 127. For illegitimate Negro births see Morison, ed., *Suffolk Court Recs.*, I, 113, 259; II, 809, 841, 1164; Dow, ed., *Essex Court Recs.*, I, 196, 323; VI, 137. Interracial bastardy cases are: Dow, ed., *Essex Court Recs.*, V, 409; VI, 23; VII, 410; Morison, ed., *Suffolk Court Recs.*, I, 185, 232; II, 809; Shurtleff, ed., *Plymouth Recs.*, VI, 177. Alice Metherill and Black Will are in Moody, ed., *Maine Recs.*, IV, 47–49, 64–66; V, 126, 169–171, 199–201; *York Deeds* (Portland, 1887–1910), VI, fol. 88.

John's penalty for attempted rape was a five pound payment to Miss Phillips, prosecution and court costs, and banishment from the colony.[15]

Whites also received stiff penalties. John Man, perhaps the Marquis de Sade of his time, for "wanton and lascivious carriages . . . and cruell beating" of his indentured servant, gave two hundred pounds sureties until the next court, paid prosecution costs and court fees, and terminated his girl's contract. John Kempe attempted rape on "3 young girles [and] was censured to bee whiped both heare [Boston], at Roxbury and at Salem very severely and was Comitted for a slave to Lieft Davenport." Two other white rapists, William Cheny and Samuel Guile, were hanged until dead.[16]

Two rapes involving Indians demonstrate important aspects of Massachusetts jurisprudence. In 1674, Tom, indicted for raping another Indian, pleaded not guilty before a "Jury of twelve men six English and six Indians against none of which he Objected." Although he was found guilty, Tom held the right to challenge a jury containing six members of his own race. The second case, from Plymouth in 1682, dealing with "Sam, the Indian," reveals a paternalistic strain in legal approaches to nonwhites. Sam was proven guilty: "although in an ordinary consideration hee deserved death, yett considering hee was but an Indian, and therefore in an incapasity [unable] to know the horibleness . . . of his abominable act . . . he was centanced . . . to be severely whipt att the post and sent out of the country." In spite of this decision, leniency for Indians and Negroes, who ordinarily met the same penalties as whites, does not appear the rule. Indeed, judges followed the argument presented by a defendant in a 1660 Essex County case, although his suggestion about Negroes was not considered valid: "the law is undeniable that the indian may have the same distribusion of Justice with our selves." John Hawthorne had argued. But "ther is as I humbly consieve not the same argument as amongst the negroes for the light of the gospell is [not] a begineing to appeare amongst them. . . ." The application of the law to Negroes followed the pattern of Tom's case and Hawthorne's suggestion for Indians—due process and equality in punishment. The courts did not consider Christianity a prerequisite for equality before the law; nor did they apply Plymouth's leniency for Sam Indian or Hawthorne's views on Negroes to the blacks in their midst.[17]

Equitable treatment for Negroes extended to other capital offenses. According to the law, murder was to be "expiated with the death of the murderer." A measure of Massachusetts's concern for justice was the care with which she appraised murder cases, often meting out punishment for manslaughter instead. Thoughtful scrutiny reflected a recognition of extenuating circumstances. And this attitude did not exclude Negro assailants of whites.

---

[15] Basto's case is in Noble and Cronin, eds., *Assistants Recs.*, I, 74, and Shurtleff, ed., *Mass. Rec.*, V, 117–118. John Negro is in Morison, ed., *Suffolk Court Recs.*, II, 1067.

[16] *Ibid.*, II, 807; Nobel and Cronin, eds., *Assistants Recs.*, I, 50, 199; II, 86; innocent whites are *ibid.*, I, 73, 158.

[17] *Ibid.*, I, 21–22; *Plymouth Recs.*, VI, 98; Hawthorne's argument is in Dow, ed., *Essex Court Recs.*, II, 240.

The average penalty for manslaughter was a twenty pound fine and the costs of prosecution, court, and detention. Depending on the circumstances, part of the fine went to the colony and part to the deceased's relatives.[18] Both instances of Negro manslaughter, originally indictments for murder against whites, were handled equitably. A 1684 defendant, "Robert Trayes, negro," wounded the "legg of Daniell Standlake ..., of which wound, and cutting the legg occationed thereby, died. ..." Since he had meant to fire at Standlake's door, the jury decided that Trayes was "an instrument of the death of Daniell Standlake by misadventure," and sentenced the defendant to pay the deceased's father five pounds or be whipped. The second case, in which the servant Robin was accused, is of particular note, not only for its dealing with manslaughter but also for its clear statement of Negro legal rights.[19]

Robin was guilty of giving John Cheeny of Cambridge "a mortall wound on the head with a stick" in 1689. His punishment was light: charges of prosecution, fees of court, and costs of prison where he was to remain until he paid. Robin had pled not guilty, but what extenuating circumstances had brought about the easy sentence are not recorded. More important, however, is that after the jury had been selected Robin was allowed to "make ... challange against any of them." In addition, one juror, feeling as Hawthorne had in 1660, that Negroes did not deserve "the same distribution of Justice with our selves," refused to appear. In reply the court fined him five shillings. Through this concrete act the court clearly stated that shirking jury duty was inexcusable and that due process extended to blacks as well as whites.

The only recorded case in which a white killed a Negro took place in Maine in 1694 when a master's continual mistreatment of his servant led to her death. In the South well before this time, as Carl Degler points out, masters were without "any fear of prosecution" if they killed slaves; the law "allowed punishment for refractory slaves up to and including accidental death. ..." But the Puritans showed more restraint. Indicted by a grand jury on suspicion of murder, Nathaniel Cane was convicted of manslaughter for "Cruelty to his Negro woman by Cruell Beating and hard usage." His fine—ten pounds ten shillings—was light. Nonetheless, a master could not mistreat, abuse, or murder his Negro without threat of legal action.[20]

Arson, an infrequent but serious offense, brought harsh penalties. Severity was demonstrated early in the colony's history when in 1640 Henry Stevens fired his master's barn and had his indenture extended by twenty-one years.

[18] Shurtleff, ed., *Mass. Recs.*, V, 50, lists penalties for manslaughter and murder. White manslaughter cases are cited in Noble and Cronin, eds., *Assistants Recs.*, I, 54, 114, 188, 358–359.

[19] The Trayes case is in Shurtleff, ed., *Plymouth Recs.*, VI, 141–142; Robin's in Noble and Cronin, eds., *Assistants Recs.*, I, 304–305, 321.

[20] Moody, ed., *Maine Recs.*, IV, 34–35. We saw no published court records convicting Negroes of murder. But note the equality of sentence in this extract from Samuel Sewall's diary, June 8, 1693: "Elisabeth Emerson of Havarill and a Negro Woman were executed after Lecture, for murdering their Infant Children." Massachusetts Historical Society, *Collections*, 5th Ser., V (1878), 379.

Throughout the century the penalties were stiff: Jack, a Negro arsonist, was hanged in 1681. Two Negroes implicated in the Maria arson case the same year were banished and Maria was burned alive, the only punishment of its kind in Massachusetts history.[21] Maria's fire had caused the death of a baby girl. She had deliberately destroyed her master's house and had not intended murder. But since she had caused a death by burning she in turn was burned. Her severe sentence may have been prompted by uneasiness over a rash of fires in the Boston vicinity. Social pressure may have induced the court to be unduly harsh in this affair but it was not stampeded. The strict sentence was a response to a specific situation and did not become a precedent for future dealings with either arsonists, murderers, or Negroes. But the case stands as an ugly blot on Puritan history.[22]

This review of legal cases indicates that throughout the seventeenth century the Negro received due process and only in isolated incidents, like the Maria case, was he given unusual treatment. But even on that occasion it is questionable to what extent skin color dictated severity. In general, the Negro held the rights of Englishmen before the courts. The legal apparatus did not undergo subtle shifts when Negroes came before it.

III

If the Negro's legal status was not circumscribed by pigmentation neither were his economic opportunities. Several black men, servant and free, accumulated real and other property; the color of their skin did not by definition render them ineligible for economic gain. Although most Negroes were members of the servant class and therefore at the bottom of the economic ladder, some were able to carve out an enviable niche in the white business world.

The story of Angola illustrates the possibilities. In 1653 he was owned by Captain Robert Keayne, who in his will in 1656 left Angola a two pound legacy. Then the free Negro Bostian Ken purchased Angola and set him free

---

[21] The Stevens case is in Noble and Cronin, eds., *Assistants Recs.*, II, 100. The documents relating to Maria, her accomplices, and Jack have been brought together by John Noble. See *Publication of the Colonial Society at Massachusetts, Transactions, 1899, 1900*, VIII (Boston, 1904), 323–336.

[22] Noble, *ibid.*, argues that Maria was hanged before burning, dismissing both Cotton and Increase Mather's assertions that she was burned alive. But Noble overlooked evidence that substantiates the Mathers' contentions: a Milton minister who had witnessed Jack's and Maria's execution noted in his diary on Sept. 22, 1681: "... two negroes burnt, one of them was first hanged." "Rev. Peter Thacher's Journal" in Albert K. Teele, ed., *The History of Milton, Mass. 1640 to 1887* (Boston, 1887), 646. Increase Mather wrote: Maria was "burned to death,—the first that has suffered such a death in New England." Mass. Hist. Soc., *Proceedings*, III (1859), 320. Edgar Buckingham's allegation that in 1675 Phillis, a Negro slave, was burned alive in Cambridge, in "Morality, Learning, and Religion, in Massachusetts in Olden Times," *History and Proceedings of the Pocumtuck Valley Memorial Association, 1880–1889* (Deerfield, Mass., 1898), II, 20, seems unsupported.

by bonding his property to Mrs. Keayne. In 1670 Governor Richard Bellingham sold a piece of land bordered "Upon the North East with the land of Angola, the Negro." Bellingham had given him this fifty-foot square piece in the late 1660's when Angola, paddling in a river, had rescued the Governor from his sinking boat. When he died in 1675 Angola's will confirmed his house, land, and other possessions upon his widow Elizabeth, her children, and her heirs forever. In the twenty years before his death Angola had paid his eighteen pound obligation to Ken and had moved from a servant with a two pound legacy to a free Negro of means.[23]

Bostian Ken, Angola's benefactor, was another prosperous Negro. In order to purchase his friend's freedom in 1656 Ken bonded his house and land in Dorchester plus four and one half acres of wheat. In 1662 he sold his one-third share of the fourteen-ton ship *Hopewell* to his "loving Friend Francis Vernon" along with "one barrell of liquor one barr of Sugar one Barr mackerell and one Barr Codfish." From 1656 to 1662 Ken dealt in considerable amounts of property.[24]

Most of the other seventeenth-century Negro landowners received their holdings from their masters. In 1677 Increase Mather bought land bordered on the "Northwest by the land of Jethro the Negro." If Governor Bellingham and the Reverend Mr. Mather owned choice land, the bordering Negro holdings may have also been desirable.[25] Other Negroes held land, houses, and small businesses. When Thomas, owner of a chair-making establishment, married Katherine in 1678, he drew up a lengthy document granting her his estate in case of his death and bound himself for one hundred pounds surety. Zippora Potter, daughter of one of Robert Keayne's Negroes, bought a twenty-eight by sixty-foot "parcell of land with a dwelling house thereupon" in 1670 for "forty Sixe pounds currant Mony of New England in hand paid." Although the number of successful Negroes was small, they came from a total Negro population in the colony that was at most only two hundred at this time.[26]

A few Negroes were property owners, but the majority were house servants living with white families. Many resided in Boston but those in the outlying areas and the Boston blacks who traveled about broadened interracial contact. Most Negroes lived in their masters' homes, were often left alone, and could

[23] *Suffolk Deeds* (Boston, 1880–1906), II, 297; III, 78; VII, 22, 144; VIII, 298–299; Morison, ed., *Suffolk Court Recs.*, II, 598; *Report of the Record Commissioners of the City of Boston Containing Miscellaneous Papers* (Boston, 1876–1909), X, 25.

[24] Bostian Ken (Kine, Kajne), also known as Sebastian and Bus Bus, probably took his surname from the Keayne family. It was common for a Negro, if he had a last name, to use his master's or former master's. *Suffolk Deeds*, II, 297; IV, 111, 113.

[25] Angola's land fronted on the main road between Boston and Roxbury and at least one man, James Pennyman, envied it. *Ibid.*, VIII, 298.

[26] Property owning Negroes and master's gifts are *ibid.*, VII, 43; X, 278, 295; Dow, ed., *Essex Court Recs.*, II, 183; VIII, 434; *York Deeds*, IV, fol. 52; Ford, ed., *Diary of Cotton Mather*, I, 278; Henry A. Hazen, *History of Billerica, Mass.* (Boston, 1883), 170–171. Charles Taussig noted a Rhode Island Negro couple that had accumulated a 300 pound fortune and in 1735 sailed back to Guinea where they were independently wealthy; see *Rum, Romance and Rebellion* (New York, 1928), 33.

come and go as they pleased when not working. They were not restricted to the towns in which they lived and in many cases moved freely about the countryside.[27]

Freedom of movement opened up certain options. One option, running away, may have been a product of working class discontent; but running away was also encouraged by alternatives that lack of repression offered.[28] Freedom of movement permitted a certain amount of fraternization between races in the lower classes; the derogatory views of most whites did not preclude informal relations. Occasionally mutual activities were forms of antisocial behavior. In 1673, for example, "John Burrington, Edward Fish, Richard Hollingworths Negro Tom, Thomas [,] Clark Cliffords Servt," and a fifth man, stole saddles and bridles and "complotted to run away." About the same time "Gregory, Nath. Emerson, Arthur Abbot and a Negro" broke into a house, took wine, and improvised a drinking party. But not all interracial mingling was mischievous. For five years in the 1690's one of Boston's four chimney sweepers was "Jeremiah the Negro"; for one year, 1693, he was joined by "Negro Will," who along with Jeremiah brought token integration to Boston's public employ. During the smallpox epidemic in the 1680's Mary Heall, a seventy-four year old widow living alone, took the Negro Zanckey into her home to watch over his recovery. On another occasion, Jack, a runaway Negro, came to Anthony Dorchester's home. Jack was a stranger but Dorchester invited him in and made him welcome:

> ... after asking for a Pipe of Tobacco which I told him there was some on the Table he tooke my knife and Cut some and then put it in his Pocket, and after that tooke downe a Cutlass and offered to draw it but it Coming out stiff I closed in upon him. ...

Jack was overpowered and taken to prison, but Dorchester's initial hospitality is noteworthy.[29]

[27] Horizontal mobility and freedom of movement are illustrated by the Maria case, discussed above; Dow, ed., *Essex Court Recs.*, VI, 255; VIII, 297–298; *Suffolk Deeds*, IV, x–xi; Ford, ed., *Diary of Cotton Mather*, II, 139; *Diary of Samuel Sewall*, Mass. Hist. Soc., *Coll.*, 5th Ser., VI (1879), 5; the travel account of an unknown Frenchman, ca. 1687, in Nathaniel B. Shurtleff, *A Topographical and Historical Description of Boston* (Boston, 1871), 48; James R. Trumbull, *History of Northampton* (Northampton, 1898), I, 376–377. Exemplifying freedom from masters' supervision is the case of a servant who persisted in wooing a young lady although repeatedly warned by her master to keep away. Both were later convicted for fornication. Dow, ed., *Essex Court Recs.*, VII, 141.

[28] Revolts were never a problem in Massachusetts but runaways were frequent. Closest to a slave revolt was an unsuccessful 1690 attempt by a New Jerseyite with abolitionist tendencies to induce Negroes, Indians, and Frenchmen to attack several Bay Colony towns. See Joshua Coffin, *A Sketch of the History of Newbury* ... (Boston, 1845), 153–154, and Sidney Perley, "Essex County in the Abolition of Slavery," *Essex County Historical and Genealogical Register*, I (1894), 2.

[29] On informal relations see Dow, ed., *Essex Court Recs.*, I, 287; V, 141; VII, 394–395; VIII, 297; Morison, ed., *Suffolk Court Recs.*, I, 249; II, 648–649; Robert F. Seybolt, *The Town Officials of Colonial Boston, 1634–1775* (Cambridge, Mass., 1939),

The colony's mechanisms of social control which permitted easy inter-racial contact did not make Negroes full fledged citizens or the social equals of whites, but neither were the blacks shunted to another realm of existence. The absence of rigid barriers in Massachusetts did not create a Negro utopia. But neither were Bay Colony blacks forced into a separate and demeaning world of their own. The Negro hovered on the fringes of full participation in social and economic life.

IV

Overcoming the obstacles of nature was of immediate importance to the first generation of Puritans; in their attempt to construct a "city upon a hill" their first concerns were the problems of building communities, of keeping their children from barbarism, and of reproducing essential and familiar institutions. But as the generations passed, as trade increased, as the frontier receded, and as the complexities of a growing colony burgeoned, the Commonwealth's problems shifted. Social order and stability had been of major importance from the beginning but during the last two decades of the seventeenth century serious social introspection increased. Ministers warned that God was angry with the people; family structure, education, the churches, and other social institutions came under closer scrutiny. It was in this context that the colony passed her first laws to regulate the Negro's behavior.

Except for militia policy, no laws were passed applying only to Negroes until the 1680's.[30] Old and New England had fitted the black man into the social system without legally recognizing slavery or a slave caste. Within the broad guidelines of the Common Law and Puritan religious views Massachusetts had extended century-old rights of Englishmen to Negroes. But in the 1680's the colony began to place restrictions upon them. The new Negro policies were responses to three social concerns: a widespread anathema for the slave trade, a pervasive uneasiness about the colony's economic future, and a grow-ing anxiety about the Negro's behavior.

In spite of the unpopularity of slaving, several Massachusetts merchants were active traders in the 1680's, selling Negroes in Virginia for three to five thousand pounds of tobacco per head. Public pressure could not prohibit businessmen from dealing with Southerners but it could discourage the prac-tice at home. Fear of public reprisal forced John Saffin, John Usher, James Wetcomb, and Andrew Belcher to import Negroes secretly in 1681. Fearing

77, 79, 83, 85, 87; Joseph Dudley to Gabriel Bernon, May 20, 1707, in George F. Daniels, *History of the Town of Oxford Massachusetts* (Oxford, 1892), 26–27. The quotation is from Smith, ed., *Colonial Justice in Western Massachusetts*, 298–299.

[30] Massachusetts never formally denied Negroes the right to bear personal arms and specifically included them in the militia in 1652. But in 1656, without ex-planation, she reversed her policy, excluding Indians and Negroes from training. Shurtleff, ed., *Mass. Records*, IV, Pt. i, 86, 257.

seizure, these merchants rerouted their Guinea trader from Swansea, Rhode Island, to Nantasket, Massachusetts, where, they wrote, "before you come in there take in such negroes . . . of ours and come up in the night with them, giveing us notice thereof wth what privacy you can. . . ." "Keepe your men Ignorant of your designe," the traders told their agent, and do nothing "prejudiciall to our mayne designe." [31]

Analyses of the economy seemed to demonstrate little benefit in the Negro's presence. In 1702 the General Court decided to promote "the bringing of White Servants and to put a period to Negroes being slaves." Beneath this admirable statement were more complex and mundane considerations. In 1708 Governor Joseph Dudley remarked that Negroes were costly to maintain during the winter months because they did little work and demanded great amounts of clothing. Negroes "are usually the worst servants," he noted. "The planters here do so much prefer white" laborers. The most complete statement of the economic disadvantages of Negroes appeared in an anonymous 1716 pamphlet. "Slaves . . . are a great hinderance to the Peopling and Improving the Country," the author began. If Negroes were excluded it "would greatly Encourage [white] Servants to come," and thereby aid the colony's growth. Since the land was "generally taken up," white servants could not acquire property and frequently became runaways and thieves. To aviod unruly indentured labor, a master could buy Negroes, and because of the tax structure, come off "cheaper than his poorer Neighbour that has an Apprentice." Apprentices cost more than slaves to maintain, were subject to regular militia training, and went to war. Slaves discouraged economic growth by draining their owners of wealth and by displacing laborers, apprentices, and craftsmen who used indenture as a stepping stone to greater things. To the author, the Negro posed a serious threat to indenture which, he felt, was the key to economic growth. [32]

The first regulations on Negroes were clauses inserted into general laws prohibiting Negroes, mulattos, Indians, servants, and apprentices from buying or being served alcoholic beverages. Later in the 1680's the same groups were warned about stealing or giving away stolen goods and whites who induced thefts or received stolen merchandise were similarly promised punishment. [33]

---

[31] William Fitzhugh, King George County Virginia, to Mr. Jackson of Piscataway, in New England, Feb. 11, 1683, in R. A. Brock, "New England and the Slave Trade," *Wm. and Mary Qtly.*, II (1894), 176–177; Saffin, Usher, Wetcomb, and Belcher to Welstead, June 12, 1681, in *New-England Historical and Genealogical Register*, XXXI (1877), 75–76.

[32] Drake, *History and Antiquities*, 525, quotes the General Court, June, 1702; Dudley to Council, Oct. 1, 1708, in Headlam, ed., *Cal. State Papers, Col. Ser., June, 1708–09*, 110; "Some Considerations Upon the several sorts of Banks Proposed as a Medium of Trade: And Some Improvements that might be made in this Province, hinted at" (Boston, 1716), in Andrew McFarland Davis, ed., *Colonial Currency Reprints, 1682–1751* (Boston, 1910–11), I, 343, 346.

[33] Acts regulating alcoholic consumption are in the Records of the Council of Massachusetts under the Administration of President Joseph Dudley, "Dudley Records," Mass. Hist. Soc., *Proceedings*, 2d Ser., XIII (Boston, 1899, 1900), 252; Ellis Ames

No further legislation appeared until after the turn of the century. In 1703 Indian, Negro, and mulatto servants and slaves could be on the streets after nine in the evening only with masters' consent. After 1703 no Negro or mulatto could be manumitted unless his master gave fifty pounds surety for the servant's welfare. The first law was directed toward night-time unrest, and the second prevented masters from throwing elderly, unemployable servants on the town charge. Both were concerned with specific and observable social problems.

The most stringent new measure, "An Act for the Better Preventing of a Spurious and Mixt Issue" of 1705, drove a deep wedge between the races. Sexual intercourse and racial intermarriage were now specifically prohibited. Fixed penalties were imposed on both races. Fornication was no longer left to judicial decision; Negro offenders were banished and the white consort, male or female, assumed responsibility for the offspring. The law reemphasized the desirability of Negro marriages, presumably as part of an effort to minimize mulatto births.

The 1705 law also placed a four pound duty on Negroes imported into the colony, and set heavy penalties on violators. The new duty aimed to discourage the slave trade. Some Puritans wished to rid the colony of Negroes or prevent any more from coming but restrictions on importation did not rest on this basis alone. Seven years later, in 1712, the General Court prohibited the trade in Indians. Revulsion for the slave trade and suspicion of outsiders worked to prevent nonwhites from coming to the Puritan Commonwealth.

A five-part law in 1707 prevented free Negroes from harboring or entertaining nonwhite servants in their homes without masters' approval and ordered them to repair highways, clean streets, or perform other tasks equal in time and amount to military duty. Since free Negroes had "a share in the benefit" of common defense, they would also go to the parade ground "in case of alarm" and "perform such tasks as the first commission of the company shall direct...." The several laws were supplemented by town ordinances which, throughout the eighteenth century, further limited Negro freedom of movement.[34]

and Abner C. Goodell, eds., *Acts and Resolves of the Province of Massachusetts Bay, 1692–1714* (Boston, 1869–1922), I, 154; Moody, ed., *Maine Recs.*, IV, 51; Edward W. Baker, "The 'Old Worcester Turnpike,'" *Proceedings of the Brookline Historical Society* (Jan. 23, 1907), 29. Laws governing stolen goods are in Ames and Goodell, eds., *Acts and Resolves*, I, 156, 325; see also Greene, *The Negro in Colonial New England*, 130. The only other seventeenth-century statute aimed at Negroes was passed in 1680: that no ship of more than 12 tons should entertain any passenger, servant or Negro, without permit from the governor. *The Colonial Laws of Massachusetts. Reprinted from the Edition of 1672, With the Supplements through 1686* (Boston, 1887), 281.

[34] The laws discussed in these paragraphs are in Ames and Goodell, eds., *Acts and Resolves*, I, 535, 578–579, 606–607; John B. Dillon, ed., *Oddities of Colonial Legislation in America...* (Indianapolis, 1879), 206–207, 211–212; *Report of the Record Commissioners of the City of Boston*, VIII, 173–177.

V

The new Massachusetts statutes dealing with Negroes were responses to specific and observable colonial problems. The measures arose from what the Puritans thought were manifestations of social disorder. The legislation was not a premeditated program to debase the Negro, for the Puritans believed that their regulations were in the Negro's best interest. Some colonial leaders like Samuel Sewall and Cotton Mather wanted to incorporate Negroes more intimately into the colony's social and religious institutions; but men of narrower vision passed laws which overruled better intentions. The Bay Colony reluctantly accepted the black man's presence but believed by the 1700's that it precipitated social disorder. Legal restrictions on Massachusetts's Negroes neither followed from nor led to slavery. In the Bay Colony these restrictions were part of a hasty problem-solving endeavor that prevalent attitudes and predispositions made possible. The Negro felt the brunt of discriminatory laws but he was not without due process and never totally removed from participation in the white social and economic orbit. These advantages reflected an attitude that later enabled the Bay Colony to lead the way in constitutional prohibitions of slavery.

Benjamin Quarles

LORD DUNMORE AS LIBERATOR

The era of the American Revolution, with its ideological com-mitment to equalitarianism and natural rights, was one of tem-porary improvement in the status of American Negroes. Antislavery societies flourished, and the northern states either outlawed slavery outright or took steps looking toward the gradual emancipation of the slaves. Though at first the Revolutionary leaders decided to exclude Negroes from the Continental Army, military exigencies led to a reversal of this policy. Except for Georgia and South Carolina, even the southern states made provisions for manumitting those slaves who fought in the Revolutionary armies.

Historians have probably exaggerated and overdramatized the improvement of the Negroes' status in this period. One example of this overdramatization has been the traditional view of the im-pact of the proclamation issued by Virginia's royal governor, Lord Dunmore, who offered to liberate those slaves joining the British forces. Not only did a number of slaves achieve their freedom in this way, but, according to most accounts, it was Dunmore's action which caused Washington and his advisors to withdraw their prohibition on Negro enlistments. In a careful study of the subject, Benjamin Quarles found no evidence that Dunmore's proclamation influenced the Revolutionary generals. Quarles concludes that most of the slaves who joined the British performed valuable services but ul-timately found death rather than freedom.

In American patriotic tradition the first full-fledged villain to step from the wings as the Revolutionary War unfolded was John Murray, Earl of Dunmore. Like other royal governors in office as the crisis reached its pitch, the Crown's

Benjamin Quarles, "Lord Dunmore as Liberator," *The William and Mary Quarterly* XV (October 1958), pp. 494–507. Reprinted with the permission of the publisher and the author.

* Mr. Quarles is a member of the Department of History at Morgan State College, Baltimore, Md.

representative in Virginia would have been a marked man no matter how circumspect his behavior. Dunmore, lacking in diplomatic skills, was destined to furnish the colonists with a convenient hate-symbol. The one act that most thoroughly defamed his name was a deed which in Negro circles cast its author in the role of liberator. This was Dunmore's proclamation inviting slaves to leave their masters and join the royal forces.

Issued as of November 7, 1775, on board the *William* in the harbor at Norfolk, the proclamation announced that in order to defeat "treasonable purposes" the governor was establishing martial law. Colonists who refused "to resort to his Majesty's standard" were to be adjudged traitors. Then came the words which were destined to be quoted far and wide: "and I do hereby further declare all indented servants, Negroes, or others, (appertaining to Rebels,) free, that are able and willing to bear arms, they joining His Majesty's Troops, as soon as may be, for the more speedily reducing the Colony to a proper sense of their duty, to His Majesty's crown and dignity." [1]

Dunmore's proclamation had its expected effect. "The colonists," wrote a contemporary, "were struck with horror," [2] the "Poet of the American Revolution" implored the heavens to deliver the colonies from the "valiant" Dunmore and "his crew of banditti" ("who plunder Virginians at Williamsburg city").[3] Taking alarm, the Continental Congress lost no time in bestirring itself. On December 2, 1775, the delegates instructed the "Committee for fitting our armed vessels" to engage ships of war for the taking or destroying of the governor's fleet,[4] and the presiding officer urged the commander in chief of the Continental Army to take such measures against his lordship as would "effectually Repel his violences and secure the peace and safety of that Colony." [5]

---

[1] Original broadside, 11 by 17 inches, in University of Virginia library. For a facsimile which Patrick Henry circulated, and which differs a little in punctuation from the original, see Francis L. Berkeley, Jr., *Dunmore's Proclamation of Emancipation* (Charlottesville, 1941), frontispiece. See also *American Archives*, comp. Peter Force, 4th Ser. (Washington, 1837–46), III, 1385.

[2] David Ramsay, *History of the American Revolution* (Philadelphia, 1789), I, 234.

[3] *The Poems of Philip Freneau*, ed. Fred Lewis Pattee (Princeton, 1902–07), I, 140. "Hell itself could not have vomitted anything more black than his design of emancipating our slaves," wrote a Philadelphia correspondent to a friend abroad. *Morning Chronicle and London Advertiser*, Jan. 20, 1776, quoted in *Letters on the American Revolution, 1774–1776*, ed. Margaret W. Willard (Boston, 1925), p. 233. It was the judgment of Edward Rutledge that the proclamation tended "more effectually to work an eternal separation between Great Britain and the Colonies,—than any other expedient, which could possibly have been thought of." Rutledge to Ralph Izard, Dec. 8, 1775, in *Correspondence of Mr. Ralph Izard* (New York, 1844), I, 165.

[4] *Journal of the Continental Congress, 1774–1789*, ed. Worthington C. Ford and others (Washington, 1904–37), III, 395.

[5] John Hancock to George Washington, Dec. 2, 1775, in *Letters of Members of the Continental Congress*, ed. Edmund C. Burnett (Washington, 1921–36), I, 267. The army commander shared the apprehension of Congress. "If," he wrote to a Virginia delegate, "that man is not crushed before spring, he will become the most formidable enemy America has; his strength will increase as a snow ball by rolling: and faster, if some expedient cannot be hit upon, to convince the slaves and servants of the impotency of his

Two days later the Congress recommended to Virginia that she resist Dunmore "to the utmost. . . ." [6]

The apprehension over Dunmore's proclamation was grounded primarily in the fear of its unsettling effect on the slaves, if not in the fear of a servile insurrection—that nightmarish dread in communities where the whites were outnumbered. A policy that would strike off their shackles would obviously have a marked appeal to the inhabitants of slave row. Moreover, there had been recent evidence that the Virginian bondmen were responsive to the offer of freedom.

Dunmore himself had furnished such evidence. For at least eight months prior to the formal proclamation, the governor had seriously considered the idea of enlisting the slaves. His reasons were plain. Rebellious planters who contemplated a resort to arms would be deprived of their workers and would be compelled to return to their homes to protect their families and their property. Moreover, the slaves would help fill the ranks of military laborers for His Majesty's forces, and such human *potential de guerre* was badly needed. And Dunmore could expect little help from British headquarters in Boston.[7] Obviously, too, the Crown supporters and their sympathizers counted on the disaffection of the Negroes in the South.[8]

Needing supporters to hold the rebellion-bent Virginians in check, Dunmore let it be known late in April 1775 that he might be driven to set up the royal standard, adding that if he did he believed that he could count on "all the Slaves on the side of Government." [9] On May 1 the governor wrote to the Earl of Dartmouth expressing confidence that, once supplied with arms and

designs." George Washington to Richard Henry Lee, Dec. 26, 1775, in R. H. Lee, *Memoir of the Life of Richard Henry Lee* (Philadelphia, 1825), II, 9. Compare Washington to Joseph Reed, Dec. 15, 1775. In *The Writings of George Washington from the Original Manuscript Sources, 1745–1799*, ed. John C. Fitzpatrick (Washington, 1931–44), IV, 167.

[6] *Journals of the Continental Congress*, III, 403.

[7] General Thomas Gage wrote to Dunmore on Sept. 10, 1775: "I can neither assist you with Men, arms or ammunition, for I have them not to spare; should you draw upon me I have not the Cash to pay your Bills." Clinton Papers, William L. Clements Library, University of Michigan. For England's continuing great difficulty in getting man power see Edward E. Curtis, *The Organization of the British Army in the American Revolution* (New Haven, 1926), pp. 51–80.

[8] "Although Virginia and Maryland are both populous," wrote Governor Josiah Martin of North Carolina to Dartmouth on June 30, 1775, "the Whites are greatly outnumbered by the Negroes, at least in the former; a circumstance that would facilitate exceedingly the Reduction of those Colonies who are very sensible of their Weakness arising from it." Clinton Papers. This idea of Negro support was a persistent one: "The Negroes may be all deemed so many Intestine Enemies, being all slaves and desirous of Freedom." Joseph Galloway to Dartmouth, Jan. 23, 1778, *Facsimiles of Manuscripts in European Archives Relating to America, 1773–1783*, ed. Benjamin F. Stevens (London, 1889–98), XXIV, no. 2079. For a similar expression from another loyalist, see "Moses Kirkland to His Majesty's Commissioners, Oct. 21, 1778," Clinton Papers.

[9] "Deposition of Dr. William Pasteur. In Regard to the Removal of Powder from the Williamsburg Magazine," in "Virginia Legislative Papers (from Originals in Virginia State Archives)," *Virginia Magazine of History and Biography*, XIII (July 1905), 49.

ammunition, he would be able "to collect from among the *Indians*,[10] negroes and other persons" a force sufficient to hold his own.[11] Two weeks later, Gage in a letter to Dartmouth touched on Dunmore's proposal: "We hear," wrote the British commander, "that a Declaration his Lordship has made, of proclaiming all the Negroes free, who should join him, has Startled the Insurgents."[12]

In late April a group of slaves, scenting freedom in the air, went to the governor's house and volunteered their services, but Dunmore had them dismissed.[13] He was then not quite ready for the open break, but it could not be long delayed. On June 8, 1775, the governor took the decisive step of quitting Williamsburg and taking asylum aboard the man-of-war *Fowey* at Yorktown, a move he had been turning over in his mind since May 15.[14] "I have thought it best for his Majesty's Service," he wrote, "to retire from amidst such hostile appearances around me." [15] The House of Burgesses, taking note of the governor's flight, assured him that his personal safety was in no danger, but pointedly noted its displeasure that "a Scheme, the most diabolical, had been meditated, and generally recommended, by a Person of great Influence, to offer Freedom to our Slaves, and turn them against their Masters." [16]

Realizing that there was no turning back, Dunmore initiated a policy of unofficial slave solicitation to augment his tiny force of three hundred white soldiers, seamen, and loyalist recruits. In early August the "Officers of the Volunteer Companies" in Williamsburg informed the Convention that the "Governour's Cutter had carried off a number of Slaves belonging to private gentlemen...." [17] Small sloops, which were employed primarily to intercept intracolonial shipments of powder, invited slaves aboard. "Lord Dunmore sails up and down the river," wrote a Norfolk correspondent on October 28, 1775, to a friend in England, "and where he finds a defenceless place, he lands, plunders the plantation and carries off the negroes." [18]

[10] Later that year Dunmore concocted a plan to raise the tribes, as Gage phrased it, "on the back Parts of the Province of Virginia, to be Joined by such Inhabitants and Indians as may be at, and about Detroit." Gage to Guy Carleton, Sept. 11, 1775, Gage MSS. (American Series), Clements Library. This so-called "Connolly Plot" is briefly described in Isaac S. Harrell, *Loyalism in Virginia* (Philadelphia, 1926), pp. 35–37.

[11] Dartmouth to Dunmore, Aug. 2, 1775, *Amer. Arch.*, 4th Ser., III, 6. In this passage Dartmouth repeats the contents of a letter from Dunmore dated May 1.

[12] Gage to Dartmouth, May 15, 1775, Gage MSS. (English Series), Clements Library.

[13] "Deposition of John Randolph in Regard to the Removal of the Powder," in "Virginia Legislative Papers," *Va. Mag. of His. and Biog.*, XV (Oct. 1907), 150.

[14] Dunmore to Gage, May 15, 1775, Gage MSS. (American Series).

[15] *Ibid.*, June 17, 1775.

[16] *Journals of the House of Burgesses of Virginia, 1773–1776*, ed. John Pendelton Kennedy (Richmond, 1905), p. 256.

[17] "Proceedings of the Virginia Convention, August 3, 1775," *Amer. Arch.*, 4th Ser., III, 373.

[18] *Morning Chronicle and London Advertiser*, Dec. 22, 1775, in Willard, *Letters on the American Revolution*, pp. 271–272. The number of slaves reaching Dunmore during the preproclamation is indeterminate; "some accounts make them about 100;

Now ready to come out into the open, Dunmore was concerned only with his timing. An apparently auspicious moment came in mid-November 1775 when a skirmish took place at Kemp's Landing on the Elizabeth River. In this action the colonial militia was routed and its two commanding colonels were captured. Entering the village in triumph, Dunmore, on November 14, ordered the publication of the proclamation he had drafted a week earlier on board the *William*. The final break had come—the governor had set up his standard and had officially called upon the slaves to join him.

Tidewater Virginia took alarm as rumors spread that the slaves were stampeding to the British.[19] But there were strong deterring factors. Foremost among these was the military alertness of the Virginians themselves. Before any substantial slave migration to Dunmore could get under way, the governor suffered a decisive defeat at arms. This occurred on December 9 at Great Bridge, a fortified span across the Elizabeth River some ten miles below Norfolk which dominated the land approach thereto. Dunmore had believed that an attack was impending and had rashly decided to take the offensive. His force of six hundred was severely repulsed, suffering sixty-one casualties, including three dead officers. Forced to retreat after twenty-five minutes of combat, Dunmore's troops hurried back to Norfolk. Feeling that he could no longer hold the city and fearing a retaliatory attack, the governor spiked his twenty pieces of cannon and ordered his followers aboard the vessels in the harbor. He was never to regain a foothold on the Virginia mainland.

The military preparation of the colonists was matched by their promptness in adopting "home front" measures to prevent slaves from joining the governor. Newspapers lost no time in publishing the proclamation in full, as information and as a warning. To deter runaways local patrol groups were doubled, highways were carefully watched, and owners of small craft were required to exercise vigilance. Since Dunmore's action had come as no surprise, the Virginians had had time to put the colony in a "tolerable state of defense."[20] Adajacent Maryland, through its Council of Safety, ordered the military to station itself in St. Mary's County "and guard the shores from thence to the river Powtowmack, to prevent any servants, negroes, or others from going on board the Fowey ship of war."[21]

To vigilance the colonists added psychological warfare. In Alexander Purdie's *Virginia Gazette* was published a letter from a subscriber urging that Negroes be cautioned against joining Dunmore. Slaves should be told that the English ministry, in refusing to stop the slave trade, had proved a far greater

others less." Edmund Pendleton and others to Virginia delegates in Congress, Nov. 11, 1775, Lee Family MSS., U. Va. library.

[19] "Letters mention that slaves flock to him in abundance, but I hope it is magnified." Edmund Pendleton to Richard Henry Lee, Nov. 27, 1775, *Amer. Arch.*, 4th Ser., IV, 202.

[20] Ramsay, *American Revolution*, I, 234.

[21] *Journal and Correspondence of the Maryland Council of Safety, Aug. 29, 1775–July 6, 1776*, ed. William H. Browne and others, *Archives of Maryland* (Baltimore, 1883—in progress), XI, 511–512.

enemy to Negroes than their American masters, and that if the colonists were defeated, their slaves would be sold to the West Indies. They should be told, too, continued Mr. Purdie's correspondent, that Dunmore was cruel to his own black servitors. And, finally, they should be urged to place their expectation on "a better condition in the next world." If this information had been spread widely, "not one slave would have joined our enemies." [22]

A week later the *Gazette* carried another letter in similar vein. Colonists were advised to inform slaves that Dunmore proposed to free only those who would bear arms for him, leaving the aged and infirm, the women and children, to bear the brunt of the shorn master's anger. Moreover, under the English flag the slaves would be much worse off than under Virginia masters, "who pity their condition, who wish in general to make it as easy and comfortable as possible, and who would willingly, were it in their power, or were they permitted, not only prevent any more negroes from losing their freedom, but restore it to such as have already unhappily lost it." Contrast this with the British, ran the *Gazette's* warning, who would sell the runaways to the sugar islands. "Be not then, ye negroes, tempted by this proclamation to ruin your selves." [23]

Official action was not long in coming. The Virginia Convention on December 8 appointed a committee to prepare an answer to Dunmore's proclamation. Five days later, when the committee made its report, it was directed to draw up a declaration stating that runaways to the British would be pardoned if they returned in ten days; otherwise they would "be liable to such punishment as shall be directed by the Convention." The following day, with the committee's report at hand, the delegates issued a declaration of policy. Beginning with a reminder that the time-honored penalty for a slave insurrection was death without benefit of clergy, the document stated that Negroes who had been "seduced" to take up arms were liable to punishment. But in order that they might return in safety to their duties, they would be pardoned if they laid down their arms forthwith. The proclamation concluded with a request to "all humane and benevolent persons in the colony" to convey to the slaves this "offer of mercy." [24] To insure a wide circulation, the proclamation was published as a broadside. [25]

The Virginians supplemented techniques of persuasion and sweet reasonableness with alternatives more forthright and punitive. In early December the Convention decreed that slaves taken in arms were to be sold to the foreign West Indies, with the sale money, minus expenses, to go to their masters. [26] Somewhat less severe was the fate of captured runaways who had failed in their

---

[22] Purdie's *Virginia Gazette*, Williamsburg, Nov. 17, 1775. Hereafter cited as Va. Gaz.

[23] *Ibid.*, Nov. 24, 1775.

[24] *Proceedings of the Convention of the Delegates in the Colony of Virginia* (Richmond, 1816), p. 62.

[25] Virginia Broadsides (V. 54), U. Va. library.

[26] William Waller Hening, *The Statutes at Large; Being a Collection of All the Laws of Virginia...* (Richmond, 1809–23), IX, 106.

attempts to reach the King's forces. Such slaves, if their masters were patriots, were returned to their home plantations, often after first serving a term of imprisonment. An owner of a captured runaway might be ordered to "convey him to some interior part of the Country as soon as may be. ...." [27] Slaves of British sympathizers were put to work in the lead mines,[28] a practice which became customary in Virginia for the duration of the war. Distrusting all Negroes who had joined the governor, the Convention recommended that military officers "seize and secure" even those who came bearing flags of truce.[29]

The death penalty was used sparingly. In Northampton County the court passed such a sentence on a group of thirteen slaves who had seized a schooner at Hungers Creek and sailed into the bay, their destination the James. Overtaken by a whale boat,[30] their execution was set for April 2, 1776. But the Northampton Committee of Safety sent word to Williamsburg inquiring whether the punishment should not be mitigated since the seizing of the boat was more "intended to effect an escape to Dunmore than any other Design of committing a felony." [31] Whenever the death sentence was passed, as in the case of two runaways who mistook an armed vessel of the Virginia navy for a British man-of-war, it was used mainly "as an example to others." [32]

Despite preventive efforts, whether an appeal to common sense or a resort to legal reprisals, many slaves made their way to the British, spurred in part by loyalist propaganda of the governor's good treatment.[33] Some two hundred "immediately joined him," [34] and within a week after the proclamation the number had reached three hundred.[35] "Numbers of Negros and

---

[27] Such was the language used by the Virginia Council to William Kirby (July 12, 1776) concerning his slave Frank. *Journals of the Council of State of Virginia*, ed. H. R. McIlwaine and Wilmer L. Hall (Richmond, 1931–32, 1952), I, 67.

[28] On Dec. 14, 1775, the Convention ordered the Committee of Safety to employ captive slaves "in working the Lead Mine in the County of *Fincastle*, for the use of this Colony." *Amer. Arch.*, 4th Ser., IV, 85. Shortly afterward four would-be followers of Dunmore who were captured at Accomac were ordered "sent up the country and employed in some publick works." *Ibid.*, VI, 1553.

[29] *Ibid.*, VI, 1524.

[30] James Kent and William Henry to Maryland Council of Safety, Feb. 28, 1776, *Arch. of Md.*, XI, 191.

[31] Northampton Committee of Safety to General Committee of Safety, Apr. 23, 1776, "Va. Leg. Papers," *Va. Mag. of Hist. and Biog.*, XV (Apr. 1908), 407.

[32] *Va. Gaz.*, Apr. 13, 1776.

[33] Northampton Committee of Safety to General Committee of Safety, Apr. 23, 1776, "Va. Leg. Papers," *Va. Mag. of Hist. and Biog.*, XV, 407. Dunmore would have every reason to welcome runaways, but perhaps his reception of them fell short of the report, circulated in the *Virginia Gazette*, that on the evening the governor's forces landed on Gwynn's Island, they amused themselves "with a promiscuous ball, which opened, we hear, by a certain spruce little gentleman, with one of the black ladies." *Vir. Gaz.*, May 31, 1776.

[34] Northampton Committee of Safety to Continental Congress, Nov. 25, 1775, "Va. Leg. Papers," *Va. Mag. of Hist. and Biog.*, XIV (Jan. 1907), 251.

[35] Andrew Sprowel to Peter Paterson, Nov. 19, 1775, *ibid.*, XIV (Apr. 1907), 387.

Cowardly Scoundrels flock to his Standard," wrote a member of the provincial Committee of Safety.[36]

Since Dunmore had no base on the mainland after mid-December 1775, the Negroes who sought his sanctuary were water-borne. Two weeks after the proclamation a group of slaves came down the James in a thirty-foot vessel, bound for the fleet off Norfolk, but they were captured near Surry.[37] Shortly afterward seven Negroes broke out of a Northampton jail and "went off in a pettinger," bound for the British ships.[38] Colonel Landon Carter of the Sabine Hall plantation made a diary notation of the break for the open water executed by ten of his retainers:

> 26 Wednesday, June, 1776. Last night after going to bed, Moses, my son's man, Joe, Billy, Postillion, John, Mullatto Peter, Tom, Panticove, Manuel & Lancaster Sam, ran away, to be sure, to Ld. Dunmore, for they got privately into Beale's room before dark & took out my son's gun & one I had there, took out of his drawer in my passage all his ammunition furniture, Landon's bag of bullets and all the Powder, and went off in my Petty Anger [pettiauger] new trimmed, and it is supposed that Mr. Robinson's People are gone with them, for a skow they came down in is, it seems, at my Landing. These accursed villians have stolen Landon's silver buckles, George's shirts, Tom Parker's new waistcoat & breeches.[39]

The Negroes who reached the British were generally able-bodied men who could be put to many uses.[40] It was as soldiers, however, that Dunmore envisioned them, and he enlisted them from the beginning. By early December he was arming them "as fast as they came in." [41] He made use of Negro privates at the rout of the colonials at Kemp's Landing; indeed, slaves had captured one of the two commanding colonels.[42] In the skirmishes preceding the action at Great Bridge, two runaways who were taken prisoner testified that the garrison was manned by thirty whites and ninety Negroes, and that "all the blacks who are sent to the fort at the great Bridge, are supplied with

[36] John Page to Thomas Jefferson, Nov. 24, 1775, *The Papers of Thomas Jefferson,* ed. Julian P. Boyd (Princeton, 1950—in progress), I, 265.

[37] *Va. Gaz.,* Jan. 10, 1776.

[38] *Maryland Gazette,* Annapolis, Feb. 22, 1776. "Pettinger" and "pettiauger" (below) are corruptions of the Spanish *piragua,* "a dugout," "a two-masted, flat-bottomed boat."

[39] "Diary of Col. Landon Carter," *William and Mary Quarterly,* 1st Ser., XX (Jan. 1912), 178–179.

[40] Two women, however, were among a party of nine slaves who were seized in mid-December after putting out to sea in an open boat in an attempt to reach Norfolk. *Pennsylvania Gazette,* Philadelphia, Dec. 20, 1775.

[41] Dunmore to Sec. of State for the Colonies, Dec. 6, 1775, Peter Force-George Bancroft Transcripts, "Virginia: Official Correspondence," Library of Congress.

[42] Edmund Pendleton to R. H. Lee, Nov. 27, 1775, *Amer. Arch.,* 4th Ser., IV, 202.

muskets, Cartridges &c strictly ordered to use them defensively & offensively." [43] By the first of December the British had nearly three hundred slaves outfitted in military garb, with the inscription, "Liberty to Slaves," emblazoned across the breast of each.[44] The governor officially designated them "Lord Dunmore's Ethiopian Regiment." [45]

The first and only major military action in which Dunmore's forces were engaged was the battle of Great Bridge.[46] Of the governor's troops of some six hundred men, nearly half were Negroes. Of the eighteen wounded prisoners taken by the Virginians in this rout, two were former slaves. James Anderson was wounded "in the Forearm—Bones shattered and flesh much torn," and Casar was hit "in the Thigh, by a Ball, and 5 shot—one lodged." [47] After the fiasco at Great Bridge, the governor was forced to operate from his ships. Taking aboard the hardiest of his Negro followers and placing them under officers who exercised them at small arms, he sanguinely awaited recruits.

Dunmore's use of Negroes also embraced sailoring services. On the six tenders sent by the governor to cannonade Hampton in late October 1775, there were colored crewman. Two of them were captured when the Virginians seized the pilot boat *Hawk Tender*.[48] To man the small craft that scurried in and out of the river settlements, harassing the plantations, the British depended largely on ex-slaves. Particularly were they needed as pilots. Joseph Harris, a runaway, served as pilot of the *Otter*, having come to Captain

[43] William Woodford to Edmund Pendleton, Dec. 5, 1775, "The Woodford, Howe, and Lee Letters," *Richmond College Historical Papers*, I (June 1915), 113. Added Woodford, "The bearer brings you one of the Balls taken out of the cartirages found upon the negro Prisoners, as they were extremely well made." *Ibid.*, p. 112.

[44] *Md. Gaz.*, Dec. 14, 1775.

[45] Dunmore to Sec. of State for Colonies, Dec. 6, 1775, Force-Bancroft Transcripts.

[46] Eyewitness accounts of the action at Great Bridge include: "...a Midshipman on board his Majesty's ship *Otter*, commanded by Captain Squires, Dec. 9," in Willard, *Letters on the American Revolution*, pp. 234–235; "...a Gentleman, dated ship *William*, off Norfolk, Virginia, Dec. 25, 1775," *ibid.*, pp. 244–245; "Thomas McKnight to Rev. Dr. McKnight, on board the King's Fisher, Dec. 26, 1775," Miscellaneous Collection, Clements Library; "Contemporary English Accounts of the Destruction of Norfolk in 1776," comp. H. S. Parsons, *Wm. & Mary Quart.*, 2d Ser., XIII (Oct. 1933), 219–224; Richard Kidder Meade to Theodorick Bland, Jr., Norfolk Town Camp, Dec. 18, 1775, in *The Bland Papers*, ed. Charles Campbell (Petersburg, 1840–43), I, 38; "The Woodford, Howe, and Lee Letters," *Richmond College Hist. Papers*, I, 96–163, passim; William Woodford to Edmund Pendleton, Dec. 10, 1775, in *Md. Gaz.*, Dec. 21, 1775, and Jan. 4, 1776. For Dunmore's account see Dunmore to Secretary of State for the Colonies, Dec. 13, 1775, Force-Bancroft Transcripts. For the story, relished by Virginians, that a well-coached slave had been sent into Dunmore's lines with instructions to misrepresent the strength of the colonial militia, see John Burk, *The History of Virginia* (Petersburg, 1805–16), IV, 85.

[47] Woodford to Pendelton, Dec. 10, 1775, "The Woodford, Howe, and Lee Letters," *Richmond College Hist. Papers*, I, 118.

[48] John Page to Thomas Jefferson, Nov. 11, 1775, *Papers of Thomas Jefferson*, ed. Boyd, I, 257.

Matthew Squire with the highest recommendation from a fellow naval officer. "I think him too useful to His Majesty's service to take away," wrote the latter, because of "his being well acquainted with many creeks in the *Eastern Shore*, at *York*, *James* River, and *Nansemond*, and many others, ..." and "accustomed to pilot. ..." [49] Two citizens on the Isle of Wight advised the chairman of the Virginia Committee of Safety to go slow on discharging "a Negro fello, named Caesar," who was not only "a very great Scoundrel" but was also "a fello' they can't do well without being an Excellent pilot." [50]

Another service performed by Dunmore's black followers was foraging. The governor's supply of provisions, particularly fresh foods, needed constant replenishing, and the Virginia leaders understandably would not permit the British to send men ashore to make purchases. "Black settlers" who might have been willing to supply his lordship with provisions had "no means of conveying them," [51] and Dunmore was driven to a dependence upon the foraging abilities of his Negro recruits. Marauding parties of predominantly ex-slave composition preyed on the countryside, making a night descent upon a plantation and making off with the choice livestock. One foraging party, captured while on its way to the Eastern Shore, was made up of "one white and sixteen blacks." [52]

Allegedly one of the services of Negroes to Dunmore was germ spreading. That the charge of germ warfare was propaganda-laden did not make it less potent in arousing indignation. The accusation was that Dunmore had inoculated two Negroes and sent them ashore at Norfolk to spread the smallpox.[53] The charge was ironic in view of the fate of the Negroes who fled to the British. The majority of them were disease fatalities. Late in March the governor informed his superior in England that the recruiting of the black regiment "would have been in great forwardness had not a fever crept in amongst them, which carried off a great many very fine fellows." He added that on advice of "medical people here," he had concluded that the trouble came from the overcrowded condition on the ships and the lack of clothing, both of which "we have now provided against." [54]

But the plague persisted, killing off the Negroes and the hope of the governor alike. Writing to Germain in June, Dunmore confessed defeat. The fever, he explained, was malignant, and had "carried off an incredible number of our people, especially blacks." Had this not happened he would have en-

---

[49] George Montague to Matthew Squire, July 20, 1775, *Amer. Arch.*, 4th Ser., II, 1692.

[50] Thomas Pierce and Thomas Smith to Edmund Pendleton, Dec. 17, 1775, "Miscellaneous Colonial Documents," *Va. Mag. of Hist. and Biog.*, XIX (July 1911), 267.

[51] "Extract of a letter to a gentleman in Scotland, dated Norfolk, Virginia, February 17, 1776," *Amer. Arch.*, 4th Ser., IV, 1166.

[52] Archibald Cary to R. H. Lee, Dec. 24, 1775, in Robert K. Brock, *Archibald Cary of Ampthill* (Richmond, 1937), p. 161.

[53] *Va. Gaz.*, June 15, 1776.

[54] Dunmore to George Germain, Mar. 30, 1776, *Amer. Arch.*, 5th Ser. (Washington, 1848–53), II, 159–160.

listed two thousand Negro followers. He was, ran his letter, separating the sick from the well and would try to keep the two groups from intermingling.[55] The governor's efforts were unavailing; by early June 1776 there were not more than "150 effective Negro men," although each day the black corps was augmented by from six to eight arrivals.[56]

The failure to arrest the smallpox, and the harassment by the Virginia and Maryland militia, finally brought an end to his lordship's stay in Chesapeake waters. In May 1776, faced with the likelihood "of a great reduction of our force" due to disease,[57] the fleet moved from their exposed quarters at Tucker's Mills near Portsmouth and took shelter on Gwynn's Island near the mouth of the Rappahannock. Nowhere were Dunmore and his "floating Town"[58] allowed peace; "we no sooner appear off the land, than signals are made from it," wrote Dunmore to Whitehall, "and if we come to anchor within cannonshot of either shore, guns are immediately brought to bear upon us. . . ."[59]

Early in July the British, after suffering an attack on their shipping, took refuge on St. George's Island in the Potomac. By the end of the month the disease-ridden corps, lacking suitable drinking water, and despairing of reenforcements, prepared to make their exit. Dismantling, burning, or running aground sixty-three out of their 103 vessels, they sailed out of the Potomac on August 6, seven of the ships bound for Sandy Hook and the others setting a southward course for St. Augustine and the Bermudas.[60] With the departing fleet went some three hundred Negroes, the healthiest going northward, destined for further military service, and Dunmore's schemes came to an inglorious end.[61]

[55] Dunmore to Germain, Mar. 30, 1776, Amer. Arch., 5th Ser., II, 162. Dunmore's policy of isolation appears to have prevented the smallpox from decimating the white troops. The monthly return of the 14th Regiment of Infantry, signed by Capt. Sam Leslie, lists a total of 128 men (with breakdowns as to rank) for Mar. 1, 1776, a total of 126 men for Apr. 1, 1776, and a total of 122 for May 1, 1776. "Monthly Return of a Detachment of His Majesty's 14th Regiment of Infantry, off Norfolk, Virginia, 1 March 1776," Clinton Papers; ibid., for Apr. 1, 1776, and for May 1, 1776. In addition to the factor of isolation, the mortality of the Negro soldiers may have been due to their performing most of the garrison and fatigue duties; at Gwynn's Island the entrenchments were guarded "chiefly by the black regiment." Va. Gaz., June 1, 1776.

[56] Entry of June 10, 1776, A. S. Hamond Diaries, 1775–77, U. Va. library. Andrew Snape Hamond, captain of the Roebuck, was the commanding officer in Virginia waters.

[57] Ibid., May 19, 1776.

[58] The descriptive phrase is Hamond's. Letter to Hans Stanley, Aug. 5, 1776, ibid.

[59] Dunmore to George Germain, July 31, 1776, Amer. Arch., 5th Ser., II, 166.

[60] Hamond Diaries, Aug. 6, 1776. Dunmore himself went to New York, arriving on Aug. 14. Journals of Lieut.-Col. Stephen Kemble, New-York Historical Society, Collections (1883–84), I, 84.

[61] Dunmore remained convinced of the soundness of his plan to arm Negroes in large numbers, reviving it even after Yorktown. See Percy Burdelle Caley, "Dunmore: Colonial Governor of New York and Virginia, 1770–1782," unpubl. diss., University of Pittsburgh, 1939, pp. 887–893.

Perhaps not more than a total of eight hundred slaves had succeeded in reaching the British,[62] and perhaps one eighth of these had been brought by loyalist masters. But Dunmore's proclamation undoubtedly had an indirect effect on thousands of additional slaves, quickening their hopes for freedom. Perhaps the imagination of colonial editors was behind such stories as that of a colored mother in New York naming her child after his lordship,[63] and that of a Negro in Philadelphia jostling whites on the streets and telling them to wait until "lord Dunmore and his black regiment come, and then we will see who is to take the wall." [64] But whether fact or fabrication, such reports reflect the attitude of expectation that Dunmore engendered among persons of color along the Chesapeake. It made no difference that he had offered freedom to the bondmen of his enemies only,[65] and that as governor he had withheld his signature from a bill against the slave trade; to those who whispered his name in slave quarters he was in truth the "African Hero" he was derisively dubbed by a Virginia patriot.[66]

If Dunmore was viewed by one group as a tyrant and by another as a liberator, this was but another paradox in a war that abounded in paradox, and another illustration of the war as a social revolution. The Negro who fled to the governor was actuated by the same love of freedom for which the colonists avowedly broke with the mother country. Dunmore's invitation to the slaves was to prefigure the thousands of runaways below the Mason-Dixon line who served as military laborers to His Majesty's forces during the Revolution and who, when peace came, sailed with them from Savannah, Charleston, and New York.

[62] Dunmore's Negro followers were computed in general terms; e.g., "...came in a great number of Black men from the Rebels." Logs of *Roebuck* and *Fowey*, in Greenwich Museum, England, entry of June 27, 1776. Photostat in A. S. Hamond MSS., U. Va. library.

[63] Taking due note, the *New York Journal* carried an occasional poem, copied in the *Va. Gaz.*, May 25, 1776:
> Hail! doughty Ethiopian Chief!
> Though ignominious Negro Thief!
> This BLACK shall prop thy sinking name,
> And damn thee to perpetual fame.

[64] *Va. Gaz.*, Supplement, Dec. 29, 1775.

[65] John King, runaway slave of a loyalist, was ordered discharged from the *King's Fisher*. Logs of *Roebuck* and *Fowey*, Feb. 23, 1776.

[66] R. H. Lee to Thomas Jefferson, July 21, 1776, in *The Letters of Richard Henry Lee*, ed. James C. Ballagh (New York, 1912–14), I, 210.

S. Sydney Bradford

THE NEGRO IRONWORKER IN
ANTE BELLUM VIRGINIA

*The vast majority of slaves cultivated staple crops—tobacco, rice,
hemp, sugar cane and, most important, cotton. Yet surprising
numbers were artisans and unskilled industrial laborers, engaged in
small-scale manufacturing on the farms and in the towns. This study
by S. Sydney Bradford offers a richly detailed description of slavery
in an industrial setting. For another type of industrial slavery, mining
in the western territories and states, the student should consult
W. Sherman Savage, "The Negro on the Mining Frontier,"
Journal of Negro History, XXX (January, 1945), pp. 30–46.*

Peculiar conditions inherent in the use of hired slave labor in industry are well illustrated in the history of colonial and ante bellum Virginia. In that state many Negroes were taken from plantations and placed in various industries to help construct canals and railroads, operate tobacco factories, and run iron furnaces and forges.[1] Slaves probably helped construct Virginia's first iron furnace, Falling Creek furnace. After this was destroyed by the Indians in 1622 the colony had no successful ironworks until 1716, when Colonel Alexander Spotswood erected the first of the several furnaces built by him. In operating his furnace at Germanna the Colonel used Negro laborers and thought them to be fairly good workers.[2]

Between 1716 and 1775 many furnaces and forges were built in Virginia,

S. Sydney Bradford, "The Negro Ironworker in Ante Bellum Virginia," *Journal of
Southern History*, XXV (May, 1959), pp. 194–206. Copyright © 1959 by the Southern
Historical Association. Reprinted by permission of the Managing Editor.

[1] Kathleen Bruce's *Virginia Iron Manufacture in the Slave Era* (New York, 1939)
treats the Tredegar Works in particular; this paper deals with Virginia's ironworks in
general.

[2] Robert Beverly, *The History and Present State of Virginia* (Chapel Hill, 1947),
49, 54–55, 126; J. M. Swank, *History of the Manufacture of Iron in All Ages* (Philadelphia, 1892), 113; Lester J. Cappon (ed.), *Iron Works at Tuball: Terms and Conditions for Their Lease . . . by Alexander Spotswood . . .* (Charlottesville, Va., 1945), 12.

and by the latter year iron was even being produced in the Shenandoah Valley. Throughout this period and during the war for independence, slaves were used both by private individuals and by the state government at ironworks all over the state, and after the war the industry continued to grow, particularly in the Valley.[3] By 1800 the iron industry had appeared in the westernmost part of Virginia, near present-day Wheeling, though the use of slaves at these works was rare since there were few Negroes in that area and those for hire in the eastern part of the state were not sent west of the Alleghenies.[4] However, slaves supplied the bulk of Virginia ironworks laborers east of the mountains.

The Revolution marked a change in practice with regard to slave labor in ironworks, for prior to that time most of such laborers were owned by the ironmaster, but the practice of hiring slaves for the furnaces began during the war and thereafter the great majority of Negroes used at ironworks in the Old Dominion were hired hands.[5] The source of the hired slaves might be either neighboring plantations or slave hiring marts; the hiring might be initiated by the ironmaster or his partner or agent or by the plantation owner. Agents received a small commission for slaves hired, and perhaps to avoid this cost plantation owners often wrote directly to the ironmasters. The usual hiring period was toward the end of the year, so ironmasters between the Blue Ridge and Allegheny Mountains travelled into the piedmont around Christmastime in order to obtain Negro workers. The hiring took about a month to complete at markets in Pittsylvania, Louisa, Spotsylvania, Orange, Albemarle, Amherst, Nelson, and Fauquier Counties.[6]

[3] J. P. Lesley, *The Iron Manufacturer's Guide to the Furnaces, Forges, and Rolling Mills of the United States* (New York, 1866), 64 and *passim*; Swank, *History*, 170 and *passim*; J. B. Pearse, *A Concise History of the Iron Manufacture of the American Colonies* (Philadelphia, 1876), 9 and *passim*; "Abstract of a Deed," *William and Mary Quarterly*, 1st series, XXII (1913), 70; Williamsburg *Virginia Gazette*, September 7, 1776, February 14, 1777; Memorandum of Negroes employed at Westham Foundry for 1781 (Virginia State Library, Richmond).

[4] Some slaves were used in the iron industry west of the Allegheny Mountains, as at G. F. Hupp's furnace in Hardy County—see deed of trust, February 6, 1852, in Deed Book Number 22 (Hardy County Clerk's Office, Moorefield, W. Va.)—but there is no evidence that Negroes were widely used. Bruce holds that no Southern ironmaster could have succeeded without using slaves (*Virginia Iron Manufacture*, 237), but her conclusion is not valid for trans-Allegheny Virginia.

[5] Swank, *History*, 264; *Virginia Gazette*, January 31, February 14, 1777; Memorandum of Negroes employed at Westham Foundry. This was unlike the situation elsewhere in the South, where the slaves were the property of the owners of the works. E. M. Lander, Jr., "The Iron Industry in Ante-Bellum South Carolina," *Journal of Southern History*, XX (August 1954), 350; Ethel Armes, *The Story of Coal and Iron in Alabama* (Birmingham, 1910), 74, 96.

[6] Deposition of G. Long in Samuel F. Jordan v. William Cash, hereafter cited as Jordan v. Cash; of William Weaver in John Doyle v. William Weaver, hereafter cited as Doyle v. Weaver; and of D. J. Willson in William Weaver v. Jordan, Davis, and Company, hereafter cited as Weaver v. Davis; bonds for Negro hire in Matthew Bryan's Administrator v. Matthew Bryan's Heirs, hereafter cited as Bryan v. Bryan, and in Enos Hord v. S. J. and W. H. Jordan, hereafter cited as Hord v. Jordan. All of the cited cases are in Case Papers of the Rockbridge County Superior Court of Chancery

The same factors determined hiring prices as sale prices of slaves. Thus, the age of a hand was a very important matter, for Negroes in their prime always brought more than boys and old men.[7] Likewise slaves with particular skills were more valuable; in the late 1830's ironmasters paid from $25 to $40 more to hire skilled Negroes than ordinary hands. Negro blacksmiths were constantly sought by furnace and forge owners, and they always commanded premium prices.[8] Competition among those who desired Negroes also influenced Negro hire. In 1830 and 1831 agents complained that the demand for slaves by the builders of canals and turnpikes had increased rates. Over twenty years later a similar objection arose because the hiring of slaves by railroads and tobacco factories had brought about a general rise in cost.[9] In addition, there was a general increase after 1800 in the amounts paid for Negroes, as the following table shows: [10]

Year	Prices Paid for Hired Negroes
1805–1807	$55–$66.98
1836	$110–$120
1840	$85–$90
1854–1855	$113.66–$134.50
1856	$150

Ironmasters usually hired slaves for the period from January 1 until the following Christmas, and shortly after the agreements had been concluded the slaves were sent to their respective ironworks. Severe winter weather oc-

(Superior Clerk's Office, Lexington, Va.). See also bonds for Negro hire in the McCormick Collection (Wisconsin State Historical Society, Madison); J. F. Tanner (for J. R. Anderson) to Col. L. Partlow, December 15, 1848, in Letter Book, Tredegar Company (Virginia State Library); D. G. Garland to William Weaver, May 23, 1828, in Weaver-Brady Collection (Duke University Library, Durham, N.C.); S. McD. Moore, to W. W. Davis, January 16, 1850, and J. L. Dickinson to Davis, February 24, 1852, in McCormick Collection.

[7] In 1838 and 1839 able-bodied Negroes were hired for $93 apiece, while old men and boys went for $63 or $64 each. Deposition of William Lusk in John Alexander v. Sidney S. Baxter, administrator of John Irvine and others, hereafter cited as Alexander v. Irvine's administrator, in Case Papers of Rockbridge County Superior Court of Chancery.

[8] Deposition of Ira F. Jordan in Weaver v. Davis. In 1808 a furnace paid $119.88 for a blacksmith and $83.25 for the next most expensive Negro, and in 1853 a forge paid $150 for a blacksmith and an average of $101.50 for unskilled workers. Ledger, Ridwell Furnace, 1805–1809 (University of North Carolina Library, Chapel Hill); bonds for Negro hire in McCormick Collection.

[9] T. Wyat to Jordans and Irvine, January 6, 1830; P. Boxley to Jordans and Irvine, January 13, 1831; Greenlee Davidson to J. D. Davidson, January 9, 1859, all in McCormick Collection.

[10] Ledger, Ridwell Furnace, 1805–1809; deposition of Matthew Bryan and report of Commissioner Chapin in Alexander v. Irvine's administrator; bonds for Negro hire in Jordan v. Cash and Bryan v. Bryan and those owned by Miss Mabel Jordan (Buena Vista, Va.); C. W. Newkirk to William Weaver, January 4, 1815, and James Coleman to William Weaver, February 19, 1856, both in Weaver-Brady Collection (Duke).

casionally delayed their departure for as much as several weeks, but this might prevent sickness arising from travel in bad weather. For example, one group of hands that crossed the Blue Ridge Mountains in stormy weather fell ill after reaching their ironworks, which upset the ironmaster since more lost time was added to the thirty days the slaves had already spent in travel. If additional workers were needed during the year they were hired for whatever time was necessary.

Unhappy incidents concerned with the hiring of Negroes often occurred. When a slave owner in 1829 allowed an ironmaster who had hired one of his Negroes for $50 to set the price for a second slave, the ironmaster named $20 as a fair price. Such an amount brought an angry protest from the slave's master, concluding with "This letter ... will close (I hope forever) my correspondence with you." On the other hand, competition for the slaves appears to have been keen, and an agent for one ironmaster failed to hire a desired Negro because an unknown individual had bribed the slave's owner to obtain him. In this case even the Negro was given a bribe to go elsewhere. The manager of another ironworks found that a slave master from whom he had hired certain Negroes for several years had increased the amount he wanted for the hands and would not lower it because, the manager believed, of a competitor's bidding. Another representative of an ironworks complained in 1855 that "You have no idea of the trouble there is in hiring hands ... there is all sorts of trickery and management." [11]

Ironmasters used Negroes for any task that needed to be done at their establishments. At the furnaces and forges slaves tended fires, worked the metal, and in fact did everything but manage the establishments, which was always the job of a white man. Elsewhere on an ironworks plantation Negroes planted and harvested crops, cut and charcoaled wood, mined iron ore, drove wagons and manned boats, made shoes, ground flour, and worked as carpenters and blacksmiths. The elite among them were the refiners, molders, and blacksmiths, and because a skilled slave was as valuable as two ordinary hands, many ironmasters owned a few skilled workers.[12] There was nothing rigid in the use of Negroes at ironworks, however, as skilled slaves were frequently used for unskilled tasks. Bob, a forge helper at Buffalo forge, for

[11] James C. Dickinson to William Weaver, January 21, 1833, in Weaver-Brady Collection (Duke); unsigned letter to W. W. Davis, January 5, 1856, in McCormick Collection; Henry A. McCormick to William Weaver, December 29, 1855, in Weaver-Brady Collection (Alderman Library, University of Virginia, Charlottesville).

[12] The following contain numerous references to work done by Negroes: deposition of Ira F. Jordan in Weaver v. Davis and of Matthew Bryan in Alexander v. Irvine's administrator; Journals, Pine Forge, 1804–1833 (University of North Carolina Library); William W. Davis Papers and Graham Ledgers and Negro Books, 1830–1840, in Weaver-Brady Collection (Virginia). With respect to skilled workers, one forge owner owned six Negro forgemen, one of whom he had purchased to prevent a competitor's buying him. J. Doyle to William Weaver, October 17, 1827, and Weaver to Doyle, October 17, 1827, in Doyle v. Weaver. The following sources also point out that ironmasters owned skilled workers: Journal, Pine Forge, 1804–1808; Negro Book, Graham Ledgers; deposition of Ira F. Jordan, in Weaver v. Davis.

example, was transferred to a chopping gang in February 1836 and stayed with that group, except for a stint at planting oats, until May 30, when he was sent back to the forge. He remained there until August 4 and was then sent back to the woodchoppers, with whom he stayed until August 22, when he returned to the forge for five days.[13]

Of all the jobs assigned to Negroes at ironworks, the two most important were mining and woodchopping. A furnace's ore banks were usually worked by slaves surpervised by a white master miner, the number of hands used in this way varying from furnace to furnace. Lucy Selina furnace used four Negroes and a white master miner in the 1830's, while Vesuvius furnace employed five or six hands, and Jane furnace worked nine or ten slaves in its pits.[14] Shafts had to be dug at some ore banks, and one furnace had holes seventy-two feet deep at its pits. In order to supply another furnace with seven to seventeen cartloads of ore a day, eight hands worked in pits that were twenty to twenty-five feet deep. The ore in the holes was first loosened by powder and then hauled to the surface in buckets. Work in such places was very often difficult because of the presence of water, and occasionally a pump was used to keep the pits as dry as possible.[15]

Vast quantities of charcoal were needed to smelt the ore brought to furnaces. Cotopaxi furnace, before it was abandoned in 1854, made 600 tons of pig iron a year, each ton of which required the burning of 200 bushels of charcoal; and a forge burned fifteen or sixteen cords of wood to make a ton of bar iron.[16] Over the years chopping gangs, usually under the supervision of a white man, denuded many wooded areas for wood to be charcoaled, for both Negro and white hands apparently had a quota to fill of nine cords a week. After the wood had been cut, about thirty cords of it would be slowly burned in a large pile; at the end of six days of smoldering approximately forty bushels of charcoal remained from each cord burned. Colliers supervised this important work, and Negro colliers were so highly valued that in the 1850's an ironmaster paid $1,000 for one.[17]

Slaveowners occasionally restricted the use of hands hired to ironmasters. Thus, some Negroes could not work at furnaces and ore mines, nor labor in

[13] Time Book, Buffalo Forge, 1830–1840, in Weaver-Brady Collection (Virginia); Patrick Brady, Home Journal, II, in McCormick Collection.

[14] Deposition of A. Campbell and of L. Shaw in Alexander v. Irvine's administrator; deposition of A. W. Templine in Weaver v. Davis.

[15] Ledger, Ridwell Furnace, 1805–1809; deposition of J. B. Johnson in Weaver v. Davis.

[16] Lesley, *Iron Manufacturer's Guide*, 70; deposition of Ira F. Jordan in Weaver v. Davis.

[17] Deposition of J. W. Schoolfield and of James Brawley in Weaver v. Mayburry; Time Book, Buffalo Forge, 1830–1840, in Weaver-Brady Collection (Virginia); deposition of A. D. Rhodes in Hord v. Jordan; agreement between John Doyle and D. Holmes, 1843, in McCormick Collection; G. P. Grimsley, *Iron Ores, Salt and Sandstones* (West Virginia Geological Survey, IV, Morgantown, W. Va., 1909), ix, 36; William L. Alexander to Col. Sam McD. Reid, August 23, 1858, in Reid-White Papers (Washington and Lee University Library, Lexington, Va.).

bad weather. One woman would not permit her slave to be worked in a mine because he had already been injured in blasting. Most Negroes, however, were sent to their hirers without any attempt being made to safeguard their welfare.[18]

It was common practice on plantations to allow slaves to do extra work for wages, and this was also permitted at ironworks, where Negroes did such labor as driving wagons, chopping wood, and making baskets, tar, spikes, and rails. Extra work could also be done at night, on Sundays, and over the Christmas holidays. This labor was credited to a slave's account, and at one works slaves earned $2.93 for threshing an extra forty-seven bushels of rye, thirty-three cents for putting a bottom in a chair and making a floor mat, and $9.70 for drawing iron on Easter Monday. Those who did additional skilled labor apparently earned the largest sums, such as $12.75, $22.02, and $25.80 for handling iron at a forge.[19] The Negroes usually spent their money at ironworks' stores, where they bought articles of all kinds, especially clothing. Sugar and coffee were also very popular purchases; one slave at a forge bought twenty-seven pounds of coffee and sixteen pounds of sugar between March 6, 1834, and January 8, 1835. Tobacco was another item very frequently purchased. The accounts of the Negroes were usually settled at the end of a year, when they received cash for the remainder of their credits. Typical payments were those of a forge in Rockbridge County, where the Negroes received from $1 to $14.83 in the years between 1834 and 1839.[20]

Although slaves were widely used in the Virginia iron industry, ironmasters did not believe they could equal the output of white laborers. No matter what type of labor they performed, Negroes were always required to work under white supervision, for it was thought that they could not be taught to do skilled work independently. This view, held by Governor Spotswood in colonial Virginia, was also expressed by a nineteenth century ironmaster: "They are not as good workmen and do not take as good care or as much pains as good white workmen." [21] Another ironmaster believed that even

[18] R. Brooks to Jordans and Irvine, January 2, 1829; [   ] to I. Y. Grevey, 1846; Nancy Matthews to Col. John Jordan, 1831, all in McCormick Collection; bond for Negro hire in Bryan v. Bryan. Only three out of fifty-two slaves hired by one furnace were prohibited from working in ore pits. Bonds for Negro hire in Bryan v. Bryan.

[19] C. S. Sydnor, *Slavery in Mississippi* (New York, 1933), 96; J. B. Sellers, *Slavery in Alabama* (Birmingham, 1950), 91; R. B. Flanders, *Plantation Slavery in Georgia* (Chapel Hill, 1933), 146; Journals, Pine Forge, 1804–1834; Graham Ledgers; Journal, Beauregard Furnace, 1861–1865 (William and Mary College Library, Williamsburg, Va.); F. T. Anderson Papers and Ledger, Union Forge, 1825–1826 (Duke University Library); Negro Books, 1830–1840, and 1844–1849, Buffalo Forge; Ledger, Union Forge, 1825–1826, all in Weaver-Brady Collection (Virginia).

[20] All records of ironworks are full of notations of such purchases. See, for example, Journals, Pine Forge, 1804–1834, and Doyle v. Kirkpatrick papers in McCormick Collection; William W. Davis Papers and Negro Book, 1830–1840, Buffalo Forge, in Weaver-Brady Collection (Virginia).

[21] Cappon (ed.), *Iron Works at Tuball*, 18; deposition of William Norcross in Alexander v. Irvine's administrator.

though Negroes could be taught to work at a forge, it was more costly to refine a ton of bar iron with slave than with white labor because slaves wasted iron ore and charcoal. Just to train Negroes took a long time. When an ironmaster was asked in 1836, "Cannot any Negro man of ordinarily good capacity be used as an underhand in a forge?" he replied, "Not with advantage without a servitude of two or three years." After one Negro had worked for five years at a forge it was still said that although he was a "first-rate" underhand for a slave, he was not an excellent worker.[22]

Perhaps naturally, the hirers of Negro ironworkers appear to have been less attentive to slaves' clothing needs than their owners would have been. The bonds for the hired Negroes stated that ironmasters were responsible for feeding and clothing the slaves concerned, and in some instances the bonds definitely prescribed what clothes were to be provided, for example two summer suits, a winter suit, a pair of shoes and socks, and a hat and blanket per man. More often, however, the bonds simply stated that the slaves would be clothed in the "usual manner," a phrase most ironmasters interpreted as they saw fit. An estimate of the clothing furnished at a forge in 1832 states that the hands received two shirts, three pairs of trousers, a coat, four pairs of shoes, a blanket, and a hat; however, they really received only a summer and winter suit, three pairs of shoes, and a hat and blanket, which was less than the amount of clothing recommended for plantation slaves.[23] Despite the rough labor at ironworks, all of the laborers at one establishment were without shoes in August 1828, and no leather had been available for five weeks. In February 1859 and June and September 1860, many slaves at another furnace were barefooted when even the manager admitted that the ore bank was so damp and rough that the workers really needed shoes. Perhaps it was this scarcity of shoes that caused the slaves to break into a building at that ironworks in March 1861 and steal clothing. As a matter of fact the manager was afraid to leave the works because he believed they would steal more.[24] The extensive purchases of clothing by slaves who did extra work also indicates that they were inadequately clothed by ironmasters.

In carrying out their responsibility for feeding the Negroes, ironmasters provided the usual basic foods, four or five pounds of bacon and a peck and half of cornmeal a week. Coffee, sugar, and molasses were not part of the

[22] Deposition of John Doyle in Weaver v. Davis; of Edwin Jordan in John Jordan's Executors v. John Jordan's Heirs, hereafter cited as Jordan v. Jordan, in Case Papers of Rockbridge County Superior Court of Chancery; and of William Norcross in Alexander v. Irvine's administrator.

[23] See, for example, bonds for Negro hire in Alexander v. Irvine's administrator, McCormick Collection, and Bryan v. Bryan; an estimate of the expense of conducting Clifton Forge for the year 1832 and deposition of Ira F. Jordan in Alexander v. Irvine's administrator. See also R. Collins, "Management of Slaves," DeBow's Review, XVII (1854), 424; Agricola, "Management of Negroes," ibid., XIX (1855), 359.

[24] John Doyle to William Weaver, August 11, 1828, in Doyle v. Weaver; W. W. Rex to D. C. E. Brady, February 25, 1859, in Weaver-Brady Collection (Virginia); Rex to Brady, June 29, September 21, 1860, March 15, 1861, in Weaver-Brady Collection (Duke).

regular ration; indeed, they were among the most popular items purchased by those who did extra work. At some ironworks individual food allotments would be distributed and the slaves would cook for themselves. At other works the food would be prepared and the Negroes would be fed as a group, a method preferable in the eyes of one ironmaster as it enabled him to keep the slaves under better supervision.[25] Negroes complained about the food situation, for furnaces and forges often were short of food, or handed out bad supplies. The records of one ironworks show that bad flour was distributed early in December 1828, that no flour was on hand by the end of that month, that roughly half a year later bacon was needed, and that between October and the end of December 1829 there was again no flour. At a second ironworks such poor beef was issued that the manager was afraid the white hands would leave. Subsequently, the bacon supply there failed, bad meat was distributed again, and at about the same time the supply of flour was exhausted.[26]

Ledgers of ironworks point to a high rate of sickness among hired Negroes. The causes of illnesses were many, but a random selection from the records of one ironworks shows that "Jack" cut his leg, "Charles" burned his leg, "Billy" was incapacitated for two weeks because of frostbite, "Tom" was visited nine times by a doctor (at $5 a visit) because of his legs and head, and three slaves received treatment for gonorrhea. At another furnace some Negroes who had gone without shoes in the fall were sick for two weeks. In at least two instances ironworks had to be closed because all the personnel had been stricken by some disease.[27] Any sickness among the hired hands was an inconvenience and expense to the ironmaster, especially as a Virginia court had ruled in 1806 that the full contract price of a hired slave who became ill had to be paid.[28] Despite that, many ironmasters adopted the practice of deducting from the hire of a sick slave the cost of medical treatment and the value of time lost. Thus, at one forge over $50 was subtracted from the hire of three slaves because of the time they had lost while sick. In order to combat

[25] Deposition of James Shank and report of Commissioner Chapin in Alexander v. Irvine's administrator. See also Ledger, Union Forge, 1825–1826, and Negro Book, 1830–1840, Buffalo Forge, in Weaver-Brady Collection (Virginia); depositions in Doyle v. Weaver and in Matthews v. McCormick in the McCormick Collection; deposition of John Doyle in Weaver v. Maybury; and Jordan, Davis and Company to William Weaver, September 8, 1832, in Weaver-Brady Collection (Virginia).

[26] John Doyle to Abraham W. Davis, December 1, 31, 1828; Charles [Gorgas] to William Weaver, March 29, April 6, 1859, and to D. C. E. Brady, August 11, 1859, and Rex to Brady, July 26, 1859, all in Weaver-Brady Collection (Virginia); and Doyle to Davis, August 25, 1829; W. W. Davis to William Weaver, December 4, 1829; and Elizabeth Matthews to Weaver, March 29, 1830; L. K. Gorgas to Brady, April 2, 1860; and W. W. Rex to Brady, May 28, 1860, all in Weaver-Brady Collection (Duke).

[27] Graham Ledgers and Miscellaneous Graham Papers and Rex to Brady, September 21, 1860, in Weaver-Brady Collection (Duke); Stephen McCormick to William Weaver, September 29, 1828, in McCormick Collection; William Viand to Joseph Marston, June 9, 1859, in Bush and Lobdell Collection (Alderman Library, University of Virginia).

[28] George v. Elliott in Helen T. Caterall's Judicial Cases Concerning American Slavery and the Negro (Washington, 1926), I, 113.

that practice some slave owners by the 1840's insisted that the hire bonds absolve them from responsibility for medical charges, and in 1854 the bonds for twenty-seven out of fifty-two hired Negroes said the slaves were to be free of medical costs.[29]

It is difficult to generalize about the discipline enforced at ironworks, but in many instances it was severe. In Rockbridge County a Negro is said to have hurled himself into a furnace rather than face a whipping. For numerous ironmasters and their managers, as well as for plantation managers, the whip was an effective "insignia of office." Although only seven slaves at the Tredegar Works were whipped within a decade, for years after the "great cat o'nine tails which hung somewhere in the yard" was still remembered. Negroes were whipped for various offenses, for example when a slave became involved in a fight over a card game and when two Negroes made a dirk.[30] It is apparent too that whipping was intended not only as a punishment for a culprit, but also as a warning to potential offenders. This was clearly the case at Buena Vista furnace in Rockbridge County when ten Negroes fled in the spring of 1855 because of whipping and generally poor treatment. After an unsuccessful attempt to take them back, their owners sent them elsewhere. This angered the furnace owners, who wanted the Negroes returned and punished before the rest of the slaves.[31] Whipping was not the only form of chastisement, however. At one furnace a slave was struck so severely on the arm that he was laid up for six days, and when another slave resisted handling by an ironworks' manager the latter simply picked up a rock and hit the Negro in the head.[32]

Despite the fear of punishment, Negroes at ironworks were perpetually running away for the same reasons that plantation hands did: to avoid hard work, to see their families, and to win freedom. Running away was a dangerous venture, for the odds against escaping were great and punishment for such boldness was severe, yet many Negroes repeatedly attempted to escape. Twelve members of a gang working on an ironworks' road attempted to run away;

[29] Bond for Negro hire in Jordan v. Jordan; Journal, Pine Forge, 1831–1834; J. R. Anderson to H. Loving, January 24, 1850, in Letter Book, Tredegar Company; and bonds for Negro hire in McCormick Collection, in Doyle v. Kirkpatrick, and in Bryan v. Bryan.

[30] John D. Capron, president, Glamorgan Pipe and Foundry Co., Lynchburg, Va., to author, July 29, 1953; Sydnor, *Slavery in Mississippi*, 71. Kenneth M. Stampp, *The Peculiar Institution* (New York, 1956), 174, says the whip was "the emblem of the master's authority. Nearly every slaveholder used it, and few grown slaves escaped it entirely." Bruce, *Virginia Iron Manufacture*, 255. See also Furnace Account Book, 1829–1832, in Graham Ledgers; R. A. Glasgow to [F. T. Anderson], February 16, 1858, in F. A. Anderson Collection. For another account of discipline by whipping, see W. W. Rex to D. C. E. Brady, October 26, 1860, in Weaver-Brady Collection (Duke).

[31] J. F. Jordan to Enos Hord, March 6, 1855; Hord to S. F. and W. H. Jordan, March 12, 1855; Hord and Tulless to S. F. and W. H. Jordan, March 21, 1855; S. F. and W. H. Jordan to Hord and Tulless, March 26, 1855, all in Hord v. Jordan. The Jordans refused to pay Hord for the Negroes for January and February, but the court in Hord v. Jordan awarded Hord $294.77 for those months.

[32] Negro Time Book, 1833–1839, in Graham Papers; John Watkins to William Weaver, July 28, 1854, in Weaver-Brady Collection (Duke).

four were successful, and of those brought back three eventually escaped after repeated attempts. Coping with this problem was both troublesome and expensive to ironmasters. In one case $37.10 was paid in costs and jail fees to retrieve a slave; in another instance it cost $110.05 to bring back four Negroes.[33]

The extensive use of Negroes by Virginia ironmasters did not prevent the industry from suffering from the competition of British and Northern iron after 1836. This was probably because with slave labor available, furnace and forge owners failed to adopt improved manufacturing methods. This conservative policy meant that the cost of making a ton of pig iron remained the same, about $15, between 1825 and 1855.[34] But English ironmasters followed the opposite path, and in 1841 a number of disturbed iron manufacturers met in Lexington, Virginia, to discuss the threat of imported iron and agreed that a new tariff was indispensable if they were to prosper. The tariff passed in the following year gave them a little help, but in 1846 duties on iron were lowered, and in 1849 a Botetourt County ironmaster declared that only his "peculiar situation" with regard to labor had kept him in business and that if a new tariff was not passed he would stop operating in 1850. The same view was expressed at a meeting of trans-Blue Ridge Mountain ironmasters in September 1849 who felt that if something was not done to relieve their distress their works would all be closed within twelve months. During the same year at least six ironmasters from Virginia attended a national iron convention that demanded added protection for the industry.[35] Another cause for despondency in these years was the fact that Pennsylvania iron undersold slave-made iron in Virginia. In 1841, 1843, and 1845 the owner of the Tredegar Works declared that he could buy Northern iron for less than or equal to what it cost to purchase locally produced iron. This was corroborated by the ironmaster who said that Northern iron at Richmond always undersold iron made in western Virginia.[36]

It is clear that Negroes supplied the bulk of the labor used at charcoal furnaces and forges in Virginia even though ironmasters criticized their ability. Most of the slaves were hired and their life was onerous, as they were worked

[33] Report of Commissioner Chapin in Alexander v. Irvine's administrator; Ledger, Ridwell Furnace, 1805–1809; receipt of jailer of Augusta County, July 27, 1831, in Alexander v. Irvine's administrator; J. Irvine's Cash Book and bond for Negro hire, both in McCormick Collection.

[34] Between 1848 and 1858, for example, apparently only three Virginia furnaces used coke. Swank, History, 371. See also deposition of John Donihoo in Weaver v. Mayburry; deposition of M. Bryan in Matthews v. McCormick; Joseph R. Anderson to F. T. Anderson, October 28, 1851, in F. T. Anderson Collection; William Mark to [   ], January 18, 1855, in McCormick Collection.

[35] Bruce, Virginia Iron Manufacture, 213, 264–65; Wheeling, W. Va., Daily Gazette, August 23, September 17, 1849; Proceedings of the Iron Convention, Held at Pittsburgh, November 21st, 22d and 23d, 1849 (Pittsburgh, 1849), 13.

[36] Letters of J. R. Anderson to Davis H. Forrer, November 10, 1841, to Col. J. Jordan, December 9, 1843, and to William Weaver, April 19, 1845, all in Letter Books, Tredegar Company; William Weaver to Wm. S. Triplett, August 25, 1862, in Weaver-Brady Collection (Virginia).

hard, were poorly fed and clothed, and were separated from their families. Contrary to Bruce, "the 'kindly relation of protector and protected, of strong and weak,' so well known to have existed on the plantation" did not exist for them, and life at an ironworks was not "a sunny rather than a dreary" thing.[37] The iron industry's continued reliance upon Negroes in the 1840's and 1850's probably contributed to the failure of ironmasters to adopt improved methods of production, and thus put them at an increasing disadvantage with regard to Northern and British iron in those decades. In general, slave labor brought neither satisfaction nor progress to Virginia's ironworkers and their industry.

[37] Bruce, *Virginia Iron Manufacture*, 249, 255–56.

E. Ophelia Settle

SOCIAL ATTITUDES DURING THE
SLAVE REGIME: HOUSEHOLD SERVANTS
VERSUS FIELD HANDS

Scholarly descriptions of the institution of slavery have generally cen-
tered on the activities of the white slaveowners and, even where dis-
cussing the Negroes' role and viewpoint, have almost invariably
depended on primary sources written by white people. In part this is
due to the nature of the source materials available. Yet the narra-
tives of fugitive slaves, and the records of interviews conducted many
years later with individuals freed by the Civil War, can, if exploited
critically, afford much useful information.

Based on interviews with ex-slaves, the article that follows de-
scribes the way in which the system of social stratification among
slaves on southern plantations—that is, the distinction between
field hands and house servants—shaped their social outlook and their
views about slavery.

T HE method of using the person's own story as the sole document in a sociological study has been questioned by social scientists all over the country. It
may seem presumptuous, therefore, to offer to a group of sociologists a paper
on social attitudes based on an analysis of 100 ex-slave documents. These were
collected intermittently over a period of four years, from 34 men and 66 women
who had been exposed to slavery for from eight to forty-five years each, and
who at the time of the interview were living in middle and west Tennessee.
These interviews were taken down by a stenographer who remained in the
background while the interviewer attempted to put the subject at ease and
allow him to tell his experiences without interruption.

E. Ophelia Settle, "Social Attitudes During the Slave Regime: Household Servants
Versus Field Hands," *Racial Contacts and Social Research,* Publications of the American
Sociological Society, XXVIII (December, 1933), pp. 95–98. Reprinted with the permis-
sion of the author and publisher.

Because the differences between the house and field slaves have been so often emphasized by writers dealing with the period of slavery, it was interesting to note these differences as presented in the attitudes shown by people who had been slaves themselves. This paper is merely an attempt to point out certain attitudes shown in documents and to indicate some possible underlying factors in the genesis of these attitudes. The latter term is here used to mean "the individual tendency to react, either positively or negatively, to a given social value." [1]

Among the group of ex-slaves interviewed, 44 were classified as house servants and 31 as field hands; 6 did both house and field work; 9 were too young to be gainfully employed; and in 10 cases the information secured did not warrant occupational classification. This division is made because the fundamental group of attitudes appear to have had their basis in occupational differences. The house slaves were thrown in close contact with their masters and mistresses and were thus exposed to the cultural influences of that group. They were usually taught to consider themselves superior to the field hands and to hold themselves apart as a group. Their dress was superior because their occupation required it; their food was often identical with that of the master; their cottages were whitewashed and built near the master's residence; their work itself was elevated above that of the toilers of the field. Add to these differences the fact that the house servants were often mulattoes, and it is easy to understand their position as a middle group in the slave régime. Above them were the masters with their families; but below them were the field hands—to whom they often felt less closely akin than to their masters.

While it is not contended that *all* house slaves held a particular set of attitudes in contradistinction to those of field hands, the contrast in these two groups is outlined sharply in the following situations:

1. Situations in which attitudes of superiority on the part of the house servant are manifested.

2. Situations in which attitudes toward runaway or unruly slaves are shown.

3. Situations in which attitudes toward the régime of slavery are presented.

An illustration of the first group of attitudes is found in the statement made by one of the Nashville house slaves who said:

> "We house slaves thought we wuz better'n the others what worked in the field; we really wuz raised a little different; fact is, I kinda think I'm better'n most folks now. Yes'm we wuz raised; they (that is, the field hands) wuzn't."

That the masters often encouraged their house slaves in their feeling of superiority to their fellow-slaves is shown by their treatment of the "play chillen"—the slave companions of the children in the master's family.

> "They wouldn't let us play with the niggers, and they wouldn't cut our hair," said one of these children, "we sat at the table and et

[1] Taken from Reuter's *Introduction to Sociology*, p. 99. Acknowledgment is made to Thomas and Znaniecki, *The Polish Peasant in Europe and America*, pp. 21–24.

after they et. We jest played with white chillen and cullud folks wuz afraid of us."

"I don't know much about the hardships of slavery because I belonged to a wealthy family and my grandmother and great grandmother lived just like the white people," declared a more cultured member of this group. "None of us were ever sold, I suppose the little cabin children had hard times; they never got to go to the big house, but I was raised right in the house."

Nowhere in the documents is the contrast between the attitudes of house and field slaves shown so well as in their statements regarding the runaway or unruly slaves who were found on every large plantation. Of course some house slaves ran away, and some field hands were more sympathetic with the master than with the runaway, but this situation is not the general rule.

A cabin child, who was 8 years old at the time of the incident narrated, said in reference to runaway slaves:

"Yes, I've seen 'em. I've stole bread out of the house and give it to 'em. I remember uncle Stephen Partee had been gone about a year in the woods, and one evenin' I went out to the barn to get some eggs, and he was hiding under the shucks; it liked to skeered me to death. He said 'Don't holler, Honey; just go back to the house and tell your mammy to send me something to eat.' I went back and got it myself and I didn't say a word, 'cause I knowed if Ole Partee (his master) caught him, he would whup him to death."

Another child of about the same age declared:

"I have carried them food and they would say 'God bless you chile,' and ask me to thank the people for them. My folks would come in the cabin and say 'there's a runaway slave' and Aunt Nancy would let me take some milk to him, and he would say 'God help you' and I would keep on taking it to him to hear him say that."

The house child, on the other hand, was usually less sympathetic and had little understanding of the conditions of these people who sought his help. One house girl, on seeing a runaway slave, was so frightened that she ran all the way to the house to tell "the white folks" what she had seen. Another joined her white "play chillen" in throwing stones at a runaway who had been caught and chained near a store. She gleefully joined in tormenting him in every possible way, and declared that she regarded him as a person entirely outside her own group.

The differences in the attitudes of these groups toward the slave régime in general is shown best in their behavior during the [civil] war. The house slave usually remained with his mistress and guarded the plantation while the cabin slave was more likely to run away to the "Yankees" if the opportunity was presented.

A typical attitude of the house servant is shown in the following document:

"I remember one that mamma always likes to tell. She said her old master was sitting on the porch with his legs crossed smoking his pipe and his old nag was tied to a post down in the yard. She looked up and saw the yankees coming with swords and guns, and everything, and she threw up her hands and shouted 'Run, Marster, the yankees are coming!' and old master got up and ran down to where the nag was tied, jumped on him and ran away. The yankees had seen him sitting there, and had seen mamma throw up her hands but they didn't see which way he went. When they got there mamma said one of them raised his gun and said 'I'm a great mind to blow your brains out,' but he didn't and she didn't care nohow because she had saved her master's life then."

One girl, when asked if the slaves on her plantation ran away, replied: "Some of 'em run away"; but added quickly "Them that lived in the quarters run away, but them that worked in the house didn't."

The maid to the wife of a "Yankee" army officer did not even know that she was a slave until her mistress told her she planned to set her free.

However, the field slave children early realized their condition and became adept at keeping secrets from the people in "the big house." They were the slaves who most frequently ran away to the "Yankees" and who, according to one slave woman, would "get out and shout" whenever the "Yankees" won a victory. Some of them ran away in families and, even if caught and returned to their masters, stayed only until they were able to arrange another escape.

Below is an example of the cleverness of these children as well as an illustration of their attitude toward the whole situation:

"I was a little gal, but I remember how the rebels would come by and ask me where the niggers was, and I would tell them I didn't know. They would keep after me and sometimes I would tell them that they went away; then they would ask where did they go and I would tell them that they went away and that was all I knowed. They used to tell me if I would tell them what they wanted to know they would give me some candy, and of course I, like other children, liked candy very much but after I got it, I would only tell them that they went away and I did not know where they went. Sometimes they would ask me 'Where is your mammy, little nigger? Ain't you got no mammy? If you will tell me I'll give you some candy.' I used to say 'Will you sho nuff?' And they would say 'Yes,' and they would give me the candy and then I would tell them that she had gone to keep the yankees from getting her.... They would ask me 'Little nigger, do you want to go to the yankees?' And I would say 'No,' because I knowed they might kill me if I said 'Yes.'"

In contrast to the field hands, then, one finds the house slaves usually a separate group, sometimes living in cabins especially built for them and their families but often living in the "big house," responsible for all household duties and taught to hold themselves superior to their brethren of the field, and to be on familiar terms with the "white folks"; always observing, however, a certain social distance in their relationship to both masters and slaves. Under these conditions it is not at all strange that with reference to most social questions the attitudes of these two groups tended to be in contradistinction to each other.

Walter Fisher

PHYSICIANS AND SLAVERY IN THE ANTEBELLUM SOUTHERN MEDICAL JOURNAL

An important aspect of slave life that has received little systematic attention has been the health and medical care of bondsmen. Walter Fisher's article on the treatment of slaves by southern physicians provides an illuminating glimpse into this largely neglected subject.

Today, even as it was generations ago, American Negro slavery is many different things to many different people, both to historians and to lay persons. These variations in views about slavery are partly reflections of what historians have written about it, and reflections, in turn, of the historians' sources. Typically, these sources have included plantation records, letters and diaries, travel accounts, newspapers and other periodicals. Traditionally, however, historians have paid little attention to medical sources, to the writings of physicians in general and, more specifically, to what they have written about slaves and slavery in antebellum medical journals. As Richard H. Shryock declared in a paper read at the meeting of the History of Science Society in 1934, while southern planters and English or northern travelers saw and described the southern scene obscurely through their respective biased glasses, the "relatively reliable professional testimony" of physicians has been neglected.[1]

Of all critics, the Southern physician was perhaps in the best position to report on the physical and moral treatment of the slaves. When he stated, as he sometimes did, that Negroes were overworked and underfed, he can hardly be suspected of antislavery bias since he was the

Walter Fisher, "Physicians and Slavery in the Antebellum Southern Medical Journal," *Journal of the History of Medicine and Allied Sciences*, XXIII (1968), pp. 36–49. Reprinted with permission of *Journal of the History of Medicine and Allied Sciences* and Walter Fisher.

[1] R. H. Shryock, "Medical sources and the social historian," *Am. hist. Rev.*, 1936, 41, 465.

friend of the planter who employed him. As a matter of fact, he usually approved of the institution. Coming into frequent contact with human bondage under the most intimate circumstances, he was in a position to understand it as few travelers could hope to do. On the other hand, his vested interest in the institution was rarely so direct or so great as was that of the planters.[2]

This paper offers a kind of demonstration-by-way-of-suggestion that the southern physicians who wrote in the medical journals published in the American South in the three decades before the Civil War are reporters and witnesses whose testimony concerning slavery should be heard, analyzed, and incorporated into the history of "the peculiar institution." [3] Their writings additionally reveal much concerning the status of medicine as science and art a century and a half ago. Within this frame of reference, the major foci of this paper will be the motives and profits involved in the medical care of slaves; and the antebellum medical practitioners—irregular, regular, and heroic.

I

The vast economic investment represented by the southern slave population was the primary reason why they were provided with medical care. Richard D. Arnold, a leading physician of Savannah, observed that slavery "as it exists with us is the only institution in which Interests and Humanity go hand in hand together." So great, he wrote, was the loss in capital by the death of a slave that a planter understood that "to save his capital was to save his negroes." [4] In correspondence between Dr. George C. Smith, of Oxford, Georgia, and Joseph A. Eve, an Augusta physician, about "a case of probable extra-uterine pregnancy," the slave patient is described as "a valuable servant" whose owners "feel great solicitude on her account, not knowing what may be the final result." [5] The feelings of a Louisiana planter who owned a slave suffering from a vesico-vaginal fistula were described by the attending physician, Dr. Samuel Cartwright of New Orleans:

> He authorized me to call in consulting physicians, and to procure for
> her all the comforts and conveniences necessary in the treatment of
> her case. He said that the patient had been pronounced incurable by

[2] Ibid.

[3] The first medical journal published south of the border states was the Southern Journal of Medicine and Surgery, begun at Augusta in 1836. In addition to those cited in this paper, other antebellum medical journals of this region were the Charleston Medical Journal and Review; the Medical Journal of North Carolina, published at Edenton and Raleigh; the Southern Medical Reformer, published at Petersburg, Virginia; and the Virginia Medical and Surgical Journal, of Richmond.

[4] R. H. Shryock, Ed., Letters of Richard D. Arnold, M.D., 1806–1876. Papers of the Trinity College Historical Society, Double Series 18–19. Durham, 1929, pp. 33–34.

[5] Sth. med. surg. J., 1845, n.s. 1, 574.

a number of physicians, but if impossible to effect a cure, he hoped that it was in the power of science to afford some relief to her intolerable sufferings.[6]

Comparable concern is revealed in the following conversation between Jim, an 18-year-old slave, "a likely and quite athletic figure," and Dr. D. Warren Brickell, of New Orleans, during a typhoid epidemic:

"What is the matter with you, Jim?" "Nothing, sir." "Well, why have you come here?" "The order of the overseer, sir, is to come to the hospital the moment we feel the least unwell: I felt a little tired just now, and thought I ought to obey orders." [7]

These incidents, and many others like them reported in the journals, also attest to the significance of their care of slaves as a source of income for southern physicians. As Dr. Arnold put it, the demand for professional attention for slaves "is the true reason why Physicians get into practice more readily at the South than at the North—and that here he stands some chance of making his bread while he has teeth to chew it." [8]

Other indications of the importance of medical care of slaves in the practice of the southern physician are to be found in the "fee bills" established by southern medical societies. Special rates for the treatment of slaves suggest that the volume of such cases may have compensated for the price differential involved. In 1851 the medical profession of Richmond, Virginia, established a table of rates in which a vaccination for a white person was charged at three dollars, or at two for five dollars, with each subsequent injection in the same family being set at one dollar. By the same schedule the vaccination of a single slave was set at two dollars; each additional vaccination on the same plantation or farm, or in the same family, cost one dollar.[9] In Nottoway County, Virginia, rates for infirmary patients were set in 1853 at seven dollars per week for whites and at five dollars for Negroes.[10]

But the profession was by no means of one mind with respect to such arrangements. The practice of attending families by the year was noticed editorially and condemned in the New Orleans Medical and Surgical Journal in 1852. In language matching that of an organized medical profession of a later day, the editors contended that

yearly practice aims at a species of miserable, petty monopoly, which is at war with the objects . . . of a liberal and enlightened profession. You may bargain with your grocer, your butcher, your laundress, and no harm comes of or by it; but for an honorable, an educated physician to hire himself by the year, like a slave; to pledge his talents and his

[6] New Orl. med. surg. J., 1859, 16, 513.
[7] New Orl. med. News Hosp. Gaz. 1856, 2, 532.
[8] Shryock, Letters of Richard D. Arnold, p. 34.
[9] Stethoscope Va. med. Gaz. 1851, 1, 178.
[10] Ibid., 3, 236.

services, for a stipulated sum, is in direct violation of the ethics of the profession.[11]

A similar criticism was voiced by a physician who signed himself "Celsus" in a Richmond, Virginia, medical journal in 1853:

> When an individual asks me to do his practice by the year, I am often inclined to return an answer a young friend of mine did on such an occasion—he indignantly replied, "whenever I am become black and am to be hired, I will let you know." [12]

The physicians of Nashville, following a similar course, agreed in 1858 not to attend either individuals or families by the year at any stipulated price nor to consult with any physician who transgressed the rule.[13]

Underlying the objections of medical practitioners to such contracts was the view, sometimes specifically stated and sometimes intimated, that annual compensation usually involved a "bargain rate." [14] Occasionally, however, another consideration entered the picture. The risks involved in collecting annual fees were greater. Moreover, the hazards involved in collecting fees for services rendered to individuals were great enough to deter the practitioner from entering into long-term group-practice agreements. For example, difficulties encountered in being paid for services furnished to slaves under mortgage or in the hands of trustees and agents led the physicians of Alabama, in a state medical convention in 1847, to recommend that practitioners seek liens on slaves so attended or furnished, "in the same manner and under the same regulations as the lien laws for the security of mechanics and laborers in relation to steamboats." [15] Unfortunately, the medical journals do not report on the implementation of this recommendation. However, the action of the Alabama group is instructive in that it points to the willingness of physicians—in their essential role as business men—to receive payment in the form of the chattels themselves.

Physicians also played an important part in the "warranty" activities associated with the sale and purchase of slaves. Juriah Harris, a professor of physiology at the Savannah Medical College, reported in 1858 that southern physicians were "daily called upon" by prospective purchasers to pronounce upon the soundness of slaves. The frequency of such requests, together with demands that physicians present medical evidence in court "in cases of prosecution for the sale of an unsound negro," led Dr. Harris to the conclusion that it was the duty of southern medical men to establish uniform rules in such practice.[16]

Harris then proceeded to outline what amounted to a code for the direction of physicians and slave-buyers. He regarded diseases of a chronic or con-

[11] *New Orl. med. surg. J.,* 1852, 8, 543.
[12] *Stethoscope Va. med. Gaz.,* 1853, 2, 238.
[13] *Nashville J. Med. Surg.,* 1860, 18, 411.
[14] *Stethoscope Va. med. Gaz.,* 1853, 2, 238.
[15] *New Orl. med. surg. J.,* 1848, 4, 678.
[16] *Savannah J. Med.,* 1858, 1, 146.

stitutional character which incapacitated the Negro "for the performance of the usual duties of his calling, viz: hard labor," as the basis for declaring the slave "unsound." Specific disqualifying diseases and ailments included the loss of arms or legs; injuries to muscles, tendons, and tissue which might prevent the dexterous handling of implements of labor; constant or recurring ulcers on the leg; malignant tumors, cancer, and scrofula; asthma; and some forms of rheumatism. Hemorrhoids, which Dr. Harris said were rare in the Negro— there were, as he put it, ten cases among whites to one in the Negro—should also be considered evidence of unsoundness. Keloid tumors, though benign, were also held to be disqualifying, Harris describing them as having the unfortunate quality of being incurable "either by the knife or medication, and having a strong tendency to scrofulous ulceration." [17]

Gonorrhea, Dr. Harris advised, was never a cause of permanent unsoundness. On syphilis, however, he suggested that the

> soundness of a negro who may be or have been affected with an infecting chancre should be looked upon with suspicion [for]...no one can tell when the constitutional effects may be developed....It is true that in this country, blessed by Providence with good air and the negro supplied with good food and clothing by his owner, that this rarely results when the chancre has been properly treated.[18]

Secondary syphilis, he continued, was "most unquestionably" a cause of unsoundness—even should the apparent symptoms be relieved by a well-directed treatment, no one could tell at what time it might reappear.[19]

Concurrence in Dr. Harris's views of the disqualifying effect of syphilis is found in the experience of other doctors. Paul F. Eve, of Augusta, reported that he was requested, in 1843, by the prospective purchaser of one Philip to give an opinion on the slave's health. "He was pronounced unsound, and to be then laboring under the tertiary effects of the venereal disease." Notwithstanding, the purchase was made. A year later Philip was "in a very desperate condition" and undergoing treatment by Dr. Eve.[20]

That determination of the soundness or unsoundness of a slave on sale was a matter requiring close attention is further revealed in the experience of "Dr. R. T. L.," of Wilkinson County, Mississippi, who was described as "a practitioner of experience" by Dr. C. S. Magoun, who reported the incident to the New Orleans Medical Journal. Dr. L. purchased, in 1844, an 18-year-old pregnant woman who was suffering with a cough. Her soundness, however, was guaranteed by the vendor, an opinion in which the physician-purchaser concurred. Three days later the slave was dead, ostensibly as a result of puerperal fever—the three-day interval between her purchase and her death being marked, however, by her giving birth to a child "of full size, healthy and vigorous."

[17] Ibid., 147, 148, 217, 218, 219, 220, 223, 292, 293.
[18] Ibid., 2, 10–11.
[19] Ibid.
[20] Sth. med. surg. J., 1845, n.s. 1, 682–83.

Moreover, a post-mortem examination disclosed that the slave had a tumor in the thorax, a condition which impelled Dr. Magoun, the reporter, to assert that the "woman was evidently unwell at the time of sale, and must have been so for weeks, if not months." "Under the circumstances," he asked, "ought the seller or buyer to be the loser?" [21]

But while the Mississippi practitioner was apparently "taking a flyer" in the slave marketplace, his brother practitioners elsewhere augmented their income by "soundness practice," asking fees of wide range. In Virginia in the 1850's charges for "an opinion of health or disease" ranged from two to ten dollars, while "an opinion involving a question of law" might cost from ten to fifty dollars.[22] And in the late fifties, post-mortem examinations in cases of legal investigation were set, in Nashville, at $25.[23]

But establishing fee schedules was one thing, collecting fees was another. Non-payment or postponement of the payment of doctors' bills was a chronic socio-economic habit of the period, whose results were felt by both the younger southern physicians and the more mature. One of the latter, Richard D. Arnold, complained that "it runs me almost crazy to think that with hundreds upon hundreds due me professionally I find the greatest difficulty in raising a simple fifty dollars." [24] And, almost wistfully, Richmond physicians were urged to seek to collect their bills at least once a year, "whenever this can be done without serious inconvenience to the patient." [25]

II

Medical care has never been the monopoly of the professional medical man. The doctor, be he wizard or scientist, has always shared his art and craft with the layman. That medical care of the slave in the antebellum South is no exception to this generalization is amply attested by a variety of data published in southern medical journals of the antebellum period. Comments of the profession on slave care by non-professionals fall into two main categories. Essentially jealous of their professional relationships to health and disease, physician-writers loudly complained of bungling by amateurs. Mistresses and overseers, and particularly midwives, were targets of professional criticism. But in his less warmly critical moments, the antebellum doctor became something of a consulting health engineer, offering in his journal articles practical suggestions for the more efficient health management of slaves.

Dr. D. Warren Brickell, a New Orleans medical editor and professor of obstetrics at the New Orleans School of Medicine, best captured the spirit of physicians who protested the "competition" by owners, overseers, and mis-

[21] *New Orl. med. J.*, 1844, 1, 434–35.
[22] *Stethoscope Va. med. Gaz.*, 1851, 1, 178.
[23] *Nashville J. Med. Surg.*, 1860, 18, 409.
[24] Shryock, Ed. (n. 4), 164.
[25] *Stethoscope Va. med. Gaz.*, 1851, 1, 180.

tresses. The physician derived no pleasure or advantage, he asserted, from treating cases which had been badly nursed. Nor had the planter "fulfilled his duty, either in point of humanity or self-interest" in allowing his slaves to be treated by amateurs. But, most of all, Brickell condemned "the almost universal practice, on the part of owners and overseers, of tampering with their sick negroes ... before applying for medical aid." A physician called to treat a slave patient "thus quacked" was compared to a man called on to stay an already rapidly falling wall. So frequently, Brickell wrote, did physicians encounter such situations that they had relapsed into a limited routine system of medication. The planter, he complained,

> has no confidence in himself or his overseer in ... putting a new spoke in a cart wheel and sends for a mechanic at once. But of the intricate mechanism of man ... their knowledge is sufficient, in their own estimation, to warrant such efforts for the restoration of the sick man as they would not ... have exerted on the comparatively worthless cart wheel.[26]

In criticism of a similar practice, Thomas S. Powell, a physician of Sparta, Georgia, lamented the treatment accorded one Mary, a slave who suffered from a chronic pain in the knee. In this case the slave's mistress, supposing the ailment to be a simple sprain, "applied vinegar and clay from the back of the chimney for several nights." More reprehensible in the eyes of this "regular" practitioner was the calling of "Dr. _____, a celebrated Thomsonian," who proceeded to vomit the patient. Notwithstanding the effects on Mary of her mistress' poultice and of the vegetable compounds which typified Thomsonian practice, Dr. Powell was able quickly to restore to health the slave whose "services were much needed in the field." [27]

Dr. H. V. Wooten, of Lowndesboro, Alabama, was called to prescribe for the slave Betty, whose owner had been treating her for what he took to be diarrhea. Wooten determined that the slave had a prolapsed uterus accompanied by profuse leucorrhoea. Subsequently an operation was performed, and the slave recovered.[28]

Still another complaint made by professional physicians had to do with the common remedies prescribed by lay practitioners. Thomas Affleck, an affluent Mississippi planter, reported to Dr. Erasmus Fenner, editor of the *Southern Medical Reports*, that overseers too often dosed "after a routine— an emetic followed by calomel and oil." [29] L. A. Dugas, professor of anatomy at the Medical College of Georgia, in treating the infant child of "Mr. L. P. D.'s negro woman Pat," for purulent ophthalmia, substituted a chloride of soda wash for the breast-milk lotion treatment which the owner had prescribed and administered.[30]

Of greater seriousness, however, were the untoward results of obstetrical

---

[26] *New Orl. med. News Hosp. Gaz.*, 1856, 2, 545–46.
[27] *Atlanta med. surg. J.*, 1856, 1, 516–18. [29] *Sth. med. Rep.*, 1849–50, 1, 436.
[28] *Sth. med. surg. J.*, 1845, n.s. 1, 845. [30] *Sth. med. surg. J.*, 1836, 1, 82–83.

practice by midwives. Dr. R. H. Whitfield, of Gainesville, Alabama, in 1855 attacked the "almost universal" employment of "negresses" as midwives. "To their bad management," he contended, "is to be attributed most of the diseases to which our females fall victim." [31] A New Orleans practitioner, alarmed by the frequency of child-birth accidents, declared that there was "probably no city of equal population in Christendom" where the male professional was less employed in obstetrical cases than in the Crescent City.

> none in which the female practitioners are less educated, being chiefly negresses or mulattresses, or foreigners without anatomical, physiological and obstetrical education.... That such uneducated persons should be generally successful is owing to the fact that in a great majority of cases no scientific skill is required, and thus a lucky negress becomes the rival of the most learned obstetrician.[32]

Luck was frequently not on the side of the midwife. A woman thought to be in labor, and so described by a midwife, was found by Dr. Richard D. Arnold to be suffering instead from an extraordinary case of rupture of the rectum and expulsion externally of the intestines.[33] Called hastily to take over where a midwife's art had failed, Dr. J. C. C. Blackburn, of Pike County, Alabama, found his slave patient suffering additionally from a prolapsed uterus.[34] Another physician complained that he owned "a valuable negress who has been made useless by the forcible extraction of the placenta immediately after the birth of her child," the act being that of "an ignorant midwife." [35] And, reporting on the diseases of Lowndesboro, Alabama, and its vicinity, Dr. H. W. Wooten observed that, although obstetrics was beginning, around 1848, to form a very important branch of practice in the region, with "very near all the white women, and many negroes calling for professional assistance in the labors," many cases involving slaves "were rendered complicated and difficult by neglect or bad management on the part of the midwives in whose hands" he found them.[36]

Loud and frequent though they may have been, physicians' complaints about midwives did not include the demand that lay accoucheurs be banned from such practice. Rather, the theme reiterated in their articles is that educational requirements and control measures be instituted for these women. The position taken by Dr. R. H. Day, of Pattersonville, Louisiana, was typical:

> If such cases must be put in the charge of women—to which I yield in hearty assent—let public opinion and the laws of our State require of all such a proper study and due qualification for their important and responsible avocation. Let not old age be their only qualification.[37]

Difficult confinement cases sometimes involved extensive treatment by

[31] New Orl. med. surg. J., 1855, 12, 196–99.
[32] Ibid., 1854, 11, 20–21.
[33] Sth. med. surg. J., 1838, 2, 79–80.
[34] Ga. Blister and Critic, 1854, 1, 133.
[35] New Orl. med. surg. J., 1855, 12, 196.
[36] Sth. med. Rep., 1851, 2, 342, 345.
[37] New Orl. med. surg. J., 1847, 4, 227.

teams of physicians. Dr. John G. Westmoreland, an Atlanta physician, was called to see one Jane, a slave, in labor. Arriving at about eight in the morning, he discovered that Jane's was a case of arm presentation. During the course of the day, until seven in the evening when a dead child was delivered, Dr. Westmoreland called three other physicians into consultation.[38] A similar case was that of Joseph P. Manly's Jane, who was described by the midwife Aunt Winney as having "the usual labor pains." Over a two-day period Jane required the services of two physicians. In Spaulding County, Georgia, Dr. E. F. Knott discovered his slave patient to be suffering from a ruptured uterus. The owner, after consultation, "immediately called my friend Dr. John R. Clark who lived within one mile . . . [and remained] until late in the afternoon." Dr. Knott meanwhile was present throughout the day, and again in the evening called for Dr. Clark. Finding that his associate had left his home to attend another patient, Knott sent for Clark's instruments and with them delivered Jane of a healthy child.[39]

III

During the 1830's James Silk Buckingham, an Englishman, traveled throughout America. In his report on his travels, published in 1841, he presented the transcript of an item appearing in a New York newspaper under the heading "More Pork for the South":

> Yesterday morning it was discovered that a barrell, which had been put into the office of the Charleston packet line . . , for the purpose of being shipped to Charleston, contained the bodies of two dead negroes. The cask and its contents were sent up to the police office and placed in the dead house for the coroner.[40]

In discussing this incident, Buckingham relates that it had lately become a common practice in New York to ship off bodies of dead Negroes "for various ports, but especially the South," to medical schools for dissection; that, to elude suspicion, these bodies were put up in salt and brine and packed in the same casks as those in which salted provisions were exported; and that the discovery reported was the third or fourth of the kind in a single month. An inquest was held and a declaration made that the Negroes had died of disease; "no further inquiry," Buckingham commented, "appears to have been made into the matter, as if it were altogether beneath the notice of white men to trace out these traders in the dead bodies of the blacks." [41]

[38] *Sth. med. surg. J.*, 1838, 2, 335.
[39] *Atlanta med. surg. J.*, 1855, 1, 11–13. See also *ibid.*, 591–94, and *New Orl. med. surg. J.*, 1845, 2, 315–16.
[40] J. S. Buckingham, *America, historical, statistic and descriptive.* London, 1841, 1, 159.
[41] *Ibid.*, 159–60.

The propaganda value of Buckingham's disclosure to the then growing American anti-slavery movement is self-evident. But the episode had a more practical significance. It connects directly with problems of medical education, medical care, and even medical experimentation. The free Negro class of the North might occasionally furnish laboratory anatomical specimens, as their persisting fear of "body-snatchers" and "night doctors" indicates. Shipping the cadavers southward, however, is another matter. No data have been uncovered to substantiate the particular Buckingham disclosures; not so, however, with regard to the general problem to which his story is related. An abundance of materials in the southern medical journals reveals that slaves had a fairly significant role in medical education and in experimental and radical medical and surgical practice of the antebellum South.

Four out of eight main articles in the August 1836 number of the *Southern Medical and Surgical Journal* deal in whole or in part with treatment furnished to slaves.[42] Four out of five operations on the eye by Professor Dugas of the Medical College of Georgia, and reported in the June 1838 number of the same journal, were performed on slaves.[43] Three of the six surgical cases reported by Professor Paul F. Eve, of the same school, involved Negroes and were performed in the presence of students in the college's anatomical theater.[44] The Louisiana Medical College, in New Orleans, advertised that among its "admirable advantages for the instruction of medical students—particularly those destined for southern practice," was "the great facility of obtaining subjects for dissection" from the New Orleans Charity Hospital, a large installation treating local patients of both races as well as a considerable transient clientele.[45]

In an editorial extolling the virtues of "Southern Institutions," the editors of the *Savannah Journal of Medicine* called particular attention to the "abundant clinical opportunities for the study of disease" in the large Negro patient population at the Savannah Medical College.[46] Students of the Atlanta Medical College examined during several weeks a slave who constituted "an interesting case" of an abscessed liver. This man was "lectured upon and prescribed for in the presence of the class." [47] And in an operation performed at the Medical College of Georgia, "assisted by the faculty" and viewed by students, Dr. Eve successfully amputated nearly one half of the lower jaw bone (four and three-quarters inches, including one of its angles) of one Dinah, who, after complaining of an aching jaw for years, was discovered to be suffering from sarcoma of the jaw.[48]

Even more dramatic is the scene described by J. Marion Sims in one of his many heroic operations. Even considering the surgical practices of the time

[42] *Sth. med. surg. J.*, 1838, 2, 335.
[43] *Ibid.*, 647–51.
[44] *Ibid.*, 643–47.
[45] *New Orl. med. surg. J.*, 1844, 1, 643–47.
[46] *Savannah J. Med.*, 1860, 2, 354.
[47] *Atlanta med. surg. J.*, 1856, 1, 329.
[48] *Sth. med. surg. J.*, 1838, 2, 120–21.

(1845), the operation was a remarkable affair. For some years Sam, a slave, had suffered from what his owner thought was a gum boil, resulting from the medicine given the slave for syphilis. Subsequently the true nature of the ailment was determined: osteo-sarcoma of the lower jaw. But Sam refused to let "one of the most distinguished surgeons of the whole region ... operate," the slave's objection being that "it would hurt too bad." Eventually Sam was sent to Montgomery to Dr. Sims, who decided that an operation was the only means of saving the life of the patient. "Determined not to be foiled in the attempt," Dr. Sims contrived an ingenious method of securing the patient. Sam was persuaded to sit in a barber's chair, to which some planks had been added at the top and bottom. He was quickly tied down by straps around thighs, knees, ankles, abdomen, thorax, shoulders, wrists, elbows, and head. Sam, Dr. Sims relates, "appeared to be very much alarmed"! Two months after the forty-minute operation Sam left Montgomery. "His mouth," the surgeon reported, "is almost always on a broad grin." [49]

Five physicians assisted Dr. Sims in this operation, while some ten medical students and fifteen other practitioners watched. The editors of the *New Orleans Medical and Surgical Journal,* in which the operation was reported, found "pleasure to record this highly creditable achievement of a Southern surgeon" and related that it had been incorporated into Mott and Velpeau's great work on operative surgery. As for Dr. Sims, among the six points which he considered significant in connection with this surgery was that it had proved its "practicability ... whether the patient is willing or not." [50]

Considered in a larger context, the Sims operation has much to say concerning the relation of the slave to the medical profession and to the problem of medical care of slaves. Sam must have been a burden to his master, having required, at the outset, treatment for venereal disease as well as for "an aching jaw." He was sent from rural Alabama into Montgomery, which suggests the owner's desperation over the constant expenditure for the care of an infirm chattel. Dr. Sims's careful preparations for the operation, the assistance that he was given, the audience which assembled to view the surgery, and the careful record he made of the operation and its results, all attest to the significance attached to the event. Sam, his owner, Dr. Sims, the surgical assistants, the practitioners, the students, and medical science generally were all benefactors—and beneficiaries—in this enterprise.

As remarkable and dramatic as the foregoing operation may be, it is not in connection with such surgery that Sims's name has become famous in modern medicine. Rather, it was as a specialist in women's diseases that he became renowned, particularly in connection with the surgical cure of vesico-vaginal fistula. This ailment, consisting of an abnormal communication between the bladder and the vagina—allowing, among other things, an involuntary discharge of urine—had long been considered incurable. Many surgeons had attempted its cure but had achieved inconclusive results.

[49] *New Orl. med. surg. J.,* 1846, 3, 126–29.
[50] *Ibid.*

In 1845, while examining a slave suffering from the ailment, Sims became convinced that an operation was practicable and perfectible. He ransacked the country for cases; found six or seven among slave women; enlarged his hospital; assumed the costs of providing for these women during their months-long stays; and then trained them to serve as his surgical assistants, for he undertook to perform the operations with only the assistance of the patients themselves. After five years and in his thirtieth operation, on the slave Anarcha in 1849, Sims perfected the surgical procedure which brought him his greatest fame. Ironically, the surgery which came to be so much acclaimed in the South and which utilized so many slaves so prominently in its perfection, was first reported not in a southern medical journal, but rather, in 1852, in the older and more prestigious *American Journal of Medical Sciences*, of Philadelphia.[51]

Another Montgomery surgeon, Dr. N. Bozeman, achieved some fame in connection with the surgical treatment of the same ailment, substituting a "button suture" for Sims's "clamp suture." Bozeman's initial operations were performed on "a young colored girl," "Kitty, a colored girl," "Dinah, a colored woman," and "a mulatto girl." [52]

The surgical cure for vesico-vaginal fistula would have been worked out in time; that it was done in 1849 is in large part a result of a medical use of "the peculiar institution" of the South, for it would have been most improbable that Sims and Bozeman could have established so remarkable a surgical schedule without the slave system which provided the experimental subjects.[53]

This relationship between surgical advance and slavery attests what Richard Shryock has called the "direct and intimate ... interplay between medical science and its social environment." [54] This interaction between society and medicine also had a corollary effect in the unintended, but nevertheless significant, role of southern physicians as sources of social history. Their professional testimony concerning the medical care of slaves, as recorded in the antebellum medical journal, provides insights and revelations important to a balanced picture of slavery and suggests, as Professor Shryock has so often urged, the efficacy and relevance of such sources for understanding other aspects of the American past.

51 See J. Marion Sims, *The story of my life*. New York, 1884, pp. 233–46.
52 *Louisville R.*, 1856, 1, 83–89.
53 An additional example of the relationship between slavery and medical development is to be found in the history of caesarian sections in the United States. In 1794 a Virginia physician performed such an operation on his wife. A quarter of a century later, Dr. François Marie Prévost, of Donaldsville, Louisiana, performed the second such operation. Regarded as the outstanding American pioneer in this specialty, Dr. Prévost completed this surgery four times between 1822 and 1831, each time upon a slave woman. *New Orl. med. surg. J.*, June, October 1879, April 1880; *Am. J. med. Sci.*, August 1835.
54 R. H. Shryock, "The significance of medicine in American history," *Am. hist. R.*, 1956, 62, 82.

Marion D. de B. Kilson

TOWARDS FREEDOM: AN ANALYSIS OF

SLAVE REVOLTS IN THE UNITED STATES

Settle's discussion focuses largely on the accommodative aspects of the Negroes' adjustment to slavery, especially on the part of the house servant class. Other scholars have emphasized resistance to the slave regime. An important early comprehensive survey of the major slave insurrections which the interested student should consult is Harvey Wish, "American Slave Insurrections before 1861," Journal of Negro History, XXII (July, 1937).

The number of slave revolts in the United States varied from period to period, and from region to region. Marion Kilson's analysis attempts to explain the factors accounting for these variations.

T HROUGHOUT the history of slavery in the United States there occurred a variety of more or less subtle expressions of opposition to the slave system by the enslaved. Opposition took many forms, ranging from individual attempts to thwart the system through negligence in work to mass endeavors to overthrow the system. One class of opposition to the status of servitude is represented by slave revolts, which may be defined minimally as attempts to achieve freedom by groups of slaves. Although the data on slave revolts are fragmentary, three types may be distinguished on the basis of sixty-five cases meeting this minimal definition. These are Systematic or Rational Revolts, Unsystematic or Vandalistic Revolts, and Situational or Opportunistic Revolts. The analysis of the characteristics of each of these types of revolt, of their distribution in time and space, of their leadership, and of their repercussions is the concern of this paper.

The three types of slave revolt differ in form, purpose, salient attributes, territorial extent, and participants. Variable aspects of these categories are expressed in Tables 1, 2, and 3. While each table summarizes the available evi-

Marion D. de B. Kilson, "Towards Freedom: An Analysis of Slave Revolts in the United States," *Phylon*, XXV (2nd Quarter, 1964), pp. 175–187. Reprinted with the permission of the publisher.

TABLE 1

TYPE I REVOLTS *

	Revolt Form	Establish Negro State	Take City	Months Preparation	For Retreat	To Spare Groups	To Allocate Tasks	Area	Leader	Insurgents
		Aim:			Plan:			Area	Participants:	
Md. 1739	C	x		several	x			1 co		200
N.Y. 1712	R			3			x	1 ci		25–30
Va. 1663	C			several				1 co		WI, S
Va. 1722	C	x						3 co	3S	
Va. 1792	C		x	several			x	4 co		600+
Va. 1793	C			4				1 ci		
Va. 1800 †	C	x	x	6		x	x	4 co	1S	c. 7,000
Va. 1816	C		x					3 co	1W	
S.C. 1720	C		x							"large"
S.C. 1816	C		x	8				1 ci		
S.C. 1822 ‡	C	x	x	7			x	80 mi	1F	c. 7,000
Ga. 1810	C			1			x	2 co		
Ga. 1819	C							1 ci	S	
Ga. 1841	C		x							S, W
La. 1837	C		x			x	x	1 co		F, S
La. 1840	C							7 co		400+S 4 W
La. 1853	C							1 ci	1S 1W	2,500 S 100W

KEY:
C: conspiracy
R: actual revolt
x: variable present

ci: city
co: county
mi: miles
F: Free Negro

S: slave
W: white
WI: indentured white

* Unless otherwise noted, the data contained in this and subsequent tables are based upon material derived from Herbert Aptheker, *American Negro Slave Revolts* (New York, 1943).

† Gabriel Prosser's Revolt. ‡ Denmark Vesey's Revolt.

TABLE 2

TYPE II REVOLTS

Revolt	Form	Aim: Destruction Property and/or Slave Holders	Unsystematic Characteristics: Lack Preparation	Gathering Recruits	Area	Leader	Participants: Insurgents
N.Y. 1708	R	x			1 to		"small"
Va. 1687	C	x			1 co		
Va. 1691	R	x			1 co	S	
Va. 1792	R	x		x	1 co		900
Va. 1831 *	R	x	x	x	1 co	S	70
N.C. 1776	C	x			3 co	1 S 1 W	
S.C. 1711	R	x				S	"several"
S.C. 1730	C		x		1 ci		
S.C. 1740	R		x	x			150–200
Ga. 1774	R	x	x		1 co		10 †
La. 1730	C	x			1 ci		
La. 1795	C	x	x		1 co		
La. 1811	R	x		x	2 co	F	400–500
Miss. 1835	C	x			1 co	W	

KEY:
C: conspiracy
R: actual revolt
x: variable present

ci: city
co: county
to: town

F: Free Negro
S: slave
W: white

* Turner's Revolt.
† Carroll, *op. cit.*, p. 38.

TABLE 3
TYPE III REVOLTS

Revolt	Form	Aim: Escape:				Armed	Participants:	
		To Free State	From Sale South	Outside U.S.A.	To Indians		Leader	Insurgents
Penn. 1734 *	C				x			
Md. 1845	R	x				x		75
Ky. 1829	R		x					90
Ky. 1848	R	x				x	1 W	75
Mo. 1836	C			x				
Mo. 1850	R	x				x	1 S	30
Va. 1799	R		x					
S.C. 1826	R				x			
Ga. 1849	C			x				300
Ga.-Md. 1826	R	x						29
La. 1840	C			x			1 S	
Texas 1851	R			x				

KEY:
C: conspiracy
R: actual revolt

x: variable present
S: slave
W: white

* Joshua Coffin, *An Account of Some of the Principal Slave Insurrections* (New York, 1860), p. 14.

dence on revolts of a particular type, further elaboration of the content and implications of these categories is necessary.

The Type I or Systematic Revolt, of which the prototypes are the conspiracies of Gabriel Prosser and Denmark Vesey, is oriented towards overthrowing the slave system itself and establishing a Negro state. It is character-ized, therefore, by careful planning and organization which necessitate a considerable period of preparation. Careful planning is evidenced by the means decided upon to realize the establishment of the Negro state. Both Prosser and Vesey planned initially to gain control of a city and thereafter to extend their operations into the surrounding area. Such a plan involves the systematic allo-cation of tasks to various groups and individuals and the calculation of the numbers of insurgents upon whom reliance could be placed. Further evidence of the rational conception of these uprisings is found in the facts that Gabriel Prosser intended to spare certain sympathetic groups of whites and hoped for aid from poor whites and Indians, and that Vesey hoped to have external aid from the West Indies and Africa to maintain his state after its establishment.[1] One corollary of such systematic planning is a long period of preparation which, in turn, increases the likelihood of discovery by the slavocracy; it is not surprising, therefore, that of the seventeen Type I Revolts [2] which have been distinguished, only one went beyond the planning phase. A second corol-lary of such rational planning is that it is likely to involve the recruitment of a large number of insurgents from a number of counties.

Two aspects of Type I Revolts merit further comment: the urban factor and armed conflict with the slavocracy. The urban factor is significant in 71 percent of the Type I Revolts, five of them occurring within an urban complex and seven others initially oriented towards gaining control of a city. The urban factor appears to have been significant as a source both of more cosmopolitan ideas and of greater role differentiation for Negroes. This does not imply that Type I Revolts are necessarily urban inspired. While Vesey was a resident of Charleston, South Carolina, Prosser lived six miles outside of Richmond, Virginia. Moreover, 29 percent of the Type I Revolts were not urban oriented. Thus the urban factor seems to facilitate rather than to determine the develop-ment of Type I Revolts. The second noteworthy aspect of Type I Revolts is that while the achievement of their ultimate goals necessitates armed conflict with members of the slavocracy potentially leading to bloodshed and property destruction, this is a secondary phenomenon rather than a primary goal.

By contrast, the Type II or Vandalistic Revolt, of which the prototype is Nat Turner's insurrection, represents a haphazard expression of opposition to the slave system aimed at the destruction of slave holders and their prop-erty. It lacks systematic preparation but may be either of lengthy or of virtually spontaneous conception. Its unsystematic character and potential spontaneity imply both that it has a greater likelihood of reaching the activist stage [3] than Type I Revolts and that reliance upon the gathering of recruits as the revolt gains momentum is of more importance than in the Type I Revolt. For example,

[1] Herbert Aptheker, *American Negro Slave Revolts* (New York, 1943), pp. 101–02, 220, 225; 272, 98, 269. Joseph Cephas Carroll, *Slave Insurrections in the United States 1800–1865* (Boston, 1938), p. 50.
[2] Table 1 summarizes the evidence for Type I Revolts.
[3] Of the fourteen Type II Revolts, 59 percent succeeded in achieving this stage.

deciding one Sunday afternoon to begin his long contemplated revolt that night, Turner set out with a handful of fellow insurgents whose numbers swelled to seventy during the course of the rising.[4] A further implication of the unsystematic nature of the Type II Revolt is that it tends to be localized within a single county and to be a rural rather than an urban-oriented phenomenon.[5] Moreover, lacking any well-defined goals beyond the immediate destruction of the life and property of the slaveholder, the Type II Revolt implies the insurgents' unconscious acceptance of ultimate capitulation to the power of the slavocracy.[6]

The Type III or Opportunistic Revolt aims at escape from servitude. It is characterized by a group of slaves attempting to escape either to a non-slave area or from removal to areas of more oppressive servitude. It tends, therefore, to be situationally determined. Given the realistic opportunity to escape to a free area by land or sea, the group attempts to realize this objective. Thus like the Type I Revolt it is rationally conceived, and like the Type II Revolt it may be virtually spontaneous.[7] Significantly, the only successful slave revolt of which there is evidence falls into the Type III category.[8]

Slave revolts of all three types occurred throughout the slave period and in all the slave regions of the United States. The distribution of types of slave revolts in time and space is summarized in Table 4. If the slave period is divided into Pre-1776 or Colonial, 1776–1800 or Revolutionary, 1801–1829 or Old South Slave, and 1830–1860 or Deep South Slave periods, a number of broad trends are observable. In the Colonial period, slave revolts occurred in Northern colonies as well as in Southern colonies; in the Southern colonies they developed primarily in Virginia and South Carolina. In the Revolutionary period with the disappearance of the slave system from the North and its extension in the South, slave revolts necessarily originated only in Southern states, primarily in Virginia, South Carolina, and Louisiana. During the predominance of slavery in the Old South, slave revolts mainly occurred there and in border states. As the New South pattern was entrenched in the final period of slavery, slave revolts took place there as well as in other parts of the slave region.[9]

[4] Aptheker, op. cit., pp. 297–98.

[5] Table 2 summarizes the data on Type II Revolts.

[6] The characterization of Type I and Type II Revolts has been based primarily on an analysis of their prototypes. Despite necessarily fragmentary evidence, it was decided to classify 28 other revolts as Type I or Type II. There are, however, 22 other conspiracies on which data are insufficient to classify as either Type I or Type II, but on which there is some useful information; they have been placed in a residual category: "?." The following conspiracies fall into Type "?": Ark.-La. 1856; D.C. 1838; Ky. 1810, 1838; La. 1812, 1835, 1856; N.C. 1825, 1835; S.C. 1713, 1829, 1835; Ga. 1835; Md. 1805; N.J. 1772; Tenn. 1856; Texas 1856; Va. 1709, 1710, 1723, 1730, 1810.

[7] Table 3 summarizes the data on Type III Revolts.

[8] Texas 1851. Aptheker, op. cit., p. 343.

[9] For relative and absolute shifts in the Negro population of various states see United States Bureau of the Census, Negro Population 1790–1915 (Washington, 1918), pp. 51, 57.

A noteworthy aspect of the distribution of slave revolts is the concentration of types of slave revolts in time. Type I Revolts occur fairly consistently throughout the slave period with slight peaks in the Colonial and Old South periods. Type II Revolts are a predominantly Colonial phenomenon (56 percent), while Type III are concentrated in the New South Period (58 percent). The predominance of Type II Revolts in the last period of slavery may be attributed to the increasingly oppressive character of slavery during this time, particularly in the New South, which made any other type of revolt virtually impracticable.

Finally, it should be mentioned that slave revolts were not evenly distributed spatially over the slave region. They were concentrated within three main areas: Virginia (25 percent), Louisiana (15 percent), and South Carolina (15.5 percent). Further, despite variations in time, within these states revolts clustered in a few counties. In Virginia revolts tended to recur in the coastal tobacco counties; Gabriel Prosser's revolt, however, encompassed the inland counties of Henrico, Louisa, Hanover, Chesterfield, and Caroline,[10] some of which were involved in another Type I Revolt in 1816. The following tabulation summarizes the agricultural situation in the eighteen insurrection counties of Virginia in 1860:

Eighteen Revolt Counties (12 percent) of Virginia—1860 [11]
percent of State total

Crop: tobacco	14	Slaves	24
Slave holders	25	Holdings (acres)	
(300–499	0	1,000+	15
200–299	50	3–9	13
1–3	24)		

The slave revolt counties of Virginia were primarily tobacco plantation counties. In tobacco culture "the great properties were usually divided ... into several plantations for more convenient operation." [12] Thus slavery under this system was less oppressive than in the Mississippi Delta region of the New South period.

With one exception the slave revolts of South Carolina was restricted to Charleston County. The principal plantation crop was rice, which involved larger plantation units and a greater number of slaves than tobacco, a task system of production, and frequently absentee landlordism.[13] The following tabulation summarizes the agricultural picture in the two insurrection counties of South Carolina in 1860:

[10] Aptheker, op. cit., p. 226.
[11] United States Census Office, Agriculture of the United States in 1860 (Washington, 1864), pp. 155, 159, 163, 218–19, 243–45.
[12] Ulrich Bonnell Phillips, American Negro Slavery (New York, 1952), p. 84.
[13] Ibid., pp. 89, 228, 250, 258.

TABLE 4
DISTRIBUTION OF SLAVE REVOLTS

Type	Pre-1776	1776–1800	1801–1829	1830–1860	Total
I	Percent	Percent	Percent	Percent	Percent
N.Y.	1.5	0.0	0.0	0.0	
Md.	1.5	0.0	0.0	0.0	
Va.	3.0	4.5	1.5	0.0	
S.C.	1.5	0.0	3.0	0.0	
Ga.	0.0	0.0	3.0	1.5	
La.	0.0	0.0	0.0	4.5	
	8.0	4.5	8.0	6.0	26.5
II	Percent	Percent	Percent	Percent	Percent
N.Y.	1.5	0.0	0.0	0.0	
Va.	3.0	1.5	0.0	1.5	
N.C.	0.0	1.5	0.0	0.0	
S.C.	4.5	0.0	0.0	0.0	
Ga.	1.5	0.0	0.0	0.0	
La.	1.5	1.5	1.5	0.0	
Miss.	0.0	0.0	0.0	1.5	
	12.0	4.5	1.5	3.0	21.5
"?"	Percent	Percent	Percent	Percent	Percent
N.J.	1.5	0.0	0.0	0.0	
Md.	0.0	0.0	1.5	0.0	
D.C.	0.0	0.0	0.0	1.5	
Ky.	0.0	0.0	1.5	1.5	
Tenn.	0.0	0.0	0.0	1.5	
N.C.	0.0	0.0	1.5	1.5	
S.C.	1.5	0.0	1.5	1.5	
Ga.	0.0	0.0	0.0	1.5	
La.	0.0	0.0	1.5	4.5	
Texas	0.0	0.0	0.0	1.5	
Va.	6.0	0.0	1.5	0.0	33.0
	9.0	0.0	9.0	15.0	
III	Percent	Percent	Percent	Percent	Percent
Penn.	1.5	0.0	0.0	0.0	
Md.	0.0	0.0	0.0	1.5	
Ky.	0.0	0.0	1.5	1.5	
Mo.	0.0	0.0	0.0	3.0	
Va.	0.0	1.5	0.0	0.0	
S.C.	1.5	0.0	0.0	0.0	
La.	0.0	0.0	0.0	1.5	
Ga.	0.0	0.0	0.0	1.5	
Ga.-Md.	0.0	0.0	1.5	0.0	
Texas	0.0	0.0	0.0	1.5	
	3.0	2.0	3.0	11.0	19.0
TOTAL	32.0%	11.0%	22.0%	35.0%	100.0%

Two Revolt Counties (7 percent) of South Carolina—1860 [14]

	percent of State total
Crop: rice	63
Slave holders	11
(1,000+	100
500–999	43
1–3	19)
Slaves	14
Holdings (acres)	
1,000+	8
3–9	17

Considering the patently oppressive nature of the slave system associated with rice culture, it does not seem accidental that slave insurrections should have taken place predominantly in Charleston County with its major urban complex.

Although a few slave revolts in Louisiana occurred in the vicinity of New Orleans, most of the revolts recurred in counties bordering the Mississippi River north and west of Baton Rouge. Although there was considerable agricultural diversification in these counties, they were primarily sugar producers. Like rice, sugar production involved large numbers of robust adult slaves.[15] The general agricultural set-up in the insurrection counties of Louisiana in 1860 is summarized in the following tabulation:

Ten Revolt Counties (21 percent) of Louisiana—1860 [16]

	percent of State total
Crops: rice	15
cotton	16
cane sugar	41
Slave holders	38
(500–999	25
300–499	35
1–3	23)
Slaves	30
Holdings (acres)	
1,000+	25
3–9	33

Among the factors which may have facilitated the development of these up-river revolts are proximity to a great communication network, agricultural diversification, and a fairly high proportion of small holdings.

Thus the pattern of a real clustering of slave revolts irrespective of temporal variations suggests that aside from the immediate catalysts which might induce a particular slave revolt, certain socio-economic variables facilitated

[14] United States Census Office, op. cit., pp. 129, 214, 237.
[15] Phillips, op. cit., pp. 164–67, 245.
[16] United States Census Office, op. cit., pp. 67, 69, 202, 230.

their occurrence and recurrence in certain areas. Fundamentally, these socio-economic factors imply an alleviation of the condition of slavery due either to the type of plantation system itself or to access to external sources of communication as inherent in propinquity to an urban center or a transportation network. These constitute a few of the factors which are considered necessary preconditions for slave revolts.

Other more immediate factors also seem to constitute preconditions for slave revolts. These may include rapid population fluctuations often leading to a significantly higher proportion of Negroes in an area [17] and revolutionary ideas current in the wider society of the time.[18] In my view, none of these possible preconditions constitute sufficient cause for the development of a slave revolt. Rather there must be a catalyst in the form of an individual or individuals.

This catalyst may arise from within or without the slave system. The leaders of slave revolts have been drawn from the social categories of free Negro, slave, and white. The type of revolt does not appear to be determined by the social type of the catalyst. Vesey (Type I) was a free Negro, Prosser (Type I) and Turner (Type II) were slaves, Boxley (Type I) and Doyle (Type III) were whites.[19] Nevertheless, Boxley is probably exceptional, as the ultimate aim of a Type I Revolt would be unlikely to appeal to many whites.

Although very little data on Negro leaders of slave revolts are available, the three leaders of the most famous revolts furnish suggestions of relevant social and personality variables. Each of these men had had opportunities which the ordinary field hand would never have experienced. Vesey had traveled extensively as a slave; as a freedman he was an urban artisan; he was literate and aware of the Haitiian success and the Missouri debate.[20] Both Prosser and Turner were slaves. Gabriel Prosser was a blacksmith and probably literate.[21] Turner was literate, had been a slave overseer, enjoyed making inventive experiments, and may have been a Baptist preacher.[22] Thus all three leaders had had opportunities to play more than one social role and had had access to a variety of ideas.

The personality of Negro leaders also appears to be a significant variable. The three major leaders were clearly charismatic individuals. They were imbued with a sense of personal destiny and considered themselves to be divinely inspired and sanctioned in their endeavors.[23] It seems likely that such charisma

[17] E.g., Turner's revolt and Mississippi Revolt of 1835; Aptheker, op. cit., pp. 293, 325.

[18] E.g., the influence of the Missouri debate on Vesey: Aptheker, op. cit., p. 270; the importance of David Walker's Appeal for Turner: Carroll, op. cit., p. 121.

[19] Aptheker, op. cit., pp. 255–56, 338. See Tables 1, 2 and 3.

[20] Carroll, op. cit., pp. 83, 85; Aptheker, op. cit., p. 270.

[21] Cf. Carroll, op. cit., p. 48 and T. W. Higginson, "Gabriel's Defeat," Atlantic Monthly X (1862), 338. Aptheker, op. cit., p. 220.

[22] William Sidney Drewry, The Southampton Insurrection (Washington, 1900), p. 28; Carroll, op. cit., p. 131. Cf. ibid., p. 130 and John W. Cromwell, "The Aftermath of Nat Turner's Insurrection," Journal of Negro History V (1920), 209.

[23] E.g., Turner: Carroll, op. cit., pp. 130–31; Gabriel: ibid., p. 149; Vesey: ibid., p. 87.

and egotism would be essential for any Negro leader to dare to challenge the power of the slavocracy. There is, however, an important personality difference between these leaders which appears to be linked to the type of revolt inspired by them. Neither Vesey nor Prosser was so self-absorbed that he could not formulate a rational plan and assign specific duties to assistants. The techniques which Vesey employed for binding the masses to his endeavor are particularly fascinating: among his lieutenants were a "sorcerer" whose charms were considered to make their wearers inviolable and a blind preacher who was believed to possess second-sight.[24] Vesey clearly understood the importance of psychological as well as technological preparation for the success of his scheme. Turner, on the other hand, seems to have been so self-absorbed that it is unlikely that he could have formulated and executed a consistent plan. Thus, there appears to be two personality types represented by these three leaders; the one in which rationality has precedence over egotistical emotionalism, and its converse. This distinction is borne out by the conduct of the men following their capture: Vesey and Prosser revealed very little about their intentions and maintained themselves stoically until their deaths; Turner met his fate no less courageously but after a lengthy and effusive confession. How many Vesey-Prosser and how many Turner personality types led slave revolts is unknown. It is hypothesized that only a Vesey-Prosser type could lead a Type I Revolt, though Types II and III might have been led by either personality type.[25]

The final aspect of slave revolts to be discussed is their repercussions both within the area of the revolt and in other areas. As shown in Table 5, throughout the slavery period the slavocracy reacted in a similar way to slave revolts. In its reactions it distinguished between Type III Revolts and the other types of revolt, but not between Type I and Type II Revolts.[26] Thus Type III Revolts always resulted in reprisals only against the immediate offenders. This is understandable as the situational and limited nature of this type of revolt was clear. Consequently, it was a phenomenon with which the slavocracy could deal in a relatively rational manner.

The reaction of the slavocracy to the Type I and Type II Revolts followed a different but consistent pattern.[27] A slave revolt resulted in a three-step syndrome within the area of revolt. There was an initial period of panic in which vengeance was wrought not only upon known insurgents but often upon innocent Negroes. During this period of mob panic and activity, aggression might also be vented upon white moderates within the area and upon outsiders who were disliked but not directly involved with the revolt. This period was followed

[24] *Ibid.*, pp. 91–93.
[25] Evidence from two Type I Revolts supports this hypothesis: Georgia 1819, Maryland 1739: Aptheker, *op. cit.*, pp. 191, 263.
[26] See Table 5 for summary of data.
[27] This analysis is based on the four reactions for which we have sufficient data: the revolts of Turner, Prosser and Vesey and the Mississippi Revolt of 1835. See Aptheker, *op. cit.*, pp. 226, 228, 271, 275, 300, 305; Carroll, *op. cit.*, pp. 57–60, 107–09, 138–39, 166, 176; Cromwell *op. cit.*, pp. 212, 214–15, 221, 225, 231; Drewry, *op. cit.*, p. 85; E. Franklin Frazier, *The Negro in the United States* (New York, 1957), p. 87; Higginson, *op. cit.*, pp. 341–44; Edwin A. Miles, "The Mississippi Slave Insurrection Scare of 1835," *Journal of Negro History*, XLII (1957), 49, 52–55.

TABLE 5

REPERCUSSIONS OF SLAVE REVOLTS WITHIN THE AREA AND IN OTHER AREAS

Revolt	Within the Area:										In Other Areas:				
	Panic and Vengeance against:				Repressive Measures:			Ameliorative Measures:			Revolt Rumors	Slave Unrest	Repressive Measures:		Ameliorative Measures:
	Insurgents	Other Negroes	White Moderates	Outsiders	Increased Armed Oppressions	Legislation Against: Slaves	Free Negro	Increased Emancipation Sentiment	Improved Conditions	Colonization Schemes			Legislation Against: Slaves	Free Negro	Anti-Slavery Sentiment
TYPE I															
Pre-1776															
Va. 1663	x														
N.Y. 1712	x	x				x									
Md. 1739	x														
1776–1800															
Va. 1792	x	x				x									
Va. 1800 *	x	x			x	x	x			x	S.C.	Va.	x	x	
1801–1829															
Va. 1816	x	?													
Ga. 1819	x														
S.C. 1822 *	x				x	x	x					no			North
1830–1860															
La. 1837	x	?			x										
Ga. 1841	x														
TYPE II															
Pre-1776															
Va. 1687	**x**					**x**									

Region / Date	1	2	3	4	5	6	7	8	9	10	11	North
N.Y. 1708	x			x								
La. 1730	x											
S.C. 1740	x						x					
1776–1800												
N.C. 1776	x											
Va. 1792	x											
La. 1795	?											
1801–1829												
La. 1811	?											
1830–1860												
Va. 1831 *	x	x		x		x		x		x	x	
Miss. 1835 *	x	x		x	x			x				
TYPE "7"												
Pre-1776												
Va. 1723	x			x	x							
Va. 1730	x											
1801–1829												
S.C. 1829	x		x									
1830–1860												
Ga. 1835	x		x									
N.C. 1835	x											
La. 1840	x											
La. 1856	x	x										
TYPE III												
1801–1829												
Ky. 1829	x											
1830–1860												
Mo. 1836	x							x		x	x	
Md. 1845	x								x			
Ky. 1848	x											
Mo. 1850	x											x

* See footnote 27.

by one in which increased armed oppression was used to enforce the threatened slave system. This second period was followed by one in which legislative measures were taken to prevent similar outbreaks. During the legislative debates ameliorative measures such as colonization schemes and proposals to reduce the oppressive character of the slave system were frequently discussed but rarely enacted. The upshot of the legislative period was invariably the harshening of repressive laws against both slaves and free Negroes.

Another aspect of the reaction of the slavocracy to a major slave revolt was the spread of the three-step syndrome, either partially or completely, to other slave areas not affected by the revolt. In part these measures may have been justified, for there is evidence that occasionally slaves in other areas were stimulated to emulate the attempts of the initial insurgents.

Nevertheless, both within the initial area of revolt and in other areas, the actual threat to the slavocracy was never great enough to invoke the exaggerated penalties which it evoked.[28] Yet indubitably the psychological threat makes this pattern comprehensible: a slave revolt whatever its form expresses the realization of the worst fears of the slavocracy and assaults its security at its most vulnerable point. These fears must be suppressed at all costs although the repressive measures taken were perceived by the slavocracy to lead to even greater threats to the system, for the members of the slavocracy assumed that an ill-treated slave was more likely to revolt than a well-treated one.

The data presented in this analysis support a rather different conclusion from that of the slavocracy as to the effect of their measures. This conclusion has been vividly expressed by Frederick Douglass and has been stated more systematically recently by Davies and Elkins.[29] In *My Bondage* Douglass wrote: " 'Beat and cuff your slave, keep him hungry and spiritless, and he will follow the chain of his master like a dog; but feed and clothe him well,—work him moderately—surround him with physical comfort,—and dreams of freedom intrude.' " [30] As has been noted in the preceding analysis, slave revolts tended to cluster in less oppressive slave areas and the catalyst for a revolt was an individual who had had opportunities to play multiple roles.[31] On the other hand, given the high rate of betrayal of conspiracies by oppressed individuals who identified themselves more closely with the master than the slave, the adverse impact upon most slaves of the repressive measures of the slavocracy, and the absolute power of the slavocracy, one can but conclude that slave revolts in the United States were doomed to failure.

[28] This fact was recognized by some contemporary observers. For example, less than ten days after Turner's bloody revolt, General Epps wrote the Governor of Virginia that local fear was exaggerated and that at no time were more than twenty men needed to put down the rebellion. Quoted in Drewry, *op. cit.*, p. 88.

[29] James C. Davies, "Toward a Theory of Revolution," *American Sociological Review*, XXVII (1962), 6; Stanley M. Elkins, *Slavery* (Chicago, 1959).

[30] Quoted in Kenneth M. Stampp, *The Peculiar Institution* (New York, 1956), p. 89.

[31] For the implications of multiple role-playing see Elkins, *op. cit.*, pp. 112 ff, 137–38.

Vincent Harding

RELIGION AND RESISTANCE AMONG ANTEBELLUM NEGROES, 1800–1860

Christianity began as a religion that appealed principally to the slaves and underprivileged freedmen of the Roman Empire. To use Friedrich Nietzsche's phrase, Christian ethics functioned as a "slave morality," sanctifying meekness and nonresistance toward the oppressor while glorifying the weak, the poor, and the humble as the "salt of the earth." For the masses of American Negroes, the Christian religion has likewise functioned principally as a compensatory escape from the harsh realities of daily life. Yet the recent prominence of Reverend Martin Luther King symbolizes the fact that religion has had a dual role. While it has served basically as a mechanism of accommodation to the American social order, it has also provided an important wellspring of Negro protest. Vincent Harding's paper is a fresh and suggestive examination of the religious motivation that often underlay resistance to bondage.

I N these days of ecumenism among the academic disciplines, it would likely be both fair and appropriate to describe the state of our historical understanding of Negro religion in America as a variety of cultural lag. This is clearly the case when we try to assess the role of black religion in the antebellum period of American history, and especially when an attempt is made to understand its relationship to acts of protest and resistance.

Stated in simplest terms, the situation may be described in this way: Thanks to the crucial work of Aptheker, the Bauers, Stampp and others we have moved beyond a naive and often distorted view of happy or indifferent Negro slaves whose docility was a sight to behold.[1] Indeed the movement to-

Printed with the permission of Vincent Harding.
[1] See especially Herbert Aptheker, *American Negro Slave Revolts*, Paperback edition

wards the new theme of slave rebellion and resistance has often been so strong that the inevitable reconsiderations and revisions have already set in.[2] But it would appear unlikely that even such fascinating and worthy caveats as those raised by Elkins, Wade and Genovese will drive us back to the old dominions— if for no other reason than the uneasiness our increasingly black-oriented age feels with such interpretations. So the new slaves seem to be a permanent fixture. On the other hand, we have not yet been released from the traditional views of black religion which supported the older generalizations concerning submissive and humble slaves. Here precisely is the lag.

Much of current historical opinion about the role of religion among antebellum southern Negroes still follows the classic lines set out in Benjamin Mays' *The Negro's God*, which claimed that the Negroes' idea of God "kept them submissive, humble and obedient." [3] Repeatedly Mays referred to this religion as "otherworldly" and "compensatory," inclining its votaries "to do little or nothing to improve their status here..." [4] Even so shrewd and perceptive a scholar as E. Franklin Frazier later adumbrated the theme in his important work on *The Negro Church*. [5] There the antebellum Negroes—especially in the South—were identified with a religion that "turned their minds from the sufferings and privations of this world to a world after death where the weary would find rest and the victims of injustice would be compensated." [6]

The views of Mays and Frazier are representative of most discussions of the black religion that developed before the Civil War. In many ways these men helped to set the theme. Their views, of course, represented an American adaptation of the classic statement by Karl Marx:

> Religion is the sign of the oppressed creature, the heart of the heartless world...the spirit of a spiritless situation. It is the *opium* of the people.[7]

In this essay what we question is not the applicability of such an understanding of religion to a majority of antebellum Negroes. Indeed, the tradi-

---

(New York: International Publishers, 1963); Raymond A. Bauer and Alice H. Bauer, "Day to Day Resistance to Slavery," *Journal of Negro History*, xxvii, 4 (October, 1942), 388–419; Kenneth M. Stampp, *The Peculiar Institution*, Paperback edition (New York: Vintage Books, 1956), particularly Chap. III.

[2] Some of the most persuasive concerns are raised in Stanley M. Elkins, *Slavery*, Paperback edition (New York: Grosset and Dunlap, 1963); Richard C. Wade, *Slavery in the Cities* (New York: Oxford University, 1964); also Wade's "The Vesey Plot: A Reconsideration," *Journal of Negro History*, xxx, 2 (May, 1964), 143–161; Eugene D. Genovese, "The Legacy of Slavery and the Roots of Black Nationalism," *Studies on the Left*, vi, 6 (November–December, 1966), 3–26.

[3] Benjamin E. Mays, *The Negro's God as Reflected in His Literature* (Boston: Chapman and Grimes, 1938), 26.

[4] *Ibid.*, 24.

[5] *The Negro Church in America* (New York: Schocken Books, 1964).

[6] *Ibid.*, 45

[7] Karl Marx and Friedrich Engels, *On Religion* (New York: Schocken Books, 1964), 42; quoted from the "Introduction to Marx's Contribution to the Critique of Hegel's Philosophy of Right."

tional view often has much support in the records. For instance, it was not accidental that a slaveholder said in the 1830's, "The deeper the piety of the slave, the more valuable he is in every respect." [8] This was a widespread opinion. Nor was that eloquent refugee from slavery, William Wells Brown, wrong when in 1850 he claimed that religious instruction for his fellow-bondsmen consisted "in teaching the slave that he must never strike a white man; that God made him a slave; and that when whipped he must find no fault ..." [9]

That was likely an accurate description of most instruction, and many slaves seemed to live by it. (Generally, of course, they had no other choice than to give at least an impression that they did.) However the present dispute does not center there. Rather this paper seeks to raise the issue of the ambiguity, the doubleness, of black religious experience, indeed of all religious experience. It seeks not to deny the opiate quality of much slave religion but to offer the suggestion that there were significant, identifiable black responses to religion which often stormed beyond submissiveness to defiance.

Perhaps Frederick Douglass best sets the scene for an understanding of this ambiguous and two-edged Negro reaction to religious teaching. In one of his autobiographical writings, this most famous of fugitive slaves, recorded words which scarcely covered his underlying scorn. He said,

> I have met, at the south, many good, religious colored people who were under the delusion that God required them to submit to slavery and to wear their chains with meekness and humility.

Then he added, "I could entertain no such nonsense as this ..." [10] For Douglass, as for countless others, the requirements of God pointed in other directions, and black religion led them away from slavery. Often it led to protest, resistance and death.

Recently a teacher of religion has tried to articulate this theme of the protest role of Negro faith. In his *Black Religion*, Joseph Washington wrote, "the religion of the Negro folk was chosen to bear roles of both protest and relief." [11] Indeed Washington went on to suggest that "the uniqueness of black religion" since the days of slavery was to be found in its constant and often risky search for "the elusive but ultimate goal of freedom and equality by means of protest and action." [12] Like so much of Washington's work, those last phrases may be overstatement, but they help to balance the scales set by Frazier, Mays and Marx.

Perhaps, then, this paper can be thought of as an attempt to suggest pathways towards an historical documentation of Joseph Washington's intuitive thesis, at least that part of it which seeks to appreciate the proper re-

[8] Quoted in Haven P. Perkins, "Religion for Slaves: Difficulties and Methods," *Church History*, x, 3 (September, 1941), 228–245.
[9] *Narrative of the Life of William Wells Brown* (London: Charles Gilpin, 1850), 82–83.
[10] *Life and Times*, Paperbook edition (New York: Crowell-Collier, 1962), 85.
[11] (Boston: Beacon Press, 1964), 33.
[12] *Ibid*

lationship of black religion to Negro protest and resistance. Without such an attempt we shall be in danger of fruitlessly trying to apply the religion of Ulrich Phillips' Negroes to the defiant men and women who often leap out of the pages of Aptheker and Stampp. To quote Douglass slightly out of context, "we can entertain no such nonsense as this . . ." (Even Marxists came to realize that religious commitment might produce revolutionary action.[13] Those who claim to be unhindered by the fetters of ideology can do no less.)

I I

It has seemed wise for the present to confine this statement to the period 1800–1860, and to focus on Negroes in the South. Therefore it may be significant to note that it was in 1800 that South Carolina's legislature indicated a keen awareness of the possible connections between black rebellion and black religion, an awareness that was apparently the property of many southern white persons. In that year the legislature passed one of the first of those countless 19th century laws restricting black religious services. This one forbade Negroes

> even in company with white persons to meet together and assemble
> for the purpose of . . . religious worship, either before the rising of the
> sun or after the going down of the same.[14]

Magistrates were given the power to break up all such gatherings. Behind the legislation was obviously a fear that these religious meetings might lead to trouble, especially if they were held at hours when they could not easily be monitored.

If the fear needed substantiation it was soon available. In Virginia's Henrico county Tom Prosser's slave, Gabriel, and Gabriel's brother, Martin, were then gathering slaves and free Negroes at strange hours and making strange uses of "religious services." Gabriel was plotting insurrection, and building a force that had evidently mounted into the thousands by 1800. At their religious services it was said that both Martin and Gabriel—what fitting names!—regularly set forth

> an impassioned exposition of Scripture . . . The Israelites were glow-
> ingly portrayed as a type of successful resistance to tyranny; and it
> was argued, that now, as then, God would stretch forth his arm to
> save, and would strengthen a hundred to overthrow a thousand.[15]

[13] See Engels on "The Peasant War in Germany," in Marx and Engels, *On Religion,* 97–118; also Eduard Bernstein, *Cromwell and Communism* (New York: Schocken Books, 1963).
[14] Quoted in W. E. B. DuBois (ed.), *The Negro Church* (Atlanta: The Atlanta University Press, 1903), 22.
[15] Harvey Wish, "American Slave Insurrections Before 1861," *Journal of Negro History,* xxii, 3 (July, 1937), 311; Thomas Wentworth Higginson, *Travellers and Outlaws* (Boston: Lee and Shepard, 1889), 1899; Aptheker, *Slave Revolts,* 220–224.

The black men of Henrico county were the new Israelites. Gabriel was their Moses. Would they follow?

It is not known how deeply this appeal from the Old Testament moved the persons who gathered in those secret meetings, nor which of them joined the attempted rebellion in response to it. But the analogy to the Israelites was a traditional one in the black community, and it continued to have great force among the slaves. Therefore it would not be too much to expect that some of the men who set themselves on the path of rebellion in those Virginia meetings were responding to a profoundly religious call, as well as to the news from Santo Domingo, or to the stirring cries of "Death or Liberty." Haiti was a good example, and the political motto was a moving cry, but it surely helped to believe as well that the God of Israel would "stretch forth his arm" to intervene on behalf of the blacks.[16]

When the insurrection was foiled by the sudden downpour of torrential rains, the white residents of Virginia would, of course, have been justified in thinking that divine intervention was indeed present—on their side.[17] But they were likely caused to be suspicious about other religious matters as the trials of the rebels revealed that Methodists and Quakers—as well as Frenchmen—were to be spared the vengeful swords of Gabriel's band.[18] What could that mean?

Religion and its relationship to black rebellion continued to be a matter for concern and for questions in Virginia, even before the coming of Nat Turner. For instance, one Richard Byrd of that state wrote to his Governor in May, 1810, to express his conviction that "slave preachers used their religious meetings as veils for revolutionary schemes," and he cited a "General Peter" from Isle of Wight as an example of the danger.[19]

Six years later this kind of fear was given solid ground in the Old Dominion again, but it was a white preacher who now seemed to be using black religion for seditious purposes. George Boxley, proprietor of a county store, was a regular participant in the religious meetings held by the Negroes of Spottsylvania and Louisa counties. Soon he began telling them "that a little white bird had brought him a holy message to deliver his fellowmen from bondage..."[20] Again the promise of divinely aided deliverance found active response, and Phillips says that Boxley "enlisted many blacks in his project" for messianic insurrection. Unfortunately for the black believers, as was so often the case, the plot was betrayed. Some Negro followers were hanged, others were sold out of the state, but Boxley escaped from jail.[21] Perhaps the message of deliverance had been meant only for him. After all, it was a white bird.

[16] *Ibid.*, 220.
[17] See citations in note 15.
[18] Aptheker, *Slave Revolts*, 224.
[19] *Ibid.*, 246.
[20] Ulrich B. Phillips, *American Negro Slavery*, Paperback edition (Baton Rouge: Louisiana State University, 1966), 476.
[21] *Ibid.*

The pattern of religious connections to rebellious movements continued consistently into South Carolina in the same year—1816. There, in Camden, a plot had evidently been maturing, and when the almost inevitable betrayal and arrests finally came, a local newspaper offered its own version of the relationship between religion and resistance:

> It is a melancholy fact [the editor said] that those who were most active in the conspiracy occupied a respectable stand in one of the churches, several were professors [i.e., avowed Christians], and one a class leader.[22]

Camden was not the only place in South Carolina where black Christians and class leaders were making life difficult for the keepers of the established order. Charleston was having its difficulties with the darker variety of Methodists, trouble that would eventually lead into deep distress.[23]

The Negroes in the port city's Methodist congregations had long outnumbered their white brethren by ten to one. They had known a sense of significant independence through their own quarterly conference and as a result of the control they exercised over finances and the discipline of their members. In 1815 alleged "abuses" had led to the loss of these privileges as well as much of the independence that went with them. But black church leaders like Denmark Vesey, Peter Poyas and Jack Pritchard (Gullah Jack) had no intentions of accepting such debilitating penalties without offering direct and open response.

They led agitation among the Negro members, rounded up a thousand new members and sent two of their leaders up to Philadelphia to be ordained by the African Methodist Episcopal bishops there. Then in 1818 a dispute over their burial ground provided the occasion for more than 4000 of the 6000 black Methodists to withdraw their membership en masse from the white Charleston congregations. With ordained ministers of their own they now moved ahead to build a meeting house and establish an independent congregation called the African Church of Charleston.

It is in this context that we may speak more precisely of rebellion. Here the crucial issue is not the nature of what happened in 1822, not the matter of whether widely organized insurrection was being planned.[24] At this juncture it is of critical importance simply to see that organized rebellion on another level had already been built deeply into the structure of black church life in Charleston. The agitation from 1815 to 1818 and the concerted withdrawal from the white congregations in the latter year took significant courage for the slaves. The raising of an independent house of worship implied not only the gathering of financial resources, but it was clearly an act of defiance for

---

[22] Aptheker, *Slave Revolts*, 258.

[23] The story of the pre-1822 struggles of the black Methodists of Charleston is developed most fully in Phillips, *American Negro Slavery*, 420–421.

[24] Richard Wade, in his works cited in note 2 above, expresses strong doubts about the extent and significance of the insurrectionary plans.

the world to see. The municipal officials knew this and responded accordingly with harassments, arrests, banishments, and finally with the closing of the church in 1821.[25] It is, then, essential to note that the sense of black solidarity was imbedded in the organization of the Negro church. Attempts to dilute this or break it down met inevitably with resistance, resistance centered in that church's life.

Did the defiance include a wider plan for insurrection? It is not the purpose of this essay to enter into the argument that has been interestingly raised by Mr. Wade. However, my own examination of available evidence leads me to suspect that the plot was "more than loose talk by aggrieved and embittered men."[26] These men had already given evidence of impressive skill in organizing black discontent for action. They had followers in their defiance, and their leadership was evidently trusted. There was no reason for them to be content with "loose talk" by 1822.

Whatever the extent of the new action being planned, it seems clear that some continuing organizing was going on, that it was centered in the membership of the African Church and that the charismatic Denmark Vesey was at the heart of the affair.[27] Now, for our purposes it is necessary only to continue to deal with the role of religion as it participated in a movement that went beyond the defense of church-oriented prerogatives to new and likely bolder concerns. If, as seems probable, an insurrection was being planned, Vesey surely knew how to continue to use themes that had led the blacks to organize for independent church status.

His focus was regularly on religion. One witness testified that this leader's "general conversation . . . was about religion, which he would apply to slavery." Indeed, "all his religious remarks were mingled with slavery," according to the testimony.[28] Was this surprising? For the most part these were church members who were being addressed, and they were also slaves. What other focus was more natural? These were also persons whose extant religious records indicate that they were profoundly attracted to the analogy between their condition and the condition of the Hebrews in Egypt. As a class leader, Vesey surely knew all this very well. So one of the alleged conspirators was probably quite accurate when he said that Denmark Vesey "read to us from the Bible, how the *children of Israel were delivered out of Egypt from bondage* . . ."[29] Nor did the persuasive exhorter stop there. It is said that he made it clear to

[25] Phillips, *loc. cit.*

[26] Wade, "The Vesey Plot," 160.

[27] See Aptheker, *Slave Revolts*, 268–276; Higginson, 215–275; John W. Lofton, Jr., "Denmark Vesey's Call to Arms," *Journal of Negro History*, xxxiii, 4 (October, 1948), 395–417; Sterling Stuckey, "Remembering Denmark Vesey," *Negro Digest*, xv, 4 (February, 1966), 28–41—a direct response to Wade's questions; Marion L. Starkey, *Striving to Make It My Home* (New York: W. W. Norton and Company, 1964), 152–210; Corporation of Charleston, *An Account of the Late Intended Insurrection* (Charleston: n.p. 1822.)

[28] Higginson, 228.

[29] Corporation of Charleston, 34 [italics in original].

the bondsmen that it was imperative to their faith that slaves "attempt their emancipation, 'however shocking and bloody might be the consequences.'" And on the strength of his magnificent authority as a class leader—and as a man—he declared that such efforts would be "pleasing to the Almighty," and that their success was thereby guaranteed.[30]

If, as we are suggesting, religion did play a critical role in the motivating of his followers, then Vesey chose wisely (or was fortunate, if he did not make the choice himself) when he gained an accomplice like Jack Pritchard, better known as Gullah Jack. This black man of Angolan background provided an excellent counterpoint to Vesey's Old Testament theme. For he was not only a member of the African Church but a conjurer, a medicine man in the African tradition. Therefore Vesey had the best of both religious worlds, and we are told that Gullah Jack exerted tremendous influence over the other members of his ancestral group.[31]

This, of course, does not mean that Vesey did not seek to rally his forces through the use of other issues as well. The tradition of Santo Domingo, the debate over Missouri, the general mistreatment of the Negroes by the city authorities and by some of their masters—these were all part of the strategy.[32] But it would be derelict to fail to note how crucial was the religious issue, especially in the light of the post-1814 church experiences. Was this not the significance of the note found in Peter Poyas' trunk after he was arrested: "Fear not, the Lord God that delivered Daniel is able to deliver us."[33]

Then in the summer of 1822, when deliverance appeared to have been aborted and the gallows were heavy with black bodies, it was fitting that the city should demolish the First African Church[34] This was not only a rehearsal of more modern southern church treatment, but it was a testimony to the significant role the people of that congregation had played in carrying the contagion of rebellion. Nor was it surprising that an Episcopalian minister boasted that such things could never happen among black Episcopalians because their Negroes "were not allowed to exhort or expound scriptures in words of their own ... and to utter ... whatever nonsense might happen into their minds."[35]

Regardless of how we see such matters now, it was evidently clear to most Charlestonians of the time that "religious enthusiasm" had been one of the motivating forces in Vesey's action. So all preachers of the gospel to slaves —white and black—were suspect.[36] And a Charleston editor condemned the white Christian missionaries who

[30] Higginson, 404.
[31] On Gullah Jack see especially Starkey and Corporation of Charleston, as cited in note 27.
[32] Corporation of Charleston, 39.
[33] Wish, 410.
[34] Phillips, 421.
[35] Quoted in Perkins, "Religion for Slaves," 232.
[36] Donald G. Mathews, *Slavery and Methodism* (Princeton: Princeton University Press, 1965), 41.

with the Sacred Volume of God in one hand scattered with the other the firebrands of discord and destruction; and *secretly* dispensed among our Negro Population, the seeds of discontent and sedition.[37]

Though he saw much, the editor did not see that the firebrands and the seeds were often in the same hand as "the Sacred Volume," but he surely must have known that the hands were often black.

At least this was the case with Nat Turner, who carried his own Volume, fire and seeds. Whatever doubts we may entertain about the authenticity of Vesey's rebellion, Turner leaves us with no choice. Even more important for our present concerns is the central theme of Turner's *Confession*—the theme of a black, avenging Messiah, urged into action by nothing less than the repeated calling of God.[38] Here was religion and resistance that would not be separated.

Based primarily on the *Confession*, the story develops. As a child he became convinced that he was "intended for some great purpose." Evidently he nurtured the search for his destiny through arduous prayer and fasting and the development of an austere personal life. Turner claimed to be directed many times by "the Spirit" as it spoke to him in his lonely vigils or as he worked in the fields. A major theme of that direction was "Seek ye the kingdom of Heaven and all things shall be added unto you." When asked later about this "Spirit," the 31-year-old prisoner made it clear that he stood self-consciously in the prophetic tradition, for he said that he had been visited by "The Spirit that spoke to the Prophets in former days."

Eventually the young mystic became fully confirmed in his sense of ordination to some "great purpose in the hands of the Almighty," and he went through his own Wilderness experience—thirty days in the forests of Virginia as a runaway slave. Then the Spirit drove him back for his great encounter with the future. In 1825 Turner saw his first major vision suggestively describing his ultimate calling. White and black spirits were battling in the air. Thunder rang out, the sun was darkened, and he watched in awe as blood flowed through the land. The same Spirit promised him the wisdom and strength needed for the task.

After a fascinating variety of other visions, the critical revelation came in May, 1828. According to Nat,

I heard a loud noise in the heavens and the Spirit instantly appeared to me and said the Serpent was loosened, and Christ had laid down the Yoke he had borne for the sins of men, and that I should take it

[37] *Ibid.*, 42.

[38] Turner's *Confession, Trial and Execution* was originally published in 1881 by T. R. Gray in Petersburg, Virginia. However it is most accessible in Herbert Aptheker, *Nat Turner's Slave Rebellion* (New York: Humanities Press, 1966). I have used the same text as it appeared in "The Confession, Trial and Execution of Nat Turner," *Negro Digest*, xiv, 9 (July, 1965), 28–48. The source will not be cited again until it seems appropriate in the development of Turner's story.

on and fight against the Serpent, for the time was fast approaching when the first should be last and the last should be first.

The Spirit also revealed to him that there would be adequate signs in nature to let him know when he should begin the messianic work for which he was ordained, when to "arise and prepare myself to slay my enemies with their own weapons." In an eclipse of the sun—that most ancient of signs— Nat Turner found his signal to begin. He ate a last supper with some of his followers and went forth to carry out his own version of the work of Christ, using the weapons of the Old Testament, drenching the ground with blood, for "neither age nor sex was to be spared." And when he was asked if he thought himself mistaken as he faced execution at the end, Turner's response came fittingly enough: "Was not Christ crucified?" To the charge of dastardly crime, his plea, of course, was "Not Guilty."

Obviously Nat Turner was one of those religious charismatics who arise in a variety of settings, from the walls of Münster to the fields of Southampton County.[39] He was not a "preacher" in any formal sense of the word, and evidently belonged to no structured church group. But he was an "exhorter," and he clearly convinced his fellow slaves by the power of his message and the strange sense of his presence that he was the anointed one of God for their deliverance—a deliverance for which slaves never ceased to yearn.

No other explanation will open the intricacies of Nat Turner. Thus when they were wounded and waiting to die, it was said of his companions that some of them "in the aggonies [sic] of Death declared that they was going happy fore that God had a hand in what they had been doing..."[40] They still believed that "Prophet Nat" was sent from God.

When all the dyings were over, after the fierce retaliations had taken place, the conviction and the legend lived on. Black people believed and remembered, and some acted. The religion of Nat Turner, the religion of black rebellion became part of their tradition.[41] Whites, on the other hand, believed variations of the black themes and acted in their own ways. Their response was well summed up by a writer in the Richmond *Enquirer* who said then:

> The case of Nat Turner warns us. No black man ought to be permitted to turn a preacher through the country. The law must be enforced—or the tragedy of Southampton appeals to us in vain.[42]

In the minds of blacks and whites alike religion and rebellion had been welded into one terrifying—or exalting—reality through the black body of Nat Turner.

[39] For the story of the Münsterites see George H. Williams, *The Radical Reformation* (London: Weidenfeld and Nicolson, 1962), 362–386.

[40] Aptheker, *Nat Turner's Slave Rebellion*, 38.

[41] From the lives of Frederick Douglass and Harriet Tubman to "The Ballad of Nat Turner" in a recently published book of poems by Robert Hayden, *Selected Poems* (New York: October House, 1966), the tradition has been carefully and faithfully maintained.

[42] Quoted in George Washington Williams, *History of the Negro Race in America*, 2 vols. (New York: G. P. Putnam's Sons, 1883), II, 90.

So the laws set off by fear swept through the states, forbidding Negroes to preach, in many places interdicting all meetings, attempting as it were to exorcise so troubling a religious spirit.[43] The Mississippi law of 1831 provided a good example when it ruled that "It is 'unlawful for any slave, free Negro, or mulatto to preach the gospel' under pain of receiving thirty-nine lashes upon the naked back of the ... preacher."[44]

The laws did not stop the strange gospel of freedom from infiltrating into the ranks of the slaves—partly because it was already there. So an insurrectionary attempt came to light in Duplin County, North Carolina, in the fall of 1831, even before Turner had been captured. In the course of its account a newspaper article revealed that "a very intelligent negro preacher named David, was put on his trial ... and clearly convicted ..." as one of the ringleaders.[45] Elsewhere in that same year another newspaper correspondent says, "It is much to be regretted that [the apparent wave of insurrectionary attempts] are instigated by fierce, ignorant fanatics, assuming to be preachers." His comment closed with this prophecy: "I forsee that this land must one day or other, become a field of blood."[46] Thus in the mind of at least one man, black preachers of religion might well lead a people to bloody revolution. Strange opium.

In 1833 when Frederick Douglass, still a slave, tried to organize a Sabbath School class among the black young people of the Eastern Shore of Maryland, he found out that this white co-religionists had not yet disassociated themselves from earlier memories and convictions. Two Methodist class leaders led the mob that stormed Douglass' Sabbath School and Douglass said he was told by one Methodist that "I wanted to be another Nat Turner, and that, if I did not look out, I should get as many balls in me as Nat did into him."[47]

Two years later, during the slave insurrection scare in Mississippi, it was again said that "suspicion centered around the 'itinerant preachers' " and other troublemakers in the neighborhood.[48] In New Orleans the newspapers were complaining in 1839 about a Negro church which was "the greatest of all public nuisances and den for hatching plots against [the] masters."[49] Seven years later the same problem existed in the city as the police arrested twelve Negroes in "a makeshift church" and charged them with "the habit of repairing to this place for ... singing hymns and cantiques which was followed by sermons the subject of which was the most inflammatory character."[50] Firebrands and sermons were continually being combined by black men whose re-

[43] DuBois (ed.), The Negro Church, 25.
[44] Ibid.
[45] Narrative of the Tragical Scene ... in Southampton County (n.p., Werner and West, 1831), 23.
[46] Ibid., 20.
[47] Douglass, 111.
[48] Quoted in Edwin A. Miles, "The Mississippi Slave Insurrection Scare of 1835," Journal of Negro History, xlii, 1 (January, 1957), 51.
[49] Quoted in Wade, Slavery in the Cities, 83.
[50] Ibid., 83–84.

ligion had not yet made them "otherworldly" enough to suit the authorities.

It may be that the ambiguous nature of American religion, as it related to antebellum blacks, was best seen by a visitor to this land, one who had become a heroic figure among abolitionists by 1841. This was Joseph Cinquez, the African who had led a rebellion aboard the vessel, *Amistad*, as it carried a load of slaves along the coast of Cuba in 1839.[51] In the course of the revolt the captain and the cook had been killed by the rebels, the ship was steered to American shores and Cinquez had been brought to New England with his fellow slaves. There they were exposed to American Christianity with all of its contradictory potentials.

Then, in 1841, just before leaving for his native continent Cinquez was given the rare opportunity to apply this nation's religion to his rebellion— after the fact. One of his fellow rebels said to a group of Christians, "We owe everything to God; he keeps us alive and makes us free." Filled with enthusiasm, another went on to claim that he would now pray for the Captain and cook rather than kill them if the rebellion were to be done over again. We are told that "Cinquez, hearing this, smiled and shook his head. When asked if we would not pray for them, he said: 'Yes I would pray for 'em, an' kill 'em too.' "[52]

III

While the religion of some slaves could lead them to pray and kill, and though the Jesus of Southampton beckoned black men through streams of the masters' blood, there were other bondsmen who were evidently no less religiously motivated but who were led to seek different alternatives in their struggle. The Bauers have reminded us of the many levels of resistance to slavery that existed in the South, and they have indicated that some slaves who shed blood as an act of protest were known to draw their own or to take the lives of their children.[53] Death and self-mutilation were preferred to slavery, and one of the accounts of such death may offer some hint concerning the religious motivation involved here.

In Kentucky it was reported that "a father and mother, shut up in a slave baracoon and doomed to the southern market ... did by mutual agreement send the souls of their children to Heaven rather than have them descend to the hell of slavery, and then both parents committed suicide." [54] No one may be sure that the theology of the contemporary writer was shared by the parents he described, but is it impossible to conceive that a religion which

[51] A brief account of the *Amistad* story is most conveniently found in Louis Filler, *The Crusade Against Slavery 1830–1860* (New York: Harper and Row, 1963), 167–168.

[52] Quoted in Williams, *History*, II, 96.

[53] See reference to the Bauer's work in note 1 above, especially pp. 415–418.

[54] *Ibid.*, 417.

stressed the reality of heaven after death might strengthen slaves to leave their bondage for the freedom they had heard was ahead? If the "other world" was really so good, why allow children to suffer the agonies that parents had known?

In spite of the possible force of such reasoning, especially in extreme situations, it is certain that the action of the Kentucky parents was not typical. Perhaps a more common religious response to slavery was simply the act of refusing to believe the Christian teachings that justified the system of exploitation. A most striking instance of this alternative was found in Georgia shortly before 1830. In Liberty County a group of slaves were listening to a white minister hold forth on a staple topic—the escaped slave, Onesimus, and his return to his master. According to the report from Georgia, half of the Negro group walked out when the point of the sermon became clear, and "the other half stayed mostly for the purpose of telling [the preacher] that they were sure there was no such passage in the Bible."[55]

Because action could often be more costly than thoughts it is likely that many more slaves were involved in the kind of resistance to such religion that was identified by a former slave who said that Negroes simply refused to believe "a pro-slavery doctrine."[56] But Henry Bibb went on to point to what might have been an even more significant kind of defiance when he said that "This kind of preaching has driven thousands into infidelity."[57] Bibb's observations were supported by a southern Presbyterian minister who noted that many white ministers had assumed that Negroes "are an unsophisticated race" only to discover among them "deism, universalism, skepticism, and all the strong objections against the truth of God ... which he may perhaps have considered peculiar only to the cultivated minds ... of critics and philosophers."[58]

May we not suggest that the turn to "deism, universalism" and other unapproved forms of southern faith on the part of the slaves was in itself a profoundly religious act of protest against a system that seemed to be supported by all the correct lines of doctrine? Thus one may possibly speak of both protest and accommodation, if the accommodation were carried out under the new religiously protestant ground rules, rules that needed perforce to remain largely interior, but nonetheless real for that.

We are, however, concerning ourselves here with the more exterior, reportable, forms of resistance, and it is clear that one of the most obvious of these was the act of running away from slavery. It was not an act lightly taken up nor easily accomplished, and a sampling of fugitive slave narratives readily reveals the level of inner conviction and strength that was most often necessary for a slave to strike out for freedom. The difficulty of the path and the dis-

---

[55] Perkins, 236.
[56] Henry Bibb, *Narrative of the Life and Adventures of* (New York: the author, 1850), 24.
[57] *Ibid.*
[58] Quoted in Perkins, 237.

obedience of the act provided good testing grounds for the nature of religious faith.

Frederick Douglass recalled his own struggle with the issue of escape as an older man continued to speak to him of the great things that he thought Douglass was meant to do in the world. Young Frederick responded: "I am a slave, and a slave for life, how can I do anything?" To this "Uncle Lawson" replied:

> The Lord can make you free, my dear; all things are possible with him ...If you want liberty, ask the Lord for it in faith, and he will give it to you.[59]

From that point on Douglass began asking—in his own unorthodox way—and planning, until he felt he had freedom grasped securely in his hands. This was why the religion of chains and submission seemed like "nonsense" to him.

Samuel Ringgold Ward, another fugitive who became a brilliant abolitionist lecturer, lived the struggle through his mother. When he was a child this matriarch had to decide whether she would remain in Maryland and likely be sold further south or whether she would encourage her husband to lead them all to freedom. The will of God was discussed at that point, and the strong, single-minded black woman decided that they should leave. As Ward later described it,

> Submission to the will of God was one thing, she was prepared for that, but submission to the machinations of Satan was quite another thing; neither her womanhood nor her theology could be reconciled to the latter.[60]

In one of the most famous of the antebellum slave narratives William Wells Brown spoke of the same issue—the relationship of his mother's God to freedom. He told of how he confided in her his own plans for escape from slavery in St. Louis just as she was being sold into the deep South. Without any hesitation she urged him to go, and her last word may have expressed her theology of slave rebellion: "God be with you."[61]

There is only one woman whose journey from Southern slavery to freedom is readily available, and that story—half legend by now—is a religious pilgrimage in itself.[62] Harriet Tubman grew up on the stories of the Hebrew

---

[59] Douglass, 91.

[60] Samuel Ringgold Ward, *Autobiography of a Fugitive Negro* (London: John Snow, 1855), 19. The family ran away in 1820.

[61] Brown, *Narrative*, 79.

[62] Three of Harriet Tubman's most widely read biographers tend to encourage the legendary aspects: Henrietta Buckmaster, *Let My People Go* (Boston. Beacon Press, 1959); Earl Conrad, *Harriet Tubman* (Washington, D.C.: Associated Publishers, 1943); and Dorothy Sterling, *Freedom Train: The Story of Harriet Tubman* (New York: Doubleday and Company, 1954). In a recent study of the Underground Railroad, Larry Gara attempts to suggest Harriett's real life size. See his *The Liberty Line* (Lexington, University of Kentucky Press, 1961).

children, heard the whispered descriptions of Nat Turner, and sang the songs of impossible hope. Like Turner she saw visions and dreamed dreams of struggle and conflict and searching for freedom. Like him she prayed and talked with God and became fully convinced that her God willed freedom. Indeed, one of her more radical biographers said that by the time she escaped from her native Maryland in 1849 "she was ready to kill for freedom, if that was necessary, and defend the act as her religious right."[63]

The year after Harriet's arrival in the North her fellow black runaways were cast in a new light as a result of the Compromise of 1850 and its Fugitive Slave law. Therefore, while Douglass and Harriet Tubman gained most lasting fame as fugitives, it was a slave who arrived north in 1854—Anthony Burns—whose case became the *cause célèbre* of his time.[64] As a result of the notoriety resulting from the Boston abolitionist furor, Burns received a letter of rebuke and excommunication from the white Baptist church he had joined as a slave in Virginia. In his response we have one of the best statements of the religious apologia for resistance through flight.

Burns wrote,

You charge me that, in escaping, I disobeyed God's law. No, indeed!
That law which God wrote upon the table of my heart, inspiring
the love of freedom, and impelling me to seek it at every hazard,
I obeyed, and by the good hand of my God upon me, I walked out
of the house of bondage.

Then, in response to the inevitable citation of Paul and Onesimus which had been in the church's letter, Burns said he would be glad to return if he had any reason to believe that he too would be received in the brotherly spirit that Paul had requested for Onesimus. But Burns said that he did not believe in such a possibility, and was staying North. Finally he stated his basic defense and comfort in the terms of his faith: "You have thrust me out of your church fellowship. So be it. You cannot exclude me from heaven ..."[65]

Such was the religion of the runaways. They were obviously a self-selective group, but an important and impressive one too. None of them was willing to wait for Frazier's "world after death" to find their rest or to gain compensation for their condition, and they had thousands of brothers in their impatience. (Even heaven-oriented Anthony Burns wanted to try out Boston before confirming his reservation in heavenly places.)

Indeed, persons like Brown, Ward, Douglass and Harriet Tubman (to say nothing of their Northern-born counterparts) seemed unwilling to accept rest anywhere. Their religion was a restless one while slavery existed in the South and segregation shamed the North. The extreme form of this eternally protesting religion was expressed, of course, by Harriet Tubman shortly after

[63] Conrad, 35.
[64] See Buckmaster for an account of Burns' situation, especially 230–236.
[65] Herbert Aptheker (ed.), A *Documentary History of the Negro People in the United States*, 2 vols. (New York: Citadel Press, 1965), I, 372.

her arrival in Philadelphia. There, upon being asked to settle in the city, she was quoted as having said,

> There are three million of my people on the plantations of the south.
> I must go down, like Moses into Egypt, to lead them out.[66]

Such a spirit breeds legends and makes history difficult to write, but Harriet Tubman did return and she delivered some small, but important fragment of the waiting people. She returned often enough to end up with rewards amounting to 40,000 dollars being offered for her. Just as her own escape from slavery was the Lord's doing in her mind, so too did a sense of divine obsession now drive Harriet Tubman to continue this strange and courageous work of deliverance.[67] She too knew how to exhort, sing spirituals and carry a gun.

If the sparse evidence available is any guide, Harriet Tubman's efforts were child's play compared to a plan that was already at work in the South when she was escaping. It was a plan that revived memories of Gabriel and Vesey and Prophet Nat, expanding them beyond imagination. According to the Reverend Moses Dickson, the founder of a post-Civil War Negro benevolent society, in 1846 he had been instrumental in forming a group of twelve young men who called themselves the twelve Knights of Tabor.[68] They vowed in that year to spend the next decade organizing an army of liberation throughout the South, and were preparing to strike for the freedom of the slaves sometime after 1856. The Old Testament name was self-consciously chosen, Dickson said, for it "gave the members courage."[69]

According to his story, they were encouraged because they knew that

> God was with Israel, and gave the victory to the bondsmen, though
> they were opposed by twenty times their number. Our cause was just,
> and we believed in the justice of the God of Israel and the rights
> of man. Under the name of Tabor we resolved to make full preparation
> to strike the blow for liberty.[70]

With this sense of divine calling the members supposedly organized within ten years more than forty thousand recruits who were "well drilled, with ample arms and ammunition." They were located in all the slave states except Texas and Missouri. The larger group was dubbed Knights of Liberty.[71]

In 1857 they were prepared, by Dickson's account, to gather more followers and converge on Atlanta with 150,000 troops. They were to spare women and children, but "march, fight, and conquer was the command, or leave their

---

[66] Sterling, 81.

[67] See references in note 62 above.

[68] For an account of this fascinating story, see Aptheker, *Documentary History*, I, 378–380 and Moses Dickson, *Manual of the International Order of Twelve* (St. Louis: A. R. Fleming, 1891), 7–17.

[69] *Ibid.*, 15.

[70] *Ibid.*, 16.

[71] Aptheker, *Documentary History*, I, 380.

bodies on the battle field." Their flag was to have a cross made up of twelve stars. Then when all was prepared, just before an unidentified "Chief" was about to give the command to march, Dickson says, "it was plainly demonstrated to [the leader] that a higher power was preparing to take part in the contest between the North and South . . ." So the group was told to hold off, and it disbanded when the Civil War came.[72]

If this account is true, America was on the verge of experiencing the work of a Holy Liberation Front. So far it has not proved possible to go beyond one or two documentary sources related to this movement. However it is important to note that if such a movement was indeed on foot, it was self-consciously arrayed in the train of Nat Turner. Event or legend, it testified to the fact that there was a strong tradition of religious rebellion among antebellum blacks.

While the Knights of Liberty failed to march, John Brown did not fail. His religious self-image is well known. Less known is the fact that many Negroes took John Brown's insurrectionary action and fitted it into their understanding of religion without any apparent difficulty.

For instance, Frances Ellen Watkins, a gifted writer who published constantly in the cause of Negro freedom, wrote these words to Brown as he awaited execution:

> The Cross becomes a glorious ensign when Calvary's . . . sufferer yields up h:s life upon it. And, if Universal Freedom is ever to be the dominant power of the land, your bodies may be only her first stepping stones to dominion.[73]

A writer representing "The Colored Women of Brooklyn" became even more explicit in setting the messianic theme as she wrote, "We . . . recognize in you a Saviour commissioned to redeem us, the American people, from the great National Sin of Slavery . . ."[74]

Harriet Tubman had meant to march with Brown, but became ill and was evidently on her way to meet him when the old man was captured. Out of the religious world in which she moved it was clear that she spoke honest words when she said after his death: "It was not John Brown that died at Charleston . . . It was Christ—it was the savior of our people."[75] The black cross had passed from Nat Turner to John Brown. Therefore it was fitting that a traditional Negro tune should be used to carry the words of "John Brown's Body."

I V

Though "John Brown's Body" is not a spiritual, its presence bears a reminder that it is impossible to conclude any discussion of black religion without at least a reference to those songs. They represent the most profound

[72] Ibid.
[73] Ibid., 441.

[74] Ibid.
[75] Sterling, 129–133.

verbal expression of Afro-American religious experience. As W. E. B. DuBois has said, they are "the siftings of centuries..."[76]

In spite of their significance it will not be fitting to attempt any lengthy exposition of them here—neither time nor skill allows that. However, it should be noted that these songs have been subjected to much of the same difficulties that we encountered at the outset of this discussion of black religion. Frazier is found again speaking of them as "essentially religious in sentiment and... otherworldly in outlook," thereby suggesting that he had missed the point of much of the greatest religious sentiments of man.[77] (Perhaps he was not blessed to hear Paul Tillich's definition of religion.)

Mays also describes most of the spirituals as expressing "compensatory" and heaven-oriented attitudes, but he faces the texts and is willing to admit that some of them clearly bespeak real protest in the present world. Especially does he cite "Go Down Moses" and "Oh Freedom" in this vein.[78] But the author of one of the most carefully wrought attempts to set the spirituals in a historical context goes much further, and develops a theme concerning the spirituals quite similar to the one being suggested here for all of Negro religion.

Miles Mark Fisher sees black religion so closely allied to protest that he suggests that some of the spirituals were likely the creation of Nat Turner, Denmark Vesey, and Harriet Tubman.[79] Especially provocative is Fisher's suggestion that "Steal Away" emerged directly out of Nat Turner's vision of 1825, when the call of God came to him through convulsions in the elements, as he grew increasingly convinced that his great future task would lead him away from all that he had known before.[80] By this Fisher does not mean to deny that many persons have sung that haunting song with longings for a heavenly place, but he affirms that it may well have originated in a marvelously earthbound experience, an experience of affirmation and rebellion.

This recognition that the spirituals surely bore many possible meanings for many persons is strongly supported by Frederick Douglass, who sang so many of them while they were yet fresh in the air. As he later recalled his youth, Douglass pointed to two examples of the potential for profound ambiguity which rested at the center of the songs. There was one with the words

> O Canaan, Sweet Canaan
> I am bound for the land of Canaan.

In Douglass' experience, as he put it, "The North was our Canaan." There

[76] DuBois, *The Souls of Black Folk* (Greenwich, Conn.: Fawcett Publications, 1961), 183. DuBois' justly famous work contains a number of important essays on black religion. See especially chapters X, XII and XIV.

[77] Frazier, 12.

[78] Mays, 28–29.

[79] Miles Mark Fisher, *Negro Slave Songs in the United States*, Paperback edition (New York: Citadel Press, 1963), 66–67, 181–185.

[80] *Ibid.*, 67.

was no doubt about that. He says, too, that a song with the words "I don't expect to stay much longer here" (probably a variant of "Steal Away") was another favorite and had "a double meaning." He explained the duality in this way: "On the lips of some it meant the expectation of a speedy summons to a world of spirits, but on the lips of our company [of young men in Maryland] it simply meant a speedy pilgrimage to a free state, and deliverance from all the evils and dangers of slavery."[81]

It would then appear that even in the midst of so community-oriented an experience as the singing of spirituals, many men may have sung out of many varied visions. For some—perhaps for most—the visions took them beyond this earth entirely, and made the experiences of their surroundings fade in importance. For other black persons the music and the faith it expressed—and engendered—filled them with a sense of God's awesome calling for their present moment, and supplied new determination to struggle, build, and resist here.

This dual function of religion should not be surprising. Speaking of another oppressed people in another time, Reinhold Niebuhr lately reminded us that "The radical sectarians [of the Reformation period] appropriated Messianism to make of it an instrument of social revolt, while the more conservative religious forces used otherworldly hopes to beguile men from injustices in history."[82]

Unless we grasp that common historical truth and apply it to the black experience in America we shall not only be unprepared to meet those Negroes who break out of the pages of Aptheker and Stampp, but we shall certainly fail to understand so recent and lately controversial a phenomenon as Martin Luther King. He stands in a long tradition of black exhorters whose lives and whose religion can neither be spiritualized, captured or denied. They can, however, be understood, and that is our task.[83]

[81] Douglass, 159–160.

[82] Introduction to Marx and Engels, On Religion, viii.

[83] After I completed this paper my attention was called to a sociological study which will attempt to relate Negro religion to protest in the modern era: Gary T. Marx, Protest and Prejudice (New York: Harper and Row, forthcoming).

PART THREE

THE ANTE-BELLUM FREE PEOPLE OF COLOR

James H. Brewer

NEGRO PROPERTY OWNERS IN SEVENTEENTH-CENTURY VIRGINIA

Early in the history of American Negroes, a group known as the "Free People of Color" emerged. James H. Brewer discusses the origins of this class of seventeenth-century Virginia, and the ironic fact that the most prosperous individuals among the free Negroes themselves cultivated staple crops with slave labor.

T HREE centuries have passed since there appeared on the Eastern Shore, along the banks of the Pungoteague River, perhaps the first community of Negro property owners in historic Virginia. Within a few years other infant black communities were to be found scattered throughout parts of Tidewater Virginia. The story concerning those forgotten African families, partially revealed by Philip Alexander Bruce nearly sixty years ago, cannot be told in its entirety. However, further light is shed on their economic pursuits in the early colonial period by a somewhat fuller exploitation of the county records of Virginia.

It is highly significant that some of the former Negro servants found the environment of seventeenth-century Virginia conducive to the amassing of property in land or chattel in various ways. For example, a few received land grants ranging from 50 to 500 acres, made possible by the head-rights system. Others acquired their property in chattel; while there were some who came into ownership of land or chattel through grants in the wills of their former masters. Through these various means a class of Negro property owners gradually came into existence. How large this class was, it is not possible to say, but the records seem to indicate that their number was relatively small.

The influx of blacks into the colony during the major part of the seventeenth century was still too meager to affect seriously the social and economic

James H. Brewer, "Negro Property Owners in Seventeenth-Century Virginia," *The William and Mary Quarterly*, XII (October, 1955), pp. 575–80. Reprinted with the permission of the publisher and author.

life of Virginia. For example, in 1625 there were only 23 Negroes in Virginia, and by the middle of the century only 300 blacks were to be found, while the whites numbered 15,000. Between 1670 and 1680 the Negro population had increased from 2,000 to 3,000. During the last two decades of the century the Negro population grew rapidly, and by 1700 there were approximately 6,000 Negroes in Virginia. It was during this period that Virginia became disturbed by the increase of blacks within her borders. Her fears were manifested by the enactment of two statutes which listed types of property the Negroes might not acquire. The first law, passed in 1670, prohibited them from owning white servants, while the second act denied to them the ownership of fire-arms or other weapons.[1]

Even though the rapid increase of the Negro population of Virginia was paralleled by certain limitations placed on their rights of ownership, the Negro never lost his right to own and to alienate his property. This is disclosed by a study of the head-rights system.[2] Beginning in 1651, a few Negro families took advantage of the head-rights custom and received acreage along the banks of the Pungoteague River on the Eastern Shore. The first of such grants was made in July, 1651, to Anthony Johnson of Northampton County, who received 250 acres of land for the importation of 5 persons into the colony.[3] At this time Anthony Johnson and his wife, Mary, were perhaps the wealthiest Negroes in Virginia.[4] After Anthony, other free blacks whose last name was Johnson procured property under the head-rights system in the forgotten Pungoteague Community. For example, John Johnson received as head-rights for the transporting of 11 persons a tract of 550 acres of land.[5] Likewise, John Johnson, Senior, was allowed his claim of 50 acres.[6] When Johnson attempted to increase his land holdings, he was summoned in 1653 to appear in court to answer proceedings instituted by his neighbor, another

[1] William W. Hening, compiler, *The Statutes at Large ... of Virginia* (Richmond, 1819–1823), II, 280, 481.

[2] This was a law designed to stimulate immigration, which stipulated that the government pledged itself to grant 50 acres of land to any person who would pay the passage of a person to Virginia. The person receiving the grant was required to record with the clerk of his respective county court the names of all persons for whose transportation the claim was made. This statute was one of the means by which the Virginia Negro was able to accumulate land of 50 acres or more. For a more detailed discussion of the head-rights system see Thomas J. Wertenbaker, *The Planters of Colonial Virginia* (Princeton, 1922), 34.

[3] Land Patents of Virginia, 1643–1651, Book No. 2, 326, Virginia State Library. Hereafter cited as Land Patents. See also Court Records of Northampton County, 1651–1654, 226; 1655–1658, 10, Virginia State Library. Hereafter cited as CRNC. The names of the five persons imported are Tho. Bembrose, Peter Bughby, Antho. Cripps, Jno. Gesorroro, and Richard Johnson.

[4] See below, p. 578.

[5] Land Patents, 1652–1655, Book No. 3, 101. The names of those imported are Jno. Edwards, William Routh, Thomas Yowell, Fra. Mayland, William Price, John Owens, Dorthy Riley, Richard Hemstead, Law. Barnes, Row. Rith, and Mary Johnson.

[6] CRNC, 1651–1654, 17.

John Johnson, to recover 450 acres of land.[7] The next member of the African community to acquire land under the head-rights was a carpenter by trade, Richard Johnson. Richard was perhaps among the 5 servants imported in 1651 by Anthony Johnson. Three years later he was assigned 100 acres adjoining the property of John and Anthony Johnson.[8]

Soon after various Johnsons had achieved a status of moderate economic importance in the historic Pungoteague Community, the records disclose that elsewhere in the colony other free Negroes had made progress in land ownership. For example, in December, 1656, Benjamin Doyle was granted a patent for 300 acres of land in Surry County "for the transportation of six persons into the colony." [9] There is also a record of a grant of 50 acres in April 18, 1667, to Emanuel Cambew of James City County.[10] In the adjoining county of York a deed dated October 28, 1668, calling for the transfer of 50 acres of land in New Kent County, was executed by Robert Jones, a white tailor of Queen's Creek, to "John Harris, a negro his heyers, Executrs, admtrs, and assigns forever."[11] On at least one occasion, a Negro leased land on a long-term basis. Philip Morgan and his heirs were "peacefully and quietly [to] enjoy the 200 acres," for 99 years, when the land was to revert to the owner's heirs.[12]

It hardly needs to be said that in sections of Tidewater Virginia there were many free blacks too poor to acquire land. As free persons, however, they inevitably acquired small amounts of personal property in various forms—cattle, household effects, and clothing. Frequently they received such items when they were freed; others, of course, earned them; and, we suspect, others came by them somewhat illegally. Manuscript records dealing with this kind of property are to be found more frequently than those dealing with land. Even the simple sale of cattle, "a black cow and a red calf" to Emanuel Dregis, is recorded.[13] Negroes were also involved in litigation, which not only became a part of the court records but also disclosed their small property holdings. Thus, in 1647 Tony Kongo was compelled by court order to pay a debt of 382 pounds of tobacco due Lewis White. The mulatto Kongo was allowed thirty days to guarantee payment out of "ye next croppe."[14] A judgment for 486 pounds of tobacco against the estate of Edward Jessop, Negro, is recorded in the court records of Northampton County.[15]

[7] *Ibid.*, 200. John Johnson sought relief from the authorities by testifying that John Johnson, Senior, "Most unrightly detayneth a pattent for 450 acres of land." The decision of the court was not revealed.

[8] Land Patents, 1652–1655, Book No. 3, 294; also 101.

[9] *Ibid.*, 1655–1664, Book No. 4, 71f.

[10] *Ibid.*, Book No. 6, 39.

[11] Court Records of York County, 1664–1672, Book No. 4, 327, Virginia State Library. Hereafter cited as CRYC.

[12] Court Records of Accomac County, 1676–1690, 185, Virginia State Library.

[13] CRNC, 1645–1651, 83. See *Virginia Magazine of History*, XI (1904), 281.

[14] CRNC, 1645–1651, 83.

[15] CRNC, 1683–1689, 258.

The most remarkable record in property holding, however, is that of Anthony Johnson, "the black patriarch" of Pungoteague Community. Within 7 months after acquiring 250 acres in July, 1651, Johnson's holdings were practically wiped out by an unfortunate fire. Johnson then petitioned the court for relief, and the judgment of the court stated, "be it therefore fitt and ordered that... (during their natural lives) the sd Mary Johnson & two daughters of Anthony Johnson be disengaged and freed from payment of taxes and leavyes in Northampton County for public use."[16] Ultimately the enterprising "black patriarch" managed to re-establish himself as a moderate property owner. In 1653 Anthony appeared as a claimant in a suit brought against Robert Parker to recover his Negro servant John Casor. Testimony in the trial discloses that Johnson attempted to show that he was intimidated by Parker to free his black servant because of threats by Parker that the servant would enter suit against Johnson to recover his master's cows as damages. The court ordered that the servant be returned to Johnson.[17] The court records also afford additional evidence as to Johnson's business transactions in an effort to replenish his losses through fire. One record shows that Anthony and his son John sold "two heifers collored black and of three years old... unto John Williams his heirs executors and assigns forever."[18] In August, 1659, Anthony managed to enlarge his land holdings when his son John "do hereby bargain and make sail of all my right title and interest of this within... patent of land to my father Anthony Johnson Negro...."[19] Finally, a chattel mortgage recorded the same year entailed the exchange of more property within the family when John transferred to his father Anthony "two heifers of two year old and four yearling heifers and one calf... and also one black cow...."[20]

The growth of a class of Negro property owners was also facilitated by the emancipation provisions of liberal and appreciative masters. Thus, former Negro servants as well as emancipated slaves did not always go forth emptyhanded from their masters' services. Many were furnished either land or chattel or both to embark upon their new life as freemen. This was true of two blacks, Philip and Nicholas, of York County. Each was bequeathed a cow and allotted a certain plot of land to cultivate for the "balance of their natural lives."[21] John, another Negro of York County, was emancipated by one Thomas Whitehead, and included among the several items he was bequeathed were the possession of a house and the use of as much land as he could cultivate.[22]

Elsewhere in Virginia other Negroes were recipients of property through wills in the seventeenth century. Notable is the will of Richard Vaughan of

16 CRNC, 1651–1654, 161.
17 Ibid., 10. See also John H. Russell, The Free Negro in Virginia, 1619–1865 (Baltimore, 1913), 33.
18 CRNC, Deeds, Wills, 1657–1666, 17.
19 Ibid., 9.
20 Ibid., 9.
21 CRYC, Will of Nicholas Martin, 1633–1694, 109.
22 Ibid., 1657–1662, 211, 217.

Northampton County, which left property to each Negro he set free. A portion of Vaughan's will reads:

> ...and for my old Negro woman...and the receive twoe Cowes with calfe (or calves by their side) two suits of clothes and bedd and a Rugge, a chest and a pott with foure Barrells of corn and a younge breedinge Sowe; Likewise my Negro girle Temperance... to bee possessed of two cowes and to have their increase male and female....[23]

Continuing, Vaughan's will stated, "that ye three Negro girls be possessed of the plantacon of John. Walthome, being to this plantacon some 144 acres of land; and he to build them a Home twenty-five feete in length and twenty feete broad, with one chimmey."[24] Under the terms of the will of John Carter, of Lancaster County, a married slave couple were to be set free and "allowed...the use of a convenient house...and as much land as they could cultivate...."[25] Robert Griggs showed equal generosity to a mulatto when he bequeathed him a home and a "certain area of ground for life...."[26] Of greater significance are the terms of the will of John Nicholls, filed in 1697, whereby the two mulatto children of one of his female slaves were to be set free and to have possession of several hundred acres of land. In addition to 310 acres left to the mulatto boy and 200 acres left to his mulatto sister, they were to receive a variety of chattel.[27]

The question concerning the economic activities of the Negro inhabitants of Pungoteague and other Virginia communities is not one of major historical significance. Yet their story in many respects parallels that of other ethnic and cultural groups in seventeenth-century Virginia. For example, some Negroes eventually became financially able to pay for the transportation of indentured servants either from Europe or Africa or both, and in this way they acquired 50 acres for each European or African they imported. Others found it more feasible to purchase their property from native Virginians. However, the bulk of the wealth among the Negro population was in chattel property. Finally, the response by the Negro to the need for economic stability resulted in the now-forgotten communities of Negro property owners in seventeenth-century Virginia.

[23] CRNC, 1654–1655, 102.
[24] *Ibid.*, Will of Richard Vaughan, 103. For a more detailed analysis of seventeenth-century wills see Philip A. Bruce, *Economic History of Virginia in the Seventeenth Century* (New York, 1896), II, 123f.
[25] Court Records of Lancaster County, original vol., 1690–1709, 3, Virginia State Library.
[26] *Ibid.*, 1674–1687, 91.
[27] Court Records of Lower Norfolk County, original vol., 1695–1703, 96, Virginia State Library. See Bruce, *Economic History of Virginia in the Seventeenth Century*, II, 125.

E. Horace Fitchett

THE TRADITIONS OF THE FREE NEGRO IN CHARLESTON, SOUTH CAROLINA [1]

If the slave population was overwhelmingly rural, the free Negroes were preeminently an urban group. There were about half a million of them in 1860, distributed roughly equally between the North and the South, and concentrated largely in coastal and river ports like Providence, New York, Cincinnati, Louisville, Baltimore, Charleston, Mobile, and New Orleans.

In the South the free Negroes lived mainly in areas of older settlement along the Atlantic Seaboard and Gulf of Mexico, where the slave system was somewhat more benevolent and paternalistic. There, a significant free population had emerged before the states, during the course of the nineteenth century, imposed practically insuperable barriers to manumission.

One of the most perceptive discussions of the ante-bellum urban free Negroes is found in the work of E. Horace Fitchett. In the article published here, he not only describes the origins, economic attainment, and social organization of the free people of color in Charleston, S.C., but he also analyzes the way they functioned as a buttress to the system of slavery.

THE free Negro in the slave system was an anomaly. The system was designed for free white men and Negro slaves. In a large measure the position of the

E. Horace Fitchett, "The Traditions of the Free Negro in Charleston, South Carolina," *Journal of Negro History*, XXV (April, 1940), pp. 139–152. Reprinted with the permission of the publisher.

[1] Paper read before the 18th Annual Institute of the Society for Social Research, August 19, 1939, at the University of Chicago. This paper was based on an investigation the writer was making of the free Negro in Charleston, S.C. It was made possible by an award from the Julius Rosenwald Fund for the year 1938–39. The writer expressed his appreciation to Professors Robert E. Park, W. Lloyd Warner, and Herbert Blumer for many stimulating and valuable suggestions.

emancipated Negro, prior to the Emancipation Proclamation, was comparable to that of the slave. Some of them preferred slavery to the type of freedom which they received.[2] They were by law deprived of education, of suffrage, and of freedom of movement; they could not testify in court against a white man, and from time to time they were prohibited from assembling in groups of more than seven without the presence of a white man.[3] However, before the slave structure was disrupted by the Civil War there were approximately one half of a million people of this class in the United States.[4] In a few communities, particularly along the seacoast, they developed into a respectable, economically independent, class-conscious group. This is notable in the case of Charleston, South Carolina.

In this discussion I shall answer briefly the following questions: (1) How did this group arise? (2) What was its economic position and how was it attained? (3) What relations did this class of people sustain with out-group members and in its own group? (4) Were there any evidences of deviations from the approved patterns of behavior? If so, what form did they take? And (5) What was the nature of the process of accommodation and social adjustment to the social system?

When the first census was taken in 1790 there were 8,089 white persons, 7,684 slaves, and 586 free Negroes in Charleston, South Carolina. Hence, the latter group constituted 3.58 per cent of the total population.[5] Many of the members of this group had no memory of a slave background or tradition. This was particularly true of the mixed bloods. Dr. Reuter advances the generalization that: "There seems to be no historical exception to the rule that when peoples come into contact and occupy the same area there is a mixture of blood that results, ultimately, in the establishment of a new modified ethnic type."[6] This condition is no less true of Charleston than of other areas. Documentary evidence may be presented to support this generalization. In 1720 one slave master, James Gilbertson, a planter, made the following provisions in his will for a mulatto woman and her children:

> My will is that my mulatto woman Ruth shall be free immediately after my Decease, & also my will is that her three female children Betty, Molly, and Keatty shall be free at the age of one and Twenty years, my will is also that Ruth have the feather bed W:ch the Indians did Cutt up, also a pot and her maintenance upon my plantation during her natural life.[7]

[2] Phillips, U. B., *American Negro Slavery* (New York, 1918), p. 446.
[3] *Ibid.*, p. 448; A Digest of the Ordinance of Charleston, 1783–1844, p. 377.
[4] *Negro Population in the United States, 1790–1915*, p. 53.
[5] *Census of Charleston*, 1848, p. 10.
[6] Reuter, E. B. (ed.), *Race and Culture Contacts* (New York, 1934), pp. 7–9.
[7] *Record of Wills of Charleston County*, Vol. 1, 1671–1724, p. 50. Through the courtesy and cooperation of Miss Parmelee Cheves of the Charleston Free Library, and Professor J. H. Easterby of the College of the City of Charleston, I was permitted to examine a large number of verbatim, typewritten copies of old wills of Charleston County.

In 1834, a prominent Charlestonian, a native of France, acknowledged in his will that the children of his housekeeper and slave were his offspring and his executors were instructed to provide for the mother and her children out of the estate. He states:

> I do hereby recognize and declare that the issue of my slave and housekeeper, Celestine, are my children and I will order and direct that my executors herein named, or such person or persons that may qualify on this will, shall and do, as soon after my death as may be convenient, send the said woman Celestine and all her said issue my children, out of this State to some other State, territory or country, where they can severally be made free and their liberty secured to them respectively; and I will, order and direct that said executors or such person or persons that may qualify and act on this will shall defray the expense of transportation or conveyance of the said Celestine and her issue to said State, territory or country as expressed from the funds of my estate.[8]

In 1826 one of the wealthiest and most influential citizens of Charleston made the following stipulation in his will for his mulatto man:

> In consideration of the good conduct and faithful valuable service of my mulatto man Toney by Trade a millwright I have for some years past given him to himself one half of his time say from the middle of May to the middle of November every year. It is my will and desire and I do direct that the same indulgence be given to him for six years from the time of my death during which time he may instruct other servants in his Profession to supply his place and at the expiration of six years from the time of my death I will and direct that his whole time be given up to him .... after the expiration of six years he may be emancipated and set free or allowed to depart from this State as (he) may ... think proper.[9]

These wills are typical of many of those which I examined. They not only provided for the freedom of a slave but also for his economic security. In a very real sense they imply that these persons were not slaves. They were in some instances recognized as the offspring of the upper caste member; they were allowed freedom of action and movement; and they were accorded special privileges. Thus they were not treated as slaves nor did they conceive of themselves as slaves. Indeed, in some of the wills the testator indicated that the servant should not be considered a slave. Such was the desire expressed in the will of Mrs. Bonneau in 1807.[10] Moreover, some of these persons obtained their freedom so early in the history of the country that the conditions of slave status could easily have been lost to their descendants. Their emancipation was indeed coeval with that of many of the white servant class. In the *South*

[8] *Record of Wills of Charleston County*, Vol. 40, Book A, 1834–1839, p. 203.
[9] *Record of Wills*, Vol. 37, Book A, 1826–1834, pp. 184–185.
[10] *Record of Wills*, Vol. 33, Book C, 1807–1818, p. 1180–1181.

Carolina Gazette for January, 1738, the following advertisement was made for a white servant girl:

> Runaway the 28th of December last, a white woman servant, about 16 years of age, named Anne Brown, born in London and can talk a little French, belonging to Edw. Townsend of Savannah, Georgia. Whoever brings the said Servant to Charleston shall have £5 in currency reward.[11]

There were also cases in which free Negroes entered Charleston from other states. Such was the case of Richard Holloway, whose citizenship papers were dated January 21, 1794. He is designated in this document as a seaman, a native of Essex County, Maryland, and a mulatto about twenty years of age.[12]

In general it is fair to say that the free Negro arose out of: (1) Children born of free colored parents; (2) Mulatto children born of free colored mothers; (3) Children of free Negro and mixed Indian parentage; (4) Manumitted slaves.[13]

In the latter part of the eighteenth and during the first part of the nineteenth centuries there emerged in Charleston a relatively economically independent group of free Negroes. They were primarily the artisans of the system. Records show, moreover, that they engaged in business transactions which made the system a going concern. In 1819 they were listed in thirty branches of work. Among them were 11 carpenters, 10 tailors, 22 seamstresses, 6 shoemakers and one owner of a hotel.[14] Thirty years later they were listed in fifty different types of work. In 1859 there were among them 50 carpenters, 43 tailors, 9 shoemakers, and 21 butchers. In these trades some of them became wealthy. In the above mentioned year, "353 persons paid taxes on property and one-hundred-and-ninety were slave holders. The property on which they paid taxes was assessed at $724,570 and the amount paid on slaves aggregated $1,170."[15] If we divide this group of taxpayers into three approximately homogeneous classes, we find that there were 192 who paid taxes on property whose assessed value ranged from $1,000 to $5,000; this group owned 105 slaves, or an average of .54 slaves each. In the second division there were 21 persons who paid taxes on property whose assessed value ranged from $5,000 to $10,000, and they owned 68 slaves, or 3¼ slaves each. And in the third bracket, there were 9 persons who paid taxes on property whose value ranged from $10,000 to $40,075. This group owned 54 slaves, an average of 6 slaves each. In this class one individual paid taxes on $23,000 worth of real estate and 14 slaves; another $33,000 worth of real estate and 5 slaves; and a third paid taxes on $40,075 worth of real estate and 14 slaves.[16]

[11] *The South Carolina Gazette*, No. 209, Jan., 1738.
[12] *Citizenship Papers of Richard Holloway*. By the courtesy of Mrs. Mae Holloway-Purcell, a descendant of the family, I was permitted to examine this document.
[13] Russell, John H., *The Free Negro in Virginia, 1619–1865*, pp. 40–41.
[14] Based on a study of the *Directory of Charleston*, 1819, pp. 21–98.
[15] *List of Taxpayers of the City of Charleston for 1860*, pp. 315–334.
[16] *Ibid.*

Moreover, the wills and deeds which they made indicate that they engaged in some of the most important business ventures of the system. In 1815, Jehu Jones bought a hotel at public auction for $13,000.[17] This hotel was located on the most important street in the city and in close proximity to the most fashionable Episcopal Church in the community.[18] It was patronized by the elite of the white society, including the governor of the state.[19]

In 1853 Joseph Dereef, another wealthy person of color, sold a piece of property to the city council for $3,600 for the extension of a street.[20] In 1870 his brother, R. E. Dereef, sold a part of his wharf to the South Carolina Rail Road Company for $17,000.[21] In 1833 Thomas Ingliss made provisions in his will for the support of a relative from the stocks which he held in the Mechanics Bank of the city.[22]

One of the characteristics of the free Negro of Charleston, which attracts the attention of the sociologists, is that it was a class-conscious group; and identified its interest, loyalties, and manners with the upper caste members of the society in so far as that behavior did not offend or disturb the *status quo*. They organized themselves into societies with high eligibility requirements. These associations were ostensibly charitable and benevolent, but in reality they were social and status organizations. In 1790 the Brown Fellowship Society was formed.[23] The preamble of this organization stated that its members were bona fide free brown men of good character. The fee of admission was $50.00 and the membership was restricted to fifty members. The society provided for the education of the children, assistance to the orphans and widows and burial grounds for their dead. They maintained a clubhouse where meetings were held monthly, and on each anniversary provisions were made for special observance. This institution had a continuous existence for more than a hundred years. In fact vestiges of it are still in evidence. There is left the cemetery, with large imposing tombstones and vaults; so is the foundation of the hall in which they met. It still has a secretary and a president. In spite of the fact that other Negro organizations, including a church, were abolished during crises periods in this slave community, the Brown Fellowship Society kept alive. The members and their organizations were careful and cautious in their conduct. We only need to remember the conflicting philosophies and the revolutionary movements of the underprivileged groups of this period to appreciate how delicate and precarious the position of this group was. At their meetings they prohibited any discussion of local or national problems. Rule XVIII of the by-laws states: "All debates on controverted points of divinity or matters of the nation, governments, states or churches, shall be excluded from the conversation of this society, and whoever shall persist in such shall be fined...."[24] The secretary

---

[17] *Register of the Mesne Conveyance Office*, Book M8, pp. 399–402.
[18] *Register of Mesne Conference Office*, pp. 21–98.
[19] Adams, F. C., *Manuel Periera* (Washington, D.C., 1853), pp. 88–89.
[20] *Conveyance Deed Book*, H13, p. 237.
[21] *Ibid.*, Deed Book, P15, p. 81.
[22] *Record of Wills*, Vol. 40, Book A, 1834–1839, pp. 289–290.
[23] *Rules and Regulations of the Brown Fellowship Society.* (1st November, 1790.)
[24] *Rules and Regulations of the Brown Fellowship Society*, p. 12.

of the organization kept very careful minutes of the proceedings of the meetings, and on one occasion when the mayor of the city asked to inspect them, because of a recently enacted law to prohibit more than seven Negroes to assemble at a time, the group was praised highly for its records and avowed objectives. So they were informed that the law was not intended for them.[25] Among other things the minutes showed that a member had been expelled from the society on April 17, 1817, for violating its rules.[26]

Now the question may be asked, what were the attitudes of this class to other groups in the community? As I envisage it, their behavior was a replica of that class in the white society which they aspired to be like. Their attitudes towards their slaves ranged from exploitation to humanitarianism. Again the wills which they left give us some indication of their position. In 1825 William Pinceel made the following stipulation in his will:

> I give and bequeath unto my Son Emanuel forever my Negro boy slave named Joe. I also give and bequeath unto Said Son for life my Negro boy slave named Tom and immediately after the death of my said Son, should the said Negro boy have conducted himself towards my Said Son as a faithful servant, then I direct that he be emancipated, but should he not have conducted himself then I give the said Negro boy to such person as my Said Son nominate and appoint in his last will and writing.[27]

The following will was made by a school teacher in 1831. He taught in Charleston between 1815 and 1830, and was one of the most active members of the Brown Fellowship Society:

> I desire that soon after my decease instruction shall be given to have all my stock and other things appertaining to my plantation in the country together with the plantation itself sold and the money arising from the same shall go to defray all expenses, taxes & provided however the said plantation cannot be sold at a fair price and it can be worked by the hands now there viz. Scipio, Abram and Peggy so as to pay expenses taxes and so forth in such case the same shall not be sold but retained for the benefit of the family if at all event, the Negroes on said plantation whose names are above mentioned be disposed of there shall be an exception of Scipio whom it is my wish shall be retained together with my slaves in town viz.: Fanny and Mary to be subservient to the wishes of my beloved wife Jennet Bonneau and children.[28]

Some of these masters also left their slaves or former slaves provided for

---

[25] Jervey, T. D., *Robert Y. Haynes and His Times*, pp. 63–69. Jervey quotes here a letter which he obtained from the minutes of the Society.

[26] *Ibid.*

[27] *Record of Wills*, Vol. 36, Book C, 1818–1826, p. 1125.

[28] *Ibid.*, Vol. 39, Book C, 1826–1834, p. 905.

economically. In 1859 John L. Francis left $1,000 to one servant and $200 to another, together with his wardrobe.[29]

The emphasis which the free Negro of this class placed upon mixed blood, free ancestry, economic position, and a devotion to the tenets of the slave system set them apart from and above other classes in the community. Moreover, their in-group tendencies were so strong that the free black people of the city were constrained to organize themselves into a society of free blacks. The first rule of this society says that it will ". . . consist of a number of respectable Free Dark men, as a majority may determine: not less than seven or more than thirty-five which number of seven shall be considered a quorum to transact business at any time. . . ." [30]

It is fair to say that the upper caste free Negro served as a custodian of the system. He interrupted plans which the detached, discontented, underprivileged Negroes designed to overthrow or to offend the mores of the system. In 1822 the Intended Denmark Vesey Insurrection [31] was circumvented by a member of this class who instructed an informed slave to go and tell his master. The insurrection had been in the process of development for four years and was considered one of the most intricate ever undertaken in this country. It had as its model the uprising of the blacks in San Domingo. Its leader had travelled through the Islands as the slave of a slave trader. Upon receiving his freedom he settled in Charleston and assumed the position of the leader of the slaves. It is estimated that from 6,000 to 9,000 slaves were identified with this movement. Only about thirty of the leaders were executed for the plot.[32] On the other hand the slave who divulged the plans was emancipated by the State of South Carolina and paid an annual stipend for the rest of his life.[33] Meantime the free Negro received $1,000 and exemption from taxation for the rest of his life.[34]

There are other evidences of unrest, but I shall take time to mention only a few of them. Between 1832 and 1853 approximately 400 free Negroes left South Carolina for Liberia, Africa.[35] They were impelled by the claims of the American Colonization Society on the one hand and the insecurity of their positions on the other. In a mass meeting which was held by this group in 1831 in the interest of emigrating to Africa, the theme was that "in Liberia

[29] *Ibid.*, Vol. 51, Book B, 1862–1868, p. 588.

[30] Browning, J. B., "The Beginnings of Insurance Enterprise among Negroes," *Journal of Negro History*, Vol. XXII, No. 4, Oct., 1937, p. 424.

[31] "Denmark Vesey," *The Atlantic Monthly*, Vol. 7, 1861, pp. 728–744.

[32] *Ibid.*, p. 740.

[33] *Statutes at Large of South Carolina*, Vol. 6, p. 194. This volume was the property of Jonathan Jasper Wright, the Negro Associate Justice of the Supreme Court of South Carolina during the Reconstruction era. He is the only Negro ever to hold such a position in the United States. His books were donated to Claflin College, S.C. by the late Dr. William Francis Holmes of Florence, S.C. Dr. Holmes read law under Judge Wright and the degree was conferred upon him at Claflin University.

[34] *Ibid.*, p. 195.

[35] *The African Repository and Colonial Journal*, Vol. III (Washington, D.C., 1833), "Opinions of a Freeman of Colour in Charleston," Oct., 1832, pp. 241–242, pp. 76–77.

you will enjoy moral and political freedom." In December, 1832, one-hundred-forty-six persons of this class departed from Charleston for Liberia.[36] As far as I have been able to ascertain none of them were members of the Brown Fellowship Society.

The relations which the aristocratic free Negro sustained in his own family and among other members of his group deserve study and analysis. They provided for the education of their children; they married inside a restricted class; dowries were apparently provided for the daughters; and great care was taken in the protection and transmission of property and slaves.

In 1794 George Bedon indicated in his will that:

> ...it is my particular desire and request that my two Sons....
> should be brought up in a Christian like manner and kept to school
> for the benefit of an Education until they arrive at the age of fifteen
> years then my two sons to be bound out during the term of six years
> to some handicraft trade under a kind and able master and in like
> manner my Daughter until she arrives at the age of fourteen years
> to be bound to a discreet and careful Mantua-maker a person of good
> character who will be so kind as to take care of an orphans morals
> as well as to teach her the trade.[37]

In 1861 Jacob Weston, one of the wealthier members of this caste, stipulated in his will that his wife and son should live in England after his death and that the son should be educated there. It was indicated that they be maintained out of the family estate.[38] The same testator designated that the support of his wife should be revoked if she married again.[39]

As was the practice generally, so it was in this group that marriage and courtship relations were expected to have the approval of the parents of the interested parties. The following letter was written in 1832, in reply to one which a young man had sent to the parents of his friend:

Charleston, March 19th, 1832

DEAR SIR:

It affords me the pleasure of giving you the approbation of Mr. Kougley and myself towards the affection you have for my daughter Cecelia. It has met her approbation for your visiting the house on her account, as to your standing in life we are perfectly acquainted with, as to objections we can have none, therefore we must join both hand and heart in wishing you all the prosperity and happiness this world can afford. I hope it is with the approbation of your family that you have addressed my daughter with respect. Dear Sir

We are yours,

Jacob and Mary Kougley [40]

---

[36] *Ibid.*, Vol. XXXIII, May, 1857, No. 5, pp. 152-155.
[37] *Record of Wills*, Vol. 25, Book A, 1793-1800, p. 208.
[38] *Records of Wills*, Vol. 50, Book A, 1860-68, p. 222.
[39] *Ibid.*
[40] *The Holloway Scrap Book.*

The Marriage Book of St. Phillip's Church, founded in 1672, shows that 168 mulattoes were married by the rectors of that institution between 1828 and 1860.[41] There were a considerable number of marriages among the families who were either business partners or who were identified with the same social and fraternal organization; in other words by usage and expectation, selections were made from in-group members. Records show that even the slaves of business partners entered into marriage relations. On November 16, 1837, Mingo, the slave of R. E. Dereef, was married to Hatira, the slave of Robert Howard.[42] These men were partners in the wood business.

The exhibition of a feeling of class-consciousness and the effort to maintain group solidarity were best exemplified in the activities of the Brown Fellowship Society. Through this medium social relations were cultivated, a system of education fostered, provisions for caring for the sick, the orphan and widow were made; and many men of wealth acted in an advisory and legal capacity as executors of the last wills of the members of the group.[43] When the Society was one hundred years old its name was changed to the *Century Fellowship Society*. Early in the twentieth century an auxiliary organization was formed which they named the *Daughters of the Century Fellowship Society*. The object of this branch of the association "... the erection of a hall to the memory of the men who won a page in the social history of the eighteenth century." [44] On the 117th anniversary of the organization, the president, in his annual address, epitomized the career of his caste in the following words: "Fortunately there were the classes in society, and as our forefathers allied themselves with them, as a consequence they had their influence and protection and they had to be in accord with them and stood for what they stood for. If they stood for high incentive so did our fathers. *If they stood for slavery so did our fathers to a certain extent but they sympathized with the oppressd,* for they had to endure some of it...." [45]

In conclusion, the free Negro of Charleston answers nicely to the "marginal man" concept.[46] By virtue of his biological characteristics; because of his partial accessibility to two social worlds; as a result of his feeling of superiority to one of these worlds, and his position of inferiority to the other, he was either constrained to become a misfit or to carve out a position which the community accepted and which he respected. Because of the nature of the social system he became a member of a separate caste which incorporated the interests, loyal-

[41] By the courtesy of Rev. Merritt Williams, Rector of St. Phillip's Church, the writer was permitted to examine the *Marriage Book* for entries of free Negroes.

[42] *Marriage Book of St. Phillip's Church.*

[43] *Minute Book of the Brown Fellowship Society,* 1869–1911. This material was made accessible through the courtesy of Mr. W. S. Montgomery, the Secretary.

[44] *The Holloway Scrapbook.*

[45] *Ibid.*

[46] Stonequist, Everett V., "The Problem of the Marginal Man," *The American Journal of Sociology,* Vol. XLI, July, 1935, pp. 3–4; and Park, Robert E., "Human Migration and the Marginal Man," *The American Journal of Sociology,* Vol. XXXIII (1928), pp. 881–893.

ties and usages of the upper caste members of the society in so far as this behavior did not offend or disturb the hierarchical arrangements. In this position he was able to circumvent the harsh ordinances which were designed to perpetuate the slave economy and to assuage the circumstances of his existence.

It is fair to say, however, that when the system was disrupted during the Civil War, this group provided the leadership, and the basis of organized, stable life for the Negro community.

This study has shown that (1) intimate human relations, whether between subordinates and superiors or between persons of equal rank, result in irresistible and inevitable *claims* [47] and *obligations* of each upon the other. In this case these relations gave rise to the emergence of a large group of free Negroes in the slave society. (2) City life with its heterogeneous population and its consequent conflict and fusion of cultures, with its competition and division of labor, tends to secularize human relations and institutions, and to facilitate freedom of movement, action and thought. Hence, if the city economy is to move on with efficiency, even the lowest servant in it must have economic value, and this is inevitably interlaced with the process of mobility. The city offered the free Negro his best opportunity for economic success. It is further shown that (3) in a society in which a group's position is not definitely defined by the mores and traditions efforts will be made to copy the patterns of conduct of those groups which have prestige, recognition and security. Lastly, it is shown that (4) the extent to which this class of Negroes in Charleston differed from similar groups in the total slave economy marked the extent to which the modes of life and patterns of conduct in the community as a whole, differed from the rest of the slave communities. The difference, in other words, is one of degree rather than kind.

[47] This idea was received from a lecture by Dr. R. E. Park in a class in collective behavior in the summer of 1935 at the University of Chicago. The course was offered by Dr. Herbert Blumer.

John Hope Franklin

THE FREE NEGRO IN THE ECONOMIC LIFE

OF ANTE-BELLUM NORTH CAROLINA

Free Negro farmers have received far less attention than their coun-
terparts in the towns. A pioneering student of the agrarian group was
the late Luther P. Jackson, who uncovered detailed evidence about
free Negro farmers through intensive research in the musty records
of Virginia county courthouses. Their ranks included laborers, tenants
and landowners.* In North Carolina, where the urban population was
small, the free Negro farmers were, relatively speaking, an even more
important segment of the population than they were in the neigh-
boring states of Virginia and South Carolina. In the selection that
follows, John Hope Franklin describes the farming operations and
property holdings of the free Negro yeomanry in North Carolina,
which, like the other older southern states, had a substantial free
Negro population that was practically absent from the Deep South,
except in Louisiana.

I N a state that was as decidedly rural as ante-bellum North Carolina, and
where the majority of the free Negroes lived in the rural areas,[1] it was only
natural that most of them made their living from the soil. The majority of the
free Negro apprentices were bound out to learn the trade of a farmer, and upon
reaching manhood they expected to pursue this occupation.[2] Since, moreover,

John Hope Franklin, "The Free Negro in the Economic Life of Ante-Bellum
North Carolina," Part II, *North Carolina Historical Review*, XIX (October, 1942),
pp. 359–375. Reprinted with the permission of the *North Carolina Historical Review*.
    * Luther P. Jackson, "The Virginia Free Negro Farmer and Property Owner,
1830–1860," *Journal of Negro History*, XXIV (October, 1939).
    [1] Only 3,197, or scarcely ten percent, of the free Negroes lived in towns in 1860.
Census Office, *The Population in 1860*, pp. 350–359.
    [2] See the occupations of free Negro apprentices in the unpublished population
schedules for the census of 1860. (Unless otherwise indicated, all manuscripts cited in
this article are in the archives of the North Carolina Historical Commission, Raleigh.)

it was extremely difficult for free Negroes to secure training in the skilled trades, many who may have had the inclination were forced into other fields. They *had* to make a living. Tradition and their meager training compelled the majority of the free Negroes to seek their living from the soil.

North Carolina was never one of the chief slaveholding states. In numbers, its slaves were fewer than those of her neighbor states of Virginia, South Carolina, and Georgia.[3] As a matter of fact, sixty-seven per cent of the slaveholding families held fewer than ten slaves in 1860, while seventy-two per cent of North Carolina's families held no slaves at all.[4] This suggests that in a state where the plantation system was only fairly well entrenched, the supply of slave labor was definitely limited. The farm labor in North Carolina was done not only by the slave but, in some areas, by the members of the white farming family, by white farm laborers, and by free Negro farm laborers.[5] In finding this work opportunity, the free Negro was extremely fortunate, and his labor was not as frequently rejected as it was in the more skilled occupations. Naturally there were objections to his presence on plantations where there were slaves, but these objections were more likely to be raised to the hiring of free Negroes on the neighbor's plantation than on one's own. Though there may have been fears that the free Negro's presence on a slave plantation might cause insolence among the slaves as well as inspire desires of freedom among them, this did not prevent the white slaveholders from hiring free Negroes to perform some of the tasks from time to time.[6]

There was, moreover, an opportunity for the free Negro to secure seasonal work on the farms of North Carolinians who had no slaves at all. The yeoman frequently harbored violent antipathies for the slave system and would refuse to hire slave labor even when it was available. He was more likely to look for assistance, during rush seasons, among the poor landless whites or among the free Negroes. The large number of free Negro farm laborers in counties where there was little or no slaveholding seems to support this point of view. In Cabarrus County, for example, where the slave population was small, there were fourteen free Negro farm laborers in 1860 and only four free Negro farmers.[7]

Naturally there were more free Negro farm hands in counties where the

[3] Census Office, *Population in 1860*, pp. 214, 452, 518.

[4] Guion G. Johnson, *Ante-Bellum North Carolina*, p. 468 ff.

[5] In describing the small farmer (white) in ante-bellum North Carolina, Dr. Guion Johnson refers to this group as the largest single class of whites in the state, and continues, "Their farms were small, and they cultivated their own land with the assistance of their families and an occasional hired hand or slave." Johnson, *Ante-Bellum North Carolina*, p. 65.

[6] See the unpublished population schedules for the census of 1860. Many free Negro farm laborers were listed as living with white families. This is all the more remarkable in view of the fact that, in such instances, the white farmer was responsible for all of the debts and obligations that were incurred by the free Negro.

[7] See the unpublished population schedules for the census of 1860. It is quite likely, moreover, that many of the free Negroes who gave their occupation as "common laborer" found work on the farms and may have been, more properly, "farm hands."

free Negro population was large. These counties, incidentally, also had a large slave population. As field hands, drivers, and all-around laborers, free Negroes found work opportunities on the largest of plantations. It was not unusual for free Negroes to live on slave plantations and to participate in the life there. Some of them had slave wives or husbands, and the benevolent master frequently permitted them to live there together, hiring the services of the free person.[8] Thomas Newton of Craven County secured his freedom from his master, Benjamin Woods, and by continuing to work for him Newton was able to purchase his wife, who had been a slave on the same plantation.[9]

Of course the number of free Negro farm laborers varied from county to county. The number to be found in any particular county depended not only upon the scarcity or abundance of farm labor, slave or free, and the attitude of the whites toward free Negro labor, but also upon the mobility of the landless free Negro population. It was extremely difficult for free Negroes, although without the trappings which usually tie people to a particular location, to move from one place to another. The reluctance of the authorities to grant passes permitting free Negroes to move about [10] and the impecunious state of a majority of the free Negroes made it quite difficult for free Negro farm laborers to migrate even to the adjoining county. It was possible, therefore, for a newly freed Negro to live and die in an area that was least suited for his advancement.

With these facts in mind, it is interesting to observe the location of the bulk of the free Negro farm hands in ante-bellum North Carolina. Of the 1,746 free Negro farm hands in the state in 1860, more than one thousand were located in the seven eastern counties which constituted the stronghold of the slave system.[11] Halifax County alone had 384 free Negro farm hands, while Pasquotank County had 284. Thirty-one counties were without any free Negro farm hands at all, while 700 were scattered among the remaining forty-eight counties.[12]

A more interesting group of free Negroes who made their living from the soil were those who either rented land or owned land and planted their own crops. They may properly be called the free Negro yeomanry. It was possible for a free Negro to obtain permission from a white landowner to live on the

[8] See, for example, the unpublished population schedules for the census of 1860 (Wake County). It seems that such a practice was quite inconsistent with the point of view that the presence of free Negroes among slaves "contributes to excite and cherish a spirit of discontent and disorder among the slaves." Petition of the citizens of New Bern to the General Assembly, December, 1831, MS. in the Legislative Papers for 1831–1832.

[9] Minutes of the Court of Pleas and Quarter Sessions for Craven County, March, 1811.

[10] After 1831 free Negroes desiring to go to other countries had to receive a license from the clerk of the Court of Pleas and Quarter Sessions of the county in which they resided. *Laws,* 1830–1831, p. 11.

[11] The seven counties were Granville, Halifax, Hertford, Northampton, Pasquotank, Perquimans, and Sampson.

[12] This information was taken from the unpublished population schedules for the census of 1860. Most of the counties with no free Negro farm hands were located in the western part of the state.

latter's land and to cultivate a portion of it and share in the returns from his labor. This, however, was looked upon with disfavor, and white owners of land were discouraged in the practice. A law of 1827 required each white person to list all free Negroes living on his land and to be responsible for the taxes which might be levied on such free Negroes.[13] Free Negro tenants who showed a disposition to work and to shoulder their responsibilities could still convince landowners that they would not be a burden to them. The tax lists of various counties and the census reports bear witness to the fact that there were free Negro tenants on the lands of white persons down to the end of the period. In the tax list for Beaufort County in 1850, for example, A. Eborn, a free Negro, was listed as the tenant of John Cutter, white. One wealthy white farmer, R. H. Reddick of Lower Broad Creek, had fourteen free Negro tenants on his land and was responsible for $143.93 in taxes for them. In the same list, F. Hackey, a free Negro, was the tenant of Samuel Swan, white.[14] At the end of the period, despite the financial risks on the part of white landowners, many free Negro tenants were still living on the land of white landowners.[15]

That the number of free Negroes who owned their farms was considerable can be seen in the real property columns of the unpublished population schedules of the census returns. Many of these individuals, like John Stanly of New Bern, had started with small holdings, and by thrift and business acumen had accumulated sizable holdings. They usually engaged in tobacco and cotton farming and marketed their crops in much the same way that other farmers in the state marketed theirs. By far the majority of the property owned by free Negroes was in the rural areas and was, of course, in the possession of free Negro farmers.

The free Negro farmer was generally in better circumstances than free Negroes in other areas of economic activity. In 1860 there were 1,047 free Negroes who gave their occupation as farmers. Of this number, approximately fifty per cent possessed some real property. In some cases they did not own an amount sufficient for their purposes, but the figures seem to suggest that the free Negro was becoming a landowner. David Reynolds, a farmer of Halifax County, owned $3,000 worth of real property in 1860. J. A. Collins of Hyde County had $1,000 worth of real property at the same time. The well known Thomas Blacknall of Franklin County owned $6,000 worth of land. Of the fifty-three Negroes with property valued at more than $2,500 each in 1860, thirty-one were farmers.[16]

In North Carolina the free Negroes who made their living from the soil numbered approximately three thousand. Doubtless this number could be augmented considerably when one takes into account the number of minors and

---

[13] *Laws,* 1827–1828, p. 21.

[14] MS. in the County Records for Beaufort County, 1850 (Beaufort County Courthouse, Washington, N.C.).

[15] See the unpublished population schedules for the census of 1860.

[16] Unpublished population schedules for the census of 1860.

housewives who assisted their fathers, brothers, and husbands in the fields. That they constituted the most important element in the economic life of the free Negro in ante-bellum North Carolina in terms of numbers and holdings is clearly shown by the facts. For the most part they went their way unnoticed. The disproportionate part of the stage occupied by the free Negroes in other pursuits was the result of the focus of light thrown upon them in the more thickly settled communities. Meanwhile the free Negro farmer, living in the inarticulate and relatively sparsely settled countryside, steadily rose in economic independence and, consequently, in the respect—somewhat disquieted, perhaps—of his fellows.

At no time during the period before the Civil War was the free Negro's right to own real property questioned. He enjoyed all the protection in the matter of acquisition, transfer, devise, and descent that other citizens of North Carolina enjoyed. The records of the county courts indicate that free Negroes used them regularly for the purpose of recording changes in ownership of real and personal property. The following record is typical of many that were found in the minutes of the county court: "A deed from Ezra F. Holmes to Southey Kease (free Negro) was proved in open court by the oath of William T. Bryan a witness thereto ordered to be registered." [17]

Having once acquired land, the free Negro could be fairly certain that the courts would protect him during his period of possession. In 1838 Benjamin Curry, a free Negro of Guilford County, was driven off the property which he had owned for twelve years. Of the four white men charged with dispossessing Curry, one claimed that the free Negro had sold him his house, land, and five slave children, and that the transaction had been executed in a deed of trust between the two parties. At the trial the solicitor for the state objected to the deed as evidence, contending that it was a slick piece of extortion and that the free Negro did not intend to give up his land. The lower court convicted the defendants of having "riotously and routously" assembled to disturb the peace of the state and with force of arms trespassed upon the property of the free Negro.

The defendants appealed the case to the Supreme Court. After making a thorough review of the facts in the case and after listening to lengthy arguments from both sides, Judge Gaston, speaking for the Court, said:

> We are of the opinion that there was no error in the conviction of which the defendant complains. In cases where the law gives to the judges a discretion over the quantum of punishment, they may, with propriety, suspend the sentence [In this case, the principal defendant had received a fine of $100.] for the avowed purpose of affording the convicted an opportunity to make restitution to the person peculiarly aggrieved by his offense.
>
> The judgment against the defendant is, therefore, reversed, and

[17] Minutes of the Court of Pleas and Quarter Sessions for Beaufort County, December, 1843 (Beaufort County Courthouse, Washington, N.C.).

this opinion is to be certified to the Superior Court—for the County of Guilford, with directions to award sentence of fine or of fine and imprisonment against the defendant agreeably thereto and to the laws of the state.[18]

The leniency of Judge Gaston was inspired by the defendant's having already restored the property to the free Negro. Though there was a reversal of the conviction, the case remains significant in that the Supreme Court went on record as being vigorously opposed to the abridgment of property rights even in the case of a free Negro.[19]

Free Negroes could sell or transfer their land at will as long as it was for a legal consideration. In 1833, for example, Benjamin Neale of Craven County sold one hundred acres of land, and the following indenture makes known the transaction:

February 4, 1833)
State of N.C.   )
County of Craven)

Be it known that Benjamin Neale (coloured man) for and in consideration of the sum of fifty dollars to me paid in hand by William B. Masters of the same State and County aforesaid, have bargained sold enfeoffed and confirmed unto the same Wm. B. Masters his heirs and assigns forever a certain parcel of land. . . . [A description of the land is given.] The said Benjamin Neale purchased of Thomas Cooke dec. containing by estimation one hundred acres be the same more or less. To have and to hold the said piece or parcel of land with all the woods ways waters and every other appurtenances thereunto belonging against the lawful claims of all and every other person.

Benjamin Neale [20]

The right of a free Negro to sell his property was confirmed by the Supreme Court in a decision of 1843. A white man, Pearson, rented a small tract of land for one year to Elijah Powell, a free Negro, who promised to give him one-half of the corn crop. The Justice of the Peace gave Pearson permission to sell Powell's crop. Powell asked that the sale be postponed until after the corn was gathered. When the corn was sold, one Hare objected, saying that he had already bought half of the crop from Powell. Pearson denied that Powell could sell his share, contending that he was only a servant. The Nash Superior Court said that Powell was a tenant and could dispose of his property as he

[18] State *v.* John H. Bennett, 20 N.C., p. 135 ff.
[19] See also the case of State *v.* Emory, 51 N.C., p. 142, in which the Supreme Court held that a free Negro could not be forcibly ejected from the possession of a house.
[20] MS. in the James W. Bryan Papers (University of North Carolina Library, Chapel Hill, N.C.). See also the deed from John and Rebecca Hambleton, free Negroes, to Churchill Moore, in the Minutes of the Court of Pleas and Quarter Sessions for Beaufort County, December, 1842 (Beaufort County Courthouse, Washington, N.C.).

pleased. In upholding this view, the Supreme Court, through Judge Daniel, said:

> Even if Powell was a servant, the division had given him a share which all would have to admit. The corn had been placed in the defendant's barn upon the naked bailment for safe-keeping. The sale of it and the demand by the purchaser put an end to the bailment.[21]

It was not at all unusual for free Negroes to direct the disposition of their property through wills. Upon the death of the testator, the will was recorded in the minutes of the county court and an executor was appointed by the court. The minutes of the Beaufort County Court for 1843 give a typical example:

> State of North Carolina)
> Beaufort County   )
> A paper writing purporting to be the last will and testament of John Hambleton deceased (free Negro) was duly proved in open court to be the last will and testament of said John Hambleton and duly executed so as to pass seal on personal estate by the oath of John W. Latham the subscribing witness thereto and ordered to be recorded and Edward Hyman the Executor named therein was qualified as Executor.[22]

An interesting case involving the will of a free Negro woman was that of the aged Mary Green of Wilmington, who left all of her property to a white attorney. She looked to him not only for counsel, the records showed, but also for protection and occasionally small sums of money. In addition to these favors, he also collected rent on the property that had been accumulated by the testator's free Negro husband. The only relative, a niece, had received a house and lot from her aunt before she died. Upon the advice of the free Negro husband, all the property was left to the white attorney. The niece went into court and contended that her aunt had been under "undue influence" and sought to have the will invalidated. Upon losing the case in the New Hanover Superior Court, the niece appealed to the Supreme Court. In upholding the decision of the lower court, Judge Manly said,

> It seems that the legatee [Joshua Wright] and the decedent [Mary Green] stood in relation of client and attorney *patron* and *dependent*, and the court below—informs the jury that persons bearing these relations are to be suspected and scrutinized more closely and carefully

[21] Hare v. Pearson, 26 N.C., p. 62.

[22] Minutes of the Court of Pleas and Quarter Sessions of Beaufort County, June, 1843 (Beaufort County Courthouse, Washington, N.C.). Free Negroes were sometimes appointed executors, as in the case of Southey Keis, of Beaufort County, who in March, 1856, appeared in court and qualified as the executor of the estate of Mary Keis. Minutes of the Court of Pleas and Quarter Sessions of Beaufort County, March, 1856 (Beaufort County Courthouse, Washington, N.C.).

than dealings between others. These relations, as facts pertinent to the issue—were submitted to the jury with proper instructions. That was all, we think, the court was authorized to do by the law of the land.

We concur with the court below that undue influence must be fraudulent and controlling and must be shown to the satisfaction of a jury, in a court of law, upon an issue of *devisavit vel nom*.[23]

Free Negroes, as other individuals, sometimes had difficulty in establishing their rightful claim to property left to them in a will. If, however, their freedom could be established and if the circumstances under which the will was made were valid, the free Negro could secure the necessary protection in the courts of the state. In 1851, one Benjamin Dicken of Edgecombe County died. His will directed his executor to free all of his slaves and send them to some free state and divide $12,000 among them. All except one woman, who died soon after, left the state. Her daughter, who had gone to Canada, claimed her mother's share of the estate for her and the other children. The executor claimed that the mother had not complied with the stipulation of the will since she had not left the state and therefore, that her heirs could claim no part of the money intended for her. Judge Pearson, of the Supreme Court, said that the removing of the Negroes was not a condition precedent to emancipation, but a condition subsequent, "by the non-performance of which they may forfeit their newly acquired freedom." The Judge was satisfied that the deceased free Negro woman had good intentions:

1. We are satisfied that Mariah the mother of the plaintiff at the time of her death—was to all intents and purposes, a free woman, and had the capacity to take property and transmit it by succession to her personal representative.

2. We are also satisfied that the children of Mariah were entitled to call upon her administrator to make distribution among them, as her next of kin—and we think it clear that all of her children are to be considered distributees.[24]

In one case several technicalities arose which made it difficult for a free Negro devisee to retain the town property that had been left her by a wealthy white man of Tarboro. In his will he said: "I give and devise to Mary Ann Jones, a free colored woman of the town of Tarboro and to her heirs and assigns forever, the lot of ground and house thereon erected on which she now lives." Since two lots belonging to the testator were adjacent, the executor interpreted the will literally and proceeded to take possession of the lot next to the one on which the devisee's house stood. Before his death, the testator had fenced in both lots together, and the free Negro woman used both lots for a garden and for other purposes. In 1860 Judge Manly of the Supreme Court awarded both lots to the estate of the free Negro woman—by that

[23] Wright *v.* Howe, 20 N.C., 318.
[24] Alvany, a free woman of color, *v.* Powell, 54 N.C., p. 34.

time deceased. He took the point of view that the gift to the free Negro woman "is not confined to the fifty yards square called a lot in the plan of the town, but extends at least to the lands enclosed and used in connection with the house." In the will the testator used the word "lot" to mean "parcel" or "piece." [25]

Perhaps the most interesting case of the period involving the inheritance of property by free Negroes arose in 1857. While a slave, a certain Miles married another slave. Afterward he was freed and subsequently purchased his wife. They had one child; then the wife was set free, and they had several other children. After this wife died, Miles married a free Negro woman by whom he had three children. When he died intestate, in 1857, a contest arose between the two sets of children over the division of the property. The children by the first wife claimed tenancy in common with the children by the second wife. When the case came before the Supreme Court, that body denied that the children by the first wife had any valid claims:

> A slave cannot make a contract. Therefore, he cannot marry legally. Marriage is based upon contract. Consequently, the relation of "man and wife" cannot exist among slaves. Neither the first nor the others of the children by the first wife were legitimate. The parties after being freed ought to have married according to law; it is the misfortune of their children that they neglected or refused to do so, for no court can avert the consequences.[26]

The possession of slaves by free Negroes was the only type of personal property holding that was ever questioned during the ante-bellum period. There may not have been much objection to the ownership of one's own family by a free Negro; but when one undertook to acquire slaves to improve his economic status, there were those who looked upon it as a dangerous trend, the legality of which was seriously questioned. If the free Negro was not a full citizen, could he enjoy the same privileges of ownership and the protection of certain types of property that other citizens enjoyed? Around this question revolved a great deal of discussion at the beginning of the militant period of the antislavery movement.[27]

When a slave was found guilty of concealing a slave on board a vessel, in violation of the act of 1825, it was contended by his owner that the prisoner, a slave, was not a person or mariner within the meaning of the act and that Green, the owner of the concealed slave, was a mulatto and hence not a citizen of the state and could not own slaves. The decision of the Supreme Court, handed down in 1833 by Judge Daniel, established once and for all the rights

[25] Doe on the demise of Mary Ann Jones v. Norfleet, 20 N.C., p. 365. A plan of the lots was included in the report of the court.

[26] Doe on the demise of Frances Howard v. Sarah Howard, 51 N.C., p. 238.

[27] Since the possession of slaves enhanced one's social position in the community, the whites may well have objected to the ownership of slaves by free Negroes on the grounds that it would tend to upset the social structure—or that by such possession the free Negroes might begin to feel that they had "arrived" socially.

of the free Negro in the matter of the ownership of slaves. He said:

> By the laws of this State, a free man of color may own land and hold lands and personal property including slaves. Without therefore stopping to inquire into the extent of the political rights and privileges of a free man of color, I am very well satisfied from the words of the act of the General Assembly that the Legislature meant to protect the slave property of every person who by the laws of the State are entitled to hold such property. I am, therefore, of the opinion that the owner is a citizen within the meaning of the Act of Assembly, and it appearing he was a mulatto is not a reason to grant a new trial to the person who concealed his slave.[28]

The decision of Judge Daniel in this case remained the accepted point of view until the very end of the period. When the hostility between the sections was developing into open conflict, the free Negro in the South witnessed an almost complete abrogation of his rights. One of the most significant laws passed during the momentous session of the legislature in 1860–1861 was the "Act to prevent free Negroes from having the control of slaves." While it did not affect a large number of free Negroes within the state,[29] it showed the extent to which the North Carolina solons were willing to go in order to combat the forces that were striking at the heart of their long-cherished system. Among other things, the law provided:

> That no free Negro, or free person of color, shall be permitted or allowed to buy, purchase, or hire for any length of time any slave or slaves, or to have any slave or slaves bound as apprentice or apprentices to him, her or them, or in any other wise to have the control, management or services of any slave or slaves, under the penalty of one hundred dollars for each offence, and shall further be guilty of a misdemeanor, and liable to indictment for the same.

Another section of the law provided that free Negroes already in the possession of slave property would not be affected by the enactment.[30]

Despite the innumerable obstacles that stood in the way of the accumulation of property by free Negroes, several amassed a considerable amount of property during their lifetime. The life of Julius Melbourn is about as interesting as one can find in the period. Born a slave in 1790 on a plantation near Raleigh, he was bought, at five years of age, by the wealthy widow of a British army official, who lived in Raleigh. When her only son was slain in a duel—said to have been fought because of some derogatory remarks concerning his mother having reared Melbourn as a gentleman—the slave was emancipated and made the sole heir to the estate of $20,000. By the time Melbourn

---

[28] State v. Edmund, a slave, 15 N.C., p. 278.
[29] The number of free Negroes who owned slaves was steadily decreasing. See below, pp. 372, 373.
[30] Laws, 1860–1861, p. 69.

was twenty-five years old his estate was worth about $30,000. By careful saving and shrewd investment, he was soon worth $50,000. When he decided that he could not live and die in a country "where the laws sustained and justified such disregard to individual rights and tolerated such inhumanity," as was manifested in the treatment of free Negroes, he sailed for England, where he spent the remainder of his life. That he was still wealthy is attested by the fact that he set up his son in a $20,000 mercantile business in London.[31]

Most of the free Negroes who owned property were possessors of small estates worth a few hundred dollars or less. These individuals, moreover, comprised only a small percentage of the total free Negro population. The great majority of free Negroes in North Carolina were, during the entire period, without any property whatsoever. At the end of the period, only 3,659, or slightly more than ten per cent, owned any property. Of this number, only 1,211 owned any real estate. In few counties did more than ten per cent of the free Negroes own property. Craven County, with 1,332 free Negroes in 1860, had only 179 free Negro property owners. Cabarrus County, with 115 free Negroes, had twelve free Negro owners of property. Halifax County, with its 3,452 free Negroes, however, had 463 free Negroes who owned property.[32] In 1860 the following free Negroes had property valued at $2,500 or more: [33] While this table does not represent the average holdings of the free Negro in ante-bellum North Carolina, it suggests that there was a number of individual cases in which free Negroes rose to a position of economic independence, despite obstacles.

In six counties in 1860 free Negroes owned no real estate.[34] While each county listed some personal property held by free Negroes, eight counties listed only one such person each.[35] Perhaps nothing is a more striking commentary on the plight of the free Negro in North Carolina than his inability to acquire property, both real and personal.

A study of the value of the property which free Negroes did possess will shed further light on the economic status of the free Negro in ante-bellum North Carolina. Of course it is difficult for one living in the fifth decade of the twentieth century to appreciate the figures which reveal the value of property owned by free Negroes in, say, 1860. Land values were so much lower at the time that it was quite possible for an individual with one hundred dollars worth of real property to have an adequate amount for farming purposes, and with a few hundred dollars he could erect a house that would be about as modern as the age could provide. There was a likelihood, however, that the land of the free Negro would be the least desirable in a given area.

[31] Julius Melbourn, *Life and Opinions of Julius Melbourn, passim.*

[32] Unpublished population schedules for the census of 1860.

[33] These statistics were compiled from the unpublished population schedules for the census of 1860.

[34] They were Alleghany, Davie, Harnett, Haywood, Jackson, and Madison. Interestingly enough, none of these counties was in the eastern part of the state.

[35] They were Catawba, Haywood, Henderson, Hyde, Jackson, Martin, McDowell, and Rutherford.

FREE NEGROES HAVING PROPERTY VALUED AT MORE THAN $2,500

Name	Occupation	Value	Name	Occupation	Value
Alee, M.	Baker	$2,750	Knight, J.	Confection	$5,905
Alston, O.	Farmer	17,644	Lan'ton, D.	Carpenter	2,500
Bell, H.		14,000	Lewis, W.	Farmer	2,750
Bethel, J.	Barber	3,550	Locklier	Farmer	5,200
Blacknall, T.	Farmer	7,300	Mangum, L.	Farmer	20,816
Bryan, C.	Farmer	2,535	Martin, W.	Farmer	2,500
Burchett, J.	Farmer	2,500	Men'hall	Farmer	3,197
Butch, H.	Farm Hand	3,450	Michael, S.	Farmer	5,000
Collins, J.	Farmer	9,000	Miller, E.	Wheelwright	8,150
Corn, D.	Farmer	5,250	Moore, D.	Barber	4,400
Corn, N.	Farmer	2,800	Norris, A.	Carpenter	3,000
Cuff, N.	Farmer	3,475	Ox'dine, J.	Farmer	9,825
Day, T.	Cab. Maker	4,000	Picar, E.		2,500
Dial, G.	Farmer	4,900	Piles, A.	Clerk	5,000
Erwin, J.	Musician	3,100	Reed, W.	Farmer	3,300
Evans, E.	Farmer	11,830	Revel, E.	Farmer	4,826
Evans, W.	Farmer	3,932	Reynolds	Farmer	4,000
Freeman, J.	Farmer	20,300	Sampson, J.	Carpenter	36,000
Graham, J.	Farmer	2,800	Scott, A.	Farmer	3,766
Green, M.	Farmer	2,600	Silvester	Farmer	2,670
Guy, W.	Farmer	2,695	Smith, N.	Farmer	2,500
Hites, E.	Carpenter	4,000	Stanly, C.	Dress Maker	4,000
Howard, J.		2,500	Steward, W.	Farmer	3,000
Jacobs, J.	Farmer	3,712	Taboon, A.	Farm Hand	5,554
Jones, M.	Housekeeper	5,500	Webb, S.	Farmer	2,810
Jones, T.		6,700	Winn, C.	Blacksmith	2,800
Jordan, J.	Farmer	4,700			

Since the majority of free Negroes were small farmers, they faced the same difficulty that other North Carolina yeomen faced: that of trying to obtain satisfactory property in the same market where the more resourceful plantation owner was making his purchases. It is a point of interest, therefore, that some free Negroes, like John C. Stanly of New Bern and James D. Sampson of New Hanover, were able to acquire some of the most desirable land in their respective communities.

On the whole, a larger number of free Negroes possessed some type of personal property, ranging from silver watches to farming tools. Thus, in the larger number of counties, the value of personal property was higher than the value of real property. But the poverty of the free Negro group can be seen clearly through this study of the value of the property of the group. They possessed an aggregate wealth of $1,045,643. (See table below.) When one considers that more than 30,000 people had to share in this wealth of slightly more than one million dollars, the realization of their plight is inescapable. The per capita wealth of the free Negroes of North Carolina was only $34 in 1860. Thousands of these were landless and without any kind of property. Even when one ascertains the per capita wealth of the free Negro property owners, the picture remains gloomy, for they had a per capita wealth of $287.

It must be remembered that fifty-three were worth more than $2,500, while several were worth more than $15,000.[36] The following table shows the value of real and personal property of free Negroes in 1860.[37]

AGGREGATE VALUE OF PROPERTY OWNED BY FREE NEGROES					
County	Real	Personal	County	Real	Personal
Alamance	$13,500	$7,415	Jackson		$125
Alexander	500	390	Johnston	$4,060	4,853
Alleghany		600	Jones	1,500	1,875
Anson	3,798	7,660	Lenoir	625	2,250
Ashe	2,200	2,495	Lincoln	100	270
Beaufort	12,410	6,960	Macon	4,050	5,100
Bertie	1,280	3,615	Madison		615
Bladen	6,289	5,112	Martin	5,549	1,200
Brunswick	6,487	6,239	McDowell	4,000	1,000
Buncombe	3,540	3,184	Mecklenburg	8,875	3,720
Burke	200	785	Montgomery	362	1,285
Cabarrus	1,072	2,050	Moore	550	1,975
Caldwell	1,295	1,284	Nash	8,939	10,889
Camden	1,000	768	New Hanover	37,720	35,060
Carteret	3,150	950	Northampton	12,824	15,359
Caswell	4,208	5,530	Onslow	1,735	3,475
Catawba	50	75	Orange	2,800	13,375
Chatham	1,680	2,960	Pasquotank	20,440	22,195
Cherokee	350	515	Perquimans	5,000	8,601
Chowan	3,600	2,793	Person	5,180	3,080
Cleveland	3,150	4,652	Pitt	2,100	5,560
Columbus	9,135	8,990	Polk	700	1,446
Craven	29,865	21,137	Randolph	5,290	8,745
Cumberland	11,500	7,722	Richmond	10,750	20,930
Currituck	1,270	1,745	Robeson	37,555	42,159
Davidson	1,200	1,428	Rockingham	2,750	1,900
Davie		1,040	Rowan	1,300	970
Duplin	3,360	3,777	Rutherford	225	100
Edgecombe	7,100	10,350	Sampson	10,014	4,742
Forsyth	1,530	1,665	Stanly	950	835
Franklin	6,535	6,013	Stokes	325	550
Gaston	2,700	2,300	Surry	925	1,144
Gates	5,125	18,755	Tyrrel	725	1,615
Granville	15,987	13,845	Union	300	975
Greene	2,475	2,920	Wake	22,204	45,362
Guilford	5,425	13,445	Warren	9,931	13,935
Halifax	30,948	42,778	Washington	5,843	5,077
Harnett		375	Watauga	475	595
Haywood		75	Wayne	13,380	9,900
Henderson	150	100	Wilkes	2,710	3,835
Hertford	15,482	16,624	Wilson	4,984	3,999
Hyde	1,000	8,000	Yadkin	840	2,912
Iredell	330	150	Yancey	1,525	1,803

[36] Unpublished population schedules for the census of 1860.

[37] These statistics were compiled from the unpublished population schedules for the census of 1860.

One area in which considerable interest has always been manifested is the ownership of slaves by free Negroes. At no time during the ante-bellum period were free Negroes in North Carolina without some slaves. The motives for such ownership were perhaps varied, as in other groups. Without a doubt there were those who possessed slaves for the purpose of advancing their economic well-being. With such a view in mind, these free Negro slaveholders were more interested in making their farms or carpenter shops "pay" than they were in treating their slaves humanely. The enterprising free Negro owners of slaves can usually be identified because of their extensive holdings of real and personal property and because of their inactivity in the manumission movement. For thirty years Thomas Day, the free Negro cabinet maker of Milton, used slaves to help him in his business. In 1830 he had two;[38] by 1860 he had three.[39] For thirty years Thomas Blacknall of Franklin County kept slaves, though the number fell from seven to three between 1830 and 1860.[40] It seems clear that these enterprising free Negroes were at least as deeply interested in the labor of their slaves as they were in their comfort.

It seems that by far the larger portion of free Negro owners of slaves were possessors of this human chattel for benevolent reasons. There are numerous examples of free Negroes having purchased relatives or friends to ease their lot. Many of them manumitted such slaves,[41] while others held title to slaves who were virtually free. An examination of the slaveholding by free Negroes seems to bear out this point. Slave Richard Gaston ran away from his master and remained in the woods until his free Negro wife had saved the necessary funds for his purchase.[42] Lila Abshur continued to hold title to her father when the legislature acted unfavorably on her petition to emancipate him.[43] While John S. Stanly undoubtedly held some slaves with the view to increasing his wealth,[44] he held others purely out of benevolence.[45]

The fluctuation in the number of free Negro owners of slaves during the period under observation is an interesting development. At the time of the taking of the first census in 1790, twenty-five free Negroes in eleven counties owned seventy-three slaves.[46] In 1830 the number of free Negro slaveholders had increased to 191, distributed in thirty-seven counties, while their human

---

[38] C. G. Woodson, *Free Negro Owners of Slaves in 1830*, p. 24.

[39] Unpublished population schedules for the census of 1860.

[40] Woodson, *Free Negro Owners*, p. 25, and the unpublished population schedules for the census of 1860.

[41] See the Minutes of the Court of Pleas and Quarter Sessions of Craven County, March, 1811. These records show that Thomas Newton, a free Negro, liberated his slave wife.

[42] C. D. Wilson, "Negroes Who Owned Slaves," *Popular Science Monthly*, LXXXI, p. 485.

[43] MS. in the Legislative Papers for 1856.

[44] In 1830 he held eighteen slaves. Woodson, *Free Negro Owners*, p. 24.

[45] In 1815 Stanly emancipated a slave woman and her five children, as well as a slave man. Minutes of the Court of Pleas and Quarter Sessions of Craven County, March, June, 1815.

[46] Census Office, *Heads of Families in the United States in 1790*, *passim*.

chattel numbered 620.[47] Interestingly enough, by 1860 there were only eight free Negro owners of slaves, the latter numbering only twenty-five.[48]

Several observations can now be made. In the first place, the number of slaves held by free Negroes was usually small. Notable exceptions are the eleven slaves held by Samuel Johnston of Bertie County in 1790;[49] the forty-four slaves each owned by Gooden Bowen of Bladen County and John Walker of New Hanover County in 1830; and the tweny-four slaves owned by John Chrichlon of Martin County in 1830.[50] Free Negroes usually held one, two, or three slaves; and the petitions of free Negroes to manumit relatives suggest that a sizable number of slaves had been acquired as a result of benevolence.

In the second place, the increase in the number of free Negroes with an accompanying increase in economic independence on the part of some caused a larger number of Negro slaves to be acquired by free Negroes. No doubt, moreover, there was some effort to conform to the pattern established by the dominant slaveholding group within the state in the effort to elevate themselves to a position of respect and privilege. Thus by 1830 more than 600 slaves were held by free Negroes. Finally, the remarkable decline both in the number of free Negro slave owners and in the number of slaves held toward the end of the period suggests the increasing economic and political difficulty that the free Negro was encountering. Many of those slaves held in 1830 had been manumitted according to the plans of the free Negro owners. Other slaves had been lost in the maze of the economic setbacks that many free Negroes were experiencing.[51] Perhaps also the fervor to acquire slave relatives and set them free was waning, as the free Negro himself began to doubt the blessings of freedom.[52] Thus even before it became illegal for free Negroes to acquire slaves—in 1861—the group had ceased to make such acquisitions. In this case the enactment made legally impossible that which the free Negro had already ceased to do.

Surrounded on all sides by a legal system which denied them the opportunity to seek a livelihood where they could and by a hostile community that often made them as unwelcome as a contagious disease, the free Negroes tried to find their place in the economic life of ante-bellum North Carolina. If they were "idle, thievish, roguish, and indolent"—a sweeping generalization that can reasonably be doubted—they merely reflected the restraints and

[47] Woodson, *Free Negro Owners*, pp. 24–26, and the unpublished population schedules for the census of 1830.

[48] The list was compiled by the writer from the unpublished population schedules for the census of 1860.

[49] *State Records*, XXVI, 278.

[50] Woodson, *Free Negro Owners*, pp. 24–25.

[51] In such cases the free Negro was losing his slaves in much the same way that the white slaveholder was losing his. By 1860 the rate of increase of slaves in North Carolina was noticeably declining. Taylor, *Slaveholding, passim.*

[52] By 1858 free Negroes had begun to send petitions to the General Assembly asking to be reenslaved. See the MSS. in the Legislative Papers for 1958, 1859, and 1860.

stigma that society had placed upon them, and their reactions were no more than natural. In view of the circumstances, it is not surprising that they were not a more powerful economic force than they were. The amazing thing is that under such adverse circumstances they were able to acquire more than a million dollars worth of property by the end of the period and to have possessed several hundred slaves during the seventy-year period ending in 1860.

Dixon Ryan Fox

THE NEGRO VOTE IN OLD NEW YORK

*Though less proscribed than the Free People of Color in the South,
northern Negroes also suffered many forms of racism and discrimination, and in most states did not enjoy full citizenship rights. For
example, though most of the New England states did accord them
the franchise, they were excluded from the ballot box in all the
states of the Old Northwest and, after 1837, in Pennsylvania. New
York was unique, providing in its constitution of 1821 for universal
white manhood suffrage, with a discriminatory property qualification
for Negroes.*

*Dixon Ryan Fox's article describes the political and social forces
that produced this partial disfranchisement of the black population. His description is especially timely because it presents early examples both of Negro bloc voting and of a white backlash.*

THE attachment of the colored citizen to the Republican party is usually
explained by reference to the memory of Lincoln, Stevens, Grant and Sumner;
but in New York, at least, the freedman learned to vote against St. Tammany
before most of those apostles of his "rights" were born, and the jealous hatred
of poor mechanics helps far more than reconstruction policies to account for
the attitude of New York Democrats towards Negro suffrage.

The appearance of the Negro in the Hudson River region is no novelty
of recent years. The Dutch brought the *swarten* to the colony before Manhattan houses were a decade old; [1] when the English made Fort Amsterdam
Fort James, the encouragement of the slave trade with New York became an
object of solitude in London.[2] The demand for "negears" was larger and more
steady here than in other colonies of the same latitude,[3] yet slaves were not

Dixon Ryan Fox, "The Negro Vote in Old New York," *Political Science Quarterly,*
XXXII (June, 1917), pp. 252–75. Reprinted with permission of *Political Science Quar-
terly.*
    [1] Mrs. S. Van Rensselaer, *History of the City of New York in the Seventeenth
Century*, N.Y., 1909, vol. i, pp. 191–195.
    [2] Instructions to Governors Bellomont, Hunter etc., in *N.Y. Colonial Documents*.
    [3] H. R. Stiles, *History of the City of Brooklyn*, Albany, 1869, vol. i, p. 231.

massed in large plantations but scattered by twos and threes as household servants among the well-to-do, chiefly in the houses of the aristocracy.[4] They were treated with a careful kindliness, and in return they developed an affection for the master that no shock of fortune could disturb.[5]

What was the partizan connection of New York slave owners? The Federalist party was the party of the aristocracy, especially in large communities,[6] the party of the wealth won by a century of trade. Since slaves in this colony were a luxury rather than an investment in agriculture, we should expect to find them belonging largely to members of this party; the records show such to have been the case.[7]

A great historian has truly remarked: "That New York is not a slave state like South Carolina is due to climate and not to the superior humanity of the founders." [8] Slavery for them did not pay. The Federalist masters preferred to see their Negroes free, and led the movement in New York state for their betterment. Governor John Jay organized the Society for Promoting the Manumission of Slaves and became its first president in 1785; [9] he was succeeded by Alexander Hamilton.[10] It was Rufus King who had moved "that there shall be neither slavery nor involuntary servitude in any of the states described in the resolve of Congress of 23rd of April, 1784," dealing with the Northwest Ordinance.[11] General Schuyler was found, when the time came, voting for

[4] In the *Documentary History of New York* (edition of 1850), vol. iii, pp. 505–521, is a list of slave-holders in the colony in 1755. Few masters had more than five slaves. The rolls of New York city and Albany have been lost, but we are able to form some estimate of the distribution of slaves in the "Wills on File in the Surrogate's Office," abstracts of which have been printed in the *Collections of the New York Historical Society*, volumes from 1900 to 1906 dealing with the years 1780 to 1800. See also Stiles, *op. cit.*, vol. ii, p. 65, and J. Munsell, *Collections on the History of Albany*, vol. i, p. 60, vol. ii, pp. 49, 382.

[5] C. F. Hoffman, *The Pioneers of New York* (delivered before St. Nicholas Society), N.Y., 1848, pp. 30–33; T. E. V. Smith, *The City of New York in the Year of Washington's Inauguration*, N.Y., 1889, p. 122. For legal status of slaves see E. V. Morgan, "Slavery in New York," *Papers of the American Historical Association*, vol. v, pp. 337–380.

[6] A. C. McLoughlin, *The Confederation and the Constitution*, N.Y., 1905, pp. 290–291. C. A. Beard, *Economic Interpretation of the Jeffersonian Democracy*, N.Y., 1915, *passim*. On the New York aristocracy, see T. Roosevelt, *Gouverneur Morris*, Boston, 1892, pp. 17 *et seq*.

[7] E.g., "Wills" as cited, liber xxxix, p. 127; xli, pp. 48, 128, 141; xlii, p. 191; N.Y. *Doc. Hist.*, vol. iii, pp. 510, 512, 514, 519, for well-known Federalist names.

[8] George Bancroft, *History of the United States* (edition 1883), vol. i, p. 513.

[9] Wm. Jay, *Life of John Jay*, N.Y., 1833, vol. i, pp. 229–235; vol. ii, p. 406. It was Jay's custom to purchase slaves of promise that he might, after due instruction, set them free. G. Pellew, *John Jay*, p. 294. See also *Correspondence of John Jay*, N.Y., 1893, vol. iv, p. 320.

[10] For Hamilton on slavery see "A Full Vindication," in *Works* (edited by J. C. Hamilton), N.Y., 1851, vol. ii, p. 9, and vol. vi, p. 298. See also F. G. Mather, "Slavery in the Colony and State of New York," in *Magazine of American History*, vol. ix, p. 408.

[11] *The Life and Correspondence of Rufus King* (edited by C. R. King), N.Y., 1900, vo. i, pp. 39, 268–292. On King's later stand against slavery see J. Q. Adams, *Memoirs*, Philadelphia, 1877, vol. vi, p. 467.

emancipation of the Negroes of the state.[12] Next to Jay in his importance in the constituent convention at White Plains in 1776 was Gouverneur Morris, who made earnest efforts for some scheme of gradual emancipation.[13] Party editors from Noah Webster [14] to William L. Stone [15] took up the cause with much enthusiasm. Certainly the leaders of the party might lay a claim to the black man's loyalty, and the party followed their leaders on this question. They finally enacted a well-calculated scheme of gradual emancipation which prevented the distress of any sudden readjustment.[16] The measure was opposed by the party of the small tradesman and the mechanic, for reasons of economic jealousy as we shall see. The workman did not like to see the Negro change his butler's coat for cap and jeans, and his salver for pick and shovel. It was a Federalist legislature and a Federalist governor who enacted the law of 1799, by almost a straight party vote of sixty-eight to twenty-three.[17] The Negroes had been reared in Federalist households; their cause had been advocated by distinguished Federalists, and now under the auspices of that party, freedom was provided. When they reached the estate of citizens, their political attachment could be easily foretold.

In numbers they were not to be neglected. New York had been the most important slave state in the North, and continued to have more Negroes than any other state in that section.[18] In New York city the proportion of Negroes to whites at the beginning of the nineteenth century was several times larger than now.[19] As soon as any slave was freed he became a voter, on the same terms as a white man, namely, if he paid taxes to the state, if he owned a freehold of the value of twenty pounds, or if he rented a tenement of the yearly

[12] N.Y. Assembly Journal, 1799, pp. 47, 49, 77.

[13] Jared Sparks, Life of Gouverneur Morris, Boston, 1841, vol. i, p. 125. See also his speeches in the Federal Convention of 1786, The Records of the Federal Convention (edited by Max Farrand), New Haven, 1911, vol. ii, pp. 221, 415, 417, 574. See also A. J. Northrup, "Slavery in New York," in N.Y. State Library Bulletin, History, no. 4, 1900.

[14] See his Effects of Slavery on Morals and Industry (pamphlet), Hartford, 1793; see also Frederick Hudson, Journalism in the United States, N.Y., 1873, p. 192.

[15] W. L. Stone, Jr., Life and Writings of William Leete Stone (bound with W. L. Stone, Life of Red Jacket, 1866), pp. 41–42.

[16] After July 4, 1799, no man or woman was to be born a slave; C. Z. Lincoln, Constitutional History of New York, Rochester, 1906, vol. i, 658; also comment in J. H. Dougherty, Legal and Judicial History of New York, N.Y., 1911, vol. ii, p. 94. Those who set free their slaves had to guarantee that their freedmen would not become public charges.

[17] See on the principle of general emancipation, N.Y. Assembly Journal, 1799, p. 77. Comparing the names of the minority with those who voted for Addison and Haight, the candidates of the opposition for members of the Council of Appointment (cf. J. D. Hammond, History of Political Parties in the State of New York, N.Y., 1842, vol. i, p. 122), we see that of those who objected to the measure all but three were Republicans.

[18] U.S. Census of 1790; Census of 1820, supplement, p. 1.

[19] See table in Mary W. Ovington, Half a Man, N.Y., 1911, p. 10; and Analectic Magazine, vol. xiii (1819), p. 279.

fee of forty shillings.[20] In the eighteenth century manumission had not been uncommon, and it became more general after 1800. The erstwhile slave became in politics a client of his former master. To say that Jay or Hamilton in urging manumission had been largely moved by the hope of adding to the Federalist vote would be not only ungenerous but absurd. Yet it was only natural that in his voting, as well as in his talk and dress, the Negro should follow the example of his former master. In Brooklyn, for example, five of the thirteen Federalist candidates in 1810 were men who had set free their slaves, while there was but one such among their opponents.[21] The credit for the first manumission under the new law in this community goes to John Doughty, who served his generation as town clerk from 1796 to 1830,[22] who registered the birth of every child of slave parents after 1799, and in whose ceremonious presence almost every manumitted slave was given his certificate of liberty.[23] Is it to be expected that the freedmen who came into Albany from Rensselaerwyck where they had been so kindly treated,[24] or those who came from the great house of General Schuyler where so many had been granted freedom,[25] would vote against "the lord"? [26]

On this question the political philosophers of Tammany Hall had entertained but little doubt; they soon saw their forebodings realized. When in 1808 the colored voters in a meeting held in New York city voiced unanimous approval of the "old party." Republicans prepared a campaign song beginning "Federalists with blacks unite." [27] In 1809 a Negro orator drew applause from a large audience when, after picturing the sad conditions under Jefferson, he exclaimed, "How important then, that we, my countrymen, should unite our efforts with those of our Federal friends in endeavoring to bring about this desirable change, so all-important to commerce, to our own best interests, and the prosperity and glory of our country." [28] Republican inspectors at the polls, to minimize the danger of this co-operation, presumed as slaves all

[20] Constitution of 1777, article vii, in U.S. House Documents, vol. xci, part 1, pp. 2630–2631. The New York pound was the equivalent of $2.50.

[21] Compare the ticket printed in the N.Y. Herald, April 7, 1810, with the list of manumissions, 1797 to 1825, as printed in the Corporation Manual of the City of Brooklyn, 1864, pp. 153–165. Jacob Hicks, the Quaker, was the single Republican nominee who had held slaves.

[22] Corporation Manual of the City of Brooklyn, 1864, pp. 167–179.

[23] T. F. DeVoe, in Historical Magazine, Second Series, vol. ii, p. 342. E. A. Doty, "The Doughty Family on Long Island," in the N.Y. Genealogical and Biographical Record, vol. xliii, p. 321; H. R. Stiles, op. cit., vol. ii, p. 65.

[24] M. Van Rensselaer, Annals of the Van Rensselaers, Albany, 1888, p. 170.

[25] G. W. Schuyler, Colonial New York, N.Y., 1885, vol. ii, p. 497.

[26] Had the promising movements toward gradual emancipation by state action in the South in the early part of the nineteenth century succeeded, no doubt the same conditions would have followed there.

[27] From a broadside quoted in T. E. V. Smith, Political Parties and Their Places of Meeting in New York City (pamphlet), N.Y., 1893, p. 10.

[28] Joseph Sydney, An Oration Commemorative of the Abolition of the Slave Trade in the United States (delivered before the Wilberforce Philanthropic Association), N.Y., 1809, a pamphlet in the N.Y. Historical Society Collection.

black men who could not prove their freedom by sufficient evidence. The Federalists denounced this practice,[29] and organized among the Negroes a chapter of their partizan fraternity, the Washington Benevolent Society.[30] In 1811 a Republican legislature drew up a drastic law as to the suffrage of the blacks,[31] which passed in spite of the objections of the Federalist Council of Revision.[32]

The election of 1813 in the midst of "Mr. Madison's war" was closely contested; for some time the returns for members of assembly were in doubt.[33] The result was long remembered. Eight years afterward in the constitutional convention, General Root, speaking for the limitation on the franchise for men of color, recalled that "the votes of three hundred Negroes in the city of New York, in 1813, decided the election in favor of the Federal party, and also decided the political character of the legislature of this state." [34] Not the number of the Negroes who were qualified made them formidable, but the strategic strength of their location. At the next election, however, the Federalist majority was overturned, and it is not surprising to find soon presented before the reformed legislature a more severe measure to limit the political influence of the Negro in New York city. This not only provided for the elaborate registration of every freedman, but obliged him always to bring full copies of such registration to the officers of election.[35] Yet these laws were made effective with much difficulty; in spite of all precautions, "Negro ballots" had to be accepted. When Clinton brought to his standard the majority of Federalists he gained the colored men as well.[36] Therefore in 1821 the Republicans were in no mood to trifle with this question.

[29] N.Y. *Commercial Advertiser*, April 26, 1809. See resolutions, Federalist meeting, *ibid.*, May 22, also N.Y. *Spectator*, April 29, 1809. The practice was defended the following year by the Republican N.Y. *Advertiser*, April 26, 1810.

[30] *Analectic Magazine*, vol. xiii (1819), p. 287.

[31] J. D. Hammond, *Political History*, vol. i, p. 296.

[32] See objections stated in N.Y. *Spectator*, May 8, 1811. The N.Y. *Evening Post* called in an "Act to prevent people of colour from voting at the next election"; see issues of April 16, 22, 1811. The official caption was "An Act to prevent frauds at election and slaves from voting"; *Laws of New York, Revision of 1813*, vol. ii, p. 253. See N.Y. Assembly Journal, 1811, pp. 251, 310 etc., and N.Y. Senate Journal, 1811, pp. 143, 163.

[33] Hammond, vol. i, p. 357.

[34] Carter, Stone and Gould, *Reports of the Proceedings and Debates of the Convention of 1821 etc.*, Albany, 1821, p. 212. In 1813 there was a bill providing for a very strict superintendence of the colored voters, which passed the senate only. The six senators who voted against it were Federalists; N.Y. Senate Journal, 1813, p. 120.

[35] See N.Y. Assembly Journal, 1814–1815, pp. 469 *et seq.*, and N.Y. Senate Journal, 1814–1815, p. 326. At a large Negro meeting in New York city thanks were voted to the Federalist Judges Kent and Platt for their spirited opposition in the Council of Revision, the Republicans were berated, and continued support was promised to those "whose opinions appear more consonant to our own." N.Y. *Spectator*, April 19, 1815. This matter was made an issue in the next campaign and was the subject of the longest of the resolutions of a Federalist meeting; see N.Y. *Commercial Advertiser*, April 11, 1816.

[36] "Extracts from the minutes of the Electors Of the People of Colour of the 5th Ward at a Meeting to Express Congratulations to his Excellency. Resolve[d] that we

The convention of 1821 has been called with somewhat pompous phraseology "a dominant emancipating agent in American democracy." [37] That one of its major purposes was to extend the suffrage to new classes was realized by friend and foe alike. "This is one of the crying evils for which we were sent here to provide a remedy," said Mr. Ross, of the committee to which this subject was referred.[38] Old qualifications of property, the remnant of the English practice of colonial days, were to be swept away, and it was known that the question of Negro suffrage would be an important subject of debate. The members of the convention were chosen on party grounds, and a large majority of them were Democrats.[39] The convention was conducted on party principles; the chairmen of all committees were appointed by the president, ex-Governor Tompkins, from his own supporters. These gentlemen differed sharply with the Federalist minority on the extension of the suffrage to poor white men, and to Negroes also. The committee in charge proposed, not to continue a twenty-pound qualification for the Negro, while giving the indigent white the vote, but actually to take away the privilege that the Negro already had.

At the opening of the debate, Mr. Ross laid down the doctrine of the Democracy: "They are a peculiar people, incapable, in my judgment, of exercising that privilege with any sort of discretion, prudence, or independence." Probably the last-named quality gave him most concern, for later he complained that the black vote was a controlled vote. A petition in behalf of Negro voters "now on your table, in all probability had been instigated by gentlemen of a different colour who expect to control their votes." [40] For others the test of contribution to the state might be sufficient, but not so for the colored men.[41] There were reasons enough why the franchise should be denied the Negro altogether, said Colonel Young, a leading Democrat from Saratoga County; and if reasons did not prove sufficient, one could easily

the People of Colour present Our humble Congratulations to his Excellency's Veneration of Being Reelected By our utmost Endeavors as our Chief Commander and Governor of the State of New York"; N.Y., June 15, 1820, DeWitt Clinton MSS., Columbia University.

[37] F. N. Thorpe, *Constitutional History of the American People*, Chicago, 1901, vol. ii, p. 354. *Cf.* E. Olbrich, *The Development of Sentiment on Negro Suffrage to 1860*, University of Wisconsin, 1912, p. 38.

[38] Carter, Stone and Gould, *Debates etc.*, pp. 180, 193. The report of the debates on Negro suffrage is quoted extensively in C. Z. Lincoln, *Constitutional History of New York*, vol. i, pp. 661–668, and in the admirable monograph of E. Olbrich, pp. 30–39. But neither of these authors has given his attention to the connection between the arguments and the partizan allegiance of the members. The same is true of Dr. H. L. Young's dissertation on *The New York Constitutional Convention of 1821*, which may be consulted in manuscript in the library of Yale University.

[39] J. D. Hammond, *Political History*, vol. ii, p. 2. Judge Hammond from this date uses the designation "Democratic" to describe the old Republican party.

[40] *Debates*, pp. 180, 181.

[41] The suffrage was extended by this constitution to all male residents of proper age who paid taxes (or were exempt by law), who did militia duty (or were exempt), or who worked at call upon the highways (or paid an equivalent), except Negroes, for whom, as we shall see, special provision was made.

fall back on prejudice. The Negro should be entirely shut out.[42] Jacob Radcliff, who now represented the Tammany Society, "considered the privilege of exclusion to be derived, not from the distinction of color—but resorted to as a rule of designation between those who understand the worth of the privilege, and those who are degraded, dependent, and unfit to exercise it." [43] Here was a scholastic refinement that would have graced a medieval disputation. As to the Negro voter having by the exercise of the franchise for forty years and more acquired a *vested* right to such exercise, as was maintained by Abraham Van Vechten, a leader of the Albany Federalists, it was answered that the sovereign people in convention could do anything.[44]

Again and again the complaint was heard that the Negro lacked independence, that he was amenable to other influences than argument. The contention, significantly enough, came from one party only.[45] The Democrats had every reason to subscribe to the opinion that the Negroes, born in slavery, and accustomed to take orders, would now vote according to the dictates of their employers.[46] To extend to blacks the same provisions as were contemplated for whites would, as Mr. Radcliff well observed, be attended with most serious results. It would let loose two thousand five hundred Negro voters in the city of New York, and a small part of these might determine the result in such close state elections as, for example, that of 1801.[47] General Root declared himself an abolitionist as to slavery [48]—for now, as later, we find opinion upon slavery and upon the suffrage bearing small relation—but he was aware of the dangerous importance of the Negro vote. He said:

> At present the number of blacks who are voters is so small, that if they were scattered all over the state, there would not be much danger to be apprehended, but if we may judge of the future by the past, I should suppose that there was some cause for alarm, when a few hundred Negroes of the city of New York, following the train of those who ride in their coaches, and whose shoes and boots they had so often blacked, shall go to the polls of the election and change the political condition of the whole state. A change in the representation of that city may cause a change in your assembly, by giving a majority to a particular party, which would vary your council of appointment, who make the highest officers of your government. Thus would the whole

[42] *Debates*, pp. 190–191. Colonel Young criticized the argument for suffrage from natural right when Dr. Clarke quoted the Declaration of Independence. It was a question of expediency. Democratic doctrine was beginning to be modified in statement.

[43] *Debates*, p. 190.

[44] *Ibid.*, p. 193; see Hammond, vol. ii, pp. 3 etc., on Van Vechten's importance in the party.

[45] One Federalist opposed his colleagues—Chief Justice Ambrose Spencer, who, however, classed the improvident mechanic with the Negro. With him it was not a matter of race; *ibid.*, p. 377.

[46] *Ibid.*, p. 185.

[47] *Ibid.*, pp. 198, 199 (Livingston).

[48] D. S. Alexander, *Political History of New York State*, N.Y., 1906, vol. i, p. 229.

state be controlled by a few hundred of this species of population in the city of New York.[49]

The Federalist members did not content themselves with silence. The committee had scarcely presented their report, in which there appeared no provision for any Negro vote, when Peter Augustus Jay, an able father's able son, arose to ask an explanation why, while extending the privilege of the franchise to some men, "they deny it to others who actually possess it." Though he abhorred slavery, he was not, he said, what was called an abolitionist; yet he would not stand by and hear it said that this denial was made "because all who were not white ought to be excluded from political rights, because such persons were incapable of exercising them discretely, and because they were peculiarly liable to be influenced and corrupted." [50] Mr. Van Vechten had not understood that the convention was expected "except by some of the citizens of New York to disfranchise anybody." Why should the Negro voters be attacked? "Have they done anything to forfeit the right of suffrage? This has has not been shown." [51] Dr. Clarke, a Federalist from Delaware County, desired to learn why Negro soldiers should not vote as well as whites; there had been nothing but applause for their service as state troops in the War of 1812. The fact that they were not liable to militia duty had made their volunteering in that crisis all the more occasion for respect and gratitude.[52] General Van Rensselaer thought any man of either race should vote, provided he had property and paid taxes.[53]

Mr. Jay moved that the word "white" be struck out of the committee's proposed amendment. After due debate the matter was referred to a select committee,[54] which finally proposed:

> That no male citizen, other than white, shall be subject to taxation, or entitled to vote at any election, unless in addition to the qualifications of age and residence, last above mentioned, he shall be seised and possessed in his own right of a freehold estate of the value of two hundred and fifty dollars, over and above all debts and incumbrances charged thereon, and shall have been, within the next year preceding the election, assessed, and shall have actually paid a tax to the state or county.[55]

Judge Jonas Platt, who had been the Federalist candidate for governor in 1810, moved to strike out the words, "other than white." The qualification of

---

[49] *Debates*, pp. 185–186.
[50] *Debates*, p. 180 (Ross), and p. 183 (Jay).
[51] *Ibid.*, pp. 193, 195.
[52] *Ibid.*, p. 187.
[53] *Ibid.*, p. 182.
[54] *Cf.* Olbrich, *op. cit.*, p. 36. Ex-Governor Tompkins, who presided, contrary to parliamentary usage appointed as nine of the thirteen members men who had voted against the Jay motion; *Debates*, p. 298.
[55] *Debates*, p. 329.

two hundred and fifty dollars freehold he thought might be applied to white and black alike; if poor Negroes were to be excluded, then he would have the same exclusion for poor white men. He declared:

> I am not disposed, sir, to turn knight-errant in favour of the men of color. But the obligations of justice are eternal and indispensable. ... The real object is, to exclude the oppressed and degraded sons of Africa, and, in my humble judgment, it would better comport with the dignity of this Convention to speak out, and to pronounce the sentence of perpetual degradation on Negroes and their posterity forever, than to establish a test, which we know they cannot comply with, and which we do not require of others.[56]

No man was more opposed to running after the *ignis fatuus* of universal suffrage than Chancellor Kent, but he could see no proper reason for discrimination against the Negro.[57] Rufus King believed that "universal suffrage was perilous to us and to the country" and yet took this same position.[58] But the majority were not moved by Federalist oratory. The qualification of two hundred and fifty dollars passed into the fundamental law to remain until 1870.[59]

The difference regarding Negro suffrage between the opposing parties was not fortuitous; their contemporaries noticed the alignment. The careful Hammond writes:

> It is somewhat curious that General Root, Colonel Young, Mr. Livingston, Mr. Briggs, &c., who were most anxious to abolish the property qualification and extend the right of suffrage to all white men, were equally zealous to exclude black citizens from the right to exercise the elective franchise; while those who most strenuously contended for retaining the freehold qualification as respected white citizens, were very solicitous to prevent an exclusion of the blacks from an equal participation with the whites. Of this last description of members, Chancellor Kent, Mr. Van Rensselaer, Mr. Jay, Mr. Van Vechten and Judge Platt were the most prominent.[60]

We have seen that the Negro had been a Federalist.[61] As soon as an ambitious freedman gained the prescribed amount of property—and we shall

[56] *Ibid.*, pp. 374, 375. Two hundred and fifty dollars had been the sum qualifying for the vote for governor, lieutenant-governor and senators. It was now extended in the Negro's case to that for member of assembly.

[57] *Ibid.*, pp. 190, 191, 221, 377.

[58] *Ibid.*, pp. 191, 287. King, though elected with the help of Democratic votes, was still a Federalist.

[59] The qualification was removed only with the passage of the Fifteenth Amendment to the Constitution of the United States. The New York Democrats protested bitterly against this amendment.

[60] *Political History*, vol. ii, p. 21.

[61] "The Negroes, with scarcely an exception, adhered to the Federalists. Their number in the city of New York was very great, and parties in that city were so

see that this group grew—he would now hesitate still less in choosing between the two parties. We are not to understand that the Negro was a lover of strong government in the abstract, or that he admired the British Constitution or suspected Jacobinical innovation; his Federalism was in his feeling. As long as the party lasted under the old designation, he voted faithfully for its candidates; and we have traced, it is hoped sufficiently, the considerations that commanded his allegiance.

The Federalist party as an organization was in 1821 already passing into history, but the feud between Van Buren's "Bucktails" [62] and all others was kept up. When in 1826 the few restrictions on white suffrage which had survived five years before were swept away, it was a Democratic legislature which retained the qualification for the blacks.[63] This fact was probably not lost upon the colored voter; and despite the hope and expectation of the convention of 1821, his tribe increased in thrift,[64] so that his political importance was not lost. In the decade after 1830, in three contests for governor, in New York city, always of such critical importance, the fifth ward—where the Negroes were most largely settled—was carried against Tammany, apparently by Negro influence.[65] The same result was brought about here in at least three municipal elections, and likewise in the eighth ward, next to the fifth in Negro population, in 1834, 1837 and 1838.[66] The sachems had little reason to look with complacency upon the slowly growing Negro influence. In Brooklyn, the fourth, ninth and seventh wards, where the Negroes were most numerous, yield corroborative evidence.[67] In Albany, a little later, it was probably Negroes in the first and tenth wards who swelled the Whig majorities.[68]

When the people of New York voted that a convention for the revision

---

evenly divided, that it was often sufficient to hold the balance between them, at times, too, when the vote of New York, in the legislature, not unfrequently decided the majority of that body"; *Life of Martin Van Buren*, a campaign pamphlet, published in Philadelphia in 1844 (in N.Y. Public Library), p. 6.

[62] The bucktail was the badge of the Tammany Society.

[63] The six senators (out of twenty-eight) who voted for equal suffrage were all anti-Tammany men; N.Y. Senate Journal, 1825, p. 147. For names *cf.* Hammond, vol. i, pp. 235, 237; vol. ii, pp. 139, 175, 193; and Alexander, vol. i, p. 156.

[64] See the testimony of W. E. Shannon, formerly of New York, in the *Report of the Debates in the Convention of California etc.*, 1849, Washington, 1850, p. 143. Much was accomplished in New York city by the Phoenix Societies; see *Minutes and Proceedings of the Third Annual Convention for the Improvement of Free People of Color etc.* (pamphlet), N.Y., 1833, pp. 36–40; F. Bancroft, *Life of Seward*, vol. i, p. 139; C. C. Andrews, *History of the New York African Free Schools etc.*, N.Y., 1830.

[65] E. Williams, New York Annual Register, 1835, p. 52; *ibid.*, 1840, p. 224; N.Y. *Evening Post*, Nov. 26, 1836; Census of N.Y. State, in O. C. Holley, *New York State Register*, p. 109.

[66] Williams, 1834, p. 279; *ibid.*, 1837, p. 348; *ibid.*, 1840, p. 225; Holley, *loc. cit.*

[67] *Cf.* N.Y. *Evening Post*, Nov. 4, 1836; Williams, 1836, p. 95; *ibid.*, 1840, p. 222; Holley, 1843, p. 82; *ibid.*, 1846, p. 107.

[68] *Cf.* J. Munsell, *Annals of Albany*, Albany, 1870, vol. ii, pp. 361–362; Holley, 1846, p. 107; *ibid.*, 1843, p. 69; *ibid.*, 1845, p. 69; N.Y. *Tribune*, Nov. 4, 1846.

of the constitution should be held in 1846, no gift of prophecy was needed to foretell that Negro suffrage would again furnish a theme of bitter controversy. The movement to take away the privilege altogether was begun before the delegates were chosen. A pamphleteer [69] who declared himself "a steady supporter of the principles and regular nominations of the Democratic party" urged the complete exclusion of all men of color from the right to vote. "Some of our people, from false notions of benevolence, or political hypocrisy, deny the natural inferiority of the black race," but as for himself he would maintain that their political proscription was in no way inconsistent with good Democratic doctrine:

> In the country, where there are but few Negroes, the danger of encouraging them to remain in the State, invite others from adjacent States and fugitive slaves to join them, and interfere in our political affairs, through the aid of a fanatical party of whites, is not so apparent as in our great cities where they are already numerous.

This broad distinction founded on geography we shall later put to test. On the other hand, the Whigs, in a mass meeting in New York city, October 28, 1845, presided over by the venerable Federalist, Philip Hone,[70] resolved that one of the first reasons for holding a convention was that "the inestimable Right of Suffrage is not secured equally to all citizens, but is clogged as to a part with a proscriptive and anomalous Property Qualification." [71]

Horace Greeley, publishing an address from colored men who asked the return of equal suffrage, endorsed their claim that manhood alone must be the test for the elective franchise,[72] and later printed this demand at the head of seven reforms that must be struggled for.[73] He bewailed "the Colorphobia which prevails so extensively in the ranks of our modern 'Democracy,' " [74] and declared that the "body of the People are divided into two great parties, one of which is generally favorable, and the other notoriously hostile to the extension of the Right of Suffrage to every peaceable, orderly citizen, without regard to the color of his skin or the amount of his property." He urged the

[69] H. P. Hastings, *An Essay on Constitutional Reform*, N.Y., 1846, in N.Y. Public Library.

[70] To see how important a part Hone played in carrying this measure through, consult report in N.Y. *Evening Post*, Oct. 29, 1845; yet Hone had no sympathy with abolitionism. See *Diary of Philip Hone*, N.Y., 1889, vol. i, p. 79. (The full manuscript is in the N.Y. Historical Society Collections.)

[71] N.Y. *Tribune*, October 30, 1845. It must be said that this was not the unanimous opinion of those attending. Col. Webb, of the *Courier and Enquirer*, who had written very gingerly about the Texas question and was anxious that the party in New York should commit itself to no principle distasteful to the southern Whigs, was able at a subsequent smaller meeting to have all such resolutions stricken out.

[72] N.Y. *Tribune*, January 23, 1846. The address itself is interesting, apparently in the hope of proselyting among Democrats its authors recalled general statements of D. D. Tompkins and Silas Wright about slavery and the rights of man.

[73] *Ibid.*, March 23, 1846.

[74] *Ibid.*, Feb. 12.

Birneyites, the members of the small and struggling group of abolitionists, to name no candidates for the convention, but to vote for Whigs, who, however they might differ with these enthusiasts as to the proper way to deal with slavery, were one with them upon the poorest Negro's right to vote.[75] As to the candidates the colored voters would themselves prefer, he, of course, had little doubt. He knew they would recall that it was the Democrats of 1821 who had excluded them, when "every Federalist in the Convention strenuously opposed the proscription." [76] And the Negro voter seemed to understand. "The Democratic party of this City," wrote one of them, "with the loud profession of the largest liberty, is the first and the only one to announce its determination to go for the curtailment of Human Freedom." [77]

It must not be considered that this was but a passing crotchet of Greeley's. The other most important Whig editor in the state was Thurlow Weed, who attempted to lead no forlorn hopes. For universal suffrage in the abstract he had no approval; [78] that was one thing in which he would if necessary stand alone. He did not care to jeopardize the union of the party and of the nation [79] by stirring up trouble in the South, and he made no secret of his hatred for the fanatical zeal of northern abolitionists.[80] Indeed, in after years Greeley charged him with a "poor white" prejudice against the black.[81] Yet at the very outset of this contest he had written, "Above all, let the class of our fellow-citizens, whose intellectual capacities are measured under our present Constitution by *property*, be relieved from the stigma under which they rest, and be placed on the footing where they belong—that of men." [82] Seward, the other member of that famous firm, likewise favored equal suffrage.[83] And despite the opposition of a few, the majority of Whigs seem to have stood behind the trusted leaders.[84]

There was as little doubt as to the policy of the Democrats. The *Journal of Commerce*, the *Argus* and the *Evening Post* had no word to say for the extension of the franchise. Bryant, who in his vagarious days of Equal Rights had brought upon his own head round condemnation for countenancing

[75] *N.Y. Tribune*, Feb. 17. It seems that the inference as to a connection between these sentiments was unwarranted.

[76] *Ibid.*, March 23.

[77] *Ibid.*, April 28.

[78] *Life of Thurlow Weed* (Autobiography), Boston, 1884, pp. 89–90. For his later revision of opinion, see *ibid.* (Memoir), p. 561.

[79] Cf. W. E. Dodd, *Expansion and Conflict*, N.Y., 1915, p. 171.

[80] *Albany Evening Journal*, Nov. 30, 1860; also Autobiography, p. 98.

[81] Horace Greeley, *Recollections of a Busy Life*, N.Y., 1873, p. 313. This reference to Weed's humble origin was no less ungenerous than unfair. See Weed's Memoir, p. 297.

[82] *Albany Evening Journal*, Oct. 30, 1845.

[83] See his "Reply to the Colored Citizens of Albany," *Works*, N.Y., 1853–1854, vol. iii, pp. 437–438.

[84] *N.Y. Evening Post*, Oct. 6, 1845. See Greeley's comment on the Webb faction, "so utterly out of place in our party"; *N.Y. Tribune*, April 1, 1846. After the election the Young Men's General County Committee of the Whigs tried to read Webb out of the party.

abolition, who had pointed out with all Cassandra's certainty the danger which followed in the train of the "domestic institution," and had stood among the staunchest in support of Adams in his fight for freedom of petition, now wrote with care to establish the doctrine that civil freedom and the suffrage presented two quite different questions. The Negro as a voter was the Negro as a peril.[85] Bennett, who in spite of claims of independence was at heart a Tammany man, complained in the *Herald* of "the detestable cry of Negro suffrage raised as a rallying cry for the election of delegates to the Convention"; [86] the *Globe* expressed a similar sentiment; [87] and the *Morning News* attributed all the Whigs' zeal to an appetite for votes.[88] This view is doubtless exaggerated; yet the hope of party gain certainly performed its part.

The election of the delegates to the convention of 1846, as a quarter of a century before, was made a party question, and again the Democrats were represented by the large majority.[89] In the course of time the matter of the franchise was presented and a long debate was begun.[90] There was no doubt as to how the parties stood. The committee report, presented by its chairman, ex-Governor Bouck, recommended suffrage for white men only; [91] if the convention should desire, it might offer unrestricted color suffrage as a separate option. If this report were adopted by the delegates, the proposition of the black man's complete exclusion, as the majority of Democrats in 1821 had wished, would go before the people with the prestige of the approval of the convention. No provision was here made for the continuation of the existing limitation of two hundred and fifty dollars, but the minority report called for equal suffrage. Mr. Bruce, a Whig from Madison County, moved to strike out the word "white," and the contest was begun. J. Leslie Russell, of St. Lawrence, took up the challenge:

> For one, he knew . . . that nine-tenths of the people in St. Lawrence county—abolitionists and all—were opposed to the admission of the Negroes to the right of suffrage. . . . He agreed in this perfectly with his constituents. This was the only issue in St. Lawrence at the Convention election. He was interrogated on this subject, and informed them expressly that he should vote against suffrage to the Negro.[92]

[85] Parke Godwin, A *Biography of William Cullen Bryant*, N.Y., 1883, vol. i, pp. 327–331, and N.Y. *Evening Post*, April 21, 1836.

[86] He "was a recognized member of the Tammany party"; *Memoirs of James Gordon Bennett and His Times*, N.Y., 1855, p. 80. He was not complimentary to the Negro, "on whom education, and every other means of moral enlightenment have been tried in vain"; N.Y. *Herald*, March 17, 1846.

[87] Quoted in N.Y. *Tribune*, Feb. 12, 1846.

[88] March 24, 1846. See Frederic Hudson, *Journalism in the United States*, pp. 576, 667.

[89] Hammond, *op. cit.*, vol. iii, p. 605.

[90] Croswell and Sutton, *Debates and Proceedings in the New York State Convention etc.*, Albany, 1846, pp. 246, 775, 782 etc. See also C. Z. Lincoln, *Constitutional History*, vol. ii, pp. 118–123 and E. Olbrich, *op. cit.*, pp. 72–78.

[91] No. 51 in Documents of the Convention of the State of New York, 1846, vol. i.

[92] *Debates*, p. 777. Mr. Russell, like the majority of the voters of St. Lawrence County, was an ardent Democrat. He was in the complete confidence of his fellow-

He was answered by Mr. Strong, a Whig member from Monroe, who declared himself no abolitionist, but who knew this question would never be finally settled until right should be done all classes of the citizens of the state.[93] Mr. Kirkland from Oneida wanted at least to save the Negro what he had.[94] But Mr. Kennedy, a Democrat from New York city, declared that a holding of real property or any other kind was no fit test for the franchise; in any change only character and manhood should be considered; but

> the females of mature age, of our own race, were entitled to a preference, when we were prepared to make such an extension. [A gentleman had] remarked that delicacy should prevent females from uniting in the exercise of political power, but what sort of delicacy was that which ... would squander it upon those whom nature had marked as a distinct race; and who were merely an excrescence upon our society! ... Nature revolted at the proposal.

He claimed that the freedmen in New York were more degraded than the like class in the South. He had statistics to prove Negroes far more vicious than whites.[95]

Federal Dana, Mr. Bruce's colleague, said if the Negro were but given decent opportunities in life like the suffrage, he would not be so vicious. Mr. Young, a Wyoming Whig, contended that colored people were as intelligent as immigrants from foreign countries and as much entitled to the elective franchise. He regretted that statistics of the good portion of those other groups had not been furnished also. Mr. Rhoades, of Onondaga, scouted a so-called democracy that would deprive men of rights simply on the ground of a difference in complexion. Mr. Waterbury, of Delaware, reverted to the case of women. "The wives and children of all our white citizens were protected in their rights and privileges by husbands and brothers. Where do you find anyone to stand up for the colored man?—Not one." But Mr. Hunt, from Tammany Hall, would listen to no such talk. "His doctrine and that of his constituents, in relation to the right of suffrage, was briefly this: We want no masters and least of all no Negro masters, to reign over us."

It was Mr. Hunt who introduced a new note in the debate. In 1821 the franchise question had been settled without reference or citation beyond the plain facts of social prudence and the experience of this world. But a new day of religious enthusiasm had come since then, and the simple words of

---

citizen of Canton, Governor Wright, who had taken a deep interest in his career; R. H. Gillett, *Life and Times of Silas Wright*, N.Y., 1874, vol. ii, p. 1727; J. D. Hammond, *Life of Silas Wright*, Syracuse, 1849, p. 730; and Russell to A. C. Flagg, Flagg MSS., N.Y. Public Library. We may infer that Wright's opinions were similar to Russell's.

[93] *Debates*, p. 777.

[94] *Ibid.*, p. 778. It may be said here that no Democrat spoke for the extension of the franchise, and no Whig against it, except Mr. Kirkland and Mr. Stow, who were content with a restricted suffrage, and Mr. Harrison, who stood with the Tammany men in the desire to shut out the Negro altogether.

[95] *Debates*, pp. 782–786, for this and the speeches in the next paragraph.

scripture were frequently taken as the unfailing guide of life.[96] In the view of most men, "common sense, reason and reflection pronounced a solemn amen to every doctrine taught in that fearful and precious book" and it was held "that all the truth to which reason ever assented had been first taught by revelation." [97]

Mr. Hunt appealed to Leviticus: "The Jews were forbidden to yoke animals of different kinds together; and if it were wrong to unite the cow and the ass in the same yoke, would it be right to unite the Caucasian and the Negro race in the same government?" [98] In some way equal suffrage was considered to imply social equality as well. Mr. Perkins, of St. Lawrence, said he should not enter the controversy further than to say that if there were any verity in scripture, mankind were at Babel divided into separate classes, "that it was the fiat of the Almighty that they should remain separate nations— that he put his mark on these creatures, that it might be known that it was a violation of the law of God to commingle our blood with them in marriage." —"Does the gentleman find that in the Bible?" asked Mr. Dana.—"Yes," was the reply; "not in those words, however." Mr. Waterbury wished to know, "If they were thus separated at Babel, how came they to go through the ark with the rest?" [99] Pausing for a moment's comment on the limitations of the gentleman from Delaware in the field of sacred chronology, the debate went forward. Mr. Dana remembered nothing in the account of Babel that properly could be cited against the right of the colored man to vote. "And before he could be convinced of that, he must have chapter and verse." Mr. Harrison, of Richmond, offered specific reference to Ham and Canaan: "Cursed be Canaan; a servant of servants shall he be to his brethren." [100] Yet Mr. Dana recalled that Noah was at this time intoxicated, and that at any rate this had no bearing upon political rights. Mr. Perkins "laid it down as the economy of Providence that there should be separate races and grades of beings on earth." The great offense that had brought on the flood had been the commingling of races. He maintained his exegesis that the female progeny of Cain, lately damned with a black mark, had as partners to this indiscretion occasioned that calamity.[101] Mr. Simmons, of Essex, on the other hand, attributed the deluge to God's wrath at slavery. "My Bible says so," he exclaimed; but he was interrupted by a voice, "Yours is a Whig Bible." [102]

When the vote was taken on Mr. Bruce's proposition to strike out the word "white," there were thirty-seven for and sixty-three against. Among the

[96] W. Walker, *History of the Congregational Churches in the United States*, N.Y., 1894, p. 320; R. E. Thompson, *History of the Presbyterian Churches in the United States*, N.Y., 1895, pp. 129–149.

[97] David Nelson, *The Cause and Cure of Infidelity*, N.Y., 1841, p. 351. This was one of the most popular and influential of the volumes issued by the American Tract Society.

[98] *Debates*, p. 786.

[99] *Debates*, p. 789.

[100] *Ibid.*, p. 790.

[101] *Ibid.*, p. 796.

[102] *Ibid.*

thirty-seven that favored equal suffrage there were two Democrats; while among the sixty-three opposed there were eight Whigs.[103] But when a member of the latter party proposed that the property qualification for the Negro be lowered from two hundred and fifty to one hundred dollars, seven of these eight were willing to make this reduction.[104] The Democrats were in the majority, however, and the Whigs had to be satisfied with a separate submission to the people of the paragraph on equal suffrage.[105]

The Democrats had won a party victory. But since 1842 at least, there had been internal strife. Because of differences about canal expenditures or the Texas annexation, or from jealousies in office-holding, there had been developing a breach within the Democratic party of the state.[106] The Conservatives, or "Hunkers," abhorred the radical "Barnburners," and were themselves despised in turn. Yet faction made no break in this alignment in the convention. Bouck, the foremost Hunker, was no more against the Negro voter than was Michael Hoffman, the Barnburners' champion.[107] It was as straight a party question as one often finds. The charge that the country districts, ignorant of the true nature of the Negro, would unite in his behalf,[108] could not be sustained. Six counties were divided in their delegation—Albany, Greene, Wayne, Dutchess, Onondaga and Schoharie, and in every one the Whig members voted on the one side and the Democrats, if present, on the other. Acquaintance with the black man seemed to count for little. In St. Lawrence, where there were thirty-seven Negroes,[109] it had been "the only issue" and the delegates had been instructed to exclude them altogether. At the election in the autumn their position was maintained in that county by a vote of nearly two to one. Neighboring Franklin county gave equal suffrage a majority of seven hundred and thirty-two.[110] Essex county had forty Negroes; the adjacent Warren, with a population somewhat less, had thirty-five. Essex went for equality; Warren, by nearly the same majority, against.[111] Livingston, with about the same proportion of colored population as Steuben, next to it in the south, went in favor, and Steuben against.[112] The same was true of Oneida and Herkimer, Cortland and Tioga, and other pairs of counties in the different sections of the state. Yet when one looks at the political complexion of these counties the inference

[103] *Ibid.*, p. 788. The party affiliation of each member of the convention may be learned from the list published in the *N.Y. Tribune*, May 5, 1846.

[104] *Debates*, p. 790.

[105] The proposition was heavily defeated at the polls, especially in New York city.

[106] J. S. Jenkins, *Lives of the Governors of New York State*, Auburn, 1851, p. 705; D. S. Alexander, *op. cit.*, vol. ii, pp. 56–76.

[107] J. S. Hammond, *Political History*, vol. iii, p. 314, 387. In the partial list published in the *N.Y. Herald*, May 1, 1846, the Hunkers and Barnburners among the Democrats are differentiated. No relation to the vote on suffrage is observable.

[108] H. P. Hastings, *loc. cit.*

[109] *Census of the State of New York, 1845*, in O. L. Holley, *New York State Register*, 1846, p. 115.

[110] Table in *N.Y. Tribune*, Nov. 19, 1846.

[111] Holley, *op. cit.*, pp. 104, 119.

[112] *Ibid.*, pp. 108, 117.

is plain. Whig counties followed the direction of their leaders, and Democratic counties did the same. When Washington gave its vote in favor, Greeley wrote, "This Washington is called a *Federal* county, while the party which has polled ninety-nine hundredths of its vote *against* Equal Rights vaunts itself *Democratic*." [113]

Nor did abolitionism play a considerable part in the opinion on Negro suffrage. St. Lawrence abolitionists, if Mr. Russell is to be credited, were emphatically against all concession in the franchise. Men who did not follow Birney, like Mr. Strong and Dr. Backus,[114] were in favor of equality. It has been said that there was a connection between equal-suffrage sentiment and that which produced the Free-Soil party in 1848.[115] Yet in the convention no man was more steadily opposed to Negro suffrage than Samuel J. Tilden,[116] who became a pillar of that party: [117] and in the test of the ballot box such an hypothesis fails utterly. In 1848 seven counties voted for Van Buren, but only one of these had desired equal suffrage, and the county which by far surpassed all others in affection for Free Soil was none other than St. Lawrence.[118] The ward in New York city most favorable to equal suffrage was the fifteenth, always Whig,[119] which in 1844 had given Birney but twelve votes out of three thousand, and which in 1848 gave Van Buren a lower fraction of its votes than almost any other ward.[120] The sixth, which gave the largest vote against the Negro, was the very citadel of Tammany. Horace Greeley, long afterward at a public meeting, recalled that election: "Twenty-five years ago, I stood at the poll of the nineteenth ward of this city all one rainy, chilly November day, peddling ballots for Equal Suffrage. I got many Whigs to take them, but not one Democrat." [121] In this recollection he no doubt was right. It was a party matter in which personalities or the fortunes of slavery in southern states or in the territories had but little bearing.

The traditional alliance between the well-to-do and the Negroes was maintained. This of itself would pique the fear of Tammany and sharpen its attack, but this was not all. The Democratic party in the cities was the party of the little man, the day worker and the mill-hand. The laborers of the forties certainly prized the luxury of feeling themselves better than the Negro; on his

---

[113] N.Y. *Tribune*, Nov. 14, 1847.

[114] Thurlow Weed, Autobiography, p. 98.

[115] E. Olbrich, *Negro Suffrage before 1860 etc.*, p. 77.

[116] At least as indicated by his votes; *Debates*, pp. 788, 790, 791.

[117] John Bigelow, *The Life of Samuel J. Tilden*, N.Y., 1908, vol. 1, p. 119. Tilden wrote much of the address called "The Corner Stone of the Free Soil Party."

[118] See returns of election of 1846 in N.Y. *Tribune*, Nov. 14, 1846, and those of 1848 in *Whig Almanac*, N.Y., 1849, p. 54.

[119] Table in N.Y. *Evening Post*, Nov. 7, 1846, and election tables in E. Williams, *New York Annual Register*, 1832–1840.

[120] *Whig Almanac, loc. cit.*

[121] In a speech at a meeting of welcome after his southern journey of 1871; *Mr. Greeley's Record on the Question of Amnesty and Reconstruction* (pamphlet), N.Y., 1872, p. 21. As to exactly where he stood, Mr. Greeley's memory must have been at fault, as there was in 1846 no nineteenth ward.

subordination hung their pride. And then there was the economic danger of too much encouragement. In Tammany Hall it had been resolved that suffrage for the Negro was "fraught with incalculable evil and mischief, both in a social and political point of view," [122] but this organization had reasons, based on work and wages, to fear the Negro's rise. It had likewise laid down the doctrine "that the inevitable result of the success of abolitionism would be to create a pinching competition between the labor of the Negro and that of the white man. Thus the aspiration of the blacks for suffrage met with the "steady and determined opposition of Tammany Hall." [123] Reason was supported by race prejudice in the heart of the mechanic. It was in the sixth and fourteenth wards of New York city that the anti-Negro vote was strongest, and here were found the largest number of immigrant citizens.[124] The connection of these facts was plain, and it was accepted as a large factor in the explanation of the outcome.[125]

Though the average Negro did not think of the connection, there was doubtless, now and then, a leader to whom these things were clear. Allied by long tradition to the Federalist Whig party, he accepted its direction with docility. As to the charge that the Whigs were low-hearted opportunists on the slavery issue he made no extensive inquiry. In feeling more concern about his own improvement than about the labor system beyond the Mississippi, he presented no exception to the custom of mankind. The Wilmot Proviso was interesting in its way, but Texas was a long way off. Since the leaders of the Free-Soil party had been Democrats, he felt no strong enthusiasm to march behind their banner. In the abolitionists he no doubt felt an interest, but there was little use in casting votes for them.[126] When the Whigs made their transition to the Republican party he of course followed, but he had no hunger for third parties. "For the last five or six years before I left New York," testified a witness in far-away Iowa, "their votes were deposited sometimes for the third-party candidate, but most generally for the old Whig party." [127] They were Whigs because their fathers had been Federalists. If there had never been a Negro south of the Potomac, still the Negro in New York would never have voted the Democratic ticket.

[122] Report of meeting, N.Y. *Evening Post*, Oct. 31, 1846.

[123] *Ibid.*, Oct. 31, 1845.

[124] Greeley claimed this question brought out extra thousands of Tammany votes; N.Y. *Tribune*, Nov. 7, 1846.

[125] N.Y. *Tribune*, Nov. 8. Yet Greeley was a steady opponent of nativism.

[126] Compare Birney's total vote in New York city in 1844 with the Negroes' voting strength; *Constitutional Debates*, 1846, p. 790, and Holley, *op. cit.*, 1845, p. 85.

[127] Mr. Clarke in the *Debates of the Constitutional Convention of the State of Iowa, 1857*, Davenport, 1857, vol. ii, p. 671. Mr. Clarke had left New York in 1831; *ibid.*, vol. i, p. 4 (biographical table).

Robert Ernst

THE ECONOMIC STATUS OF
NEW YORK CITY NEGROES, 1850–1863

Even in the North the ante-bellum free people of color were, to use John Hope Franklin's words, "quasi-free Negroes." Though conditions were on the whole better in the Northeast than in the old Northwest, in most states Negroes faced disfranchisement, mob violence, economic discrimination, and varying degrees of exclusion and segregation, especially in regard to schools, places of recreation, and transportation. Nevertheless, as in the South, a few achieved a modicum of prosperity. Robert Ernst's article describes the role of Negroes in the economic life of the nation's leading seaport, and the degree of progress which they made in view of the many obstacles facing them.

"THERE is now in session in this City a Convention composed entirely of colored citizens. The object of the Convention is to consider the present condition of the Negro race, and to devise means for its improvement." In an obscure column of Horace Greeley's *Tribune*, March 20, 1851, these words introduced a remarkable Report on the Social Condition of the Colored Race, delivered at the meeting by James McCune Smith, one of the best educated Negroes in the metropolis, a physician and civic leader. Smith weighed the advantages and disadvantages of city life for the Negro and offered a plan whereby, through their own efforts, the free Negroes of the Empire City might improve their lot.

However optimistic Smith may have seemed, he painted a dismal picture of actual conditions. New York offered small comfort to its two thousand colored families. "Our lives are much shortened. Look at the preponderance of widows and children among us. They so far exceed the calamities of mere sickness, that our benevolent societies have been obliged to cut off the widows

Robert Ernst, "The Economic Status of New York City Negroes, 1850–1863," published by the Association for the Study of Negro Life and History in Vol. XII of *Negro History Bulletin*, pp. 131–132, 139–143 (March, 1949). Reprinted by permission of the publisher.

and orphans, in order to help the sick. . . . Next, the seductions of the City—policy gambling, porter houses . . . create a gang of lazaroni of both sexes . . . signs which our foes call the type of our condition."[1]

Of more importance was the reflection in this report of an awakening race consciousness, born of discrimination and segregation, and an emerging class consciousness born of the failure to maintain status in a growing industrial society. "City life shuts us from general mechanical employment; while journeymen in the cities refuse to work with us, and colored bosses have either too little capital, or too little enterprise, to bring up and employ apprentices and journeymen." Only menial jobs were left to the Negro. Relentlessly, the uncontrollable, impersonal forces of industrialism affected the Negro as a wage earner. "The enormous combination of capital, which is slowly invading every calling in the city, from washing and ironing to palace steamers," the report asserted, "must tend more and more to grind the face of the poor in the cities, and render them more and more the slaves of lower wages and higher rents."

Of these restrictions upon the Negro's freedom, discrimination was much the older. Racial prejudice and custom had erected an almost impenetrable barrier between whites and Negroes. If some colored person were found to be ignorant, dirty, or boisterous, shiftless or lacking in ambition, pleasure-loving or an inveterate gambler, his traits were allegedly due to the inferiority of his race. An intelligent Englishman remarked during the Civil War that some whites "would shoot a black man with as little regard to moral consequences as they would a wild hog."[2] Even immigrants, themselves held in contempt by the natives, looked down upon the Negroes. When the colored people tried to better their condition, the German *Staats-Zeitung* called them "apes of the white race" who belonged in Africa and not in the United States; equality of blacks and whites was "unnatural" in a country which belonged to the whites.[3] As early as 1833 an English traveller noted that Negroes could not sit in any public assembly, court or church, except in a special section "generally in the most remote or worst situation."[4] In 1843 the New York Zoological Institute announced that "PEOPLE OF COLOR [were] not permitted to enter, EXCEPT WHEN IN ATTENDANCE UPON CHILDREN AND FAMILIES."[5] During the fifties, Negroes were refused passage on omnibuses and street railroads, and attempts to eject colored persons from the cars sometimes resulted in violence.[6]

[1] New York Daily *Tribune*, March 20, 1851. The report, including its plan of a mutual savings association, is fully presented.

[2] [James D. Burn], *Three Years among the Working Classes in the United States during the War* (London, 1865), p. xiv. For the Negro reaction, cf. Carter G. Woodson (ed.), *The Mind of the Negro as Reflected in Letters written during the Crisis* (Washington, 1926), pp. 276–280.

[3] New Yorker *Staats-Zeitung*, March 29, 1851.

[4] [James Boardman], *America and the Americans* (London, 1833), p. 311.

[5] *Colored American*, March 25, 1843.

[6] *Courrier des Etats-Unis*, April 25, 1856; New York *Tribune*, September 18, 24, December 20, 1855. By 1861 such discrimination had all but disappeared, although one

In employment, as in transportation, discrimination was customary. White artisans in skilled occupations would have little or nothing to do with the Negroes. In the year 1833 a French traveller wrote that in not a single trade in New York City were colored persons allowed to work with whites.[7] Almost thirty years later Henry Ward Beecher averred that there was "not a foundary, a machine shop, a shipyard, a carpenter's shop, a cabinet shop, a blacksmith shop" which a Negro could enter.[8] The refusal of the whites to let Negroes work with them often forced the colored artisans to accept menial occupations, and it precluded any serious organization of skilled Negro craftsmen. When, for example, Negro and white barbers planned to create a mutual protective association with the object of raising the price of shaves to 8c and haircuts and shampoos to 15c each, the white barbers urged separate associations for each race.[9]

Segregation was partly responsible for the "Harlem" of the time, although it must be conceded that many colored people normally and voluntarily lived in their own communities. The Negro section harbored only the poorest white persons, usually foreign-born. Despite the political emancipation of the Negro in New York State in 1827, a large part of the city's colored population had long lived apart from the white—at least since 1800.[10] In 1825 more than one-fifth of Manhattan's Negroes inhabited the unhealthy sixth ward, spreading from the notorious slums of the Five Points north and west to the Hudson River. Individuals and some families, however, were scattered throughout the city, many as servants in white homes.[11] A decade later the fifth and eighth wards near the Hudson had become the center of the colored population; in West Broadway and in Thomas, Leonard, Sullivan, Greene, Mercer, and Mulberry streets the Negro inhabitants remained well beyond the middle of the century.[12]

The Negroes were slow to follow the northward trend of migration on Manhattan. Dispersion was blocked on the north for decades by Greenwich

line still posted signs reminding Negroes that riding in its cars was a privilege, not a right. Anglo-African, October 19, 1861, July 16, 1864.

[7] E. S. Abdy, Journal of a Residence and Tour in the United States (London, 1835), Vol. I, p. 358.

[8] New York Daily Tribune, December 1, 1862.

[9] Anglo-African, November 28, 1863.

[10] George E. Haynes, The Negro at Work in New York City (New York, 1912), pp. 48, 144. I cannot wholly agree with Mary Ovington's statement (Half a Man, New York, 1911, p. 26) that "until 1860 the race was infrequently segregated, and black and white were neighbors, not only in their homes but in business."

[11] New York State Census, 1825 and 1835. The loss in the sixth ward is accounted for by the fact that the northern part of this ward became in 1827 the fourteenth ward. Although its growth as a Negro area never equalled that of the fifth and eighth wards, the fourteenth continued to attract Negroes.

[12] Longworth's Directory, 1832–33; Staats-Zeitung, April 7, 1860; New York Herald, July 15, 16, 1863; Anglo-African, August 22, 1863. On the occasion of the riot of 1834, a note from Joseph Curtis introducing a colored woman to Mayor Lawrence referred to "many families of color" living in the neighborhood of Sullivan Street. This note, dated July 12, is now in the possession of the New York Historical Society.

Village, where an exclusive if somewhat impoverished Knickerbocker element held sway.[13] To a lesser extent the fashionable Washington Square neighborhood also limited Negro expansion. By 1860, however, a large colored settlement had appeared far to the north near the Hudson between Twenty-Sixth and Fortieth streets, and some Negroes had already filtered into the Greenwich and Washington Square strongholds.[14]

If the city's colored inhabitants spread gradually over a wider area on the island, their ranks were thinned by migration elsewhere. While Manhattan's population as a whole rose steadily throughout the period, its Negro population grew only until 1840. Thereafter the colored folk lost ground. The 13,358 of 1840 shrank to 12,574 at the outbreak of the Civil War, owing probably to the higher death rate of the Negro than of the white, the strong hostility toward the blacks aroused by anti-slavery agitation, and the flights of southern fugitive slaves who had settled in the city and were terrified at the passage of the Fugitive Slave Law of 1850.[15]

Living conditions of the Negroes were shaped largely by the growth of the city. During the forties and fifties commercial New York was becoming industrial New York. Warehouses along the crowded South Street wharves and the stores and factories in lower Manhattan obscured the gracious old private homes, and hordes of European immigrants streamed into the Empire City, marking the end of an era. Almost overnight the city felt a housing shortage. Speculators and property owners partitioned old mansions into tenements to accommodate three or more families. The newcomers and the Negroes, including some from the South, poured into these reconstructed buildings, sometimes "swarming from cellar to garret," as unscrupulous owners divided their space into "the smallest proportions capable of containing human life within four walls." [16] Property values soared; rents were raised. Housing failed to meet the demand for shelter at low rentals despite the erection of new buildings designed especially as tenement houses.

The new type of tenement building often contained a narrow hall with access to two suites of rooms on each of three or four floors, all of which had inadequate light, air, and sanitary facilities. Indeed, washing and toilet conveniences were rarely, if at all, available inside these barracks. Frequently another tenement was built in the rear of the same lot, accessible only through a narrow alley. Along such buildings and in the yards were the privies and

[13] Citizens' Association of New York, *Report of the Council of Hygiene and Public Health* (New York, 1865), pp. 120–121.

[14] *Eighth Census of the United States*, 1860, population schedule, p. 337.

[15] Leo H. Hirsch, Jr., "New York and the Negro, from 1783 to 1865," *Journal of Negro History*, Vol. XVI, No. 4, October 1931, p. 415, citing census figures. (In 1850 some 2,120 of the 13,815 New York City Negroes were born in the South. *Ibid.* Haynes, *op. cit.*, pp. 46–47, gives Manhattan's Negro population as 18,600 in 1840 and 15,000 in 1860; however, in less densely settled Brooklyn the Negro population increased from 2,000 in 1840 to 5,000 in 1860. *ibid.*

[16] New York State Assembly, *Report of the Select Committee . . . to Examine into the Condition of Tenant Houses in New York and Brooklyn* (Albany, 1857), p. 22.

flimsy frame sheds and shanties, some inhabited by the overflow of the tenements living amid an accumulation of stinking filth and rubbish.[17] Here it was that most of the Negroes lived—in the poorest houses in the poorest neighborhoods. Rent gouging was common, as agents leased from the owners and collected enough in tenants' rents to purchase the properties in a short time. Many such speculators in human misery were enriched by charging $3 to $13 per month for apartments and 75c to $1.25 per week for single rooms twelve feet square.[18]

The Negro could ill afford high rents, especially when the cost of living rose to unprecedented heights in the middle of the century, since occupations open to Negroes were severely limited and the chances of advancement were poor. The majority of colored workers were unskilled. In 1850 nearly three-quarters of all gainfully employed Negroes (exclusive of seamen) were servants, laborers, and other unskilled or occasional workers.[19] Most of the rest were men of varying skills, including barbers and coachmen. Each of these two occupations alone attracted over a hundred persons. In business and the professions, Negroes were almost unrepresented. A mere sixty colored men were clerks, merchants, druggists, doctors, lawyers, ministers, teachers, and students, or, according to the census analysis, only one in about fifty-five.[20]

Five years later, in 1855, the situation was even worse. Of 3,688 gainfully employed colored persons for whom information is available, fully 3,225, or

[17] Ibid., p. 23; Reports of the United States Industrial Commission (Washington, 1901), Vol. XV, p. 453.
[18] New York State Assembly, Report of the Select Committee ... [op. cit.], pp. 15–19.
[19] Computed from figures in J. D. B. DeBow, Statistical View of the United States ...Compendium of the Seventh Census (Washington, 1854), pp. 80–81. I have not included "mariners" in this computation because they were an unstable floating element of the city's population. Of course, many "mariners" were unskilled seamen. DeBow's statistics are not absolutely accurate; they do not agree precisely with data gleaned from the New York City directory (Cf. Charles H. Wesley, Negro Labor in the United States, New York, 1927, p. 39), but they may be regarded as the best available approximations. A total of 3,337 individuals were classified:

1,144 laborers	21 ministers	4 printers
808 servants	21 boarding	3 barkeepers
434 mariners	house keepers	3 druggists
122 barbers	12 carpenters	3 jewelers
107 coachmen	12 sextons	3 merchants
95 cooks	11 hostlers	2 apprentices
44 stewards	9 doctors	2 confectioners
39 carmen	8 teachers	2 hatters
33 butchers	8 cigar makers	2 mechanics
28 boatmen	7 clerks	("generally")
24 farmers	7 gardners	1 blacksmith
24 musicians	5 ink makers	1 gunsmith
23 shoemakers	4 bakers	1 student
23 tailors	4 painters	Also 207 other occupations
		(sweeps, scavengers, etc.)

[20] Ibid., p. 81.

87½ per cent, were engaged in menial or unskilled employment.[21] Of these, one-third were domestic servants, another third were laborers (including "whitewashers"), and about one-tenth were laundresses. The remainder consisted largely of seamstresses and dressmakers, cooks, porters, teamsters, coachmen, hackmen and drivers of other types of vehicles. Among the reasons for the Negroes' depressed status were the tradition of servitude, the continuing stigma of inferiority, the lack of education and opportunity to develop skills, and, as Dr. Smith pointed out to the Negro convention in 1851, the dearth of capital and the small number of colored employers.

The large proportion of Negroes who were servants, waiters, and laundresses, moreover, is partly attributable to their relative docility: they were frequently hired in preference to the Irish and German immigrants who were pouring into the city. Irish "turbulence" was contrasted with Negro "humility." Colored domestics usually were regarded as more tractable and better mannered than the children of Erin, while Negro waiters were "quicker in manipulation" and "less doggedly independent" than whites. Sometimes the favoritism in hiring was clearly reflected in the want ads of the newspapers:
WANTED—A Cook, Washer, and Ironer; one who perfectly understands her business; any color or country except Irish . . .[22]
WOMAN WANTED—To do general housework . . . English, Scotch, Welsh, German, or any country or color will answer except Irish . . .[23]
COACHMAN WANTED—A Man who understands the care of horses and is willing to make himself generally useful, on a small place six miles from the city. A colored man preferred. No Irish need apply . . .[24]

The Negroes could welcome this preference as long as they remained docile. As a perspicacious Englishman later remarked, much of their civility was "forced upon them by the circumstances of their helpless and degraded condition." [25] Meanwhile, immigrants were taking jobs which traditionally had been reserved for the colored folk.

As the Empire City grew wealthy on commerce and industry, much of the necessary labor was supplied by the foreign-born. Some 156,000 of these newcomers lived and worked on Manhattan in 1855; in comparison, the 3,688 gainfully employed Negroes were numerically insignificant.[26] Colored workers gradually were supplanted not only in a few of the better-paid posi-

---

[21] Statements in this paragraph are based upon my analysis of the manuscript schedules of the census marshals for New York City in the New York State Census of 1855. These volumes are now located in the county clerk's office, Hall of Records, New York City. My tabulation was limited, of course, to residents of Manhattan Island. Despite the exclusion of data from small portions of two of the volumes illegible because of their fragile condition, I believe the figures here given are reasonably accurate. In this article all further references to this material appear as: MSS., *New York State Census*, 1855.

[22] New York *Herald*, May 13, 1853.

[23] New York Daily *Sun*, May 11, 1853, as quoted by the *Irish American*, May 28, 1853.

[24] New York Daily *Tribune*, May 14, 1852.

[25] [Burn], *Three Years among the Working Classes, op. cit.*, p. xiii.

[26] MSS., *New York State Census*, 1855.

tions but as menial workers of all sorts, laborers, porters, dock hands, waiters, cooks, and maids.[27]

Even as colored domestics remained in demand, the Irish quickly surpassed them in numbers. Whereas in 1833 a traveller observed that the servants in New York City were "generally blacks," two decades later the city's Irish servants outnumbered by ten to one its entire Negro population.[28] At the same time, about 500 colored laborers and an equal number of colored waiters competed for employment with over 17,000 laborers and about 1,500 waiters born in the Emerald Isle.[29]

Economic rivalry between Negroes and immigrants intensified racial prejudices. The superior training and experience of many whites enabled them to obtain positions in most of the trades, while the black man found himself the eternal laborer. For him it was usually a question of manual labor or no job at all. This explains in part the willingness of Negroes to be hired on occasion as strikebreakers, should white laborers become unruly and demand higher wages. In 1853, for example, when Irish laborers at the Erie Railroad depot struck for $1.25 a day and a working limit of ten hours, Negroes, allegedly armed with revolvers, were hired in their places.[30] Whenever employers used colored men as scabs, mistrust and smouldering fears were fanned into passionate hatred.

The unrest of white workers was further fomented during the Civil War by the Conscription Act of 1863, which permitted the rich to exempt themselves from the draft by money payments. Many workers, including the foreignborn—who constituted half the city's population—believed that when they were drafted employers would replace them with Negroes. Fearing that newly emancipated southern Negroes might join with the colored workers of the North in taking away their jobs, the whites vented their blind rage in assaults upon innocent Negro citizens.[31] Native, German, and French workingmen were aroused by rumors of the importation of colored men to displace them at lower wages, and during a strike on the docks Irish longshoremen assaulted Negro strikebreakers.[32]

[27] Charles H. Wesley, Negro Labor in the United States (New York, 1927), p. 76; Arnett G. Lindsay, "The Economic Condition of the Negroes of New York Prior to 1861," Journal of Negro History, Vol. VI, No. 2, April 1921, p. 194; J. H. Harmon, Jr., "The Negro as a Local Business Man," Journal of Negro History, Vol. XIV, No. 2, April 1929, p. 119.

[28] John Finch, Travels in the United States of America and Canada (London, 1833), p. 35; MSS., New York State Census, 1865.

[29] MSS., New York State Census, 1855.

[30] Irish American, July 9, 1853.

[31] Freeman's Journal, August 16, 18, 1862; Courrier des Etats-Unis, August 16, October 7, 1862, April 14, 1863; Albion, November 18, 1863. Cf. Madeleine H. Rice, American Catholic Opinion in the Slavery Controversy (New York, 1944), pp. 124, 154; Basil L. Lee, Discontent in New York City, 1861–1865 (Washington, 1943), chapter IV, passim.

[32] Staats-Zeitung, April 18, 1863; Criminal-Zeitung, April 24, 1863; Andreas Dorpalen, "The German Element and the Issues of the Civil War," Mississippi Valley

Racial hatred and class consciousness, inflamed by the Emancipation Proclamation and the enforcement of conscription, burst into flames during the hectic week of July 11, 1863 as the enrollment of conscripts touched off the furious draft riots. For several days the metropolis was thrown into an uproar. Desperate mobs attacked the registry offices, sacked the residence of anti-slavery agitators, intimidated peaceable workingmen, assaulted and lynched Negroes, wrecked their homes and places of business, and burned the Colored Orphan Asylum into a shambles of blackened ruins. After an orgy of pillage and destruction, the police and militia finally restored order.[33]

While these riots were clear evidence of working class discontent, more important though less spectacular instances are afforded by the efforts of workingmen to improve their status by concerted action. During the fifties and sixties workers in nearly every industry struck for higher wages and fewer working hours. Some, like the German tailors, shoemakers, and bakers, tried to by-pass the wage system by organizing co-operative shops, and a number turned to Marxian socialism introduced at New York by the German, Joseph Weydemeyer. No Negroes joined the attacks upon capitalism, and, despite the formation in New York City of an American League of Colored Laborers in 1850, the Negro workers seem to have taken a negligible part in the labor struggles of the time.[34]

Apparently in only one instance did colored and white workers co-operate in the battle for higher wages. It was an exceptional situation, involving the hotel waiters, most of whom were Irish-born. Because the Negroes were fewer in number and more tractable (and hence more desirable from

Historical Review, Vol. XXIX, No. 1, June 1942, p. 68; George E. McNeill, _The Labor Movement: The Problem of Today_ (Boston, 1887), p. 126.

[33] Joel T. Headley, _The Great Riots of New York, 1712–1873; Including a Full and Complete Account of the Four Days' Draft Riot of 1863_ (New York, 1873), pp. 136–289; Wesley, _op. cit._, pp. 100–101; _Albion_, July 18, 1863; _Messager Franco-Américain_, July 15, 1863. My forthcoming _Immigrant Life in New York City_ shows that the European newcomer took part in the riots not as immigrants but as members of the white working classes. The twentieth annual report of the Association for Improving the Conditions of the Poor (1863, pp. 44–45) refers to Irish rowdies as the instigators of the violence but absolves from blame the immigrants as a group. The confused character of the riots is indicated by the fact that German grocery, liquor store, and beer garden proprietors suffered injury and property losses at the hands of the mob. Persuaded that the Orientals were but a "modification" of the Negro, a crowd of whites launched an attack upon the Chinese. New York _Herald_, July 16, 1863; _Anglo-Africa_, July 25, 1863; Lee, _op. cit._, p. 195; County of New York, Board of Supervisors, _Document No. 13_, December 27, 1867 (New York, 1868), Vol. I, pp. 90–91, 101, 111, 193, 207, 222–224, 424–425, 465, 507, 550–552, 684–686, 694–696.

[34] The league was a philanthropic and educational enterprise rather than a typical labor union. Headed by S. R. Ward, Lewis Woodson, Frederick Douglass, James McCune Smith, and others, its object was to promote union of skilled colored workmen, to improve their "social and physical condition," and to recommend commercial, mechanical, and agriculture education to Negro youth. It also planned a fund which would assist Negroes to go into business. New York _Daily Tribune_, July 30, 1850. An industrial fair which it contemplated for 1852 does not seem to have taken place. I have found no further mention of this organization.

the proprietors' viewpoint) they were paid more than the whites. In 1853, when Negro waiters were receiving $16 a month and white waiters only $12, the whites gathered to discuss means of equalizing their wages. A colored delegate to the meeting advised the group to hold out for $18 a month, hoping thereby to aid Negroes in raising their own pay (or perhaps to dupe the whites into making impossible demands!). A strike ensued, but it was a miserable failure. Some employers retained their best white waiters at higher wages but fired the rest, replacing them with women or Negroes.[35]

In skilled occupations Negroes and whites made no common efforts to improve conditions of work. Had Negro cooperation been desired by the whites, it would have been of no material help. There were too few skilled colored workers. Of 3,688 gainfully employed Negroes in 1855, about 200, or only four tenths of one per cent were engaged in the skilled trades.[36] In a traditionally Negro calling, 74 colored barbers and 4 hairdressers were easily outnumbered by Germans, Irishmen, English and French, together with a small but growing number of Italians.[37] Tailors, shoemakers, carpenters, sawyers, tinsmiths, coopers, cabinetmakers and upholsterers, nurses, cigar makers, and jewellers accounted for another 107 Negro working people of varying degrees of skill, while some of the 73 colored boatmen (of whom 56 were stewards) may have been partly skilled.[38]

Not only were the Negro artisans few in number; most of them were geographically isolated from the white artisans. Perhaps the main reason for

[35] New York *Herald*, March 31, 1853, as cited by the *European*, May 2, 1857; New York *Tribune*, April 26, May 3, 1853.

[36] MSS., *New York State Census, 1855*. Cf. *supra*, note 21; *infra*, note 38. In the late 1830's the city's Negro community included 3 carpenters and joiners, 5 boot and shoemakers, 5 tailors, an engraver, a watch and clock maker, a sign painter, and 2 dress and cloak makers. Haynes, *op. cit.*, p. 67.

[37] MSS., *New York State Census*, 1855; *Staats-Zeitung*, April 7, 1860.

[38] From the manuscript schedules of the *New York State Census* of 1855. Excluding professionals, I tabulated occupations of some 204 Negroes who, it seemed to me, possessed some degree of occupational skill. These are listed here (the figures in parentheses show the total number of whites and Negroes in the several occupations, as listed in the printed version of the census):

78 barbers (including 4 hairdressers) (997)
19 tailors (12,609)
13 boot and shoemakers (6,745)
13 nurses (636)
12 carpenters (excluding ship carpenters) (6,901)
10 sawyers (285)
8 cigar makers (1,996 "tobacconists")
6 coopers (1,018)
5 jewelers (1,099)
5 tinsmiths (897)
3 cabinetmakers (2,606)
3 masons, plasterers, bricklayers (3,634)

2 moulders (593)
2 bakers (2,856)
2 clock makers (79)
2 printers (1,901)
2 sail makers (281)
2 upholsterers (711)
1 each of the following: boat builder, blacking maker, blacksmith, confectioner, carver and gilder, cage maker, chandler, "cutter," gold and silversmith, hat and cap maker, iron worker, painter, roofer and slater, ship carpenter, shirt and collar maker, tool maker.

the existence of this class of colored workers was the fact that, with a few exceptions, they served the Negro community almost exclusively. In this respect they resembled the German shoemakers, carpenters, painters, and masons who catered to the needs of the German immigrants and seldom were found outside New York City's "Little Germany." Each Negro craftsman had his own clientele which, if not entirely colored, included immigrants of little means who usually shared the same slum areas.

In some respects the Negro population developed a degree of self-sufficiency. Negro shops and services were available in the community. About 1840, Negroes published a newspaper and operated two first-class restaurants, two dry goods stores, a hairdressing establishment, three tailor shops, four "pleasure gardens," a confectionery, a fruit store, and two coal yards.[39] The restaurants and the richer stores were in the financial district or in the white shopping neighborhoods, but most were in localities where Negroes congregated. The smallest shops which did not advertise were probably in run-down localities inhabited chiefly by the colored people themselves. Among these were numerous second-hand clothing stores and barber shops. Fifteen years later, some 31 Negroes were dealers in foodstuffs, mostly butchers, while 11 were peddlers and traders, 4 were retail shopkeepers, and 18 served as clerks; there were also 5 merchants, agents, or salesmen, a contractor, a distiller or brewer, an express man, a clothier, an undertaker, and a stable keeper.[40] Colored persons were proprietors of 14 hotels and boarding houses and 5 restaurants in 1855.[41] On the whole, however, the small number of Negro businesses reflected a lack of opportunity, while such colored enterprises as existed showed the courage of Negro businessmen who risked their capital in property which might be damaged or ruined by a race riot.

Few Negroes entered the professions. Considering the difficulties in the way of Negro self-improvement, however, it is remarkable that approximately 50 colored professional men were reported by the state census marshals in 1855. Exactly half were teachers and clergymen. Fifteen Negro musicians included, no doubt, dancers and minstrel singers. Five physicians, a dentist, a lawyer, and an artist complete the list.[42]

[39] Haynes, op. cit., pp. 96–97.
[40] MSS., New York State Census, 1855. Among the more prominent Negro enterprises were Thomas Dowling's restaurant near the corner of Wall and Broad streets, Edward Bidwell's two thriving stores in Broadway, Austin Steward's liquor business, Henry Scott's pickling business, and James McCune Smith's drug store. Lindsay, "The Economic Condition of the Negroes . . . ," loc. cit., pp. 106, 139, 197–198; Harmon, "The Negro as a Local Business Man," loc. cit., p. 120. Cf. Martin R. Delany, The Condition, Elevation, Emigation, and Destiny of the Colored People . . . (Philadelphia, 1852), chapter X.
[41] MSS., New York State Census, 1855. Others in supervisory occupations were 7 housekeepers and janitors, 2 watchmen and 8 miscellaneous superintendents. In addition there were 7 farmers, 4 gardeners, florists, and nurserymen, and 4 fishermen.
[42] Ibid. There were 13 teachers and 12 clergymen; 3 "engineers" and a student were also reported. Cf. Delany, op. cit., chapter XI.

Perhaps more important as an index of the well-being of any community is the degree to which real and personal property is owned. Colored folk sometimes acquired real estate despite their lowly position in society. In 1837, before the famous panic of that year, the *Colored American* asserted that Negro freeholders to the amount of $250 did "not fall far short of 300."[43] Twelve years later such freeholders represented 2.2 per cent of the Negro population; in 1855 this percentage had risen to 8.7, and by 1865 to 10.5.[44] As to the dollar value of real estate, only one estimate seems to be available: in 1859 the taxed real estate owned by Negroes on Manhattan amounted to $1,400,000, while perhaps a like amount was owned in Brooklyn.[45] The value of personal property owned by Negroes is harder to assess. An indication, at least, is afforded by savings bank deposits. In 1837 the *Colored American* claimed that the colored folk had from $50,000 to $80,000 in New York City savings banks, an amount which seems grossly exaggerated when compared with James McCune Smith's estimate in 1851 of "$40,000 or $50,000 belonging to the colored people invested in savings banks in Wall-st."[46] By 1855 the Negro deposits reached $60,000.[47] Apart from savings, colored businessmen and artisans acquired property and equipment necessary for their work, and in 1861 Smith stated that the Negroes of the Empire City had invested in their own businesses some $755,000.[48]

While we may conclude from this evidence that a colored aristocracy had appeared by the middle of the century, the great mass of Negro families saw no improvement of their lot. Wages failed to keep pace with rising rents and the prices of provisions, while in depression years, as in 1857, unemployment swelled the relief rolls. Hard times, the many disabilities of colored workers, heightened prejudice aroused by abolitionist propaganda, and the filling of unskilled and semiskilled occupations by immigrants contributed more than

[43] *Colored American*, July 22, 1837. One of these was probably E. Davis who, during the abolitionist riot of 1834, owned the brick buildings at 121 Broome and 123 Forsyth streets. MS letter from H. and A. Averill to Mayor Lawrence, July 12, 1834, now in the possession of the New York Historical Society.

[44] Hirsch, "New York and the Negro . . . ," *loc. cit.*, p. 434, which cites census figures and yearbooks as sources. By Article II, Section 1, of the State Constitution of 1821, Negro freeholders to the value of $250 were permitted to vote; they also were taxed, while Negroes possessing less than this were exempted from taxation.

[45] Wesley, *op. cit.*, p. 49. In Philadelphia, Negroes owned real estate amounting to $400,000 in 1847 and $800,000 in 1856. Abram L. Harris, *The Negro as Capitalist* (Philadelphia, 1936), p. 6. For mention of Negro-owned houses in New York in 1864 cf. the Citizens Association's *Report of the Council of Hygiene, op. cit.*, p. 240.

[46] *Colored American*, May 22, 1837; New York Daily *Tribune*, March 20, 1851.

[47] Harris, *op. cit.*, p. 23. According to a report published in the *African Repository*, Vol. XXXI, January 1856, p. 8, "free persons of color" had $600,000 deposited in savings fund institutions in New York, a figure which I consider highly dubious. Cf. Arnett G. Lindsay, "The Negro in Banking," *Journal of Negro History*, Vol. XIV, No. 2, April 1929, p. 159.

[48] Wesley, *op. cit.*, pp. 49–50, citing Clark, *The Condition of the Colored People of the United States*, p. 11; cf. Harris, *op. cit.*, p. 6. The Brooklyn figure was $76,200, and in Williamsburg, $4,900.

anything else to the remarkable decline in the Negro population of Manhattan during the 1850's. New York might afford the first step toward the foreigner's fortune, but for the colored man it held out little hope.

SPECIAL STATISTICAL NOTE. The following material, made available for the first time, shows occupations in which ten or more Negroes were engaged in 1855 (derived from the manuscript schedules of the *New York State Census of 1855*):

1,025 domestic servants	17 boatmen
536 laborers (including carpet shakers)	16 longshoremen
499 waiters	15 chimney sweeps
366 laundresses	15 musicians
176 porters	14 hotel and boarding house keepers
151 cooks	13 boot and shoemakers
129 whitewashers	13 nurses
111 dressmakers, seamstresses	13 teachers
102 drivers, coachmen, hackmen	12 clergymen
78 barbers (including 4 hairdressers)	12 carpenters
56 stewards	12 wine and liquor dealers
55 cartmen, draymen, teamsters	11 peddlers, traders
19 butchers	11 farmers, gardeners, florists,
19 tailors	nurserymen
18 clerks	10 sawyers

Louis Ruchames

JIM CROW RAILROADS IN MASSACHUSETTS

Segregation, with its diverse manifestations, had its beginnings more in the North than in the South. Especially in the northeastern states, Negroes mounted indignant protests against the practice. They achieved their greatest measure of success in Massachusetts, where white sentiment was more sympathetic to their cause than in any other state. Louis Ruchames' article describes one of these early Negro protests against segregation. As he shows, their tactics were quite similar to those employed by civil rights organizations today.

Massachusetts is today in the forefront of those states that have sought to achieve equality of status and opportunity for all racial groups. Its fair employment and fair educational practice laws are among the finest in the country and have achieved notable successes in opening up new opportunities for racial and religious groups within the state. Segregation of Negroes and whites, although it still exists to some extent, is a steadily shrinking element in the social structure of Massachusetts.

How different is this situation from what obtained a century or more ago. In the 1830's and 1840's segregation was the dominant pattern in the state. As late as 1843 Negroes were forbidden to marry whites; they were segregated in the churches, where they occupied the "Negro pew"; they were confined to the most menial occupations; they could not attend the same schools as white children—in Boston this situation continued to 1855; they were segregated on stagecoaches, railroads and steam boats. Writing in 1836, Lydia Maria Child, a prominent author and Abolitionist, charged that "our prejudice against colored people is even more inveterate than it is at the South. The planter is often attached to his Negroes, and lavishes caresses and kind words upon them, as he would on a favorite hound: but our cold-hearted, ignoble prejudice admits of no exception—no intermission."[1]

Louis Ruchames, "Jim Crow Railroads in Massachusetts," *American Quarterly*, VIII (Spring, 1956), pp. 61–75. Reprinted with permission of *American Quarterly* and Louis Ruchames.

[1] *An Appeal in Favor of That Class of Americans Called Africans* (New York, 1836), p. 195.

The basic causes of this change are well known. The expansion of industry and the rise of large urban centers seriously weakened the system of caste. The growth of a large middle class whose interests and ideals favored individual freedom and equality before the law was a no less significant factor. Less well known, however, is the day to day activity of a large body of men and women, enrolled in the Abolitionist movement under the leadership of William Lloyd Garrison, whose self-sacrificing efforts on behalf of racial equality in the North, in addition to their efforts against slavery in the South, provided the motive power for the changes that did take place. It was they who exposed segregation and discrimination to the public eye, condemned them unreservedly and organized the campaigns which helped to diminish or eliminate such practices from significant areas of public life.

The first important Abolitionist campaign against segregation began with the appearance of the *Liberator*, edited and published by Garrison, in 1831. In its third issue it called attention to the existing law prohibiting the marriage of Negroes and whites, and demanded its repeal. The movement for repeal reached its peak in the 1840's, and success was finally achieved in 1843. It was in the midst of this campaign that the question of "Jim Crow" cars on certain of the railways of Massachusetts came to the fore.

Railroads had first come into public use in Massachusetts in 1836. Following existing customs on many stagecoaches and passenger vessels, several railroads instituted the practice of segregating Negroes in a separate car. These were the Eastern Railroad, extending at first from Boston to Salem and later reaching the New Hampshire border; the New Bedford and Taunton trunk line; and the Boston and Providence Railroad.

At first, the car for Negroes had no definite name. A letter to the *Massachusetts Spy* of Worcester in 1838, referred to it as a "dirt car." [2] In 1841, however, it came to be referred to quite widely as the "Jim Crow" car. The name was taken from a song and dance routine popularized during the 1830's by Thomas D. Rice, "the father of American Minstrelsy." The routine was called "jumping Jim Crow" and was an imitation, by a white, of a Negro referred to as Jim Crow, doing a song and dance. Reflecting prevailing white prejudices, it caricatured the Negro as an inferior and ignorant creature. Thus, the application of "Jim Crow" to the cars for Negroes on the railroads of Massachusetts was a natural development, and Massachusetts has come to have the dubious distinction of first using the term with reference to a segregated Negro car.

Before 1841 there were occasional references in the press of the Commonwealth to instances of enforced segregation on the railroads. There was no discernible public agitation on the subject, however, until the early part of 1841, when the issue came to a head through a series of incidents involving Negro and white leaders of the Abolitionist movement.

David Ruggles, a Negro Abolitionist of New York, who had played a prominent part in the Underground Railway and had helped more than five

[2] Reprinted in the *Liberator*, VIII (December 14, 1838), 197.

hundred Negro slaves to escape to the North, was ordered by a conductor, while going from New Bedford to Boston on the New Bedford and Taunton branch railroad on July 6, to leave the car in which he was seated and to move to another set aside for Negroes. On refusing, he was dragged out by the railroad superintendent and several others employed by the company, his clothing torn in the process, and thrown off the train. Ruggles brought suit for assault and battery against those who were involved in removing him.

The trial took place in New Bedford before Justice Henry A. Crapo on July 19 and 20. The company based its eviction of Ruggles on a regulation issued by its agent, William A. Crocker, on January 1, 1841, which read: "Passengers who go in the cars of the Taunton and New Bedford branch railroad, will take such seats as may be assigned them by the conductor." The company contended that a copy of the regulation had been pointed out to Ruggles when he had been asked to move to the Negro car. He had refused, and was then ejected. In delivering his opinion, Justice Crapo suggested that two issues were involved: (1) the right of the company to issue the regulation in question; and (2) whether or not undue force had been used to put the regulation into effect. On the first issue, he ruled that the railroad was the private property of the company, which therefore had the right to issue such regulations ensuring the welfare and comfort of its passengers as were not forbidden by the existing law of the state. The regulation in question, he ruled, was not contrary to the law of the state. As to the question of undue force, he ruled that such had not been proven. The charges brought by Ruggles were thereupon dismissed and the defendants adjudged not guilty.[3]

A few weeks later, on September 8, Frederick Douglass, the Negro Abolitionist, and J. A. Collins, the General Agent of the Massachusetts Anti-Slavery Society, a white man, were the center of another violent fracas. They had purchased tickets in Newburyport and were on their way, together, to the annual meeting of the Strafford County Anti-Slavery Society. On taking seats side by side in a car of the Eastern Railroad, they were approached by the conductor, who ordered Douglass to move into the Jim Crow car. Collins and several of the other passengers objected to the conductor's demand. Collins was ordered to leave his seat, the better to enable the conductor to drag or "snake" Douglass out of the car. He refused, remarking, "If you haul him out, it will be over my person, as I do not intend to leave this seat." The conductor left and returned with four or five men who seized Douglass and carried him into the Jim Crow car. In the process, Collins was injured and Douglass had his clothing torn.

About three weeks later, Collins, Douglass, J. M. Buffum, a white Abolitionist, and an unidentified woman were travelling on the Eastern Railroad to Newburyport. Collins and Douglass occupied one seat, with Buffum sitting behind them and the woman in front. In Lynn the conductor approached

[3] For a summary of the proceedings and the ruling see the *New Bedford Mercury*, July 22, 1841; also the *Liberator*, XI (August 6, 1841), 165.

Douglass and ordered him out. The following colloquy, reported in detail in the *Liberator,* then took place:

Buffum: Can't I ride with him, if he goes into the forward car! I want to have some conversation with him, and I fear I shall not have another opportunity so favorable.

The Conductor: No! I'd as soon haul you out of his car, as I'd haul him from this.

Douglass: There are but very few in this car, and why, since no objection has been made, do you order me out?

A Passenger: I've no objection to riding with him—let's take a vote on the question.

Buffum: That's just what I want—let us have a vote on the question.

A second passenger: I've no objection to that step.

The conductor remained adamant.

Douglass: If you will give me any good reason why I should leave this car, I'll go willing; but, without such reason, I do not feel at liberty to leave; though, you can do with me as you please, I shall not resist.

The Conductor: You have asked that question before.

Douglass: I mean to continue asking the question over and over again, as long as you continue to assault me in this manner.

Others took up the cry and called out: "Give him one good reason." Finally, forced to speak, the conductor muttered. "Because you are black."

Finding himself unequal to the task of dragging Douglass out, the conductor secured the help of eight or ten toughs. What happened next is vividly described by Collins:

"Snake out the d - - - - d nigger," cried one. "Out with him," responded another guardian of the "peculiar institution" of the South. The gang of men stood in a leaping posture, with their hands extended and fingers half bent, ready for the going forth of the command of the captain to seize him. The word was given—"Take him out!" Five or six, like so many tigers, laid hold of Douglass, but he happened to be exceedingly heavy, as the laws of gravity were in full force. His attachment to his seat was so great, that these half dozen bullies found it no easy task to snake him out over me. "Damm that Collins," cried out one of them, "out with him, out with him." Whereupon five or six laid violent hands upon me. One gave me a severe blow upon the back part of my head, and another hit me in my face, cutting my lip considerably. Like my friend Douglass, I did not feel inclined to part with my seat at the command of these ruffians, if I may be allowed the use of such an expression; in consequence of which, our seat gave way, and we, with five or six of these villains laying hold of our head, arms and legs, were dragged out head foremost, and deposited upon the ground in no very gentle manner. One of the gang gave me a very severe kick in my back, in consequence of which, I am lame at the present time. I was so badly bruised that my person, in various parts, is now black and blue. Buffum remained behind with Douglass, whose baggage was thrown out after him. I was allowed to pass on in the same train. Soon after the cars started, the conductor approached me, and made use of the most abusive language. I asked him if he was employed by the company to insult passengers; and, if so, I considered him the most faithful servant I ever met with; and then turned myself around, and began to read. He shook his little fist about my head a few times, and was greatly enraged because I would hold no conversation with him. I was now left to myself until we arrived at Salem.[4]

On arriving in Salem, Collins was accosted by the conductor and other officials of the railroad, including its president, Mr. Neal, and was ordered to leave the train because of his earlier defence of Douglass. After some remonstrance and only when it became clear that he would be dragged out if he failed to leave peacefully, he walked out of the train and took a private conveyance to Newburyport.

In the ensuing months, there occurred numerous other incidents. One morning, at the end of September, Mrs. Mary Newhall Green, the secretary of the Lynn Anti-Slavery Society, a light-complexioned Negro, who had previously without incident used the Eastern Railroad for trips from Lynn to Boston, was dragged out of the white car, with a baby in her arms. In the process, the baby was injured, and Mrs. Green's husband, who had sought to defend her, was badly beaten.

On the evening of that day, some three or four white men, who had boarded the train of the Eastern Railroad in East Boston, were dragged out of their car, together with a Negro whose ejection they had protested.[5] One of the whites, Dr. Daniel Mann, a dentist of Boston, brought charges of assault and battery against George Harrington, the conductor, who had led the assault. The trial took place in the Boston Police Court before a Justice Simmons. The lawyer for the defense was a Mr. Lord of Salem; Dr. Mann's counsel was Samuel E. Sewall, a well-known Abolitionist who was a descendant of Massachusetts Chief Justice Samuel Sewall, an outspoken opponent of Negro slavery in Colonial days.[6]

Lord argued that "all corporations in the Commonwealth have power to make such reasonable and proper by-laws for the management of their business as their own interests and the public good may require; that the established usage and the public sentiment of this community authorise a separation of the

4 *Liberator*, XI (October 15, 1841), 165.
5 *Ibid.*, XI (October 15, 1841), 165.
6 *Ibid.*, XI (November 5, 1841), 180.

blacks from the whites in public places; that the regulation adopted by the Eastern Railroad Corporation was reasonable and proper, and such as they had a perfect right to adopt; that if the rule was unreasonable, neither Dr. Mann nor any other person had power to take the law into their own hands, and to right the wrong; and that he and his friends formed a conspiracy to prevent the execution of this rule; and in this they were trespassers." [7]

On the other hand, Sewall argued that the directors of the railroad did not have the legal right to authorize a conductor to separate passengers on the basis of color; that a rule of that kind was arbitrary and unlawful, as was the attempt to enforce it; that the conductor had no right to evict any person by force without first notifying him of the company's regulation—which had not been done in this case; and that the conductor had no right to evict passengers who had merely expressed their objections to his action.

Justice Simmons decided, however, "that the conductor was justified by the disorderly and unlawful conduct of Dr. Mann and his friends in ejecting them from the cars—and ordered that the defendant be discharged." [8]

Toward the end of the year, there occurred an incident that had a strong impact upon public opinion. It involved Charles Lenox Remond, a Negro Abolitionist who had been chosen one of the American delegates to the World Anti-Slavery Convention held in London in June, 1840. Endowed with an attractive personality and eloquence of speech, Remond had been warmly received by the foremost leaders of English society. He returned to America in December, 1841, carrying with him the signatures of 60,000 Irishmen urging their countrymen in America to oppose slavery. On his arrival in Boston, Remond boarded a train of the Eastern Railroad to visit his parents, who were living in Salem. The conductor ordered him into the "Jim Crow" car. When several white friends, who had just welcomed him in Boston and were eager to hear the story of his visit abroad, moved to the "Jim Crow" car with him, they were ordered by the conductor to leave immediately or be dragged out.

In describing the incident, the Abolitionists were not slow to point out the difference between Remond's insulting reception in his own country and the love and respect accorded him in Europe. "In England, Scotland, and Ireland, Mr. Remond was received into the best circles, and treated with the utmost courtesy and respect. In Exeter Hall, London, with a royal duke in the chair, and succeeding Daniel O'Connell as one of the speakers on that occasion, he was listened to with admiration, and elicited thunders of applause. . . . But, in his own land, as soon as he steps his foot on the shore, he is treated more vilely than a dog, and prohibited from enjoying the society even of those who have crucified their own prejudices, and whose hearts are touched with sympathy for his lot! And America is the land of liberty and equality—the land which cannot tolerate a nobility—the land which scoffs at monarchy!" [9]

[7] Massachusetts Anti-Slavery Society, *Tenth Annual Report*, January 26, 1842.
[8] *Liberator*, XI (November 5, 1841), 180.
[9] Massachusetts Anti-Slavery Society, *Tenth Annual Report*, January 26, 1842.

As these incidents came to their notice, the Abolitionists expressed their indignation and took steps to combat the policy of the railroads.[10] A speech in the state legislature, in March, 1841, by Representative George Bradburn, who had been leading the campaign for repeal of the marriage law, helped bring the problem to public attention.[11] Speaking on a bill to authorize the owners of the Eastern Railroad to extend their wharves, Bradburn surprised the House when he announced that, despite his interest in railroad expansion, he would vote against the bill because of the Eastern Railroad's policy of segregation. It was not until the attack upon David Ruggles, however, that public opinion was really aroused. On July 12, a mass meeting of protest, attended by prominent residents of the city, was held in New Bedford. Ruggles presented his version of the attack upon him and was followed by several other speakers. The meeting adjourned and reconvened the following day to hear the report of an investigating committee appointed to look into the incident. After hearing the report, those assembled resolved "that as citizens of a free and enlightened community, and descendants of those Revolutionary worthies who poured out their hearts' blood in the cause of our civil liberty, we do remonstrate in the most solemn manner against those inhuman proceedings as took place at the railroad depot, in this town on the 6th of the present month, in expelling David Ruggles of New York, from the car, for the unworthy cause of his having a color which the God of Nature was pleased to give him." [12]

The failure of Ruggles' suit against the New Bedford and Taunton Railroad outraged the Abolitionists and stimulated their campaign for further action. Soon after the trial, the *Liberator* printed a letter from Ruggles, dated July 24, giving his version of the proceedings before Justice Crapo. He charged that, "It was hardly to be supposed that his honor could give an equitable decision in this case—himself being a stockholder in said company, and therefore lawfully rendered incapable of occupying the bench of justice under such circumstances. In relation to Justice Crapo's court, I must confess, he rendered it the greatest farce I ever witnessed. In giving his opinion, he declared his

[10] Even before railroads had come into use, Abolitionists had condemned segregation on public conveyances. In 1834, the *Liberator* had characterized the treatment of Negroes on stagecoaches and steamboats as "vulgar and shameful in the extreme." (*Liberator*, IV [June 4, 1834], 91.) In 1836, Lydia Maria Child, the prominent Abolitionist author, had asked in her famous *Appeal*: "Will any candid person tell me why respectable colored people should not be allowed to make use of public conveyances, open to all who are able and willing to pay for the privilege? Those who enter a vessel, or a stagecoach, cannot select their companions. If they can afford to take a carriage or boat for themselves, then, and then only, they have a right to be exclusive." (*An Appeal in Favor of That Class of Americans Called Africans* [New York, 1836], p. 206.) In the ensuing years, the *Liberator*, from time to time, reported instances of segregation, which it condemned in no uncertain terms. See VIII (December 14, 1838), 197; IX (July 19, 1938), 116; IX (October 18, 1839), 167; IX (October 25, 1839), 170; X (June 26, 1840), 101.

[11] The marriage law, first enacted in 1705–6, and revised in 1834, forbade the intermarriage of whites with Negroes, Indians or Mulattoes. It was repealed in 1843 after a long struggle which began in 1831.

[12] *Liberator*, XI (July 24, 1841), 118.

ignorance of the law in the case, and, of course, adhered to the authority of Judge Lynch." Entitling the letter "Lynching in New Bedford, Justice Henry A. Crapo and Lynch Law," the *Liberator* commented: "The conduct of Justice Crapo, in giving his legal sanction to the dastardly assault and battery upon the person of Mr. Ruggles at the New Bedford depot by the conductors of the railroad train, is in our view, unspeakably atrocious." [13]

As the attacks upon Negroes and their white sympathizers in the railroad cars continued, other newspapers besides the *Liberator* condemned them, and public demand for action began to intensify. The Boston *Daily Times*, the Lynn *Record*, the Dover *Morning Star*, the Quincy *Patriot* and the Massachusetts *Spy* printed reports of incidents and letters from readers, and forcefully denounced the conduct of the railroad companies and the courts. The Dover *Morning Star* actually called for a boycott of the Eastern Railroad. [14] The *Liberator* emphasized that Stephen Chase, the superintendent of the Eastern Railroad, was a member in good standing of the Society of Friends, and called upon the Society to "disown" him or "be willing to lie under the imputation of conniving at the sanctioning of high-handed villainy and brutal ruffianism." [15]

The Abolitionists of Massachusetts initiated a concerted campaign against the railroads at a meeting of the Massachusetts Anti-Slavery Society on August 17, 1841. It was decided that in addition to the petitions for repeal of the marriage law, which they were circulating, they would also distribute petitions "for a law declaring equal rights of persons in the use of the means of conveyance furnished under charters from the State." [16] In September, three large public meetings were held in Lynn, with people of all shades of political opinion attending. At one of the meetings, in the First Universalist meeting house, resolutions were unanimously adopted condemning the attack upon Collins and Douglass as "a gross violation of our State constitution as well as of all law and decency," "the substitution of Lynch law and mobocracy for order and decorum," and asserting that those present would "use all the means in their power, consistent with their views of law and christianity, to defend the colored people who may see fit to take their seats in the long cars, in the enjoyment of their rights." [17]

At a meeting on September 30, it was further resolved that the attacks "demand the interference of Legislative authority," and that petitions to that effect be presented to the legislature. In order to secure the widest public support, another resolution affirmed that the Eastern Railroad's practices "be viewed not as a question between Abolitionists and Anti-Abolitionists, but as a matter connected with the freedom of every citizen." [18]

The campaign for legislative action quickly gathered momentum. On

[13] *Ibid.*, XI (August 6, 1841), 127.
[14] *Ibid.*, XI (October 1, 1841), 157.
[15] *Ibid.*, XI (October 8, 1841), 163.
[16] *Ibid.*, XI (August 20, 1841), 139.
[17] *Ibid.*, XI (October 15, 1841), 166.
[18] *Ibid.*, XI (October 15, 1841), 166.

October 15, the *Liberator* printed a copy of a petition that was being circulated by the Board of Managers of the Massachusetts Anti-Slavery Society. The petition requested the legislature "to pass a law declaring and defining the rights of the people of this Commonwealth in the use of the means of conveyance furnished by the Railroad companies therein, in order that the officers of said companies may no longer claim the right of depriving any class of persons of the use of any of their cars, on the sole ground of color, and of insulting, assaulting and ejecting white passengers, merely for claiming the equal means of conveyance for persons of color." [19] Anti-Slavery societies throughout the state quickly swung into action and tied this campaign in with the already powerful one against the marriage law. Thus, the Norfolk County Anti-Slavery Society, at its quarterly meeting, resolved to "recommend to the Abolitionists of the several towns in this county, to interrogate the candidates of the whig and the democratic parties, of their respective towns, for the State Legislature, as to their view for the repeal of the marriage law, and for defining the powers of Rail-Road Corporations." [20] The quarterly meeting of the Worcester North Division Anti-Slavery Society passed a resolution and added the recommendation "to those who may be travelling to New York or Portland, to patronize the Boston and Norwich in preference to the Providence and Stonington Railroad, the Boston and Exeter in preference to the Boston and Newburyport Railroad, inasmuch as colored people are, by these companies respected and treated as equal human beings." [21]

In their public pronouncements, the Abolitionists kept repeating a number of points which proved to be extremely effective in swinging public opinion to their side. They emphasized, for instance, that the railroads which forcefully prevented whites and Negroes from sitting together were most solicitous in permitting Southern slaveholders to keep their Negro slaves by their side when travelling in those very same cars. It was only the free Negro who was segregated, not the slave. Thus, the author of a letter to the *Massachusetts Spy* of Worcester, wrote: "That Corporation [the Eastern Railroad] consider this 'Jim Crow' car good enough for a 'Nigger,' if said 'Nigger' be a *free* man or woman. Let a southern slaveholder, however, get into one of their first class cars, accompanied by his 'chattels personal,' and no matter how black those 'chattels' may be, not a word will be uttered against the arrangement. After all, then, it is *not* color alone which excludes a man from the best car. The colored person to be excluded must also be *free!!* I ask every man or woman who may see these lines, if this be consistent? If it be right? I ask them if they are willing such an insult should be offered to freedom in Massachusetts? Ay, and in sight of Bunker Hill?" [22]

[19] *Ibid.*, XI (October 15, 1841), 166.
[20] *Ibid.*, XI (October 29, 1841), 175.
[21] *Ibid.*, XI (October 29, 1841), 175.
[22] Reprinted in the *Liberator*, XI (November 5, 1841), 177. Similarly, James Buffum, in a letter to the *National Anti-Slavery Standard*, extracts from which were printed in the *Liberator*, XI (November 12, 1841), 184, noted: "Let it be observed that

Another point stressed by the Abolitionists was the repression of freedom of speech by the railroad corporations, whose procedure it was to attack all those who protested the forcible evictions of Negroes from white cars. Dr. Daniel Mann, the white dentist who had been assaulted, emphasized this when he asked, in a letter to the *Liberator:* "But, *reader* are *you* willing to ride in the cars under the cringing sense that a padlock is on your lips, and that a power as despotic as that of the Turk, wielded by hands far less responsible and far more degraded, is ready to insult and trample upon your rights, and can do so with impunity, if by any censure of their abuse, you should provoke their rage?" [23]

A third argument, no less important than the others, concerned the wealth and power of the railroads, which had enabled them to flout public opinion and to secure the sympathetic decisions of those court justices before whom suits had been brought. The spectacle of judges justifying the evictions of Negroes and the attacks upon their white sympathizers strengthened the conviction that only through the power of popular protest, directed into legislative action, could the railroads' arrogance be curbed. As Dr. Daniel Mann emphasized in his letter to the *Liberator*, after Judge Simmons had dismissed his suit against the Eastern Railroad, "Justice was foiled and overcome in her own temple by the power and management of wealth, vested in a corporation which the people have established. The serpent hatched by their kindness has become a boa constrictor, to crush them in its folds. No court can guard the rights of the people against such a power. The people alone who created the power can prescribe its limits, and defend themselves from its encroachments. The need of their action is now demonstrated. . . . It is the contest of the unguarded rights of American citizenship with an overgrown, overbearing and unprincipled monopoly of wealth and power and wrong . . . In short, let all the ready means by which a wealthy corporation can socially violate private rights with impunity, by force of arms, and force of falsehood, purchased by the form of wealth, be guarded against by law; and let every man feel that he is a member of a republic in which an injury offered to the meanest citizen is an insult to the whole community." [24]

The effect of Judge Simmons' decision upon the people and press of Massachusetts is illustrated by the reaction of the Lynn *Record*, which urged that "if the 'Great and General Court of Massachusetts' is not disfranchised, but has yet the power of *making laws* in favor of *the people*, without regard to the color of the skin, the color of the hair, the *breadth of the shoulders*,

---

this murderous prejudice, in reality, exists against *condition* more than against *color*. . . .
Slaves can travel beside their masters in all our public vehicles without offending northern nerves; why, then, is such a fuss made about colored *freemen?* Our merchants and sea captains can trade with Africans for gold dust and ivory, in exchange for rum and trinkets; they do not shudder at striking heads for such profitable bargains; how is it that they bear such hatred to the colored man in their own country? The plain truth is, it arises from contempt for their *condition.*"

[23] *Liberator*, XI (November 12, 1841), 182.
[24] *Ibid.*, XI (November 12, 1841), 182.

or the quality of the clothes, we trust, in the name of liberty, (if it is yet lawful to speak that word) that the independent voters at the coming election will see to it that men are chosen who will define the powers of corporations somewhat differently from the New Bedford Justice (Judge Crapo) or the Boston Justice." [25]

The movement against the "Jim Crow" car reached its peak at the beginning of 1842. As petitions demanding legislative action poured into the legislature, a joint legislative committee of both houses under the chairmanship of Seth Sprague, Jr., of Boston, was appointed to study the problem and bring in a report. It held a public meeting in February; those who appeared before it were Remond and two of the most prominent white anti-slavery lawyers of Massachusetts, Wendell Phillips and Ellis Gray Loring. The *Bay State Democrat*, reporting that the State House, the scene of the meeting, "was crowded with a large audience, consisting of the members of the two houses, and ladies and gentlemen generally," noted that Remond's speech, "coming as it did from one of the proscribed race, and delivered in a manner at once graceful and pointed, seemed to produce much effect upon the assembly." [26]

Phillips, in his testimony, affirmed the right of the legislature to end segregation on the railroads. The railroad corporations, he argued, were created and protected by the legislature "in the exercise of special privileges and franchises. The legislature creates—of course, it can control them. They are bound to make reports, from time to time, of their proceedings to it. The fact presupposes the right to regulate their proceedings, if need be." The railroad corporations were in duty bound to observe the laws and constitution of the Commonwealth, and to do nothing to contravene "the equal rights of all the people which that Constitution was framed to secure." Declaring that it was "a right, not a privilege to be transported in the cars of the corporations, upon payment of a certain sum," he affirmed that such payment "and conformity to the usual and decent rules of society, *entitle* a man to the use of this conveyance." As a right, therefore, "it surely ought to be an equal right." But forcing a colored man to ride in a "Jim Crow" car constitutes "an injury to his rights, and insult to his person," and should therefore not be permitted by the legislature. Noting that segregation was confined to three roads and that "on the largest and most frequented of the railroads, no such regulation has obtained"—an indication that there was no general public opinion demanding such regulation—he emphasized that "we ask not for the *writing* of law;—we ask the Legislature to say *what is law*." By affirming that the railroads were acting contrary to the constitution and the laws of Massachusetts, the legislature would not only acknowledge the equal rights of all citizens of the Commonwealth but would also end the violence prevailing on those roads. "A most definite action in the case is required," he continued. "If the Legislature be not ready to affirm and defend the rights of all, let them make it law that

25 Reprinted in *ibid.*, XI (November 12, 1841), 184.
26 *Ibid.*, XII (February 25, 1842), 32.

color is an important particular in the tenure of rights. Let that be clearly known, and it may be submitted to—till such a demonstration of the sense of the people as no Legislature can mistake, shall procure its repeal. But while uncertainty prevails, there will be continued brawls and breaches of the peace. What the petitioners do claim is action,—on one side or on the other." [27]

Remond argued that complexion could not "be rightfully made the criterion of rights"; he would oppose such a criterion, he said, even if the Negro were in the majority. What he was asking for was justice "and not favor for either complexion"; the regulations in question "do not end with the termination of the route, but, in effect, tend to discourage, disparage and depress this class of citizens"; it means treating all Negroes as though they are one uniform mass. "No distinction is made by the community in which we live. The most vicious is treated as well as the most respectable, both in public and private . . . and I submit, whether this unkind and unchristian policy is not well calculated to make every man disregardful of his conduct, and every woman unmindful of her reputation"; the degrading treatment of the Negro in America, "finds a counterpart in no other"; the Negro does not deny to any man the social right of selecting his "society and associates, but he does demand equality of civil rights—such as on the railroads—where one man has not the prerogative to define rights for another. For instance, sir, in public conveyances, for the rich man to usurp the privileges to himself, to the injury of the poor man, would be submitted to in no well regulated society. And such is the position suffered by persons of color." [28]

Loring pointed out, in words that have a contemporary ring as we think of the recent Supreme Court decision in the education cases, that although the accommodations given the Negro were inferior, it was immaterial whether they were or not. "To give inferior accommodations might be an injury; but to make any distinction whatever *is an insult*; one which men of color will suffer more from, than from an injury, if their feelings are what they ought to be. . . . Distinctions made between parties that are socially held to be unequal, are always an insult to the reputedly inferior party. If the peer's daughter be forbidden to marry the peasant's son, common sense tells us that the peasant is the insulted party, however plausibly it may be argued that the prohibition touches both alike." As common carriers the railroad corporations "have the right to make any regulations for the management of their business, which are not inconsistent with the public good." The regulations in question, however, are not consistent with the public good. Even if public opinion of the majority of the people of the state approved of the regulations, they would still not have the right to make them. "Are all our rights then at the mercy of a majority? Our Constitution and our laws are framed mainly to protect the rights of the *minority*, and to say to the majority, 'Thus far shalt thou go, and no further.' " [29]

[27] *Ibid.*, XII (February 18, 1842), 26.
[28] *Ibid.*, XII (February 25, 1842), 30.
[29] *Ibid.*, XII (March 4, 1842), 34.

Following the hearing, the joint legislative committee submitted a report which condemned the policy of segregation on the railroads, affirmed the need of remedial action through legislation and the right of the legislature to take such action, and presented a bill which declared that "no rail-road corporation shall... make or establish any by-law or regulation which shall make any distinction, or give a preference in accommodation to any one or more persons over others on account of descent, sect, or color." Moreover, "Any officer or servant of any rail-road corporation, who shall assault any person for the purpose of depriving him of his right or privilege in any car or other rail-road accommodation, on account of descent, sect, or color, or shall aid or abet any other person in committing such assault, shall be punished by imprisonment in the county jail not less than six days, or by fine not less than ten dollars; and shall also be answerable to the person assaulted, to the full amount of his damage in an action of trespass." [30]

However, notwithstanding strong public sentiment and a unanimous committee recommendation, the bill was defeated in the Senate.[31] Despite this setback, the demands for legislative action continued. Petitions were again circulated and presented to the legislature at the beginning of the next session in January, 1843, and a bill similar to that of the previous year was reintroduced. It passed the Senate but was victimized by a maneuver in the House by Representative Park of Boston. Park moved the deletion of the words "rail-road," so that the bill applied to all corporations—he indicated that he planned to vote against the bill after his amendment was accepted, thus admitting that the purpose of the amendment was to increase opposition to the bill—the amendment was passed by a vote of 164 to 67, and the bill itself indefinitely postponed by a vote of 171 to 61.[32]

The vote was not taken by yeas and nays, which meant that the vote of each legislator was not made public. Apparently, public opinion was too strongly opposed to the policy of the railroads to be openly defied. The Liberator was undoubtedly correct in its observation, after characterizing the result as "inexcusable and dastardly," that the legislators "refused to allow the vote to be taken by yeas and nays, in order that they might not be identified." [33]

But the bill's defeat in the legislature actually marked the final stages in the resistance of the railroads to public pressure. During the debate, Representative Adams of Boston, a member of the committee submitting the bill, had observed that he preferred a voluntary abandonment by the railroads of their policy, rather than the passage of legislation. With public pressure rising all about them, and faced with the certainty that the legislation would be enacted the following year if segregation continued, the railroads accepted

[30] Ibid., XII (March 4, 1842), 33.
[31] Henry Wilson, History of the Rise and Fall of the Slave Power in America (Boston, 1872), I, 494.
[32] Liberator, XIII (February 17, 1843), 21.
[33] Ibid., XIII (February 10, 1843), 23.

Representative Adams' advice and abolished segregation during the ensuing weeks. Although Remond did write, in a letter to the *Liberator* dated April 25, 1843, that on boarding a train in Salem for Boston he had been ordered by the conductor into a separate car, he did admit that for the past three weeks he had had no difficulty at any other point.[34] Thereafter, all discrimination and segregation on the railroads of Massachusetts ended and no further incidents were reported. The *Twelfth Annual Report* of the Massachusetts Anti-Slavery Society observed that "We are happy to have reason to believe that . . . no distinctions any longer exist upon any of the Railways of Massachusetts." [35]

One last incident in this drama of the railroads took place in November, 1843. Nathaniel Barney of Nantucket, a member of the Society of Friends, and an Abolitionist, was a stockholder of the New Bedford and Taunton railroad. As long as the company maintained its regulation, Barney refused to accept his dividends. With the regulation abandoned, Barney ordered the company to pay the sum due him—$22.50—"to the order of Francis Jackson for William Lloyd Garrison, in view of his faithful and undeviating advocacy of the rights of humanity." Garrison accepted the sum as a contribution to the *Liberator*, thanked Barney, and noted that "no odious proscription now obtains on that railroad." [36]

[34] *Ibid.*, XIII (April 28, 1843), 67.
[35] Massachusetts Anti-Slavery Society, *Twelfth Annual Report*, January 24, 1844 (Boston, 1844), p. 7.
[36] *Liberator*, XIII (December 1, 1843), 190.

Dorothy Porter

THE ORGANIZED EDUCATIONAL ACTIVITIES
OF NEGRO LITERARY SOCIETIES, 1828–1846

*Meeting discrimination in the public school systems and exclusion
from many lectures and lyceums, Negroes often organized their own
schools and adult literary societies. The selection from Dorothy
Porter's study illustrates the character of these efforts.*

• • • THE evolution of the early American Negro literary societies, which
like the other organizations were expressions of the free Negro's impulses toward
organization and improvement, forms an interesting chapter in the cultural
and educational history of the American Negro. They began to appear over one
hundred years ago when certain Negroes living in Northern cities took definite
steps to improve their mental and moral condition through the medium of
these societies. These organizations were known not only as literary societies,
but also as debating and reading-room societies.

Some of the expressed reasons for the organization of these institutions
were the stimulation of reading and the spreading of useful knowledge by
providing libraries and reading rooms, the encouragement of expressed literary
efforts by providing audiences as critics and channels of publication for their
literary productions and the training of future orators and leaders by means
of debates. Thus, their activities as a whole were educational. Apart from this,
there were certain existing conditions inherent in the race relations of the times
which led to the establishment of these societies. The Reverend Theodore S.
Wright, a prominent Negro of the day, was thrown out of a white literary
meeting of the Alumni of Nassau Hall in New York City.[9] The presence of

From Dorothy Porter, "The Organized Educational Activities of Negro Literary
Societies, 1828–1846," *Journal of Negro Education*, V (October, 1936), pp. 556–66,
568–69, 574–76. Reprinted with the permission of *Journal of Negro Education* and
Mrs. Dorothy Porter.

[9] American Anti-Slavery Society, *Fourth Annual Report.* New York: William S.
Dorr. 1837. p. 110.

Negroes in white literary organizations was not wanted. Even in Massachusetts, often referred to as the "birthplace of freedom," this condition was true. In New Bedford, Massachusetts, Charles Sumner and Ralph Waldo Emerson recalled their engagements to speak at a Lyceum when they learned that colored patrons were not to share the same privileges as the white members.[10] At Lynn, Massachusetts, there was opposition to Charles Lenox Remond, a Negro lecturer, who was to address a white group.[11] New institutions were formed in these places as a result of this discrimination. Thus, Negroes began to form societies of their own, in which they could have fuller and freer discussions and freedom of activity and control. A list of the more important societies which flourished during this period follows:

Negroes Literary Societies Listed by States and Cities
With Dates of Formation

PENNSYLVANIA
Philadelphia
Demosthenian Institute, 1837.
Edgeworth Society. Before 1837.
Female Literary Society, 1831.
Gilbert Lyceum, 1841.
Library Company of Colored Persons, 1833.
Minerva Literary Association, 1934.
Philadelphia Association for Moral and Mental Improvement of the People of Color, 1835.
Reading Room Society, 1828.
Rush Library and Debating Society, 1836.
Pittsburgh
Theban Literary Society, 1831.
Young Men's Literary and Moral Reform Society of Pittsburgh and Vicinity, 1837.
NEW YORK
New York City
Female Literary Society. Before 1836.
Ladies Literary Society, 1834.

New York African Clarkson Society, 1829.
New York Garrison Literary Association, 1834.
New York Philomathean Society, 1830.
Phoenix Society, 1833.
Albany
Literary Societies (two). Before 1843.
Buffalo
Debating Society. Before 1837.
Young Ladies Literary Society. Before 1837.
Poughkeepsie
Literary Society. Before 1837.
Rochester
Debating Society. Before 1843.
Ladies Literary and Dorcas Society, 1833.
Schenectady
Debating Society. Before 1843.
Troy
Debating Society. Before 1837.
Literary Society. Before 1837.
Mental and Moral Improvement Society. Before 1837.

[10] William C. Nell, *The Colored Patriots of the American Revolution.* Boston: R. F. Wallcut. 1855. p. 114.
[11] *Ibid.,* p. 115.

MASSACHUSETTS
  Boston
    Adelphic Union for the Promotion of Literature and Science, 1836.
    Afric-American Female Intelligence Society, 1832.
    Boston Philomathean Society, 1836.
    Thompson Literary and Debating Society. Before 1835.
    Young Men's Literary Society. Before 1845.
  New Bedford
    Debating Society. Before 1837.
CONNECTICUT
  Hartford
    Literary and Religious Institution, 1834.
RHODE ISLAND
  Providence
    Literary Society, 1833.
    Debating Society. Before 1837.
NEW JERSEY
  Newark
    Tyro and Literary Association, 1832.

MARYLAND
  Baltimore
    Young Men's Mental Improvement Society for the Discussion of Moral and Philosophical Questions of all kinds. Before 1835.
    Phoenix Society. Before 1835.
WASHINGTON, D.C.
    Debating Society. Before 1837.
    Literary Society. Before 1837.
    Washington Conventional Society, 1834.
OHIO
  Cincinnati
    Literary Society. Before 1843.
  Columbus
    Literary Society. Before 1843.
MICHIGAN
  Detroit
    Young Men's Lyceum and Debating Society. Before 1846.

THE PHILADELPHIA SOCIETIES

The free Negroes in Philadelphia seem to have taken the lead in the establishment of literary societies among Negroes. On the evening of March 20, 1828, group of free men of color gathered together to organize a society that in some way would have as its purpose "the mental improvement of the people of color in the neighborhood of Philadelphia." [12] William Whipper, one of the most prominent Negroes of the day, was the guiding spirit of the group. In a short address to the men present, he urged them not to sit, "as idle spectators to the movement being carried on by nations to improve themselves," but because of their limited opportunities to "feel bound to open an institution to which they may repair and qualify themselves for future usefulness." A com-

---

[12] Educational societies were organized much earlier than the literary societies. Their efforts embodied some of those of the literary societies, in that they spread "useful knowledge" and collected books for the use of the members. See the Constitution of the Pittsburgh African Education Society, *Hazard's Register of Pennsylvania*. Philadelphia. V. 9., p. 115.

mittee was formed to draw up a constitution for the society which was to be known as the "Reading Room Society" for young men in Philadelphia. The library was to consist of some books treating on the subject of ancient, modern, and ecclesiastical history, the *Laws of Pennsylvania, The Freedom's Journal, The Genius of Universal Emancipation,* and other works. For reasons which are not given, all books, "chimerical or visionary," were to be excluded.[13] The public received benefits from this organization, as well as the members. This is evidenced in the appointment of William Whipper, the Secretary, at a meeting held May 2, 1828 to deliver to the public an address on the evening of May 12th, in the African Methodist Episcopal Church, in Lombard Street.[14]

From Whipper's address, we learn that members of the society were required to have certain moral qualifications in order to secure the protection and welfare of the society. Monthly dues and an initiation fee were exacted. All of the money received except that which went for wood, light, and rent was to be expended for the purpose of securing books. These books were to be placed in the care of a librarian who was instructed that "it shall be the duty to deliver to said members alternately such books as they shall demand with strict regard that no member shall keep a book out of the library longer than a week, without paying a fine prescribed in the constitution, unless an apology for sickness, or absence be given—those shall be the only excuses." [15] Meetings were held weekly, at which time members returned and received books. At the meetings they read and expressed among themselves whatever sentiments they may have received from their readings.

Early in the year 1832, William Lloyd Garrison addressed the Female and Literary Society of Philadelphia. He found the group a most interesting and alert one, and writing of it in the *Liberator* said: "If the traducers of the Negro race could be acquainted with the moral worth, just refinement, and large intelligence of this association their mouths would be hereafter dumb." The members of this organization met every Tuesday night for the purpose of "mental improvement in moral and literary pursuits." The majority of the ladies wrote original literary pieces which were placed anonymously in a box and later criticized. The society in 1832 was composed of about twenty members, having been organized in 1831.... Scattered through the files of the *Liberator* are found many poems and essays written by members of this society and by members of other female societies organized in other cities. For the most part these writings were signed with just a forename, pseudonym, or simply by "A Lady of Color." This makes the identification of the authors difficult, if not impossible.

There had existed since 1731, a Library Company in Philadelphia, which had its beginning in the "Junto Club" founded by Benjamin Franklin "for literary and scientific discussion, the reading of original essays, poems, etc."

[13] *Freedom's Journal.* New York. 1828. V. 2. p. 98.
[14] *Ibid.,* p. 83.
[15] *Ibid.,* p. 306.

It was called the "club of mutual improvement" and was the forerunner of subscription libraries in the United States. This Library Company is still in existence today.[18] The colored people of Philadelphia, no doubt, attempted to form an organization similar to this one, for on January 1, 1833 the Philadelphia Library Company of Colored Persons was established. Nine members were present at its formation and signed its constitution. The society composed of free colored males grew very rapidly in membership and soon after its establishment applied to the legislature for an act of incorporation, which was granted in 1836.[19]. . .

The main object of this society was to build up a collection of useful books on every subject for the benefit of its members and to enlighten the group by means of weekly lectures on literary and scientific subjects. The lectures were given by the members of the society and others from the first week in October to the following May of each year.[21] Books were made accessible with comparatively little cost. A systematic order for reading was adopted by those interested. To stimulate reading and research a series of debates was introduced. These debates gave the members practice in the art of public speaking. From time to time the society received books, pamphlets, and maps as gifts. By 1838, the library had 600 volumes and the society had about 150 members who took an active part in the organization.[22] The Right Reverend Bishop White of the Protesant Episcopal Church was a frequent contributor to the collection. There was an admission fee to the society of one dollar and a monthly assessment of twenty-five cents. The meetings were held in the basement of the St. Thomas Episcopal Church.[23]

An editorial appeared in the *Genius of Universal Emancipation* during the year 1833 which summed up the progress of the colored people of Philadelphia and credited them with the establishment of libraries, reading rooms, and debating societies. According to the editorial, a gentleman who was present at the regular meeting of one of the debating clubs included the following information in his report: "Discussions were conducted with a degree of spirit and propriety and displayed a cogency and acuteness of reasoning, and an elevation and elegance of language for which he was little prepared. The subjects of discussion generally relate to their own rights and interests and frequently result in decisions from which the prejudiced mind of the white man would startle and shrink with apprehension." The editorial further states:

> They are numerous [the societies], united and bitterly conscious of
> the degradation and their power. To this let the pride, the inde-

[18] George M. Abbott, *A Short History of the Library Company of Philadelphia.* Philadelphia: 1913. p. 3.

[19] Joseph Wilson, *Sketches of the Higher Classes of Colored Society in Philadelphia.* (By a Southerner.) Philadelphia: Merrihew and Thompson, 1841. p. 98.

[21] Hazard's *Register of Pennsylvania, op. cit.,* 1833, v. 11, p. 186.

[22] Pennsylvania Society for the Promotion of the Free People of Color of the City of Philadelphia, *op. cit.,* p. 30.

[23] Wilson, *op. cit.,* pp. 99–100.

pendence and ambition which science ever imparts be added, and the consequences though beyond the reach of conjecture would doubtless be such as to involve the character, and condition of the whole country."[24]

The Minerva Literary Association organized in October 1834, with thirty ladies present at its first meeting, was immediately a successful organization and from all indications seems to have been a real "school for the encouragement and promotion of polite literature." The programs consisted of "readings and recitations of original and selected pieces, together with appropriate matters." Many of the essays and other original productions, in both prose and poetry which were written by these ladies, were of sufficient merit to be used in the Poets Corner and other publications of the day. These ladies held their meetings weekly.[25]

On December 16, 1836 the Rush Library and Debating Society was founded in Philadelphia and was incorporated March 1, 1837. Seven men were responsible for its formation and they had in mind the same purposes as those who had formed the Philadelphia Library Company.[26] In 1838 there were forty-one members who belonged to it, and the library contained 132 volumes.[27] By 1841, its library had 200 volumes. The books were all useful although of a miscellaneous character. Regular meetings were held in Salter's Hall.[28]

The Demosthenian Institute, formed at the home of John P. Burr, January 10, 1837, was organized primarily to prepare its members for the public platform. Addresses were made, discussions took place and questions were answered in the presence of the members. The members had planned that the society should be made into a preparatory school until the members had gained sufficient confidence and experience to fit them for public appearances. In 1841 this organization had forty-two members, and the library contained over one hundred scientific and historical works. The *Demosthenian Shield*, a weekly paper, first published on June 29, 1841, was the organ of the society. Its subscription list numbered over one thousand persons before the first issue appeared.[29] According to Wilson, it had a neat typographical appearance and it showed dignity and ability in the editorial department. No information seems available concerning the possible existence of any printed organs for the other literary societies,[30] although a poem "To George Thompson" "By a Lady of Philadelphia" was reprinted in *Human Rights*, which had been taken from

[24] *Genius of Universal Emancipation. op. cit.*, v. 3, p. 90.
[25] Wilson, *op. cit.*, p. 108.
[26] *Ibid.*, p. 101.
[27] Pennsylvania Society for the Promotion of the Abolition of Slavery. *Present State and Condition of the People of Color. op. cit.*, p. 3.
[28] Wilson, *op. cit.*, p. 102.
[29] Wilson, *op. cit.*, pp. 105–106.
[30] There is no mention of any other such publications in I. G. Penn. *The Afro-American press and its Editors*, 1891; F. G. Detweiler, *The Negro Press in the United States*, 1922; or in Charles S. Johnson's article "The Rise of the Negro Magazine," *Journal of Negro History*, v. 13, 1928.

The Struggler, "a newspaper edited in Philadelphia by an Association of Colored men."[31] This would seem to indicate that *The Struggler* was an organ of one of the literary societies.

At a meeting of the Council of the Philadelphia Association for the Moral and Mental Improvement of the People of Color, held in Philadelphia June 5th to June 9th, 1837, much attention was given to the "mental state" of the Negro. This association which was incorporated on February 28, 1835, met annually with delegates coming from the various churches, literary and beneficial societies.[32] Among the various resolutions submitted at a meeting held in 1837 was one which called for a survey to be made by a committee of the number of children who were members of their respective churches and who attended daily and weekly schools. Other committees were appointed to ascertain and report on the number and names of moral, literary, and beneficial societies in the City of Philadelphia, in order to have a historical record of the instruments that were being used to elevate the colored people.[33] Other committees were to correspond with similar societies organized in other cities in order to determine the educational progress of the people. Reports were to be made from time to time through the newspapers concerning the progress of the various groups....

The Gilbert Lyceum, which was organized for literary and scientific purposes, seems to have been the first and only society which admitted individuals of both sexes. The society was named after the man who had first suggested its formation. The initial meeting took place on January 31, 1841 under the leadership of Robert Douglass, Jr., a Philadelphia painter of some note. Among the twelve persons present at the first meeting were Joseph Cassey, John C. Bowers, Robert Purvis, Sarah M. Douglass and Harriet Purvis.[37] A series of lectures was delivered before the group, which for the most part was well attended. In 1841, there were forty-one members who belonged to the lyceum. It is stated that these members planned to collect a cabinet of minerals and curiosities for their organization.

The free people of color, as a whole, owe some of their educational progress to the efforts of these societies. A report made in 1836 on the condition of the Negroes who lived in the Districts of Southwark and Northern Liberties, shows that out of 2,560 adults 1,030 could read and 92 could write; and that there were 970 children out of 1,945 who could read. The Negroes supported the following number of churches at this time: 6 Methodist, 2 Presbyterian, 3 Baptist, and 1 Lutheran. In addition to the literary societies, they maintained sixty beneficial societies, two tract societies, two Bible societies, two temperance societies and one moral reform society. Their combined property

[31] *Human Rights,* New York. Published for the American Anti-Slavery Society. V. 1, No. 5. Nov., 1835.

[32] *Minutes and Proceedings of the Philadelphia Council of the Philadelphia Association for the Moral and Mental Improvement of the People of Color.* (June 5th–9th, 1837.) Philadelphia: Merrihew and Gunn, 1837, p. 14.

[33] *Ibid.,* p. 6.

[37] Wilson, *op. cit.,* p. 110.

holdings were valued at $200,000.[38] Similar efforts were successful in the organization of societies in the cities of New York, Boston, Hartford, Cincinnati, Washington, D.C., Providence; and in the East and West this movement developed rapidly.

THE NEW YORK SOCIETIES

In New York City, Rochester, and other cities in the State of New York similar endeavors were made to form literary societies and debating clubs for the purpose of self-education. The young women, in particular, in these cities who organized these groups frequently combined the desire to learn with the desire to perform work of an altruistic nature in behalf of those in slavery, as well as for the many destitute Negro children.

In 1829, in New York City, one year after the organization of the first literary society in Philadelphia, the New York African Clarkson Society, composed of the young men of the city, was established. On the evening of April 23, 1834, the society celebrated its fifth anniversary and from the published reports it appears to have been a great occasion. The affair was held in the Abyssinia Baptist Church, with tickets of admission available at six cents. The members of the society arrived on this particular evening in a body and seated themselves together on the rostrum. The program consisted for the most part, of music, furnished by a union band, speech-making and the reading of the constitution. The young men sang *The Clarkson Ode*, which was composed probably when the society was organized and was as follows:

> With joyful hearts join hand in hand,
> And celebrate the Clarkson band.
> This day by legislative aid,
> A corporate body made.
> Prosperity attend our band,
> And gratitude this will demand:
> And let out thankful lays be heard,
> On every April twenty-third.

The church was filled with spectators and it was said that the members who were present were proud of their organization on this occasion.[39]

The leading literary society in New York City was the New York Philomathean Society which was organized in 1830.[40] At a later period in 1843, this society developed into the Odd Fellow's Lodge and became the Philomathean Lodge, No. 646.[41] These facts seem to indicate that the members of the society were all men. The Philomathean Society was "devoted to the improvement of

[38] The *Emancipator*. New York: R. G. Williams. V. 2, Nov. 10, 1836, p. 112.

[39] *Emancipator, op. cit.*, v. 2, May 6, 1834. (Frequently there is no pagination given on the newspapers. It will be given where found.)

[40] *Colored American*. New York: R. Sears. V. 1. No. 27. July 8, 1837.

[41] Charles H. Brooks, *A History and Manual of the Grand United Order of Odd Fellows in America*. Philadelphia: 1893, p. 21.

literature and useful knowledge." In 1837 it had acquired about six hundred volumes for its circulating library. It solicited donations of books and money to be used for the purchase of books and for subscriptions to periodicals. The society asked that books be loaned to the library and it promised that they would be well cared for and returned when wanted.[42] At a meeting held August 18, 1837, the society decided that members of all literary institutions of color would be admitted to all of its meetings, with the exception of the business meeting, and that they would be permitted to take part in the general debates.[43]

There was provided for the members a series of lectures on literary and historical subjects, which took place twice a week. The services of the outstanding men in the fields of science and literature were secured for these lectures. An admission fee was charged. The programs were arranged by a Board of Associates. The chairman of this board was Phillip A. Bell and the secretary was Thomas Jennings, Jr. The society had the following officers: Ransome F. Wake, Prefect; George W. Moore, Scribe; William Garribrance, Treasurer; James Fields, Librarian; Timothy Seamon, Recorder; Henry Williams, Curator.

The society which exerted the widest influence and which had the largest membership was the Phoenix Society, organized in New York City in 1833.[44] The Negroes in New York City had been spiritually and educationally helped by the ministers and by the establishment of Sabbath and day schools; but the Negro population which numbered about 20,000 was excluded from "instruction in its popular and inviting forms." A pamphlet containing the history and describing the animals in the Zoological Institute in New York City was distributed in 1834. This pamphlet included the following statement: "The proprietors wish it to be understood that the people of color are not permitted to enter except when in attendance upon children and families."[45] The colored people felt that until they were able to attend public meetings and places of interest that they should provide a building and appropriate means for self-improvement.

The above type of prejudice toward the Negro was one of the causes for the organization of the Phoenix Society. It was composed chiefly of young colored men, but it had some white members who gave whatever assistance they could. The society was "designed to be the soul of the entire population and their friends in the city." Its primary object was "to promote the improvement of the coloured people in morals, literature, and the mechanical arts." All persons who wished to promote the objects of the society and who were of good "moral character" could become members by paying one dollar joining fee and twenty-five cents quarterly. The applicants had to be accepted, however, by the board of directors. Many prominent men, white and colored, were officers to the society. Some of these persons were also members and officers of the various anti-slavery societies. The constitution and by-laws, published in

[42] *Colored American, op. cit.*, v. 1, No. 27, July 8, 1837.

[43] *Ibid.*, v. 1, No. 31, August 5, 1837.

[44] Arthur Tappan, *The Life of Arthur Tappan.* New York: Hurd and Houghton, 1870, p. 158.

[45] *Emancipator, op. cit.*, v. 1 (new series) March 9, 1837.

1835 listed the officers at that time: Rev. Christopher Rush, President; Rev. Theodore S. Wright, 1st Vice-President; Thomas L. Jennings, 2nd Vice-President; Rev. Peter Williams, Corresponding Secretary; and Arthur Tappan, Treasurer. David Ruggles, William Hamilton, Charles B. Ray, Dr. John Brown and Samuel E. Cornish were on the Board of Directors.

The Phoenix Society attempted large projects which involved many duties for its members. It wished to exploit all possibilities of the situation it had set out to alleviate. One cannot but admire the forthrightness that launched such a program as the following: First of all an attempt to raise $10,000 for the purpose of erecting a public edifice to be appropriated to the use of a library, reading room, museum or exhibition room, hall, etc., where colored youth and others might enjoy the benefit of such courses of lectures and other instruction on morals, literature and the mechanic arts, as are enjoyed by the white community.[46] The Ward Societies were inaugurated whose functions laid a considerable obligation upon every member. Members of the Ward Societies were to visit the various families within the Ward vicinity and make a registry of every colored person, ascertaining his age, sex, occupation and his ability to read or write. They were to induce the old and young to become members of the society. Adults were to be urged to attend school and were to be impressed with the importance of sending their children to school regularly and punctually. Furthermore, each Ward group was organized to maintain a circulating library for the use of the people of color at a moderate fee, to organize lyceums to serve the advantages of public speaking and to promote lectures on science. Finally and characteristically, they were to form moral reform societies and to seek young men of "good moral character" as members whom they could expect to assist ultimately in getting a good liberal education. The Ward Societies served a further general interest by reporting to the board all members who were skilled and capable of conducting trades, by procuring places at trade with respectable farmers for them, and by giving preference in employment to those who could "read and cipher." In addition they encouraged people of color, whenever they could to improve their minds and to abstain from every vicious and demoralizing practice.[47]

The rapid growth of the Phoenix Society made it necessary to abandon the first rented rooms and to hire a hall in which to hold meetings. A course of lectures was given by several clergymen of the city on morals, scientific, and historical subjects. An evening school for adults was started with both white and colored teachers. A high school for colored youth was begun and continued for two years or more."[48]

Samuel E. Cornish, at one time librarian of the society, made strenuous attempts to build up the library. . . .[49] The first annual report of the Board of

[46] *Constitution and By-Laws of the Phoenix Society of New York.* New York: H. R. Piercy, 1835, p. 5.

[47] *Ibid.*, p. 6.

[48] Tappan, *op. cit.*, p. 162.

[49] *Colonizationist and Journal of Freedom.* Boston: George W. Light, February, 1834, p. 307.

Directors of the Phoenix Society shows that the general operations of the Board were confined principally to the "organization of Ward Societies, the institution of historical and scientific lectures, the establishment of reading rooms and libraries and the formation of temperance societies which existed in great numbers." The report indicates that through the organization of the Phoenix Society there was "produced a more intimate and extensive union, and a more anxious concern for the general improvement among the young people of every denomination than had existed at any former period in the city." More public spirit was exhibited and many contributions were made to objects of public utility. The cause of temperance was greatly advanced. Expensive entertainments were less frequent and a desire to acquire useful knowledge was increased. Throughout the year the scientific lectures had brought together four or five hundred persons. In the report much credit was given to Samuel E. Cornish for his services in arranging the lectures, in planning and establishing the library and reading rooms and for promoting the interests of the society generally.[51]

The New York Garrison Literary Association sometimes called the New York Garrison Literary and Benevolent Society seems to be the only institution of its kind, in that it was maintained primarily for the colored youth. Anybody of "good moral character" between the ages of "four and twenty by subscribing to the constitution and by paying 12½ cents admission and 1 cent per week could become a member." The society was formed early in 1834, and its members were primarily interested in religion, virtue, literature, the downfall of prejudice, and slavery and oppression in any form. They desired that the organization would be a means of spreading "useful knowledge." Probably because of the large size of the organization, it had many officers, a board of managers, an executive committee, a visiting committee and other assistants for managing it. These officers were elected annually. John W. Lewis was President; Henry Garnett, Secretary; and Prince Loveridge, Librarian. David Ruggles was a member of the executive committee in the year 1834.[52]

Education and liberty formed the main topics for discussion at their meetings which were devoted to singing, praying, and the reading of original compositions. The meetings were attended by over one hundred and fifty children and were at first held in the public school rooms in Laurens Street. P. Loveridge, a teacher in the public school, stated at one of the early meetings held in April 1834, that one of the trustees of the school objected to the use of the name of Garrison for the society and suggested that it be changed to Finley. The young men insisted, however, on retaining the name of Garrison. At a meeting on the night of April 19, 1834, David Ruggles, who had been appointed to find a new place in which to hold meetings, reported that he had received a letter from Phillip A. Bell, Chairman of the Board of Associates of the Philomathean Society, permitting them to use the Philomathean Hall for

[51] *Ibid.*, v. 2, May 20, 1834.
[52] *Ibid.*, April, 1834.

one year. At this same meeting it was resolved that the anti-slavery hymn book should be adopted for the use of the society and that each member should be supplied with a copy of it.[53]

There existed in New York as in other cities a female literary society. Abigail M. Mathews was one of the founders of the New York Female Literary Society[54] and Henrietta D. Ray, the wife of Charles B. Ray, was the president.[55] The Ladies Literary Society of the City of New York, as it was styled, was started in 1834. At its third anniversary held September 23, 1837, a very lengthy and elaborate program was held. In order to render financial aid to the *Colored American*, a new newspaper, and the New York Vigilance Committee, the society held fairs.[56] Thus its purpose was extended beyond the literary and educational aim to the larger social objectives....

THE DECADENCE OF THE LITERARY SOCIETIES

The efforts of these literary societies deserve recognition and praise for they not only actually helped to disseminate knowledge among a people for the most part poorly educated, but they taught the Negro how to use his leisure time to advantage. The lecturers who addressed these societies chose not only literary topics, but also scientific and educational ones. These lectures were said to be stimulating to the hearers. They prompted many Negroes who could read to read further, and those who were unable to read to learn to read. Many of these addresses were printed and widely circulated throughout several states. Some of them have been preserved and handed down to us as rare items of the book-collecting field. The lecture platform of these societies was the workshop and the preparatory school for many of the Negro anti-slavery lecturers who later won fame in America and England as public speakers.

As a result of the activities of these societies many Negroes started private libraries. In Philadelphia and nearby cities there were 8,333 volumes in private libraries in 1838.[85] David Ruggles, a Negro printer and abolitionist, was probably the earliest Negro book-collector. He maintained a circulating library and made available to many readers anti-slavery and colonization publications. He charged a fee which was less than twenty-five cents a month for the renting of books for the year. He sold books and printed at frequent intervals in the various newspapers lists of books relating to the Negro and to slavery.[86] In this

[53] *Ibid.*, May 27, 1834.
[54] *Ibid.*, v. 1, June 9, 1836 (new series), p. 23.
[55] *Ibid.*, v. 1, No. 24, 1936 (new series) p. 119.
[56] *Colored American, op. cit.*, v. 2, No. 1, Jan. 20, 1838, p. 7.
[85] Robert Purvis, *Appeal of Forty Thousand Citizens, Threatened with Disfranchisement, to the People of Pennsylvania*. Philadelphia: Merrihew and Gunn, 1838, p. 11.
[86] See advertisement column of the *Emancipator*, Vol. 4, No. 22, May 31, 1834, p. 87.

same connection, *The Colored American,* a Negro newspaper first published in 1837, maintained a reading room.[87]

With a few exceptions these societies had to struggle to continue their activities. The existence of several societies in one city caused competition for membership. Several of the leaders of the Philadelphia societies felt that the various societies should merge into one large organization which would include men and women of all ages, regardless of their learning. A plan for such an organization was drawn up by Mr. James Needham which proposed "to have lectures by competent persons at stated intervals, to encourage men of color to become professors in particular branches of science, to establish a library, collect a cabinet of minerals and procure philosophical apparatus as soon as its permanent organization might allow of so doing.[88] No evidence has been found to indicate that this society was ever organized.

The various anti-slavery organizations weakened the strength of the literary and debating societies in that they called constantly on the members of the literary societies to furnish audiences for their lectures and some of the leaders in these societies were pressed into service as speakers and workers for the emancipation programs. In many instances members of the literary societies were officers and members of the anti-slavery societies. William Whipper, Samuel E. Cornish, James C. Bowers, Robert and Harriet Purvis, Sarah Douglass and numerous others listed above were members and officers of the literary and also the anti-slavery organizations.[89]

For the most part, these societies were short-lived. Some existed actively for ten or twelve years, others died an early death. As is still true of many organizations, the members became lax in their membership and in the payment of their assessments. Some years later, after the particular societies mentioned in this article had served their purposes and passed out of existence, other organizations with similar purposes were set up, and in turn existed for brief periods. Many of these were influenced by the anti-slavery struggle and were in the main anti-slavery societies until around 1857 when they took on a more definite literary aspect.

These organizations are indications of the activity of self-educative influences in Negro life. They worked from within the group and showed their results not only in organized action but also in trained individuals who joined hands with the white leadership in other religious and philanthropic societies working for the improvement of Negro life. The story of the development of Negro education in its broader implications would be incomplete without some reference to these endeavors of the Negro literary societies. They were frequently the background for the organization of the Negro school. They were the supporters of the educative life among Negroes in a day when there were few formal instruments of education in existence for their use.

[87] *Colored American,* v. 2, No. 5, Feb. 10, 1838, p. 18.
[88] Wilson, *op. cit.,* p. 112.
[89] See the Reports of the American Anti-Slavery Societies 1835–1845.

Ray Allen Billington

JAMES FORTEN: FORGOTTEN ABOLITIONIST

The fact that many Negroes participated in the abolitionist move-
ment has often been "forgotten." Ray Allen Billington has presented
a portrait of James Forten, one of the most prominent of the
Negro abolitionists. While Billington's article may exaggerate some-
what the extent of Forten's influence upon Garrison, nevertheless
during the early years of the Liberator Forten was an important
source of financial and moral support for the noted white leader.
Moreover Forten's career illustrates the antislavery activities of
many free Negroes, most notably their criticism of the American
Colonization Society many years before prominent white antislavery
advocates like Garrison became disillusioned with its program. Bil-
lington's article also touches on another phase of Negro protest
activity: the Negro ante-bellum convention movement, which opposed
the southern slavery system and attempted to improve the status of
free Negroes in the North.

THE most important single incident in the American antislavery crusade
was the conversion of William Lloyd Garrison and Theodore Dwight Weld
to a belief in racial equality. These two men, and the thousands who flocked
to their standards, held that no biological differences distinguished Negroes
from whites. As this was the case, they argued, the slaves should be emancipated
either immediately or gradually, then educated and equipped to share the responsibilities of society with their fellow citizens. Social and political equality
for all Americans was the objective of abolitionists from the day that Garrison
proclaimed his intention to be "as harsh as truth and as uncompromising as
justice" until the last slave was freed.[1]

The Garrisonian doctrine of equality was completely antagonistic to the
generally accepted racial views of both northerners and southerners in the
early nineteenth century. Enlightened men on both sides of the Mason-Dixon
line had, since the Revolution, detested the institution of slavery, yet few

Ray Allen Billington, "James Forten: Forgotten Abolitionist," published by the
Association for the Study of Negro Life and History in Vol. XIII of *Negro History
Bulletin*, pp. 31–36, 45 (Nov., 1949). Reprinted by permission of the publisher.
[1] *The Liberator*, January 1, 1831.

among them were willing to concede that Negroes were physically or intellectually equal to whites. Instead they believed that the blacks were inferior creatures, halfway between animals and humans, who were fit only for the barbarism of Africa or servile life in the United States. The popular attitude was typified in the objectives of the American Colonization Society upon its formation in 1817. Members recognized the evils of slavery but insisted they should be shipped back to the African jungles for which nature had fitted them.

To men who held these views the concepts of Garrisonianism were thoroughly shocking. Between them and the abolitionists there was no compromise. The "colonizers" based their platform on a belief in racial inequality; the "abolitionists" built their program about a belief in racial equality For the next thirty years northerners debated these two beliefs, as abolitionism slowly gained supporters and strength. Southerners, however, moved in the opposite direction. Driven to greater conservatism by the northern attack on white supremacy, they had by the 1850's ceased to apologize for slavery as a necessary evil, viewing the institution instead as a positive good. When a Republican victory in 1860 warned them that the concept of racial equality was to be enshrined in the White House they deserted the Union.

Viewed in this light the doctrines of abolitionism become important in explaining the course of American history. Where did those views originate? Who first suggested that the races were equal, and that Negroes should be accorded the same legal and social status as whites? Doubtless a handful of forward-looking reformers from the days of antiquity onward had preached equality, but their opinions were of little importance; concepts only deserve recognition when they influence man's behavior. Avowals of racial equality, no matter how sincere, had no impact on American life until they fell on the ears of the humanitarians who launched the abolition crusade. Apparently the doctrine, in usable form, was first suggested to Garrison and his followers by a small group of Negro reformers whose contribution has been largely overlooked by historians of antislavery. Of these none was more important than James Forten, a wealthy free Negro of Philadelphia, whose efforts in behalf of the slaves launched pre-Garrisonian abolitionism in the United States.

Born in Philadelphia on September 2, 1766, James Forten was the son of Negro parents whose ancestors had lived in Pennsylvania as freemen for at least two generations.[2] His education was unusually scant even for that day; after a brief introduction to learning in the school of the famed Quaker philanthropist, Anthony Benezet, the death of his father in 1775 forced him to assume his share of the family's financial burdens.[3] For a few years he worked

---

[2] A close friend of Forten's, Lydia Maria Child, is authority for the statement that so far as he could recollect, no member of his family had been slaves. *The Freedmen's Book* (Boston, 1865), 100. Another friend, however, later quoted Forten as saying that his great-grandfather had been brought from Africa as a slave, and that his grandfather had obtained his freedom. Samuel J. May, *Some Recollections of the Antislavery Conflict* (Boston, 1869), 287.

[3] For accounts of Forten's boyhood see Child, *Freedmen's Book*, 101–102; William C. Nell, *Colored Patriots of the American Revolution* (Boston, 1855), 166–167; and Robert Purvis, *Remarks on the Life and Character of James Forten, Delivered at*

in a grocery store, but the outbreak of the Revolution turned his thoughts to a more adventurous career. After repeated pleadings broke down his mother's opposition, the fifteen year old Forten in 1781 enlisted as powder boy aboard the *Royal Louis*, a Pennsylvania privateer commanded by Stephen Decatur, Sr.[4]

The next year was crammed with excitement for the young Philadelphian. The *Royal Louis*, was a formidable vessel, mounting twenty-two guns and carrying a crew of two hundred men, twenty of whom were colored.[5] Its commander, the father of the naval hero of the War of 1812, was already a seasoned privateer, having commanded the *Comet* and the *Fair American* in successful forays against English shipping.[6] Surely with his stout new ship he could surpass the feats of his last voyage when his *Fair American* brought to bay no less than three British merchantmen, four brigs, and a packet.[7] Little wonder that the youthful Forten looked forward to rollicking adventure and handsome profits as Decatur's ship sailed smoothly down the Chesapeake Bay on a warm July day in 1781.

For a time his bright hopes seemed about to come true. Scarcely had the *Royal Louis*, put to sea when a lookout sighted fair game, the English brig-of-war *Active*, which struck its colors after a sharp skirmish.[8] On the next cruise, however, fate was less kind. Once more a sail was sighted; once more Decatur gave chase. This time the expected victim turned out to be a powerful enemy frigate, the *Amphyon*. Undaunted, the crew of the *Royal Louis* prepared to give battle, only to see the sails of two other war vessels, the *Nymph* and the *Pomona*, loom over the horizon. Hopelessly outclassed, Decatur was forced to surrender.[9]

That was a sickening moment for young Forten. Negro prisoners, he knew, were seldom exchanged; instead they were sent in chains to the West Indies to be sold into slavery. That he escaped this grim fate was due to a fortunate

Bethel Church, March 30, 1842 (Philadelphia, 1842), 4. A brief sketch of Forten's career is in the *Dictionary of American Biography* (New York, 1928–1937), VI, 536–537.

[4] All contemporary biographers of Forten place the date of his enlistment in 1780 and state that he was fourteen years old. Nell, *Colored Patriots*, 166; Child, *Freedmen's Book*, 101; Purvis, *Remarks on the Life and Character of James Forten*, 4. Actually the *Royal Louis* was not commissioned until July 23, 1781, and sailed from Philadelphia at once. *Naval Records of the American Revolution* (Washington, 1906), 449. Apparently his early biographers based their accounts on Forten's memory, which was faulty. He was also responsible for the statement that the ship mounted twenty-six guns rather than twenty-two. William C. Nell, *Services of Colored Americans in the Wars of 1776 and 1812* (Boston, 1851), 16.

[5] Forten is responsible for the latter statement, as no list of the crew has been located. Nell, *Services of Colored Americans*, 16.

[6] Information about Stephen Decatur will be found in Alexander S. Mackenzie, *Life of Stephen Decatur* (Boston, 1846), 9–10; William Decatur Parsons, *The Decatur Genealogy* (New York, 1921), 10; and the *Dictionary of American Biography*, V, 186–187.

[7] A record of Decatur's previous conquests is in the *Naval Records of the American Revolution*, 445; and more fully in J. Thomas Scharf and Thomas Wescott, *History of Philadelphia* (Philadelphia, 1884), I, 423.

[8] *Pennsylvania Archives, Second Series* (Harrisburg, 1874), I, 373.

[9] Scharf and Wescott, *History of Philadelphia*, 423; Nell, *Colored Patriots*, 168.

circumstance. Aboard the *Amphyon* was the youthful son of its commander, Sir John Beasly, thirsting for the companionship of some one his own age. The two boys, so unlike in background, struck up an immediate friendship. Young Beasly was particularly intrigued by his companion's skill at marbles, and the two spent much time together at the game. According to legend, Sir John was so impressed with Forten's character that he offered to take him to England for an education. This offer, Forten later testified, was haughtily refused. "No, No!" he reported himself as saying. "I am here as a prisoner for the liberties of my country; *I never, never, shall prove a traitor to her interests.*"[10] Thus rebuffed, the British commander transferred the fifteen year old powder boy, with a number of other captives to the prison ship *Jersey*, which was anchored in Wallabout Bay on the lonely shore of Long Island. "Thus," Forten often remarked in later life, "did a game of marbles save me from a life of West Indian servitude."[11]

During the next seven months, however, he probably had occasion to wish that his fingers were less skilled. The *Jersey* was a rotting old hulk, so leaky that pumps ran constantly to keep her afloat and so decayed that snow drifted through the cracks in her hull. A thousand prisoners were crowded into her stinking hold without light, ventilation, or sanitation, there to exist on food condemned as unfit for the English forces; frequently the starving captives had to knock worms from the biscuits or shred mahogany-colored meat that was too hard to cut. Thanks to his youth and stamina, Forten escaped the fate of the ten thousand prisoners who died aboard the ship during the war.[12] So unquenchable was his spirit that on one occasion he even gave up an opportunity to escape in favor of a companion worse off than himself.[13] He was finally released in a general exchange of prisoners, reaching home safely as the Revolution was drawing to a close.[14]

Although still in his teens, Forten was ready to exhibit the freedom-loving spirit that marked his later years. Why, he asked himself, should he stay in a

---

[10] Child, *Freedmen's Book*, 101–102; Nell, *Colored Patriots*, 168. These two accounts, which agree in substance, were apparently based on Forten's reminiscences.

[11] Nell, *Colored Patriots*, 169.

[12] Descriptions of the *Jersey* are in Gardner W. Allen, *A Naval History of the American Revolution* (Boston, 1913), II, 631–637; Edgar A. Maclay, *A History of the United States Navy* (New York, 1904), I, 138–139; and John R. Spears, *The History of Our Navy* (New York, 1899), I, 223–224. The reminiscences of several prisoners confined to the ship while Forten was aboard fail to mention him, but add colorful details of life aboard. These include Thomas Andros on Board the Old Jersey Prison Ship (Boston, 1833), 1–80; Captain Thomas Dring, *Recollections of the Jersey Prison-Ship* (Providence, 1829); and Ebenezer Fox, *The Revolutionary Adventures of Ebenezer Fox* (Boston, 1839), 93–228.

[13] The youth who escaped was Daniel Brewton who was carried from the ship in a sea chest in which Forten had planned to escape. Later steward of the *Lazaretto* in Philadelphia, Brewton showed both William Nell and Robert Purvis a certificate testifying that he had been aboard the *Jersey* with Forten, and described the rescue. Nell, *Colored Patriots*, 170–172; Purvis, *Remarks on the Life and Character of James Forten*, 7–8.

[14] Forten was released after seven months on the *Jersey*. His mother had given him up for dead when he finally reached Philadelphia.

land that proclaimed all men equal yet condemned those with dark skins to second-class citizenship? Why not escape to England where men were judged by character rather than color? These were the motives that sent him overseas for one of the most important twelve-month periods of his career. The slavery question was just beginning to captivate public interest at that time; the Somerset case[15] had already decreed that any slave touching English soil became free but the slave trade still flourished and the first reformers were lifting their voices against the evil. Forten lent an avid ear to their arguments, particularly to the pleas of Granville Sharp, a humanitarian who led the parliamentary assault on bonded servitude.[16] During the year that he listened young Forten became an avowed abolitionist, ready to dedicate his life to the crusade for freedom.

Back in Philadelphia once more he was apprenticed to Robert Bridges, a sailmaker whose loft was a landmark on the south wharves of the city. With a lack of prejudice all too rare in that day, Bridges in 1786 elevated his twenty-year-old helper to a position as foreman; twelve years later, when the owner died, Forten assumed control of the establishment. For the next forty years he conducted the business successfully, employing as many as forty men at times and amassing a comfortable fortune in the process. According to contemporary accounts many of his profits originated in a device to handle sails which he perfected and patented.[17] The popularity of his invention allowed him to provide a comfortable home for his widowed mother, a sister, a wife, and a growing family of eight children.[18]

The passing years not only assured James Forten economic security but gave him an opportunity to shine as a civic leader among Philadelphia's Negroes. On at least four occasions he rescued persons from drowning near his sail loft, a service that was recognized in 1821 when the managers of the Humane Society presented him with an Honorary Certificate "as a testimony of their approbation of his meritorious conduct." [19] During the War of 1812,

[15] The Somerset case arose in 1771 when a slave, James Somerset, was taken by his master from Virginia to England. Refusing to serve his owner there, he obtained a writ of habeas corpus which allowed him to carry his case before the British courts. They eventually held that slavery was contrary to the laws of England and that Somerset was a free man. John W. Cromwell, *The Negro in American History* (Washington, 1914), 245.

[16] Purvis, *Remarks on the Life and Character of James Forten*, 8–9.

[17] Henry E. Baker, "The Negro in the Field of Invention," *Journal of Negro History*, II (January, 1917), 25. A search of patent lists for the period, however, fails to reveal any patent issued either to Forten or to his employer, Robert Bridges. Apparently the invention was never patented, but was still immensely profitable. See *A Digest of Patents, Issued by the United States from 1790 to January 1, 1839* (Washington, 1840); *A Classified Index of Subjects of Inventions* (Washington, 1872); *A list of Patents Granted by the United States for the Encouragement of Arts and Sciences, alphabetically arranged, from 1790 to 1820; Continued by Supplements to April, 1823* (Washington, 1823); *List of Patents and Inventions and Designs issued by the United States from 1790 to 1847* (Washington, 1847); *Subject-Matter Index of Patents for Inventions issued by the United States Patent Office from 1790 to 1873, Inclusive* (Washington, 1874).

[18] Nell, *Colored Patriots*, 172–174; Child, *Freedmen's Book*, 102–103.

when British troops pressed close on Philadelphia, he enlisted 2,500 colored patriots to improve the city's defenses. Marching with them from the State House yard to Gray's Ferry, Forten directed earthworks construction for two uninterrupted days.[20] Nor did he neglect the spiritual welfare of his race. When the St. Thomas' African Episcopal Church was incorporated in Philadelphia in 1796 he was among the pioneer members, serving on the first vestry. He remained active in the church from that day until his death.[21]

These activities prepared James Forten for a role in the cause that interested him most—abolitionism. His interest in the problem was awakened in 1800 when two of Philadelphia's most prominent Negroes, the Reverend Richard Allen, pastor of the African Methodist Church, and Absalom Jones, a founder of the St. Thomas' African Episcopal Church, circulated a petition among the city's colored citizens, urging Congress to modify the Fugitive Slave Act of 1793 and to adopt "such measures as shall in due course emancipate the whole of their brethren from their present situation."[22] Forten, as a signer, watched the fate of the petition with interest. To his disgust only one congressman sympathized with the petitioners. Representative George Thatcher of Massachusetts[23] supported their request in language faintly prophetic of that used by abolitionists a generation later; the remainder not only refused to listen but resolved that such petitions had a "tendency to create disquiet and jealousy, and ought therefore to receive no encouragement or countenance from this House." When this resolution was adopted by a thumping vote of eighty-five to one (with Thatcher casting the lone ballot in opposition),[24] James Forten wrote a letter of appreciation to the champion of his cause.[25] From that time on he was resolved to change the attitude of his unsympathetic fellow-countrymen.

His next opportunity came in 1813 when the Pennsylvania legislature considered a bill to bar free Negroes from the state. Forten, in a series of five letters published in pamphlet form, led the attack on the measure. "Has the

[19] The certificate, which was dated May 9, 1821, is printed in Nell, *Colored Patriots*, 174–175. Nell states that Forten rescued seven persons during his lifetime; Mrs. Child sets the number at twelve. Child, *Freedmen's Book*, 103.

[20] Scharf and Wescott, *History of Philadelphia*, I, 573–574; Neil, *Colored Patriots*, 191.

[21] William Douglass, *Annals of the First African Church in the United States of America, now styled the African Episcopal Church of St. Thomas* (Philadelphia, 1862), 107. When, in 1804, a school was established by the church, Forten was chosen one of the Board of Trustees. *Ibid.*, 110.

[22] The petition from the "free blacks" of Philadelphia was laid before Congress on January 2, 1800, by Robert Waln, a representative from Pennsylvania. *Annals of Congress*, 6th Cong., 1st Sess., 232.

[23] George Thatcher, a Federalist, represented Massachusetts in Congress between March 4, 1789, and March 3, 1801. *Biographical Directory of the American Congress* (Washington, 1928).

[24] The petition was debated on January 2 and January 3. *Annals of Congress*, 6th Cong., 1st Sess., 239–246.

[25] Nell, *Colored Patriots*, 176. The letter is printed in Purvis, *Remarks on the Life and Character of James Forten*, 12–14.

God who made the white man and the black left any record declaring us a different species?" he asked. "Are we not sustained by the same power, supported by the same food, hurt by the same wounds, wounded by the same wrongs, pleased with the same delights, and propagated by the same means? And should we not then enjoy the same liberty, and be protected by the same laws?" He passionately "hoped that the legislators who have hitherto guarded their fellow creatures, without regard to the colour of their skin, will still stretch forth the wings of protection to that race, whose persons have been the scorn, and whose calamities have been the jest of the world for ages."[26]

The importance of Forten's views on racism cannot be overestimated. Unlike most reformers, even among Negroes, he was convinced that no biological differences distinguished whites and blacks. In this conviction he anticipated the abolitionists of a later day; indeed the basic concept underlying abolitionism was nowhere better expressed before 1820 than in his outspoken letters.

Like most intellectual pioneers, Forten was far ahead of his time. This was demonstrated three years later when the American Colonization Society was formed.[27] This antislavery organization was based on the concept—then generally accepted in North and South alike—that the Negro was fit only for the barbarism of Africa or the servile life of an American slave; its objective was gradual emancipation followed by a wholesale deportation of the freedmen to the land of their ancestors. Despite this, many prominent northerners of both races gave colonization their unqualified support. James Forten, however, refused to be misled. Believing unreservedly in the equality of the races, he hewed to the line later held by William Lloyd Garrison and Theodore Dwight Weld; the slaves, he insisted, should be freed, educated, and fitted to take their rightful place in American society. His views stamp him as one of the first true abolitionists in the United States.

He first made himself heard on the subject in 1817 when supporters of the American Colonization Society, recognizing his influence among the freemen of Philadelphia, asked him to endorse their program. They dangled a tempting bait before him; a man of his prestige, they said, could become the Lord Mansfield of the society's Colony of Liberia if he cast his lot with them. Forten refused to listen. He would, he reputedly told them, "rather remain as James Forten, sailmaker, in Philadelphia, than enjoy the highest offices in the gift of their society."[28]

To a man of such sincere conviction a mere refusal to support colonization was not enough; his fellow countrymen must be warned against a plan that might eventually drive all Negroes from their adopted land. With this in mind Forten sought the support of the Reverend Richard Allen, Absalom Jones, Robert Douglass, and others prominent in Philadelphia's colored population,

[26] James Forten, *Letters from a Man of Colour, on a Late Bill before the Senate of Pennsylvania* (Philadelphia [1813]), 3–4, 7. One of the letters is reprinted in Carter G. Woodson, *Negro Orators and Their Orations* (Washington, 1925), 42–51.

[27] For an account of this organization see Early L. Fox, *The American Colonization Society, 1817–1840* (Baltimore, 1919).

[28] Nell, *Colored Patriots*, 177.

with them arranging a mass meeting of protest at the Bethel Church in January, 1817. The hall was crowded that night when Forten mounted the rostrum to serve as chairman; speeches were heard and then previously prepared resolutions were adopted by a unanimous vote:[29]

Whereas, our ancestors (not of choice) were the first successful cultivators of the wilds of America, we, their descendants, feel ourselves entitled to participate in the blessing of her luxuriant soil, which their blood and sweat enriched; and that any measure or system of measures, having a tendency to banish us from her bosom, would not only be cruel, but in direct violation of those principles which have been the boast of this republic.

Resolved, That we view with deep abhorrence the unmerited stigma attempted to be cast upon the reputation of the free people of color by the promoters of this measure, "that they are a dangerous and useless part of the community," when, in the state of disfranchisement in which they live, in the hour of danger they ceased to remember their wrongs, and rallied around the standard of their country.

Resolved, That we will never separate ourselves voluntarily from the slave population of this country; they are our brethren by the ties of consanguinity, suffering, and wrong; and we feel there is more virtue in suffering privations with them, than fancied advantages for a season.

Resolved, That without arts, without science, or a proper knowledge of government, to cast into the wilds of Africa the free people of color, seems to us the circuitous route by which they must return to perpetual bondage.

Resolved, That, having the strongest confidence in the justice of God and the philanthropy of the free states, we cheerfully submit our destinies to the guidance of Him who suffers not a sparrow to fall without His special providence.

Persuasive as these resolutions were, they failed to check a mounting interest in colonization among Philadelphia's citizens. By July 23, 1817, the society's leaders felt confident of enough support to call a preliminary meeting to plan a local branch for the city.[30] This stirred Forten into action once more. The protest meeting that he arranged was held on August 10, 1817, in the

---

[29] A full account of the meeting, together with the text of the resolutions adopted, is in G. B. Stebbins, Facts and Opinions Touching the Real Origin, Character, and Influence of the American Colonization Society (Boston, 1853), 194–196. For briefer accounts of the meeting see: Nell, Colored Patriots, 177–178; William Lloyd Garrison, Thoughts on African Colonization (Boston, 1832), Pt. II, 9–10; Lewis Tappan, Life of Arthur Tappan (New York, 1870), 135–136; Booker T. Washington, The Story of the Negro (New York, 1909), I, 290; Cromwell, Negro in American History, 28; and Louis R. Mehlinger, "The Attitude of the Free Negro toward African Colonization," Journal of Negro History, I (June, 1916), 276–301.

[30] Scharf and Wescott, History of Philadelphia, I, 590.

school house at Green Court with a crowd of almost three thousand present. Again James Forten was in the chair; again enthusiastic speakers denounced colonization before a lengthy "Address to the humane and benevolent inhabitants of the city and county of Philadelphia" was adopted. This able document argued that colonization would doom free Negroes and ex-slaves alike to the hazards of a life for which they had no training, as well as depriving them of the benefits of religious instruction. Liberia, the writers predicted, would soon be the "abode of every vice, and the home of every misery." Furthermore, they believed that wholesale deportations would raise the price of slaves still in bondage, thus tending to perpetuate the institution. "Let not a purpose be assisted which will stay the cause of the entire abolition of slavery in the United States," the Address concluded, "and which may defeat it altogether; which proffers to those who do not ask for them benefits, but which they consider *injuries*, and which must insure to the multitude, whose prayers can only reach through us, *misery, sufferings, and perpetual slavery.*"[31]

Printed copies of this appeal were spread throughout Philadelphia and sent to Joseph Hopkinson, the Federalist representative serving Pennsylvania in Congress.[32] Despite a favorable reaction among Negroes, the Philadelphia Colonization Society was formed on August 12 as an auxiliary of the American Colonization Society.[33]

Undaunted by this defeat, Forten continued the attack with renewed vigor, certain that colonization would collapse when his countrymen learned the true nature of the movement. In November, 1819, he again presided over a large meeting of Philadelphia Negroes which condemned the American Colonization Society's efforts to "perpetuate slavery in the United States:"[34]

> *Resolved,* That the people of color of Philadelphia now enter and proclaim their most solemn protest against the proposition to send their people to Africa, and against every measure which may have a tendency to convey the idea that they give the project a single particle of countenance or encouragement.

A decade later Forten was primarily responsible for a national convention of Negro delegates which assembled at Philadelphia on September 15, 1830, to oppose colonization. Similar conventions were held yearly thereafter, usually in Philadelphia but occasionally in other cities, and in all Forten played a leading role. Due to his influence, as much as any other thing, the free Negroes of the North were arrayed in a solid phalanx against colonizers by the time abolitionism demanded their support.[35]

[31] The meeting is described in Garrison, *Thoughts on African Colonization*, Pt. II, 10–13. The Address is printed in Mehlinger, "Attitude of the Free Negro toward African Colonization," *loc. cit.*, 278–279, and in Woodson, *Negro Orators*, 52–55. See also Herbert Aptheker, *The Negro in the Abolitionist Movement* (New York, 1941), 3–32.

[32] A search of the *Annals of Congress*, 14th Cong., 2nd Sess., and 15th Cong., 1st Sess., failed to reveal any mention of the petition.

[33] Scharf and Wescott, *History of Philadelphia*, I, 591.

[34] *Niles Register*, XVII (November 27, 1819), 201–202.

[35] Carter G. Woodson, *The Negro in Our History* (Washington, 1941 edn.), 271–273.

Nor did the passing years alter his views. In 1833, when nearly sixty years of age, he spoke with all the fire of youth when a companion asked his views on colonization. "My great-grandfather," he said, "was brought to this country a slave from Africa. My grandfather obtained his own freedom. My father never wore the yoke. He rendered valuable service to his country in the war of our Revolution; and I, though then a boy, was a drummer in that war. I was taken prisoner, and was made to suffer not a little on board the Jersey prison-ship. I have since lived and labored in a useful employment, have acquired property, and have paid taxes in this city. Here I have dwelt until I am nearly sixty years of age, and have brought up and educated a family, as you see, thus far. Yet some ingenious gentlemen have recently discovered that I am still an African; that a continent, three thousand miles, and more, from the place where I was born is my native country. And I am advised to go home. Well, it may be so. Perhaps if I should only be set on the shore of that distant land, I should recognize all I might see there, and run at once to the old hut where my forefathers lived a hundred years ago."[36]

James Forten's attack on the concept of racial inequality which underlay colonization had important results. In all probability his unwavering belief in the equality of the races helped convince William Lloyd Garrison that colonization was not the answer to the slavery problem, thus laying the basis for the rise of abolitionism.[37] This, in turn, gave Forten the reforming opportunity he had long sought; he threw himself into the Garrisonian crusade with a zeal that belied both his advancing years and his upper class position.

For by the 1830's Forten was a man of substance. His sailmaking shop, where as many as forty white and Negro workmen were enployed,[38] had by 1832 rewarded him with a fortune of $100,000, a sizeable sum for that day.[39] This he used "to live in as handsome a style as anyone could wish to live"[40] in a spacious house on Lombard Street in Philadelphia.[41] Under his roof were gathered his ever-growing family: his wife, his eight children and other relatives; at times no less than twenty-two persons gathered about the family board.[42] A man of "commanding mind and well informed," he was highly respected by Negroes and whites alike. Particularly admired were the moral causes to which

[36] May, Some Recollections of the Antislavery Conflict, 287.

[37] Archibald H. Grimké, William Lloyd Garrison (New York, 1891), 144, holds that Garrison's conversations with Forten helped convince him that colonization was an evil, thus laying the basis for the beginnings of abolitionism. This is also the thesis of Clarice A. Richardson, The Anti-Slavery Activities of Negroes in Pennsylvania (unpublished master's thesis, Howard University, 1937), 10–11.

[38] May, Some Recollections of the Antislavery Conflict, 286.

[39] Carter G. Woodson, The Works of Francis J. Grimké (Washington, 1942), IV, 96n.

[40] Some Recollections of the Antislavery Conflict, 286.

[41] Forten occupied a house at 92 Lombard Street through most of his life. Philadelphia Directory for 1813 (Philadelphia, 1813); Philadelphia Directory for 1842 (Philadelphia, 1842), 88.

[42] According to the Census of 1830. Carter G. Woodson, Free Negro Heads of Families in the United States in 1830 (Washington, 1925).

he dedicated his life. He never drank, and was a steadfast supporter of temperance societies. His liberal contributions gave strength to the movements for universal peace and women's rights.[43] Forten was also the guiding spirit behind the American Moral Reform Society, an agency of colored men dedicated to the "promotion of Education, Temperance, Economy, and Universal Liberty."[44] As a founder and perennial president of that organization he directed its efforts toward bettering the standards of Negroes in Philadelphia and the nation.[45]

All this security and comfort James Forten was willing to sacrifice to aid the slaves. Recognizing that abolitionism was the nation's most unpopular cause; knowing that mobs might damage his property or threaten his aging limbs if he persisted in its support, he still showed no hesitation when the banner was unfurled by William Lloyd Garrison. To him the Boston leader was a "chosen instrument, in the Divine hand, to accomplish the great work of the abolition of American slavery,"[46] and must be aided without regard to cost. Even before the first issue of *The Liberator* appeared, Forten solicited subscriptions among Philadelphia Negroes; on December 31, 1830, he could send Garrison money from twenty-seven subscribers and a pledge of continued support. "I hope your efforts may not be in vain," he wrote "and that 'The Liberator' be the means of exposing more and more the odious system of Slavery, and of raising up friends to the oppressed and degraded People of Colour, throughout the Union. Whilst so much is doing in the world, to ameliorate the condition of mankind, and the spirit of Freedom is marching with rapid strides, and causing tyrants to tremble; may America awake from the apathy in which she has long slumbered. She must sooner or later fall in with the irresistible current. Great efforts are now making in the cause of Liberty; the people are becoming more interested and determined on the subject."[47]

Forten did not relax his efforts after the launching of *The Liberator* on January 1, 1831. A month later he sent Garrison twenty additional subscriptions;[48] on March 1 he arranged a mass meeting of Philadelphia Negroes where the paper's purposes were explained and unanimously endorsed.[49] From that time on he was a regular contributor to *The Liberator* and to abolition societies; with the exception of the wealthy New York merchants, Arthur and

[43] Child, *Freedmen's Book*, 103; Purvis, *Remarks on the Life and Character of James Forten*, 17.
[44] The objectives of the society are described in its monthly publication, the *National Reformer*, I (February, 1839), 81.
[45] Nell, *Colored Patriots*, 181; Cromwell, *The Negro in American History*, 35.
[46] Nell, *Colored Patriots*, 178.
[47] James Forten to William Lloyd Garrison, December 31, 1830. Dorothy B. Porter, ed., "Early Manuscript Letters Written by Negroes," *Journal of Negro History*, XXIV (April, 1939), 199–200.
[48] James Forten to William Lloyd Garrison, February 2, 1831. *Ibid.*, 200–201.
[49] The meeting was held on March 1, 1831. *The Liberator*, March 12, 1831. See also Herbert Aptheker, "The Negro in the Abolitionist Movement," *Science and Society*, V (Spring, 1941), 162.

Lewis Tappan, Forten was probably the most generous supporter of the radical antislavery cause.[50] His only reward was the mounting strength of Garrison-ianism. "It has," he wrote Garrison jubilantly during the spring of 1831, "roused up a spirit in our Young People, that has been slumbering for years, and we shall produce writers able to vindicate our cause." [51] Garrison, in turn, developed a warm affection for "the greatly esteemed and venerable sail-maker of Philadelphia," as he called Forten.[52] Seldom did he pass through Philadelphia without visiting the spacious house on Lombard Street, to dine with the family, spend the night, or simply engage in an hour's conversation on abolitionism. Such visits, wrote the elderly Forten after one of them, "are cheering, they are as green spots in the journey of life." [53]

His early contacts with Garrison allowed Forten to play a significant role when the American Anti-Slavery Society was formed. Many of the reformers who gathered in Philadelphia for the organizational meeting in December, 1833, made the Forten home their headquarters; about the family table plans were discussed and strategy mapped.[54] Until forced to retire from active labors by advancing age, he served frequently on the society's Board of Managers,[55] as well as collecting subscriptions for *The Liberator* [56] and lending the paper needed financial support.[57] Little wonder that members of the American Anti-Slavery Society, while recognizing the contributions of leading members during the 1840 meeting, lauded Forten with:

> James Forten, right well
> I love to hear tell,
> Of thy aid in our much boasted war;
> And mark with what scorn
> Does thy noble heart spurn
> The friends of Liberia's shore
> James Forten!
> The friends of Liberia's shore.[58]

[50] Woodson, *Works of Francis J. Grimké*, IV, 96n.

[51] James Forten to William Lloyd Garrison, March 21, 1831. Porter, "Early Manuscript Letters Written by Negroes," *loc. cit.*, 201–202.

[52] Washington, *The Story of the Negro*, 290.

[53] James Forten to William Lloyd Garrison, July 28, 1832. "Early Manuscript Letters Written by Negroes," *loc. cit.*, 204–205. For an account of one of Garrison's visits to the Forten home see Anna D. Hallowell, ed., *James and Lucretia Mott. Life and Letters* (Boston, 1884), 119.

[54] May, *Some Recollections of the Antislavery Conflict*, 286. May reported that he and several other convention delegates dined at Forten's home and "were entertained with as much ease and elegance as I could desire to see."

[55] His name appears in the *Second Annual Report of the American Anti-Slavery Society, May 12, 1835* (New York, 1835), 12; *Fifth Annual Report of the Executive Committee of the American Anti-Slavery Society, May, 1839* (New York, 1839), 13.

[56] *The Liberator*, September 17, 1841, contained a letter from Forten stating that he was sending additional subscriptions.

[57] Woodson, *Works of Francis J. Grimké*, IV, 96n.

[58] *The Liberator*, May 22, 1840.

Nor did national acclaim blind Forten to the local aspects of abolitionism during his declining years. In 1832 he circulated a petition among Philadelphia Negroes, praying that the Pennsylvania legislature take steps to prevent the return of escaped slaves.[59] A year later he presided over a large meeting of colored people where resolutions were adopted expressing sympathy for education, antislavery, and anticolonialization.[60] In 1836 he prepared a memorial to the legislature urging the members to condemn slavery and wipe out distinctions against men of color in the state. "Let our motto be," he pleaded, "the Law Knows No Distinction." [61] During the following year he served as one of two delegates from Philadelphia to a convention at Harrisburg which urged the end of slavery and colonization.[62] Undeterred by criticism or advancing age, James Forten gave unstintingly to the day's most unpopular cause. Few men, either white or colored, could boast such an outstanding record.

Only with death could his followers show the full measure of their appreciation. Ill health beset him increasingly in his declining years; by the fall of 1841 he was forced to write Garrison that he could exert himself in the cause of abolition no longer, but that his interest was as firm and ardent as ever.[63] A year later he died at the ripe age of seventy-six. His funeral, held on February 24, 1842, was one of the largest in the history of Philadelphia; several hundred whites and several thousand Negroes marched in the procession that followed his body to the grave.[64] At a public meeting to honor his memory a large group of friends, without distinction of color, paid him tribute in the eulogies common to that day.[65]

James Forten passed from the scene with the cause that he sponsored still in its infancy. Yet even on his deathbed he could take solace in the fact that his children were equipped to carry on the crusade with a zeal matching his own.[66] To them, if not to their father, came the privilege of seeing his fondest dreams fulfilled when Abraham Lincoln's Emancipation Proclamation completed the reform to which he had devoted his life.

[59] *Ibid.*, April 14, 1832.

[60] The meeting was held on April 1, 1833. *Ibid.*, April 13, 1833.

[61] *Human Rights*, II (September 4, 1836).

[62] Forten and Robert Purvis, his son-in-law, were the two delegates from Philadelphia. *Proceedings of the Pennsylvania Convention at Harrisburg* (Philadelphia, 1837).

[63] *The Liberator*, September 17, 1841.

[64] Accounts of the funeral are in *ibid.*, March 18, 1842, and in the *National Anti-Slavery Standard*, March 24, 1842. Briefer descriptions by those who attended are in Child, *Freedmen's Book*, 103; and Hallowell, *James and Lucretia Mott*, 232.

[65] *National Anti-Slavery Standard*, March 24, 1842.

[66] Among Forten's children who were active in abolitionism were Margaretta, who served as secretary of the Philadelphia Female Anti-Slavery Society, James, who spoke and sang in the cause of freedom, Robert, who refused to live in a United States that condoned slavery, Harriet, who was married to the well-known reformer, Robert Purvis, who was one of the organizers of an antislavery convention that met in New York in 1837.

William H. Pease and Jane H. Pease

ANTISLAVERY AMBIVALENCE:
IMMEDIATISM, EXPEDIENCY, RACE *

If Forten was indeed a "forgotten abolitionist," as Billington refers to him, the fault lies in part with white historians who have ignored the role of Negroes in the abolitionist movement. Yet it also lies in part with the white abolitionists themselves. Generally far in advance of most of the American public in their racial attitudes, few of them —even among the most prominent—were fully emancipated from the prejudices of their age. In recent years a spirited discussion has engaged historians concerning whether or not the white abolitionists, who practically excluded Negroes from decision-making positions in antislavery societies, were genuinely racial equalitarians. William and Jane Pease have explored this subject in a penetrating manner.

O<small>F</small> constant distress to students of the American antislavery movement has been its ambivalence, especially its ambivalence over the term Immediatism. The term had originally defined a means to end British colonial slavery, but it failed to be similarly applicable to emancipation in the American South. Therefore the antislavery movement strained to give new meaning to emancipation *"instant and universal."* Did it not really mean gradual emancipation immediately begun or, perhaps, immediate emancipation gradually achieved? But no less than over immediatism, antislavery crusaders were beset by a fundamental ambivalence in their attitude toward the Negro himself. At the simplest level there was no issue. Slavery was sin; and the crusaders were moved to free the

William H. Pease and Jane H. Pease, "Antislavery Ambivalence: Immediatism, Expedience, Race." *American Quarterly*, XVII (Winter, 1965), pp. 682–695. Reprinted with permission of *American Quarterly*, and William H. and Jane H. Pease.
* This article was read, in a slightly modified form, at the annual meetings of the Mississippi Valley Historical Association, April 1965.

slave by a humanitarianism too genuine to be doubted.[1] Yet, sympathetic as they might appear and believe themselves to be toward the Negro, the abolitionists were, as Leon Litwack and others have shown, in part at least prejudiced against him.[2] And the variety of their response toward him demonstrates the ambivalence so characteristic of the antislavery movement as a whole.

Endemic was the abolitionists' tendency toward abstraction. Frequently they so abstracted both the "Negro" and the "Crusade" that they dealt not with people in a situation but only with intellectualizations in a vacuum. John Thomas has recently noted that William Lloyd Garrison failed "to understand people, black or white" and used them simply "as counters in the grim business of reform."[3] His analysis echoes publisher James Gordon Bennett's conclusion made one hundred years earlier that to Garrison "nothing [was] sacred ... but the ideal intellect of the negro race."[4]

This preoccupation with the ideal is reflected by the American Anti-Slavery Society, which, at its inception in 1833, resolved that to guarantee education to the Negro was more important than to end "corporeal slavery itself, inasmuch as ignorance enslaves the mind and tends to the ruin of the immortal soul."[5] And, on the very eve of Emancipation, Philadelphia antislavery leader James Miller McKim, although emphasizing the importance of slave rehabilitation and active in prosecuting it, thought that it was "not the place ... of [the] abolitionists to descend to the details of th[e] work, teaching and the like; let this," he added, "be attended to by the neophytes and others. We are to continue to be what we always have been," he concluded, "a wheel within a wheel; an original motive power."[6] Thus for thirty years abolitionists, to a greater or lesser extent, heeded the kind of exhortation which Henry C. Wright enunciated so forcefully:

[1] The abolitionists were defined and set off from their contemporaries by their opposition to slavery and their concern for the welfare of the slaves, a concern which usually embraced the free Negroes as well. This article is not, however, designed to compare abolitionists as a group with nonabolitionists but rather to explore the variations within the group.

[2] See, for example, Leon Litwack, "The Abolitionist Dilemma: The Antislavery Movement and the Northern Negro," *New England Quarterly*, XXXIV (1961), 50–73; and his *North of Slavery: The Negro in the Free States, 1790–1860* (Chicago, 1961). See also Larry Gara, Louis Filler, Gerda Lerner, Stanley Elkins for considerations of prejudice. For psychological probing see David Donald, Hazel Wolf, Clifford Griffin, Martin Duberman.

[3] John L. Thomas, *The Liberator, William Lloyd Garrison, A Biography* (Boston, 1963), p. 153.

[4] Quoted in Wendell Phillips Garrison and Francis Jackson Garrison, *William Lloyd Garrison, 1805–1879; The Story of His Life as Told by His Children* (4 vols.; New York, 1885–89), III, 283.

[5] American Anti-Slavery Society, *Proceedings of the Anti-Slavery Convention, Assembled at Philadelphia, Decembr 4, 5, and 6, 1833* (New York, 1833), p. 19.

[6] James Miller McKim to Samuel J. May, May 20 [1862], in Samuel J. May Papers, Cornell University.

Watch, Sister, & pray that you enter not into temptation. *Watch, not* ... for Abolition as an Organization, not even for our millions of crushed & bleeding slaves ..., but watch *for* the eternal, immutable Principles of Justice & Right—watch for *Humanity*. ... We are seeking an object that must command the respect of the world—i e *the redemption of man from the dominion of man*. This is Abolition.[7]

The abolitionists did, of course, at least partly understand their own position. They may not have realized just how fully they were depersonalizing the Negroes; but they were quite aware that they had difficulties in matching their protestations to their actions. "We are," said the Connecticut crusader Samuel J. May with a Zolaesque directness, "culpably ignorant of, or shamefully indifferent to the wrongs which are inflicted upon our colored brethren. ... We are prejudiced against the blacks; and our prejudices are indurated ... by the secret, vague consciousness of the wrong we are doing them. Men are apt to dislike those most, whom they have injured most."[8] And despite the teaching of the antislavery periodical, the *Abolitionist*, that the antislavery enthusiast ought "to banish from his own mind the unworthy feelings which would lead him to regard any human being with contempt merely on account of his color," New York abolitionist Lewis Tappan admitted "that when the subject of acting out our profound principles in treating men irrespective of color is discussed heat is always produced."[9]

This much, then, the abolitionists themselves perceived. But for the student of the antislavery movement it is also imperative to recognize that prejudice and abstraction were but the obvious symptoms of an ambivalence which gives to the antislavery crusade in the expediency and temporizing of its actions and in the complexity of its thought an architecture baroque in the richness of its variations.[10]

It was, for example, relatively simple to accept the humanity of the

---

[7] Henry C. Wright to Maria Weston Chapman, May 2, 1839, in Weston Papers, Antislavery Collection, Boston Public Library.

[8] Samuel J. May, Sermon delivered May 29, 1831, in Boston, as reported in *Liberator*, July 23, 1831.

[9] *Abolitionist*, I (Jan. 1833), as quoted in Merton L. Dillon, "'The Failure of the American Abolitionists," *Journal of Southern History*, XXV (1959), 167. Lewis Tappan, Diary entry [Apr. 1836], as quoted in Litwack, *North of Slavery*, p. 218. See also Garrison's July 4, 1829 oration (*Garrison* I, 133–34); Susan Cabot, *What Have We, as Individuals, to Do with Slavery* (American Anti-Slavery Society, *Anti-Slavery Tract No. 15*. New York, 1855), pp. 3–4; Beriah Green, *American Anti-Slavery Reporter*, I (June 1834), 88; and Birney to William Wright, June 20, 1845, in *Letters of James Gillespie Birney, 1831–1857*, ed. Dwight L. Dumond (2 vols.; New York, 1938), II, 947.

[10] This ideological ambivalence is reflected in the cleavages within the antislavery movement over the appropriate courses of action to be pursued. These cleavages have already been well examined in a variety of studies on antislavery published since 1935. Whether to take political action or to regard it as damaging to the requisite moral fervor, whether to expend time and funds on schools, give aid to fugitives and buy freedom for individual slaves or to work exclusively to propagate the antislavery faith are debates not only about means but also about the basic concepts of antislavery.

Negro; but then how did one account for his patently submerged position vis-à-vis the whites? Abolitionists like Lydia Maria Child of Northampton, Massachusetts, tried to link the two elements by admitting that, while all Negroes were not "Scotts or Miltons," they were "*men,* capable of producing their proportions of Scotts and Miltons, if they could be allowed to live in a state of physical and intellectual freedom." [11] At the other extreme the New York Whig politician, William Henry Seward, defending the mentally deranged William Freeman in 1846, tried to subordinate intellectual lack to simple humanity and to separate it from race. He pleaded with the jury that

> the color of the prisoner's skin, and the form of his features, are not impressed upon the spiritual, immortal mind which works beneath. In spite of human pride, he is still your brother, and mine, in form and color accepted and approved by his Father, and yours, and mine, and bears equally with us the proudest inheritance of our race—the image of our Maker. Hold him then to be a MAN.[12]

In denying, furthermore, that the apparent differences between Negroes and whites were not inherent the abolitionists became environmentalists. John Rankin, ex-slaveholder from Virginia and an ardent abolitionist, asserted with good will but dubious logic that, if racial inferiority were a valid criterion, then all Negroes would be inferior to all whites if but one was. Clearly this was not so. Therefore existing inferiority was explainable only in environmental terms.[13] Slavery it was, asserted German refugee Charles Follen of Boston, that debased and degraded the Negroes and generated among whites an "absurd and cruel prejudice against color." [14] The antislavery solution to prejudice was clear once the cause was thus linked to slavery. Charles Calistus Burleigh of Connecticut optimistically exhorted his fellow whites to "give [the Negro] his liberty, and as strong a motive to exertion as you have;—a prospect of reward as sure and ample; not only wages for his toil, but respect and honor and social standing according to his worth, and see what he can then become." [15]

[11] Lydia Maria Child, *An Appeal in Favor of that Class of Americans Called Africans* (orig. ed. 1833. New York, 1836), p. 171.
[12] William Henry Seward, *Argument in Defense of William Freeman on His Trial for Murder . . .* (4th ed.; Auburn, N.Y., 1846), pp. 8–9. See also C. T. C. Follen, *Works, with a Memoir of His Life* [by Mrs. E. L. Follen] (5 vols.; Boston, 1841), I, 627–28.
[13] John Rankin, *Letters on American Slavery Addressed to Mr. Thomas Rankin . . .* (5th ed.; Boston, 1838), pp. 10–11. See also Lewis Tappan, *The Life of Arthur Tappan* (New York, 1870), p. 131; James A. Thome and J. Horace Kimball, *Emancipation in the West Indies. A Six Months Tour in Antigua, Barbadoes, and Jamaica in the Year 1837* (American Anti-Slavery Society, Anti-Slavery Examiner No. 7. New York, 1838), p. 75; and Sallie Holley to Gerrit Smith, Nov. 17, 1865, in the Smith Miller Papers, Syracuse University.
[14] Charles Follen, "The Cause of Freedom in Our Country," *Quarterly Anti-Slavery Magazine,* II (Oct. 1836), 65.
[15] Charles Calistus Burleigh, *Slavery and the North* (New York [1855]), p. 4. Rankin essentially held the same view, but thought that it would take a long time to raise the Negro; see *Letters on American Slavery,* pp. 10–11.

Yet, for all their exuberance, for all their belief in equality, for all their efforts to raise the Negro above the debilitating influences of adverse environment, the abolitionists were never wholly convincing. Much of what they said betrayed an implicit and at times explicit belief in racial inferiority. Here again ambivalence emerged. That the abolitionists themselves were usually unconscious of their expression of prejudice and that they denied it when challenged should surprise no one. Nor, indeed, is the thoughtful student surprised to learn that such prejudice did in fact exist. Occasionally crude, more often hidden in underlying assumptions or in appeals to science, prejudice played a more pervasive role than the logic of consistency would admit.

Exasperated by poor printing, inferior paper and numerous misprints, and spurred on by his own literary pride, Edmund Quincy lashed out in a letter to Caroline Weston in 1846 at "Wendell's nigger," whom he held responsible for botching an Antislavery Report. Never, he urged, let the printing out to "*Smart people*"; they get things up so poorly.[16] Here clearly was not only a rather vulgar display of prejudice but also of a value structure in which the typography of a convention's report weighed more heavily than economic opportunity for the free Negro.

The acerbity of these outbursts may be attributed to Quincy alone. The subterranean import, however, was common property among antislavery people. As late as 1860 Theodore Parker, a backer of John Brown, observed that "the Anglo-Saxon with common sense does not like this Africanization of America; he wishes the superior race to multiply rather than the inferior." [17] His neighbor, Samuel Gridley Howe, known for his multiple reform interests, accepted Parker's assumptions but rejected his predictions by observing that, particularly among young Canadian refugee Negroes, many succumbed to "mesenteric and other glandular diseases" and suffered from "phthisical diseases" and a "softening of tubercles." "Many intelligent physicians," he stated, "who have practiced among both [white and Negro] classes, say that the colored people are feebly organized; that the scrofulous temperament prevails among them; that the climate tends to development of tuberculous diseases; that they are unprolific and short-lived." [18]

Whether feebly organized in physique or not, the Negroes were certainly docile in temperament. "It is paying a very poor compliment, indeed, to the courage and superiority of us whites," Richard Hildreth said through the sympathetically portrayed Mr. Mason in Archy Moore, "to doubt whether we, superior as well in numbers as in every thing else, could not inspire awe enough to maintain our natural position at the head of the community, and to keep

[16] Edmund Quincy to Caroline Weston, Feb. 1, 1846, in Weston Papers. A year later Quincy complained about Frederick Douglass' independence (what he thought was Douglass' overcharging the American Anti-Slavery Standard for copy supplied) by observing that "These niggers, like Kings, are kittle cattle to shoe behind." Quincy to Caroline Weston, July 2, 1847, in Weston Papers.

[17] Theodore Parker, John Brown's Expedition Reviewed in a Letter from Theodore Parker, at Rome, to Francis Jackson, Boston (Boston, 1860), p. 14.

[18] Samuel Gridley Howe, The Refugees from Slavery in Canada West. Report to the Freedmen's Inquiry Commission (Boston, 1864), pp. 21–22.

these poor people in order without making slaves of them." [19] But, if Hildreth's Mason was fictional, the Lane Rebels were not. They had concluded, in their famous debates on slavery, that *"the blacks are abundantly able to take care of and provide for themselves"*; but had added immediately that they *"would be kind and docile if immediately emancipated."* [20] This emphasis on docility is important, for quite openly it reduced the status of the Negro below that of the white man. J. Miller McKim, for example, negated American standards of self-reliance and manly independence when he praised Negroes for "their susceptibility to control." [21]

Not unreasonably, many Negroes actively resented this abolitionist presumption about their "susceptibility to control." During the 1850s, in fact, this resentment was in large part responsible for the growth and activity of the Negro Convention movement, whose purpose it was to do for the Negroes themselves what they feared the whites, at last, would not accomplish for them. Frederick Douglass and Henry Highland Garnet, two Negro leaders of marked undocility, both took umbrage at Maria Weston Chapman for her paternal concern about their appropriate behavior; and Douglass, disillusioned with radical abolitionism in the face of growing political antislavery activity and ambitious himself to assert his independence from white abolitionist domination, defied the Boston hierarchy by establishing his own newspaper in Rochester, New York. Likewise, Martin Delany, a successful Negro doctor, resented the Negroes' exclusion from antislavery leadership and was highly dubious about the abolitionists' touted support of economic opportunity for free Negroes. Delany's disillusionment led him to abandon America as a viable home for the Negro and in the late 1850s to sponsor projects for African colonization.[22]

Despite concepts of racial inferiority, further borne out by an almost universal preference for the lighter-skinned over the darker-skinned Negro,[23] abo-

[19] Richard Hildreth, *Archy Moore: The White Slave* (1st ed.; 1836. New York, 1856), p. 264.

[20] As reported in Henry B. Stanton to Joshua Leavitt, Mar. 10, 1834, in *American Anti-Slavery Reporter*, I (Apr. 1834), 54.

[21] James Miller McKim, *The Freedmen of South Carolina* ... (Philadelphia, 1862), p. 9. See also *Letters from Port Royal. Written at the Time of the Civil War*, ed. Elizabeth Ware Pearson (Boston, 1906), pp. 102–03, 315–16; The *Anti-Slavery Record* III (Feb. 1837), 15; *Letters of Theodore Dwight Weld, Angelina Grimké Weld and Sarah Grimké, 1822–1844*, eds. Gilbert H. Barnes and Dwight L. Dumond (2 vols.; New York, 1934), II, 524; and Leon Litwack, *North of Slavery*, p. 223.

[22] In the Weston Papers one may find numerous examples of the patronizing antislavery attitude and of Negro response to it. See also Filler, *Crusade Against Slavery*, p. 143. In particular note Frederick Douglass to Maria Weston Chapman, Mar. 29, 1846, Weston Papers; and Martin Robinson Delany, *The Condition, Elevation, Emigration, and Destiny of the Colored People of the United States Politically Considered* (Philadelphia, 1852), pp. 25–29.

[23] Antislavery literature contains many illustrations of the preference for lighter-skinned Negroes. See Samuel May Jr., *The Fugitive Slave Law and Its Victims* (American Anti-Slavery Society, Anti-Slavery Tract No. 18 [New York, 1855]); George Bourne, *Slavery Illustrated in its Effects Upon Woman and Domestic Society* (Boston, 1837); Hildreth's *Archy Moore*; and William I. Bowditch, *White Slavery in the United States*

litionists in fact did demand just and equitable civil liberties for colored persons. "The oppressive civil disabilities laid upon them in the non-slaveholding States, and the settled opposition to their education and elevation...," said the Andover Theological Seminary antislavery society,

> are but glaring indications of the prevalent spirit of slavery. The same contempt of the black man—the same disposition to trample on his rights and to lord it over his person, follows him, whatever *degree* of emancipation he may have obtained, and in whatever part of the nation he takes his refuge. Though we had in view only the wrongs of the colored people in New-England, we should feel ourselves compelled to take our present stand, and vindicate their rights as brethren, as men, and as Americans.[24]

Abolitionists everywhere asserted that Negroes and whites should be judged and treated according to the same standards in the apportioning not only of civil rights but also of economic and educational opportunities. In its Declaration of Sentiments the American Anti-Slavery Society announced in 1833 that

> all persons of color who possess the qualifications which are demanded of others, ought to be admitted forthwith to the enjoyment of the same privileges, and the exercise of the same prerogatives, as others; and... the paths of preferment, of wealth, and of intelligence, should be opened as widely to them as to persons of a white complexion.[25]

Schools, like Oberlin College and the Noyes Academy in New Hampshire, which admitted Negroes on equal terms with whites,[26] bore out these principles as did Charles Sumner's argument in the Roberts Case in 1849 that separate schools were unequal and threatened cleavages in society.[27] And Samuel J. May, summing up the concept in a statement which avoided many of the pitfalls of prejudice into which his colleagues fell, averred that "all we demand for them is that negroes shall be permitted, encouraged, assisted to become as wise, as virtuous, and as rich as they can, and be acknowledged to be just what they have become, and be treated accordingly." [28]

(American Anti-Slavery Society, *Anti-Slavery Tract No. 2* [New York, 1855]); see also in this connection Theodore Dwight Weld, *American Slavery as it is: Testimony of a Thousand Witnesses* (New York, 1839); and the juvenile [Jonathan Walker], *A Picture of Slavery, for Youth. By the Author of "The Branded Hand" and "Chattelized Humanity"* (Boston, n.d.).

[24] This is a summary given by D. T. Kimball and F. Laine to *Genius of Temperance*, Aug. 22, 1833, as reported in *Liberator*, Sept. 28, 1833. Similar demands for equality of treatment can be found in Child, *Appeal*, pp. 195–208.

[25] American Anti-Slavery Society, *Proceedings of the Anti-Slavery Convention, Assembled at Philadelphia*, contains the Declaration of Sentiments.

[26] See *Liberator*, Oct. 25, 1834, for information about the Noyes Academy.

[27] Charles Sumner, "Equality before the Law: Unconstitutionality of Separate Colored Schools in Massachusetts. Argument before the Supreme Court of Massachusetts, in the Case of Sarah C. Roberts v. The City of Boston...," in *The Works of Charles Sumner* (Boston, 1872), II, 327–76.

[28] Samuel Joseph May, *Some Recollections of Our Anti-Slavery Conflict* (Boston, 1869), p. 29. See also Birney, *Letters*, II, 945; and Garrison, *Garrison*, I, 148.

Yet these appeals to the efficacy of education and economic betterment reveal the middle-class values to which almost all abolitionists subscribed and which both compound and explain much of the ambivalence in the antislavery movement. As middle-class Americans, abolitionists, naturally enough, measured the Negroes against middle-class standards, and to those standards they expected the Negroes to conform—Negroes who were generally ex-slaves from the lowest and most abject class in America. Assuredly the American Anti-Slavery Society was eager to uplift them to "an equality with the whites" but only after carefully disclaiming that it approved any such non-middle-class shenanigans as adopting colored children, encouraging interracial marriages or "exciting the people of color to assume airs." [29]

It was expected, then, that the Negroes should adapt themselves to the values of the white community, should, as one abolitionist advised, submit to prejudice "with the true dignity of meekness" so that their critics might be stilled. Thus was fulfilled the stereotype of the malleable, willing and docile colored man. Still, on limited occasions, the same writer observed, the Negroes should take a positive stand. They should demand admission to the public schools, they should organize or join lyceum groups, they should acquire knowledge and education. And, he said in a condensed version of a middle-class *Poor Richard's*, they should organize uplifting visits to their poor and degraded brethren and teach them "temperance . . . cleanliness, neatness, strict honesty, and all that belong to good morality." [30] In addition to these virtues, the American Anti-Slavery Society agents were admonished to instill in the free people of color

> the importance of domestic order, and the performance of relative duties in families; of correct habits; command of temper and courteous manners. Also the duty and advantages of industry and economy; promptness and fidelity in the fulfillment of contrasts or obligations, whether written or verbal; and encourage them in the acquisition of property, especially of real estate in fee simple, particularly dwellings for their own families. Present their duties and privileges as citizens, and encourage them to become voters, and to secure equal privileges with other citizens. . . . [31]

Others, varying little from the standard reforming attitudes of the day but less optimistic about raising the Negro to the middle-class, urged him to adopt their own conception of lower-class standards. He should learn a trade and become a mechanic. Since these abolitionists categorized the social strata in

[29] Executive Committee of the American Anti-Slavery Society to Mayor Cornelius Lawrence of New York, July 16, 1834, included in the microfilm printing of *Liberator*, between 1833 and 1834, reel 1.

[30] This entire argument appeared in a series of articles, signed "S. T. U.," which appeared in *Liberator*, Feb. 11, 18, 25, and Mar. 3, 1832. The quotations are from the first and last issues, respectively.

[31] Executive Committee of the American Anti-Slavery Society to its agents, n.d. [1834–5?], included in the microfilm printing of *Liberator*, between 1833 and 1834, reel 1.

such a way that the hardy mechanic always fell comfortably below the solid middle class, the Negro was bracketed, at worst, with the Irish hod carrier, and at best only identified with the honest toiler.[32]

Sometimes in the abolitionists' arguments one discovers strong overtones of ordinary self-interest. The *Anti-Slavery Almanac* assured its readers, for example, that emancipated Negroes would not flock to the North. Let no one be perturbed, the *Almanac* urged in unctuous tone. "If the slaves are gradually set free, they must leave the place where they are, (and will be likely to go to the north,) that they may not interfere with the slavery which remains. But if they are all set free at once, they may continue where they are." Putting the argument in other terms, emancipated Negroes would be a great boon to the economy not only in the South but in the North as well.[33] "The southern laborers, when free and paid," C. C. Burleigh had said, "would buy of us many comforts and conveniences not allowed them now ... which would give new activity to our shops and mills and shipping, and steadier employment, and, most likely, higher wages, to all kinds of labor here." [34] Thus emancipation would not inconvenience the North with a mass of freed slaves; it would rather prove quite profitable.

Still, there was the thorny issue of defining the social position of the Negro in a predominantly white society. Many of the same abolitionists who demanded so unfalteringly no association with slaveholders found it ticklishly difficult to espouse social intercourse with Negroes and almost impossible to champion holy wedlock with those of black skin. In theory and in conscience, of course, they deplored the bans on interracial marriage; yet in practice they as often betrayed an opposite sentiment.[35] For his own part, Garrison defended the ideal goal but reconciled it with practical reality. "At the present time," he said expediently, "mixed marriages would be in bad taste...." [36] Elizur

[32] See, for example, the *Anti-Slavery Record*, I (June 1835), 68, urging that Negroes be apprenticed at good trades. And see also the commentary reprinted by *Liberator*, Mar. 31, 1837, from the Bangor *Mechanic*, in which it is made quite clear that the laborer is quite aware that the middle class looks down on the working class. See also, for comparisons with the Irish, Hildreth, *Archy Moore*, p. 264; Sarah Grimké to Elizabeth Pease [May 20? 1938], in *Weld-Grimké Letters*, II, 679; William Allen Diary, Nov. 10, 1863, State Historical Society of Wisconsin.

[33] The *Anti-Slavery Almanac* (1837 and 1839). The quotation is from the earlier volume, p. 44. The self-interest showed in other ways as well. Defending what later became Radical Republican doctrine, Maria Weston Chapman wrote to Lizzy (Chapman) Laugel (Sept. 24, 1862) that "black *soldiers* would save our Armies, & black *citizens* our *republican institutions*" (Weston Papers). And Wendell Phillips also unconsciously suggested the same prior self-concern when he spoke at the *Liberator's* 20th anniversary celebration: "My friends, if we never free a slave, we have at least freed ourselves in the effort to emancipate our brother man." (Quoted in Garrison, *Garrison*, III, 320.)

[34] Burleigh, *Slavery and the North*, pp. 8–9.

[35] See Birney, *Letters*, I, 397; Garrison, *Garrison*, II, 356; *Anti-Slavery Record*, I (June 1835), 71; and Gilbert H. Barnes, *The Antislavery Impulse, 1830–1844* (New York, 1933), p. 274, note 20. See also Louis Ruchames, "Race, Marriage and Abolition in Massachusetts," *Journal of Negro History*, XL (1955), 250–73, on the fight for repeal of discriminatory marriage laws.

[36] *Liberator*, Aug. 13, 1831.

Wright, however, scornfully ridiculed such temporizing over prejudice. "Pray, what is the matter? we ask of a generous and enlightened public," he snapped viciously.

> The reply is couched with quaking apprehension, in the appalling interrogatory; *would you have your daughter marry a negro?* And the utter slavery to which this tyrant prejudice has reduced everything that is noble and good in the land, is evinced by nothing more clearly than by the pains taking of even abolitionists to show that colored men *may be* enfranchised and elevated without bringing on the dreaded consequence.[37]

It seemed necessary, in the end, to plaster over the issue and to allay white fears. Mrs. Child, echoing the frequent antislavery assertion that there were scarcely enough abolitionists in the South to account for the evidences of miscegenation there, insisted that to say that abolitionists wished amalgamation was "a false charge, got up by the enemies of the cause, and used as a bugbear to increase the prejudices of the community." In fact, she added, "by universal emancipation we want to *stop* amalgamation." [38] More reassuring to those who hoped that the issues raised by social equality would fail to materialize was Samuel G. Howe's commentary made after a close study of Canadian Negroes. "Upon the whole," he observed,

> ... the experience of the Canadian refugees goes to show that there need be no anxiety upon the score of amalgamation of races in the United States. With freedom, and protection of their legal rights; with an open field for industry, and opportunities for mental and moral culture, colored people will not seek relationship with whites, but will follow their natural affinities, and marry among themselves.[39]

The social distance decreed by class identification provided perhaps the most common and satisfactory framework for abolitionists' contacts with free Negroes. Thus, steeped in middle-class values and having identified the Negroes with the laboring classes, the antislavery band frequently assumed the patronizing air of the uplifter and the saved toward the downtrodden and unwashed. James G. Birney, speaking for a slaveholding background, observed that without question emancipation would, "where the superior intelligence of the master was acknowledged, produce on the part of the beneficiaries, the most entire and cordial reliance on his counsel and friendship." [40] And Sumner, in the Roberts Case, urged that "the vaunted superiority of the white race imposes corresponding duties. The faculties with which they are endowed, and

[37] [Elizur Wright Jr.], "Caste in the United States: A Review," *Quarterly Anti-Slavery Magazine*, II (Jan. 1837), 177.

[38] Lydia Maria Child, *Anti-Slavery Catechism* (Newburyport, 1836), pp. 31–32.

[39] Howe, *Refugees from Slavery*, p. 33.

[40] Quoted in *The Legion of Liberty and Force of Truth, Containing the Thoughts, Words, and Deeds, of Some Prominent Apostles, Champions and Martyrs* (New York, 1843), n.p.

the advantages they possess, must be exercised for the good of all. If the colored people are ignorant, degraded, and unhappy," he asserted with a fine sense of noblesse oblige, "then should they be especial objects of care." [41]

Such paternalism was, to be sure, most benign. At times, however, it was most insufferable. "The more I mingle with your people," Angelina Grimké wrote to Sarah Douglass in a display of tactlessness as gargantuan as it was overbearing,

> the more I feel for their oppressions and desire to sympathize in their sorrows. Joshua Leavitt threw out a new and delightful idea on this subject on our way to Bloomfield. He said he believed the Lord had a great work for the colored people to do, and that your long con-tinued afflictions and humiliations was the furnace in which He was purifying you from the dross[,] the tin[,] and the reprobate silver, that you might come out like gold seven times refined. I Hav[e] thought of this and fully believ[e] you will after all get up abov[e] us and be the favored instruments [to?] carry pure and undefiled Religion to the Heathen World. May the Lord lift you from the dung hill and set you among princes....[42]

Helping the Lord hoist the poor Negroes off the dung hill was, as it often turned out, an arduous and dangerous chore, but one which gave the abolition-ists a chance many of them coveted to become martyrs in the cause. To de-fend the Negro in court, to speak on his behalf before hostile audiences, to be harried from town after town by the frenzied mob was the stuff of which martyrdom was made. And the genuine joy in the experience of such martyr-dom only enhanced the rewards of protective guardianship, as those who braved the mob when Pennsylvania Hall was burned well knew. Confronting the hostile elements, the stalwart women of the Female Anti-Slavery Conven-tion "maintain[ed] the perilled cause to the last." As they adjourned "the col-ored members of the convention were protected by their white sisters, and Oh! Shame to say," one of the white sisters wrote, "at both were thrown a shower of stones." [43] And then, Oh! Shame to say, the brand new hall was set ablaze and totally destroyed.

In their enthusiasm to elevate the Negro, the abolitionists frequently carried on their shoulders an early version of the White Man's Burden. They taught their children in heavily freighted moral tales that "negroes, even poor, degraded, despised slaves, are not without reason and understanding. [And that] many of them have a large share of sagacity." Go forth, they directed even the toddlers, instruct the poor and ignorant; become teachers, and help train the Negroes themselves to become missionaries that they may enlighten

[41] Sumner, "Equality before the Law," II, 376.

[42] In Angelina and Sarah Grimké to Sarah Douglass, Feb. 22, 1837, *Weld-Grimké Letters*, I, 364–65. Gerda Lerner contends that the Grimké sisters were almost if not totally above prejudice in "The Grimké Sisters and the Struggle against Race Prejudice," *Journal of Negro History*, XLVIII (1936), 277–91.

[43] Letter from a New York woman, May 18, 1838, in *Liberator*, May 25, 1838.

"their countrymen who are in ignorance and darkness." [44] The adults themselves set the initial example. When Helen Benson, daughter of Rhode Island abolitionist George Benson, was married to Garrison, she refused to allow cake at her wedding or to wear fancy clothes lest she be a poor model for the Negroes to follow.[45] Theodore Weld also cast himself as an exemplar of the good. "I attend Church with our colored friends," he wrote; "but," he honestly admitted, "I do it to cast my lot with them; and," he contentedly concluded, "tho not spiritually edified, I find joy and peace in it." [46]

It was, however, a far more difficult thing for the same abolitionists to follow through, unhesitatingly and courageously, the implications of their theories, to work unfalteringly and without equivocation, straight on to free the slave and obtain equality for the free Negro. Certainly the abolitionists were almost universally too forthright and too dedicated to be faithless to their ideals; certainly they did not knowingly forsake their plighted word. Still it was a constant fact of the antislavery crusade that it was clearly marked by the constant temporizing of its participants.[47] In Ohio, some Lane students objected when one of their number took up residence with Cincinnati Negro families while he was working among them because they thought it would be harmful to their project.[48] Throughout the North antislavery societies debated the questions "Ought abolitionists to encourage colored persons in joining Anti-Slavery Societies?" or "Is it expedient for Abolitionists to encourage social intercourse between white and colored families?" And their composite response was at best an equivocal "perhaps." [49]

This political temporizing was not, of course, without its reasons, particularly in the light of mobs and physical violence provoked by extremists. Some abolitionists, of course, merely thought of public relations and how best to draw support to the cause. Birney, for his part, thought it enough to strive for equal civil rights without, at the same time, trying for social equality. Too much too soon, he argued, would mean a denial of all rights to the Negro.[50] So too the American Anti-Slavery Society, after the serious antiabolitionist riots in New York in 1834, rejected charges that they supported amalgamation or

[44] From a story in the Juvenile Department, signed "H. Sabbath School Treasury," *Liberator*, Jan. 14, 1832. The Juvenile column was a regular feature in the early years of the *Liberator*. Henry C. Wright was designated American Anti-Slavery Society agent to children.

[45] Garrison, *Garrison*, I, 427.

[46] Weld to Sarah and Angelina Grimké, Dec. 15 [1837], in *Weld-Grimké Letters*, I, 496. A similar viewpoint turns up in Unitarian observations quite frequently as a rejection of emotional-evangelical enthusiasms.

[47] In a letter to Lewis Tappan, Weld, for example, wrote concerning a slave case in Connecticut that "not one of the Abolitionists here [in Hartford] was willing to appear *openly* in the matter as the friend of the compla[i]nant. Brother Tyler and myself who are the only persons known publickly in the case as friends of the compla[i]nant, have been and are still plentifully threatened with mob vengeance." June 8, 1837, *Weld-Grimké Letters*, I, 399.

[48] *Liberator*, Jan. 10, 1835.

[49] From Litwack, *North of Slavery*, p. 218.

[50] Birney to Weld, July 26, 1834, *Weld-Grimké Letters*, I, 163.

attacked the Constitution. "We disclaim, and entirely disapprove," they asserted, "the language of a hand-bill recently circulated in this City the tendency of which is thought to be to excite resistance to the Laws. Our principle is, that even hard laws are to be submitted to by all men, until they can by peaceable means be altered." [51]

The abolitionists were painfully aware of their actions, yet in good conscience they believed that their course was the better part of wisdom and thus did not compromise their valor. Arthur Tappan for one was so fearful lest his earlier activities be misconstrued that he assured A. F. Stoddard of Glasgow in 1863 that "if . . . you should know of any one's charging me with any gross assault on the fastidiousness of the age, when I became the avowed friend of the colored man, you may set it down to the score of ignorance or malignant falsehood." [52] But Sarah Forten, member of the actively antislavery Negro family of Philadelphia, understood. "How much of this leaven still lingers in the hearts of our white brethren and sisters is oftentimes made manifest to us," she wrote, referring specifically to an abolitionist who was comfortable with Negroes only under cover of night; "but when we recollect what great sacrifices to public sentiment they are called upon to make," she generously added, "we cannot wholly blame them." [53]

Briefly, then, the antislavery movement was beset, throughout its history, by a fundamental ambivalence. Never could the abolitionists decide collectively, and infrequently individually, whether the Negro was equal or inferior to the white; whether social equality for the Negro should be stressed or whether it should be damped; whether civil and social rights should be granted him at once or only in the indefinite and provisional future; whether, in fact, social and civil rights should be granted or whether only civil rights should be given him. The abolitionists, furthermore, were torn between a genuine concern for the welfare and uplift of the Negro and a paternalism which was too often merely the patronizing of a superior class. And their forthright concern for the Negro was still more qualified by an unhappy degree of temporizing.

These are the hallmarks of a critical and fundamental ambivalence. When such a quandary existed over the position and treatment of the free Negro and over the very nature of the beings to be freed, abolitionist temporizing becomes understandable. When immediate emancipation as a plan of abolition was translated to mean only immediate repentance of the sin of slavery, the needs of the human beings who were slaves were ignored. The abolitionists had sought solace in abstractions about humanity. And their hesitancy and confusion about the question of race illuminate much of the contention and indecision within the antislavery movement—a movement baffled and torn by ambivalence.

[51] *Liberator*, July 19, 1834.
[52] Arthur Tappan to A. F. Stoddard, Aug. 27, 1863, in Tappan, *Tappan*, pp. 201–2.
[53] Sarah Forten to Angelina Grimké, Apr. 15, 1837, *Weld-Grimké Letters*, I, 380.

Howard H. Bell

NATIONAL NEGRO CONVENTIONS OF THE MIDDLE 1840'S: MORAL SUASION VS. POLITICAL ACTION

Between 1830 and 1835 Negro leaders held annual conventions to protest against conditions oppressing the race. Excluded from the inner councils of the antislavery societies, they revived the convention movement during the middle forties. At the same time they were still ideologically involved in the mainstream of abolitionism. When the American Antislavery Society split in 1839–1840 over philosophical and tactical issues, the Negro members were found on both sides. Howard H. Bell analyzes the divergent Negro views on this matter. He also describes the many other proposals for racial advancement—ranging from cultivation of the middle-class virtues to the advocacy of slave insurrection—made at the conventions, and introduces the reader to many of the prominent Negro protest leaders of the ante-bellum generation.

B<small>Y</small> 1840 militant abolitionism was a way of life widely accepted by many people in the North. To that date those championing moral persuasion as the best means of abolishing slavery had been the dominant group. But with the advent of the Liberty Party many turned to political action as more effective in accomplishing that end. By 1843 many Negro leaders, especially in the areas outside of New England, were ardent admirers of the new party since it offered an opportunity for a type of action which had previously been denied them. It was therefore to be expected that national conventions meeting in upstate New York during the middle 'forties would be influenced by Liberty Party ideals.

Howard H. Bell, "National Negro Conventions of the Middle 1840's: Moral Suasion vs. Political Action," *Journal of Negro History,* XLII (October, 1957), pp. 247–60. Reprinted with permission of *Journal of Negro History.*

The annual national conventions which had been carried on for six consecutive years during the early 'thirties had died out when New York and Philadelphia began championing different ways of meeting the problems facing the Negro in the United States. By the end of that decade, however, there was a demand for a revival of the national conventions.[1] In the autumn of 1841 a number of men from Philadelphia set their names to a call for such an assembly. Among the items on the agenda were issues such as temperance, education, economy, agricultural and mechanical trades, and the development of a manual labor school. A new and previously unpopular feature was the consideration of petitioning for a grant of land from Congress for agricultural and other purposes for the use of the Negro.[2] Not content with petitioning for a grant of land, the subject of emigration was also listed for discussion.[3] To say the least the proposed assembly was set to deal with an ambitious schedule and one that might be expected to draw the fire of some abolitionists, especially those opposed to separate Negro organizations and to emigration.

One of the leading abolitionist journals asked God's blessing upon the new enterprise;[4] another was open in its criticism of the proposed convention and carried also in its columns the disapproval of at least two Negro newspapers.[5] As it turned out, both encouragement and criticism were wasted. Shortly before the proposed gathering, a Negro procession celebrating temperance and British West Indian emancipation was broken up by white boys in the streets of Philadelphia, and a protracted riot ensued. Some attempt was made to show that the proposal for the assembly was responsible for the riot,[6] but there were many other factors contributing to the outbreak. Due to the unsettled conditions following this unfortunate but not unusual affair, it was considered ill-advised to hold the convention, and the plans were dropped.[7]

One might speculate endlessly on what turn history would have taken if the convention had been held. Its agenda was broad enough that, if intelligently handled, it could have resulted in much good. And the men who called the convention were not of the same convictions as were those responsible for the revived national convention in 1843. The call for a national convention in 1843 [8] was the signal for opposition from certain Boston Negroes, who distrusted the politics of the New Yorkers responsible for the invitation.[9] The Bostonians decided, however, to participate in the convention "as a medium through which we may deliberately devise means to operate and cooperate with

[1] The Colored American, September 23, 1837; December 30, 1837; April 12, 1838; April 19, 1838; May 3, 1838.
[2] The Liberator, November 5, 1841.
[3] The Pennsylvania Freeman, December 8, 1841.
[4] The Liberator, November 5, 1841.
[5] National Anti-Slavery Standard, July 28, 1842. The Negro newspapers involved were The Northern Star and Freemen's Advocate and the Journal and Messenger, two of those short-lived publications so characteristic of the era.
[6] Ibid., August 11, 1842.
[7] The Liberator, August 19, 1842.
[8] The Liberator, July 28, 1843; National Anti-Slavery Standard, July 27, 1843.
[9] The Liberator, July 28, 1843.

our white friends, against TWO of the greatest evils ever inflicted upon an innocent and inoffensive people—slavery and prejudice." [10] Negroes of New Bedford, Massachusetts, were not so tractable; they branded the backers of the convention as deserters of the Garrisonian tradition [which they were] and held that a good dose of real anti-slavery teaching of the old tradition was the only cure for the world's evils.[11]

Despite opposition, the convention assembled on August 15, 1843, at Buffalo, New York. Thirty of the delegates were from the Mohawk River area, five from Michigan, three from the New York metropolitan section, two from Massachusetts, two from Connecticut, and eight from Ohio. In addition, several states were represented by one person each.[12] The tone of the convention was set by a speech from the president *pro tem*, Samuel H. Davis, of Buffalo. He hailed the Constitution of the United States as a document guaranteeing freedom and equality to all citizens.[13] But Davis was not fully supported on this issue,[14] perhaps because those dictating policy were willing to let the constitutional question lie quiescent in the interest of pushing the matter of alignment with the Liberty Party.[15] Nor was Davis himself interested in putting all his faith in the Constitution. Before he had finished, he had hinted at military action by an oppressed people. His speech was aggressive enough to pave the way for any radical action the delegates might choose to take.

Like most of the others of the period the convention was interested in encouragement of accepted patterns of self-improvement—temperance, moral reform, support of mechanical trades and of antislavery.[16] The members spent some time on plans for the establishment of a national Negro press [17] and stressed the development of a frontier agricultural community. But education was neglected "until it was too late for a committee to report upon it, and do the subject justice, as was intended." [18] All of these subjects could be handled with a reasonable degree of unanimity and equanimity, but the more controversial problems were hotly debated.

It was a foregone conclusion that some attempt would be made to pay homage to the new religion of political affiliation (chiefly the Liberty Party);

[10] *Ibid.*, August 4, 1843.

[11] *National Anti-Slavery Standard*, September 7, 1843.

[12] National Negro Convention, 1843, *Minutes of the National Convention of Colored Citizens: Held at Buffalo, on the 15th, 16th, 17th, 18th and 19th of August, 1843, For the Purpose of Considering Their Moral and Political Condition as American Citizens* (New York: Piercy and Reed, printers, 1843), p. 10.

[13] *Ibid.*, p. 4.

[14] *Ibid.*, pp. 16–17, 24.

[15] The Liberty Party was founded in 1840 by abolitionists who believed in political action. Its concentration on antislavery, however, was not conducive to attracting a large following. During the years that the party remained active (1840–1848) it usually played into the hands of its worst enemies, the slave-holders. Nevertheless, it attracted many idealists and was especially appealing to Negroes because of its antislavery ideals.

[16] *National Negro Convention*, 1843, pp. 15–16.

[17] *Ibid.*, pp. 27–30.

[18] *Ibid.*, p. 21, footnote.

but when such a resolution was proposed, Frederick Douglass and Charles L. Remond, both moral suasionists at the time, leaped to spearhead the opposition. Of the two men, Remond had already attained a certain degree of prominence as an antislavery speaker in the Garrisonian tradition, while Douglass, later to become the greatest Negro orator and leader of the antebellum era, was but a few years removed from slavery. Chief supporters of the resolution were listed as Henry H. Garnet, William C. Munro, J. N. Gloucester, Theodore S. Wright, David Lewis, and Charles B. Ray. These men, with the possible exception of Lewis, were ministers, and all lived in the area of the Hudson River or west as far as Ohio and Michigan. They were, therefore, more inclined to the beliefs of western abolitionists than to those of the Garrisonians. Party affiliation, to the Garrisonians, meant affiliation with corruption; they contended, moreover, that it was unwise to tie the abolitionists to any one party. But few at the convention were of like belief, and the Liberty Party received the sanction of the assembly with but seven dissenting votes.[19] Not content with this victory, Liberty Party adherents revived the subject later in the convention and pronounced a second blessing upon the political party which stood for allowing the vote to all free men, regardless of color.[20]

As is evident, a large majority of the delegates at the Buffalo National Convention stood for radical political action, if measured by the Garrisonian standard. The scales, however, were more evenly balanced when it came to the consideration of endorsement of physical violence in the overthrow of slavery. Resort to such means had been much in the minds of the more aggressive Negroes for several years. Samuel E. Cornish had felt called upon in 1838 to criticize an ardent young man who had considered the matter favorably in a public speech.[21] Somewhat later a convention of Maine and New Hampshire Negroes had refused to condemn those who resorted to bloodshed for the sake of freedom.[22] It is not surprising, then, that Samuel H. Davis, when opening the Buffalo National Convention in 1843, should have hinted at using other than peaceful means to obtain rights long overdue, or that Henry Highland Garnet—spectacular, persuasive, and appealing—should have prepared an address to the slaves which he sought to have the convention sanction.

The speech was so effectively presented that he had his audience laughing or crying, almost at will.[23] In fact, one enthusiastic reporter went so far as to contend that Garnet had so swayed the audience that "for one hour of his life his [the reporter's] mind had not been his own, but wholly at the control of the eloquent negro." [24] This address, suppressed by the narrow margin of one

[19] *Ibid.*, pp. 15–16.

[20] *Ibid.*, pp. 21–22.

[21] *The Colored American*, March 3, 1838.

[22] Negro State Convention, Maine and New Hampshire, 1841, *Minutes of the First Colored Convention, Held in the City of Portland, October 6–[9], 1841* (Portland, [Maine]: 1842), p. 7.

[23] *Buffalo Commercial Advertiser*, August 23, 1843. Title varies.

[24] *Emancipator*, October 12, 1843. Title varies, as do the organizations sponsoring the paper.

vote, was not printed until five years later, and then, admittedly, with some modifications, "retaining, however, all of its original doctrine." [25] Much of the address, as printed, is plain antislavery argument. But directed to the slaves as it was, it might have been expected to attract more attention than it otherwise would. Add to this the championship of physical violence in securing freedom,[26] and it is easy to understand why the address could set off such a furor as it did on the convention floor.

Having worked up slowly to the subject of violence, Garnet suggested that the slaves go to their masters and demand their freedom, then refuse to work if that freedom were denied.

> If they then commence the work of death, they and not you, will be responsible for the consequences. You had better all die, *die immediately*, than live slaves, and entail your wretchedness upon your posterity.... However much you and all of us may desire it there is not much hope of Redemption without the shedding of blood. If you must bleed, let it all come at once—rather *die freemen than live to be slaves*.[27]

Although the printed version has some moderating passages at the close, indicating that the speaker did not advocate an insurrection, the slaves were, even there, reminded that they were three million in number, and that resistance should be the motto.[28]

Despite the growing radicalism of the age, the preponderance of Liberty Party sympathizers in the assembly, and the eloquence of the speaker, the convention was not ready to assume the responsibility for such a message. It was turned over to a revision committee consisting of Garnet, Douglass, A. M. Sumner, S. N. [probably S. H.] Davis, and R. Banks.[29] With the exception of Douglass, these men were all from the area west of the Hudson River, and it is probable that not too much revision was made in the text. When the document was once more before the assembly, it was rejected but with the bare majority of one vote.[30] The episode was enlivened by the sardonic remark of Charles L. Remond to Charles B. Ray "not to try to sit on two stools," when Ray asked that his vote be added in support of the address after he had with-

---

[25] Henry Highland Garnet, *An Address to the Slaves of the United States of America (Rejected by the National Convention of 1843)*, as printed in David Walker's *Walker's Appeal, in Four Articles, Together with a Preamble, to the Colored Citizens of the World, but in Particular, and Very Expressly to Those of the United States of America. Written in Boston, in the State of Massachusetts, Sept[ember] 28, 1829* (2nd ed., with corrections, etc.; [n.p.], 1830), p. 89. In this case Garnet's *Address* was merely added to Walker's *Appeal*, using consecutive pagination, or both articles were printed together in 1848, using the 1830 edition of the *Appeal*.

[26] *Ibid.*, p. 93.

[27] *Ibid.*, p. 94.

[28] *Ibid.*, p. 96.

[29] *National Negro Convention, 1843*, pp. 12–14.

[30] *Ibid.*, pp. 17–19.

held his ballot on the first round.[31] It was not until public opinion had come around to a more aggressive attitude in 1848 that the address received the support of the free Negro community.

The Garrisonian press was bitterly opposed both to the Liberty Party tendencies of the convention and to Garnet's speech. Maria Weston Chapman, ardent Anti-Slavery Society worker, and sometimes relief editor for Garrison on *The Liberator*, was glad to see that the convention had had the good sense to reject the address. She felt that Garnet must have fallen under evil advisers, and she hoped the speech was for effect, rather than in demonstration of Garnet's real attitude. In commenting upon the current tendency to resort to ballots, she held that such action might easily lead to an exchange of bullets.[32] And at least one Negro newspaper was reported to be in accord with Mrs. Chapman's views concerning the Liberty Party.[33] But Garnet showed his readiness to defend himself against all comers when he wrote, "If it has come to this, that I must think and act as you do, because you are an abolitionist, or be exterminated by your thunder, then I do not hesitate to say that your abolitionism is abject slavery." [34] There was little in 1843 which would identify the national convention with those of the early 'thirties. Instead of serious consideration of emigration to Canada, this convention came within a trifle of advocating an insurrection of slaves. Instead of spending extensive time on a plan for a Negro college, it demanded emphatically that Negroes refrain from worshiping in churches where absolute equality was not allowed. Instead of timidly asserting that the Negro should have equality in the suffrage but admitting that there was not much to be done about it, the convention listened respectfully to a proposition for violence if equality were not forthcoming.

Here for the first time the moral suasionists, representing the old order, met in national convention with men who championed the newer confidence in political action as the means by which the salvation of all the people was to be accomplished. Though seriously outnumbered, the moral suasionists were not without modifying influence. The presence of Frederick Douglass and Charles L. Remond, along with a few others, was probably responsible for the rejection of Garnet's address to the slaves. Moreover, the two groups found that they had something in common in hatred of prejudice within the churches. And if Douglass and Remond in 1843 could not stem the tide of the Liberty Party in the West, they could at least hold up the avalanche long enough to make their opponents argue their cause and thus work for the enlightenment of the public.

As the delegates parted to go to their homes, some of them carried with them plans for state conventions which, it was expected, would advance the cause of the Negro. In other cases state conventions had been proposed before

[31] *The Liberator*, September 8, 1843.
[32] *Ibid.*, September 22, 1843.
[33] *Ibid.*, September 29, 1843.
[34] *Ibid.*, December 8, 1843.

the national assembly had gathered. Indiana Negroes issued a call for a state assembly to convene at Indianapolis on September 4, 1843,[35] while to the east in Ohio plans had been set on foot as early as March for such a convention at Columbus.[36] Michigan [37] and New York [38] both held state gatherings shortly after the Buffalo National Convention, and it seems more than probable that Connecticut, and the coalition of Maine and New Hampshire were doing the same.

In 1847 upstate New York leaders once more urged the necessity of a national convention. Scheduled at first for mid-August,[39] the time of meeting was later extended to October. An examination of the list of delegates who gathered at Troy, New York, on October 6, 1847, reveals a surprising number from the state of New York (forty-six of a total of sixty-six). Of the rest, Massachusetts sent fourteen and Connecticut two, while single delegates were present from scattered states.[40] Connecticut was represented by two able ministers, Amos G. Beman, who had encouraged Negro state convention activities in his state for a decade, and J. W. C. Pennington, who had helped in getting the national convention organized in the early 'thirties. Massachusetts sent Frederick Douglass, Leonard Grimes, Boston minister, and William Wells Brown who was soon to attain some prominence as the first Negro novelist and historian. New York City commanded the services of James McCune Smith; Thomas Van Rensselaer, editor of The Ram's Horn, a new Negro newspaper; and Alexander Crummell, known chiefly for his interest in, and affiliation with, Liberia.[41] The brilliant and showy but somewhat erratic Henry Highland Garnet was, as usual, the chief spokesman for the upstate third party men.

The idea of a national press which had been considered favorably in 1843 was revived and debated at length [42] and eventually decided in the affirmative. A separate manual labor college for the Negro was also considered favorably by the majority of those present.[43] But the subject of temperance, assigned to two ministers and an editor for recommendations, was side-stepped by the suggestion from these gentlemen that the matter be turned over to the tem-

[35] The Philanthropist, August 16, 1843. No record of this convention found.
[36] Ibid., March 29, 1843. No record of this convention found.
[37] Negro State Convention, Michigan, 1843, Minutes of the State Convention of the Colored Citizens of the State of Michigan, Held in the City of Detroit, on the 26th & 27th of October, 1843, for the Purpose of Considering Their Moral & Political Condition as Citizens of the State (Detroit: Printed by William Harsha, 1843), p. 4.
[38] National Anti-Slavery Standard, October 17, 1844.
[39] The Liberator, July 23, 1847.
[40] National Negro Convention, 1847, Proceedings of the National Convention of Colored People, and Their Friends, held in Troy, N[ew] Y[ork] on 6th, 7th, 8th, and 9th October, 1847 (Troy, N[ew] Y[ork]: J. C. Kneeland & C[ompany], 1847), p. 3.
[41] Ibid., pp. 8–9.
[42] Ibid., pp. 6–9; The North Star, January 14, 1848. (This paper was founded and edited by Frederick Douglass; the name was later changed to Frederick Douglass' Paper); The Liberator, November 19, 1847.
[43] The North Star, December 3, 1847; National Negro Convention, 1847, pp. 9–11; The Liberator, November 19, 1847.

perance convention to meet at Great Barrington, Massachusetts, almost a year hence.[44]

The committee appointed to express the sentiments of the convention on matters of freedom and slavery was headed by Frederick Douglass. Other members included Thomas Van Rensselaer, John Lyle, R. D. Kenny, and Alexander Crummell. Their report was moral suasionist in tone and incurred the criticism of Garnet who took exception to such terms as "sanctity of religion," when used in the sense of protecting slavery. As a minister, he felt that religion was being blamed too much when it was represented as supporting slavery. It was for this reason that he urged the qualifying phrase, "falsely so called," to identify the brand of religion meant. He also took exception to sole reliance on moral suasion as a means of securing freedom for the slave. He contended that political action should be added as a legitimate means of securing the end in view.

It seems that the attack by Garnet and others was successful, and the report was canceled. Later it was reconsidered and placed in the hands of a new committee, of which Douglass and Garnet were both members.[45] When the report once more appeared, there was no reference to the term "moral suasion"; it was, nevertheless, a decidedly moral suasionist document. It abounded with such declarations as "the best means of abolishing slavery is the proclamation of the truth, and the best means of destroying caste is the mental, moral and industrial improvement of our people." And again,

> Liberty is always sufficient to grapple with tyranny. Free speech—
> free discussion—peaceful agitation—the foolishness of preaching—
> these, under God, will subvert this giant crime, and send it reeling to
> its grave, as if smitten by a voice from the throne of God.[46]

This victory for moral suasionist doctrines at the Troy National Convention—a convention with a strong bent toward radical action—showed Frederick Douglass at his best as a champion of Garrisonian doctrines before he had come under the influence of the western abolitionists of the Gerrit Smith school of thought. Douglass was only then preparing to leave the East and to establish himself at some point in the area of the Great Lakes. It was Douglass who headed the first committee which brought in a report highly moral suasionist in tone. It was Douglass who defended it and when the report had been rejected, Douglass was appointed as one of the members of the new committee. Garnet, as chief spokesman for the opposition group, and thereby a representative of the majority of the delegates attending the convention, was unable to command more than the hollow appearance of victory in the elimination of such specific terms as "moral suasion," and in the softening of the attack on the church—an attack which had become a favorite sport of the Garrisonians.

[44] National Negro Convention, 1847, p. 11.
[45] Ibid., pp. 13–15.
[46] Ibid., pp. 31–32.

There remains Garnet's triumph—the renewed address to the slaves, first delivered in 1843 at the Buffalo National Convention, and suppressed by that body. In describing Garnet's speech, William C. Nell, strong and loyal Garrisonian and opponent of physical force, incorporated much into the statement: "To those acquainted with his talent and eloquence, it will be unnecessary to mention that the address produced much sensation." [47] Reaction was not so intense as it had been four years earlier, partly because public opinion had moved rapidly toward accepting a more aggressive attitude in the intervening years. Moreover, Douglass's encouragement of the use of education and propaganda had its influence in softening the effect of Garnet's militancy.[48]

In the field of agriculture, various communal experiments on the American frontier were common, and some were to be found in the older settled communities. Emphasis was placed upon going to the farm as a kind of panacea for the ills of society. It was to be expected, then, that this attitude would be reflected in the Negro conventions of the period. In 1843 an able committee headed by Charles B. Ray presented a convincing address on the merits of an agricultural life. Possession of the soil was represented as giving an independence not easily attainable elsewhere. This committee was well informed. They had a report from a group in Mercer County, Ohio, who had refused to come to the convention but who were happy and reasonably prosperous on the farms which they had taken up only six years earlier.

In keeping with the communal experimentation of the times, it was recommended that agricultural communities be built up by banding together in units of about twenty family groups. These families were to settle on adjacent land, cooperate on matters of common interest such as schools, churches, roads, flour and saw mills, and share in any profits from such ventures —according to the amount of individual investment. A gesture toward erasure of the color line, or at least toward avoiding the accusation of planning a segregated community, was made by the provision that a few carefully selected white families might be accepted in the organization.[49]

When the convention met at Troy four years later the subject of agriculture was handled in much the same manner, except that Gerrit Smith, philanthropist, humanitarian, and dabbler in practically every phase of the reform movement, had meantime made land in New York available for the asking. His generosity had placed 140,000 acres of land at the disposal of some 3,000 Negroes, and in so doing had made many of them eligible for the suffrage for the first time.[50] This was enough to divert the interest of the New Yorkers from such a communal frontier settlement as had been proposed in 1843. The new landholders were anxious to do something to show their appreciation to their benefactor, but Douglass and Garnet agreed that they could best accomplish that end by moving onto the land and improving it.[51]

[47] The North Star, December 3, 1847.
[48] The Liberator, November 19, 1847.
[49] National Negro Convention, 1843, pp. 30–36.
[50] National Negro Convention, 1847, pp. 25–30.
[51] Ibid., p. 13.

The matter of a national press received favorable attention in the middle 'forties. Negroes had long been aware of the urgency for an organ which would be devoted entirely to the uplift of the race. *Freedom's Journal* and *The Rights of All* had attempted in the late 'twenties to fulfill such a need. *The Liberator* had served in that capacity in the early 'thirties. But as Garrison began to embrace other reforms or fads, the Negro once more sought an organ which he could call his own. To this end Philip A. Bell of New York started an ephemeral newspaper called *The Struggler*, to be followed in January, 1837, by *The Weekly Advocate*. This paper, after some reorganization, became *The Colored American*, and for several years was the chief organ of the colored people. With the opening of the decade of the 'forties, however, there were several struggling papers, and not one was receiving adequate support. It needed no prophet to foretell that all were likely to fail and that the cause of the Negro would suffer accordingly. This was one of the problems which faced the Buffalo National Convention in 1843.[52]

A committee appointed to deal with the subject held that a press could be used to build up or to tear down; that it could, if properly used, act as an agency for enlightenment and for getting acquainted; and that it could be utilized as an aid in the building of character. They recommended that a national press be established, either by the creation of a new weekly newspaper or by the support of one already set up.[53] This recommendation was followed by official action in the appointment of able men—Philip A. Bell, Samuel E. Cornish, Charles B. Ray, Amos G. Beman, Theodore S. Wright, and others— to look into the possibilities for establishing such an organ.[54] Most, if not all, of this group were experienced in the editorial field, but if they were successful in organizing a national publication it has not come to light.

Four years later at Troy the subject was again up for discussion. Again there were several Negro publications, and more in the planning stage.[55] Again a committee reported in favor of a national press. This time it was James McCune Smith, once associated with Samuel E. Cornish in editing *The Colored American*, who led the drive for such a publication.[56] Thomas Van Rensselaer had recently set up *The Ram's Horn*, and Frederick Douglass was soon to establish *The North Star*; both men were opposed to the national press. It was Douglass's opinion that such an arrangement would soon result in its being the press of a clique, rather than that of the Negro public.[57]

Opponents of the scheme, including Douglass and Van Rensselaer, came in for some of Garnet's witty sarcasm when that gentleman pointed out that those indisposed were chiefly in the newspaper business, or about to go into it. "Of course," he opined, "there was nothing of selfishness in all this." [58]

[52] *The Liberator*, July 28, 1843; *National Anti-Slavery Standard*, July 27, 1843.
[53] *National Negro Convention*, 1843, pp. 27–30.
[54] *Ibid.*, p. 25.
[55] *National Negro Convention*, 1847, pp. 6–7.
[56] *The North Star*, January 14, 1848.
[57] *National Negro Convention*, 1847, pp. 6–8.
[58] *Ibid.*, p. 6.

But self-interest, it seems, may have colored Garnet's own reaction in favor of the press. Douglass, writing three months later, implied that there had been some thought of appointing a foreign agent to go to England to raise funds for the project.[59] But Garnet, if he was angling for such an appointment from the convention, was unsuccessful. He was awarded the place of home agent.[60]

When the vote was finally taken, less than one-fourth of those casting their ballots were opposed to the press.[61] Of the twenty from New York who voted, sixteen were in favor; of the four opposed, at least one, if not two, was involved in a current newspaper project. The total New York vote, however, was less than half of those recorded as delegates, and among those not voting were such men as William H. Topp, Albany businessman, Charles B. Ray, and Stephen Myers, Albany editor. Nine of the fourteen delegates from Massachusetts voted for the national press. Of the three who refrained from voting, Douglass was about ready to establish his own publication; Nathan Johnson was in the chair; and William Wells Brown was a loyal Garrisonian and therefore opposed to "complexional projects" of any kind. Only two from Massachusetts, William C. Nell and Charles Weeden, voted against the proposition.[62] With the vote of Massachusetts running so favorably for a Negro press, it might appear that the Garrisonian hold was not so strong as it might have been, even in the home state.

When the Cleveland National Convention met in the following year (September 6, 1848) there seem to have been but few present who had been at Troy. In the meantime, Frederick Douglass had established his *The North Star* at Rochester, New York, and it had surged rapidly to front rank among Negro publications. Furthermore, Douglass was present at the convention. And finally, the interest of the assembly was geared to the coming elections. Under these circumstances the press was dealt with effectively but perfunctorily by declaring that Douglass's publication was serving the need of a national press.[63] Thus at last, by official action but without assuming control, the Negro in convention had an official national press.

The conventions of the middle 'forties represent a definite gain for independent Negro leadership. By 1847 the break in the ranks of Negro abolitionists had been partially healed. By that time two national conventions had been held in which Garrisonian moral suasionists and ballot-minded Liberty Party adherents had worked on the problems facing the Negro and had found that they had much in common. Powerful moral suasionists of the Douglass-Nell variety had done business with the strident Garnet and the impatient Charles B. Ray of Liberty Party sympathies. This encounter demonstrated beyond a reasonable doubt that although the greatest of the giants still lived in the house of Garrison, the sheer force of numbers was slowly winning the argument for greater militancy and more dependence upon the ballot. By 1847

---

[59] *The North Star*, January 14, 1848.
[60] *National Negro Convention*, 1847, p. 9.
[61] *The Liberator*, November 19, 1847.
[62] *National Negro Convention*, 1847, pp. 8–9.
[63] *The North Star*, September 29, 1848.

even the scoffers were forced to admit that the National Negro Convention was once more the most powerful voice in Negro affairs—a voice that had a militant ring which was absent from the deliberations of the 'thirties, a voice commanding the confidence of the Negro masses and the respect of all men of good will.

Larry Gara

WILLIAM STILL AND THE

UNDERGROUND RAILROAD *

One area of antislavery activity in which Negroes took the lead was Underground Railroad work. In a recent revisionist study entitled The Liberty Line (1961), Larry Gara has discounted the traditional emphasis upon the role of white abolitionists. Most of the fugitive slaves, he points out, escaped from the South on their own, without assistance; and once they arrived in the North they were helped chiefly by free Negroes, who in many cities organized vigilance committees to assist the fugitives. One of the most noted of the northern Negro Underground Railroad agents was William Still, secretary of the Philadelphia Vigilance Committee. Gara's account of Still is illustrative of the activities of the northern vigilance committees.

THE writer of a popular account of the underground railroad in Pennsylvania stated in his preface that "it required the manhood of a man and the unflinching fortitude of a woman, ... to be an abolitionist in those days, and especially an Underground Railroad agent." [1] He was referring to the noble minority who stood firm when the abolitionists were being "reviled and persecuted" in both the North and the South. Other underground railroad books—some of them written by elderly abolitionists—put similar emphasis on the heroic conductors of the mysterious organization. They reflected the history of the underground railroad from the vantage point of the abolitionist con-

Larry Gara, "William Still and the Underground Railroad," *Pennsylvania History*, XXVIII (January, 1961), pp. 33–44. Reprinted with permission of *Pennsylvania History* and Larry Gara.

* A grant from the Penrose Fund of the American Philosophical Society made it possible to complete the research upon which this article is based. A shorter version was read at the annual meeting of the Pennsylvania Historical Association on October 14, 1960.

[1] Robert C. Smedley, *History of the Underground Railroad in Chester and the Neighboring Counties of Pennsylvania* (Lancaster, Pa., 1883), preface, xv.

ductor. They also contributed to the growth of a favorite American legend, which is as much a part of folklore as of history. Two of the forgotten characters in the popular legend are the Negro members of various vigilance committees and the fugitives themselves. If it required strong character to be an abolitionist, it took even more courage to become a hunted fugitive or one of his colored abettors. William Still's work with the Philadelphia vigilance committee called attention to both of these neglected groups.

William Still's parents were both born slaves, and they left slavery at considerable personal sacrifice: his father purchased his freedom, and his mother, after one unsuccessful attempt to escape, finally ran away with two of her four children. They later farmed a forty-acre plot in the New Jersey pines near Medford. William was born there on October 7, 1821, the youngest of eighteen children. With a bare minimum of formal schooling he continued his own education by extensive reading. When he was twenty he left home, and three years later he moved to Philadelphia. He held a number of jobs before joining the staff of the Pennsylvania Society for Promoting the Abolition of Slavery in the fall of 1847.[2]

Still began working with the abolition society as a combination janitor and mail clerk. After several years, both his duties and his salary were increased. He took a special interest in the society's efforts to assist slaves who had run away from the South. They were often boarded at his home before resuming their journey towards Canada. For fourteen years Still served the society. During that time he worked with such well known anti-slavery advocates as Robert Purvis, who was also colored, Lucretia and James Mott, Sarah Pugh, Thomas Garrett, and J. Miller McKim, who was the agent in charge of the Philadelphia office.[3]

In 1838 Philadelphia abolitionists had organized a vigilance committee to assist fugitives coming into the city. There was some underground railroad activity in the area. Thomas Garrett of Wilmington, the more militant anti-slavery Quakers of Philadelphia and the neighboring counties, and the vigilance committee were primarily responsible for the work. Although there was a semblance of organization to these efforts, much of the aid given the fugitive slaves was on a haphazard basis. By 1852 even the vigilance committee had disintegrated. In December of that year a group of abolitionists reported that the old committee "had become disorganized and scattered" and that for several years its duties "had been performed by individuals on their own responsibility, and sometimes in a very irregular manner," causing "much dissatisfaction and complaint." The group decided to organize a new vigilance committee, with an acting committee of four members, which should have the authority to attend "to every case that might require aid," to raise necessary funds, and "to keep a record of all their doings," and especially of their receipts and ex-

---

[2] James P. Boyd, "William Still: His Life and Work to This Time," in William Still, *Still's Underground Rail Road Records* (3rd ed., Phila., 1883), iii–xvii. The title page varied somewhat in each edition of Still's book, but the pagination of the text remained the same.

[3] Boyd, "Still," in Still, *Underground Rail Road*, xviii.

penditures. They appointed William Still chairman of the acting committee.[4]

One of the principal activities of the new Philadelphia vigilance committee was to extend financial aid to fugitives. The committee provided money to board fugitives with families of free Negroes, sometimes for as long as thirteen days but usually for only a few days. As a Negro, William Still easily gained the confidence of the new arrivals and knew where to find them board and lodging among the colored population of Philadelphia. The committee also purchased clothing, medicine, and the fugitives' railroad fares to Canada. It advertised anti-slavery meetings in the newspapers and on one occasion spent twenty dollars for handbills and other expenses of a meeting. Mostly, the committee spent money in small amounts; very few items in its financial reports involved more than five dollars.[5]

At times William Still and other members of the acting vigilance committee were very busy with their labor on behalf of the fugitives. Late in 1857 J. Miller McKim wrote another abolitionist, "Other rail-roads are in a declining condition and have stopped their semi annual dividends, but the Underground has never before done so flourishing a business." He further reported, "Exactly fifty—men, women and children—have passed through the hands of our Vigilance Committee in the last fortnight." [6] It was a dramatic time and a most unusual amount of work for the vigilance committee. According to the committee's journal it assisted approximately 495 fugitives between December, 1852, and February, 1857. In his later published account, covering eight years of vigilance committee activity, Still listed approximately eight hundred fugitives, including sixty children, who had received aid from the committee.[7]

Although a great deal of William Still's work was of such a routine nature as answering correspondence or meeting new arrivals at the railroad station, he had some moments of high adventure too. One arrival from the South, who had purchased his freedom, contacted Still for information about his family. Upon investigation he proved to be Still's own brother, left in slavery forty years earlier when his mother fled to the North. Still also witnessed the arrival of the famous Henry "Box" Brown, who had literally had himself crated and sent north via the Adams' Express Company, and of the clever William and Ellen Craft. The Crafts had traveled all the way from Georgia with the nearly-white Ellen disguised as an ailing planter and William playing the part of the faithful servant. Still observed a number of other unusual and interesting cases, though none got the public attention given to Henry "Box" Brown and the Crafts.[8]

[4] Still, *Underground Rail Road*, 611–12.

[5] Journal of the Philadelphia Vigilance Committee, 1852–1857, in the Historical Society of Pennsylvania.

[6] J. Miller McKim to Mrs. M. W. Chapman, November 19, 1857, in the Weston Papers in the Boston Public Library. McKim's letter was published in the 1858 edition of the *Liberty Bell*.

[7] Journal of the Philadelphia Vigilance Committee; Still, *Underground Rail Road*, passim.

[8] Lucretia Mott to Joseph and Ruth Dugdale, March 28, 1849, in the Lucretia Mott MSS in the Friends Historical Library of Swarthmore College; Still, *Underground Rail Road*, 81–86, 368–377.

One of William Still's duties was to ask the newly arrived slaves their names, the names of their masters and where they had come from, and to question them about their escape experiences and the severity of their servitude. In part the interrogation was meant to protect the vigilance committee from the imposters who not infrequently found the abolitionists easy prey for a handout. Still not only recorded the data but carefully preserved the records. In his book he wrote that he had kept the documents for possible use in helping to reunite relatives and friends.[9] In 1884 he told a meeting of aged abolitionists that he had kept them because they were interesting, and because his family had been connected with the underground railroad.[10] Possibly, too, the records were a protection for him in case any of the Philadelphia abolitionists had requested a detailed accounting of Still's work for the anti-slavery society. To Still the vigilance committee was synonymous with the underground railroad. In 1893 he informed historian Wilbur H. Siebert that his "were the only records that were kept of the U.G.R.R.," and that when he collected them he had never dreamed that they could be published in his lifetime.[11]

Still's voluminous record books were a rich source of indisputable evidence had the government been inclined to invoke the Fugitive Slave Law against him or the vigilance committee. He hid the records after the Harpers Ferry fiasco and for a while they were stored in the loft of the Lebanon Cemetery building.[12] In a number of instances he faced possible prosecution. It was Still and others at the anti-slavery office who had warned the Negroes of Christiana that warrants were out for two slaves hiding there. The slave hunt resulted in a mob scene in which the slaves' master was murdered and his nephew seriously wounded. Several abolitionists and thirty-four Negroes were indicted for treason but none were convicted.[13] Still was not indicted with the Christiana rioters but the government brought charges against him for helping to entice Jane Johnson away from her master, Colonel John H. Wheeler, the American minister to Nicaragua. Still was acquitted, but two of five other Negroes indicted were sentenced to a week in jail on a charge of assault and battery, and Passmore Williamson, a Philadelphia Quaker, spent three months in jail for contempt of court.[14] John Brown had confided his plans to William Still six months before his raid on Harpers Ferry and a memorandum found among the papers of Brown's lieutenant, John Henry Kagi, seemed to implicate Still in the scheme.[15] In all these cases Still avoided punishment, but

[9] Still, *Underground Rail Road*, preface; Boyd, "Still," in Still, *Underground Rail Road*, xxxiv.

[10] *Commemoration of the Fiftieth Anniversary of the Organization of the American Anti-Slavery Society, in Philadelphia* (Philadelphia, 1884), 39–40.

[11] William Still to Wilbur H. Siebert, November 18, 1893, in scrapbook "The Underground Railroad in Pennsylvania, vol. 3," in the Wilbur H. Siebert Papers in the Ohio Historical Society.

[12] Boyd, "Still," in Still, *Underground Rail Road*, xxiii, xxxiv.

[13] Still, *Underground Rail Road*, 348–368.

[14] Still, *Underground Rail Road*, 86–95.

[15] Boyd, "Still," in Still, *Underground Rail Road*, xxii–xxiv.

when a woman sued him for libel in 1860 he was not so fortunate.

The woman, a Mrs. Ellen Wells, who was a former slave from St. Louis, was traveling throughout the country raising money to purchase her mother, her children, and several other relatives from slavery. She stayed at William Still's rooming house in Philadelphia, but he did not encourage her project. When a Boston abolitionist wrote for information about Ellen Wells, Still answered that she was an imposter and a prostitute. The letter fell into Mrs. Wells' hands and she sued Still for scandalous and malicious libel. He pleaded guilty to having written the letter and the court sentenced him to ten days in jail and fined him a hundred dollars. Boston abolitionists supported Still and paid the fine from the treasury of the Massachusetts Anti-Slavery Society.[16]

A year later, with the Civil War in progress, Still resigned his position with the Pennsylvania Anti-Slavery Society.[17] He had already ventured into some real estate transactions, and he then bought and managed first a store and later a very successful retail coal business. In 1872 he published *The Underground Rail Road*. The book was another of William Still's contributions to the progress of his race. His work with the fugitive slaves had impressed upon him the need for Negroes to take the initiative to improve their condition. In August of 1860 he told a Negro audience at Kennett Square celebrating the anniversary of West Indian emancipation, "The hundreds of heroic fugitives who yearly throw off their yokes, ... seem to cry aloud in our ears—'Hereditary bondmen! know ye not who would be free themselves must strike the blow?' "[18]

In 1855 William Still had visited the former slaves who had settled in Canada, and he later wrote a strong defense of their conduct and achievements, answering those who maintained that slaves could not meet the responsibilities of free citizens. In 1859 he initiated a successful eight-year campaign to secure equal service for Negroes in the Philadelphia streetcars. In 1861 he helped organize an association for the purpose of collecting and disseminating accurate information about the American Negro population in order to improve its position.[19] These and many other activities stemmed from Still's determination to help improve the status of the colored people.[20] So did his book. He wanted to make the underground railroad "a monument to the heroism of the bondmen under the yoke." Their "heroism and desperate struggles," said Still, as well as "the terrible oppression that they were under, should be kept green in the memory of this and coming generations." He also believed that books written

[16] J. Miller McKim to R. S. Webb, June 23, 1860, and Samuel May, Jr., to McKim, May 23, 1860, in the Garrison Papers in the Boston Public Library; New York *National Anti-Slavery Standard*, April 28, May 5, 1860.

[17] Boyd, "Still," in Still, *Underground Rail Road*, xxx.

[18] New York *National Anti-Slavery Standard*, August 18, 1860.

[19] Boyd, "Still," in Still, *Underground Rail Road*, xxv–xxviii, li–lvii; Harrod G. Villard, "Wiliam Still," in the *Dictionary of American Biography*, 18:23.

[20] For Still's other activities see Alberta S. Norwood, "Negro Welfare Work in Philadelphia, Especially as Illustrated by the Career of William Still, 1775–1930," unpublished thesis in the Library of the University of Pennsylvania (1931).

by Negroes would prove their mental ability and provide an effective answer to those who argued that the colored people were inferior. "We very much need works on various topics from the pens of colored men to represent the race intellectually," he wrote.[21]

He received added encouragement from the Philadelphia abolitionists. At a meeting in May, 1871, the Pennsylvania Anti-Slavery Society passed a resolution requesting Still to publish his reminiscences relating to the underground railroad. That same year there was a seven-months coal strike in Pennsylvania which made his business very dull but gave him the leisure he needed to prepare his material for publication. Still worked diligently in the preparation of his book, a task which was made more difficult by the bitter division in the anti-slavery movement. He corresponded with old acquaintances, put his own records in order and collected material from others. The Philadelphia abolitionists with whom he had worked were all Garrisonians, but he included the political abolitionist Lewis Tappan among those whom he asked for information. One of the difficult tasks was to write a sketch of J. Miller McKim, his superior in the anti-slavery office. When McKim asked Still to outline the material concerning him, Still tactfully replied that "it would not be just to confine [McKim] to any special department of the work but to represent [him] as a general laborer," with many services in the anti-slavery cause.[22] Frederick Douglass, however, got no mention in Still's book, except in material reprinted from a British pamphlet. In 1893 Douglass boasted of his long service in the underground railroad and claimed that Still had omitted him because he had criticized Still's conduct toward the fugitives.[23]

William Still's book on the underground railroad is unique in that it emphasized the courage and ingenuity of the fugitives. White conductors are the heroes in the accounts which the abolitionists recorded for posterity; in Still's account, the daring fugitives are the heroes. Scattered throughout the volume are legal documents, letters, and newspaper items, but the focus of the narrative is always on the slaves themselves. Still placed his sketches of the abolitionist conductors at the end of the book, after the great bulk of material on the passengers. The book's numerous illustrations also focus the spotlight on the absconding slaves and on their heroic struggle for freedom.

In Still's book the vast majority of the fugitive slaves came from the neighboring border states. Most of them were young men, of more than average intelligence, though there were some women and children too. Although they were all considered underground railroad passengers, many of them had

[21] William Still to Dr. Henry Charles, June 6, 1873, to J. W. Jones, November 4, 1873, and to J. C. Price, June 3, 1873, in the William Still Papers in the Historical Society of Pennsylvania.

[22] Boyd, "Still," in Still, *Underground Rail Road*, xxxv; William Still to J. Miller McKim, November 10, 1871, in the J. Miller McKim Papers in the New York Public Library.

[23] Frederick Douglass to Wilbur H. Siebert, March 27, 1893, in scrapbook, "The Underground Railroad in New York, vol. 2," in the Siebert Papers in the Ohio Historical Society.

received little or no assistance before they contacted the vigilance committee. Some passed as white or as free Negroes, some traveled on foot at night, some adopted clever disguises, and more than a few hid or were hidden on steamers running from southern ports. Much of the escape drama was a self-help affair.

Although never a slave himself, William Still hated the South's peculiar institution. Not only did he have the zeal of the abolitionists, but as a Negro he was able to identify himself emotionally with the bondsmen. "The half will never be told of the barbarism of Slavery," he wrote. He described one fugitive as a "decided opponent to the no-pay system, to flogging, and selling likewise." Still said he had taken care "to furnish artless stories, [and] simple facts," and had resorted "to no coloring to make the book seem romantic." He took great care to be factual but his bias was apparent throughout the book. In his preface Still commented that those who sought information regarding "the existence, atrocity, struggles and destruction of Slavery" would have no trouble finding the "hydra-headed monster ruling and tyrannizing over Church and State, North and South, white and black, without let or hindrance for at least several generations." [24]

The fugitives whom Still and the vigilance committee interviewed had confirmed his prejudice against the slave system. Although a few maintained that they had been treated well, the great majority testified to many hardships. Some were probably aware of the committee's preference for cruel and libertine masters. One slave from Maryland said that he had been "treated as bad as a man could be," another had been "allowed no privileges of any kind, Sunday or Monday," and a woman had "endured all outraged nature could endure and survive." The fugitives described their former owners with an abundance of such terms as "always a big devil—ill-grained," an "ill-natured man," and "a notorious frolicker." One described a cruel master who "made a common practice of flogging females when stripped naked." Still and the other committee members were also temperance advocates and duly noted in their records when a master was described as "given to 'intemperance'" and to "gross 'profanity,'" "a gambler and spree'r," and a man "devoted to card playing, rum-drinking and fox-hunting." [25]

Occasionally the committee sharply questioned fugitives whose stories did not seem plausible, but they sometimes took obviously exaggerated statements at face value. After trying to dispute her testimony, the committee gave "the benefit of the doubt" to Amarian, a good-looking girl of twenty-one who said she had always been treated very well. Similarly, they doubted Washington Somlor's description of inhuman treatment at the hands of a master who "believed in selling, flogging, cobbing, paddling, and all other kinds of torture...." Yet they accepted the statements of William Jordon who said that he had lived three months in a cave "surrounded with bears, wild cats, rattle-snakes and the like." Theophilus Collins testified that he was brutally punished for

---

[24] William Still, *The Underground Rail Road* (Philadelphia, 1872), 144, 290, preface, 3, 5. This preface appears only in the first edition.

[25] Still, *Underground Rail Road*, 185, 260, 307, 383, 388, 416, 480, 519, 533, 754.

attending a Sunday night religious meeting. His master called him in for a whipping and when he refused to remove his shirt, gave him twenty blows on the head with the butt of a cowhide, struck him on the head with fire-tongs, beat him with a parlor shovel until the handle broke, jabbed the shovel blade at his head with all his might, and, when the slave tried to make for the door, stabbed him in the head and stomach with a pocket knife. Nevertheless, Theophilus escaped and ran sixteen miles carrying a part of his entrails in his hands for the whole journey.[26]

William Still believed that a book containing such thrilling tales as the one Theophilus told to the vigilance committee should certainly sell many copies. His previous business experience enabled him to plan and promote the sale of his book to good advantage. He decided to sell it only by subscription and carefully supervised his sales campaign.[27]

Prospective agents for a particular territory had to apply personally to Still. If no suitable person applied, Still preferred to leave the area temporarily unsolicited. He had two editions, one in plain English cloth which sold for five dollars, and a sheepskin edition priced at five-fifty. Still prepared a full set of instructions for his agents and sold each of them a kit with sample copies. He gave them forty or fifty per cent of the purchase price as commission, but they had to adhere strictly to his terms. During the financial panic of 1873 he permitted them to sell on the installment plan, but they were not to deliver the book until the last payment had been made. All of his agents had to submit weekly reports.[28]

Still preferred to hire colored men to sell his book, but he realized that few of his race had the necessary experience. He was confident it would be well received among the Negroes and among the Republicans, if the agents did their part well. "The book only needs to be presented by a man who appreciates and comprehends the value and importance of having our heroes and Martyrs under Slavery well represented in the history of our times—to make the work take exceedingly well," he wrote a representative in Kansas in 1873.[29] And the work took well indeed. A salesman in Pittsburgh cleared about a hundred dollars a week for six weeks. His best agent followed five others who had sold only a few copies in Baltimore, and at the end of six weeks he had more than three hundred subscriptions. In 1873 Still reported, "Agents are doing well with the U.G.R.R. this summer. East, West, North and South, wherever competent persons are presenting it." He first printed ten thousand copies but hoped to sell a hundred thousand before the demand ceased.[30] The

[26] Ibid., 130, 304, 435, 495–496.

[27] Boyd, "Still," in Still, Underground Rail Road, xlvi–xlix, lxi–lxii.

[28] Still to T. L. W. Titus, January 7, 1874, to W. D. Teister, June 10, 1873, to Robert Furnas, June 18, 1873, to James E. Thompson, July 9, 1873, and to J. C. Price, June 23, 1873, all in the Still Papers.

[29] Still to Thomas E. Franklin, April 9, 1874, and the Rev. J. C. Embry, October 14, 1873, in the Still Papers.

[30] Still to W. H. Jones, June 3, 1873, the Rev. Jones, November 12, 1873, and to E. Sanborn, June 11, 1873, in the Still Papers.

first edition sold out completely, as did a second edition in 1879. In 1883 Still published a third edition with a new title, *Still's Underground Rail Road Records,* and with a sketch of the author written by James P. Boyd.

William Still's book undoubtedly circulated more widely than any other firsthand account of the underground railroad. In writing and distributing it Still proved that a Negro author could produce a creditable book and sell it on a large scale. He proudly exhibited it at the Philadelphia Centennial Exposition in 1876. It was a fitting tribute to his race. He hoped it would inspire other Negroes to greater efforts until they could exhibit such fruits "of their newly gained privileges" as "well-conducted shops and stores; lands acquired and good farms" well-managed, and "valuable books produced and published on interesting and important subjects." [31] It is not possible to evaluate the book's effect on American Negroes, but in one respect it failed to make its mark. William Still put the courageous fugitive slaves at the center of his stage. His book provided an excellent corrective for the many abolitionist-centered accounts. Yet in the popular mind, the white conductor of the underground railroad remains the leading figure in the drama. Despite Still's financial success, his message has been hidden under a mass of literature written by the abolitionists, their descendants, and admirers.

[31] William Still, *The Underground Rail Road* (Philadelphia and Cincinnati, 1879), preface. This preface appears in the second and third editions.

PART FOUR

CIVIL WAR
AND
RECONSTRUCTION

Benjamin Quarles

THE ABDUCTION OF THE "PLANTER"

The participation of black men in the Civil War, though mostly ignored by the standard histories, has received considerable attention from those scholars who have been interested in the study of the Negroes' past in the United States. In the following selection Benjamin Quarles gives a detailed account of a famous incident in the struggle that resulted in the emancipation of the slaves.

To the confederate capital on a spring afternoon in the second year of the war came a one-sentence dispatch addressed to General R. E. Lee: "I have just learned by telegraph that [the] steamer 'Planter,' with five guns aboard, intended for the harbor, was stolen in Charleston this morning." Dated May 13, 1862, from the Savannah headquarters of the Department of South Carolina and Georgia, the terse report concluded with a "Very respectfully," and bore the name of the commanding officer, J. C. Pemberton.

Pemberton's dispatch referred to the "abduction" by a group of slaves of a Confederate vessel, a dramatic deed which made its instigator, Robert Smalls, "an object of interest in Dupont's fleet," as Admiral David D. Porter phrased it. The spectacular escape of Smalls and his party became one of the war's oft-told stories. Requiring careful planning and brilliant execution, the feat in truth was unparalleled in audacity. "I thought," said Smalls, as he delivered the vessel to the Union Navy, "that the 'Planter' might be of some use to Uncle Abe."

A native South Carolinian, Smalls was born in Beaufort in 1839. When he was twelve his master brought him to Charleston, where, after a succession of occupations, he finally became a rigger and began to learn boating and the twisting coastal waters. When the war came, the stockily built young slave was impressed into the Confederate service, and in March, 1862, he was made a member of the crew of the "Planter."

Formerly a cotton steamer plying the Pee Dee River and capable of

Benjamin Quarles, "The Abduction of the 'Planter,'" *Civil War History,* IV (March 1958), pp. 5–11. Reprinted with the permission of Benjamin Quarles and of *Civil War History.*

carrying 1,400 bales, the "Planter" had been chartered by the war government and converted into a transport running from point to point in the Charleston harbor and the neighboring waters. Built of live oak and red cedar, the boat measured 150 feet in length, had a 30 foot beam, a depth of 7 feet 10 inches, and drew 3 feet 9 inches of water. As a Confederate dispatch boat, she mounted two guns for her own use, a 32-pounder pivot gun and a 24-pounder howitzer. Attached to the engineering department at Charleston, the "Planter" carried a crew of eleven, of whom three were whites—captain, mate, and engineer—and the remainder slaves.

By far the ablest of the slave crew was Smalls. Determined to escape, Smalls hit upon the idea of making off with the "Planter." Wherever the Union Navy extended its blockade along the Southern seacoast, freedom-minded Negroes had sensed a new opportunity. By scow, oyster boat, barge, homemade canoe, or anything that would float, they made their way to the Union men-of-war. But no plan of escape was as imaginative and as daring as Smalls's.

The young wheelsman worked out the details in his mind. The escaping party would number sixteen, of whom half would be women and children, including Smalls's wife and their two young ones. The "Planter" would put out to sea casually, as though making a routine run to reconnoiter. Knowing they could expect little mercy if caught, Smalls bound the party to agree that if they were unable to make good their flight, they would blow up the vessel rather than be taken alive. Smalls's plan embraced one final but essential detail—all three white officers would have to remain ashore for the night. Such an absence would be contrary to standing general orders which stipulated that officers of light draft vessels were to remain "on board day and night" when their boat was docked at the wharf.

Finally came such a night as Smalls waited for—the night of May 12. Coincidentally, on the afternoon of that day, 200 pounds of ammunition and four guns—"a banded rifle 42, one 8-inch columbiad, one 8-inch seacoast howitzer, and one 32-pounder"—had been loaded on the "Planter" for transport to the harbor battery, Fort Ripley.

With the white officers ashore, Smalls began to put his plan into operation. The sixteen slaves got aboard in the crisp early morning, the women and children being led below deck in pin-drop quiet. Smalls broke into Captain C. J. Relyea's cabin and took the captain's hat. At 3:00 a.m. one of the fugitives struck a match and set the kindlings on fire under the boilers; twenty-five minutes later the hawsers which moored the boat to Southern Wharf were cast off. From the pilothouse Smalls sounded the wharf signal. The shore sentinel at his post some fifty yards distant noticed the ship gliding away but sensed nothing afoot; he "did not think it necessary to stop her, presuming that she was but pursuing her usual business," in the language of an official report issued later that day.

Now to run the many fortifications in the harbor. Bristling with sea defenses, the defiant city was ringed with forts and batteries on constant alert.

But for the runaway slaves there was no turning back. Hoisting the ship's two flags, Confederate and Palmetto, Smalls eased into the inner channel. He geared the "Planter" to its customary pace, although not to dash at full speed required the utmost self-control.

The critical minutes of the great deception had arrived. Wearing the captain's hat and mimicking his gait, Smalls stood in the pilothouse with the cord in his hand. As the vessel passed Fort Johnson, he pulled the lanyard on the steam whistle and gave the proper salute. All went well.

Finally the abductors approached the last hurdle, historic Fort Sumter. Thirteen months ago it was here that the opening shots of the war had been fired, and at the identical morning hour. One of the four transport guns on the "Planter" belonged originally, as Smalls well knew, to Fort Sumter, having been struck on the muzzle during the bombardment of that bastion and now having been repaired because of the Confederacy's scarcity of heavy guns.

Abreast of Sumter, Smalls sounded the private signal, three shrill whistles followed by a hissing one. "The sentinel on the parapet called for the corporal of the guard and reported the guard-boat going out," stated the official report of Major Alfred Rhett. In turn, the corporal of the guard relayed the intelligence to the officer of the day, Captain David G. Fleming. The information had been passed along in routine fashion since it was, in Major Rhett's words, "by no means unusual for the guard-boat to run out at that hour." Then came the fateful order to permit the halted vessel to go on her way; by signal Sumter answered, "All right." The "Planter" had been taken for the guard boat and hence allowed to pass!

The slave-manned steamer moved in a southeasterly direction and entered the main ship channel, maintaining her leisurely pace until she had outdistanced the line of fire of the Confederate battery. Then she got up steam, lowered her guns, and ran up a white flag.

Not a minute too soon was the flag of truce hoisted. Off Charleston was a Union blockading fleet of ten warships, and the "Planter" had been spied by the lookout on the inside ship, "Onward." The commander, J. F. Nickels, had ordered his ship swung around so as to train the maximum gunfire on the approaching craft. Just as the "Onward" succeeded in bringing her port guns to bear on the oncoming steamer, Commander Nickels caught sight of the white flag. The gunners relaxed.

Unmolested, the harbor boat drew up alongside the armed sailing vessel. A prize crew boarded the "Planter" and greeted its crew. Down came the white flag, and up went the American ensign. Then and there in the outer harbor the ownership of the captive boat was transferred from the Confederate States of America to the Union Navy.

Later that morning the senior officer commanding the blockading squadron off Charleston, E. G. Parrott, taking advantage of the good weather, ordered the prize crew to take the "Planter" and its captors to Port Royal, and there to report the incident to Flag Officer S. F. Du Pont. No order could have pleased Smalls and his companions more, most of them having originally come from the Sea Island region.

The "Planter" made the sixty-mile trip to Port Royal by way of St. Helena Sound and Broad River, reaching her destination shortly after ten in the evening. Word awaited Smalls that he was to report directly to Du Pont, and the next morning he was ushered aboard the flagship "Wabash." There the elderly admiral, "that stately and courteous potentate, elegant as one's ideal French marquis," listened attentively as the ex-slave told his story.

Later that day, in a lengthy report to the Secretary of the Navy, Du Pont summed up the exploit: "The bringing out of this steamer, under all the circumstances, would have done credit to anyone." The admiral also jotted down another conclusion: "This man, Robert Smalls, is superior to any who have yet come into the lines, intelligent as many of them have been."

Back in Charleston the news was received with consternation not unmingled with disbelief. In a front-page story devoted to the "extraordinary occurrence," the *Courier* reported that "our community was intensely agitated Tuesday morning by the intelligence that the steamer 'Planter' ... had been taken possession of by her colored crew, steamed up and boldly ran [*sic*] out to the blockaders." Added the daily, "The news was not at first credited." Another Charleston newspaper, the *Mercury*, concluded its descriptive story of the escape by explaining that "the run to Morris Island goes out a long way past the fort, and then turns. The 'Planter' did not turn."

Voicing the general indignation of Confederate South Carolina over the negligence of the white officers of the boat, the *Columbia Guardian* expressed a fervent wish that the "recreant parties will be brought to speedy justice, and the prompt penalty of the halter rigorously enforced." From army headquarters in Richmond came a dispatch to General Pemberton stating that General Lee had received the papers relative to the "Planter's" escape and that "he very much regrets the circumstances, and hopes that necessary measures will be taken to prevent any repetition of a like misfortune."

News of Smalls's feat quickly spread throughout the North, and public sentiment became strong for awarding prize money to the "Planter's" crew. Congress responded, moving with unusual speed. Two weeks from the day of the seizure, that body passed a bill ordering the Secretary of the Navy to have the vessel appraised and "when the value thereof shall be thus ascertained to cause an equitable apportionment of one-half of such value ... to be made between Robert Smalls and his associates who assisted in rescuing her from the enemies of the Government." Within another week Lincoln had signed the bill.

Smalls turned out to be right in believing that the "Planter" might be of some use to the North. Admirably suited to the shallow waters of the Sea Island region, she was immediately equipped with musket-proof bulwarks and converted into a navy transport, carrying upwards of seventy men. Exactly one month after the abduction, Admiral Du Pont, in acknowledging two letters from naval officer A. C. Rhind, wrote that he was "glad that the 'Planter' has proved so useful a transport, and that we have again been able so materially to aid the army, especially at a critical time, when its generals were almost helpless for want of transports."

Early in September, 1862, the "Planter" was sold to the army, which could make much better use of a wood-burner than could the sister service. The quartermaster's department welcomed the addition, "as we have comparatively no vessels of light draft." Until she was decommissioned and sold at Baltimore in September, 1866, the "Planter" remained in military service, being used mainly as a troop transport, but seeing occasional service as a supply boat.

During most of its period of use by the armed forces, the "Planter" was piloted or commanded by Smalls. Over the four months the boat remained under navy supervision, the young Negro was employed as pilot. During the year 1863 and for the first two months in 1864, the army employed him in a like capacity, paying him $50 a month until September 30, 1863, then $75 a month from October 1 to November 30, 1863, and thenceforth $150 a month. On March 1, 1864, he was made captain.

The pilot was promoted to master as a reward for bravery under fire (before the war was over, Smalls had fought in seventeen engagements), but the appointment was merited on other grounds. For the fugitive slave brought much with him. His knowledge of the coastline of South Carolina and Georgia was intimate; few men were more familiar with the sinuous windings of those waters, and no hand was more skilled in their navigation. Indeed, "the accession of Smalls is deemed of more importance than the heavy guns of the 'Planter,'" wrote a reporter for the *Philadelphia Inquirer* (May 17, 1862), "as Smalls is thoroughly acquainted with all the intricacies of navigation in that region." Smalls also brought a knowledge of where the torpedoes had been planted to destroy the Union gunboats and where the masked batteries were located.

The intelligence he furnished was so valuable that the Secretary of the Navy, in his annual report to President Lincoln, made it a point to describe them:

> From information derived chiefly from the contraband Pilot, Robert Smalls, who has escaped from Charleston, Flag Officer Du Pont, after proper reconnaissance, directed Commander Marchand to cross the bar with several gun-boats and occupy Stono. The river was occupied as far as Legarville, and examinations extended further to ascertain the position of the enemy's batteries. The seizure of Stono Inlet and river secured an important base for military operations, and was virtually a turning of the forces in the Charleston harbor.

At the war's end Smalls was among the thousands who witnessed the re-raising of the American flag at Fort Sumter. This event had been scheduled for April 14, four years to the day after the one on which the Union forces had been forced to haul down the colors. Present at the flag-raising ceremonies was a distinguished roster of reformers and public notables, including William

Lloyd Garrison, Judge Advocate General Joseph Holt, Supreme Court Justice N. H. Swayne, Senator Henry Wilson, and the chief speaker, Henry Ward Beecher. On hand also was Robert Anderson, brought back to Sumter to raise the very shot-pierced flag which the Southerners had forced him to lower four years previously. But perhaps the most symbolic figure present was Captain Robert Smalls, who that morning had left Charleston, Sumter bound, at the helm of the "Planter," profusely decorated with the Stars and Stripes and loaded down with hundreds "of the emancipated race."

After the war Smalls had fifty years to live, many of them spent in the public eye—as a member of the South Carolina legislature, a five-term United States Congressman, and Collector of the Port at Beaufort. But no moment of his eventful life could ever match that memorable dawn when he abducted the "Planter."

Louis R. Harlan

DESEGREGATION IN NEW ORLEANS PUBLIC SCHOOLS DURING RECONSTRUCTION

One of the achievements of the Radical Reconstruction regimes was the inauguration of a system of free public schools in the southern states. Of the state constitutions passed under Radical auspices, only those of Louisiana and South Carolina required legally nonsegregated schools. Yet even in these two states Jim Crow schools were the rule. The only integrated public educational institutions were the University of South Carolina and the public school system of New Orleans. Louis R. Harlan has examined the history of integration in the New Orleans public schools during Reconstruction. His article is of far broader scope than its title indicates, because he also touches upon many aspects of the life of the New Orleans free Negroes.

I⊤ is a fact not generally known even to historians that the New Orleans public schools during the Reconstruction period underwent substantial racial desegregation over a period of six and a half years, an experience shared by no other southern community until after 1954 and by few northern communities at the time. This essay is limited to a summary of the evidence that there was indeed desegregation in New Orleans in the 1870's and to an effort to explain it chiefly in terms of circumstances in New Orleans at the time. It is obvious that New Orleans, as the only real urban center in the overwhelmingly rural South, could not be an example from which any general conclusions can be drawn about Reconstruction in the region or even in Louisiana as a whole. The experience of one southern urban community during Reconstruction, however, may hold interest for students of the rapidly urbanizing contemporary South.

For a generation of historians rather suddenly concerned with past strug-

Louis R. Harlan, "Desegregation in New Orleans Public Schools During Reconstruction," *American Historical Review*, LXVII (April, 1962), pp. 663–75. Reprinted with permission of the author and publisher.

gles over civil rights, the interest of this study lies partly in the new crop that it makes in the much-plowed field of Reconstruction history. The historians both of Louisiana Reconstruction [1] and of southern education [2] have pronounced the desegregation experiment of New Orleans an almost total failure. The conclusions of historians of the Dunning school may be explained by their preoccupation with political themes or their racialistic and sectional blind spots, but perhaps a better explanation is that they read in the partisan press the headlined stories of white walkouts and Negro evictions, but failed to note the undramatic evidence of the return of most of these pupils in the following days and months. Historians of southern education seem to have relied too heavily on a secondary source by the Louisiana educational historian Thomas H. Harris, who in turn depended vaguely on the "testimony of men who lived through the period." Harris declared in 1924: "The schools were never mixed. The law was evaded from the first, and the negroes were about as active in evading it as the whites." [3]

It is with some surprise, therefore, that we read the testimony in 1874 of Thomas W. Conway, the Radical state superintendent and prime mover of New Orleans desegregation:

> I had fully concluded to put the system of mixed schools to a thorough, practical test, and I did. The white pupils all left . . . and the school-house was virtually in the hands of the colored pupils. This was the picture one day. What will you think when I tell you that before I reached my office that day, the children of both races who, on the school question, seemed like deadly enemies, were, many of them, joined in a circle, playing on the green, under the shade of the wide-spreading live oak. In a few days I went back to see how the school was progressing, and, to my surprise, found nearly all the former pupils returned to their places; and that the school, like all the schools in the city, reported at the close of the year a larger attendance than at any time since the close of the war. The children

---

[1] Alcée Fortier, *Louisiana Studies* (New Orleans, 1894), 267–68; John R. Ficklen, *History of Reconstruction in Louisiana* (Baltimore, 1910), 207–208; Ella Lonn, *Reconstruction in Louisiana after 1868* (New York, 1918), 54–55, 357; John S. Kendall, *History of New Orleans* (3 vols., Chicago, 1922), I, 331, 665; Roger W. Shugg, *Origins of Class Struggle in Louisiana* (University, La., 1939), 226; Garnie W. McGinty, *Louisiana Redeemed* (New Orleans, 1941), 24. George W. Cable, *Strange True Stories of Louisiana* (New York, 1889), 221–32, is more accurate, though limited to a single public school.

[2] Horace M. Bond, *The Education of the Negro in the American Social Order* (New York, 1934), 52; Charles W. Dabney, *Universal Education in the South* (2 vols., Chapel Hill, N.C., 1936), I, 368–71; Harry S. Ashmore, *The Negro and the Schools* (Chapel Hill, N.C., 1954), 7–8; John Hope Franklin, "Jim Crow Goes to School," *South Atlantic Quarterly*, LVIII (Spring 1959), 225–35; Alfred H. Kelly, "The Congressional Controversy over School Segregation, 1867–1875," *American Historical Review*, LXIV (Apr. 1959), 537–63.

[3] Thomas H. Harris, *The Story of Public Education in Louisiana* (New Orleans, 1924), 30; an undocumented work.

were simply kind to each other in the school-room as in the streets and elsewhere! A year ago I visited the same school and saw therein about as many colored children as whites, with not a single indication of any ill-feeling whatever.

All that is wanted in this matter of civil rights is to let the foes of the measure simply understand that we mean it. Do this, and as in the case of the enemies of free schools in Louisiana, they will be quiet.[4]

The whole truth, of course, embraces both the historians' evidence of evasion and strident resistance and Conway's idyl of dancing on the green. Evasion lasted for three years, until the last legal recourse was exhausted, and then desegregation began. As desegregation spread slowly into more and more schools, as Conway said, there was indeed resistance, but it was fruitless, sporadic, separated by long periods of tacit acceptance, and successful in the end only because Reconstruction itself failed.

The forces of evasion were in effect even before the state constitution in 1867 prohibited the establishment of separate schools and required that no public school should deny admission on account of race or color.[5] On the eve of the constitutional convention the city hastily established its first Negro schools to give credibility to its stand for "separate but equal" rather than desegregated schools,[6] and Freedmen's Bureau officials opposed to mixed schools [7] hastily transferred their local schools to the city board.[8] State Superintendent Robert M. Lusher resigned before the end of his term to become the state agent of the Peabody Education Fund, which spent more money in Louisiana than in any other state to aid a system of private white schools.[9]

In New Orleans, where whites outnumbered Negroes nearly three to one, white Republicans in the city government cooperated with the city school board in efforts to thwart Superintendent Conway in his equally determined effort to give desegregation a thorough trial in that city. The city's news-

[4] Conway to the editor of the Washington *National Republican*, in Washington *New National Era*, June 4, 1874.

[5] New Orleans *Tribune*, Oct. 27, 1867 [all New Orleans newspapers hereafter cited without place name].

[6] *Tribune*, July 24, 1867; *Times*, July 31, Sept. 19, Oct. 1, 9, 11, 15, 16, 20, 1867; *Crescent*, Sept. 15, 17, 1867; Minutes of New Orleans City Board of School Directors [hereafter cited as Sch. Bd. Min.] Sept. 16, Oct. 2, 9, 1867 (VII, 203–14, 219–26), MSS volumes in Orleans Parish School Board Office, New Orleans.

[7] L. Jolissaint, Parish of Orleans School Report, Sept. 15, 1868, Tri-Monthly Report Book of Office of Assistant Sub-Assistant Commissioner, Parish of Orleans, Louisiana, Bureau of Refugees, Freedmen, and Abandoned Lands, National Archives; *Crescent*, Sept. 17, 1867; *Picayune*, Dec. 4, 1867.

[8] Sch. Bd. Min., Nov. 6, Dec. 4, 1867 (VII, 235–37, 251–53); *Times*, Dec. 25, 1867.

[9] *Picayune*, Apr. 14, 1868; Peabody Education Fund, *Proceedings of the Trustees* (6 vols., Boston, 1867–1914), I, 91, 262–63, 408–12, 434–39 (July 1868, Feb. 1871, Oct. 1874).

papers meanwhile undertook to create an atmosphere of resistance and fear, advocating desertion of the schools en masse by the whites, establishment of private schools, and refusal to pay school taxes, and predicting the destruction of the public schools and race war.[10] The city school board resorted to a pupil placement system [11] and all of the legal stratagems so familiar today. The loopholes of every school law were sought out, and a bewildering succession of suits and injunctions cluttered the courts. At one time five school cases were simultaneously on the dockets. Finally the sands of delay ran out; a court decision of December 1870 was acknowledged by all parties to be decisive, and desegregation began within a month.[12]

To overcome the forces of delay and evasion, the Radicals found it necessary to centralize and strengthen the school system. The city school board was replaced by another appointed by the state board of education, which in turn was appointed by the governor. The city board was allowed by state law to estimate its annual needs and require the city governments to levy and collect a local tax sufficient to supply the amount. The high salaries that this arrangement made possible, though often tardily paid, attracted good local teachers and created a reasonably good *esprit de corps*.

The extent of desegregation cannot be measured precisely because the official reports made no separate accounting of the races and because the population of New Orleans was so peculiarly mixed, with so many very light colored persons and swarthy white ones, that observers often found it impossible to distinguish between them.[13] Nevertheless, there is considerable evidence of desegregation in official records and in newspapers, particularly in the reports of the annual examinations or closing exercises of the schools. From such sources it is possible to identify by name twenty-one desegregated schools and some others that may have been desegregated, about one-third of the city's public schools.[14] The school authorities at no time initiated desegre-

---

[10] See, e.g., *Picayune*, Oct. 22, 1867, Aug. 13, 1868, Nov. 24, 1870; *Commercial Bulletin*, Feb. 7, 1870; *Times*, May 2, 1868, Feb. 17, Apr. 10, 1870.

[11] Sch. Bd. Min., May 21, 27, 1868 (VII, 323, 327–28). According to the *Picayune*, Jan. 12, 1871, "everything worked smoothly, attempts at mixing the schools being frustrated by the plan adopted by Mr. Van Norden, the President of the Board, who issued permits on which alone admission could be gained, to applicants, and taking good care that no negroes were admitted into white schools."

[12] *Annual Report of the State Superintendent of Public Education for the Year 1870* [hereafter cited as *Annual Report*] (New Orleans, 1871), 17–28; *Picayune* and *Times* throughout 1869–1870, esp. *Times*, Dec. 20, 1870; *Picayune*, Jan. 12, 1871; *Commercial Bulletin*, Jan. 11, 12, 1871. On earlier desegregation efforts, see *ibid.*, Apr. 27, 30, May 17, 18, June 30, 1870; Sch. Bd. Min., May 21, 27, June 3, 1868 (VII, 322–28, 336–37).

[13] *Times*, Oct. 6, 1873; *Louisianian*, Sept. 4, 1875.

[14] These were: Barracks, Bayou Bridge, Bayou Road, Beauregard, Bienville, Central Boys' High, Claiborne, Fillmore, Fisk, Franklin, Keller, Lower Girls' High, Madison, Paulding, Pontchartrain (Milneburg), Rampart, Robertson, St. Anne, St. Philip, Spain, Webster schools certainly desegregated, and Cut-off Road, Dunn, Gentilly, McDonoghville vaguely reported to be so. See *Bulletin*, Jan. 11, Feb. 1, 1871, Dec. 11, 18, 19, 1874; *Republican*, Apr. 12, 1873, Dec. 12, 1874; *Picayune*, June 23, 1871, Dec. 11, 12,

gation, but simply required the admission of Negro children to white or mixed schools whenever they applied. Thus by choice or social pressure a majority of the city's school children attended either the separate Negro schools or white schools.[15] A surprising number of colored children, nevertheless, entered mixed schools under this arrangement. In 1877 the number was estimated at three hundred,[16] but that was some six months after the end of Reconstruction. Other evidence indicates that between five hundred and one thousand Negroes and several thousand whites attended mixed schools at the height of desegregation.[17] Light colored children, who could move about more easily in the white world, were usually the first to enter mixed schools and the last to leave them after Reconstruction, but children "as black as ebony" were reported "side by side with the fairest Caucasians" in the same classrooms.[18]

All of the five mixed schools with seventy-five or more Negroes enrolled were in the Second and Third Districts, below Canal Street, where descendants of the original French and Spanish inhabitants and the Irish, German, and Italian immigrants predominated. In this downtown area there was no rigid residential separation, and the houses of prostitution as well as schoolhouses were desegregated, though without causing as much public excitement. Since nearly all of the schools in these districts were desegregated,[19] one might assume that the character of the Latin or immigrant population explained everything. But this is not so. Negro residential areas were dispersed throughout the city, and some of the largest schools in the so-called American districts, the First and Fourth, contained Negro children.[20] One of these, the Fisk School, contained "a considerable number." [21] Below New Orleans proper, in the Fifth and Seventh Districts, the scattered settlements on both sides of the river contained some desegregated primary schools.[22] Of the city's three

---

19, 1874, Feb. 19, Nov. 10, 1875, Nov. 20, 1876, Dec. 6, 1877; *Times*, Apr. 10, June 7, Oct. 6, Dec. 13, 1873, Dec. 18, 19, 1874, Feb. 19, 1875, Sept. 20, 22, 1876; *L'Abeille*, Dec. 18, 1874; report on Claiborne Boys' School, Mar. 10, 1873, Special Reports of Principals, Louisiana Department of Education Miscellaneous Papers, Department of Archives and Manuscripts, Louisiana State University; *Annual Report*, 1872, 242–43. Contemporaries estimated that between one-third and one-half of the schools were desegregated. *Annual Report*, 1872, 18; *Republican*, July 18, 1873, Sept. 16, 1875; Edward Lawrence, "Color in the New Orleans Schools," *Harper's Weekly*, XIX (Feb. 13, 1875), 147–48; *Louisiana*, Feb. 13, 1875.

[15] *Annual Reports*, 1869, 13, 1871, 308.

[16] City Superintendent William O. Rogers, in *Annual Report*, 1877, 303.

[17] The six leading desegregated schools alone were reported to have more than five hundred Negro pupils. *Picayune*, Dec. 11, 1874; *Times*, June 7, Dec. 13, 1873, Dec. 18, 1874; *Bulletin*, Dec. 19, 1874; *Republican*, Apr. 12, 1873; report on Claiborne Boys' School, Mar. 10, 1873, Education Archives, LSU.

[18] *Bulletin*, Dec. 15, 1874.

[19] *Ibid.*, Oct. 22, 1874; *L'Abeille*, Apr. 16, 1876.

[20] Fisk, Franklin, Madison, Paulding, and Webster Schools in the First District and Keller School in the Fourth District.

[21] *Times*, Dec. 18, 1874.

[22] Pontchartrain, Cut-off Road, Dunn, Gentilly, and McDonoghville.

public high schools, two were desegregated. At the Lower Girls' High School, desegregation proceeded peacefully for years, about one-fifth of the students being colored.[23] At the Central Boys' High several Negro pupils attended after 1875,[24] and a Negro was professor of mathematics there for two years, until after the end of Reconstruction.[25]

Desegregation caused only a temporary decline of enrollment in the schools as a whole and in the mixed schools themselves. Enrollment dropped from 24,892 to 19,091 in the first year of desegregation, but then rose steadily to 26,251 in 1875, which was higher than at any other time in the nineteenth century.[26] The report that 21,000 of these were white and 5,000 colored [27] indicates that there were actually more white pupils in the public schools during desegregation than either before or after.

In the desegregated schools the same trend was evident. The Fillmore Boys' School in the Third District, for example, was desegregated in 1871, when its enrollment was 377, and soon contained 100 colored pupils. In 1873 the conservative New Orleans *Times* reported 700 enrolled, "wonderful" attendance, and good discipline. Fillmore School was the largest in the city, crowded to capacity. In 1874 its enrollment reached 890, and the following year more of its graduates qualified for the high school, through competitive examinations, than those of any other boys' school.[28] Other mixed schools with large Negro enrollments had similar records of increasing enrollment and high academic standing. At the Bienville School, where attendance was cut in half in 1871 by desegregation and a river flood, both enrollment and average attendance by 1874 exceeded the levels prior to desegregation. It sent more of its graduates to high school in 1873 than any two other boys' schools.[29]

Why would desegregated schools be so crowded in a community as race conscious as New Orleans? The explanation seems to be that the quality of instruction was higher in those schools than in most of the others, because of the system of classification of elementary schools. Nearly all the mixed schools

[23] Cable, *Strange True Stories of Louisiana*, 219–32; Dora R. Miller to Cable, May 31, 1889, Feb. 10, May 5, 1890, George W. Cable Papers, Howard-Tilton Memorial Library, Tulane University; *Republican*, Apr. 12, 1873; *Times*, Dec. 17, 18, 1874.

[24] *Ibid.*, Jan. 12, 13, Feb. 4, 1875; *Bulletin*, Jan. 13, 1875; *Picayune*, Feb. 19, 1875; *Republican*, Mar. 3, 1875.

[25] Harris, *Public Education in Louisiana*, 46; Sch. Bd. Min., Sept. 11, 1875, Dec. 6, 1876, Nov. 7, 1877 (VIII, 60, 200, IX, 174, 177).

[26] *Annual Reports*, 1871, 321, 326, 1875, 12, 1877, 289, 1879, 13; Robert M. Lusher, MSS autobiography, June 1890, Robert M. Lusher Papers, LSU. Kendall, *History of New Orleans*, II, 531, reported 23,668 enrolled in 1899.

[27] *Picayune*, Jan. 12, 1875, as reported in *Times-Picayune*, Jan. 25, 1937, clipping in New Orleans Public Schools vertical file, Louisiana Room, LSU; *Times*, Oct. 6, 1873; *Annual Report*, 1877, 303.

[28] *Picayune*, June 23, 1871, Dec. 12, 1874; *Times*, Dec. 13, 1873; *Annual Reports*, 1874, 183, 1875, 208.

[29] *Commercial Bulletin*, Jan. 12, 31, 1871; *Picayune*, June 23, Dec. 11, 1871; *Republican*, June 23, 1871; *Times*, June 7, Oct. 6, Dec. 12, 1873; *Annual Reports*, 1871, 375, 1874, 183, 1875, 208–10.

were classified as Grammar A schools, which had more teachers and a higher salary scale, and sent more graduates to the high schools than the Grammar B schools and Primary schools. Apparently this was why Negro children chose to enter them and why whites also attended them regardless of color, so that their enrollment steadily increased. Most of the Negro schools were Grammar B, and, according to report, "the mixed schools are the best in the city, and the colored schools the poorest—the poorest in quarters, furniture, text-books, and in every way." [30]

Desegregation of the public schools caused enrollment in private and parochial schools to increase, but not enough to damage the public schools. The most ambitious plan of the period, "an elaborate design for the establishment of schools by private enterprise," was presented to a mass meeting of citizens of the Second and Third Districts by former state superintendent Robert M. Lusher.[31] It temporarily evoked much enthusiasm, but Lusher later wrote: "The failure of the Canvassers appointed to raise means for making the plan effectual, to collect a sufficient amount, unfortunately caused the plan to be abandoned." [32] No coordination of private school efforts was ever developed.

Existing Catholic parochial schools, new Presbyterian and Episcopalian parochial schools, and the old and new private schools all expanded. Enrollment in these schools rose from about ten thousand in 1869 to seventeen thousand in 1873, but then declined to fourteen thousand the next year and subsequently even further.[33] "Parochial schools on the pay system are virtually a failure," confessed Father Abram J. Ryan, editor of the local Catholic weekly; the reason he gave was economic: "poor families who have three or four, sometimes eight or ten children . . . cannot possibly send them to the parochial schools at the rate of $2 or even $1 per month, each." [34] This consideration applied with even greater force to the private schools, where tuition was normally twice as high.[35]

Predicted racial violence and tax resistance did not materialize, and after experimenting with walkouts from mixed schools and with private schools, the people of New Orleans learned to live with the change. For three years, from the fall of 1871 until the fall of 1874, the tumult and the shouting

---

[30] *Republican*, July 18, 1873; *Times*, June 18, 1870.

[31] *Commercial Bulletin*, May 25, June 8, 1870; *Times*, May 25, 1870; *Picayune*, June 8, 1870.

[32] Lusher, autobiographical MSS, May 31, 1889, Lusher Papers; Harris, *Public Education in Louisiana*, 56.

[33] *Annual Reports*, 1869, 27, 76, 1873, 72, 284; *Morning Star and Catholic Messenger*, Jan. 31, 1869, Oct. 18, 1874. The figure for 1869 is a compromise between the state report, which estimated 1,200 in parochial schools, the Catholic press, which estimated 5,000 to 6,000, and the city superintendent, who estimated 15,000. *Reports of the United States Commissioner of Education*, 1873, 547, 1874, 535, 1877, 315 (Washington, D.C., 1874, 1875, 1879), estimate 13,779 enrolled in 1873, 14,235 in 1874, 12,000 in 1877.

[34] *Morning Star and Catholic Messenger*, May 22, 1870, July 4, 1875.

[35] *Picayune*, Sept. 17, 1875.

diminished.[36] At the risk of oversimplification, two explanations may be suggested. First, desegregation was administered with such skill that the opposition was disarmed, but foremost, for reasons largely political thousands of New Orleans whites and the leading newspapers actually sought to win the Negro's vote on a basis of recognizing his civil rights.

Though statesmanlike qualities are not generally attributed to Reconstruction leaders, and the school officials were certainly not plaster saints, they administered the New Orleans school efficiently and without major scandal. "If an irrational prejudice is exhibited on one side of this question," said Superintendent Conway, "let it not be met by an equally irrational precipitancy on the other side. This great question of education for the people ... should not be imperiled by injudicious action, even in behalf of a principle confessedly just and equitable." [37] Though rewarded with diatribes for their pains,[38] Conway, his Negro successor William G. Brown, and City Superintendent Charles W. Boothby pursued a "firm and yet moderate course" and conducted a school system good enough to win loyalty from the teachers and even occasional compliments from the opposition.[39]

The complex reasons why many New Orleans whites embraced or acquiesced in Negro civil rights between 1871 and 1874 have been treated elsewhere by T. Harry Williams [40] and can only be outlined here. The central fact was that Louisiana Negroes had a majority of the votes and were protected against intimidation by federal troops. As Reconstruction continued in Louisiana after its demise in other states, native whites realized that they had to win a substantial segment of the Negro vote if they hoped to oust the carpetbaggers. The Negroes were ably led, not so much by the white carpetbaggers as by their own well-educated New Orleans persons of color and Negro carpetbaggers. It was to these colored leaders that the white conservatives made overtures when the inevitable conflicts of interest developed between the white and colored wings of the Radical Republicans.

In 1871 and 1872 New Departure Democrats and new parties that abandoned the Democratic label partly because of its unpopularity among Negroes made bids for Negro votes by platform promises of recognition of civil rights and by parading a few Negro speakers at their rallies.[41] The vague commitments

---

[36] There were a few exceptions, such as editorials in *Picayune*, Jan. 4, 1872; *Times*, Apr. 10, 1873. Their news columns, however, reported favorably on desegregated schools. See *Times*, Dec. 13, 1872, June 7, 1873; *Picayune*, Sept. 29, Dec. 11, 1872.

[37] *Annual Reports*, 1869, 12–13, 1871, 47.

[38] *Times*, Nov. 24, 1870; *Bulletin*, Oct. 22, 1874; *L'Abeille*, Feb. 21, 1875.

[39] The moderation was owing partly to opposition and occasional insubordination. M. C. Cole to Thomas W. Conway, Sept. 9, 1871, William G. Brown to City Board of School Directors, June 1873, Department of Education Archives, LSU; Conway to Henry C. Warmoth, Nov. 18, 1871, Henry C. Warmoth Papers, Southern Historical Collection, University of North Carolina; *Republican*, Oct. 7, 1870; *Commercial Bulletin*, Apr. 27, 1870; *Times*, May 6, 1870, July 3, 1873.

[40] T. Harry Williams, "The Louisiana Unification Movement of 1873," *Journal of Southern History*, XI (Aug. 1945), 349–69.

[41] E. John Ellis to Thomas C. W. Ellis, Feb. 29, 1872, E. John and Thomas C. W. Ellis Papers, LSU.

were insufficient to win the Negro vote in the election of 1872, and this failure led to the specific commitments of the unification movement of 1873. Simply stated, the unification movement proposed a fusion of the native white and Negro voters in which the Negroes would promise to assist in ousting the carpetbaggers and cutting the taxes and the whites would guarantee the Negroes full civil rights: suffrage, office holding, desegregated transportation and places of public resort, and mixed schools. Confederate General P. G. T. Beauregard, the merchant Isaac N. Marks, and a thousand other New Orleans citizens of both races signed a unification manifesto endorsing desegregated schools in unmistakable terms and presented it for endorsement to cheering crowds. In this atmosphere it is understandable that the press and pulpits ceased to thunder against desegregation. After Marks had read the school clause of the manifesto to a mass meeting and a voice interrupted to ask, "Will you send your children to the public schools?" that is, to desegregated schools, the question was greeted with "hisses and other demonstrations" and an invitation to leave the hall.[42] The unification movement failed to achieve the interracial political alliance it sought, because of the reluctance of many whites, particularly in the rural areas, to concede so much to the Negroes, and because of Negro suspicion that the white unificationists would be unwilling or unable to make good their commitments. The movement did give desegregation a breathing spell, however, and its spirit continued to animate some New Orleans whites. Marks, stating his freedom of racial bias, took a seat on the city school board and helped to administer school desegregation.[43] In 1875 George W. Cable sent carefully reasoned arguments for mixed schools to a New Orleans paper,[44] and in the same year David F. Boyd, president of the state university, tried to publish a proposal to desegregate his school.[45]

To most New Orleans whites, however, the failure of unification was the signal for a change in policy and leadership. If Negroes could not be persuaded to vote with the whites, then enough Negroes had to be kept from the polls to ensure a white majority. The White League arose in 1874, spread quickly from the rural parishes to New Orleans, staged a three-day *coup d'état* in September until the arrival of federal troops, and installed a Conservative city government in December. In the same period the position of mixed schools was weakened by the removal from the congressional civil rights bill of the school desegregation clause.[46] The stage was set for the well-known school riots of December 1874, which reflected the momentary political climate of that period as clearly as the acquiescent mood of the previous three years reflected an opposite policy.

[42] *Times,* July 16, 1873; *Picayune,* July 16, 1873.
[43] Sch. Bd. Min., Jan. 12, 1876 (VIII, 125).
[44] These are in George W. Cable, *The Negro Question,* ed. Arlin Turner (Garden City, N.Y., 1958), 26–36.
[45] David F. Boyd, "Some Ideas on Education: The True Solution of the Question of 'Color' in Our Schools, Colleges & Universities, &c, &c," [Dec. 12 or 13] 1875, Walter L. Fleming Collection, LSU.
[46] Kelly, "Congressional Controversy over School Segregation," 558; *Picayune,* Dec. 18, 1874.

During three days of rioting, mobs often described as high school boys or "boy regulators" rudely ejected from mixed schools colored children who had been peacefully attending for years, insulted teachers, beat and threatened to hang the city superintendent.[47] What is not generally understood is that the White League and its newspaper supporters instigated and directed the mobs, which were composed mostly of men and adolescents not enrolled in the high schools, using a handful of high school rowdies as fronts.[48] Moreover, the riots failed to achieve their objective. Sober citizens persuaded the White League to call off "the boys," and the schools reopened after the holidays on a desegregated basis,[49] remaining so for another two and a half years, until after Reconstruction.

Even after the end of Reconstruction, it appeared at first that desegregation might survive the change. The schools remained mixed through the remainder of the term, and Negroes were appointed to the school boards.[50] But when the city school board voted to segregate the schools the following fall, the governor gave a Negro delegation neither aid nor comfort.[51] Resort to the state and federal courts proved equally futile. The Negroes lost three test cases despite the mandatory provisions of the state constitution,[52] and the constitution itself was rewritten in 1879 to permit separate schools and in 1898 to require them.

An obvious conclusion is that the southern devices of evasion and resistance broke down, largely through their own internal weaknesses. On the other hand, New Orleans whites never really surrendered their concept of the public school as a sort of private club. The chief significance of the New Orleans experiment with desegregation, however, centers around the fact, which was not merely incidental, that it occurred in a deep southern state with a large Negro population.

It was really universal suffrage—Negro suffrage protected by strong federal sanctions—that produced the mixed schools and sustained them through the years of trial. Negro votes in the constitutional convention secured the

[47] *Times, Picayune, Bulletin, L'Abeille, Republican, Louisianian* for Dec. 15–19, 1874; a convenient summary is *Annual Report*, 1874, liii–lxxxvi.

[48] "Notes on Mixed School Embroglio Dec. 1874," at end of Ephraim S. Stoddard diary for 1874–75, Ephraim S. Stoddard Collection, Tulane University; Dora R. Miller to Cable, Feb. 10, May 5, 1890, Cable Papers; Lawrence, "Color in the New Orleans Schools," 147–48; Cable, *Strange True Stories of Louisiana*, 223–32; *Times*, Dec. 19, 20, 1874, Jan. 3, 1875; *Republican*, Dec. 19, 1874; *Picayune*, Dec. 20, 1874; *Louisianian*, Dec. 26, 1874.

[49] *Bulletin*, Jan. 13, 1875; *Times*, Feb. 4, 19, 1875; *Republican*, Mar. 3, 1875; *L'Abeille*, Apr. 16, 1876.

[50] Lusher Diary, Mar. 31, 1877, Lusher Papers; Barnes F. Lathrop, ed., "An Autobiography of Francis T. Nicholls, 1834–1881," *Louisiana Historical Quarterly*, XVII (Apr. 1934), 257, 261.

[51] Sch. Bd. Min., June 22, July 3, 1877 (IX, 56–60, 63–64); *Picayune*, June 27, 1877; *Democrat*, June 27, 28, 1877.

[52] See *Times*, Sept. 27, 28, 30, Oct. 3, 24, 31, Nov. 29, 1877, May 22, 1878; *Picayune*, Oct. 6, 24, 1877; *Louisianian*, Sept. 29, 1877, Nov. 29, 1879.

mixed school clause, and Negro votes elected school officers who would carry it out. Negro votes were the consideration for which whites were willing to bargain acquiescence in desegregation. And when the compromise of 1877 removed the federal sanctions for Negro suffrage, the mixed schools were an early casualty. Desegregation was only part of a broader social struggle in which the ballot was the primary lever of power.

New Orleans desegregation is not entirely explained by Negro votes, however, since the Negro majority was in rural Louisiana, where schools were only rarely desegregated.[53] In the adjacent rural state of Mississippi, the Negro majority permitted separate schools to be established by a local-option school law.[54] It would seem that any rural effort at mixed schools in the lower South was foredoomed by the weak economic position of Negro share-croppers, the lack of demand for educated labor in the cotton fields, and the desire of white planters to maintain racial segregation as a means of social control. In southern states outside of the cotton belt, of course, the Negro minority was too weak politically to win desegregation against almost unanimous white opposition.[55]

If the key to desegregation was to be found in the city, then why was the New Orleans experience so different from that of Charleston, South Carolina?[56] The South Carolina constitution of 1868 also required desegregation, and that state also had a Negro majority of voters. Yet the state officials successfully opposed desegregation, and neither the Negro legislators nor the Charleston Negro community pressed the issue.[57] Explanation of the difference between these two urban centers involves consideration of such intangible but very real influences as the singular character of New Orleans and the structure of leadership in the New Orleans Negro community.

With a population of 200,000, New Orleans was metropolitan in size and in the radiating influence of its river trade and railroad connections. Linked with continental Europe by its Creole tradition, its large and diverse immigrant population, and the cultural ties of more recent French *émigrés*, and

[53] *Annual Reports*, 1871, 120, 189; *Louisianian*, Mar. 13, 1875.

[54] Governor James L. Alcorn defending this policy in Washington *New Era*, June 2, 1870; *Congressional Globe*, 42 Cong., 2 sess., 3258 (May 9, 1872). Some Negro dissatisfaction is indicated in Vernon L. Wharton, *The Negro in Mississippi, 1865–1890* (Chapel Hill, N.C., 1947), 243–46; correspondence from Mississippi in Washington *New National Era*, Apr. 4, May 2, June 6, 1872, Apr. 10, 1873, July 2, 1874.

[55] See William G. Brownlow in *Congressional Record*, 43 Cong., 1 sess., 4144 (May 27, 1874). Only in Louisiana, Mississippi, and South Carolina, states with Negro majorities, did the Reconstruction constitutions contain school desegregation clauses.

[56] This was suggested by Professor August Meier, Morgan State College, in floor discussion of this paper at the Southern Historical Assocation meetng, Tulsa, Okla., Nov. 11, 1960.

[57] Francis B. Simkins and Robert H. Woody, *South Carolina during Reconstruction* (Chapel Hill, N.C., 1932), 434–39; Dabney, *Universal Education in the South*, I, 234–35; Richard H. Cain in *Congressional Record*, 43 Cong., 1 sess., 565 (Jan. 10, 1874); *ibid.*, 43 Cong., 2 sess., 957, 960, 981 (Feb. 3, 4, 1875). South Carolina did experiment with desegregating its state university.

linked by trade with racially complex Latin America, it was in many respects
the nation's most cosmopolitan city. Travelers, immigrants, and clients frequently reminded New Orleans citizens that southern racial attitudes and
practices were not widely accepted.[58]

In many other ways New Orleans was unique among southern cities.
Desegregated worship in the Catholic churches, which claimed about half
of the city's population, possibly modified racial attitudes.[59] The colored
population was residentially dispersed throughout the city and was only
about one-fourth of the total population; it was not so large as to induce in
whites the fear of being engulfed if racial barriers were lowered. The city
had opposed secession and was part of the Confederacy less than two years,
whereas it underwent Reconstruction for almost nine years prior to desegregation and for some fifteen years in all. The interest of many New Orleans
leaders in sugar protection and in federal subsidies for river and harbor improvement and railroads made them ideologically more amenable to Whig-
gish Republicanism than the cotton planters of the Charleston area. The
prominence of New Orleans merchants in the unification movement of 1873
suggests that many of them were more concerned with economic development than with social control. They were willing to compromise on racial
issues in order to free themselves from a political regime on which they
blamed the city's economic plight. Thus political polarization by race was incomplete and ephemeral.

The vigorous and ambitious leadership of the New Orleans Negro community was also a powerful stimulus to desegregation. The basis for the high
quality of this leadership was laid during the slavery period, when the free
Negroes of New Orleans enjoyed a status "probably unequaled in any other
part of the South." [60] Whereas the Charleston free Negroes formed a truncated
social pyramid in which artisans were the highest large class,[61] the New
Orleans *gens de couleur* included a number of substantial merchants, cotton
factors, caterers, doctors, and lawyers, even newspaper editors and poets.
Negroes also had much social freedom in cosmopolitan New Orleans. "The
whole behavior of the Negro toward the whites," says Joseph G. Tregle,
"was singularly free of that deference and circumspection which might have
been expected in a slave community." [62] Though the social weather became

[58] See "A Frenchman" to the editor, *Times*, July 1, 1877.

[59] George Rose, *The Great Country* (London, 1868), 191.

[60] Joseph G. Tregle, Jr., "Early New Orleans Society: A Reappraisal," *Journal of
Southern History*, XVIII (Feb. 1952), 34.

[61] E. Horace Fitchett, "The Traditions of the Free Negro in Charleston, South
Carolina," *Journal of Negro History*, XXV (Apr. 1940), 142–43; George B. Tindall,
South Carolina Negroes, 1877–1900 (Columbia, S.C., 1952), 129–52; Simkins and
Woody, *South Carolina*, 26, 91; E. Franklin Frazier, *Black Bourgeoisie* (Glencoe, Ill.,
1957), 32.

[62] Tregle, "Early New Orleans Society," 33; Donald E. Everett, "Free Persons of
Color in New Orleans, 1803–1865," unpublished doctoral dissertation, Tulane Uni-
versity, 1953; Annie L. W. Stahl, "The Free Negro in Ante-Bellum Louisiana,"
Louisiana Historical Quarterly, XXV (Apr. 1942), 301–96.

stormier in the last years of slavery, the colored elite regained self-confidence during the Union occupation, serving as officers in the Union army and eventually as officeholders in the state government. Soon after the war they won a crucial struggle for desegregation of streetcars against almost the same arguments and dire predictions later used to obstruct school desegregation.[63]

The light-skinned New Orleans Negroes, abandoning an early effort to be classed legally as whites, merged their lot with that of the Negro masses and forged an impressive Negro solidarity on racial questions. Since New Orleans was the state capital in this period, they were able to incorporate the darker skinned rural political leaders into their upper-class circle.[64] There is little evidence in the Reconstruction period that the colored bourgeoisie of New Orleans was as isolated from the Negro masses as E. Franklin Frazier has found the same class in the mid-twentieth century.[65] Well educated in private schools, in the North, and in France, they maintained a highly articulate newspaper press and an efficient if opportunistic political organization. They held about half of the seats on the city school board and protected the desegregation experiment against occasional desertion and failure of nerve on the part of their white colleagues. Sharing with most professional men the belief that "knowledge is power," these Negro leaders pressed their own children steadily into desegregated schools in search of equal educational opportunities.

New Orleans desegregation, then, achieved its successes in the 1870's through a unique conjunction of circumstances. A political coalition was temporarily created between the rural Negro majority, the urban Negro minority, and northern Republicans in control of federal and state governments. New Orleans was a metropolitan and cosmopolitan, not merely polyglot, center, in which the southern rural mores were challenged by other traditions, values, and interests. The prior development of a free Negro elite in New Orleans provided the leadership and steadfastness which outsiders could not furnish. Such a fortuitous convergence, however, depended too heavily on one *sine qua non*, the temporary sojourn of federal power in the South. Not until the whole region came more closely to resemble New Orleans, not until an urban South and a more strongly based Negro community emerged, could the experiment be renewed auspiciously.

[63] *Tribune*, June 25, 1865, May 4, 7, 9, 12, 1867.
[64] Donald E. Everett, "Demands of the New Orleans Free Colored Population for Political Equality, 1862–1865," *Louisiana Historical Quarterly*, XXXVIII (Apr. 1955), 55–64; Germaine A. Memelo [Reed], "The Development of State Laws Concerning the Negro in Louisiana 1864–1900," unpublished master's thesis, Louisiana State University, 1956, 72–82; unanimous petition of Louisiana Negro legislators for passage of the civil rights bill, in *Congressional Globe*, 42 Cong., 2 sess., 815 (Feb. 5, 1872).
[65] Frazier, *Black Bourgeoisie*, 24–26.

Philip Durham

THE NEGRO COWBOY [1]

While Negroes in the South were grappling with the problems of land, education, and politics, other black men were participating in the final phases of the American frontier experience. One phase of this little-known side of Negro Life has been treated in W. Sherman Savage's "The Negro on the Mining Frontier," Journal of Negro History, Vol. XXX (January, 1945), pp. 30–46. In the article reprinted below, Philip Durham has demonstrated that, contrary to popular stereotypes, Negroes played a key role in the history of the cattle kingdom, from its beginning in the 1850's until its demise late in the nineteenth century.

Who knows, today, about the Negro cowboy and his contribution to the making of the West? Ask anyone. Or read some of the thousands of "Western Stories" which have appeared during the last fifty years; if the Negro cowboy is in one, he is very well hidden. Apparently, then, the existence of the Negro cowboy is currently unknown because the writers of Western stories did not include him: his non-existence is due to the vagaries of fiction. One important reason for his exclusion may have been discovered by Professor Walter P. Webb, who asked several Western story magazine editors to give their reasons for the popularity of the type, and here is an answer:

> The Western story is the most popular type of action story. In order to give reasons for this, one thing must be recognized immediately: it is understood by us, and should be understood by everyone, that we are dealing with the popularity of Western stories as concerns readers who are white, who may be called Nordics, using this term advisedly.

Philip Durham, "The Negro Cowboy," *American Quarterly*, VII (Fall, 1955), pp. 291–301. Reprinted with permission of *American Quarterly*.
[1] A paper from this article was read before the American Studies Association Group at the Modern Language Association meeting in Chicago on December 28, 1953.

The white race has always been noted for being hard-drinking, hard-fighting, fearless, fair and square.[2]

Quite obviously, the Negro cowboy, in fiction, was confronted with a color line over which he could not ride.

The American cowboy has been described, by men who actually knew him, in these terms: he was independent, loyal, impulsive, generous; he had a hot and hasty temper, a strong sense of right and wrong; and he took his liquor straight. This description is not, however, peculiar to the Anglo-Saxon cowboy; it applies equally to the Negro cowboy, who, after the Civil War, moved out across the plains to play a significant rôle in the development of the cattle industry and became a part of the spirit of the West—a spirit which demanded a conscience but cared little for color.

Western autobiography, which unfortunately has a limited audience, includes the Negro cowboy, and in sufficient numbers to establish his active presence and contributions. Of the three non-fiction books published during the nineteenth century which dealt with the cowboy, two of them included the Negro. The first, Joseph McCoy's *Historic Sketches of the Cattle Trade of the West and Southwest*, published in Kansas City, Missouri, in 1874, describes the cowboys generally, as a type, and does not differentiate among them. The second, however, an autobiographical account, *A Texas Cowboy*, by Charles A. Siringo, refers to the Negro cowboy. This story of range life is accurate, and one senses the authenticity, the realistic approach, without literary affectation. In recording his day-to-day activities, Siringo makes no attempt to set apart the Negro cowboy; rather he is mentioned casually as is everyone else. He writes, for example, "At another time, on the same day, I roped a large animal and got my horse jerked over backwards on top of me and in the horse getting up he got me all wound up in the rope, so that I couldn't free myself until relieved by 'Jack,' a negro man who was near at hand." [3] Or, on another occasion, "Henry Coats was in the lead of the herd. Asa Dawdy and Otto Draub on the left point, while Negro 'Gabe' and I kept them from turning to the right." [4]

The third non-fiction cowboy book of the nineteenth century was *The Story of the Cowboy* by Emerson Hough. This book describes a symbolic cowboy which would include them all:

> Rude and unlettered though he be, and treating his companions with a rough and ready familiarity, the cowpuncher yet accords to his neighbour the right to live the life and go the gait which seems most pleasing to himself. One does not intrude upon the rights of others in the cow country, and he looks to it very promptly that no one shall

[2] Walter Prescott Webb, *The Great Plains* (New York: Ginn and Company, 1931), p. 467.

[3] Charles A. Siringo, *A Texas Cowboy* (New York: New American Library, 1951), p. 43.

[4] Siringo, *A Texas Cowboy*, p. 64.

intrude upon his. In the cow towns or at the cow camps one never hears the abusiveness or rude speech common in the older settlements.[5]

With this attitude Hough did not need to identify the Negro cowboy more than to say, when speaking of breaking horses, "Some of the early Southern busters were negroes, and very good breakers they made." [6]

Although there is, in twentieth-century publications, ample evidence of the Negro cowboy in the biographical, autobiographical, and historical accounts of the West, there has been no attempt on my part, of course, to search these books merely to find his presence. But a few examples are necessary to indicate the manner in which the Negro was treated or referred to in these accounts. Also, it is not only possible but, of course, probable that the Negro was often included in a group of cowboys without being specifically identified. There was no particular reason why he should have been. In *The Cowboy*, Philip Rollins comments on the nationality of the cowboy.

> While the men of the Range were mainly English or Irish descent or birth, and had, in frequent instances, claim to early American ancestors of Scottish origin, the Southwest added to its quota of such bloods numerous men of Mexican extraction, and a more than occasional negro, with here and there men of strain partly Indian. The majority of all the men were American born.[7]

Although Rollins lists national and color types, his interest is in what makes up an American cowboy.

Charles Siringo's twentieth-century autobiography, *Riata and Spurs*, is a re-write of his earlier work with more literary pretensions. Yet he continues to write casually of the Negro cowboy and reports incidents not recorded in the first book. In referring to a time when he was riding herd with Negro cowboys, he tells how he was being dragged by a horse and Lige saved his life.[8] Again he wrote, "I hunted up Babe Fisher, a yellow negro whom I knew could be trusted, and who afterward became a noted outlaw...." [9] One of the episodes concerns a Negro cowboy in the rôle of a peace officer, losing his life in an attempt to bring in the notorious outlaw, John Wesley Harden.[10]

The Negro cowboy serving as a peace officer was not unusual. Frank Eaton, more colorfully known on the range as Pistol Pete, includes in his autobiography an incident in which a Negro marshal was successful.

[5] Emerson Hough, *The Story of the Cowboy* (New York and London: D. Appleton and Company, 1927), p. 203.

[6] Hough, p. 91.

[7] Philip Ashton Rollins, *The Cowboy* (New York: Charles Scribner's Sons, 1922), p. 22.

[8] Charles A. Siringo, *Riata and Spurs* (Boston and New York: Houghton Mifflin Company, 1931), p. 18.

[9] Siringo, *Riata and Spurs*, p. 6.

[10] Siringo, *Riata and Spurs*, p. 145.

We were just leaving the livery barn when I saw Charlie Pettit walking up to me. Charlie was a big Negro Deputy United States Marshal, from the Wichita Court.

"Frank," he said, "Ernest Lewis is up at the hotel and I have a warrant for him. He may have a gang up there. Come up and help me get him."

We started up to the hotel together. Lewis was sitting on the porch. He started like he was going to make a gunplay, but I put my hand on my gun and shook my head at him and he stopped. He and I had played with guns and he knew I was the best shot.

"Sorry, Mr. Lewis," Pettit said, "but I have a warrant for you and it's a fugitive warrant."

By that he meant that Lewis was paid for if anything went wrong. He had committed a crime that was punishable by death. Pettit's orders were to bring him in dead or alive.[11]

Eaton was, of course, glorifying himself, but it was the Negro ex-cowboy who completed the assignment of taking in a white outlaw.

A book in which the Negro cowboy figures quite prominently is J. Frank Dobie's *A Vaquero of the Brush Country, Partly from the Reminiscences of John Young*. At the outset the word "cowboy" is defined, and the author seeks out its derivation. In Southwest Texas the cowboys were generally referred to as "vaqueros," a term originally applied only to Spanish or Mexican cowboys. "But from an early day," writes the author, "Texans, especially those near the border have used the word without reference to race." Thus in one outfit would be found Mexican, Negro, and white "vaqueros." [12] The Negroes in this book range from comic to heroic. When a Negro cowpuncher went on guard he was told to call the next watch by the stars. Not being able to read the stars properly, he did not know when to call his successor, so he rode herd all night.[13]

Living up to the requirements of the Western Code was naturally expected of the Negro cowboy, and this story illustrates that he did not shirk his duty.

Not alone was it his breed that made the American cowboy stick to herd and horse until only death could drag him loose; it was his occupation.

"We had a negro cowboy named George," says an old time Plains cowman, "who was not very well clad because he liked to pike at monte too well to buy clothes. We all had colds and coughs till it was like a bunch of Texas pot hounds baying a 'possum' when we tried to sleep. One bitter night I was near George on herd and tried

---

[11] Frank Eaton, *Pistol Pete* (Boston: Little, Brown, 1952), p. 267.

[12] J. Frank Dobie, *A Vaquero of the Brush Country, Partly from the Reminiscences of John Young* (Dallas: The Southwestern Press, 1929), p. 1.

[13] *Ibid.*, p. 97.

to get him to go to the chuck wagon and turn his horse loose, but
he was too game for that. His teeth were chattering as he said to me
'I can stand it if the rest of you all can.' Presently I saw him lean
over his saddle horn, coughing, and he looked like he was losing his
breath. By the time I got to him he was off his horse, as dead as a
mackerel and stiff as a poker. He had simply frozen to death sitting
on that horse. We placed his body in the chuck wagon on his bed and
drove to the Palo Duro and on the highest hill we could find we
planted the poor black boy, rolled in his blankets. The ground was
sandy; so we could dig a grave deep enough that the coyotes would
not claw into it." [14]

Perhaps it is not unusual that an old time cowboy should recall, for the purpose of illustrating the loyalty of the cowboy, an example which just happened
to be a Negro.

The inevitable cook must always figure in cowboy yarns. However, for the
moment, we are interested in the real kind, not the storybook kind. The
cooks were either white or colored, it did not matter which, and they were
ex-cowboys. When a cowboy was no longer able to do his share in riding
herd, for "physical injury, ordinarily the gift of bucking, and in the form of
hernia, allowed to the average man but seven years of active riding," [15] he
often preferred to become a cook rather than to leave the range. He was occasionally unhappy because his life became less active, but his position as a
cook was not necessarily a degraded one, nor was he helpless. One of the tales
in The Trail Drivers of Texas is the story of a shooting match between a
white cowboy and the Negro cook—a two-year-old heifer against five dollars.
The cook was hard to beat and the cowboy won only on a fluke.[16] Reminiscing
with John Young provides another sketch:

The one man in our outfit that I recall most often and most vividly
was Sam, the negro cook. He always had a cheerful word or cheerful
song, and he seemed to have an affection for every one of us. When
we camped in the vicinity of brush every cowboy coming in would
rope a chunk of wood and snake it up to the chuck wagon. That wood
always made Sam grinning happy whether he needed it or not. He
was about thirty-five years old, as black as a crow, and weighed
around 225 pounds. As he had been raised on a ranch, he was a
good rider, and frequently one of the boys would get him to "top
off" (ride first) a bad horse.[17]

In those days Sam could hold his own among the men of the West.

It would be unforgivable to discuss the cattle range and the cowboy with-

    [14] Ibid., p. 100.
    [15] Rollins, The Cowboy, p. 305.
    [16] J. Marvin Hunter, ed., The Trail Drivers of Texas (Nashville: Cokesbury Press,
1925), pp. 484–88.
    [17] Dobie, A Vaquero of the Brush Country, Partly from the Reminiscences of John
Young, p. 137.

out including at least one stampede. The following, from the "Recollections" of Charles Goodnight—one of the most famous of the rangemen of the Southwest—has a Negro cowboy and also a touch of frontier humor. Charlie Goodnight and his cowboys were driving a herd through the Pecos country of New Mexico in 1867, where they had been constantly harassed by Indians who stampeded the cattle, shot one of the cowboys, and stole part of the heard. A severe lightning storm added to the difficulties of driving. The heard was in an extremely nervous condition as Goodnight rode along one side of it with "Bose Ikard, an ex-slave and one of the best night riders he ever had." [18]

"The cattle had been so shot to pieces," said Goodnight, "and so badly spoiled that they continued stampeding, and after we had passed through Buffalo Gap we had a run which I shall never forget. They had been quiet all night, and at daybreak I told Bose, who was on guard with me, to watch them and I would wake the cook. I reached camp and tied my horse to the wagon wheel, giving him some rope so he could get a little grass. Then I commenced to wake the men who were asleep around the wagon on the side next the herd. Something happened, in an instant the herd stampeded right down on the camp, and it looked as though the men would be trampled to death. There certainly was some scrambling, as most of them had not got out of bed.

"I jerked a blanket off one of the beds, jumped in front of the cattle that were coming at full speed, and by waving the blanket and doing all the yelling I could, succeeded in splitting the herd around the wagon and beds. Charlie, powerful, fast, and the best-trained horse I ever rode in a stampede, was still tied to the wagon. He knew his business, of course, wanted to go, and got to the end of his rope, where the stampede knocked him down and many cattle went over him. I had my belt knife ready, and as the last steer cleared him, I cut the rope and he got up with me on him. I supposed he would be scared out of his wits and run from the cattle, but at once he struck out at full speed with the herd.

"By this time it was light enough to see. I kept going up the side of the cattle as fast as possible, wondering why Bose had not turned the front. When I had almost caught up with him, he looked back and saw me, and immediately his horse shot out like lightning and he threw the leaders around. After we got them circled I asked him why he had not turned them sooner.

" 'I'll tell you sah,' answered the cautious Bose. 'I wuzn't sartin who had dis herd 'till I saw you. I t'ought mabe de Indians had 'um.' " [19]

[18] J. Evetts Haley, *Charles Goodnight, Cowman and Plainsman* (Boston and New York: Houghton Mifflin Company, 1936), p. 166.
[19] *Ibid.*, pp. 166–67.

A Negro cowboy who commanded great respect both as a man and cow-puncher is in "Jack" Thorp's book of the old range days. "Cowmen from Toyah, Texas, to Las Vegas, New Mexico, knew Add, and most of them at different times had worked on round-ups with him." The L F D outfit's range boss, Add, was well liked and was "one of the best hands on the Pecos River." [20] Among other accomplishments, "Nig Add" was a "dictionary on earmarks an' brands," [21] which "in due time [caused him to become the] hero of a cowboy song...." [22] On one occasion, however, Add's popularity created a good deal of embarrassment. "Everybody knew him. When he got married each cow-man wanted to give him a present, no one knowing what the other man had sent him, 'as ranches were far apart.' He received nineteen stoves and ranges for wedding presents." [23]

Perhaps the most interesting of all books dealing with the Negro cowboy is an autobiography written by one. It is the story of Deadwood Dick of Deadwood, South Dakota fame, a name well known in Western lore; the full title reads *The Life and Adventures of Nat Love Better Known in the Cattle Country as "Deadwood Dick"—By Himself.* Born in 1854, sometime in June he thought, in Davidson County, Tennessee, Nat was the son of slave parents who had positions of responsibility on a plantation. From Nat Love one must expect some exaggeration, as one must expect it from every cowboy who wrote his autobiography, especially after he had left the range and had time to dream through his experiences, but in his "Preface" Love writes, "I have tried to record events simply as they are, without attempting to fill out a chapter at the cost of the truth." [24] As a boy he had had plenty of riding experience on the plantation, so with his freedom and a growth of fifteen years he decided to increase his opportunities by going West. Arriving in a Kansas cattle town, in 1869, Nat sought work from Duval, a Texas outfit which had just brought in a herd and was preparing to return to the home ranch. "There were several colored cowboys among them," according to Nat, "and good ones too." Before he could be hired he had to prove his ability, so the boss of the outfit had a colored cowboy named Bronko Jim get Nat the roughest horse they had, which he rode and earned the name "Red River Dick." [25]

With his first range outfit Nat Love began a successful and venturesome career. "By strict attention to business, born of a genuine love of the free and

[20] N. Howard Thorp, *Pardner of the Wind* (Caldwell: The Caxton Printers, 1945), p. 22.
[21] N. Howard Thorp, *Songs of the Cowboys* (Boston and New York: Houghton Mifflin Company, 1921), p. 166.
[22] Thorp, *Pardner of the Wind,* p. 22.
[23] Thorp, *Songs of the Cowboys,* p. 166. See also John A. Lomax, *Adventures of a Ballad Hunter* (New York: The Macmillan Company, 1947), p. 46. Mr. Lomax writes that on the big ranches he had trouble getting the cowboys to sing for him, but with "smaller groups on remote ranches I enjoyed better fortune. Two or three Negro cow-boys sang lustily when I got them away from the crowd."
[24] Nat Love, *The Life and Adventures of Nat Love* (Los Angeles: Wayside Press, 1907), preface.
[25] *Ibid.,* p. 41.

wild life of the range, and absolute fearlessness, I became known throughout the country as a good all around cowboy and a splendid hand in a stampede." After three years with Duval, Nat signed on with the Pete Gallinger Company, "whose immense range was located on the Gila River in southern Arizona." There he stayed "for several years and soon became one of their most trusted men, taking an important part in all the big round-ups and cuttings throughout western Texas, Arizona and other states where the company had interests to be looked after." [26] And the Gallinger Company eventually made Nat their chief brand reader.

Love took part in all of the cowboys' activities, and his manner in relating these events is no different from that found in any other cowboy autobiography. He knew, for example, that the "test of a cowboy's worth is in his gameness and his nerve." [27] One of the favorite sports was roping and riding steers, which, thought Nat, "is done more for the sport's sake than anything else, and the love of showing off, a weakness of all cowboys more or less." [28] It was not uncommon for them to become involved in shooting trouble over brands, and death was frequently the result. On Christmas Day, 1872,

> I and a number of friends were in a place called Holbrook, Ariz. A dispute started over a saddle horse with the following result. Arizona Bob drew his forty-five Colt revolver, but before he had time to fire he was instantly killed by A. Jack. Then a general fight ensued in which five horses and three men were killed.[29]

After delivering a herd, at the end of a trail, Nat was always ready to "see the elephant" with the rest of the boys.

> Then we all headed for Dodge City to have a good time, and I assure you we had it. It was our intention and ambition to paint the town a deep red color and drink up all the bad whiskey in the city. Our nearly two months journey over the dusty plains and ranges had made us all inordinately thirsty and wild, and here is where we had our turn, accordingly we started out to do the town in true western style, in which we were perfectly successful until the town had done us, and we were dead broke.... While our money lasted we would certainly enjoy ourselves, in dancing, drinking and shooting up the town.[30]

Every old cowhand who has written about his days on the range has included at least one episode of this sort.

During a trip to old Mexico to pick up a herd, Love's outfit had an opportunity to meet Mexican cowboys. "These men were for the most part typ-

[26] *Ibid.*, p. 43.
[27] *Ibid.*, p. 50.
[28] *Ibid.*, p. 49.
[29] *Ibid.*, p. 51.
[30] *Ibid.*, pp. 54–55.

ical greasers, but they proved to us that they knew a thing or two about the cattle business, and all the things considered they were a jolly companionable sort of an oufit." [31] Along with the other cowboys of the time, Nat went through the usual adventures which appear to have happened to them all. Once, after he had put up a terrific fight, he was captured by Yellow Dog's tribe. They would normally have killed him, he thought, but they did not because there was colored blood in the tribe; "and as I was a colored man they wanted to keep me, as they thought I was too good a man to die." [32] With pride in his ability to more than hold his own among the cowboys, Nat swaggered a bit when he admitted to being "naturally tough," for he "carried the marks of fourteen bullet wounds." He confessed, also, that he had been a "dare devil" cowboy, "wild, reckless, free" and "afraid of nothing," but he did not want to leave an impression that he was a heartless killer.

> It was not with any sense of pride or in bravado that I recount here the fate of the men who have fallen at my hand.
> It is a terrible thing to kill a man no matter what the cause. But as I am writing a true history of my life, I cannot leave these facts out. But every man who died at my hands was either seeking my life or died in open warfare, when it was a case of killing or being killed.[33]

Like other cowboys writing "true life" stories, Nat also happened to meet the famous men of the plains, including Buffalo Bill, Billy the Kid, and Bat Masterson, the renowned marshal of Dodge City.

The high point, however, in the career of Nat Love came on July 4, 1876, in Deadwood, South Dakota. In the spring of that year the home ranch had received an order to drive three thousand head to a point near Deadwood. After the cattle had been delivered, the boys headed for town to celebrate. On the morning of the Fourth the gamblers and mining men of Deadwood collected a purse of $200 as first prize for a roping contest. There were about twelve contestants, "six of them being colored cowboys." Not only did Nat win, but he set a record. The morning event had been so successful that another purse was made up for a shooting contest in the afternoon. Again Nat won, but with the purse came the biggest prize of all: he was given the title of "Deadwood Dick," a distinction and honor which he was still proudly carrying when he wrote his book thirty years later. Love found freedom and happiness as a cowboy on the Western range, for he came into his own at a time and place where to be "all man" was the most important requisite of the West. As Nat expressed it, "What man with the fire of life and youth and health in his veins could not rejoice in such a life?" [34] Color was no barrier to fame for Nat Love.

At this point these autobiographical data raise a historical question in

81 *Ibid.*, p. 31.
82 *Ibid.*, p. 99.
83 *Ibid.*, p. 105.
84 *Ibid.*, p. 70.

Western literature: why did the fame achieved by the Negro cowboy not carry over into fiction? That the Negro cowboys were on the range in considerable numbers, and doing a creditable job, is, as has been pointed out, a historical fact. However, the day of the range cowboy was over before his fiction began. There is a difference of opinion as to which is the first Western story, but all students of the genre agree that it came between 1902 and Zane Grey's *Riders of the Purple Sage* in 1912.[35] And the comparatively short period of the range cowboy, approximately thirty-five years, had ended by 1900. We have no cowboy statistics, but the evidence indicates that the greatest percentage of Negro cowboys were on the Western plains, particularly in Texas, immediately after the Civil War, and that their number was dwindling rapidly by the end of the century. The Texas Rangers had been dissolved during the war, and in 1870 the governor of Texas set up the state police. Many Negroes were state police officers in a body which soon became so hated that it was considered a duty to shoot them on sight, for they were set up to enforce Reconstruction measures. The state police lasted for only three years, with the Rangers being reëstablished in 1874—excluding the Negro. The Negro began moving farther west, into New Mexico and Arizona, and on up into the northern range. Nat Love left Texas for Arizona in 1872. Gradually, as the century moved on, and the West became more populated, the Negro cowboy was forced into other occupations. In 1890 Deadwood Dick became a Pullman porter.

It is possible that the earliest writers of Western stories, during the first decade of this century, attributed the then existing conditions to an earlier period. These writers knew the West only after it had become populated, and they knew but little of those days when a cowboy was paid and valued for skill, not color.

It is quite obvious that the Romantic tradition in fiction laid its heavy hand on the Western story. In Southern fiction the Negro was cast as a "faithful retainer." In the Western story the same attitude prevailed, for the Negro could be a cook but he could not be a cowboy. The earliest Westerns unrealistically included women; the capable but pure, white kind, gracefully riding across the plains, into the sunset and the purple sage, admired from afar by all the cowboys, and won at the end of the hard riding, hard shooting heroes. In the words of a tall puncher called Jess Hill:

> Punchin' cows in these mountains ain't like it is in a book I read before I left the ranch, where all the cute waddie had ter do was ride slick fat horses, sleep on a geese-hair bed, set the boss' daughter en afterwards marry her, en she the prettiest girl in the West. I wonder why some sure-enough cowhand don't write the truth about it, heh? [36]

[35] Some candidates for the first Western story are Owen Wister, *The Virginian* (1902); Bertha M. Bower, *Chip of the Flying U* (1904); and Zane Grey, *Riders of the Purple Sage* (1912).
[36] Thorp, *Pardner of the Wind*, p. 13.

The fact that truth is stranger than fiction is one of the reasons why the Western romance prevailed in its present form. Fiction was what the East had been brought up on, a romantic concept of the West, and the Western writers saw no reason to write fact when fiction paid. The Negro cowboy did not fit into the romantic concept, and once the Western story stereotype was formed, during its first decade, it became impervious to change.

It is possible, however, that because so many of the Westerns were written by people who did not know the West, that these writers were unaware of the contribution of the Negro cowboy to the opening up of the range. When Owen Wister, Bertha Bower, and Zane Grey arrived in the West they saw only the saffron after-glow; had they been in time to witness the West's high noon, the Western story might never have come into existence. Fiction writers could see only a particular kind of man silhouetted against the skyline, and they chose to ignore the fact that "chaps" were worn by men of many nationalities and colors and that these were also included with the "men who made the spirit of the West, who forbade Mason and Dixon's line to extend, who harnessed democracy." [37] But now we know that pioneering, according to tradition, is an Anglo-Saxon job, and the Western myth is sometimes stronger and more important than reality.

In all fairness to those serious novelists of the West who write realistically, it should be said that when their setting and time includes him they can accord the Negro proper treatment. This is in the novel of the West—not the Western story—, and two of this type who come to mind are Walter Van Tilburg Clark and Tom Lea.[38] But where is the Negro cowboy in the Western story, in these thousands of books in this multi-million dollar business? The Negro was part of the spirit of the West, but he is not included in its fiction. The early West had a tradition which asked of a man only that he be capable and have courage and loyalty: where he came from and what he looked like was immaterial. That same West is represented in fiction by an Anglo-Saxon tradition which implies that all readers are white and that only a white cowboy can be a hero who is "fearless, fair and square."

[37] Rollins, *The Cowboy*, p. 383.
[38] Walter Van Tilburg Clark, *The Ox-Bow Incident* (New York: Random House, 1940). Tom Lea, *The Wonderful Country* (Boston: Little, Brown, 1952).

Vernon L. Wharton

THE RACE ISSUE IN THE OVERTHROW OF RECONSTRUCTION IN MISSISSIPPI

Under the provisions of the Reconstruction Act of 1867, Negroes in the southern states were enfranchised, and for the next several years they played an important political role. Whites resented the activities of Negroes in politics and accused Negro voters and office-holders of venality and ignorance. Using a variety of stratagems, the whites overturned the Reconstruction regimes and by 1877 eliminated Negroes from effective political participation in all of the southern states.

The late Vernon L. Wharton's discussion of the race issue in Reconstruction Mississippi is a superb case study of how Negroes actually functioned politically, and how the whites used intimidation to overthrow an essentially honest and effective government which was based largely on black votes.

ON the questionable theory that man is a rational being, students of the overthrow of the Republican governments in the South have usually placed heavy emphasis on the real or alleged inefficiency, dishonesty, and extravagance of those governments. It may be that such weaknesses have from time to time resulted in great popular upheavals or violent revolutions against parties in power, although much evidence to the contrary might be presented from present conditions and from history. Be that as it may, the multitude of stories about the degradation of the Reconstruction governments must not blind us to the significance in the situation of U. B. Phillips' "central theme of Southern history," the relations of the races.

For the study of the influence of race feeling in the undoing of Recon-

Vernon L. Wharton, "The Race Issue in the Overthrow of Reconstruction in Mississippi," *Phylon*, II (Fourth Quarter, 1941), pp. 362–370. Reprinted with permission of *Phylon*.

struction, the state of Mississippi offers a story that in some respects is unique. As Howard K. Beale,[1] and Francis B. Simkins,[2] and others have recently pointed out, we are not yet prepared to offer intelligent judgment as to the significance or quality of Reconstruction governments in any of the Southern states. Whatever this judgment may be for the rest of the South, that for Mississippi must take a peculiar form. In this state, Negroes made up a large majority of the electorate. Yet the effort to discover the accepted pattern of Negro domination, inefficiency, extravagance, and corruption meets with failure.

In the first place, Negroes, in spite of their majority, never endeavored to take control of any branch of the state government. To the convention of one hundred men who drew up the Reconstruction constitution they elected only sixteen of their number. Never at any time did they have a majority in either house of the state legislature. Never did they hold more than three of the seven major state offices. No Negro held any judicial office above that of justice of the peace. During the seven years of Republican power, a total of only twelve Negroes held the office of sheriff. Furthermore, although Negroes in some of the Delta counties outnumbered the whites more than ten to one, there were only a few instances in which Negroes held a majority of the offices in such counties, and even then the white officials seem to have had the dominant part in all decisions.

At no time was there any effort on the part of the Negroes to use their political power to gain special advantages for their race in state legislation. One of their first acts was to petition Congress to remove the political disabilities of the Southern whites. At no time was there any effort to set up schools in which Negro children would mingle with whites. Throughout the Republican regime, per capita appropriations to white schools were larger than those for Negroes.[3] Although Negro legislators succeeded in gaining the passage of a state civil rights act in 1873, cases in which Negroes strove to maintain their equal privileges under this act were rare indeed. Officials of public conveyances and places of entertainment simply disregarded the act,[4] and even a Negro congressman and the Negro Secretary of State accepted discrimination without protest.[5]

It is undoubtedly true that many of the Negroes who held local and county offices were ignorant and incompetent, although general contemporary charges of illiteracy are open to question, and in some cases can be shown to be

[1] Howard K. Beale, "On Rewriting Reconstruction History," *American Historical Review*, Vol. XLV, 1940, No. 4, pp. 807–833.

[2] Francis B. Simkins, "New Viewpoints of Southern Reconstruction," *Journal of Southern History*, Vol. V, 1939, No. 1, pp. 49–61.

[3] Stuart G. Noble, *Forty Years of the Public Schools in Mississippi*, New York, 1918, pp. 34, 39.

[4] John S. McNeily, "War and Reconstruction in Mississippi," *Publications of the Mississippi Historical Society*, Centenary Series, Vol. LI, pp. 414–415.

[5] Hinds County *Gazette*, January 25, 1871, February 11, 1874.

incorrect. Altogether, little difference can be discovered in the administration of counties that had Negro office-holders and those in which such officials were never elected.

Mississippi was also fortunate in the Negro membership of its legislatures. Much evidence might be introduced to uphold this declaration, but the testimony of Edward King, everywhere critical of Negro office-holders, will serve the purpose:

> I wish here to avow ... that those of the Negroes in office, with whom I came in contact in Mississippi, impressed me much more powerfully as worthy, intelligent, and likely to progress, than many whom I saw elsewhere in the South. There are some who are exceedingly capable, and none of those immediately attached to the government at Jackson are incapable. In the Legislature there are now and then Negroes who are ignorant; but of late both branches have been freer of this curse than have those of Louisiana or South Carolina.[6]

In regard to the three powerful Negro leaders of the state, we may consider the testimony of Alexander K. McClure, who at the time of his visit to the South had abandoned the Republican Party to become a leader in the fight against Grant and his henchmen. After a study of the entire Southern situation, McClure wrote:

> Mississippi is exceptionable also in the reputable character of her most prominent colored leaders. In all the other Southern states the Negro leaders have rivaled the white adventurers in reckless and bewildering robbery, but they have not done so in Mississippi. Three black men here have reached national fame as leaders of their race, and they are all esteemed as honest men.[7]

In dispassionate moments, Democratic leaders and editors joined freely in this estimate of John R. Lynch, Blanche K. Bruce, and Hiram Revels.[8]

The generally accepted estimate of the Reconstruction governments also fails to hold in Mississippi in respect to governmental taxes, expenditures, and bonded debt. For various reasons, including the reconstruction of public property destroyed during the war, the new program of public education, and the loss of revenue from the head tax on slaves, all units of the state experienced a rise in the tax rate as compared to that before the war. But the significant fact is that there was no correlation at all between the rates of taxation in the various counties and the political or racial character of those counties. In 1874,

[6] Edward King, *The Great South*, Hartford, Connecticut, 1875, p. 314.
[7] Alexander K. McClure, *The South*, Philadelphia, 1886, p. 314.
[8] Franklin A. Montgomery, *Reminiscences of Mississippians in Peace and War*, Cincinnati, 1901, pp. 279, 292; Jackson *Clarion*, April 24, 1873, January 20, 1881; Hinds County *Gazette*, October 2, 1872.

at the height of Negro-Republican control, the average rate for the thirty-nine Democratic counties was 12 7/13 mills. That for the thirty-four Republican counties was 13 7/17, a difference of less than one mill.[9]

It is also true that the expenditures of the state government almost exactly doubled under the Republican regime as compared to the average of the years immediately preceding the war. But it must be noted that the average annual expenditure of the Republican regime was only $1,400,000, for a state with a population of more than 900,000. This represented a per capita cost of less than $1.50 a year, one of the very lowest in the Union, and one that was negligible according to modern standards. The greater part of the increase in state costs went for educational expenditures, the absorption of court costs formerly borne by the counties, and the establishment or expansion of state institutions for the care of defectives. Furthermore, these costs were met without any significant increase in the debt of the state. The actual debt at the end of the Republican regime was less than one million dollars.[10]

In their administration of state affairs, the Republicans left a remarkable record of honesty. The conclusion of J. W. Garner in his *Reconstruction in Mississippi* seems to be approximately correct:

> So far as the conduct of state officials who were entrusted with the custody of public funds is concerned, it may be said that there were no great embezzlements or other cases of misappropriation during the period of Republican rule.... The treasurer of the Natchez hospital seems to have been the only defaulting official during the administration of Governor Ames. He was a "carpet bagger," and the amount of the shortage was $7,251.81. The colored state librarian during Alcorn's administration was charged with stealing books from the library. The only large case of embezzlement during the postbellum period was that of the Democratic treasurer in 1866. The amount of the shortage was $61,962.[11]

It may be added that the next embezzlement of any importance was that of the Democratic "redemption" treasurer who was elected in 1875. His shortage was $315,612.19.[12]

Altogether, as governments go, that supplied by the Negro and white Republicans in Mississippi between 1870 and 1876 was not a bad government, and, in several important respects, it possessed distinct superiority over those that preceded it and followed it. But one problem it could not solve. For various reasons, the Republican Party came to be branded as the party of Negroes, and it was apparent that Negroes were demanding more and more

[9] Jackson *Mississippi Weekly Pilot*, January 23, 1875; James W. Garner, *Reconstruction in Mississippi*, New York, 1901, p. 313.
[10] Mississippi House of Representatives *Journal*, 1876, p. 9; *Annual Report of the State Treasurer*, 1875, pp. 19–21.
[11] James W. Garner, *Reconstruction in Mississippi*, pp. 322–323.
[12] Hinds County *Gazette*, March 22, 1890.

recognition within the party. It was also true that many of the Negroes favored a further expansion of the functions of the state, entirely at the expense, according to the whites, of white tax-payers. The way was open for the formation of a "white-line" party, and this project was more significant than any other in the so-called "campaign of liberation" of 1875.

From the beginning of Reconstruction, there were in Mississippi, as in the other Southern states, a large number of white men who insisted on the necessity of accepting the results of the war and of complying with the requirements of the national government. In the forefront of this group were a number of ante-bellum leaders of the state, many of them old-line Whigs. With the apparent inevitability of Negro suffrage, they insisted that the only intelligent course was to grant to Negroes all rights extended to them by the Federal government, and to persuade them to follow native white leadership.

Two factors doomed these men to failure. The first was the determined opposition of a majority of the white population to their program. The other lay in the fact that almost none of these men could bring himself to deal with a Negro, however honest or able that Negro might be, as a political or social equal. The same attitude was held by such Northern leaders in the state as H. R. Pease, G. C. McKee, and R. C. Powers. By 1874, men of this class had to recognize either their failure to make Democrats of the Negroes, or the repudiation of their leadership in the Republican Party.

The majority of the white citizens, with a semi-religious belief that the Negro was an inferior who must be kept in subjection, had found themselves from the beginning unable to endorse the program of the conservatives. As early as December, 1869, the editor of the Columbus *Index* made a bid for the leadership of this group with the declaration: "We have given the Negro a fair trial. He has voted solidly against us, and we hoist, from this day, the white man's flag, and will never take it down so long as we have a voice in the government of this state." [13] The year 1870 saw the organization of a number of "White Men's Clubs," especially in the counties where there were large numbers of both races. These clubs were pledged to labor unceasingly for the restoration of white supremacy in Mississippi and in the nation. The Columbus *Democrat*, advocating the union of these groups in a revitalized Democratic Party, declared: "Its leading ideas are, that white men shall govern. . . . Nigger voting, holding office, and sitting in the jury box, are all wrong, and against the sentiment of the country." Here was sheer racial antagonism. There was no consideration of the undesirability of the participation of ignorant and poverty-stricken masses in the government of the state; the line was drawn on the basis of race, and it was chiefly toward the propagation of this feeling that the Democratic campaign of 1875 was directed.

With the rejection by the Republicans of the gubernatorial bid of the conservative J. L. Alcorn in 1873, and the significant increase in office holding by Negroes after that election, the movement gained new strength. Native and Northern whites whose leadership had been rejected joined in the demand for

[13] Hinds County *Gazette*, December 15, 1869, quoting the Columbus *Index*.

white supremacy. When Democrats gained control of the national House of Representatives in 1874, the powerful conservative leaders in Mississippi agreed at last to abandon their caution. The word went out that the time for revolution was at hand, and the efforts of such men as A. G. Brown, and L. Q. C. Lamar to temper the movement were of no avail.

Greater and greater numbers of the white Republicans in Mississippi were now deserting the party and joining the Democratic clubs. As Charles Nordhoff was told in the spring of 1875, the Democrats were making it "too damned hot for them to stay out." [14] At the same time, more and more conservative Democratic newspapers were openly accepting the "white-line" program. The transition could be seen clearly in most cases, and was especially noticeable in the powerful Hinds County *Gazette* and Jackson *Clarion*. Editors who had strongly condemned the Black Code and who had for several years written of Negroes in varying terms of sympathy, impatience, or friendly ridicule, and who had even praised them at times, during the summer of 1874 came to speak of them with open dislike, and finally to devote column after column to efforts to stir up hatred against them.

As time went on, the attack became ever more bitter, and by mid-summer practically every paper in the state except the official Republican organ was supporting a campaign based on the color line as the predominant issue.[15] The Forest *Register* carried at its masthead the slogan: "A white man in a white man's place. A black man in a black man's place. Each according to the eternal fitness of things." The Yazoo City *Banner* declared: "Mississippi is *a white mans country, and by the Eternal God we'll rule it.*" [16] The Handsboro *Democrat* called for "A white man's government, by white men, for the benefit of white men." [17] All these papers justified their stand in editorials declaring the depravity and innate bestiality of the Negro. These attacks reached a climax in one published by the Forest *Register*.

> A Negro preacher is an *error loci*. God Almighty, in farming out his privileges to mankind, drew a line as to qualifications.
> ...Does any sane man believe the Negro capable of comprehending the Ten Commandments? The miraculous conception and birth of our Saviour? The high moral precepts taught from the temple on the mount? Every effort to inculcate these great truths but tends to bestialize his nature, and by obfuscating his little brain unfits him for the duties assigned him as a hewer of wood and drawer of water.

[14] Charles Nordhoff, *The Cotton States*, p. 77.

[15] See files of Vicksburg *Herald*, Handsboro *Democrat*, Yazoo City *Banner*, Vicksburg *Monitor*, Okolona *Southern States*, Newton *Ledger*, Brandon *Republican*, Columbus *Index*, Columbus *Democrat*, Jackson *Clarion*, Hinds County *Gazette*, and Meridian *Gazette*.

[16] Jackson *Mississippi Weekly Pilot*, July 31, 1875, quoting the Yazoo City *Banner*.

[17] Jackson *Mississippi Weekly Pilot*, April 10, 1875, quoting the Handsboro *Democrat*.

The effort makes him a demon of wild, fanatical destruction, and consigns him to the fatal shot of the white man.[18]

Declarations by the rapidly dwindling group of conservative Democrats that the votes of the Negroes could be obtained by treating them fairly and reasoning with them met the scorn of the white-liners.[19] Furthermore, when Lamar succeeded in inserting in the Democratic-Conservative platform a vague statement recognizing "the civil and political equality of man" and inviting the Negro to vote, white-liners were quick to deny allegiance.[20]

As the campaign progressed, charges of inefficiency, extravagance, and corruption were almost completely dropped by the Democrats. Later testimony by Democratic leaders before Congressional investigating committees has led historians to picture these considerations as the real issues of the campaign, but the picture is not a true one. More accurate was the statement given by W. A. Montgomery, leader of the Democratic military forces in the central portion of the state. In his testimony, Montgomery declared: "... [The] only issue in the election was whether the whites or the blacks should predominate; there was no other politics that I could see in it. Men that had been Republicans all their lives just laid aside republicanism and said that they had to go into the ranks then."[21] In the words of J. S. McNeily, chief contemporary Democratic historian of the state: "It was a part of the creed of a desperate condition, one easily understood, that any white man, however odious, was preferable ... to any Negro however unobjectionable individually."[22]

In a state where a frontier code still held much influence, it was inevitable that a campaign appealing to prejudice and hatred should result in much violence, and, in the end, it was violence that carried the campaign for the Democrats. In this violence thousands of young men and boys of all classes, a large part of the farm element, and many local political leaders took active part. By September, the Hinds County *Gazette* was able to announce: "The people of this State are now fully armed, equipped, and drilled...."[23]

With powerful military forces at its command, the white Democracy was ready for its campaign against Negroes who were timorous, unarmed, and largely unorganized. As the campaign of intimidation went on, Negro Republicans were ostentatiously enrolled in "dead books."[24] Negro political leaders were warned that another speech would mean death.[25] Republican

---

[18] Forest *Register*, September 15, 1875.

[19] James B. Ranck, *Albert Gallatin Brown*, p. 275; Jackson *Mississippi Weekly Pilot*, May 29, 1875, quoting the Vicksburg *Herald*.

[20] Columbus *Democrat*, August 21, 1875.

[21] Testimony, *Senate Reports*, 44th Congress, 1st session, No. 527, p. 542.

[22] J. S. McNeily, "Climax and Collapse of Reconstruction in Mississippi," *Publications of the Mississippi Historical Society*, XII, p. 405.

[23] Hinds County *Gazette*, September 29, 1875.

[24] W. Calvin Wells, "Reconstruction in Hinds County," *Publications of the Mississippi Historical Society*, IX, p. 102.

[25] John W. Kyle, "Reconstruction in Panola County," *Publications of the Mississippi Historical Society*, XIII, p. 71.

political meetings were broken up by violent attacks, or were prevented, by armed force.[26] Committees of "active young men" waited on Negroes who tried to prevent others of their race from deserting their party.[27] Negroes were prevented from registering by sham battles and the firing of pistols at registration points, or by armed pickets who met them on the roads.[28] Thickly populated Negro sections heard nightly the booming of Democratic cannon. Democrats adopted as a policy the practice of appearing in force at such Republican meetings as were held, and of demanding the privilege of presenting Democratic speakers, and of compelling Republican speakers to "tell the truth or quit the stand." [29]

By far the most effective weapon at the disposal of the whites, however, was the so-called "race riot." The first of these "riots" occurred in Meridian early in the period of Reconstruction. It resulted in the death of twenty or thirty Negroes, and in the complete breakdown of the Republican organization in the surrounding area. Democratic leaders of the time later declared that the lesson learned at Meridian made such riots an intentional and essential part of the campaign of 1875, and that they were the decisive factor.[30] It was immediately learned that the Negroes, timid and unresourceful after generations of servitude, could offer no effective resistance. During the year before the election, at least fifteen affairs of this type occurred, bringing death to three white Republicans, five Democrats, and at least 150 Negroes. After each incident of this type, white vigilante companies took command of the surrounding region, and in several cases systematically lynched Negro leaders in each district.[31] In each case the encounter marked the end of effective Republican activity over a large area.

The effect of the campaign of violence and intimidation on the Negroes is clearly revealed in their letters to Governor Adelbert Ames. These ranged from the perplexed inquiries of intelligent leaders to the frantic appeals of representatives of the ignorant and terrified majority. From bloody Yazoo

[26] Fred M. Witty, "Reconstruction in Carroll and Montgomery Counties," *Publications of the Mississippi Historical Society*, X, p. 123; Jackson *Mississippi Weekly Pilot*, October 2, 1875; *United States Senate Reports*, 44th Congress, 1st session, no. 527, pp. 196–197.

[27] Hinds County *Gazette*, July 28, August 18, September 23, 1875.

[28] Jackson *Mississippi Weekly Pilot*, October 9, 1875; *United States Senate Reports*, 44th Congress, 1st session, No. 527, p. 1718.

[29] Kyle, XIII, p. 72; Julia Kendel, "Reconstruction in Lafayette County," *Publications of the Mississippi Historical Society*, XIII, p. 244; Hinds County *Gazette*, August 4, 1875.

[30] Dunbar Rowland, *History of Mississippi* (Chicago, 1929), II, p. 172; William H. Hardy, "Recollections of Reconstruction in East and Southeast Mississippi," *Publications of the Mississippi Historical Society*, VII, pp. 205–206. For evidence that the same policy was followed in South Carolina, on the basis of information from Mississippi, see Francis B. Simkins and Robert H. Woody, *South Carolina During Reconstruction*, note p. 487, and p. 496.

[31] Hardy, VII, p. 206; Jackson *Mississippi Weekly Pilot*, March 20; September 4, 11, 25; October 2, 1875; Albert T. Morgan, *Yazoo* (Washington, 1884), pp. 465–484.

came the plea: "I beg you most fulley to send the United soldiers here; they have hung six more men since the hanging of Mr. Fawn; they won't let the Republican have no ticket. . . . Send help, help, troops. . . ." [32] From Noxubee County there was the cry:

> Last Saturday, the 30th, the democrats was in Macon town in high rage, raring around and shooting of their cannons up and down the streets, and shooting all their pistols also . . . and there was Richard Gray shot down walking on the pavements, shot by the democrats, and he was shot five times, four times after he fell, and he was shot because he was nominated for treasurer, and fothermore, because he made a speech and said he never did expect to vote a democratic ticket, and also advised the colored citizens to do the same. [33]

From Warren County there was letter after letter, including one that declared: "The rebles turbulent; are arming themselves here now to-day to go to Sartartia to murder more poor negroes. Gov. aint the no pertiction." [34]

There was no protection; frantic efforts of the Governor brought mocking laughter from the triumphant Democrats. [35] When President Grant refused aid, the election became a formality. In many of the black counties armed whites took charge of the polls. Yazoo County, center of an overwhelming Negro majority, reported only seven Republican votes. The Democratic Legislature quickly secured the resignation of the Republican Governor, Lieutenant-Governor, and Superintendent of Education, and in Mississippi the Reconstruction experiment was over.

From the story, obvious conclusions may be drawn. Race prejudice, with a few contributing factors, was sufficient to bring about violent overthrow of the Reconstruction government in Mississippi. Stories of dishonesty and inefficiency in other Southern states, and to a lesser extent in Mississippi, certainly have their place in the history of Reconstruction. It is an error, however, to exhibit them as prime causes for the Democratic counter-revolutions, the establishment of Jim Crow laws, and the legal and extra-legal denial of rights of citizenship to Negroes. This conclusion is not a happy one. Righteous wrath aroused by the abuse of public trust may be assuaged, but race hatred, in any time or any land, is a mysterious force, easily stirred to greater intensity. It stands as perhaps the greatest problem that can be offered to the student of social science.

[32] *Senate Reports*, 44th Congress, 1st session, "Documentary Evidence," p. 9.
[33] *Ibid.*, p. 73.
[34] *Ibid.*, p. 89.
[35] Jackson *Mississippi Weekly Pilot*, September 11, 1875, quoting the Jackson *Clarion*.

August Meier

August Meier is University Professor of History and Senior Research Fellow, Center for Urban Regionalism, at Kent State University. He is the author of *Negro Thought in America, 1880–1915*. Professor Meier is the General Editor of Atheneum's paperback reprints on American Negro Life as well as a forthcoming series of original studies of the Negro in America.

Elliott Rudwick

Elliott Rudwick, Professor of Sociology and Senior Research Fellow, Center for Urban Regionalism, at Kent State University, has written *W. E. B. Du Bois: Propagandist for the Negro Protest*, currently reprinted by Atheneum Paperbacks. He will be co-author, with August Meier, of a history of CORE, to be published by Atheneum.